PHIL 350 Philosophy of Religion

American River College Custom Edition

POJMAN | REA

D0884871

CENGAGE
Learning·

Australia • Brazil • Japan • Korea • Mexico • Singapore • Spain • United Kingdom • United States

PHIL 350 Philosophy of Religion

Philosophy of Religion: An Anthology, 6th Edition
Louis P. Pojman | Michael Rea

Executive Editors:
 Maureen Staudt
 Michael Stranz

Senior Project Development Manager:
 Linda deStefano

Marketing Specialist:
 Courtney Sheldon

Senior Production/Manufacturing Manager:
 Donna M. Brown

PreMedia Manager:
 Joel Brennecke

Sr. Rights Acquisition Account Manager:
 Todd Osborne

Cover Image:
 Getty Images*

*Unless otherwise noted, all cover images used by Custom Solutions, a part of Cengage Learning, have been supplied courtesy of Getty Images with the exception of the Earthview cover image, which has been supplied by the National Aeronautics and Space Administration (NASA).

For product information and technology assistance, contact us at
Cengage Learning Customer & Sales Support, 1-800-354-9706

For permission to use material from this text or product,
submit all requests online at **cengage.com/permissions**
Further permissions questions can be emailed to
permissionrequest@cengage.com

This book contains select works from existing Cengage Learning resources and was produced by Cengage Learning Custom Solutions for collegiate use. As such, those adopting and/or contributing to this work are responsible for editorial content accuracy, continuity and completeness.

Compilation © 2010 Cengage Learning

ISBN-13: **978-1-133-83742-8**

ISBN-10: 1-133-83742-5

Cengage Learning
5191 Natorp Boulevard
Mason, Ohio 45040
USA

Cengage Learning is a leading provider of customized learning solutions with office locations around the globe, including Singapore, the United Kingdom, Australia, Mexico, Brazil, and Japan. Locate your local office at:
international.cengage.com/region.

Cengage Learning products are represented in Canada by Nelson Education, Ltd.
For your lifelong learning solutions, visit **www.cengage.com/custom.**
Visit our corporate website at **www.cengage.com.**

Printed in the United States of America

Table of Contents

PART VI

Death and Immortality

Of all the many forms which natural religion has assumed none probably has exerted so deep and far-reaching an influence on human life as the belief in immortality and the worship of the dead; hence [a discussion] of this momentous creed and of the practical consequences which have been deduced from it can hardly fail to be at once instructive and impressive, whether we regard the record with complacency as a noble testimony to the aspiring genius of man, who claims to outlive the sun and the stars, or whether we view it with pity as a melancholy monument of fruitless labour and barren ingenuity expended in prying into that great mystery of which fools profess their knowledge and wise men confess their ignorance.

SIR JAMES FRAZIER, *THE BELIEF*
IN IMMORTALITY, VOL. 1
(LONDON: MACMILLAN, 1913), VII–VIII.

IS THERE LIFE AFTER DEATH? Few questions have troubled humans as deeply as this one. Is this finite, short existence of three score and ten years all that we have? Or is there reason to hope for a blessed postmortem existence where love, justice, and peace, which we now experience in Fragmented forms, will unfold in all their fullness and enable human existence to find fulfillment? Are we merely mortal or blessedly immortal?

Anthropological studies reveal a widespread and ancient sense of immortality. Prehistoric societies buried their dead with food so that the deceased would not be hungry in the next life. Most cultures and religions have some version of a belief in another life, whether it be in the form of a resurrected body, a transmigrated soul, reincarnation, or an ancestral spirit present with the tribe.

Let us begin by understanding what we mean by immortality. Being immortal is not simply a matter of living on through our works or in the memories of our loved ones. Rather, for our purposes, immortality involves freedom from death. To be immortal is to be the sort of being who will never undergo the permanent cessation of one's conscious existence.

For most people, death is the ultimate tragedy. It is the paramount evil, for it deprives us of all that we know and love on earth. Our fear of death is profound; we have a passionate longing to live again and to be with our loved ones. And yet there isn't a shred of direct empirical evidence that we shall live again. As far as we can tell scientifically, mental function is tied to brain function, so that when the latter comes permanently to an end, the former does as well. Some claim to have experienced the afterlife, but there are naturalistic explanations for such experiences and, in any case, their veridicality cannot be confirmed by empirical means.

Many have thought, however, that philosophical argument can shed light on the question of immortality. In the Western tradition three views have dominated, one denying life after death and two affirming it. The negative view, going back to the ancient Greek atomist philosophers Democritus and Leucippus, holds that we are identical with our bodies (including our brains), so that when the body dies, the self does as well. We may call this view materialist monism, because it does not allow for the possibility of a soul or spiritual self that can live without the body.

The positive views divide into dualist and monist theories of life after death. The dualist views separate the body from the soul or self of the agent and affirm that it is the soul or self that lives forever. This view was held by the pre-Socratic philosopher Pythagoras (570–500 BCE) and is developed by Plato (427–347 BCE). In modern philosophy it is represented by René Descartes (1596–1650). It is sometimes referred to as the Platonic-Cartesian view of immortality. These philosophers argue that we are essentially spiritual or mental beings and that our bodies are either unreal or not part of our essential selves. Death is merely the separation of our souls from our bodies, a sort of spiritual liberation.

Many in the dualist tradition maintain that the (typical) soul will be reincarnated several, perhaps many, times before attaining the final goal of permanent separation from the body. On this view—found in various strands of Pythagoreanism, Platonism, Buddhism, and Hinduism—embodiment is an undesirable state, and only those who lead the right sort of lifestyle have any hope of freeing themselves from the cycle of reincarnation. By way of contrast, Christian dualists deny reincarnation and maintain instead that the ultimate destination for the soul (after becoming disembodied at death) is to be re-embodied in one's *resurrected* earthly body. The difference between reincarnation and resurrection is just the difference between getting a brand new body (reincarnation) after death and getting one and the same body (resurrection). This is not to say, of course, that our bodies in the afterlife will have exactly the same properties—flaws, limitations, and so on—as our present earthly bodies. Indeed, according to the Christian tradition anyway, quite the opposite is the case: Our resurrected bodies will be greatly improved, or glorified. But the point is that the body you have in the afterlife will be the *same* body that you have now, despite its differences—much like your body after a successful diet or workout regimen is the same body you had before, albeit healthier, stronger, and in other respects better.

Although the Christian tradition has been predominantly dualistic, many Christians endorse a monistic view of immortality. This is the second of the two positive views on immortality just mentioned. On this view, either there is no soul or else the soul is not the sort of thing that can properly be said to "live" apart from the body. Either way, then, the afterlife can never be a disembodied life. Our hope for an afterlife is nothing other than a hope for our own resurrection—for the reconstitution or re-creation or miraculous resuscitation of our present earthly bodies (albeit, again, in an improved or glorified form).

We begin this section with a selection from Plato defending the view that the soul can exist apart from the body. Although Plato has many arguments for this thesis, one of the most famous is found in the *Phaedo,* it is included in our first reading. One section is worth quoting in full:

> When the soul employs the body in any inquiry, and makes use of sight, or hearing, or any other sense—for inquiry with the body must signify inquiry with the senses—she is dragged away by the body to the things which are impermanent, changing, and the soul wanders about blindly, and becomes confused and dizzy, like a drunken man, from dealing with things that are changing.... [But] when the soul investigates any question by herself, she goes away to the pure and eternal, and immortal and unchangeable, to which she is intrinsically related, and so she comes to be ever with it, as soon as she is by herself, and can be so; and then she rests from her wandering and dwells with it unchangingly, for she is related to what is unchanging. And is not this state of the soul called wisdom?★

The argument may be reconstructed as follows:

1. If a person's soul while in the body is capable of any activity independently of the body, then it can perform that activity in separation from the body (i.e., after death, surviving death).

2. In pure or metaphysical thinking (i.e., in contemplating the forms and their interrelationships), a person's soul performs an activity independently of the body. No observation is necessary for this investigation.

3. Therefore, a person's soul can engage in pure or metaphysical thinking in separation from the body. That is, it can and must survive death.

This is a positive argument for the existence of the soul. Unfortunately, the second premise is dubious, for it could be the case that the mind's activity is dependent on the brain. And it is precisely this latter claim that is defended by Bertrand Russell in the second reading in this section. According to Russell, there is no reason at all to believe in the immortality of the soul because all of the best empirical evidence points to the conclusion that a person's mental life comes to an end with the death of her brain.

★*Phaedo,* 79 c–d, trans. Louis Pojman.

In our third reading, John Hick rejects the Platonic notion of an immortal and separable soul and urges instead a view according to which life after death requires the resurrection of the body, where resurrection is conceived as "God's re-creation or reconstitution of the human psychophysical individual." He briefly considers the question of what it would take to re-create a human body—that is, the question of what criteria have to be satisfied for a new body created at "resurrection time" to be the *same* body as the one that died—and then moves on to a discussion of what evidence we might have for believing in such an afterlife.

In our fourth reading, Jeffrey Olen devotes considerably more attention to questions about criteria of identity. He examines two views on the matter: the "memory criterion" and the "bodily criterion." According to the memory criterion, person A is the same person as person B if and only if A and B have the right sort of overlap in their memories and the right sort of continuity between their memories and other psychological states. For example, if B exists later than A, then B should remember a lot of what A remembers; furthermore, B should remember at least some of what A takes to be "present experience." There should also be some continuity among their goals, beliefs, desires, and other mental states. (This isn't to deny that goals, beliefs, and desires change over time. But the idea is that if B exists, say, a mere ten seconds later than A, and if B has beliefs, desires, goals, and memories virtually *none* of which overlap with A's, then B just isn't the same person as A.) Olen favors the psychological continuity criterion, and he argues furthermore in favor of the possibility of life after death. On his view, the mind is like computer software: Just as the same software can be transferred to different hardware, so too a mind can be transferred to a different brain (or other supporting medium). But to say that the mind can be transferred to a different medium is just to say that the mind can *change bodies*; and if it can change bodies, he contends, then the mind can survive the death of the body.

Finally, we close this section with an essay on the Hindu view of life, death, and reincarnation by Prasannatma Das.

VI.1

Immortality of the Soul

PLATO

Plato (c. 427–347 BCE) lived in Athens, was a student of Socrates, and is almost universally recognized as one of the most important philosophers who ever lived. Indeed, it

Reprinted from *Alcibiades I* and the *Phaedo*, translated by William Jowett (New York: Charles Scribner's Sons, 1889).

has been remarked that the entire history of Western philosophy is but a footnote to Plato. The excerpts that comprise the following selection concern Plato's views about the soul. According to Plato, human beings are composed of two substances: body and soul. Of these, the true self is the soul, which lives on after the death of the body. All of Plato's writings are in the form of dialogues. In the first dialogue (from Alcibiades I) Socrates argues with Alcibiades about the true self. The second dialogue (from the Phaedo) takes place in prison, where Socrates awaits his execution. He is offered a way of escape but rejects it, arguing that it would be immoral to flee such a fate at this time and that he is certain of a better life after death.

FROM ALCIBIADES I

Soc. And is self-knowledge an easy thing, and was he to be lightly esteemed who inscribed the text on the temple at Delphi? Or is self-knowledge a difficult thing, which few are able to attain?

Al. At times, I fancy, Socrates, that anybody can know himself; at other times, the task appears to be very difficult.

Soc. But whether easy or difficult, Alcibiades, still there is no other way; knowing what we are, we shall know how to take care of ourselves, and if we are ignorant we shall not know.

Al. That is true.

Soc. Well, then, let us see in what way the self-existent can be discovered by us; that will give us a chance to discover our own existence, which without that we can never know.

Al. You say truly.

Soc. Come, now, I beseech you, tell me with whom you are conversing?—with whom but with me?

Al. Yes.

Soc. As I am with you?

Al. Yes.

Soc. That is to say, I, Socrates, am talking?

Al. Yes.

Soc. And I in talking use words?

Al. Certainly.

Soc. And talking and using words are, as you would say, the same?

Al. Very true.

Soc. And the user is not the same as the thing which he uses?

Al. What do you mean?

Soc. I will explain: the shoemaker, for example, uses a square tool, and a circular tool, and other tools for cutting?

Al. Yes.

Soc. But the tool is not the same as the cutter and user of the tool?

Al. Of course not.

Soc. And in the same way the instrument of the harper is to be distinguished from the harper himself?

Al. He is.

Soc. Now the question which I asked was whether you conceive the user to be always different from that which he uses?

Al. I do.

Soc. Then what shall we say of the shoemaker? Does he cut with his tools only or with his hands?

Al. With his hands as well.

Soc. He uses his hands too?

Al. Yes.

Soc. And does he use his eyes in cutting leather?

Al. He does.

Soc. And we admit that the user is not the same with the things which he uses?

Al. Yes.

Soc. Then the shoemaker and the harper are to be distinguished from the hands and feet which they use?

Al. That is clear.

Soc. And does not a man use the whole body?

Al. Certainly.

Soc. And that which uses is different from that which is used?

Al. True.

Soc. Then a man is not the same as his own body?

Al. That is the inference.

Soc. What is he, then?

Al. I cannot say.

Soc. Nay, you can say that he is the user of the body.

Al. Yes.

Soc. And the user of the body is the soul?

Al. Yes, the soul.

Soc. And the soul rules?

Al. Yes.

Soc. Let me make an assertion which will, I think, be universally admitted.

Al. What is that?

Soc. That man is one of three things.

Al. What are they?

Soc. Soul, body, or the union of the two.

Al. Certainly.

Soc. But did we not say that the actual ruling principle of the body is man?

Al. Yes, we did.

Soc. And does the body rule over itself?

Al. Certainly not.

Soc. It is subject, as we were saying?

Al. Yes.

Soc. Then that is not what we are seeking?

Al. It would seem not.

Soc. But may we say that the union of the two rules over the body, and consequently that this is man?

Al. Very likely.

Soc. The most unlikely of all things: for if one of the members is subject, the two united cannot possibly rule.

Al. True.

Soc. But since neither the body, nor the union of the two, is man, either man has no real existence, or the soul is man?

Al. Just so.

Soc. Would you have a more precise proof that the soul is man?

Al. No; I think that the proof is sufficient.

Soc. If the proof, although not quite precise, is fair, that is enough for us; more precise proof will be supplied when we have discovered that which we were led to omit, from a fear that the inquiry would be too much protracted.

Al. What was that?

Soc. What I meant, when I said that absolute existence must be first considered; but now, instead of absolute existence, we have been considering the nature of individual existence, and that may be sufficient; for surely there is nothing belonging to us which has more absolute existence than the soul?

Al. There is nothing.

Soc. Then we may truly conceive that you and I are conversing with one another, soul to soul?

Al. Very true.

Soc. And that is just what I was saying—that I, Socrates, am not arguing or talking with the face of Alcibiades, but with the real Alcibiades; and that is with his soul.

Al. True ....

FROM THE PHAEDO

SOCRATES: What again shall we say of the actual acquirement of knowledge?—is the body, if invited to share in the inquiry, a hinderer or a helper? I mean to say, have sight and hearing any truth in them? Are they not, as the poets are always telling us, inaccurate witnesses? and yet, if even they are inaccurate and indistinct, what is to be said of the other senses?—for you will allow that they are the best of them?

Certainly, he replied.

Then when does the soul attain truth?—for in attempting to consider anything in company with the body she is obviously deceived.

Yes, that is true.

Then must not existence be revealed to her in thought, if at all?

Yes.

And thought is best when the mind is gathered into herself and none of these things trouble her— neither sounds nor sights nor pain nor any pleasure,— when she has as little as possible to do with the body, and has no bodily sense or feeling, but is aspiring after being?

That is true.

And in this the philosopher dishonors the body; his soul runs away from the body and desires to be alone and by herself?

That is true.

Well, but there is another thing, Simmias: Is there or is there not an absolute justice?

Assuredly there is.

And an absolute beauty and absolute good?

Of course.

But did you ever behold any of them with your eyes?

Certainly not.

Or did you ever reach them with any other bodily sense? (and I speak not of these alone, but of absolute greatness, and health, and strength, and of the essence or true nature of everything). Has the reality of them ever been perceived by you through the bodily organs? or rather, is not the nearest approach to the knowledge of their several natures made by him who so orders his intellectual vision as to have the most exact conception of the essence of that which he considers?

Certainly.

And he attains to the knowledge of them in their highest purity who goes to each of them with the mind alone, not allowing when in the act of thought the intrusion or introduction of sight or any other sense in the company of reason, but with the very light of the mind in her clearness penetrates into the very light of truth in each; he has got rid, as far as he can, of eyes and ears and of the whole body, which he conceives of only as a disturbing element, hindering the soul from the acquisition of knowledge when in company with her—is not this the sort of man who, if ever man did, is likely to attain the knowledge of existence?

There is admirable truth in that, Socrates, replied Simmias.

And when they consider all this, must not true philosophers make a reflection, of which they will speak to one another in such words as these: We have found, they will say, a path of specula- tion which seems to bring us and the argument to the conclusion, that while we are in the body, and while the soul is mingled with this mass of evil our desire will not be satisfied, and our desire is of the truth. For the body is a source of endless trouble to us by reason of the mere requirement of food; and also is liable to diseases which over- take and impede us in the search after truth: and by filling us so full of loves, and lusts, and fears, and fancies, and idols, and every sort of folly, prevents our ever having, as people say, so much as a thought. From whence come wars, and fightings, and factions? whence but from the body and the lusts of the body? For wars are occasioned by the love of money, and money has to be acquired for the sake and in the service of the body; and in consequence of all these things the time which ought to be given to philosophy is lost. Moreover, if there is time and an inclination toward philosophy, yet the body introduces a turmoil and confusion and fear into the course of speculation, and hinders us from seeing the truth; and all experience shows that if we would have pure knowledge of anything we must be quit of the body, and the soul in herself must behold all things in themselves: then I suppose that we shall attain that which we desire, and of which we say that we are lovers, and that is wisdom; not while we live, but after death, as the argument shows; for if while in company with the body, the soul cannot have pure knowledge, one of two things seems to follow—either knowledge is not to be attained at all, or, if at all, after death. For then, and not till then, the soul will be in herself alone and without the body. In this present life, I reckon that we make the nearest approach to knowledge when we have the least possible concern or interest in the body, and are not saturated with the bodily nature, but remain pure until the hour when God himself is pleased to release us. And then the foolishness of the body will be cleared away and we shall be pure and hold converse with other pure souls, and know of ourselves the clear light everywhere; and this is surely the light of truth. For no impure thing is allowed to approach the pure. These are the sort of words, Simmias, which the true lovers of wisdom cannot help saying to one another, and thinking. You will agree with me in that?

Certainly, Socrates.

But if this is true, O my friend, then there is great hope that, going whither I go, I shall there be satisfied with that which has been the chief concern of you and me in our past lives. And now that the hour of departure is appointed to me, this is the hope with which I depart, and not I only, but every man who believes that he has his mind purified.

Certainly, replied Simmias.

And what is purification but the separation of the soul from the body, as I was saying before; the habit of the soul gathering and collecting herself into herself, out of all the courses of the body; the dwelling in her own place alone, as in another life, so also in this, as far as she can; the release of the soul from the chains of the body?

Very true, he said.

And what is that which is termed death, but this very separation and release of the soul from the body?

To be sure, he said.

And the true philosophers, and they only, study and are eager to release the soul. Is not the separation and release of the soul from the body their especial study?

That is true.

And as I was saying at first, there would be a ridiculous contradiction in men studying to live as nearly as they can in a state of death, and yet repining when death comes.

Certainly.

Then Simmias, as the true philosophers are ever studying death, to them, of all men, death is the least terrible. Look at the matter in this way: how inconsistent of them to have been always enemies of the body, and wanting to have the soul alone, and when this is granted to them, to be trembling and repining; instead of rejoicing at their departing to that place where, when they arrive, they hope to gain that which in life they loved (and this was wisdom), and at the same time to be rid of the company of their enemy. Many a man has been willing to go to the world below in the hope of seeing there an earthly love, or wife, or son, and conversing with them. And will he who is a true lover of wisdom, and is persuaded in like manner that only in the world below he can worthily enjoy her, still repine at death? Will he not depart with joy? Surely, he will, my friend, if he be a true philosopher. For he will have a firm conviction that there only, and nowhere else, he can find wisdom in her purity. And if this be true, he would be very absurd, as I was saying, if he were to fear death.

SOCRATES: And were we not saying long ago that the soul when using the body as an instrument of perception, that is to say, when using the sense of sight or hearing or some other sense (for the meaning of perceiving through the body is perceiving through the senses),—were we not saying that the soul too is then dragged by the body into the region of the changeable, and wanders and is confused; the world spins round her, and she is like a drunkard when under their influence?

Very true.

But when returning into herself she reflects; then she passes into the realm of purity, and eternity, and immortality, and unchangeableness, which are her kindred, and with them she ever lives, when she is by herself and is not let or hindered; then she ceases from her erring ways, and being in communion with the unchanging is unchanging. And this state of the soul is called wisdom?

That is well and truly said, Socrates, he replied.

And to which class is the soul more nearly alike and akin, as far as may be inferred from this argument, as well as from the preceding one?

I think, Socrates, that, in the opinion of every one who follows the argument, the soul will be infinitely more like the unchangeable,—even the most stupid person will not deny that.

And the body is more like the changing?

Yes.

Yet once more consider the matter in this light: When the soul and the body are united, then nature orders the soul to rule and govern, and the body to obey and serve. Now which of these two functions is akin to the divine? and which to the mortal? Does not the divine appear to you to be that which naturally orders and rules, and the mortal that which is subject and servant?

True.

And which does the soul resemble?

The soul resembles the divine, and the body the mortal,—there can be no doubt of that, Socrates.

VI.2

The Finality of Death

BERTRAND RUSSELL

Bertrand Russell (1872–1970), once a student and tutor at Cambridge University, was one of the most significant philosophers and social critics of the twentieth century. In this short essay, Russell outlines some of the major objections to the idea of life after death. He argues that it is not reasonable to believe that our personality and memories will survive the destruction of our bodies. He claims that the inclination to believe in immortality comes form emotional factors, notably the fear of death.

Before we can profitably discuss whether we shall continue to exist after death, it is well to be clear as to the sense in which a man is the same person as he was yesterday. Philosophers used to think that there were definite substances, the soul and the body, that each lasted on from day to day, that a soul, once created, continued to exist throughout all future time, whereas a body ceased temporarily from death till the resurrection of the body.

The part of this doctrine which concerns the present life is pretty certainly false. The matter of the body is continually changing by processes of nutriment and wastage. Even if it were not, atoms in physics are no longer supposed to have continuous existence; there is no sense in saying: this is the same atom as the one that existed a few minutes ago. The continuity of a human body is a matter of appearance and behavior, not of substance.

The same thing applies to the mind. We think and feel and act, but there is not, in addition to thoughts and feelings and actions, a bare entity, the mind or the soul, which does or suffers these occurrences. The mental continuity of a person is a continuity of habit and memory: there was yesterday one person whose feelings I can remember, and that person I regard as myself of yesterday; but, in fact, myself of yesterday was only certain mental occurrences which are now remembered and are regarded as part of the person who now recollects them. All that constitutes a person is a series of experiences connected by memory and by certain similarities of the sort we call habit.

If, therefore, we are to believe that a person survives death, we must believe that the memories and habits which constitute the person will continue to be exhibited in a new set of occurrences.

No one can prove that this will not happen. But it is easy to see that it is very unlikely. Our memories and habits are bound up with the structure of the brain, in much the same way in which a river is connected with the riverbed. The water in the river is always changing, but it keeps to the same course because previous rains have worn a channel. In like manner, previous events have worn a channel in the brain, and our thoughts flow along this channel. This is the cause of memory and mental habits. But the brain, as a structure, is dissolved at death, and memory therefore may be expected to be also dissolved. There is no more reason to think otherwise than to expect a river to persist in its old course after an earthquake has raised a mountain where a valley used to be.

All memory, and therefore (one may say) all minds, depend upon a property which is very noticeable in certain kinds of material structures but exists little if at all in other kinds. This is the property of forming habits as a result of frequent similar occurrences. For example: a bright light makes the pupils of the eyes contract; and if you repeatedly flash a light in a man's eyes and beat a gong at the same time, the gong alone will, in the end, cause his pupils to contract. This is a fact about the brain and nervous system—that is to say, about a certain material structure. It will be found that exactly similar facts explain our response to language and our use of it, our memories and the emotions they arouse, our moral or immoral habits of behavior, and indeed everything that constitutes our mental personality, except the part determined by heredity. The part determined by heredity is handed on to our posterity but cannot, in the individual, survive the disintegration of the body. Thus both the hereditary and the acquired parts of a personality are, so far as our experience goes, bound up with the characteristics of certain bodily structures. We all know that memory may be obliterated by an injury to the brain, that a virtuous person may be rendered vicious by encephalitis lethargica, and, that a clever child can be turned into an idiot by lack of iodine. In view of such familiar facts, it seems scarcely probable that the mind survives the total destruction of brain structure which occurs at death.

It is not rational arguments but emotions that cause belief in a future life.

The most important of these emotions is fear of death, which is instinctive and biologically useful. If we genuinely and wholeheartedly believed in the future life, we should cease completely to fear death. The effects would be curious, and probably such as most of us would deplore. But our human and subhuman ancestors have fought and exterminated their enemies throughout many geological ages and have profited by courage; it is therefore an advantage to the victors in the struggle for life to be able, on occasion, to overcome the natural fear of death. Among animals and savages, instinctive pugnacity suffices for this purpose; but at a certain stage of development, as the Mohammedans first proved, belief in Paradise has considerable military value as reinforcing natural pugnacity. We should therefore admit that militarists are wise in encouraging the belief in immortality, always supposing that this belief does not become so profound as to produce indifference to the affairs of the world.

Another emotion which encourages the belief in survival is admiration of the excellence of man. As the Bishop of Birmingham says, "His mind is a far finer instrument than anything that had appeared earlier—he knows right and wrong. He can build Westminster Abbey. He can make an airplane. He can calculate the distance of the sun…. Shall, then, man at death perish utterly? Does that incomparable instrument, his mind, vanish when life ceases?"

The Bishop proceeds to argue that "the universe has been shaped and is governed by an intelligent purpose," and that it would have been unintelligent, having made man, to let him perish.

To this argument there are many answers. In the first place, it has been found, in the scientific investigation of nature, that the intrusion of moral or aesthetic values has always been an obstacle to discovery. It used to be thought that the heavenly bodies must move in circles because the circle is the most perfect curve, that species must be immutable because God would only create what was perfect and what therefore stood in no need of improvement, that it was useless to combat epidemics except by repentance because they were sent as a punishment for sin, and so on. It has been found, however, that, so far as we can discover, nature is indifferent to our values and can only be understood by ignoring our notions of good and bad. The Universe may have a purpose, but nothing that we know suggests that, if so, this purpose has any similarity to ours.

Nor is there in this anything surprising. Dr. Barnes tells us that man "knows right and wrong." But, in fact, as anthropology shows, men's views of right and wrong have varied to such an extent that no single item has been permanent. We cannot say, therefore, that man knows right and wrong, but only that some men do. Which men? Nietzsche argued in favor of an ethic profoundly different from Christ's, and some powerful governments have accepted his teaching. If knowledge of right and wrong is to be an argument for immortality, we must first settle whether to believe Christ or Nietzsche, and then argue that Christians are immortal, but Hitler and Mussolini are not, or vice versa. The decision will obviously be made on the battlefield, not in the study. Those who have the best poison gas will have the ethic of the future and will therefore be the immortal ones.

Our feelings and beliefs on the subject of good and evil are, like everything else about us, natural facts, developed in the struggle for existence and not having any divine or supernatural origin. In one of Aesop's fables, a lion is shown pictures of huntsmen catching lions and remarks that, if he had painted them, they would have shown lions catching huntsmen. Man, says Dr. Barnes, is a fine fellow because he can make airplanes. A little while ago there was a popular song about the cleverness of flies in walking upside down on the ceiling, with the chorus: "Could Lloyd George do it? Could Mr. Baldwin do it? Could Ramsay Mac do it? Why, no." On this basis a very telling argument could be constructed by a theologically-minded fly, which no doubt the other flies would find most convincing.

Moreover, it is only when we think abstractly that we have such a high opinion of man. Of men in the concrete, most of us think the vast majority very bad. Civilized states spend more than half their revenue on killing each other's citizens. Consider the long history of the activities inspired by moral fervor: human sacrifices, persecutions of heretics, witch-hunts, pogroms leading up to wholesale extermination by poison gases, which one at least of Dr. Barnes's episcopal colleagues must be supposed to favor, since he holds pacifism to be un-Christian. Are these abominations, and the ethical doctrines by which they are prompted, really evidence of an intelligent Creator? And can we really wish that the men who practiced them should live forever? The world in which we live can be understood as a result of muddle and accident; but if it is the outcome of deliberate purpose, the purpose must have been that of a fiend. For my part, I find accident a less painful and more plausible hypothesis.

VI.3

Immortality and Resurrection

JOHN HICK

A short biographical sketch of John Hick precedes selection IV.C.2. In the present article, Hick examines the Platonic notion of the immortality of the soul and argues that it is filled with problems. In its place he argues for the New Testament view of the re-creation of the psychophysical person, a holistic person who is body–soul in one. He then offers a thought experiment involving "John Smith" reappearances to show that re-creation is conceivable and worthy of rational belief. In the last part of this essay, Hick considers whether parapsychology can provide evidence for our survival of death.

THE IMMORTALITY OF THE SOUL

Some kind of distinction between physical body and immaterial or semimaterial soul seems to be as old as human culture; the existence of such a distinction is indicated by the manner of burial of the earliest human skeletons yet discovered. Anthropologists offer various conjectures about the origin of the distinction: perhaps it was first suggested by memories of dead persons, by dreams of them, by the sight of reflections of oneself in water and on other bright surfaces, or by meditation upon the significance of religious rites which grew up spontaneously in face of the fact of death.

It was Plato (428/7–348/7 B.C.), the philosopher who has most deeply and lastingly influenced western culture, who systematically developed the bodymind dichotomy and first attempted to prove the immortality of the soul.[1]

Plato argues that although the body belongs to the sensible world[2] and shares its changing and impermanent nature, the intellect is related to the unchanging realities of which we are aware when we think not of particular good things but of

Goodness itself, not of specific just acts but of Justice itself, and of the other "universals" or eternal Ideas by participation in which physical things and events have their own specific characteristics. Being related to this higher and abiding realm rather than to the evanescent world of sense, the soul is immortal. Hence, one who devotes one's life to the contemplation of eternal realities rather than to the gratification of the fleeting desires of the body will find at death that whereas the body turns to dust, one's soul gravitates to the realm of the unchanging, there to live forever. Plato painted an awe-inspiring picture, of haunting beauty and persuasiveness, which has moved and elevated the minds of men and women in many different centuries and lands. Nevertheless, it is not today (as it was during the first centuries of the Christian era) the common philosophy of the West; and a demonstration of immortality which presupposes Plato's metaphysical system cannot claim to constitute a proof for a twentieth-century person.

Plato used the further argument that the only things that can suffer destruction are those which are composite, since to destroy something means to disintegrate it into its constituent parts. All material

John Hick, *Philosophy of Religion*, 4th ed., copyright 1990, pp. 122–32. Reprinted by permission of Pearson Education, Inc., Upper Saddle River, N.J. Footnotes edited.

bodies are composite; the soul, however, is simple and therefore imperishable. This argument was adopted by Aquinas and became standard in Roman Catholic theology, as in the following passage from the Catholic philosopher Jacques Maritain:

> A spiritual soul cannot be corrupted, since it possesses no matter; it cannot be disintegrated, since it has no substantial parts; it cannot lose its individual unity, since it is self-subsisting, nor its internal energy, since it contains within itself all the sources of its energies. The human soul cannot die. Once it exists, it cannot disappear; it will necessarily exist for ever, endure without end. Thus, philosophic reason, put to work by a great metaphysician like Thomas Aquinas, is able to prove the immortality of the human soul in a demonstrative manner.[3]

This type of reasoning has been criticized on several grounds. Kant pointed out that although it is true that a simple substance cannot disintegrate, consciousness may nevertheless cease to exist through the diminution of its intensity to zero.[4] Modern psychology has also questioned the basic premise that the mind is a simple entity. It seems instead to be a structure of only relative unity, normally fairly stable and tightly integrated but capable under stress of various degrees of division and dissolution. This comment from psychology makes it clear that the assumption that the soul is a simple substance is not an empirical observation but a metaphysical theory. As such, it cannot provide the basis for a general proof of immortality.

The body–soul distinction, first formulated as a philosophical doctrine in ancient Greece, was baptized into Christianity, ran through the medieval period, and entered the modern world with the public status of a self-evident truth when it was redefined in the seventeenth century by Descartes. Since World War II, however, the Cartesian mind–matter dualism, having been taken for granted for many centuries, has been strongly criticized.[5] It is argued that the words that describe mental characteristics and operations—such as "intelligent," "thoughtful," "carefree," "happy," "calculating," and the like—apply in practice to types of human behavior and to behavioral dispositions. They refer to the empirical individual, the observable human being who is born and grows and acts and feels and dies, and not to the shadowy proceedings of a mysterious "ghost in the machine." An individual is thus very much what he or she appears to be—a creature of flesh and blood, who behaves and is capable of behaving in a characteristic range of ways—rather than a nonphysical soul incomprehensibly interacting with a physical body.

As a result of this development, much mid-twentieth-century philosophy has come to see the human being as in the biblical writings, not as an eternal soul temporarily attached to a mortal body, but as a form of finite, mortal, psychophysical life. Thus, the Old Testament scholar J. Pedersen said of the Hebrews that for them "the body is the soul in its outward form."[6] This way of thinking has led to quite a different conception of death from that found in Plato and the Neoplatonic strand in European thought.

THE RE-CREATION OF THE PSYCHOPHYSICAL PERSON

Only toward the end of the Old Testament period did afterlife beliefs come to have any real importance within Judaism. Previously, Hebrew religious insight had focused so fully upon God's covenant with the nation, as an organism that continued through the centuries while successive generations lived and died, that the thought of a divine purpose for the individual, a purpose transcending this present life, developed only when the breakdown of the nation as a political entity threw into prominence the individual and the question of personal destiny.

When a positive conviction arose of God's purpose holding each man and woman in being beyond the crisis of death, this conviction took the non-Platonic form of belief in the resurrection of the body. The religious difference between the Platonic belief in the immortality of the soul, and the Judaic Christian belief in resurrection is that the latter postulates a special divine act of re-creation. This produces a sense of utter dependence upon God in the hour of death, a feeling that is in accordance with the biblical understanding of the human being as having been formed out of "the dust of the earth,"[7] a product (as we say today) of the slow evolution of life from its lowly beginnings in the primeval slime. Hence, in the Jewish and Christian conception, death is something real and fearful. It is not thought to be like walking from one room to another, or like taking off an old coat and putting on a new one. It means sheer unqualified extinction—passing out from the lighted circle of life into "death's dateless night." Only through the sovereign creative love of God can there be a new existence beyond the grave.

What does "the resurrection of the dead" mean? Saint Paul's discussion provides the basic Christian answer to this question.[8] His conception of the general resurrection (distinguished from the unique resurrection of Jesus) has nothing to do with the resuscitation of corpses in a cemetery. It concerns God's re-creation or reconstitution of the human psychophysical individual, not as the organism that has died but as a *soma pneumatikon*, a "spiritual body," inhabiting a spiritual world as the physical body inhabits our present material world.

A major problem confronting any such doctrine is that of providing criteria of personal identity to link the earthly life and the resurrection life. Paul does not specifically consider this question, but one may perhaps develop his thought along lines such as the following.[9]

Suppose, first, that someone—John Smith— living in the United States were suddenly and inexplicably to disappear before the eyes of his friends, and that at the same moment an exact replica of him were inexplicably to appear in India. The person who appears in India is exactly similar in both physical and mental characteristics to the person who disappeared in America. There is continuity of memory, complete similarity of bodily features including fingerprints, hair and eye coloration, and stomach contents, and also of beliefs, habits, emotions, and mental dispositions. Further,

the "John Smith" replica thinks of himself as being the John Smith who disappeared in the United States. After all possible tests have been made and have proved positive, the factors leading his friends to accept "John Smith" as John Smith would surely prevail and would cause them to overlook even his mysterious transference from one continent to another, rather than treat "John Smith," with all of John Smith's memories and other characteristics, as someone other than John Smith.

Suppose, second, that our John Smith, instead of inexplicably disappearing, dies, but that at the moment of his death a "John Smith" replica, again complete with memories and all other characteristics, appears in India. Even with the corpse on our hands, we would, I think, still have to accept this "John Smith" as the John Smith who had died. We would just have to say that he had been miraculously re-created in another place.

Now suppose, third, that on John Smith's death the "John Smith" replica appears, not in India, but as a resurrection replica in a different world altogether, a resurrection world inhabited only by resurrected persons. This world occupies its own space distinct from that with which we are now familiar. That is to say, an object in the resurrection world is not situated at any distance or in any direction from the objects in our present world, although each object in either world is spatially related to every other object in the same world.

This supposition provides a model by which one may begin to conceive of the divine re-creation of the embodied human personality. In this model, the element of the strange and mysterious has been reduced to a minimum by following the view of some of the early Church Fathers that the resurrection body has the same shape as the physical body,[10] and ignoring Paul's own hint that it may be as unlike the physical body as a full grain of wheat differs from the wheat seed.[11]

What is the basis for this Judaic-Christian belief in the divine re-creation or reconstitution of the human personality after death? There is, of course, an argument from authority, in that life after death is taught throughout the New Testament (although very rarely in the Old Testament). More basically, though, belief in the resurrection arises as a corollary of faith in the sovereign purpose of God, which is not restricted by death and which holds us in being beyond our natural mortality. In a similar vein it is argued that if it be the divine plan to create finite persons to exist in fellowship with God, then it contradicts both that intention and God's love for the human creatures if God allows men and women to pass out of existence when the divine purpose for them still remains largely unfulfilled.

It is this promised fulfillment of God's purpose for the individual, in which the full possibilities of human nature will be realized, that constitutes the "heaven" symbolized in the New Testament as a joyous banquet in which all and sundry rejoice together. As we saw when discussing the problem of evil, it is questionable whether any theodicy can succeed without drawing into itself this eschatological[12] faith in an eternal, and therefore infinite, good which thus outweighs all the pains and sorrows that have been endured on the way to it.

Balancing the idea of heaven in Christian tradition is the idea of hell. This, too, is relevant to the problem of theodicy. Just as the reconciling of God's goodness and power with the fact of evil requires that out of the travail of history there shall come in the end an eternal good for humanity, so likewise it would seem to preclude eternal human misery. The only kind of evil that is finally incompatible with God's unlimited power and love would be utterly pointless and wasted suffering, pain which is never redeemed and worked into the fulfilling of God's good purpose. Unending torment would constitute precisely such suffering; for being eternal, it could never lead to a good end beyond itself. Thus, hell as conceived by its enthusiasts, such as Augustine or Calvin, is a major part of the problem of evil! If hell is constructed as eternal torment, the theological motive behind the idea is directly at variance with the urge to seek a theodicy. However, it is by no means clear that the doctrine of eternal punishment can claim a secure New Testament basis.[13] If, on the other hand, "hell" means a continuation of the purgatorial suffering often experienced in this life, and leading eventually to the high good of heaven, it no longer stands in conflict with the needs of theodicy. Again, the idea of hell may be deliteralized and valued as a powerful and pregnant symbol of the grave responsibility inherent in our human freedom in relation to our Maker.

DOES PARAPSYCHOLOGY HELP?

The spiritualist movement claims that life after death has been proved by cases of communication between the living and the "dead." During the closing quarter of the nineteenth century and the decades of the present century this claim has been made the subject of careful and prolonged study by a number of responsible and competent persons.[14] This work, which may be approximately dated from the founding in London of the Society for Psychical Research in 1882, is known either by the name adopted by that society or, more commonly today, as parapsychology.

Approaching the subject from the standpoint of our interest in this chapter, we may initially divide the phenomena studied by the parapsychologist into two groups. There are those that involve no reference to the idea of a life after death, chief among these being psychokinesis (PK) and extrasensory perception (ESP) in its various forms (such as telepathy, clairvoyance, and precognition). There are also those phenomena that raise the question of personal survival after death, such as the apparitions and other sensory manifestations of dead persons and the "spirit messages" received through mediums. This division is, however, only of preliminary use, for ESP has emerged as a clue to the understanding of much that occurs in the second group. We shall begin with a brief outline of the reasons that have induced the majority of workers in this field to be willing to postulate so strange an occurrence as telepathy.

Telepathy is a name for the mysterious fact that sometimes a thought in the mind of one person apparently causes a similar or associated thought to occur to someone else when there are no normal means of communication between them, and under circumstances such that mere coincidence seems to be excluded.

For example, one person may draw a series of pictures or diagrams on paper and somehow transmit an impression of these to someone else in another room who then draws recognizable reproductions of them. This might well be a coincidence in the case of a single successful reproduction; but can a series consist entirely of coincidences?

Experiments have been devised to measure the probability of chance coincidence in supposed cases of telepathy. In the simplest of these, cards printed in turn with five different symbols are used. A pack of fifty, consisting of ten bearing each symbol, is then thoroughly shuffled, and the sender concentrates on the cards one at a time while the receiver (who of course can see neither sender nor cards) tries to write down the correct order of symbols. This procedure is repeated, with constant reshuffling, hundreds or thousands of times. Since there are only five different symbols, a random guess would stand one chance in five of being correct. Consequently, on the assumption that only "chance" is operating, the receiver should be right in about 20 percent of his or her tries and wrong in about 80 percent; the longer the series, the closer should be the approach to this proportion. However, good telepathic subjects are right in a larger number of cases than can be reconciled with random guessing. The deviation from chance expectation can be converted mathematically into "odds against chance" (increasing as the proportion of hits is maintained over a longer and longer series of tries). In this way, odds of over a million to one have been recorded. J. B. Rhine (Duke University) has reported results showing "antichance" values ranging from seven (which equals odds against chance of 100,000 to one) to eighty-two (which converts the odds against chance to billions).[15] The work of both these researchers has been criticized, and a complex controversy surrounds them; on the other hand,

other researchers have recorded similar results.[16] In the light of these reports, it is difficult to deny that some positive factor, and not merely "chance," is operating. "Telepathy" is simply a name for this unknown positive factor.

How does telepathy operate? Only negative conclusions seem to be justified to date. It can, for example, be said with reasonable certainty that telepathy does not consist of any kind of physical radiation analogous to radio waves. First, telepathy is not delayed or weakened in proportion to distance, as are all known forms of radiation; second, there is no organ in the brain or elsewhere that can plausibly be regarded as its sending or receiving center. Telepathy appears to be a purely mental occurrence.

It is not, however, a matter of transferring or transporting a thought out of one mind into another—if, indeed, such an idea makes sense at all. The telepathized thought does not leave the sender's consciousness in order to enter that of the receiver. What happens would be better described by saying that the sender's thought gives rise to a mental "echo" in the mind of the receiver. This "echo" occurs at the unconscious level, and consequently the version of it that rises into the receiver's consciousness may be only fragmentary and may be distorted or symbolized in various ways, as in dreams.

According to one theory that has been tentatively suggested to explain telepathy, our minds are separate and mutually insulated only at the conscious (and preconscious) level, but at the deepest level of the unconscious we are constantly influencing one another, and it is at this level that telepathy takes place.[17]

How is a telepathized thought directed to one particular receiver among so many? Apparently the thoughts are directed by some link of emotion or common interest. For example, two friends are sometimes telepathically aware of any grave crisis or shock experienced by the other, even though they are at opposite ends of the earth.

We shall turn now to the other branch of parapsychology, which has more obvious bearing upon our subject. The *Proceedings of the Society for Psychical*

Research contain a large number of carefully recorded and apparently satisfactorily attested cases of the appearance of the figure of someone who has recently died to living people (in rare instances to more than one at a time) who were, in many cases, at a distance and unaware of the death. The S.P.R. reports also establish beyond reasonable doubt that the minds that operate in the mediumistic trance, purporting to be spirits of the departed, sometimes give personal information that the medium could not have acquired by normal means, and at times even give information, later verified, that had not been known to any living person.[18]

On the other hand, physical happenings such as the "materializations" of spirit forms in a visible and tangible form, are much more doubtful. However, even if we discount the entire range of physical phenomena, it remains true that the best cases of trance utterance are impressive and puzzling, and taken at face value are indicative of survival and communication after death. If, through a medium, one talks with an intelligence that gives a coherent impression of being an intimately known friend who has died and who establishes identity by a wealth of private information and indefinable personal characteristics—as has occasionally happened—then we cannot dismiss without careful trial the theory that what is taking place is the return of a consciousness from the spirit world.

However, the advance of knowledge in the other branch of parapsychology, centering upon the study of extrasensory perception, has thrown unexpected light upon this apparent commerce with the departed, for it suggests that unconscious telepathic contact between the medium and his or her client is an important and possibly a sufficient explanatory factor. This was vividly illustrated by the experience of two women who decided to test the spirits by taking into their minds, over a period of weeks, the personality and atmosphere of an entirely imaginary character in an unpublished novel written by one of them. After thus filling their minds with the characteristics of this fictitious person, they went to a reputable medium, who proceeded to describe accurately their imaginary friend as a visitant from beyond the grave and to deliver appropriate messages from him.

An even more striking case is that of the "direct voice" medium (a medium in whose séances the voice of the communicating "spirit" is heard apparently speaking out of the air) who produced the spirit of one "Gordon Davis," who spoke in his own recognizable voice, displayed considerable knowledge about Gordon Davis, and remembered his death. This was extremely impressive until it was discovered that Gordon Davis was still alive; he was a real-estate agent and had been trying to sell a house at the time when the séance took place![19]

Such cases suggest that genuine mediums are simply persons of exceptional telepathic sensitiveness who unconsciously derive the "spirits" from their clients' minds.

In connection with "ghosts," in the sense of apparitions of the dead, it has been established that there can be "meaningful hallucinations," the source of which is almost certainly telepathic. To quote a classic and somewhat dramatic example: a woman sitting by a lake sees the figure of a man run toward the lake and throw himself in. A few days later a man commits suicide by throwing himself into this same lake. Presumably, the explanation of the vision is that the man's thought while he was contemplating suicide had been telepathically projected onto the scene via the woman's mind.[20]

In many of the cases recorded there is delayed action. The telepathically projected thought lingers in the recipient's unconscious mind until a suitable state of inattention to the outside world enables it to appear to the conscious mind in a dramatized form—for example, by a hallucinatory voice or vision—by means of the same mechanism that operates in dreams.

If phantoms of the living can be created by previously experienced thoughts and emotions of the person whom they represent, the parallel possibility arises that phantoms of the dead are caused by thoughts and emotions that were experienced by the person represented when he or she was alive. In other words, perhaps ghosts may be "psychic footprints," a kind of mental trace left behind by the dead but not involving the presence or even the continued existence of those whom they represent.

RESUSCITATION CASES

Yet another range of phenomena that have recently attracted considerable interest consists of reports of the experiences of people who have been resuscitated after having been declared dead.[21] The periods during which they were apparently dead vary from a few seconds to twenty minutes or even more. These reports include the following elements, though not usually all on the same occasion: an initial loud noise; a sensation as of being drawn through a dark tunnel-like space; emergence into a "world" of light and beauty; meeting with relatives and friends who had died; encounter with a "being of light" of immense moral or spiritual impressiveness, who is assumed by Christians to be Christ and by others to be an angel or a deity; an extremely vivid and almost instantaneous visual review of one's life; approach to a border, sensed to be the final division between this life and the next; and being sent or drawn back to the earthly body. Generally, those who have had this kind of experience are reluctant to speak about such hard-to-describe and hard-

to-believe phenomena, but characteristically their attitude toward death has changed and they now think of their own future death without fear or even with positive anticipation.

Prior to such visual and auditory sequences there is also often an "out-of-the-body" experience, a consciousness of floating above one's own body and seeing it lying in bed or on the ground or the operating table. There is a growing literature concerning such "out-of-the-body" experiences, whether at the time of death or during life.[22]

Whether or not the resuscitation cases give us reports of the experiences of people who have actually died, and thus provide information about a life to come, it is at present impossible to determine. Do these accounts describe the first phase of another life, or perhaps a transitional stage before the connection between mind and body is finally broken; or do they describe only the last flickers of dream activity before the brain finally loses oxygen? It is to be hoped that further research may find a way to settle this question.

All these considerations suggest the need for caution in assessing the findings of parapsychology.[23] However, this caution should lead to further investigations, not to a closing of the issues. In the meantime one should be careful not to confuse absence of knowledge with knowledge of absence.

NOTES

1. *Phaedo*.
2. The world known to us through our physical senses.
3. Jacques Maritain, *The Range of Reason* (London: Geoffrey Bles Ltd. and New York: Charles Scribner's Sons, 1953), p. 60.
4. Kant, *Critique of Pure Reason, Transcendental Dialectic*, "Refutation of Mendelssohn's Proof of the Permanence of the Soul."
5. Gilbert Ryle's *The Concept of Mind* (London: Hutchinson & Co., Ltd., 1949, and New York: Barnes & Noble Books, 1975) is a classic statement of this critique.

6. J. Pedersen, *Israel* (London: Oxford University Press, 1926), I, 170.
7. Genesis 2:7; Psalm 103:14.
8. I Corinthians 15.
9. The following paragraphs are adapted, with permission, from a section of my article, "Theology and Verification," published in *Theology Today* (April 1960) and reprinted in *The Existence of God* (New York: The Macmillan Company, 1964) and elsewhere. A fascinating recent argument for the personal identity of an original and his or her replica is offered by Derek Parfitt in *Reasons and Persons* (New York: Oxford University Press, 1985).

10. For example, Irenaeus, *Against Heresies*, Book II, Chap. 34, para. 1.

11. I Corinthians 15:37.

12. From the Greek *eschaton*, end.

13. The Greek word *aionios*, which is used in the New Testament and which is usually translated as "eternal" or "everlasting," can bear either this meaning or the more limited meaning of "for the aeon, or age."

14. The list of past presidents of the Society for Psychical Research includes the philosophers Henri Bergson, William James, Hans Driesch, Henry Sidgwick, F. C. S. Schiller, C. D. Broad, and H. H. Price; the psychologists William McDougall, Gardner Murphy, Franklin Prince, and R. H. Thouless; the physicists Sir William Crookes, Sir Oliver Lodge, Sir William Barrett, and Lord Rayleigh; and the classicist Gilbert Murray.

15. J. B. Rhine, *Extrasensory Perception* (Boston: Society for Psychical Research, 1935), Table XLIII, p. 162. See also Rhine, *New Frontiers of the Mind* (New York: Farrar and Rinehart, Inc., 1937) pp. 69f.

16. The most comprehensive up-to-date account of the evidence for ESP, together with competent discussions of its significance, is to be found in Benjamin Wolman, ed., *Handbook of Parapsychology* (New York: Van Nostrand, 1977). For the important Russian work see L. L. Vasiliev, *Experiments in Distant Influence* (previously *Experiments in Mental Suggestion*, 1963) (New York: E. O. Dutton, 1976).

17. Whateley Carington, *Telepathy* (London: Methuen, 1945), Chaps. 6–8. See also H. L. Edge, R. L. Morris, J. H. Rushand, and J. Palmer, *Foundations of Parapsychology* (London: Routledge, 1986).

18. A famous example is the Chaffin will case, recounted in many books, such as C. D. Broad, *Lectures on Psychical Research* (London: Routledge & Kegan Paul and New York: Humanities Press, 1962), pp. 137–39. (This, incidentally, remains one of the best books on parapsychology.)

19. S. G. Soal, "A Report of Some Communications Received through Mrs. Blanche Cooper," Sec. 4, *Proceedings of the Society for Psychical Research*, XXXV, 560–89.

20. F. W. H. Myers, *Human Personality and Its Survival of Bodily Death* (London: Longmans, Green, & Co., 1903 and New York: Arno Press, 1975), I, 270–71. This is a classic work, still of great interest.

21. The recent wave of interest began with the publication in 1975 of Raymond Moody's *Life after Life* (Atlanta: Mockingbird Books), and has been fed by a growing number of other books, including Raymond Moody, *Reflections on Life after Life* (New York: Bantam Books, 1977); Karlis Otis and Erlendur Haraldsson, *At the Hour of Death* (New York: Avon Books, 1977); Maurice Rawlings, *Beyond Death's Door* (Nashville: Thomas Nelson, Inc., 1978, and London: Sheldon Press, 1979).

22. For example, Sylvan Muldoon and Hereward Carrington, *The Phenomena of Astral Projection* (London: Rider, 1951); Robert Crookall, *The Study and Practice of Astral Projection* (London: Aquarian Press, 1961); Celia Green, *Out-of-the-Body Experiences* (London: Hamish Hamilton, 1968); *Journeys Out of the Body* (New York: Doubleday & Co., Inc., 1971, and London: Souvenir Press, 1972); Benjamin Walker, *Beyond the Body* (London: Routledge & Kegan Paul, 1974).

23. Philosophical discussions of parapsychology can be found in: C. D. Broad, *Religion, Philosophy and Psychical Research* (London: Routledge & Kegan Paul, 1953); James Wheatley and Hoyt Edge, eds., *Philosophical Dimensions of Parapsychology* (Springfield, III.; C Thomas, 1976); Shivesh Thakur, ed., *Philosophy and Psychical Research* (New York: Humanities Press, 1976); Jan Ludwig, ed., *Philosophy and Parapsychology* (Prometheus, 1978); Stephen Braude, *ESP and Psychokinesis: A Philosophical Examination* (Philadelphia: Temple University Press, 1980).

VI.4

Personal Identity and Life After Death

JEFFREY OLEN

Jeffrey Olen (1946–) is a writer-philosopher who for many years taught philosophy at the University of Wisconsin at Stevens Point. In this essay he discusses the criteria of personal identity in order to determine what would have to survive our death if we were to be able to say that it is truly we who survive. Through some intriguing thought experiments, Olen builds a case for the possibility of survival. Olen has a functionalist view of personhood, believing that "the human brain is analogous to a computer." On this view, a given brain state is also a given mental state because it performs the appropriate function in the appropriate "program." Olen argues that just as different computers can run the same program, so too different brains (or other media) can "run" the same mind. So we can change bodies and therefore survive the death of our own body just as long as our personalities and memories are preserved intact.

It is Sunday night. After a long night of hard drinking, John Badger puts on his pajamas, lowers the heat in his Wisconsin home to fifty-five degrees and climbs into bed beneath two heavy blankets. Meanwhile, in Florida, Joe Everglade kisses his wife goodnight and goes to sleep.

The next morning, two very confused men wake up. One wakes up in Wisconsin, wondering where he is and why he is wearing pajamas, lying under two heavy blankets, yet shivering from the cold. He looks out the window and sees nothing but pine trees and snow. The room is totally unfamiliar. Where is his wife? How did he get to this cold, strange place? Why does he have such a terrible hangover? He tries to spring out of bed with his usual verve but feels an unaccustomed aching in his joints. Arthritis? He wanders unsurely through the house until he finds the bathroom. What he sees in the mirror causes him to spin around in sudden fear. But there is nobody behind him. Then the fear intensifies as he realizes that it was his reflection that had stared back at

him. But it was the reflection of a man thirty years older than himself, with coarser features and a weather-beaten face.

In Florida, a man awakens with a young woman's arm around him. When she too awakens, she snuggles against him and wishes him good morning. "Who are you?" he asks. "What am I doing in your bed?" She just laughs, then tells him that he will have to hurry if he is going to get in his ten miles of jogging. From the bathroom she asks him about his coming day. None of the names or places she mentions connect with anything he can remember. He climbs out of bed, marveling at the ease with which he does so, and looks first out the window and then into the mirror over the dresser. The sun and swimming pool confound him. The handsome young man's reflection terrifies him.

Then the phone rings. The woman answers it. It is the man from Wisconsin. "What happened last night, Mary? How did I get here? How did I get to look this way?"

"Who is this?" she asks.

"Don't you recognize my voice, Mary?" But he knew that the voice was not his own. "It's Joe."

"Joe who?"

"Your husband."

She hangs up, believing it to be a crank call. When she returns to the bedroom, the man in her husband's robe asks how he got there from Wisconsin, and why he looks as he does.

PERSONAL IDENTITY

What happened in the above story? Who woke up in Joe Everglade's bed? Who woke up in John Badger's? Which one is Marys's husband? Has Badger awakened with Everglade's memories and Everglade with Badger's? Or have Badger and Everglade somehow switched bodies? How are we to decide? What considerations are relevant?

To ask such questions is to raise the problem of *personal identity*. It is to ask what makes a person the same person he was the day before. It is to ask how we determine that we are dealing with the same person that we have dealt with in the past. It is to ask what constitutes personal identity over time. It is also to ask what we mean by the same person. And to answer this question, we must ask what we mean by the word "person."

Persons

In the previous chapter, we asked what a human being is. We asked what human beings are made of, what the nature of the human mind is, and whether human beings are part of nature or distinct from it.

To ask what a *person* is, however, is to ask a different question. Although we often use the terms "person" and "human being" interchangeably, they do not mean the same thing. If we do use them interchangeably, it is only because all the persons we know of are human beings, and because, as far as we know, whenever we are confronted with the same human being we are confronted with the same person.

But the notion of a human being is a *biological* notion. To identify something as a human being is to identify it as a member of *Homo sapiens*, a particular species of animal. It is a type of organism defined by certain physical characteristics.

The notion of a person, on the other hand, is not a biological one. Suppose, for instance, that we find life on another planet, and that this life is remarkably like our own. The creatures we discover communicate through a language as rich as our own, act according to moral principles, have a legal system, and engage in science and art. Suppose also that despite these cultural similarities, this form of life is biologically different from human life. In that case, these creatures would be persons, but not humans. Think, for example, of the alien in *E.T.* Since he is biologically different from us, he is not human. He is, however, a person.

What, then, is a person? Although philosophers disagree on this point, the following features are relatively noncontroversial.

First, a person is an intelligent, rational creature. Second, it is a creature capable of a peculiar sort of consciousness—self-consciousness. Third, it not only has beliefs, desires, and so forth, but it has beliefs about its beliefs, desires, and so forth. Fourth, it is a creature to which we ascribe moral responsibility. Persons are responsible for their actions in a way that other things are not. They are subject to moral praise and moral blame. Fifth, a person is a creature that we treat in certain ways. To treat something as a person is to treat it as a member of our own moral community. It is to grant it certain rights, both moral and legal. Sixth, a person is a creature capable of reciprocity. It is capable of treating us as members of the same moral community. Finally, a person is capable of verbal communication. It can communicate by means of a *language*, not just by barks, howls, and tail-wagging.

Since, as far as we know, only human beings meet the above conditions, only human beings are considered to be persons. But once we recognize that to be a person is not precisely the same thing that it is to be a human being, we also recognize that other creatures, such as the alien in *E.T.*, is also a person. We also recognize that perhaps not all human beings are persons—human fetuses, for example, as some have argued. Certainly, in the American South before the end of the Civil War, slaves were not considered to be persons. We might also mention a remark of D'Artagnan, in Richard Lester's film version of *The Three Musketeers*. Posing as a French nobleman, he attempted to cross the English Channel with a companion. When a French official remarked that his pass was only for one person, D'Artagnan replied that he was only one person—his companion was a servant.

Moreover, once we recognize the distinction between human beings and persons, certain questions arise. Can one human being embody more than one person, either at the same time or successive times? In the example we introduced at the beginning of this chapter, has Badger's body become Everglade's and Everglade's Badger's? Can the person survive the death of the human being? Is there personal survival after the death of the body?

Concerning identity through time in general, two issues must be distinguished. First, we want to know how we can *tell* that something is the same thing we encountered previously. That is, we want to know what the *criteria* are for establishing identity through time. Second, we want to know what *makes* something the same thing it was previously. That is, we want to know what *constitutes* identity through time.

Although these issues are related, they are not the same, as the following example illustrates. We can *tell* that someone has a case of the flu by checking for certain symptoms, such as fever, lack of energy, and sore muscles. But having these symptoms does not *constitute* having a case of the flu. It is the presence of a flu virus—not the symptoms—that makes an illness a case of the flu.

We commonly use two criteria for establishing personal identity. The first is the *bodily criterion*, the second the *memory criterion*. How do we apply them?

We apply the bodily criterion in two ways. First, we go by physical resemblance. If I meet someone on the street who looks, walks, and sounds just like Mary, I assume that it is Mary. Since the body I see resembles Mary's body exactly, I assume that the person I see is Mary. But that method can sometimes

fail us, as in the case of identical twins. In such cases, we can apply the bodily criterion in another way. If I can discover that there is a continuous line from one place and time to another that connects Mary's body to the body I now see, I can assume that I now see Mary. Suppose, for example, that Mary and I went to the beach together, and have been together all afternoon. In that case, I can say that the person I am now with is the person I began the day with.

There are, however, times when the bodily criterion is not available. If Mary and Jane are identical twins, and I run across one of them on the street, I may have to ask who it is. That is, I may have to rely on Mary's memory of who she is. And, if I want to make sure that I am not being fooled, I may ask a few questions. If Mary remembers things that I believe only Mary can remember, and if she remembers them as happening to *her*, and not to somebody else, then I can safely say that it really is Mary.

Generally, the bodily criterion and the memory criterion do not conflict, so we use whichever is more convenient. But what happens if they do conflict? That is what happened in our imagined story. According to the bodily criterion, each person awoke in his own bed, but with the memories of someone else. According to the memory criterion, each person awoke in the other's bed with the body of someone else. Which criterion should we take as decisive? Which is fundamental, the memory criterion or the bodily criterion?

The Constitution of Personal Identity

To ask the above questions is to ask what *constitutes* personal identity. What is it that makes me the same person I was yesterday? What makes the author of this book the same person as the baby born to Sam and Belle Olen in 1946? Answers to these questions will allow us to say which criterion is fundamental.

Perhaps the most widely discussed answer to our question comes from John Locke (1632–1704), whose discussion of the topic set the stage for all future discussions. According to Locke, the bodily criterion cannot be fundamental. Since the concept of a person is most importantly the concept of a conscious being who can be held morally and legally responsible for past actions, it is *continuity of consciousness* that constitutes personal identity. The bodily criterion is fundamental for establishing sameness of *animal*, but not sameness of *person*.

Suppose, for instance, that John Badger had been a professional thief. If the person who awoke in Badger's bed could never remember any of Badger's life as his own, but had only Everglade's memories and personality traits, while the man who awoke in Everglade's bed remembered all of Badger's crimes as his own, would we be justified in jailing the man who awoke in Badger's bed while letting the man who awoke in Everglade's go free? Locke would say no. The person who awoke in Badger's bed was not Badger.

If we agree that it is sameness of consciousness that constitutes personal identity, we must then ask what constitutes sameness of consciousness. Some philosophers have felt that it is sameness of *mind*, where the mind is thought of as a continuing nonphysical substance. Although Locke did not deny that minds are nonphysical, he did not believe that sameness of nonphysical substance is the same thing as sameness of consciousness. If we can conceive of persons switching *physical* bodies, we can also conceive of persons switching *nonphysical* ones.

Then what does Locke take to be crucial for personal identity? *Memory.* It is my memory of the events of Jeffrey Olen's life as happening to me that makes me the person those events happened to. It is my memory of his experiences as *mine* that makes them mine.

Although Locke's answer seems at first glance a reasonable one, many philosophers have considered it inadequate. One reason for rejecting Locke's answer is that we don't remember everything that happened to us. If I don't remember anything that happened to me during a certain period, does that mean that whoever existed "in" my body then was not me? Hardly.

Another reason for rejecting Locke's answer is that memory is not always accurate. We often sincerely claim to remember things that never happened. There is a difference, then, between *genuine* memory and *apparent* memory. What

marks this difference is the *truth* of the memory claim. If what I claim to remember is not true, it cannot be a case of genuine memory.

But that means that memory cannot constitute personal identity. If I claim to remember certain experiences as being my experiences, that does not make them mine, because my claim may be a case of apparent memory. If it is a case of genuine memory, that is because it is true that the remembered experiences are mine. But the memory does not *make* them mine. Rather, the fact that they are mine makes it a case of genuine memory. So Locke has the situation backward. But if memory does not constitute personal identity, what does?

Some philosophers have claimed that, regardless of Locke's views, it *must* be sameness of mind, where the mind is thought of as a continuing nonphysical entity. This entity can be thought of as the self. It is what makes us who we are. As long as the same self continues to exist, the same person continues to exist. The major problem with this answer is that it assumes the truth of mind-body dualism, a position we found good reason to reject in the previous chapter. But apart from that, there is another problem.

In one of the most famous passages in the history of philosophy, David Hume (1711–1776) argued that there is no such self—for reasons that have nothing to do with the rejection of dualism. No matter how hard we try, Hume said, we cannot discover such a self. Turning inward and examining our own consciousness, we find only individual experiences—thoughts, recollections, images, and the like. Try as we might, we cannot find a continuing self. In that case, we are justified in believing only that there are *experiences*—not that there is a continuing *experiencer*. Put another way, we have no reason to believe that there is anything persisting through time that underlies or unifies these experiences. There are just the experiences themselves.

But if we accept this view, and still require a continuing nonphysical entity for personal identity, we are forced to the conclusion that there is no such thing as personal identity. We are left, that is, with the position that the idea of a person existing through time is a mere fiction, however useful in daily life. And that is the position that Hume took. Instead of persons, he said, there are merely "bundles of ideas."

Thus, the view that personal identity requires sameness of mind can easily lead to the view that there is no personal identity. Since this conclusion seems manifestly false, we shall have to look elsewhere? But where?

The Primacy of the Bodily Criterion

If neither memory nor sameness of mind constitutes personal identity, perhaps we should accept the view that sameness of *body* does. Perhaps it is really the bodily criterion that is fundamental.

If we reflect on the problem faced by Locke's theory because of the distinction between genuine and apparent memory, it is tempting to accept the primacy of the bodily criterion. Once again, a sincere memory claim may be either genuine memory or apparent memory. How can we tell whether the claim that a previous experience was mine is genuine memory? By determining whether I was in the right place in the right time to have it. And how can we determine that? By the bodily criterion. If my *body* was there, then I was there. But that means that the memory criterion must rest on the bodily criterion. Also, accepting the primacy of the bodily criterion gets us around Hume's problem. The self that persists through and has the experiences I call mine is my physical body.

This answer also has the advantage of being in keeping with materialism, a view accepted in the previous chapter. If human beings are purely physical, then persons must also be purely physical, whatever differences there may be between the notion of a person and the notion of a human being. But if persons are purely physical, what makes me the same person I was yesterday is no different in kind from what makes my typewriter the same typewriter it was yesterday. In both cases, we are dealing with a physical object existing through time. In the latter case, as long as we have the same physical materials (allowing for change of ribbon, change of keys, and the like) arranged in the same way, we have the same typewriter. So it is with persons. As long as we have the same physical materials (allowing for such

changes as the replacement of cells) arranged in the same way, we have the same person.

Although this answer is a tempting one, it is not entirely satisfactory. Suppose that we could manage a brain transplant from one body to another. If we switched two brains, so that all the memories and personality traits of the persons involved were also switched, wouldn't we conclude that the persons, as well as their brains, had switched bodies? When such operations are performed in science-fiction stories, they are described this way.

But this possibility does not defeat the view that the bodily criterion is fundamental. It just forces us to hold that the bodily criterion must be applied to the brain, rather than the entire body. Personal identity then becomes a matter of brain identity. Same brain, same person. Unfortunately, even with this change, our answer does not seem satisfactory. Locke still seems somehow right. Let us see why.

Badger and Everglade Reconsidered

Returning to our tale of Badger and Everglade, we find that some troubling questions remain. If Mrs. Everglade continues to live with the man who awoke in her bed, might she not be committing adultery? Shouldn't she take in the man who awoke in Badger's bed? And, once again assuming that Badger was a professional thief, would justice really be served by jailing the man who awoke in his bed? However we answer these questions, one thing is certain—the two men would always feel that they had switched bodies. So, probably, would the people who knew them. Furthermore, whenever we read science-fiction stories describing such matters, we invariably accept them as stories of switched bodies. But if we accept the bodily criterion as fundamental, we are accepting the impossible, and the two men in our story, Mrs. Everglade, and their friends are mistaken in their beliefs. How, then, are we to answer our questions?

If we are unsure, it is because such questions become very tricky at this point. Their trickiness seems to rest on two points. First, cases like the Badger-Everglade case do not happen in this world. Although we are prepared to accept them in science-fiction tales, we are totally unprepared to deal with them in real life.

Second, and this is a related point, we need some way of *explaining* such extraordinary occurrences. Unless we know how the memories of Badger and Everglade came to be reversed, we will be unable to decide the answers to our questions. In the movies, it is assumed that some nonphysical substance travels from one body to another, or that there has been a brain transplant of some sort. On these assumptions, we are of course willing to describe what happens as a change of body. This description seems to follow naturally from such explanations.

What explains what happened to Badger and Everglade? We can rule out change of nonphysical substance, because of what was said in the previous chapter and earlier in this chapter. If we explain what happened as the product of a brain switch, then the bodily criterion applied to the brain allows us to say that Badger and Everglade did awaken in each other's bed, and that Mrs. Everglade would be committing adultery should she live with the man who awoke in her bed.

Are there any other possible explanations? One that comes readily to mind is hypnotism. Suppose, then, that someone had hypnotized Badger and Everglade into believing that each was the other person. In that case, we should not say that there had been a body switch. Badger and Everglade awoke in their own beds, and a wave of the hypnotist's hand could demonstrate that to everyone concerned. Their memory claims are not genuine memories, but apparent ones.

But suppose it was not a case of hypnotism? What then? At this point, many people are stumped. What else could it be? The strong temptation is to say nothing. Without a brain transplant or hypnotism or something of the sort, the case is impossible.

Suppose that we accept this conclusion. If we do, we may say the following: The memory criterion and the bodily criterion cannot really conflict. If the memories are genuine, and not apparent, then whenever I remember certain experiences as being mine, it is possible to establish that the same brain is involved in the original experiences and the memory of them. Consequently, the memory

criterion and the bodily criterion are equally fundamental. The memory criterion is fundamental in the sense that consciousness determines what part of the body is central to personal identity. Because sameness of consciousness requires sameness of brain, we ultimately must apply the bodily criterion to the brain. But the bodily criterion is also fundamental, because we assume that some physical object—the brain—must remain the same if the person is to remain the same.

The Memory Criterion Revisited

Although the answer given above is a tidy one, it may still seem unsatisfactory. Perhaps it is a cheap trick just to dismiss the Badger-Everglade case as mere fantasy and then ignore it. After all, if we can meaningfully describe such cases in books and films, don't we have to pay some attention to them? As long as we can imagine situations in which two persons can switch bodies without a brain transplant, don't we need a theory of personal identity to cover them?

Philosophers are divided on this point. Some think that a theory of personal identity has to account only for what can happen in this world, while others think it must account for whatever can happen in any conceivable world. Then again, some do not believe that there is any conceivable world in which two persons could change bodies without a brain switch, while there are others who are not sure that such things are impossible in the actual world.

Without trying to decide the matter, I can make the following suggestion for those who demand a theory of personal identity that does not rely on the assumption that genuine memory is tied to a particular brain.

In the previous chapter, I concluded that functionalism is the theory of mind most likely to be true. To have a mind, I said, is to embody a psychology. I also said that we don't merely move our bodies, but write poetry, caress the cheek of someone we love, and perform all sorts of human actions. I might have expressed this point by saying that we are not just human beings, but persons as well. What makes a human being a person? We are persons because we embody a psychology.

If that is true, then it may also be true that we are the persons we are because of the psychologies we embody. If it is a psychology that makes a human being a person, then it is a particular psychology that makes a particular human being a particular person. Sameness of psychology constitutes sameness of person. In that case, we can agree with this much of Locke's theory—it is continuity of consciousness that constitutes personal identity. But what is continuity of consciousness, if not memory?

An answer to this question is provided by the contemporary British philosopher Anthony Quinton. At any moment, we can isolate a number of mental states belonging to the same momentary consciousness. Right now, for instance, I am simultaneously aware of the sound and sight and feel of my typewriter, plus the feel and taste of my pipe, plus a variety of other things. Such *momentary* consciousnesses belong to a continuous series. Each one is linked to the one before it and the one following it by certain similarities and recollections. This series is my own *continuity* of consciousness, my own *stream* of consciousness. It is this stream of consciousness that makes me the same person I was yesterday.

If we accept Quinton's theory, we can then say that the memory criterion, not the bodily criterion, is fundamental. We can also say that, even if in this world continuity of consciousness requires sameness of brain, we can conceive of worlds in which it does not. To show this, let us offer another possible explanation of the Badger-Everglade situation.

Suppose a mad computer scientist has discovered a way to reprogram human beings. Suppose that he has found a way to make us the embodiment of any psychology he likes. Suppose further that he decided to experiment on Badger and Everglade, giving Badger Everglade's psychology and Everglade Badger's and that is why the events of our story occurred. With this explanation and the considerations of the previous paragraphs, we can conclude that Badger and Everglade did change bodies. By performing his experiment, the mad scientist has made it possible for a continuing stream of consciousness to pass from one body to another. He has, in effect, performed a body transplant....

Should we accept Quinton's theory? There seems to be no good reason not to. In fact, there are at least two good reasons for accepting it. First, it seems consistent with a functionalist theory of the mind. Second, it allows us to make sense of science fiction stories while we continue to believe that in the real world to be the same person we were yesterday is to have the same brain.

LIFE AFTER DEATH

Is it possible for the person to survive the death of the body? Is there a sense in which we can continue to live after our bodies have died? Can there be a personal life after death?

According to one popular conception of life after death, at the death of the body the soul leaves the body and travels to a realm known as heaven. Of course, this story must be taken as metaphorical. Does the soul literally leave the body? How? Out of the mouth? Ears? And how does it get to heaven? By turning left at Mars? Moreover, if the soul remains disembodied, how can it perceive anything? What does it use as sense organs? And if all souls remain disembodied, how can one soul recognize another? What is there to recognize?

As these questions might suggest, much of this popular story trades on a confusion. The soul is thought of as a translucent physical substance much like Casper the ghost, through which other objects can pass as they do through air or water. But if the soul is *really* nonphysical, it can be nothing like that.

If this story is not to be taken literally, is there some version of it that we can admit as a possibility? Is there also the possibility of personal survival through reincarnation as it is often understood—the re-embodiment of the person without memory of the former embodiment?

Materialism and the Disembodied Soul

So far, we have considered both the mind and the body as they relate to personal identity. Have we neglected the soul? It may seem that we have, but philosophers who discuss the mind-body question and personal identity generally use the terms "mind" and "soul" interchangeably. Is the practice legitimate, or is it a confusion?

The practice seems to be thoroughly legitimate. If the soul is thought to be the crucial element of the person, it is difficult to see how it could be anything but the mind. If it is our character traits, personality, thoughts, likes and dislikes, memories, and continuity of experience that make us the persons we are, then they must belong to the soul. If they are taken to be crucial for one's personal identity, then it seems impossible to separate them from one's soul.

Moreover, people who accept some version of the popular conception of life after death noted above believe in certain continuities between earthly experiences and heavenly ones. In heaven, it is believed, we remember our earthly lives, we recognize friends and relatives, our personalities are like our earthly personalities, and we are judged by God for our actions on earth. But if we believe any of this, we must also believe that the soul cannot be separated from the mind.

If that is the case, it is difficult to accept the continued existence of a disembodied soul. Once we accept some form of materialism, we seem compelled to believe that the soul must be embodied. Does that rule out the possibility of any version of the popular story being true?

Some philosophers think that it does. Suppose, for instance, that the mind-brain identity theory is true. In that case, when the brain dies, so does the mind. Since the mind is the repository of memory and personality traits, it is identical with the soul. So when the brain dies, so does the soul.

This is a powerful argument, and it has convinced a number of people. On the other hand, it has also kept a number of people from accepting materialism of any sort. If it is felt that materialism and life after death are incompatible, and if one is firmly committed to the belief in life after death, then it is natural for one to reject materialism.

Is there a way of reconciling materialism and life after death? I think so.

Although it seems necessary that persons must be embodied, it does not seem necessary that the same person must be embodied by the same body. In our discussion of personal identity, we allowed that Badger and Everglade might have changed bodies, depending on our explanation of the story. Let us try a similar story.

Mary Brown is old and sick. She knows she will die within a couple of weeks. One morning she does die. At the same time, in some other world, a woman wakes up believing herself to be Mary. She looks around to find herself in a totally unfamiliar place. Someone is sitting next to her. This other woman looks exactly like Mary's mother, who died years earlier, and believes herself to be Mary's mother. Certainly, she knows everything about Mary that Mary's mother would know.

Before the woman believing herself to be Mary can speak, she notices some surprising things about herself. She no longer feels old or sick. Her pains are gone, and her mind is as sharp as ever. When she asks where she is, she is told heaven. She is also told that her husband, father, and numerous old friends are waiting to see her. All of them are indistinguishable from the persons they claim to be. Meanwhile, back on earth, Mary Brown is pronounced dead. Is this woman in "heaven" really Mary Brown? How could we possibly explain the phenomenon?

Suppose we put the story in a religious context. Earlier, we saw that one possible explanation of the Badger-Everglade case is that some mad computer scientist had reprogrammed the two so that each embodied the psychology of the other. Suppose we replace the mad scientist with God, and say that God had kept a body in heaven for the purpose of embodying Mary's psychology when she died, and that the person believing herself to be Mary is the new embodiment of Mary's psychology. Would this count as a genuine case of life after death?

If we accept the Badger-Everglade story, appropriately explained, as a case of two persons switching bodies, there seems no reason to deny that Mary has continued to live "in" another body. But even if we are unsure of the Badger-Everglade case, we can approach Mary Brown's this way. What is it that we want to survive after death? Isn't it our memories, our consciousness of self, our personalities, our relations with others? What does it matter whether there is some nonphysical substance that survives? If that substance has no memories of a prior life, does not recognize the soul of others who were important in that earlier life, what comfort could such a continuing existence bring? In what sense would it be the survival of the *person*? How would it be significantly different from the return of the lifeless body to the soil?

If we assume that our story is a genuine case of personal survival of the death of the body, we may wonder about another point. Is it compatible with Christian belief? According to John Hick, a contemporary British philosopher who imagined a similar story, the answer is yes. In I Corinthians 15, Paul writes of the resurrection of the body—not of the physical body, but of some spiritual body. Although one can think of this spiritual body as a translucent ghost-like body that leaves the physical body at death, Hick offers another interpretation.

The human being, Hick says, becomes extinct at death. It is only through God's intervention that the spiritual body comes into existence. By the resurrection of this spiritual body, we are to understand a *recreation* or *reconstitution* of the person's body in heaven. But that is precisely what happened in our story.

Thus, a materialist view of the nature of human beings is not incompatible with the Christian view of life after death. Nor, for that matter, is it incompatible with the belief that the spiritual body is nonphysical. If we can make sense of the claim that there might be such things as nonphysical bodies, then there is no reason why a nonphysical body could not embody a psychology. Remember— according to functionalism, an abstract description such as a psychology is independent of any physical description. Just as we can play chess using almost anything as chess pieces, so can a psychology be embodied by almost anything, assuming that it is complex enough. So if there can be nonphysical bodies, there can be nonphysical persons. Of course, nothing said so far assures us that the Christian story—or any other story of life after death—is true. That is another matter....

Reincarnation

Much of what has been said so far does, however, rule out the possibility of reincarnation as commonly understood. If human beings are purely physical, then there is no nonphysical substance that is the person that can be reincarnated in another earthly body. Moreover, even if there were such a substance, it is difficult to see how its continued existence in another body could count as the reincarnation of a particular person, *if* there is no other continuity between the old life and the new one. Once again, personal survival requires some continuity of consciousness. It is not sameness of *stuff* that constitutes personal identity, but sameness of consciousness. This requirement is often overlooked by believers in reincarnation.

But suppose that there is some continuity of consciousness in reincarnation. Suppose that memories and the rest do continue in the next incarnation, but that they are not easily accessible. Suppose, that is, that the slate is not wiped completely clean, but that what is written on it is hard to recover. In that case, the passage of the soul into a new incarnation would count as personal survival *if* there were such a soul to begin with.

Assuming, again, that there is not, what can we say about the possibility of reincarnation? To conceive of such a possibility, we must conceive of some very complicated reprogramming by God or some mad scientist or whatever. I shall leave it to you to come up with such a story, but I shall say this much. There does not seem to be any good reason to think that any such story is remotely plausible, least of all true.

The Final Word?

In this chapter we looked at two closely related questions: What constitutes personal identity? And is it possible for a person to survive the death of her own body?

The answer to the second question depended on the first. If we had concluded that the basis of personal identity is sameness of body, then we would have been forced to conclude that life after death is impossible. And there did seem to be good reason to come to these conclusions. How, we asked, could we assure that any memory claim is a case of genuine memory? Our answer was this. In the cases likely to confront us in our daily lives, we must establish some physical continuity between the person who had the original experience and the person who claims to remember it.

But the problem with this answer is that it is too limited. Because we can imagine cases like the Everglade-Badger example, and because our science-fiction tales and religious traditions offer stories of personal continuity without bodily continuity, we can say the following. Regardless of what happens in our daily lives, our concept of a person is a concept of something that does not seem tied to a particular body. Rather, our concept of a person seems to be tied to a particular stream of consciousness. If there is one continuing stream of consciousness over time, then there is one continuing person. Our question, then, was whether we can give a coherent account of continuity of consciousness from one body to another.

The answer was yes. Using the computer analogy of the functionalist, we can explain such continuity in terms of programming. If it is possible to "program" another brain to have the same psychology as the brain I now have, then it is possible for me to change bodies. And if it is possible for me to change bodies, then it is also possible for me to survive the death of my body.

VI.5

A Hindu Theory of Life, Death, and Reincarnation

PRASANNATMA DAS

When he wrote this article, Prasannatma Das was a young Hindu philosopher studying at the Krishna Temple in Vrindavan, India. In this essay he describes the basic Hindu view of karma—the doctrine that says the way we live in this life will determine our initial state in the next life—and reincarnation—the notion that the same person lives in a different body in future lives based on the idea of karma. Prasannatma Das appeals to the Bhagavad Gita, the most sacred of Hindu scriptures, for his exposition. Lord Krishna, the main speaker in that work, is viewed by Hindus as an avatar (manifestation) of God. You should be aware that, as with most major religions, there are many versions of Hinduism. This is one important Hindu version of the meaning of life and death, but not the only one. The term cosmogonal in the quotation from Thoreau refers to the origin of the world.

This essay was commissioned for the first edition of *Life & Death*, ed. Louis Pojman (Jones & Bartlett, 1993) and is reprinted here by permission of the author. All references are to the *Bhagavad Gita*, translated by A. C. Bhaktivedanta Swami Prabbupada (Los Angeles: The Bhaktivedanta Book Trust, 1983).

A HINDU VIEW OF LIFE AND DEATH

In a previous age, there lived a wise king named Yudhisthira. Having been banished by an evil cousin, he and his four brothers were wandering in a forest. One day the youngest brother went to get water from a nearby lake. When, after a time, he did not come back, the next brother went. He did not come back either. Twice more this happened until finally Yudhisthira himself went. He came to the lake and was about to drink from it when suddenly a voice boomed forth, "Do not drink this water. I am the owner of this lake, and if you drink this water, you shall die like your brothers have before you!" Yudhisthira then saw the lifeless bodies of his brothers lying nearby. The voice continued. "You may drink of this water only on the condition that you answer my questions. If you answer them correctly, you and your brothers shall live. If you fail, then you too shall die."

The voice then presented a series of questions to the king, all of which he answered perfectly. One of these questions was, "Of all the amazing things in this world, what is the most amazing?" The king replied, "The most amazing thing is that although everyone sees his parents dying, and everything around him dying, still we live as though we will live forever. This is truly amazing."

It is indeed amazing that even in the face of inevitable death, few perceive the urgency of our predicament; however, in every culture and tradition there have been those thoughtful souls who have done so. Within the Hindu tradition many such seekers have found the teachings of Lord Krishna as presented in the *Bhagavad Gita* to be a source of knowledge and inspiration. Appearing as an episode in the great epic of ancient India, the *Mahabharata*, the *Bhagavad Gita* is one of the most profound theological dialogues known to man. Henry David Thoreau once said, "In the morning I bathe my intellect in the stupendous and cosmogonal philosophy of the *Bhagavad Gita*, in comparison with which our modern world and its literature seem puny and trivial."

The first message of Lord Krishna's teaching in the *Bhagavad Gita* is that we are not these bodies.

The body is constantly changing; we once had the body of a small baby, then that of a child, of an adult, of an old person, and eventually the body will return to the dust from whence it came. Yet when we look in the mirror we think that this body is what we are.

But what are we really? Krishna explains that we are the eternal soul within the body and what we call death is merely the soul leaving one body and going elsewhere:

> Never was there a time when I did not exist, nor you, nor all these kings; nor in the future shall any of these cease to be.
>
> As the embodied soul continuously passes, in this body, from boyhood to youth to old age, the soul similarly passes into another body at the time of death. A sober person is not bewildered by such a change.
>
> For the soul there is neither birth nor death at any time. He has not come into being, does not come into being, and will not come into being. He is unborn, eternal, ever-existing, and primeval. He is not slain when the body is slain.
>
> As a person puts on new garments, giving up old and useless ones, the soul similarly accepts new material bodies, giving up old and useless ones. (2.12–13, 20, 22)

Krishna is explaining that we are not these bodies; we are the soul inside. I am not a twenty-year-old college student about to fail his philosophy course, but rather I am an eternal spirit-soul who, out of ignorance of his true nature, now identifies himself with the temporary forms of this world. When I enter a new body, I remain the same person.

For example, imagine a candle over which a series of filters are placed; the light appears to be changing according to the color of the filter obscuring it—blue, green, etc. But the original source of the light, the flame, is not changing, only the covering is. In the same way, the soul does not change, only the covering, the body, changes.

Sometimes at night we look up at the sky and see that the clouds are luminous. From the glowing of the clouds we can understand that because the moon is behind them, the clouds themselves appear to be luminous. Similarly when examining this body we can infer the existence of the soul by its symptom consciousness, which pervades the body and gives it the appearance of being alive.

Another basic teaching of the *Bhagavad Gita* is the law of karma, which states that for every action there is a corresponding reaction, or "whatever goes around, comes around." Our situation in this life was caused by the activities and desires of our previous lives. Similarly our future existence—our body, education, amount of wealth, happiness and distress, etc., will be determined by how we live now. If we harm others then we must suffer in return, and if we do good then we correspondingly enjoy. Moreover, we are given a body which suits our consciousness. If, like an animal, a human spends his life eating, sleeping, mating, and defending, ignoring his higher capacities, then he may be placed into the body of an animal. At the time of death the consciousness we have cultivated during our life will carry us, the soul, to our next body. "Whatever state of being one remembers when he quits his body, that state he will attain without fail." (8.6)

The goal is not to come back to this world at all but to attain the supreme destination:

> From the highest planet in the material world down to the lowest, all are places of misery wherein repeated birth and death take place. But one who attains to My abode ... never takes birth again. (8.16)

Death is perceived according to the quality of one's existence. The ignorant see death as something to be feared. They have material desires, and death will defeat them. Those who are seeking wisdom understand death as an impetus to live correctly, as a time when their knowledge will be put to test. The most amazing thing in this world is that although everyone knows they are going to die, they still act as though they will live forever. Imagine a person who has received an eviction notice—he must vacate his apartment in two weeks. If he promptly prepared for this, and found another place to go, he would not be in anxiety. Unfortunately, even though our eviction notice was given at the time of birth, very few take heed.

Krishna states:

> What is night for all living beings is the time of awakening for the self-controlled, and the time of awakening for all beings is the night for the introspective sage. (2.69)

There are different types of activities which have different values. There are pious activities which lead to taking birth in a situation of relative enjoyment, there are impious activities which lead to suffering and ignorance, and there are spiritual activities which lead one to God. Such spiritual activities are called *yoga*. (*yoga* does not mean Indian gymnastics but actually refers to the process of reuniting one's self with God.)

This yoga, or real religious life, is not just a passive activity, but is an active cultivation. If a farmer wants to harvest crops, he must begin working early in the season; plowing the fields, planting seeds, watering, weeding, etc. The fruits of his labor will manifest themselves at harvest time. Similarly, one who desires to attain to perfection must engage in a cultivation of the soul which will yield the harvest of spiritual perfection. When death comes, he will taste the fruit of his endeavor.

In this world there is nothing so sublime and pure as transcendental knowledge. Such knowledge is the mature fruit of all mysticism. One who has become accomplished in the practice of devotional service enjoys this knowledge within himself in due course of time. "That is the way of the spiritual and godly life, after attaining which a person is not bewildered. If one is in this situation even at the hour of death, one can enter into the kingdom of God." (4.38; 2.72)

Death will come. No situation in this world is permanent. All changes. Whether a table, a car, a human body, a civilization, or a mountain, everything comes into being, remains for some time, and then finally dwindles and disappears. What of this world can survive the passage of time? As Krishna says, "One who has been born is sure to die." (2.27) Of this there is no doubt.

Yet many people do not see the urgency of our situation. "Yes, I know one day I shall have to die;

but for now let me eat, drink, have fun, and get a big bank balance," they think. Dedicated to the pursuit of the temporary phenomena of this world, living a life of vanity, they die like ignorant animals without higher knowledge. They and their fantasies are put to ruin. Their valuable human form of life with its great potential of knowledge and self-realization is wasted.

On the other hand, a thoughtful person understands the reality of this world, and, like a student who knows he must pass a test before he can graduate, prepares himself. This process of preparation begins with inquiry. Who am I? When this body is finished, what happens to me? Why do I exist? How can I be happy? By nature the eternal soul is full of happiness and knowledge. But now that eternal, blissful, fully cognizant being is something like a fish out of water. The lost creature will not be happy until it is placed back into the water. Giving the fish a new car or expensive jewelry will not rectify its problem; it will not become happy in this way. So too, no degree of rearranging this material world will solve our problems; we will not be satisfied until we are back in the spiritual world. Thus a wise person is not interested in attaining any of the tempting but temporary offerings of this world, knowing that they have a beginning and an end. As the founder of Christianity pointed out, "Seek ye first the kingdom of God, and all these things will be added unto you" (Luke 12.31). Therefore, "The yogis, abandoning attachment, act ... only for the sake of purification." (5.11). [Yogis are holy men. Ed.]

The sage is not interested in attaining temporary things like fame, adoration or distinction.

> An intelligent person does not take part in the sources of misery, which are done to contact with the material senses ... such pleasures have a beginning and an end, and so the wise man does not delight in them. (5.22)

He does not mind leaving this world because he is not attached to it. Rather he is interested in things with real value. Krishna lists some qualities which a thoughtful person might cultivate:

> Humility; pridelessness; non-violence; tolerance; simplicity approaching a bona fide spiritual master; cleanliness; steadiness; self-control; the perception of the evil of birth, death, old age, and disease; detachment; freedom from entanglement with children, wife, home and the rest; even-mindedness amid pleasant and unpleasant events; constant and unalloyed devotion to Me; aspiring to live in a solitary place; detachment from the general mass of people; accepting the importance of self-realization; and philosophical search for the Absolute Truth.... (13.8–12)

A yogi has no desire to fulfill in this world. Thus he is not attached to it. Thus he does not mind leaving it. Thus he has no fear of death.

Since he has no personal desire in this world and has faith in God, he welcomes death in the same way that the kitten welcomes the jaws of the mother cat, whereas they are feared by the mouse. Krishna states:

> To those who are constantly devoted to serving Me with love, I give the understanding by which they can come back to Me.
>
> To show them special mercy, I, dwelling in their hearts, destroy with the shining lamp of knowledge the darkness born of ignorance. (10.10–11)

For those of us who are not enlightened beings, the fact that we must die can serve as an impetus to reach that higher transcendental state; what have we to lose? If we are wrong in our hopes, and death does indeed end all, then have we lost anything by our effort? And if our hopes are correct, then certainly we have all to gain.

A faithful man who is dedicated to transcendental knowledge and who subdues his senses is eligible to achieve such knowledge, and having achieved it he quickly attains the supreme spiritual peace.

When one is enlightened with the knowledge by which [ignorance] is destroyed, then his knowledge reveals everything, as the sun lights up everything in the daytime. (4.39, 5.16)

PART II

Traditional Arguments for the Existence of God

CAN THE EXISTENCE OF GOD be demonstrated or made probable by argument? The debate between those who believe that reason can demonstrate that God exists and those who do not has an ancient lineage, going back to Protagoras (ca. 450 BCE) and Plato (427–347 BCE). The Roman Catholic church has traditionally held that the existence of God is demonstrable by human reason. The strong statement of the First Vatican Council (1870) indicates that human reason is adequate to arrive at a state of knowledge:

> If anyone says that the one and true God, our creator and Lord, cannot
> be known with certainty with the natural light of human reason by
> means of the things that have been made: let him be anathema.

Many others, including theists of various denominations, among them Catholics, have denied that human reason is adequate to arrive at knowledge or demonstrate the existence of God.

Arguments for the existence of God divide into two main groups: a priori and a posteriori arguments. An *a priori argument* is one whose premises one can justifiably believe without having experiences of the world beyond what is needed to acquire the concepts involved in the premises. An a posteriori argument, on the other hand, is an argument with at least one premise that can be justifiably believed only on the basis of experience. In this work we consider one a priori argument for the existence of God and two a posteriori arguments. The a priori argument is the ontological argument. The a posteriori arguments are the cosmological argument and the teleological argument.

The question before us in this part of our work is, What do the arguments for the existence of God establish? Do any of them demonstrate beyond reasonable doubt the existence of a supreme being or deity? Do any of them make it probable (given the evidence at hand) that such a being exists?

II.A THE ONTOLOGICAL ARGUMENT FOR THE EXISTENCE OF GOD

THE ONTOLOGICAL ARGUMENT for the existence of God is the most intriguing of all the arguments for theism. It is one of the most remarkable arguments ever set forth. First devised by St. Anselm (1033–1109), Archbishop of Canterbury in the eleventh century, the argument has continued to puzzle and fascinate philosophers ever since. Let the testimony of the agnostic philosopher Bertrand Russell serve as a typical example here:

> I remember the precise moment, one day in 1894, as I was walking along Trinity Lane [at Cambridge University where Russell was a student], when I saw in a flash (or thought I saw) that the ontological argument is valid. I had gone out to buy a tin of tobacco; on my way back, I suddenly threw it up in the air, and exclaimed as I caught it: "Great Scott, the ontological argument is sound!"[*]

The argument is important not only because it claims to be an a priori proof for the existence of God but also because it is the primary locus of such philosophical problems as whether existence is a property and whether the notion of necessary existence is intelligible. Furthermore, it has special religious significance because it is the only one of the traditional arguments that clearly concludes to the necessary properties of God, that is, his omnipotence, omniscience, omnibenevolence, and other great-making properties.

Although there are many versions of the ontological argument and many interpretations of some of these, most philosophers agree on the essential form of Anselm's version in the second chapter of his *Proslogion*. Anselm believes that God's existence is absolutely certain. Yet he desires understanding to fulfill his faith. Thus he writes: "Therefore, Lord, you who grant understanding to faith, grant that, insofar as you know it is useful for me, I may understand that you exist as we believe you exist, and that you are what we believe you to be. Now we believe that you are something than which nothing greater can be thought. So can it be that no such nature exists, since 'The fool has said in his heart, "There is no God."'"?

The argument that follows may be treated as a reductio ad absurdum argument. That is, it begins with a supposition (*S*: suppose that the greatest conceivable being exists in the mind alone) that is contradictory to what one desires to prove. One then goes about showing that (*S*) together with other certain or self-evident assumptions yields a contradiction, which in turn demonstrates that the contradictory of (*S*) must be true: A greatest possible being must exist in reality. You, the reader, can work out the details of the argument.

A monk named Gaunilo, a contemporary of Anselm's, sets forth the first objection to Anselm's argument. Accusing Anselm of pulling rabbits out of

---

[*]*Autobiography of Bertrand Russell* (New York: Little, Brown & Co., 1967).

hats, he tells the story of a delectable lost island, one that is more excellent than all lands. Since it is better that such a perfect island exist in reality than simply in the mind alone, this Isle of the Blest must necessarily exist. Anselm's reply is that the analogy fails, for unlike the greatest possible being, the greatest possible island can be conceived as not existing. More recently, Alvin Plantinga has clarified Anselm's point. The idea is that some properties have intrinsic maximums and others do not. No matter how wonderful we make the Isle of the Blest, we can conceive of a more wonderful island. The greatness of islands is like the greatness of numbers in this respect. There is no greatest natural number, for no matter how large the number we choose, we can always conceive of one twice as large. On the other hand, the properties of God have intrinsic maximums. For example, perfect knowledge has an intrinsic maximum: For any proposition, an omniscient being knows whether it is true or false.

Our next reading is the critique by Immanuel Kant (1724–1804), who accused the proponent of the argument of defining God into existence. Kant claims that Anselm makes the mistake of treating "exists" as a first-order predicate like "blue" or "great." When we say that the castle is blue, we are adding a property (viz., blueness) to the idea of a castle, but when we say that the castle exists, we are not adding anything to the concept of a castle. We are saying only that the concept is exemplified or instantiated. In Anselm's argument "exists" is treated as a first-order predicate, which adds something to the concept of an entity and makes it *greater*. This, according to Kant, is the fatal flaw in the argument.

There are many considerations involved in the ontological argument that are not dealt with in our readings. For a clear discussion of the wider issues involved in this argument, see William Rowe's introductory work, *Philosophy of Religion* (Chapter 3, "The Ontological Argument").

II.A.1

The Ontological Argument

ST. ANSELM

St. Anselm (1033–1109), Abbot of Bec and later Archbishop of Canterbury, is the originator of one of the most intriguing arguments ever devised by the human mind, the ontological argument for the existence of a supremely perfect being. After the short selection from Anselm's Proslogion, *there*

From *Monologion and Proslogion, with the replies of Gaunilo and Anselm*, trans. with introduction and notes by Thomas Williams. (Indianapolis, IN: Hackett Publishing Company, 1996.) © 1996 by Thomas Williams. Used with permission.

follows a brief selection from Gaunilo's reply, In Behalf of the Fool, *and a counterresponse by Anselm.*

[ST. ANSELM'S PRESENTATION]

Therefore, Lord, you who grant understanding to faith, grant that, insofar as you know it is useful for me, I may understand that you exist as we believe you exist, and that you are what we believe you to be. Now we believe that you are something than which nothing greater can be thought. So can it be that no such nature exists, since "The fool has said in his heart, 'There is no God'" (Psalm 14:1; 53:1)? But when this same fool hears me say "something than which nothing greater can be thought," he surely understands what he hears; and what he understands exists in his understanding,[1] even if he does not understand that it exists [in reality]. For it is one thing for an object to exist in the understanding and quite another to understand that the object exists [in reality]. When a painter, for example, thinks out in advance what he is going to paint, he has it in his understanding, but he does not yet understand that it exists, since he has not yet painted it. But once he has painted it, he both has it in his understanding and understands that it exists because he has now painted it. So even the fool must admit that something than which nothing greater can be thought exists at least in his understanding, since he understands this when he hears it, and whatever is understood exists in the understanding. And surely that than which a greater cannot be thought cannot exist only in the understanding. For if it exists only in the understanding, it can be thought to exist in reality as well, which is greater. So if that than which a greater cannot be thought exists only in the understanding, then that than which a greater *cannot* be thought is that than which a greater *can* be thought. But that is clearly impossible. Therefore, there is no doubt that something than which a greater cannot be thought exists both in the understanding and in reality....

This [being] exists so truly that it cannot be thought not to exist. For it is possible to think that something

exists that cannot be thought not to exist, and such a being is greater than one that can be thought not to exist. Therefore, if that than which a greater cannot be thought can be thought not to exist, then that than which a greater cannot be thought is *not* that than which a greater cannot be thought; and this is a contradiction. So that than which a greater cannot be thought exists so truly that it cannot be thought not to exist.

And this is you, O Lord our God. You exist so truly, O Lord my God, that you cannot be thought not to exist. And rightly so, for if some mind could think something better than you, a creature would rise above the Creator and sit in judgment upon him, which is completely absurd. Indeed, everything that exists, except for you alone, can be thought not to exist. So you alone among all things have existence most truly, and therefore most greatly. Whatever else exists has existence less truly, and therefore less greatly. So then why did "the fool say in his heart, 'There is no God,'" when it is so evident to the rational mind that you among all beings exist most greatly? Why indeed, except because he is stupid and a fool?...

But how has he said in his heart what he could not think? Or how could he not think what he said in his heart, since to say in one's heart is the same as to think? But if he really—or rather, *since* he really—thought this, because he said it in his heart, and did not say it in his heart, because he could not think it, there must be more than one way in which something is "said in one's heart" or "thought." In one sense of the word, to think a thing is to think the word that signifies that thing. But in another sense, it is to understand what exactly the thing is. God can be thought not to exist in the first sense, but not at all in the second sense. No one who understands what God is can think that God does not exist, although he may say these words in his heart with no signification at all, or with some peculiar signification. For God is that than which a greater cannot be thought. Whoever understands this properly, understands that this being exists in such a way that he cannot, even in thought, fail to exist. So whoever understands that God exists in this way cannot think that he does not exist.

Thanks be to you, my good Lord, thanks be to you. For what I once believed through your grace, I now understand through your illumination, so that even if I did not want to *believe* that you exist, I could not fail to *understand* that you exist....

[GAUNILO'S CRITICISM]

"For example, there are those who say that somewhere in the ocean is an island, which, because of the difficulty—or rather, impossibility—of finding what does not exist, some call 'the Lost Island'. This island (so the story goes) is more plentifully endowed than even the Isles of the Blessed with an indescribable abundance of all sorts of riches and delights. And because it has neither owner nor inhabitant, it is everywhere superior in its abundant riches to all the other lands that human beings inhabit.

"Suppose someone tells me all this. The story is easily told and involves no difficulty, and so I understand it. But if this person went on to draw a conclusion, and say, 'You cannot any longer doubt that this island, more excellent than all others on earth, truly exists somewhere in reality. For you do not doubt that this island exists in your understanding, and since it is more excellent to exist not merely in the understanding, but also in reality, this island must also exist in reality. For if it did not, any land that exists in reality would be greater than it. And so this more excellent thing that you have understood would not in fact be more excellent.'–If, I say, he should try to convince me by, this argument that I should no longer doubt whether the island truly exists, either I would think he was joking, or I would not know whom I ought to think more foolish: myself, if I grant him his conclusion, or him, if he thinks he has

established the existence of that island with any degree of certainty, without first showing that its excellence exists in my understanding as a thing that truly and undoubtedly exists and not in any way like something false or uncertain."...

[ST. ANSELM'S REJOINDER]

But, you say, this is just the same as if someone were to claim that it cannot be doubted that a certain island in the ocean, surpassing all other lands in its fertility (which, from the difficulty—or rather, impossibility—of finding what does not exist, is called "the Lost Island"), truly exists in reality, because someone can easily understand it when it is described to him in words. I say quite confidently that if anyone can find for me something existing either in reality or only in thought to which he can apply this inference in my argument, besides that than which a greater cannot be thought, I will find and give to him that Lost Island, never to be lost again. In fact, however, it has already become quite clear that that than which a greater cannot be thought cannot be thought not to exist, since its existence is a matter of such certain truth. For otherwise it would not exist at all.

Finally, if someone says that he thinks it does not exist, I say that when he thinks this, either he is thinking something than which a greater cannot be thought, or he is not. If he is not, then he is not thinking that it does not exist, since he is not thinking it at all. But if he is, he is surely thinking something that cannot be thought not to exist. For if it could be thought not to exist, it could be thought to have a beginning and an end, which is impossible. Therefore, someone who is thinking it, is thinking something that cannot be thought not to exist. And of course someone who is thinking this does not think that that very thing does not exist. Otherwise he would be thinking something that cannot be thought. Therefore, that than which a greater cannot be thought cannot be thought not to exist....

NOTE

1. The word here translated "understanding" is "*intellectus.*" The text would perhaps read better if I translated it as "intellect," but this would obscure the fact that it is from the same root as the verb "*intelligere,*" "to understand." Some of what Anselm says makes a bit more sense if this fact is constantly borne in mind.

II.A.2

A Critique of the Ontological Argument

IMMANUEL KANT

The German philosopher Immanuel Kant (1724–1804) in his remarkable work Critique of Pure Reason *(1781), from which our selection is taken, set forth a highly influential critique of the ontological argument. Essentially, the objection is that "existence is not a predicate," whereas the opposite is assumed to be true in the various forms of the ontological argument, that is, when you say that Mary is my mother, you are noting some property that describes or adds to who Mary is. But when you say, "Mary, my mother, exists," you are not telling us anything new about Mary; you are simply affirming that the concepts in question are exemplified. "Existence" is a second-order predicate or property, not to be treated as other first-order, normal predicates or properties are.*

THE IMPOSSIBILITY OF AN ONTOLOGICAL PROOF OF THE EXISTENCE OF GOD

It is evident from what has been said, that the conception of an absolutely necessary being is a mere idea, the objective reality of which is far from being established by the mere fact that it is a need of reason. On the contrary, this idea serves merely to indicate a certain unattainable perfection, and rather limits the operations than, by the presentation of new objects, extends the sphere of the understanding. But a strange anomaly meets us at the very threshold; for the inference from a given existence in general to an absolutely necessary existence, seems to be correct and unavoidable, while the conditions of the *understanding* refuse to aid us in forming any conception of such a being.

Philosophers have always talked of an absolutely necessary being, and have nevertheless declined to take the trouble of conceiving whether—and how—a being of this nature is even cogitable, not to mention that its existence is actually demonstrable. A verbal definition of the conception is certainly easy enough; it is something, the non-existence of which is impossible. But does this definition throw any light upon the conditions which render

From Kant's *Critique of Pure Reason*, translated by J. M. D. Meiklejohn (New York: Colonial Press, 1900). Translation revised by Louis Pojman.

it impossible to cogitate the non-existence of a thing—conditions which we wish to ascertain, that we may discover whether we think anything in the conception of such a being or not? For the mere fact that I throw away, by means of the word *Unconditioned*, all the conditions which the understanding habitually requires in order to regard anything as necessary, is very far from making clear whether by means of the conception of the unconditionally necessary I think of something, or really of nothing at all.

Nay, more, this chance-conception, now become so current, many have endeavored to explain by examples, which seemed to render any inquiries regarding its intelligibility quite needless. Every geometrical proposition—a triangle has three angles—it was said, is absolutely necessary; and thus people talked of an object which lay out of the sphere of our understanding as if it were perfectly plain what the conception of such a being meant.

All the examples adduced have been drawn, without exception, from *judgments*, and not from *things*. But the unconditioned necessity of a judgment does not form the absolute necessity of a thing. On the contrary, the absolute necessity of a judgment is only a conditioned necessity of a thing, or of the predicate in a judgment. The proposition above-mentioned, does not enounce that three angles necessarily exist, but, upon condition that a triangle exists, three angles must necessarily exist—in it. And thus this logical necessity has been the source of the greatest delusions. Having formed an *à priori* conception of a thing, the content of which was made to embrace existence, we believed ourselves safe in concluding that, because existence belongs necessarily to the object of the conception (that is, under the condition of my positing this thing as given), the existence of the thing is also posited necessarily, and that it is therefore absolutely necessary—merely because its existence has been cogitated in the conception.

If, in an identical judgment, I annihilate the predicate in thought, and retain the subject, a contradiction is the result; and hence I say, the former belongs necessarily to the latter. But if I suppress both subject and predicate in thought, no contradiction arises; for there is *nothing* at all, and therefore no means of forming a contradiction. To suppose the existence of a triangle and not that of its three angles, is self-contradictory; but to suppose the non-existence of both triangle and angles is perfectly admissible. And so is it with the conception of an absolutely necessary being. Annihilate its existence in thought, and you annihilate the thing itself with all its predicates; how then can there be any room for contradiction? Externally, there is nothing to give rise to a contradiction, for a thing cannot be necessary externally; nor internally, for, by the annihilation or suppression of the thing itself, its internal properties are also annihilated. God is omnipotent—that is a necessary judgment. His omnipotence cannot be denied, if the existence of a Deity is posited—the existence, that is, of an infinite being, the two conceptions being identical. But when you say, *God does not exist*, neither omnipotence nor any other predicate is affirmed; they must all disappear with the subject, and in this judgment there cannot exist the least self-contradiction.

You have thus seen, that when the predicate of a judgment is annihilated in thought along with the subject, no internal contradiction can arise, be the predicate what it may. There is no possibility of evading the conclusion—you find yourselves compelled to declare: There are certain subjects which cannot be annihilated in thought. But this is nothing more than saying: There exist subjects which are absolutely necessary—the very hypothesis which you are called upon to establish. For I find myself unable to form the slightest conception of a thing which, when annihilated in thought with all its predicates, leaves behind a contradiction; and contradiction is the only criterion of impossibility, in the sphere of pure *à priori* conceptions.

Against these general considerations, the justice of which no one can dispute, one argument is adduced, which is regarded as furnishing a satisfactory demonstration from the fact. It is affirmed, that there is one and only one conception, in which the non-being or annihilation of the object is self-contradictory, and this is the conception of an *ens realissimum.*[*] It possesses, you say, all reality, and you feel yourselves justified in admitting the

---

[*]Latin: "most real being."

possibility of such a thing. (This I am willing to grant for the present, although the existence of a conception which is not self-contradictory, is far from being sufficient to prove the possibility of an object.[1]) Now the notion of all reality embraces in it that of existence; the notion of existence lies, therefore, in the conception of this possible thing. If this thing is annihilated in thought, the internal possibility of the thing is also annihilated, which is self-contradictory.

I answer: It is absurd to introduce—under whatever term disguised—into the conception of a thing, which is to be cogitated solely in reference to its possibility, the conception of its existence. If this is admitted, you will have apparently gained the day, but in reality have enounced nothing but a mere tautology. I ask, is the proposition, *this or that thing* (which I am admitting to be possible) exists, an analytical or a synthetical proposition? If the former, there is no addition made to the subject of your thought by the affirmation of its existence; but then the conception in your minds is identical with the thing itself, or you have supposed the existence of a thing to be possible, and then inferred its existence from its internal possibility—which is but a miserable tautology. The word *reality* in the conception of the thing, and the word *existence* in the conception of the predicate, will not help you out of the difficulty. For, supposing you were to term all positing of a thing, reality, you have thereby posited the thing with all its predicates in the conception of the subject and assumed its actual existence, and this you merely repeat in the predicate. But if you confess, as every reasonable person must, that every existential proposition is synthetical, how can it be maintained that the predicate of existence cannot be denied without contradiction—a property which is the characteristic of analytical propositions, alone.

I should have a reasonable hope of putting an end forever to this sophistical mode of argumentation, by a strict definition of the conception of existence, did not my own experience teach me that the illusion arising from our confounding a logical with a real predicate (a predicate which aids in the determination of a thing) resists almost all the endeavors of explanation and illustration. A *logical predicate* may be

what you please, even the subject may be predicated of itself; for logic pays no regard to the content of a judgment. But the determination of a conception is a predicate, which adds to and enlarges the conception. It must not, therefore, be contained in the conception.

Being is evidently not a real predicate, that is, a conception of something which is added to the conception of some other thing. It is merely the positing of a thing, or of certain determinations in it. Logically, it is merely the copula of a judgment. The proposition, *God is omnipotent*, contains two conceptions, which have a certain object or content; the word *is*, is no additional predicate—it merely indicates the relation of the predicate to the subject. Now, if I take the subject (God) with all its predicates (omnipotence being one), and say, *God is*, or *There is a God*, I add no new predicate to the conception of God, I merely posit or affirm the existence of the subject with all its predicates—I posit the *object* in relation to my *conception*. The content of both is the same; and there is no addition made to the conception, which expresses merely the possibility of the object, by my cogitating the object—in the expression, it *is*—as absolutely given or existing. Thus the real contains no more than the possible. A hundred real dollars contain no more than a hundred possible dollars. For, as the latter indicate the conception, and the former the object, on the supposition that the content of the former was greater than that of the latter, my conception would not be an expression of the whole object, and would consequently be an inadequate conception of it. But in reckoning my wealth there may be said to be more in a hundred real dollars, than in a hundred possible dollars—that is, in the mere conception of them. For the real object—the dollars—is not analytically contained in my conception, but forms a synthetical addition to my conception (which is merely a determination of my mental state), although this objective reality—this existence—apart from my conception, does not in the least degree increase the aforesaid hundred dollars.

It does not matter which predicates or how many of them we may think a thing possesses, I do not make the least addition to it when we further declare that this thing exists. Otherwise, it would not be the exact same thing that exists, but something more than we had thought in the idea or concept; and hence, we could not say that the exact object of my thought exists. On the contrary, it exists with the same defect with which I have thought it, since otherwise what exists would be something different from what I thought. So when I think of a being as the highest reality, without any imperfection, the question still remains whether or not this being exists. For although, in my idea, nothing may be lacking in the possible real content of a thing in general, something is still lacking in its relation to my mental state; that is, I am ignorant of whether the object is also possible *à posteriori*. It is here we discover the core of our problem. If the question regarded an object of sense merely, it would be impossible for me to confuse the idea of a thing with its existence. For the concept of the object merely enables me to think of it according to universal conditions of experience; while the existence of the object permits me to think of it within the context of actual experience. However, in being connected with the content of experience as a whole, the concept of the object is not enlarged. All that has happened is that our thought has thereby acquired another possible perception. So it is not surprising that, if we attempt to think existence through the pure categories alone, we cannot specify a single mark distinguishing it from mere possibility.

Whatever be the content of our conception of an object, it is necessary to go beyond it, if we wish to predicate existence of an object. In the case of sensuous objects, this is attained by their connection according to empirical laws with some one of my perceptions; but when it comes to objects of pure thought, there is no means whatever of knowing of their existence, since it would have to be known in a completely *à priori* manner. But all our knowledge of existence (be it immediately by perception or by inferences connecting some object with a perception) belongs entirely to the sphere of experience—which is in perfect unity with itself—and although an existence out of this sphere cannot be absolutely declared to be impossible, it is a hypothesis the truth of which we have no means of discovering.

The idea of a supreme being is in many ways a very useful idea; but for the very reason that it is an idea, it is incapable of enlarging our knowledge with regard to the existence of things. It is not even sufficient to instruct us as to the possibility of a being which we do not know to exist. The analytical criterion of possibility, which consists in the absence of contradiction in propositions, cannot be denied it. But the connection of real properties in a thing is a synthesis of the possibility of which an *à priori* judgment cannot be formed, because these realities are not presented to us specifically; and even if this were to happen, a judgment would still be impossible, because the criterion of possibility of synthetical cognitions must be sought for in the world of experience, to which the object of an idea cannot belong. And thus the celebrated Leibniz has utterly failed in his attempt to establish upon *à priori* grounds the possibility of this sublime ideal being.

The celebrated ontological or Cartesian argument for the existence of a supreme being is therefore insufficient; and we may as well hope to increase our stock of knowledge by the aid of mere ideas, as the merchant to increase his wealth by adding a few zeros to his bank account.

NOTE

1. A conception is always possible, if it is not self-contradictory. This is the logical criterion of possibility, distinguishing the object of such a conception from *the nihil negativum*. But it may be, notwithstanding, an empty conception, unless the objective reality of this synthesis, by which it is generated, is demonstrated; and a proof of this kind must be based upon principles of possible experience, and not upon the principle of analysis or contradiction. This remark may be serviceable as a warning against concluding, from the possibility of a conception—which is logical, the possibility of a thing—which is real.

II.B THE COSMOLOGICAL ARGUMENT FOR THE EXISTENCE OF GOD

ASKING PEOPLE WHY THEY BELIEVE in God is likely to evoke something like the following response: "Well, things didn't just pop up out of nothing. Someone, a pretty powerful Someone, had to cause the universe to come into existence. You just can't have causes going back forever. God must have made the world. Nothing else makes sense."

All versions of the cosmological argument begin with the *a posteriori* assumptions that the universe exists and that something outside the universe is required to explain its existence. That is, it is *contingent*, depending on something outside of itself for its existence. That "something else" is logically prior to the birth of the universe. It constitutes the reason for the existence of the universe. Such a being is God.

One version of the cosmological argument is called the "first-cause argument." From the fact that some things are caused, we may reason to the existence of a first cause. The Dominican friar St. Thomas Aquinas (1225–1274) gives a version of this argument in our first reading. His "second way" is based on the idea of causation:

> We find that among sensible things there is an ordering of efficient causes, and yet we do not find—nor is it possible to find—anything that is an efficient cause of its own self. For if something were an efficient cause of itself, then it would be prior to itself—which is impossible.
>
> But it is impossible to go on to infinity among efficient causes. For in every case of ordered efficient causes, the first is a cause of the intermediate and the intermediate is a cause of the last—and this regardless of whether the intermediate is constituted by many causes or by just one. But when a cause is removed, its effect is removed. Therefore, if there were no first among the efficient causes, then neither would there be a last or an intermediate. But if the efficient causes went on to infinity, there would not be a first efficient cause, and so there would not be a last effect or any intermediate efficient causes, either—which is obviously false. Therefore, one must posit some first efficient cause—which everyone calls God.

The general outline, focusing on the second argument, goes something like this:

1. There exist things that are caused.
2. Nothing can be the cause of itself.
3. There cannot be an infinite regress of causes.
4. Therefore, there exists an uncaused first cause.
5. If there is an uncaused first cause, then the uncaused first cause is God.
6. Therefore, God exists.

What can we say of this argument? Certainly the first premise is true—some things have causes. Indeed, we generally believe that every event has a cause that explains why the event happened. The second premise seems correct, for how could something that didn't exist cause anything, let alone its own existence? Note that premise 2 and premise 4 do not contradict one another. There is nothing obviously incoherent about the idea that something or someone existed from eternity and so is uncaused, whereas there is something incoherent about the idea that something nonexistent caused itself to come into being.

One difficulty with the argument is premise 3: There cannot be an infinite regress of causes. Why can't there be such a regress? You might object that there is an infinite regress of numbers, so why can't there be an infinite regress of causes?

One response to this objection is that there is a significant difference between numbers and events and persons. Numbers are just abstract entities, whereas events and persons are concrete, temporal entities, the sorts of things that need to be brought into existence. Numbers exist in all possible worlds. They are eternal, but Napoleon, Mt. Everest, and you are not eternal but need a causal explanation. The child asks, "Mommy, who made me?" and the mother responds, "You came from my womb." The child persists, "Mommy, who made you and your womb?" The mother responds that she came from a fertilized egg in her mother's womb, but the child persists in the query until the mother is forced to admit that she doesn't know the answer or perhaps says, "God made the world and all that is in it." God may be one explanatory hypothesis, answering the question why the world came to be, but the question is, Are there other, equally good explanatory hypotheses? In other words, does the argument from first cause, *even if it is valid*, give us reason to think that *God* is the first cause?

In our second reading, the eighteenth-century philosopher Samuel Clarke sets forth a different version of the cosmological argument, the argument from contingency (Aquinas's third way). Clarke, like Aquinas before him, identifies the independent and necessary being with God. We are dependent, or contingent, beings. Reducing the argument to the bare bones, the argument from contingency is this:

1. Every being that exists is either contingent or necessary.
2. Not every being can be contingent.
3. Therefore, there exists a necessary being upon which the contingent beings depend.
4. A necessary being on which all contingent beings exist is what we mean by *God*.
5. Therefore, God exists.

A necessary being is self-existing, independent, and has the explanation of its existence in itself, whereas contingent beings do not have the reason for their existence in themselves but depend on other beings and, ultimately, depend on a necessary being.

In our third reading, William Rowe examines the cosmological argument, and especially versions like the argument from contingency based on the *principle of sufficient reason* (PSR)—the thesis that everything must have an explanation to account for it. He points out problems connected with this principle.

In our fourth reading, William Lane Craig and J. P. Moreland defend the *kalām* cosmological argument, an argument first set forth by Arab Islamic scholars, al-Kindi and al-Ghazali, in the Middle Ages.

In our final reading, Paul Draper analyzes the *kalām* argument and claims that, Craig's defense of the cosmological argument fails, both because it fails to establish that the universe had a beginning and because it rests on an equivocation of the phrase 'begins to exist.'

II.B.1

The Five Ways

THOMAS AQUINAS

The Dominican friar Thomas Aquinas (1225–1274) is considered by many to be the greatest theologian in Western religion. The five ways of showing the existence of God given in this selection are versions of the cosmological argument. The first way concerns the fact that there is change (or motion) and argues that there must be an Unmoved Mover that originates all change but itself is not moved. The second way is from the idea of causation and argues that there must be a first, uncaused cause to explain the existence of all other causes. The third way is from the idea of contingency. It argues that because there are dependent beings (e.g., humans), there must be an independent or necessary being on whom the dependent beings rely for their subsistence. The fourth way is from excellence, and it argues that because there are degrees of excellence, there must be a perfect being from whence all excellences come. The final way is from the harmony of things. There is a harmony of nature, which calls for an explanation. The only sufficient explanation is that there is a divine designer who planned this harmony.

ARTICLE 3: DOES GOD EXIST?

It seems that God does not exist:

Objection 1: If one of a pair of contraries were infinite, it would totally destroy the other contrary. But by the name 'God' one means a certain infinite good. Therefore, if God existed, there would be nothing evil. But there is evil in the world. Therefore, God does not exist.

Objection 2: What can be accomplished with fewer principles is not done through more principles.

But it seems that everything that happens in the world could have been accomplished through other principles, even if God did not exist; for things that are natural are traced back to nature as a principle, whereas things that are purposeful are traced back to human reason or will as a principle. Therefore, there is no need to claim that God exists.

But contrary to this: Exodus 1:14 says under the personage of God, "I am Who am."

I respond: There are five ways to prove that God exists.

Printed with the permission of the translator, Alfred J. Freddoso. This translation is being published by Saint Augustine's Press.

The *first* and clearest way is that taken from motion:

It is certain, and obvious to the senses, that in this world some things are moved.

But everything that is moved is moved by another. For nothing is moved except insofar as it is in potentiality with respect to that actuality toward which it is moved, whereas something effects motion insofar as it is in actuality in a relevant respect. After all, to effect motion is just to lead something from potentiality into actuality. But a thing cannot be led from potentiality into actuality except through some being that is in actuality in a relevant respect; for example, something that is hot in actuality—say, a fire—makes a piece of wood, which is hot in potentiality, to be hot in actuality, and it thereby moves and alters the piece of wood. But it is impossible for something to be simultaneously in potentiality and in actuality with respect to same thing; rather, it can be in potentiality and in actuality only with respect to different things. For what is hot in actuality cannot simultaneously be hot in potentiality; rather, it is cold in potentiality. Therefore, it is impossible that something should be both mover and moved in the same way and with respect to the same thing, or, in other words, that something should move itself. Therefore, everything that is moved must be moved by another.

If, then, that by which something is moved is itself moved, then it, too, must be moved by another, and that other by still another. But this does not go on to infinity. For if it did, then there would not be any first mover and, as a result, none of the others would effect motion, either. For secondary movers effect motion only because they are being moved by a first mover, just as a stick does not effect motion except because it is being moved by a hand. Therefore, one has to arrive at some first mover that is not being moved by anything. And this is what everyone takes to be God.

The *second* way is based on the notion of an efficient cause:

We find that among sensible things there is an ordering of efficient causes, and yet we do not find—nor is it possible to find—anything that is an efficient cause of its own self. For if something

were an efficient cause of itself, then it would be prior to itself—which is impossible.

But it is impossible to go on to infinity among efficient causes. For in every case of ordered efficient causes, the first is a cause of the intermediate and the intermediate is a cause of the last—and this regardless of whether the intermediate is constituted by many causes or by just one. But when a cause is removed, its effect is removed. Therefore, if there were no first among the efficient causes, then neither would there be a last or an intermediate. But if the efficient causes went on to infinity, there would not be a first efficient cause, and so there would not be a last effect or any intermediate efficient causes, either—which is obviously false. Therefore, one must posit some first efficient cause—which everyone calls God.

The *third* way is taken from the possible and the necessary, and it goes like this:

Certain of the things we find in the world are able to exist and able not to exist; for some things are found to be generated and corrupted and, as a result, they are able to exist and able not to exist.

But it is impossible that everything should be like this; for that which is able not to exist is such that at some time it does not exist. Therefore, if everything is such that it is able not to exist, then at some time nothing existed in the world. But if this were true, then nothing would exist even now. For what does not exist begins to exist only through something that does exist; therefore, if there were no beings, then it was impossible that anything should have begun to exist, and so nothing would exist now—which is obviously false. Therefore, not all beings are able to exist [and able not to exist]; rather, it must be that there is something necessary in the world.

Now every necessary being either has a cause of its necessity from outside itself or it does not. But it is impossible to go on to infinity among necessary beings that have a cause of their necessity—in the same way, as was proved above, that it is impossible to go on to infinity among efficient causes. Therefore, one must posit something that is necessary *per se*, which does not have a cause of its necessity from outside itself but is instead a cause of necessity for the other [necessary] things. But this everyone calls God.

The *fourth* way is taken from the gradations that are found in the world:

In the world some things are found to be more and less good, more and less true, more and less noble, etc. But *more* and *less* are predicated of diverse things insofar as they approach in diverse ways that which is maximal in a given respect. For instance, the hotter something is, the closer it approaches that which is maximally hot. Therefore, there is something that is maximally true, maximally good, and maximally noble, and, as a result, is a maximal being; for according to the Philosopher in *Metaphysics* 2, things that are maximally true are maximally beings.

But, as is claimed in the same book, that which is maximal in a given genus is a cause of all the things that belong to that genus; for instance, fire, which is maximally hot, is a cause of all hot things. Therefore, there is something that is a cause for all beings of their *esse*, their goodness, and each of their perfections—and this we call God.

The *fifth* way is taken from the governance of things:

We see that some things lacking cognition, viz., natural bodies, act for the sake of an end. This is apparent from the fact that they always or very frequently act in the same way in order to bring about that which is best, and from this it is clear that it is not by chance, but by design, that they attain the end.

But things lacking cognition tend toward an end only if they are directed by something that has cognition and intelligence, in the way that an arrow is directed by an archer. Therefore, there is something intelligent by which all natural things are ordered to an end—and this we call God.

Reply to objection 1: As Augustine says in the *Enchiridion*, "Since God is maximally good, He would not allow any evil to exist in His works if He were not powerful enough and good enough to draw good even from evil." Therefore, it is part of God's infinite goodness that He should permit evils and elicit goods from them.

Reply to objection 2: Since it is by the direction of a higher agent that nature acts for the sake of a determinate end, those things that are done by nature must also be traced back to God as a first cause. Similarly, even things that are done by design must be traced back to a higher cause and not to human reason and will. For human reason and will are changeable and subject to failure, but, as was shown above, all things that can change and fail must be traced back to a first principle that is unmoved and necessary *per se*.

II.B.2

The Argument from Contingency

SAMUEL CLARKE

Samuel Clarke (1675–1729), an English philosopher and Anglican minister, one of the first to appreciate the work of Isaac Newton, here sets forth a version of the argument from contingency. It is based on the idea that if some beings are dependent, or contingent, there must of necessity be an independent being upon which all other beings are dependent.

Reprinted from *A Discourse Concerning Natural Religion* (1705).

There has existed from eternity some one unchangeable and independent being. For since something must needs have been from eternity; as hath been already proved, and is granted on all hands: either there has always existed one unchangeable and *independent* Being, from which all other beings that are or ever were in the universe, have received their original; or else there has been an infinite succession of changeable and *dependent* beings, produced one from another in an endless progression, without any original cause at all: which latter supposition is so very absurd, that tho' all atheism must in its account of most things (as shall be shown hereafter) terminate in it, yet I think very few atheists ever were so weak as openly and directly to defend it. For it is plainly impossible and contradictory to itself. I shall not argue against it from the supposed impossibility of infinite succession, *barely and absolutely considered in itself,* for a reason which shall be mentioned hereafter: but, if we consider such an infinite progression, as *one* entire endless *series of dependent* beings; 'tis plain this whole series of beings can have no cause *from without,* of its existence; because in it are supposed to be included *all things* that are or ever were in the universe: and 'tis plain it can have no reason *within itself,* of its existence; because no one being in this infinite succession is supposed to be self-existent or necessary (which is the only ground or reason of existence of any thing, that can be imagined *within the thing itself,* as will presently more fully appear), but every one *dependent* on the foregoing: and where *no part* is necessary, 'tis manifest *the whole* cannot be necessary; absolute necessity of existence, not being an outward, relative, and accidental determination; but an inward and essential property of the nature of the thing which so exists. An infinite succession therefore of merely *dependent beings,* without any original independent cause; is a *series* of beings, that has neither necessity nor cause, nor any reason *at all* of its existence, neither *within itself* nor *from without:* that is, 'tis an express contradiction and impossibility; 'tis a supposing *something to be caused,* (because it's granted in every one of its stages of succession, not to be necessary and from itself); and yet that in the whole it is caused *absolutely by nothing:* Which every man knows is a contradiction to be done *in time;* and because duration in this case makes no difference, 'tis equally a contradiction to suppose it done from eternity: And consequently there must *on the contrary,* of necessity have existed from eternity, *some one* immutable and *independent* Being: Which, what it is, remains in the next place to be inquired.

II.B.3

An Examination of the Cosmological Argument

WILLIAM ROWE

Brief biographical remarks about William Rowe appear before selection I.B.9. In the present selection, taken from the second edition of his Philosophy of Religion: An Introduction *(1993), Rowe begins by distinguishing between a priori and a posteriori arguments and setting the cosmological argument in historical perspective. Next, he divides the argument into two parts: that which seeks to prove the existence of a self-existent being and that which seeks to prove that this self-existent being is the God of theism. He introduces the principle of sufficient reason—"There must be an explanation (a) of the existence of any being and (b) of any positive fact whatever"—and shows its role in the cosmological argument. In the light of this principle, he examines the argument itself and four objections to it.*

STATING THE ARGUMENT

Arguments for the existence of God are commonly divided into *a posteriori* arguments and *a priori* arguments. An *a posteriori* argument depends on a principle or premise that can be known only by means of our experience of the world. An *a priori* argument, on the other hand, purports to rest on principles all of which can be known independently of our experience of the world, by just reflecting on and understanding them. Of the three major arguments for the existence of God—the Cosmological, the Teleological, and the Ontological—only the last of these is entirely *a priori*. In the Cosmological Argument one starts from some simple fact about the world, such as that it contains things which are caused to exist by other things. In the Teleological Argument a somewhat more complicated fact about the world serves as a starting point, the fact that the world exhibits order and design. In the Ontological Argument, however, one begins simply with a concept of God....

Before we state the Cosmological Argument itself, we shall consider some rather general points about the argument. Historically, it can be traced to the writings of the Greek philosophers, Plato and Aristotle, but the major developments in the argument took place in the thirteenth and in the eighteenth centuries. In the thirteenth century Aquinas put forth five distinct arguments for the existence of God, and of these, the first three are versions of the Cosmological Argument.[1] In the first of these he started from the fact that there are things in the world undergoing change and reasoned to the conclusion that there must be some ultimate cause of change that is itself unchanging. In the second he started from the fact that there are things in the world that clearly are caused to exist by other things and reasoned to the conclusion that there must be some ultimate cause of existence whose own existence is itself uncaused. And in the third argument he started from the fact that there are things in the world which need not have existed at all, things which do exist but which we can easily imagine might not, and reasoned to the conclusion that there must be some being that had to be, that exists and could not have failed to exist. Now it might be objected that even if Aquinas' arguments do prove beyond doubt the existence of an unchanging changer, an uncaused cause, and a being that could not have failed to exist, the arguments fail to prove the existence of the theistic God. For the theistic God, as we saw, is supremely good, omnipotent, omniscient, and creator of but separate from and independent of the world. How do we know, for example, that the unchanging changer isn't evil or slightly ignorant? The answer to this objection is that the Cosmological Argument has two parts. In the first part the effort is to prove the existence of a special sort of being, for example, a being that could not have failed to exist, or a being that causes change in other things but is itself unchanging. In the second part of the argument the effort is to prove that the special sort of being whose existence has been established in the first part has, and must have, the features—perfect goodness, omnipotence, omniscience, and so on—which go together to make up the theistic idea of God. What this means, then, is that Aquinas' three arguments are different versions of only the first part of the Cosmological Argument. Indeed, in later sections of his *Summa Theological* Aquinas undertakes to show that the unchanging changer, the uncaused cause of existence, and the being which had to exist are one and the same being and that this single being has all of the attributes of the theistic God.

We noted above that a second major development in the Cosmological Argument took place in the eighteenth century, a development reflected in the writings of the German philosopher, Gottfried

Leibniz (1646–1716), and especially in the writings of the English theologian and philosopher, Samuel Clarke (1675–1729). In 1704 Clarke gave a series of lectures, later published under the title *A Demonstration of the Being and Attributes of God*. These lectures constitute, perhaps, the most complete, forceful, and cogent presentation of the Cosmological Argument we possess. The lectures were read by the major skeptical philosopher of the century, David Hume (1711–1776), and in his brilliant attack on the attempt to justify religion in the court of reason, his *Dialogues Concerning Natural Religion*, Hume advanced several penetrating criticisms of Clarke's arguments, criticisms which have persuaded many philosophers in the modern period to reject the Cosmological Argument. In our study of the argument we shall concentrate our attention largely on its eighteenth-century form and try to assess its strengths and weaknesses in the light of the criticisms which Hume and others have advanced against it.

The first part of the eighteenth-century form of the Cosmological Argument seeks to establish the existence of a self-existent being. The second part of the argument attempts to prove that the self-existent being is the theistic God, that is, has the features which we have noted to be basic elements in the theistic idea of God. We shall consider mainly the first part of the argument, for it is against the first part that philosophers from Hume to Russell have advanced very important objections.

In stating the first part of the Cosmological Argument we shall make use of two important concepts, the concept of a *dependent being* and the concept of a *self-existent being*. By a *dependent being* we mean *a being whose existence is accounted for by the causal activity of other things*. Recalling Anselm's division into the three cases: "explained by another," "explained by nothing," and "explained by itself," it's clear that a dependent being is a being whose existence is explained by another. By a *self-existent being* we mean *a being whose existence is accounted for by its own nature*. This idea … is an essential element in the theistic concept of God. Again, in terms of Anselm's three cases, a self-existent being is a being whose existence is explained by itself. Armed with

these two concepts, the concept of a dependent being and the concept of a self-existent being, we can now state the first part of the Cosmological Argument.

1.   Every being (that exists or ever did exist) is either a dependent being or a self-existent being.

2.   Not every being can be a dependent being.

Therefore,

3.   There exists a self-existent being.

DEDUCTIVE VALIDITY

Before we look critically at each of the premises of this argument, we should note that this argument is, to use an expression from the logician's vocabulary, *deductively valid*. To find out whether an argument is deductively valid, we need only ask the question: If its premises were true, would its conclusion have to be true? If the answer is yes, the argument is deductively valid. If the answer is no, the argument is deductively invalid. Notice that the question of the validity of an argument is entirely different from the question of whether its premises are in fact true. The following argument is made up entirely of false statements, but it is deductively valid.

1.   Babe Ruth is the President of the United States.

2.   The President of the United States is from Indiana.

Therefore,

3.   Babe Ruth is from Indiana.

The argument is deductively valid because even though its premises are false, if they were true its conclusion would have to be true. Even God, Aquinas would say, cannot bring it about that the premises of this argument are true and yet its conclusion is false, for God's power extends only to what is possible, and it is an absolute impossibility that Babe Ruth be the President, the President be from Indiana, and yet Babe Ruth not be from Indiana.

The Cosmological Argument (that is, its first part) is a deductively valid argument. If its premises are or were true, its conclusion would have to be true. It's clear from our example about Babe Ruth, however, that the fact that an argument is deductively valid is insufficient to establish the truth of its conclusion. What else is required? Clearly that we know or have rational grounds for believing that the premises are true. If we know that the Cosmological Argument is deductively valid, and can establish that its premises are true, we shall thereby have proved that its conclusion is true. Are, then, the premises of the Cosmological Argument true? To this more difficult question we must now turn.

PSR AND THE FIRST PREMISE

At first glance the first premise might appear to be an obvious or even trivial truth. But it is neither obvious nor trivial. And if it appears to be obvious or trivial, we must be confusing the idea of a self-existent being with the idea of a being that is not a dependent being. Clearly, it is true that any being is either a dependent being (explained by other things) or it is not a dependent being (not explained by other things). But what our premise says is that any being is either a dependent being (explained by other things) or it is a self-existent being (explained by itself). Consider again Anselm's three cases.

a. explained by another
b. explained by nothing
c. explained by itself

What our first premise asserts is that each being that exists (or ever did exist) is either of sort *a* or of sort *c*. It denies that any being is of sort *b*. And it is this denial that makes the first premise both significant and controversial. The obvious truth we must not confuse it with is the truth that any being is either of sort *a* or not of sort *a*. While this is true it is neither very significant nor controversial.

Earlier we saw that Anselm accepted as a basic principle that whatever exists has an explanation of its existence. Since this basic principle denies that any thing of sort *b* exists or ever did exist, it's clear that Anselm would believe the first premise of our Cosmological Argument. The eighteenth-century proponents of the argument also were convinced of the truth of the basic principle we attributed to Anselm. And because they were convinced of its truth, they readily accepted the first premise of the Cosmological Argument. But by the eighteenth century, Anselm's basic principle had been more fully elaborated and had received a name, the *Principle of Sufficient Reason*. Since this principle (PSR, as we shall call it) plays such an important role in justifying the premises of the Cosmological Argument, it will help us to consider it for a moment before we continue our enquiry into the truth or falsity of the premises of the Cosmological Argument.

The Principle of Sufficient Reason, as it was expressed by both Leibniz and Samuel Clarke, is a very general principle and is best understood as having two parts. In its first part it is simply a restatement of Anselm's principle that there must be an explanation of the existence of any being whatever. Thus if we come upon a man in a room, PSR implies that there must be an explanation of the fact that that particular man exists. A moment's reflection, however, reveals that there are many facts about the man other than the mere fact that he exists. There is the fact that the man in question is in the room he's in, rather than somewhere else, the fact that he is in good health, and the fact that he is at the moment thinking of Paris, rather than, say, London. Now, the purpose of the second part of PSR is to require an explanation of these facts, as well. We may state PSR, therefore, as the principle that *there must be an explanation (a) of the existence of any being, and (b) of any positive fact whatever*. We are now in a position to study the role this very important principle plays in the Cosmological Argument.

Since the proponent of the Cosmological Argument accepts PSR in both its parts, it is clear that he will appeal to its first part, PSRa, as justification for the first premise of the Cosmological Argument. Of course, we can and should enquire into the deeper question of whether the proponent of the argument is rationally justified in accepting PSR itself. But we shall put this question aside for the moment. What we need to see first is whether he is correct in thinking that *if* PSR is true then both of the premises of the Cosmological Argument are true. And what we have just seen is that if only the first part of PSR, that is, PSRa, is true, the first premise of the Cosmological Argument will be true. But what of the second premise of the argument? For what reasons does the proponent think that it must be true?

THE SECOND PREMISE

According to the second premise, not every being that exists can be a dependent being, that is, can have the explanation of its existence in some other being or beings. Presumably, the proponent of the argument thinks there is something fundamentally wrong with the idea that every being that exists is dependent, that each existing being was caused by some other being which in turn was caused by some other being, and so on. But just what does he think is wrong with it? To help us in understanding his thinking, let's simplify things by supposing that there exists only one thing now, A_1, a living thing perhaps, that was brought into existence by something else, A_2, which perished shortly after it brought A_1 into existence. Suppose further that A_2 was brought into existence in similar fashion some time ago by A_3, and A_3 by A_4, and so forth back into the past. Each of these beings is a *dependent* being, it owes its existence to the preceding thing in the series. Now if nothing else ever existed but these beings, then what the second premise says would not be true. For if every being that exists or ever did exist is an A and was produced by a preceding A, then every being that exists or ever did exist would be dependent and, accordingly, premise two of the Cosmological Argument would be false. If the proponent of the Cosmological Argument is correct there must, then, be something wrong with the idea that

every being that exists or did exist is an A and that they form a causal series: A_1 caused by A_2, A_2 caused by A_3, A_3 caused by A_4, ... A_n caused by A_{n+1}. How does the proponent of the Cosmological Argument propose to show us that there is something wrong with this view?

A popular but mistaken idea of how the proponent tries to show that something is wrong with the view, that every being might be dependent, is that he uses the following argument to reject it.

1. There must be a *first* being to start any causal series.

2. If every being were dependent there would be no *first* being to start the causal series.

Therefore,

3. Not every being can be a dependent being.

Although this argument is deductively valid, and its second premise is true, its first premise overlooks the distinct possibility that a causal series might be *infinite*, with no first member at all. Thus if we go back to our series of A beings, where each A is dependent, having been produced by the preceding A in the causal series, it's clear that if the series existed it would have no first member, for every A in the series there would be a preceding A which produced it, *ad infinitum*. The first premise of the argument just given assumes that a causal series must stop with a first member somewhere in the distant past. But there seems to be no good reason for making that assumption.

The eighteenth-century proponents of the Cosmological Argument recognized that the causal series of dependent beings could be infinite, without a first member to start the series. They rejected the idea that every being that is or ever was is dependent not because there would then be no first member to the series of dependent beings, but because there would then be no explanation for the fact that there are and have always been dependent beings. To see their reasoning let's return to our simplification of the supposition that the only things that exist or ever did exist are dependent beings. In our simplification of that supposition only one of the dependent beings exists at a time, each one perishing as it produces the next in the series. Perhaps the first thing to note about this supposition is that there is no individual A in the causal series of dependent beings whose existence is unexplained—A_1 is explained by A_2, A_2 by A_3, and A_n by A_{n+1}. So the first part of PSR, PSRa, appears to be satisfied. There is no particular being whose existence lacks an explanation. What, then, is it that lacks an explanation, if every particular A in the causal series of dependent beings has an explanation? It is the *series itself* that lacks an explanation, or, as I've chosen to express it, *the fact that there are and have always been dependent beings.* For suppose we ask why it is that there are and have always been As in existence. It won't do to say that As have always been producing other As—we can't explain why there have always been As by saying there always have been As. Nor, on the supposition that only As have ever existed, can we explain the fact that there have always been As by appealing to something other than an A— for no such thing would have existed. Thus the supposition that the only things that exist or ever existed are dependent things leaves us with a fact for which there can be no explanation; namely, the fact that there are and have always been dependent beings.

QUESTIONING THE JUSTIFICATION OF THE SECOND PREMISE

Critics of the Cosmological Argument have raised several important objections against the claim that if every being is dependent the series or collection of those beings would have no explanation. Our understanding of the Cosmological Argument, as well as of its strengths and weaknesses, will be deepened by a careful consideration of these criticisms.

The first criticism is that the proponent of the Cosmological Argument makes the mistake of treating the collection or series of dependent beings as though it were itself a dependent being, and,

therefore, requires an explanation of its existence. But, so the objection goes, the collection of dependent beings is not itself a dependent being any more than a collection of stamps is itself a stamp.

A second criticism is that the proponent makes the mistake of inferring that because each member of the collection of dependent beings has a cause, the collection itself must have a cause. But, as Bertrand Russell noted, such reasoning is as fallacious as to infer that the human race (that is, the collection of human beings) must have a mother because each member of the collection (each human being) has a mother.

A third criticism is that the proponent of the argument fails to realize that for there to be an explanation of a collection of things is nothing more than for there to be an explanation of each of the things making up the collection. Since in the infinite collection (or series) of dependent beings, each being in the collection does have an explanation—by virtue of having been caused by some preceding member of the collection—the explanation of the collection, so the criticism goes, has already been given. As David Hume remarked, "Did I show you the particular causes of each individual in a collection of twenty particles of matter, I should think it very unreasonable, should you afterwards ask me, what was the cause of the whole twenty. This is sufficiently explained in explaining the cause of the parts."[2]

Finally, even if the proponent of the Cosmological Argument can satisfactorily answer these objections, he must face one last objection to his ingenious attempt to justify premise two of the Cosmological Argument. For someone may agree that if nothing exists but an infinite collection of dependent beings, the infinite collection will have no explanation of its existence, and still refuse to conclude from this that there is something wrong with the idea that every being is a dependent being. Why, he might ask, should we think that everything has to have an explanation? What's wrong with admitting that the fact that there are and have always been dependent beings is a *brute fact*, a fact having no explanation whatever? Why does everything have to have an explanation anyway?

We must now see what can be said in response to these several objections.

Responses to Criticism

It is certainly a mistake to think that a collection of stamps is itself a stamp, and very likely a mistake to think that the collection of dependent beings is itself a dependent being. But the mere fact that the proponent of the argument thinks that there must be an explanation not only for each member of the collection of dependent beings but for the collection itself is not sufficient grounds for concluding that he must view the collection as itself a dependent being. The collection of human beings, for example, is certainly not itself a human being. Admitting this, however, we might still seek an explanation of why there is a collection of human beings, of why there are such things as human beings at all. So the mere fact that an explanation is demanded for the collection of dependent beings is no proof that the person who demands the explanation must be supposing that the collection itself is just another dependent being.

The second criticism attributes to the proponent of the Cosmological Argument the following bit of reasoning.

1. Every member of the collection of dependent beings has a cause or explanation.

Therefore,

2. The collection of dependent beings has a cause or explanation.

As we noted in setting forth this criticism, arguments of this sort are often unreliable. It would be a mistake to conclude that a collection of objects is light in weight simply because each object in the collection is light in weight, for if there were many objects in the collection it might be quite heavy. On the other hand, if we know that each marble weighs more than one ounce, we could infer validly that the collection of marbles weighs more than an ounce. Fortunately, however, we don't need to decide whether the inference from 1 to 2 is valid or invalid. We need not decide this question because

the proponent of the Cosmological Argument need not use this inference to establish that there must be an explanation of the collection of dependent beings. He need not use this inference because he has in PSR a principle from which it follows immediately that the collection of dependent beings has a cause or explanation. For according to PSR, every positive fact must have an explanation. If it is a fact that there exists a collection of dependent beings then, according to PSR, that fact too must have an explanation. So it is PSR that the proponent of the Cosmological Argument appeals to in concluding that there must be an explanation of the collection of dependent beings, and not some dubious inference from the premise that each member of the collection has an explanation. It seems, then, that neither of the first two criticisms is strong enough to do any serious damage to the reasoning used to support the second premise of the Cosmological Argument.

The third objection contends that to explain the existence of a collection of things is the same thing as to explain the existence of each of its members. If we consider a collection of dependent beings where each being in the collection is explained by the preceding member which caused it, it's clear that no member of the collection will lack an explanation of its existence. But, so the criticism goes, if we've explained the existence of every member of a collection, we've explained the existence of the collection—there's nothing left over to be explained. This forceful criticism, originally advanced by David Hume, has gained considerable support in the modern period. But the criticism rests on an assumption that the proponent of the Cosmological Argument would not accept. The assumption is that to explain the existence of a collection of things it is *sufficient* to explain the existence of every member in the collection. To see what is wrong with this assumption is to understand the basic issue in the reasoning by which the proponent of the Cosmological Argument seeks to establish that not every being can be a dependent being.

In order for there to be an explanation of the existence of the collection of dependent beings, it's clear that the eighteenth-century proponents would require that the following two conditions be satisfied:

C1. There is an explanation of the existence of each of the members of the collection of dependent beings.

C2. There is an explanation of why there are any dependent beings.

According to the proponents of the Cosmological Argument, if every being that exists or ever did exist is a dependent being—that is, if the whole of reality consists of nothing more than a collection of dependent beings—C1 will be satisfied, but C2 will not be satisfied. And since C2 won't be satisfied, there will be no explanation of the collection of dependent beings. The third criticism, therefore, says in effect that if C1 is satisfied, C2 will be satisfied, and, since in a collection of dependent beings each member will have an explanation in whatever it was that produced it, C1 will be satisfied, So, therefore, C2 will be satisfied and the collection of dependent beings will have an explanation.

Although the issue is a complicated one, I think it is possible to see that the third criticism rests on a mistake: the mistake of thinking that if C1 is satisfied C2 must also be satisfied. The mistake is a natural one to make for it is easy to imagine circumstances in which if C1 is satisfied C2 also will be satisfied. Suppose, for example that the whole of reality includes not just a collection of dependent beings but also a self-existent being. Suppose further that instead of each dependent being having been produced by some other dependent being, every dependent being was produced by the self-existent being. Finally, let us consider both the possibility that the collection of dependent beings is finite in time and has a first member, and the possibility that the collection of dependent beings is infinite in past time, having no first member. Using G for the self-existent being, the first possibility may be diagramed as follows:

G, we shall say, has always existed and always will. We can think of d_1 as some presently existing dependent being, d_2, d_3, and so forth as dependent beings that existed at some time in the past, and d_n as the first dependent being to exist. The second possibility may be portrayed as follows:

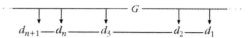

On this diagram there is no first member of the collection of dependent beings. Each member of the infinite collection, however, is explained by reference to the self-existent being G which produced it. Now the interesting point about both these cases is that the explanation that has been provided for the members of the collection of dependent beings carries with it, at least in part, an answer to the question of why there are any dependent beings at all. In both cases we may explain why there are dependent beings by pointing out that there exists a self-existent being that has been engaged in producing them. So once we have learned that the existence of each member of the collection of dependent beings has its existence explained by the fact that G produced it, we have already learned why there are dependent beings.

Someone might object that we haven't really learned why there are dependent beings until we also learn *why* G has been producing them. But, of course, we could also say that we haven't really explained the existence of a particular dependent being, say d_3, until we also learn not just that G produced it but *why* G produced it. The point we need to grasp, however, is that once we admit that every dependent being's existence is explained by G, we must admit that the fact that there are dependent beings has also been explained. So it is not unnatural that someone should think that to explain the existence of the collection of dependent beings is nothing more than to explain the existence of its members. For, as we've seen, to explain the collection's existence is to explain each member's existence and to explain why there are any dependent beings at all. And in the examples we've considered, in doing

55

PART II • TRADITIONAL ARGUMENTS FOR THE EXISTENCE OF GOD

the one (explaining why each dependent being exists) we've already done the other (explained why there are any dependent beings at all). We must now see, however, that on the supposition that the whole of reality consists *only* of a collection of dependent beings, to give an explanation of each member's existence is not to provide an explanation of why there are dependent beings.

In the examples we've considered, we have gone outside of the collection of dependent beings in order to explain the members' existence. But if the only beings that exist or ever existed are dependent beings then each dependent being will be explained by some other dependent being, ad infinitum. This does not mean that there will be some particular dependent being whose existence is unaccounted for. Each dependent being has an explanation of its existence; namely, in the dependent being which preceded it and produced it. So C1 is satisfied: there is an explanation of the existence of each member of the collection of dependent beings. Turning to C2, however, we can see that it will not be satisfied. We cannot explain why there are (or have ever been) dependent beings by appealing to all the members of the infinite collection of dependent beings. For if the question to be answered is why there are (or have ever been) any dependent beings at all, we cannot answer that question by noting that there always have been dependent beings, each one accounting for the existence of some other dependent being. Thus on the supposition that every being is dependent, it seems there will be no explanation of why there are dependent beings. C2 will not be satisfied. Therefore, on the supposition that every being is dependent there will be no explanation of the existence of the collection of dependent beings.

THE TRUTH OF PSR

We come now to the final criticism of the reasoning supporting the second premise of the Cosmological Argument. According to the criticism, it is admitted that the supposition that every being is dependent implies that there will be a *brute fact* in the universe, a fact, that is, for which there can be no explanation whatever. For there will be no explanation of the

fact that dependent beings exist and have always been in existence. It is this brute fact that the proponents of the argument were describing when they pointed out that if every being is dependent, the series or collection of dependent beings would lack an explanation of *its* existence. The final criticism asks what is wrong with admitting that the universe contains such a brute, unintelligible fact. In asking this question the critic challenges the fundamental principle, PSR, on which the Cosmological Argument rests. For, as we've seen, the first premise of the argument denies that there exists a being whose existence has no explanation. In support of this premise the proponent appeals to the first part of PSR. The second premise of the argument claims that not every being can be dependent. In support of this premise the proponent appeals to the second part of PSR, the part which states that there must be an explanation of any positive fact whatever.

The proponent reasons that if every being were a dependent being, then although the first part of PSR would be satisfied—every being would have an explanation—the second part would be violated; there would be no explanation for the positive fact that there are and have always been dependent beings. For first, since every being is supposed to be dependent, there would be nothing outside of the collection of dependent beings to explain the collection's existence. Second, the fact that each member of the collection has an explanation in some other dependent being is insufficient to explain why there are and have always been dependent beings. And, finally, there is nothing about the collection of dependent beings that would suggest that it is a self-existent collection. Consequently, if every being were dependent, the fact that there are and have always been dependent beings would have no explanation. But this violates the second part of PSR. So the second premise of the Cosmological Argument must be true: Not every being can be a dependent being. This conclusion, however, is no better than the principle, PSR, on which it rests. And it is the point of the final criticism to question the truth of PSR. Why, after all, should we accept the idea that every being and every positive fact must have an explanation? Why, in short, should we believe PSR? These are important questions, and any final judgment of the Cosmological Argument depends on how they are answered.

Most of the theologians and philosophers who accept PSR have tried to defend it in either of two ways. Some have held that PSR is (or can be) known *intuitively* to be true. By this they mean that if we fully understand and reflect on what is said by PSR we can see that it must be true. Now, undoubtedly, there are statements which are known intuitively to be true. "Every triangle has exactly three angles" or "No physical object can be in two different places in space at one and the same time" are examples of statements whose truth we can apprehend just by understanding and reflecting on them. The difficulty with the claim that PSR is intuitively true, however, is that a number of very able philosophers fail to apprehend its truth, and some even claim that the principle is false. It is doubtful, therefore, that many of us, if any, know intuitively that PSR is true.

The second way philosophers and theologians who accept PSR have sought to defend it is by claiming that although it is not known to be true, it is, nevertheless, a presupposition of reason, a basic assumption that rational people make, whether or not they reflect sufficiently to become aware of the assumption. It's probably true that there are some assumptions we all make about our world, assumptions which are so basic that most of us are unaware of them. And, I suppose, it might be true that PSR is such an assumption. What bearing would this view of PSR have on the Cosmological Argument? Perhaps the main point to note is that even if PSR is a presupposition we all share, the premises of the Cosmological Argument could still be false. For PSR itself could still be false. The fact, if it is a fact, that all of us *presuppose* that every existing being and every positive fact has an explanation does not imply that no being exists, and no positive fact obtains, without an explanation. Nature is not bound to satisfy our presuppositions. As the American philosopher William James once remarked in another connection, "In the great boarding house of nature, the cakes and the butter and the syrup seldom come out so even and leave the plates so clear."

Our study of the first part of the Cosmological Argument has led us to the fundamental principle on which its premises rest, the Principle of Sufficient Reason. Since we do not seem to know that PSR is true, we cannot reasonably claim to know that the premises of the Cosmological Argument are true. They might be true. But unless we do know them to be true they cannot *establish* for us the conclusion that there exists a being that has the explanation of its existence within its own nature. If it were shown, however, that even though we do not *know* that PSR is true we all, nevertheless, *presuppose* PSR to be true, then, whether PSR is true or not, to be consistent we should accept the Cosmological Argument. For, as we've seen, its premises imply its conclusion and its premises do seem to follow from PSR. But no one has succeeded in *showing* that PSR is an assumption that most or all of us share. So our final conclusion must be that although the Cosmological Argument might be a *sound* argument (valid with true premises), it does not provide us with good rational grounds for believing that among these beings that exist there is one whose existence is accounted for by its own nature. Having come to this conclusion, we may safely put aside the second part of the argument. For even if it succeeded in showing that a self-existent being would have the other attributes of the theistic God, the Cosmological Argument would still not provide us with good rational grounds for belief in God, having failed in its first part to provide us with good rational grounds for believing that there is a self-existent being.

NOTES

1. See St. Thomas Aquinas, *Summa Theologica*, IIa. 2, 3.

2. David Hume, *Dialogues Concerning Natural Religion*, Part IX, ed. H. D. Aiken (New York: Hafner Publishing Company, 1948), pp. 59–60.

II.B.4

The *Kalām* Cosmological Argument

WILLIAM LANE CRAIG AND J. P. MORELAND

William Lane Craig (1949–   ) is a research professor of philosophy at Biola University in Los Angeles. He received his Ph.D. in philosophy from the University of Birmingham (England) and a Th.D. from the University of Munich (Germany). J. P. Moreland (1948–   ) is distinguished professor of philosophy at Biola University. He received his Ph.D. in philosophy from the University of Southern California. Professors Craig and Moreland are the authors of numerous works in philosophy of religion, including Philosophical Foundations for a Christian Worldview *(2003), from which the following selection is taken. The* kalām *argument is a version of the cosmological argument developed by the Arab Islamic scholars al-Kindi and al-Ghazali in the Middle Ages. In this article Craig and Moreland develop two versions of the* kalām *argument, both aiming to prove that the universe must have a cause of its existence.*

The cosmological argument is a family of arguments that seek to demonstrate the existence of a Sufficient Reason or First Cause of the existence of the cosmos. The roll of the defenders of this argument reads like a *Who's Who* of western philosophy: Plato, Aristotle, ibn Sina, Al Ghazali, Maimonides, Anselm, Aquinas, Scotus, Descartes, Spinoza, Leibniz and Locke, to name but some. The arguments can be grouped into three basic types: the *kalām* cosmological argument for a First Cause of the beginning of the universe, the Thomist cosmological argument for a sustaining a Ground of Being of the world, and the Leibnizian cosmological argument for a Sufficient Reason why something exists rather than nothing.

The *kalām* cosmological argument derives its name from the Arabic word designating medieval Islamic scholasticism, the intellectual movement largely responsible for developing the argument. It aims to show that the universe had a beginning at some moment in the finite past and, since something cannot come out of nothing, must therefore have a transcendent cause, which brought the universe into being. Classical proponents of the argument sought to demonstrate that the universe began to exist on the basis of philosophical arguments against the existence of an infinite, temporal regress of past events. Contemporary interest in the argument arises largely out of the startling empirical evidence of astrophysical cosmology for a beginning of space and time. Today the controlling paradigm of cosmology is the standard big bang model, according to which the space-time universe originated *ex nihilo* about fifteen billion years ago. Such an origin *ex nihilo* seems to many to cry out for a transcendent cause.

By contrast the Thomist cosmological argument, named for the medieval philosophical theologian Thomas Aquinas, seeks a cause that is first, not in the temporal sense, but in the sense of rank. Aquinas agreed that "if the world and motion have a first beginning, some cause must clearly be posited for this origin of the world and of motion" (*Summa contra gentiles* 1.13.30). But since he did not regard the *kalām* arguments for the past's finitude as demonstrative, he argued for God's existence on the more difficult assumption of the eternity of the world. On Aquinas's Aristotelian-inspired metaphysic, every existing finite thing is composed of essence and existence and is therefore radically contingent. A thing's essence is an individual nature which serves to define what that thing is. Now if an essence is to exist, there must be conjoined with that essence an act of being. This act of being involves a continual bestowal of being, or the thing would be annihilated. Essence is in potentiality to the act of being, and therefore without the bestowal of being the essence would not exist. For the same reason no substance can actualize itself; for in order to bestow being on itself it would have to be already actual. A pure potentiality cannot actualize itself but requires some external cause. Now although Aquinas argued that there cannot be an infinite regress of causes of being (because in such a series all the causes would be merely instrumental and so no being would be produced, just as no motion would be produced in a watch without a spring even if it had an infinite number of gears) and that therefore there must exist a First Uncaused Cause of being, his actual view was that there can be no intermediate causes of being at all, that any finite substance is sustained in existence immediately by the Ground of Being. This must be a being that is not composed of essence and existence and, hence, requires no sustaining cause. We cannot say that this being's essence includes existence as one of its properties, for existence is not a property, but an act, the instantiating of an essence. Therefore, we must conclude that this being's essence just *is* existence. In a sense, this being has no essence; rather, it is the pure act of being, unconstrained by any essence. It is, as Thomas says, *ipsum esse subsistens*, the act of being itself subsisting. Thomas identifies this being with the God whose name was revealed to Moses as "I am" (Ex 3:14).

The German polymath Gottfried Wilhelm Leibniz, for whom the third form of the argument is named, sought to develop a version of the cosmological argument from contingency without the Aristotelian metaphysical underpinnings of the Thomist argument. In his essay "The Principles of Nature and of Grace, Based on Reason," Leibniz wrote, "The first question which should rightly be asked is this: why is there something rather than nothing?" Leibniz meant this question to be truly universal, not merely to apply to finite things. On the basis of his principle of sufficient reason, as stated in his treatise *The Monadology*, that "no fact can be real or existent, no statement true, unless there be a sufficient reason why it is so and not otherwise," Leibniz held that his question must have an answer. It will not do to say that the universe (or even God) just exists as a brute fact, a simple fact that cannot be explained. There must be an explanation why it exists. He went on to argue that the sufficient reason cannot be found in any individual thing in the universe, nor in the collection of such things which comprise the universe, nor in earlier states of the universe, even if these regress infinitely. Therefore, there must exist an ultramundane being that is metaphysically necessary in its existence, that is to say, its nonexistence is impossible. It is the sufficient reason for its own existence as well as for the existence of every contingent thing.

In evaluating these arguments, let us consider them in reverse order. A simple statement of a Leibnizian cosmological argument runs as follows:

1. Every existing thing has an explanation of its existence, either in the necessity of its own nature or in an external cause.

2. If the universe has an explanation of its existence, that explanation is God.

3. The universe is an existing thing.

4. Therefore the explanation of the existence of the universe is God.

Is this a good argument? One of the principal objections to Leibniz's own formulation of the argument is that the principle of sufficient reason as stated in The *Monadology* seems evidently false. There cannot be an explanation of why there are any contingent states of affairs at all, for if such an explanation is contingent, then it too must have a further explanation, whereas if it is necessary, then the states of affairs explained by it must also be necessary. Some theists have responded to this objection by agreeing that one must ultimately come to some explanatory stopping point that is simply a brute fact, a being whose existence is unexplained. For example, Richard Swinburne claims that in answering the question "Why is there something rather than nothing?" we must finally come to the brute existence of some contingent being. This being will not serve to explain its own existence (and, hence, Leibniz's question goes unanswered), but it will explain the existence of everything else. Swinburne argues that God is the best explanation of why everything other than the brute Ultimate exists because as a unique and infinite being God is simpler than the variegated and finite universe.

But the above formulation of the Leibnizian argument avoids the objection without retreating to the dubious position that God is a contingent being. Premise (1) merely requires any existing *thing* to have an explanation of its existence, either in the necessity of its own nature or in some external cause. This premise is compatible with there being brute *facts* about the world. What it precludes is that there could exist things—substances exemplifying properties—that just exist inexplicably. This principle seems quite plausible, at least more so than its contradictory, which is all that is required for a successful argument. On this analysis, there are two kinds of being: necessary beings, which exist of their own nature and so have no external cause of their existence, and contingent beings, whose existence is accounted for by causal factors outside themselves.

Premise (2) is, in effect, the contrapositive of the typical atheist response to Leibniz that on the atheistic worldview the universe simply exists as a brute contingent thing. Atheists typically assert that, there being no God, it is false that everything has an explanation of its existence, for the universe, in this case, just exists inexplicably. In so saying, the atheist implicitly recognizes that if the universe has an explanation, then God exists as its explanatory ground. Since, as premise (3) states, the universe is obviously an existing thing (especially evident in its very early stages when its density was so extreme), it follows that God exists.

It is open to the atheist to retort that while the universe has an explanation of its existence, that explanation lies not in an external ground but in the necessity of its own nature. In other words, (2) is false; the universe is a metaphysically necessary being. This was the suggestion of David Hume, who demanded, "Why may not the material universe be the necessarily existent being?" Indeed, "How can anything, that exists from eternity, have a cause, since that relation implies a priority in time and a beginning of existence?" (*Dialogues Concerning Natural Religion*, Part 9).

This is an extremely bold suggestion on the part of the atheist. We have, we think we can safely say, a strong intuition of the universe's contingency. A possible world in which no concrete objects exist certainly seems conceivable. We generally trust our modal intuitions on other matters; if we are to do otherwise with respect to the universe's contingency, then atheists need to provide some reason for such skepticism other than their desire to avoid theism. But they have yet to do so.

Still, it would be desirable to have some stronger argument for the universe's contingency than our modal intuitions alone. Could the Thomist cosmological argument help us here? If successful, it would show that the universe is a contingent being causally dependent on a necessary being for its continued existence. The difficulty with appeal to the Thomist argument, however, is that it is very difficult to show that things are, in fact, contingent in the special sense required by the argument. Certainly things are naturally contingent in that their continued existence is dependent on a myriad of factors including particle masses and fundamental forces, temperature, pressure, entropy level and so forth, but this natural contingency does not suffice to establish things' metaphysical contingency in the sense that being must continually be added to their essences lest they be spontaneously annihilated. Indeed, if Thomas's argument does ultimately lead to an absolutely simple being whose essence is existence, then one might well be led to deny that beings are metaphysically composed of essence and existence if the idea of such an absolutely simple being proves to be unintelligible....

But what about the *kalām* cosmological argument? An essential property of a metaphysically necessary and ultimate being is that it be eternal, that is to say, without beginning or end. If the universe is not eternal, then it could not be, as Hume suggested, a metaphysically necessary being. But it is precisely the aim of the *kalām* cosmological argument to show that the universe is not eternal but had a beginning. It would follow that the universe must therefore be contingent in its existence. Not only so, the *kalām* argument shows the universe to be contingent in a very special way: it came into existence out of nothing. The atheist who would answer Leibniz by holding that the existence of the universe is a brute fact, an exception to the principle of sufficient reason, is thus thrust into the very awkward position of maintaining not merely that the universe exists eternally without explanation, but rather that for no reason at all it magically popped into being out of nothing, a position which might make theism look like a welcome alternative. Thus the *kalām* argument not only constitutes an independent argument for a transcendent Creator but also serves as a valuable supplement to the Leibnizian argument.

The *kalām* cosmological argument may be formulated as follows:

1. Whatever begins to exist has a cause.
2. The universe began to exist.
3. Therefore, the universe has a cause.

Conceptual analysis of what it means to be a cause of the universe then aims to establish some of the theologically significant properties of this being.

Premise (1) seems obviously true—at the least, more so than its negation. It is rooted in the metaphysical intuition that something cannot come into being from nothing. Moreover, this premise is constantly confirmed in our experience. Nevertheless, a number of atheists, in order to avoid the argument's conclusion, have denied the first premise. Sometimes it is said that quantum physics furnishes an exception to premise (1), since on the subatomic level events are said to be uncaused (according to the so-called Copenhagen interpretation). In the same way, certain theories of cosmic origins are interpreted as showing that the whole universe could have sprung into being out of the subatomic vacuum. Thus the universe is said to be the proverbial free lunch.

This objection, however, is based on misunderstandings. In the first place, not all scientists agree that subatomic events are uncaused. A great many physicists today are quite dissatisfied with the Copenhagen interpretation of subatomic physics and are exploring deterministic theories like that of David Bohm. Thus subatomic physics is not a proven exception to premise (1). Second, even on the traditional, indeterministic interpretation, particles do not come into being out of nothing. They arise as spontaneous fluctuations of the energy contained in the subatomic vacuum, which constitutes an indeterministic cause of their origination. Third, the same point can be made about theories of the origin of the universe out of a primordial vacuum. Popular magazine articles touting such theories as getting "something from nothing" simply do not understand that the vacuum is not nothing but rather a sea of fluctuating energy endowed with a rich structure and subject to physical laws. Thus there is no basis for the claim that quantum physics proves that things can begin to exist without a cause, much less that the universe could have sprung into being uncaused from literally nothing.

Other critics have said that premise (1) is true only for things *in* the universe, but it is not true *of* the universe itself. But the argument's defender may reply that this objection misconstrues the nature of the premise. Premise (1) does not state merely a physical law like the law of gravity or the laws of thermodynamics, which are valid for things within the universe. Premise (1) is not a physical principle. Rather, premise (1) is a metaphysical principle: being cannot come from nonbeing; something cannot come into existence uncaused from nothing. The principle therefore applies to all of reality, and it is thus metaphysically absurd that the universe should pop into being uncaused out of nothing. This response seems quite reasonable: for on the atheistic view, there was not even the *potentiality* of the universe's existence prior to the big bang, since nothing is prior to the big bang. But then how could the universe become actual if there was not even the potentiality of its existence? It makes much more sense to say that the potentiality of the universe lay in the power of God to create it.

Recently some critics of the *kalām* cosmological argument have denied that in beginning to exist the universe *became actual* or *came into being*. They thereby focus attention on the theory of time underlying the *kalām* argument (see chap. 18). On a static or so-called B-theory of time (according to which all moments of time are equally existent) the universe does not in fact come into being or become actual at the big bang; it just exists tenselessly as a four-dimensional space-time block that is finitely extended in the *earlier than* direction. If time is tenseless, then the critics are right that the universe never really comes into being, and therefore the quest for a cause of its coming into being is misconceived. Although Leibniz's question, "Why is there (tenselessly) something rather than noting?" should still rightly be asked, there would be no reason to look for a cause of the universe's beginning to exist, since on tenseless theories of time the universe did not truly begin to exist by virtue of its having a first event, any more than a meter stick begins to exist by virtue of its having a first centimeter. In affirming that things which begin to exist need a cause, the proponent of the *kalām* cosmological argument assumes the following understanding of that notion, where x ranges over any entity and t ranges over times, whether instants or moments of nonzero finite duration:

A. x begins to exist at t if and only if x comes into being at t.

B. x comes into being at t if and only if (i) x exists at t, and the actual world includes no state of affairs in which x exists timelessly, (ii) t is either the first time at which x exists or is separated from any $t' < t$ at which x existed by an interval during which x does not exist, and (iii) x's existing at t is a tensed fact.

The key clause in (B) is (iii). By presupposing a dynamic or so-called A-theory of time, according to which temporal becoming is real, the proponent of the *kalām* cosmological argument justifiably assumes that the universe's existing at a first moment of time represents the moment at which the universe came into being. Thus the real issue separating the proponent of the *kalām* cosmological argument and critics of the first premise is the objectivity of tense and temporal becoming.

Premise (2), *The universe began to exist*, has been supported by both deductive philosophical arguments and inductive scientific arguments. The first of four arguments for this premise that we will consider is the argument based on *the impossibility of the existence of an actual infinite*. It may be formulated as follows:

1. An actual infinite cannot exist.

2. An infinite temporal regress of physical events is an actual infinite.

3. Therefore an infinite temporal regress of physical events cannot exist.

In order to assess this argument, it will be helpful to define some terms. By an actual infinite, the argument's defender means any collection having at a time t a number of definite and discrete members that is greater than any natural number $\{0, 1, 2, 3, \ldots\}$. This notion is to be contrasted with a potential infinite, which is any collection having at any time t a number of definite and discrete members that is equal to some natural number but which over time increases endlessly toward infinity as a limit. By *exist* proponents of the argument mean "have extra-mental existence," or "be instantiated in the real world." By a "physical event," they mean any change occurring within the space-time universe. Since any change takes time, there are no instantaneous events. Neither could there be an infinitely slow event, since such an "event" would in reality be a changeless state.

Therefore, any event will have a finite, nonzero duration. In order that all the events comprising the temporal regress of past events be of equal duration, one arbitrarily stipulates some event as our standard and, taking as our point of departure the present standard event, we consider any series of such standard events ordered according to the relation *earlier than*. The question is whether this series of events is comprised of an actually infinite number of events or not. If not, then since the universe is not distinct from the series of past physical events, the universe must have had a beginning, in the sense of a first standard event. It is therefore not relevant whether the temporal series had a beginning *point* (a first temporal instant). The question is whether there was in the past an event occupying a nonzero, finite temporal interval that was absolutely first, that is, not preceded by any equal interval.

Premise (1) asserts, then, that an actual infinite cannot exist in the real, spatiotemporal world. It is usually alleged that this sort of argument has been invalidated by Georg Cantor's work on the actual infinite and by subsequent developments in set theory. But this allegation misconstrues the nature of both Cantor's system and modern set theory, for the argument does not in fact contradict a single tenet of either. The reason is this: Cantor's system and set theory are simply a universe of discourse, a mathematical system based on certain adopted axioms and conventions. The argument's defender may hold that while the actual infinite may be a fruitful and consistent concept within the postulated universe of discourse, it cannot be transposed into the spatiotemporal world, for this would involve counterintuitive absurdities. This can be shown by concrete examples that illustrate the various absurdities that would result if an actual infinite were to be instantiated in the real world.

Take, for example, Hilbert's Hotel, a product of the mind of the great German mathematician David Hilbert. As a warm-up, let us first imagine a hotel with a finite number of rooms. Suppose, furthermore, that all the rooms are full. When a new guest arrives asking for a room, the proprietor apologizes, "Sorry, all the rooms are full," and that is the end of the story. But now let us imagine a hotel with

an infinite number of rooms and suppose once more that *all the rooms are full*. There is not a single vacant room throughout the entire infinite hotel. Now suppose a new guest shows up, asking for a room. "But of course!" says the proprietor, and he immediately shifts the person in room #1 into room #2, the person in room #2 into room #3, the person in room #3 into room #4 and so on, out to infinity. As a result of these room changes, room #1 now becomes vacant, and the new guest gratefully checks in. But remember, before he arrived, all the rooms were full! Equally curious, according to the mathematicians, there are now no more persons in the hotel than there were before: the number is just infinite. But how can this be? The proprietor just added the new guest's name to the register and gave him his keys—how can there not be one more person in the hotel than before?

But the situation becomes even stranger. For suppose an infinity of new guests show up at the desk, asking for a room. "Of course, of course!" says the proprietor, and he proceeds to shift the person in room #1 into room #2, the person in room #2 into room #4, the person in room #3 into room #6 and so on out to infinity, always putting each former occupant into the room number twice his own. Because any natural number multiplied by two always equals an even number, all the guests wind up in even-numbered rooms. As a result, all the odd-numbered rooms become vacant, and the infinity of new guests is easily accommodated. And yet, before they came, all the rooms were full! And again, strangely enough, the number of guests in the hotel is the same after the infinity of new guests check in as before, even though there were as many new guests as old guests. In fact, the proprietor could repeat this process *infinitely many times*, and yet there would never be one single person more in the hotel than before.

But Hilbert's Hotel is even stranger than the German mathematician made it out to be. For suppose some of the guests start to check out. Suppose the guest in room #1 departs. Is there not now one fewer person in the hotel? Not according to the mathematicians! Suppose the guests in rooms #1, 3, 5, … check out. In this case an infinite number of people have left the hotel, but according to the mathematicians, there are no fewer people in the hotel! In fact, we could have every other guest check out of the hotel and repeat this process infinitely many times, and yet there would never be any fewer people in the hotel. Now suppose the proprietor doesn't like having a half-empty hotel (it looks bad for business). No matter! By shifting occupants as before, but in reverse order, he transforms his half-vacant hotel into one that is jammed to the gills. You might think that by these maneuvers the proprietor could always keep this strange hotel fully occupied. But you would be wrong. For suppose that the persons in rooms #4, 5, 6, ... checked out. At a single stroke the hotel would be virtually emptied, the guest register would be reduced to three names, and the infinite would be converted to finitude. And yet it would remain true that the same number of guests checked out this time as when the guests in rooms #1, 3, 5, ... checked out! Can anyone believe that such a hotel could exist in reality?

Hilbert's Hotel certainly seems absurd. Since nothing hangs on the illustration's involving a hotel, the argument, if successful, would show in general that it is impossible for an actually infinite number of things to exist in spatiotemporal reality. Students sometimes react to such illustrations as Hilbert's Hotel by saying that we really do not understand the nature of infinity and, hence, these absurdities result. But this attitude is simply mistaken. Infinite set theory is a highly developed and well-understood branch of mathematics, and these absurdities can be seen to result precisely because we *do* understand the notion of a collection with an actually infinite number of members.

Sometimes it is said that we can find counterexamples to the claim that an actually infinite number of things cannot exist, so that premise (1) must be false. For instance, is not every finite distance capable of being divided into 1/2, 1/4, 1/8, ..., on to infinity? Does that not prove that there are in any finite distance an actually infinite number of parts? The defender of the argument may reply that this objection confuses a potential infinite with an actual infinite. He will point out that while you can

continue to divide any distance for as long as you want, such a series is merely potentially infinite, in that infinity serves as a limit that you endlessly approach but never reach. If you assume that any distance is *already* composed out of an actually infinite number of parts, then you are begging the question. You are assuming what the objector is supposed to prove, namely that there is a clear counterexample to the claim that an actually infinite number of things cannot exist.

Again, it is worth reiterating that nothing in the argument need be construed as an attempt to undermine the theoretical system bequeathed by Cantor to modern mathematics. Indeed, some of the most eager enthusiasts of the system of transfinite mathematics are only too ready to agree that these theories have no relation to the real world. Thus Hilbert, who exuberantly extolled Cantor's greatness, nevertheless held that the Cantorian paradise exists only in the ideal world invented by the mathematician and is nowhere to be found in reality. The case against the existence of the actual infinite need say nothing about the use of the idea of the infinite in conceptual mathematical systems.

The second premise states that *an infinite temporal regress of events is an actual infinite.* The second premise asserts that if the series or sequence of changes in time is infinite, then these events considered collectively constitute an actual infinite. The point seems obvious enough, for if there has been a sequence composed of an infinite number of events stretching back into the past, then an actually infinite number of events have occurred. If the series of past events were an actual infinite, then all the absurdities attending the real existence of an actual infinite would apply to it.

In summary: if an actual infinite cannot exist in the real, spatiotemporal world and an infinite temporal regress of events is such an actual infinite, we can conclude that an infinite temporal regress of events cannot exist, that is to say, the temporal series of past physical events had a beginning. And this implies the second premise of the original syllogism of the *kalām* cosmological argument.

The second argument against the possibility of an infinite past that we will consider is the argument based on *the impossibility of forming an actual infinite by successive addition*. It may be formulated as follows:

1. The temporal series of physical events is a collection formed by successive addition.
2. A collection formed by successive addition cannot be an actual infinite.
3. Therefore, the temporal series of physical events cannot be an actual infinite.

Here one does not assume that an actual infinite cannot exist. Even if an actual infinite can exist, it is argued that the temporal series of events cannot be such, since an actual infinite cannot be formed by successive addition, as the temporal series of events is.

Premise (1) presupposes once again an A-theory of time. On such a theory the collection of all past events prior to any given event is not a collection whose members all tenselessly coexist. Rather, it is a collection that is instantiated sequentially or successively in time, one event coming to pass on the heels of another. Since temporal becoming is an objective feature of the physical world, the series of past events is not a tenselessly existing continuum, all of whose members are equally real. Rather, the members of the series come to be and pass away one after another.

Premise (2) asserts that a collection formed by successive addition cannot be an actual infinite. Sometimes this is described as the impossibility of traversing the infinite. In order for us to have "arrived" at today, temporal existence has, so to speak, traversed an infinite number of prior events. But before the present event could arrive, the event immediately prior to it would have to arrive, and before that event could arrive, the event immediately prior to it would have to arrive, and so on ad infinitum. No event could ever arrive, since before it could elapse there will always be one more event that had to have happened first. Thus, if the series of past events were beginningless, the present event could not have arrived, which is absurd.

This argument brings to mind Betrand Russell's account of Tristram Shandy, who, in the novel by Sterne, writes his autobiography so slowly that it takes him a whole year to record the events of a single day. Were he mortal, he would never finish, asserts Russell, but if he were immortal, then the entire book could be completed, since to each day there would correspond a year, and both are infinite. Russell's assertion is untenable on an A-theory of time, however, since the future is in reality a potential infinite only. Though he write forever, Tristram Shandy would only get farther and farther behind, so that instead of finishing his autobiography, he will progressively approach a state in which he would be *infinitely* far behind. But he would never reach such a state because the years and hence the days of his life would always be finite in number though indefinitely increasing.

But let us turn the story about: Suppose Tristram Shandy has been writing from eternity past at the rate of one day per year. Should not Tristram Shandy now be infinitely far behind? For if he has lived for an infinite number of years, Tristram Shandy has recorded an equally infinite number of past days. Given the thoroughness of his autobiography, these days are all consecutive days. At any point in the past or present, therefore, Tristram Shandy has recorded a beginningless, infinite series of consecutive days. But now the question inevitably arises: *Which* days are these? Where in the temporal series of events are the days recorded by Tristram Shandy at any given point? The answer can only be that *they are days infinitely distant from the present*. For there is no day on which Tristram Shandy is writing that is finitely distant from the last recorded day.

If Tristram Shandy has been writing for one year's time, then the most recent day he could have recorded is one year ago. But if he has been writing two years, then that same day could not have been recorded by him. For since his intention is to record *consecutive* days of his life, the most recent day he could have recorded is the day immediately after a day at least two years ago. This is because it takes a year to record a day, so that to record two days he must have two years. Similarly, if he has been writing three years, then the most recent day recorded could be no more recent than three years ago plus two days. In fact, the recession into the past of the most recent recordable day can be plotted according to the formula: (present date $-n$ years of writing) $+ (n - 1)$ days. In other words, the longer he has written the further behind he has fallen. But what happens if Tristram Shandy has, *ex hypothesi*, been writing for an infinite number of years? The first day of his autobiography recedes to infinity, that is to say, to a day infinitely distant from the present. Nowhere in the past at a finite distance from the present can we find a recorded day, for by now Tristram Shandy is infinitely far behind. The beginningless, infinite series of days which he has recorded are days which lie at an infinite temporal distance from the present. What therefore follows from the Tristram Shandy story is that an infinite series of past events is absurd, for there is no way to traverse the distance from an infinitely distant event to the present, or, more technically, for an event that was once present to recede to an infinite temporal distance.

But now a deeper absurdity bursts into view. For if the series of past events is an actual infinite, then we may ask, why did Tristram Shandy not finish his autobiography yesterday or the day before, since by then an infinite series of moments had already elapsed? Given that in infinite time he would finish the book, then at any point in the infinite past he should already have finished. No matter how far along the series of past events one regresses, Tristram Shandy would have already completed his autobiography. Therefore, at no point in the infinite series of past events could he be finishing the book. We could never look over Tristram Shandy's shoulder to see if he were now writing the last page. For at any point an actually infinite sequence of events would have transpired and the book would have already been completed. Thus at no time in eternity will we find Tristram Shandy writing, which is absurd, since we supposed him to be writing from eternity. And at no point will he finish the book, which is equally absurd, because for the book to be completed, he must at some point have finished. What the Tristram Shandy story really tells us is that an actually infinite temporal regress is absurd.

Sometimes critics indict this argument as a sleight-of-hand trick like Zeno's paradoxes of motion. Zeno argued that before Achilles could cross the stadium, he would have to cross halfway; but before he could cross halfway, he would have to cross a quarter of the way; but before he could cross a quarter of the way, he would have to cross an eighth of the way, and so on to infinity. It is evident that Achilles could not even move! Therefore, Zeno concluded, motion is impossible. Now even though Zeno's argument is very difficult to refute, nobody really believes that motion is impossible. Even if Achilles must pass through an infinite number of halfway points in order to cross the stadium, somehow he manages to do so! The argument against the impossibility of traversing an infinite past, some critics allege, must commit the same fallacy as Zeno's paradox.

But such an objection fails to reckon with two crucial disanalogies of an infinite past to Zeno's paradoxes: whereas in Zeno's thought experiments the intervals traversed are *potential* and *unequal,* in the case of an infinite past the intervals are *actual* and *equal.* The claim that Achilles must pass through an infinite number of halfway points in order to cross the stadium is question-begging, for it already assumes that the whole interval is a composition of an infinite number of points, whereas Zeno's opponents, like Aristotle, take the line as a whole to be conceptually prior to any divisions which we might make in it. Moreover, Zeno's intervals, being unequal, sum to a merely finite distance, whereas the intervals in an infinite past sum to an infinite distance. Thus his thought experiments are crucially disanalogous to the task of traversing an infinite number of equal, actual intervals to arrive at our present location.

It is frequently objected that this sort of argument illicitly presupposes an infinitely distant starting point in the past and then pronounces it impossible to travel from that point to today. But if the past is infinite, then there would be no starting point whatever, not even an infinitely distant one. Nevertheless, from any given point in the past, there is only a finite distance to the present, which is easily "traversed." But in fact no proponent of the *kalām* argument of whom we are aware has assumed that there was an infinitely distant starting point in the past. (Even the Tristram Shandy paradox does not assert that there was an infinitely distant first day, but merely that there were days infinitely distant in the past.) The fact that there is *no beginning* at all, not even an infinitely distant one, seems only to make the problem worse, not better. To say that the infinite past could have been formed by successive addition is like saying that someone has just succeeded in writing down all the negative numbers, ending at −1. And, we may ask, how is the claim that from any given moment in the past there is only a finite distance to the present even relevant to the issue? The defender of the *kalām* argument could agree to this happily. For the issue is how the *whole* series can be formed, not a finite portion of it. Does the objector think that because every *finite* segment of the series can be formed by successive addition that the whole *infinite* series can be so formed? That is as logically fallacious as saying because every part of an elephant is light in weight, the whole elephant is light in weight. The claim is therefore irrelevant.

In summary: If a collection formed by successive addition cannot be an actual infinite, then since the temporal series of events is a collection formed by successive addition, it follows that the temporal series of past physical events is not beginningless.

The third argument for the universe's beginning advanced by contemporary proponents of the *kalām* cosmological argument is an inductive argument based on the expansion of the universe. In 1917, Albert Einstein made a cosmological application of his newly discovered gravitational theory, the general theory of relativity (GTR). In so doing he assumed that the universe exists in a steady state, with a constant mean mass density and a constant curvature of space. To his chagrin, however, he found that GTR would not permit such a model of the universe unless he introduced into his gravitational field equations a certain "fudge factor" in order to counterbalance the gravitational effect of matter and so ensure a static universe. Unfortunately, Einstein's static universe was balanced on a razor's edge, and the least perturbation would cause

the universe either to implode or to expand. By taking this feature of Einstein's model seriously, the Russian mathematician Alexander Friedman and the Belgian astronomer Georges Lemaître were able to formulate independently in the 1920s solutions to the field equations which predicted an expanding universe.

In 1929 the astronomer Edwin Hubble showed that the red-shift in the optical spectra of light from distant galaxies was a common feature of all measured galaxies and was proportional to their distance from us. This red-shift was taken to be a Doppler effect indicative of the recessional motion of the light source in the line of sight. Incredibly, what Hubble had discovered was the isotropic expansion of the universe predicted by Friedman and Lemaître on the basis of Einstein's GTR.

According to the Friedman-Lemaître model, as time proceeds, the distances separating galactic masses become greater. It is important to understand that as a GTR-based theory, the model does not describe the expansion of the material content of the universe into a preexisting, empty space, but rather the expansion of space itself. The ideal particles of the cosmological fluid constituted by the galactic masses are conceived to be at rest with respect to space but to recede progressively from one another as space itself expands or stretches, just as buttons glued to the surface of a balloon would recede from one another as the balloon inflates. As the universe expands, it becomes less and less dense. This has the astonishing implication that as one reverses the expansion and extrapolates back in time, the universe becomes progressively denser until one arrives at a state of "infinite density"[1] at some point in the finite past. This state represents a singularity at which space-time curvature, along with temperature, pressure and density, becomes infinite. It therefore constitutes an edge or boundary to space-time itself. The term "big bang" is thus potentially misleading, since the expansion cannot be visualized from the outside (there being no "outside," just as there is no "before" with respect to the big bang).

The standard big bang model, as the Friedman-Lemaître model came to be called, thus describes a universe that is not eternal in the past but that came into being a finite time ago. Moreover—and this deserves underscoring—the origin it posits is an absolute origin *ex nihilo*. For not only all matter and energy, but space and time themselves come into being at the initial cosmological singularity. There can be no natural, physical cause of the big bang event, since, in Quentin Smith's words, "it belongs analytically to the concept of the cosmological singularity that it is not the effect of prior physical events. The definition of a singularity... entails that it is *impossible to extend the spacetime manifold beyond the singularity....* This rules out the idea that the singularity is an effect of some prior natural process."[2] Sir Arthur Eddington, contemplating the beginning of the universe, opined that the expansion of the universe was so preposterous and incredible that "I feel almost an indignation that anyone should believe in it—except myself."[3] He finally felt forced to conclude, "The beginning seems to present insuperable difficulties unless we agree to look on it as frankly supernatural."[4]

Sometimes objectors appeal to scenarios other than the standard model of the expanding universe in an attempt to avert the absolute beginning predicted by the standard model. But while such theories are possible, it has been the overwhelming verdict of the scientific community that none of them is more probable than the big bang theory. The devil is in the details, and once you get down to specifics you find that there is no mathematically consistent model that has been so successful in its predictions or as corroborated by the evidence as the traditional big bang theory. For example, some theories, like the oscillating universe (which expands and recontracts forever) or the chaotic inflationary universe (which continually spawns new universes), do have a potentially infinite future but turn out to have only a finite past. Vacuum fluctuation universe theories (which postulate an eternal vacuum out of which our universe is born) cannot explain why, if the vacuum was eternal, we do not observe an infinitely old universe. The quantum gravity universe theory propounded by the famous physicist Stephen Hawking, if interpreted realistically, still involves an absolute origin of the universe even if the universe does not begin in a so-called singularity, as it does in the standard big bang theory. The recent speculative cyclic ekpyrotic scenario championed by Paul Steinhardt not only leaves unresolved the difficulties facing the old oscillating universe but has also been shown to require a singular beginning in the past. In sum, according to Hawking, "Almost everyone now believes that the universe, and *time itself*, had a beginning at the Big Bang."[5]

The fourth argument for the finitude of the past is also an inductive argument, this time on the basis of the thermodynamic properties of the universe. According to the second law of thermodynamics, processes taking place in a closed system always tend toward a state of equilibrium. Now our interest in the law concerns what happens when it is applied to the universe as a whole. The universe is, on a naturalistic view, a gigantic closed system, since it is everything there is and there is nothing outside it. This seems to imply that, given enough time, the universe and all its processes will run down, and the entire universe will come to equilibrium. This is known as the heat death of the universe. Once the universe reaches this state, no further change is possible. The universe is dead.

There are two possible types of heat death for the universe. If the universe will eventually recontract, it will die a "hot" death. As it contracts, the stars gain energy, causing them to burn more rapidly so that they finally explode or evaporate. As everything in the universe grows closer together, the black holes begin to gobble up everything around them, and eventually begin themselves to coalesce. In time, all the black holes finally coalesce into one large black hole that is coextensive with the universe, from which the universe will never reemerge.

On the other hand if, as is more likely, the universe will expand forever, then its death will be cold, as the galaxies turn their gas into stars, and the stars burn out. At 10^{30} years the universe will consist of 90% dead stars, 9% supermassive black holes formed by the collapse of galaxies, and 1% atomic matter, mainly hydrogen. Elementary particle physics suggests that thereafter protons will decay into electrons and positrons so that space will be filled with a rarefied gas so thin that the distance between an electron and a positron will be about the size of the present galaxy. Eventually all black holes will completely evaporate and all the matter in the ever-expanding universe will be reduced to a thin gas of elementary particles and radiation. Equilibrium will prevail throughout, and the entire universe will be in its final state, from which no change will occur.

Now the question that needs to be asked is this: if given enough time the universe will reach heat death, then why is it not in a state of heat death now, if it has existed forever, from eternity? If the universe did not begin to exist, then it should now be in a state of equilibrium. Like a ticking clock, it should by now have run down. Since it has not yet run down, this implies, in the words of one baffled scientist, "In some way the universe must have been *wound up*."[6]

Some people have tried to escape this conclusion by adopting an oscillating model of the universe which never reaches a final state of equilibrium. But even apart from the physical and observational problems plaguing such a model, the thermodynamic properties of this model imply the very beginning of the universe that its proponents sought to avoid. Because entropy increases from cycle to cycle in such a model, it has the effect of generating larger and longer oscillations with each successive cycle. Thus, as one traces the oscillations back in time, they become progressively smaller until one reaches a first and smallest oscillation. Hence, the oscillating model has an infinite future, but only a finite past. In fact, it is estimated on the basis of current entropy levels that the universe cannot have gone through more than 100 previous oscillations.

Even if this difficulty were avoided, a universe oscillating from eternity past would require an infinitely precise tuning of initial conditions in order to last through an infinite number of successive bounces. A universe rebounding from a single, infinitely long contraction is, if entropy increases during the contracting phase, thermodynamically untenable and incompatible with the initial low-entropy condition of our expanding phase. Postulating an entropy decrease during the contracting phase in order to escape this problem would require us to postulate inexplicably special low-entropy conditions

at the time of the bounce in the life of an infinitely evolving universe. Such a low-entropy condition at the beginning of the expansion is more plausibly accounted for by the presence of a singularity or some sort of quantum creation event.

So whether one adopts a recontracting model, an ever-expanding model or an oscillating model, thermodynamics suggests that the universe had a beginning. The universe appears to have been created a finite time ago, and its energy was somehow simply put in at the creation as an initial condition.

On the basis of these four arguments for the finitude of the past, the proponent of the *kalām* argument seems to have good grounds for affirming the second premise of the *kalām* cosmological argument: that the universe began to exist. It therefore follows that the universe has a cause. Conceptual analysis enables us to recover a number of striking properties that must be possessed by such an ultramundane being. For as the cause of space and time, this entity must transcend space and time and therefore exist atemporally and nonspatially, at least without the universe. This transcendent cause must therefore be changeless and immaterial, since timelessness entails changelessness, and changelessness implies immateriality. Such a cause must be beginningless and uncaused, at least in the sense of lacking any antecedent causal conditions. Ockham's razor will shave away further causes, since we should not multiply causes beyond necessity. This entity must be unimaginably powerful, since it created the universe without any material cause.

Finally, and most remarkably, such a transcendent cause is plausibly taken to be personal. Three reasons can be given for this conclusion. First, there are two types of causal explanation: scientific explanations in terms of laws and initial conditions and personal explanations in terms of agents and their volitions. A first state of the universe *cannot* have a scientific explanation, since there is nothing before it, and therefore it can be accounted for only in terms of a personal explanation. Second, the personhood of the cause of the universe is implied by its timelessness and immateriality, since the only entities we know of that can possess such properties are either minds or abstract objects, and abstract objects do not stand in causal relations. Therefore, the transcendent cause of the origin of the universe must be of the order of mind. Third, this same conclusion is also implied by the fact that we have in this case the origin of a temporal effect from a timeless cause. If the cause of the origin of the universe were an impersonal set of necessary and sufficient conditions, it would be impossible for the cause to exist without its effect. For if the necessary and sufficient conditions of the effect are timelessly given, then their effect must be given as well. The only way for the cause to be timeless and changeless but for its effect to originate anew a finite time ago is for the cause to be a personal agent who freely chooses to bring about an effect without antecedent determining conditions. Thus we are brought, not merely to a transcendent cause of the universe, but to its Personal Creator. He is, as Leibniz maintained, the Sufficient Reason why anything exists rather than nothing.

NOTES

1. This should not be taken to mean that the density of the universe takes on a value of H_0 but rather that the density of the universe is expressed by a ratio of mass to volume in which the volume is zero; since division by zero is impermissible, the density is said to be infinite in this sense.

2. Quentin Smith, "The Uncaused Beginning of the Universe," in *Theism, Atheism and Big Bang Cosmology*, by William Lane Craig and Quentin Smith (Oxford: Clarendon, 1993), p. 120.

3. Arthur Eddington, *The Expanding Universe* (New York: Macmillan, 1933), p. 124.

4. Ibid., p. 178.

5. Stephen Hawking and Roger Penrose, *The Nature of Space and Time*, The Isaac Newton Institute Series of Lectures (Princeton, N.J.: Princeton University Press, 1996), p. 20.

6. Richard Schlegel, "Time and Thermodynamics," in *The Voices of Time*, ed. J. T. Fraser (London: Penguin, 1948), p. 511.

II.B.5

A Critique of the *Kalām* Cosmological Argument

PAUL DRAPER

Paul Draper is professor of philosophy at Purdue University and the author of several important essays in the philosophy of religion. In this article he analyzes William Lane Craig's philosophical defense of the kalam cosmological argument. Draper contends that Craig's defense fails, both because it fails to establish that the universe had a beginning and because it rests on an equivocation of the phrase 'begins to exist.'

Epistemology begins in doubt, ethics in conflict, and metaphysics in wonder.

In a recent book,[1] William Lane Craig offers a philosophical and scientific defense of a very old and very wonderful argument: the *kalām* cosmological argument. Unlike other cosmological arguments, the *kalām* argument bases its conclusion that the universe has a cause of its existence on the premise that the universe began to exist a finite time ago. Craig calls it the "*kalām*" cosmological argument because "*kalām*" is the name of a theological movement within Islam that used reason, including this argument, to defend the Muslim faith against philosophical objections. After being fully developed by Arab thinkers like al-Kindi and al-Ghazali, the argument eventually made its way to the West, where it was rejected by St. Thomas Aquinas and defended by St. Bonaventure.[2] My focus in this paper will be on Craig's philosophical defense of the argument. I will try to show that this defense fails, both because it fails to establish that the universe had a beginning and because it commits the fallacy of equivocation.

Compare the following two cosmological arguments, each of which concludes that the universe has a cause of its existence:

1. Every contingent thing (including things that are infinitely old) has a cause of its existence.

2. The universe is contingent.

3. Therefore, the universe has a cause of its existence.

1. Everything that begins to exist has a cause of its existence.

2. The universe began to exist.

3. Therefore, the universe has a cause of its existence.

The first of these arguments is sometimes called the argument from contingency. It was suggested by Aristotle, clearly formulated by Arabic philosophers like ibn Sina, and later championed in the West by St. Thomas Aquinas. I find it completely unpersuasive. For although the second premise is clearly true (so long as "contingent" means "logically contingent"), I do not find the first premise appealing at all. If something is infinitely old, then it has always existed, and it's hard to see why something that has always existed requires a cause of its existence, even if it is logically possible that it not have existed. (Indeed, it's not even clear that something that has always existed *could* have a cause of its existence.)

The second of these arguments is the *kalām* cosmological argument. This argument avoids the weakness of the argument from contingency by denying that the universe is infinitely old and maintaining that the universe needs a cause, not because it is contingent, but rather because it had a beginning. In other words, it replaces the weak premise that every contingent thing needs a cause of its existence with the compelling premise that everything that begins to exist needs a cause of its existence. Of course, a price must be paid for strengthening the first premise: the second premise—that the universe began to exist—is not by a long shot as unquestionably true as the claim that the universe is contingent.

Craig, however, provides a spirited and plausible defense of this premise. He offers four arguments in support of it, two of which are philosophical (armchair cosmology at its best) and two of which are scientific (but still interesting). Both philosophical arguments depend on a distinction between a potential infinite and an actual infinite. A potential infinite is a series or collection that can increase forever without limit but is always finite (e.g., the set of events that have occurred since the birth of my daughter or the set of completed years after 1000 BCE). An actual infinite is a set of distinct things (real or not) whose number is actually infinite (e.g., the set of natural numbers). The first philosophical argument claims that there can't be an infinite regress of events, because actual infinites cannot exist in reality. According to the second argument, an infinite regress of events is impossible because, even if actual infinites could exist in reality, they could not be formed by successive addition.

The first scientific argument is based on the evidence for the Big Bang theory, which seems to many scientists to support the view that the universe had a beginning. The second scientific argument appeals to the Second Law of Thermodynamics. According to this law, the amount of energy available to do mechanical work always decreases in a closed system. Thus, since the universe as a whole is a closed system with a finite amount of such energy, an infinitely old universe is incompatible with the fact that we have not yet run out of such energy—the universe has not yet reached its "equilibrium end state." Since I'm no scientist, I will focus my attention on Craig's philosophical arguments, beginning with the second one.

As Craig himself points out, his second philosophical argument is very similar to the argument that Immanuel Kant uses to support the thesis of his first antinomy:

> If we assume that the world has no beginning in time, then up to every given moment an eternity has elapsed and there has passed away in the world an infinite series of successive states of things. Now the infinity of a series consists in the fact that it can never be completed through successive synthesis. It thus follows that it is impossible for an infinite world-series to have passed away, and that a beginning of the world is therefore a necessary condition of the world's existence.[3]

Craig formulates the argument as follows:

(i) The temporal series of events is a collection formed by successive addition.

(ii) A collection formed by successive addition cannot be an actual infinite.

(iii) Thus, the temporal series of events cannot be an actual infinite. (from i and ii)

(iv) Therefore, the temporal regress of events is finite. (from iii)[4]

This argument is closely related to Zeno's paradoxes, which depend on the claim that one cannot complete an infinite series of tasks one at a time since that would imply an infinitieth member of the series. As it stands, the argument is unconvincing. For while it is true that one cannot start with a finite collection and then by adding one new member at a time turn it into an infinite collection (no matter how much

time one has available), nothing of the sort is required in order for the past to be infinite. For if the temporal regress of events is infinite, then the universe has never had a finite number of past events. Rather, it has always been the case that the collection of past events is infinite. Thus, if the temporal regress of events is infinite, then the temporal series of events is not an infinite collection formed by successively adding to a finite collection. Rather, it is a collection formed by successively adding to an infinite collection. And surely it is not impossible to form an infinite collection by successively adding to an already infinite collection.

One might object that, if the temporal regress of events is infinite, then there must be some event E separated from the birth of my daughter by an infinite number of intermediate events, in which case the collection containing E and all those intermediate events would have to be an actually infinite collection formed by successively adding to a finite collection of events, namely the collection containing E as its only member. This objection fails because it is simply not true that, if the temporal regress of events is infinite, then there must be two events separated by an infinite number of intermediate events. For consider the set of natural numbers. It is actually infinite, yet every member of it is such that there is a finite number of members between it and its first member.[5]

Craig's first philosophical argument is, I believe, much more promising than his second. It bases its conclusion that the temporal regress of physical events must be finite—there must have been a first physical event—on the premises that an actual infinite cannot exist in reality and an infinite temporal regress of events is an actual infinite.[6] From this and the further claim that a first physical event could not have been preceded by an eternal absolutely quiescent physical universe, the conclusion is drawn that the physical universe had a beginning. The first stage of this argument can be formulated as follows:

a. No set of real things is actually infinite.

b. If there was no first event, then the set of all real events occurring prior to the birth of my daughter is actually infinite.

c. Therefore, there was a first event.

Craig defends premise (a) of this argument by pointing out that the assumption that a set of real things is actually infinite has paradoxical implications.[7] For example, it implies that we could have a library consisting of infinitely many black books (each might be assigned an even number). We could then add infinitely many red books (each might be assigned an odd number) and yet not increase the number of books in the library by a single volume. Indeed, we could add infinitely many different colors of books with infinitely many books of each color (the red books could be assigned rational numbers between 0 and 1, the black books rational numbers between 1 and 2, and so on) and not increase our collection by a single volume.

These paradoxes arise because the following three statements constitute an inconsistent triad:

S1. A set has more members than any of its proper subsets.

S2. If the members of two sets can be placed in one-to-one correspondence, then neither set has more members than the other.

S3. There are actually infinite sets.

For example, since the set of even numbers has one-to-one correspondence with the set of natural numbers and even with the set of rational numbers, S2 implies that one could add infinitely many red books or infinitely many books of each of infinitely many different colors to the library without increasing the size of that library's collection. (One need only make sure that the additions are *denumerably* infinite.) But of course S1 implies that any such addition would increase the size of the collection since the set of even numbers is a proper subset both of the set of natural numbers and of the set of rational numbers. Thus, two intuitively appealing principles together imply a contradiction on the assumption that there can be an actually infinite collection of books. One way to avoid this contradiction is to reject the assumption that there can be an actually infinite collection of books. So the underlying argument in defense of the claim that no collection of real things is actually infinite is simply that, since S1 and S2 are both true of collections of real things, it follows that S3 is not

true of such collections—no collections of real things are actually infinite.

Craig claims that Georg Cantor's theory of transfinite numbers is consistent because it rejects the first member of the triad. But this member is not rejected because it can be proven false about actually infinite sets, nor is the second member accepted because it can be proven that if a one-to-one correspondence between the elements of two actually infinite sets can be established then the sets are equivalent. Rather, equivalent sets are simply defined as sets having one-to-one correspondence. Thus, while Cantor's theory is a consistent mathematical system, there is, according to Craig, no reason to think that it has any interesting ontological implications. In particular, it does not provide any reason to think that S1 is false about actually infinite sets and hence provides no justification for thinking that actual infinites can exist in reality.[8]

Notice that, if Craig is right that past events are real but future events are not, then his argument for a first event does not commit him to the position that there is a last event. For consider the following parallel argument for the conclusion that there will be a last event:

(a) No set of real things is actually infinite.

(b) If there will be no last event, then the set of all real events occurring after the birth of my daughter is actually infinite.

(c) Therefore, there will be a last event.

Since future events are not real, the second premise of this argument is false. If there is no last event, then the set of all real events occurring after the birth of my daughter is merely potentially infinite—not actually infinite. This collection can increase in size indefinitely, but it will always be finite. Past events, on the other hand, are all real. So if there is no first past event, then the set of all real past events is actually infinite, not potentially infinite. Craig concludes that, although there may be no last event, there must be a first event, and hence, since matter cannot exist without events occurring, it follows that the universe has not always existed—it began to exist.

Although this fascinating argument for the second premise of the *kalām* argument may be sound, Craig has not given us adequate reason to believe it is. The problem concerns the inconsistent triad mentioned above. What Craig needs to do is to show that, when it comes to collections of real things, we should reject the third member of the triad instead of S1 or S2. But he has not shown this. S1 and S2 are certainly true for finite collections. But it's far from clear that they are true for all collections. Allow me to explain why.

Consider S1, which says that a set has more members than any of its proper subsets. If "more" means "a greater number," then the claim that S1 is true for actually infinite sets requires us to make sense of claiming that actually infinite sets have a *number* of members. But an actually infinite set doesn't have a natural number of members or a rational number of members or a real number of members, so one such set can't have a greater natural or rational or real number of members than another. Of course, an actually infinite set does have a transfinite number of members. But transfinite numbers are what Cantor defines them to be. And given his definition, it simply isn't true that actually infinite sets have a greater transfinite number of members than all of their proper subsets. We could say that an actually infinite set has a greater "infinite number" of members than all of its proper subsets, but Craig gives us no theory of infinite numbers that would justify that claim.

Of course, Craig might claim that no such theory is necessary, that we don't even need to make use of the word *number* here; for it's just obvious that, in some sense of the word *more*, any set that has every member that another set has and some members it doesn't have has more members than the other set. I agree this is obvious, but in the case of infinite sets, this is obvious only because "more" can just mean "has every member the other set has and some members it doesn't have." If, however, we grant Craig that S1 is true on these grounds, then why accept S2? Why not claim instead that actually infinite collections of real objects are possible, but the fact that two of them have one-to-one correspondence is not a good reason to believe that neither has "more" members than the other? Why, for example, is it more reasonable to

believe that actually infinite libraries are impossible than to believe that, although they are possible, one such library can have "more" books than a second despite the fact that the books in the first can be placed in one-to-one correspondence with the books in the second? Craig provides no good answer to these questions. Obviously he cannot all of a sudden appeal to Cantor's theory to justify accepting S2. For that would commit him to rejecting S1. And since, when infinite sets are compared, the word *more* cannot mean what it does when finite sets are compared, the fact that S2 is true for finite sets is not by itself a good reason to believe that it is true for all sets.

So Craig fails to show that S1 and S2 are both true of all collections of real objects, and hence he fails to show that actually infinite collections of real objects are impossible. Therefore, his first philosophical argument, like his second, fails to establish that an infinite regress of events is impossible and so fails to establish that the universe began to exist. This leaves us with Craig's scientific arguments. Since I lack the expertise to evaluate these arguments, let's assume, for the sake of argument, that they succeed and hence that the universe did begin to exist. Must we then conclude that the *kalām* argument succeeds? This would be a profound result. Granted, this argument doesn't get all the way to God's existence. But accepting its conclusion does require rejecting naturalism—since nothing can be a cause of its own existence, a cause outside the natural world would be required.

As wonderful as this conclusion is, I do not believe that Craig's defense of the *kalām* argument justifies accepting it, even assuming that his scientific arguments are sound. This is because Craig commits the fallacy of equivocation. The verb "to begin" has a narrow or strict sense and a broad or loose sense. In the narrow sense, "to begin" means "to begin within time." When used in this way, "x begins to exist" implies that there was a time at which x did not exist and then a later time at which x exists. But "to begin" can also mean "to begin either within or with time." When used in this way, "x begins to exist" does not imply that there was a time at which x did not exist, because the past may itself be finite in which case something that begins to exist at the first moment in time is such that there never was a time at which it did not exist—it begins with time rather than within time. Now consider the two premises of the *kalām* argument in the fight of this distinction.

The second premise is that the universe began to exist. All of Craig's arguments in favor of this premise, including his scientific ones, would be unsound if one interpreted "began to exist" in the second premise as meaning "began to exist within time." For nothing in these arguments counts against a relational view of time. And on a relational view of time, a first temporal event is simultaneous with a first moment in time. This would mean that, if the temporal series of past events is finite, then the universe began to exist with time. Indeed, if anything, the arguments in favor of the second premise support a beginning with time. For if an infinite regress of events is an actual infinite and for that reason impossible, then it would seem that an infinite past would be an actual infinite and for that reason impossible. Moreover, one of Craig's scientific arguments appeals to an interpretation of the Big Bang Theory according to which time did not exist "before" the big bang. So the most that Craig has established is that the universe began to exist either within or with time.

The first premise is that anything that begins to exist has a cause of its existence. What does "begins to exist" mean here? Craig defends this premise by claiming that it is an "empirical generalisation enjoying the strongest support experience affords."[9] But experience only supports the claim that anything that begins to exist within time has a cause of its existence. For we have no experience whatsoever of things beginning to exist with time.[10] Such things would require timeless causes. And even if it is conceptually possible for a temporal event to have a

timeless cause, we certainly have no experience of this. Of course, Craig also claims that premise (1) is intuitively obvious—that it needs no defense at all. But it is far from obvious that a universe that begins to exist with time needs a cause of its existence. Like an infinitely old universe, a universe that begins to exist with time has always existed—for any time t, the universe existed at t. And once again, it's far from obvious that something that has always existed requires a cause for its existence. It's not even clear that such a thing *could* have a cause of its existence.

So in order to be justified in believing both of the premises of the argument—justified, that is, solely on the basis of Craig's defense of those premises—we would need to equivocate on the meaning of "begins to exist." We would need to use this term in the narrow sense in the first premise and in the broad sense in the second premise. But then the conclusion of the argument would not follow from its premises. Thus, Craig commits the fallacy of equivocation.[11]

Do my objections to Craig's defense of the *kalām* argument prove that it is doomed? I don't think so. The argument remains promising. Perhaps, for example, it could be shown that an absolute theory of time is correct, and that such a theory, together with scientific or new philosophical evidence against an infinitely old universe, implies a beginning of the universe within time. Or perhaps it could be shown that the universe began to exist with time and that even something that begins to exist with time requires a cause of its existence. So my conclusion is not that the *kalām* argument should be dismissed. It is just that it has not yet been adequately defended. I still *wonder* whether the argument is a good one.

NOTES

1. William Lane Craig, *The Kalām Cosmological Argument* (New York: Harper & Row Publishers), 1979.

2. For a brief but interesting history of the argument, see Craig, Part I.

3. Immanuel Kant, *Critique of Pure Reason*, trans. Norman Kemp Smith (London: Macmillan & Co., 1929), p. 396. Quoted by Craig on p. 189.

4. Craig, p. 103.

5. Cf. Quentin Smith, "*Infinity and the Past,*" in *Theism, Atheism, and Big Bang Cosmology*, ed. William Lane Craig and Quentin Smith (Oxford: Clarendon Press, 1993), pp. 78–83; Antony Flew, "The Case for God Challenged," in *Does God Exist?: The Great Debate*, ed. J. P. Moreland and Kai Nielsen (Nashville: Thomas Nelson Publishers,

1990), p. 164; and Keith Parsons, "Is There a Case for Christian Theism?" in *Does God Exist?: The Great Debate*, p. 187.

6. Craig, p. 69.

7. Craig, pp. 82–87.

8. Craig, pp. 94–95.

9. Craig, p. 145. Craig also suggests here that premise (1) could be defended by appealing to an a priori category of causality. Such Kantian maneuvering does not seem very promising in this context. For in order to reconcile it with the realism presupposed by the *kalām* argument, one would need to claim that the causal principle must, as a necessary precondition of thought, hold without exception in the noumenal world!

10. Cf. Quentin Smith, "The Uncaused Beginning of the Universe," in *Theism, Atheism, and Big Bang Cosmology*, p. 123.

11. In "The Caused Beginning of the Universe" (in *Theism, Atheism, and Big Bang Cosmology*) Craig denies that his inference is equivocal on the grounds that "our conviction of the truth of the causal principle is not based upon an inductive survey of existents in space-time, but rather upon the metaphysical intuition that something cannot come out of nothing" (p. 147). Of course, he did appeal to such a survey in his book, but Craig claims that this was just "a last-ditch defence of the principle designed to appeal to the hard-headed empiricist who resists the metaphysical intuition that properly grounds our conviction of the principle" (p. 147, note 13). This response to the charge of equivocation is not at all convincing. For metaphysical intuitions about contingent matters are notoriously unreliable—that's why so many contemporary philosophers are, quite justifiably, "hard-headed empiricists." Further, at the risk of committing the genetic fallacy, it is worth pointing out that it is probably our experience of things beginning to exist within time that causes some of us to have the metaphysical intuition that something cannot come out of nothing.

II.C THE TELEOLOGICAL ARGUMENT FOR THE EXISTENCE OF GOD

THE TELEOLOGICAL ARGUMENT for the existence of God begins with the premise that the world exhibits intelligent purpose, order, or other marks of design, and it proceeds to the conclusion that there must be or probably is a divine intelligence, a supreme designer, to account for the observed or perceived intelligent purpose or order. Although core ideas of the argument can be found in Plato, in the Bible (Rom. 1), and in Cicero, the most well-known treatment of it is found in William Paley's *Natural Theology* (1802). In his opening chapter, included here as our first selection, he offers his famous "watch" argument, which begins as follows:

In crossing a heath, suppose I pitched my foot against a stone, and were asked how the stone came to be there, I might possibly answer, that for anything I knew to the contrary, it had lain there for ever; nor would it, perhaps, be very easy to show the absurdity of this answer. But suppose I found a watch upon the ground, and it should be inquired how the watch happened to be in that place, I should hardly think of the answer which I had before given—that, for anything I knew, the watch might have always been there. Yet why should not this answer serve for the watch as well as for the stone? Why is it not as admissible in the second case, as in the first?

Paley argues that just as we infer the existence of an intelligent designer to account for the purpose-revealing watch, we must analogously infer the existence of an intelligent grand designer to account for the purpose-revealing world.

"Every indication of contrivance, every manifestation of design, which existed in the watch, exists in the works of nature; with the difference, on the side of nature, of being greater and more, and that in a degree which exceeds all computation." The skeleton of the argument looks like this:

1. Human artifacts are products of intelligent design (purpose).

2. The works of nature resemble these human artifacts, particularly in having parts that are functionally organized.

3. Therefore, the works of nature are (probably) products of intelligent design (purpose).

4. But these works are vastly more complex and far greater in number than human artifacts.

5. Therefore, there probably is a powerful and vastly intelligent designer who designed the works of nature.

Ironically, Paley's argument was attacked even before Paley had set it down, for David Hume (1711–1776) had long before written his famous *Dialogues Concerning Natural Religion* (published posthumously in 1779), the classic critique of the teleological argument. Paley seems to have been unaware of it. A selection from the Dialogues is included as our second reading. In it, the natural theologian, Cleanthes, debates the orthodox believer, Demea, and the skeptic or critic, Philo, who does most of the serious arguing.

Hume, through Philo, attacks the argument from several different angles. He argues first of all that the universe—which might itself be viewed as one of Paley's "works of nature"—is not sufficiently like the productions of human design to support the argument. Philo puts it as follows:

> But can you think, Cleanthes, that your usual phlegm and philosophy have been preserved in so wide a step as you have taken, when you compare to the universe, houses, ships, furniture, machines and from their similarity in some circumstances infer a similarity in their causes? ... But can a conclusion, with any propriety, be transferred from the parts to the whole? Does not the great disproportion bar all comparison and inferences? From observing the growth of a hair, can we learn anything concerning the generation of a man?

We cannot argue from the parts to the whole. You, the reader, will want to test this judgment with some possible counterexamples.

Philo's second objection is that the analogy from artifact to divine designer fails because you have no other universe with which to compare this one. We would need to make such a comparison in order to decide if it were the kind of universe that was designed or simply the kind that developed on its own. As C. S. Peirce put it, "Universes are not as plentiful as blackberries." Because there is only one of them, we have no standard of comparison by which to judge it.

Paley's answer to this would be that if we could find one clear instance of purpose-fulness in nature (e.g., the eye), it would be sufficient to enable us to conclude that there is probably an intelligent designer. Hume makes several other points against the design argument, which you will want to examine on you own.

A modern objection to the argument, one that was anticipated by Hume, is that based on Darwinian evolution, which has cast doubt upon the notion of teleological explanation altogether. In his *Origin of Species* (1859) Darwin claimed that the process of development from simpler organisms to more complex ones took place gradually over millions of years through an apparently nonpurposeful process of trial and error, of natural selection, and of survival of the fittest. As Julian Huxley put it, the evolutionary process

> results immediately and automatically from the basic property of living matter—that of self-copying, but with occasional errors. Self-copying leads to multiplication and competition; the errors in self-copying are what we call mutations, and mutations will inevitably confer different degrees of biological advantage or disadvantage on their possessors. The consequence will be differential reproduction down the generations—in other words, natural selection.[*]

As important as Darwin's contribution is in offering us an alternative model of biological development, it doesn't altogether destroy the argument from design. The theist has at least two ways of reviving the argument. First, she can argue that the process of natural selection is the *way* in which a divine designer might work out his purpose for the world, and the inference to the existence of a designer can then still be construed as an inference to the best explanation. Alternatively, she can turn her attention away from biological structures and look for marks of design elsewhere in the universe—as, for example, in the apparent "fine tuning" of the natural laws and physical constants. She might then argue that, regardless of whether a design inference is warranted as an explanation for biological purpose, such an inference is, at any rate, warranted as an explanation for these other features of the universe.

The former strategy is pursued by Richard Swinburne in the third reading in this section: "The Argument from Design," excerpted from the first edition of his *The Existence of God* (2004). The latter strategy is explained by Robin Collins in the fourth and final reading in this section, "A Scientific Argument for the Existence of God."

Swinburne, a modern Cleanthes, rejects all deductive forms of arguments for the existence of God, and in their place he sets a series of inductive arguments: versions of the cosmological argument, the teleological argument, the argument from religious experience, and others. Although none of these alone proves the existence of God or shows it to be more probable than not, each adds to the probability of God's existence. Together they constitute a cumulative case for theism. There is something crying for an explanation: Why does this grand

---

[*]*Evolution as Process* (New York: Harper & Row, 1953), 4.

universe exist? Together the arguments for God's existence provide a plausible explanation of the existence of the universe, of why we are here, of why there is anything at all and not just nothing.

Swinburne's arguments are set in terms of confirmation theory. He distinguishes arguments that are "P-inductive" (in which the premises make the conclusion probable) from those that are "C-inductive" (in which the premises confirm the probability of the conclusion or make it more probable than it otherwise would be—although without showing the conclusion to be more probable than not). The cosmological and teleological arguments are, according to Swinburne, good C-inductive arguments. Because there is no counterargument to theism (note that Swinburne believes he can successfully meet the argument from evil; see Part IV) and because religious experience offers considerable evidential force in favor of theism, the cumulative effect is to significantly increase the probability of theism.

Robin Collins likewise defends the conclusion that theism is more probable on a certain kind of evidence than atheism. In Collins's essay, the evidence in focus is the fact that the laws of nature and fundamental physical constants appear to have been "fine-tuned" so as to make it possible for living organisms to arise. To take just a few examples, Collins notes that if gravity had been stronger or weaker by one part in 10^{40}, or if the neutron were not about 1.001 times the mass of the proton, or if the electromagnetic force had been slightly stronger or weaker, life would have been impossible. In short, the likelihood of the laws and fundamental constants being so well coordinated as to allow for the possibility of life is staggeringly low; thus, Collins argues, the fact that the laws and constants *are* so well coordinated constitutes evidence that their values are not the result of chance but rather are due to the creative activity of an intelligent designer.

II.C.1

The Watch and the Watchmaker

WILLIAM PALEY

William Paley (1743–1805), Archdeacon of Carlisle, was a leading evangelical apologist. His most important work is Natural Theology, or Evidences of the Existence and Attributes of the Deity Collected from the Appearances of Nature *(1802), the first chapter of which is reprinted here. Paley argues that just as we infer the existence of an intelligent designer to explain the presence of*

From William Paley, *Natural Theology, or Evidences of the Existence and Attributes of the Deity Collected from the Appearances of Nature* (1802).

a subtle and complex artifact like a watch, so too we must infer the existence of an intelligent Grand Designer to explain the existence of the works of nature, which are far more subtle, complex, and cleverly contrived than any human artifact.

STATEMENT OF THE ARGUMENT

In crossing a heath, suppose I pitched my foot against a stone, and were asked how the stone came to be there, I might possibly answer, that, for anything I knew to the contrary, it had lain there for ever; nor would it, perhaps, be very easy to show the absurdity of this answer. But suppose I found a watch upon the ground, and it should be inquired how the watch happened to be in that place, I should hardly think of the answer which I had given—that, for anything I knew, the watch might have always been there. Yet why should not this answer serve for the watch as well as for the stone? Why is it not as admissible in the second case as in the first? For this reason, and for no other; viz., that, when we come to inspect the watch, we perceive (what we could not discover in the stone) that its several parts are framed and put together for a purpose, e.g. that they are so formed and adjusted as to produce motion, and that motion so regulated as to point out the hour of the day; that, if the different parts had been differently shaped from what they are, if a different size from what they are, or placed after any other manner, or in any other order than that in which they are placed, either no motion at all would have been carried on in the machine, or none which would have answered the use that is now served by it. To reckon up a few of the plainest of these parts, and of their offices, all tending to one result:—We see a cylindrical box containing a coiled elastic spring, which, by its endeavor to relax itself, turns round the box. We next observe a flexible chain (artificially wrought for the sake of flexure) communicating the action of the spring from the box to the fusee. We then find a series of wheels, the teeth of which catch in, and apply to, each other, conducting the motion from the fusee to the balance, and from the balance to the pointer, and, at the same time, by the size and shape of those wheels, so regulating that motion as to terminate in causing an index, by an equable and measured progression, to pass over a given space in a given time. We take notice that the wheels are made of brass, in order to keep them from rust; the springs of steel, no other metal being so elastic; that over the face of the watch there is placed a glass, a material employed in no other part of the work, but in the room of which, if there had been any other than a transparent substance, the hour could not be seen without opening the case. This mechanism being observed, (it requires indeed an examination of the instrument, and perhaps some previous knowledge of the subject, to perceive and understand it; but being once, as we have said, observed and understood,) the inference, we think, is inevitable, that the watch must have had a maker; that there must have existed, at some time, and at some place or other, an artificer or artificers who formed it for the purpose which we find it actually to answer; who comprehended its construction, and designed its use.

I. Nor would it, I apprehend, weaken the conclusion, that we had never seen a watch made; that we had never known an artist capable of making one; that we were altogether incapable of executing such a piece of workmanship ourselves, or of understanding in what manner it was performed; all this being no more than what is true of some exquisite remains of ancient art, of some lost and to the generality of mankind, of the more curious productions of modern manufacture. Does one man in a million know how oval frames are turned? Ignorance of this kind exalts our opinion of the unseen and unknown artist's skill, if he be unseen and unknown, but raises no doubt in our minds of the existence and agency of such an artist, at some former time, and in some place or other. Nor can I perceive that it varies at all the inference, whether the question arise concerning a human agent, or concerning an agent of a different species, or an agent possessing, in some respect, a different nature.

II. Neither, secondly, would it invalidate our conclusion, that the watch sometimes went wrong, or that it seldom went exactly right. The purpose of the machinery, the design, and the designer, might be evident, and, in the case supposed, would be evident, in whatever way we accounted for the irregularity of the movement, or whether we could account for it or not. It is not necessary that a machine be perfect, in order to show with what design it was made; still less necessary, where the only question is, whether it were made with any design at all.

III. Nor, thirdly, would it bring any uncertainty into the argument, if there were a few parts of the watch, concerning which we could not discover, or had not yet discovered, in what manner they conduced to the general effect; or even some parts, concerning which we could not ascertain whether they conduced to that effect in any manner whatever. For, as to the first branch of the case, if by the loss, or disorder, or decay of the parts in question, the movement of the watch were found in fact to be stopped, or disturbed, or retarded, no doubt would remain in our minds as to the utility or intention of these parts, although we should be unable to investigate the manner according to which, or the connection by which, the ultimate effect depended upon their action or assistance; and the more complex is the machine, the more likely is this obscurity to arise. Then, as to the second thing supposed, namely, that there were parts which might be spared without prejudice to the movement of the watch, and that he had proved this by experiment, these superfluous parts, even if we were completely assured that they were such, would not vacate the reasoning which we had instituted concerning other parts. The indication of contrivance remained, with respect to them, nearly as it was before.

IV. Nor, fourthly, would any man in his senses think the existence of the watch, with its various machinery, accounted for, by being told that it was one out of possible combinations of material forms; that whatever he had found in the place where he found the watch, must have contained some internal configuration or other; and that this configuration might be the structure now exhibited, viz., of the works of a watch, as well as a different structure.

V. Nor, fifthly, would it yield his inquiry more satisfaction, to be answered, that there existed in things a principle of order, which had disposed the parts of the watch into their present form and situation. He never knew a watch made by the principle of order; nor can he even form to himself an idea of what is meant by a principle of order, distinct from the intelligence of the watchmaker.

VI. Sixthly, he would be surprised to hear that the mechanism of the watch was no proof of contrivance, only a motive to induce the mind to think so.

VII. And not less surprised to be informed, that the watch in his hand was nothing more than the result of the laws of *metallic* nature. It is a perversion of language to assign any law as the efficient, operative cause of anything. A law presupposes an agent; for it is only the mode according to which an agent proceeds; it implies a power; for it is the order according to which that power acts. Without this agent, without this power, which are both distinct from itself, the *law* does nothing, is nothing. The expression, "the law of metallic nature," may sound strange and harsh to a philosophic ear; but it seems quite as justifiable as some others which are more familiar to him such as "the law of vegetable nature," "the law of animal nature," or, indeed, as "the law of nature" in general, when assigned as the cause of phenomena in exclusion of agency and power, or when it is substituted into the place of these.

VIII. Neither, lastly, would our observer be driven out of his conclusion, or from his confidence in its truth, by being told that he knew nothing at all about the matter. He knows enough for his argument: he knows the utility of the end: he knows the subserviency and adaptation of the means to the end. These points being known, his ignorance of other points, his doubts concerning other points, affect not the certainty of his reasoning. The consciousness of knowing little need not beget a distrust of that which he does know....

APPLICATION OF THE ARGUMENT

Every indication of contrivance, every manifestation of design, which existed in the watch, exists in the works of nature; with the difference, on the side of nature, of being greater and more, and that in a degree which exceeds all computation. I mean that the contrivances of nature surpass the contrivances of art, in the complexity, subtilty, and curiosity of the mechanism; and still more, if possible, do they go beyond them in number and variety; yet in a multitude of cases, are not less evidently mechanical, not less evidently contrivances, not less evidently accommodated to their end, or suited to their office, than are the most perfect productions of human ingenuity.

II.C.2

A Critique of the Design Argument

DAVID HUME

The Scottish empiricist and skeptic David Hume (1711–1776) is one of the most important philosophers who ever lived. Among his most important works are A Treatise on Human Nature, An Enquiry Concerning Human Understanding, *and* Dialogues Concerning Natural Religion *(published posthumously in 1779), from which the present selection is taken. The* Dialogues *contain the classic critique of the argument from design. Our reading is from Parts 2 and 5 of this dialogue. Cleanthes, who opens our selection, is a natural theologian, the Paley of his time, who opposes both the orthodox believer, Demea, and the skeptic, Philo. It is Philo who puts forth the major criticisms against the argument from design.*

Cleanthes: Look round the world: Contemplate the whole and every part of it: You will find it to be nothing but one great machine, subdivided into an infinite number of lesser machines, which again admit of subdivisions to a degree beyond what human senses and faculties can trace and explain. All these various machines, and even their most minute parts, are adjusted to each other with an accuracy which ravishes into admiration all men who have ever contemplated them. The curious adapting of means to ends, throughout all nature, resembles exactly, though it much exceeds, the productions of human contrivance; of human design, thought, wisdom, and intelligence. Since therefore the effects resemble each other, we are led to infer, by all the rules of analogy, that the causes also resemble, and that the Author of Nature is somewhat similar to the mind of man, though possessed of much larger faculties, proportioned to the grandeur of the work which he has executed. By this argument *a posteriori*, and by this argument alone, do we prove at once the

From David Hume, *Dialogue Concerning National Religion* (1779) London: Longman Green, 1878.

existence of a Deity and his similarity to human mind and intelligence.

Demea: I shall be so free, *Cleanthes,* said *Demea,* as to tell you that from the beginning I could not approve of your conclusion concerning the similarity of the Deity to men; still less can I approve of the mediums by which you endeavor to establish it. What! No demonstration of the Being of God! No abstract arguments! No proofs *a priori!* Are these which have hitherto been so much insisted on by philosophers all fallacy, all sophism? Can we reach no farther in this subject than experience and probability? I will say not that this is betraying the cause of a Deity; but surely, by this affected candor, you give advantages to atheists which they never could obtain by the mere dint of argument and reasoning.

Philo: What I chiefly scruple in this subject, said *Philo,* is not so much that all religious arguments are by *Cleanthes* reduced to experience, as that they appear not to be even the most certain and irrefragable of that inferior kind. That a stone will fall, that fire will burn, that the earth has solidity, we have observed a thousand and a thousand times; and when any new instance of this nature is presented, we draw without hesitation the accustomed inference. The exact similarity of the cases gives us a perfect assurance of a similar event, and a stronger evidence is never desired nor sought after. But wherever you depart, in the least, from the similarity of the cases, you diminish proportionably the evidence; and may at last bring it to a very weak *analogy,* which is confessedly liable to error and uncertainty. After having experienced the circulation of the blood in human creatures, we make no doubt that it takes place in *Titius* and *Maevius;* but from its circulation in frogs and fishes it is only a presumption, though a strong one, from analogy that it takes place in men and other animals. The analogical reasoning is much weaker when we infer the circulation of the sap in vegetables from our experience that the blood circulates in animals; and those who hastily followed that imperfect analogy are found, by more accurate experiments, to have been mistaken.

If we see a house, *Cleanthes,* we conclude, with the greatest certainty, that it had an architect or builder because this is precisely that species of effect which we have experienced to proceed from that species of cause. But surely you will not affirm that the universe bears such a resemblance to a house that we can with the same certainty infer a similar cause, or that the analogy is here entire and perfect. The dissimilitude is so striking that the utmost you can here pretend to is a guess, a conjecture, a presumption concerning a similar cause; and how that pretension will be received in the world, I leave you to consider.

Cleanthes: It would surely be very ill received, replied *Cleanthes;* and I should be deservedly blamed and detested did I allow that the proofs of a Deity amounted to no more than a guess or conjecture. But is the whole adjustment of means to ends in a house and in the universe so slight a resemblance? The economy of final causes? The order, proportion, and arrangement of every part? Steps of a stair are plainly contrived that human legs may use them in mounting; and this inference is certain and infallible. Human legs are also contrived for walking and mounting; and this inference, I allow, is not altogether so certain because of the dissimilarity which you remark; but does it, therefore, deserve the name only of presumption or conjecture?

Demea: Good God! cried *Demea,* interrupting him, where are we? Zealous defenders of religion allow that the proofs of a Deity fall short of perfect evidence! And you, *Philo,* on whose assistance I depended in proving the adorable mysteriousness of the Divine Nature, do you assent to all these extravagant opinions of *Cleanthes?* For what other name can I give them? or, why spare my censure when such principles are advanced, supported by such an authority, before so young a man as *Pamphilus?*

Philo: You seem not to apprehend, replied *Philo,* that I argue with *Cleanthes* in his own way, and, by showing him the dangerous consequences of his tenets, hope at last to reduce him to our opinion. But what sticks most with you, I observe, is the representation which *Cleanthes* has made of the argument *a posteriori;* and, finding that that argument is likely to escape your hold and vanish into air, you think it so disguised that you can scarcely believe it to be set in its true light. Now, however much I may dissent, in other respects, from the dangerous principle of *Cleanthes,* I must allow that he has fairly represented that argument, and I shall endeavor so to state the matter to you that you will entertain no further scruples with regard to it.

Were a man to abstract from everything which he knows or has seen, he would be altogether incapable, merely from his own ideas, to determine what kind of scene the universe must be, or to give the preference to one state or situation of things above another. For as nothing which he clearly conceives could be esteemed impossible or implying a contradiction, every chimera of his fancy would be upon an equal footing; nor could he assign any just reason why he adheres to one idea or system, and rejects the others which are equally possible.

Again, after he opens his eyes and contemplates the world as it really is, it would be impossible for him at first to assign the cause of any one event, much less of the whole of things, or of the universe. He might set his fancy a rambling, and she might bring him in an infinite variety of reports and representations. These would all be possible; but, being all equally possible, he would never of himself give a satisfactory account for his preferring one of them to the rest. Experience alone can point out to him the true cause of any phenomenon.

Now, according to this method of reasoning, *Demea,* it follows (and is, indeed, tacitly allowed by *Cleanthes* himself) that order, arrangement, or the adjustment of final causes, is not of itself any proof of design, but only so far as it has been experienced to proceed from that principle. For aught we can know *a priori,* matter may contain the source or spring of order originally within itself, as well as mind does; and there is no more difficulty in conceiving that the several elements, from an internal unknown cause, may fall into the most exquisite arrangement, than to conceive that their ideas, in the great universal mind, from a like internal unknown cause, fall into that arrangement. The equal possibility of both these suppositions is

allowed. But, by experience, we find, according to *Cleanthes,* that there is a difference between them. Throw several pieces of steel together, without shape or form; they will never arrange themselves so as to compose a watch. Stone and mortar and wood, without an architect, never erect a house. But the ideas in a human mind, we see, by an unknown, inexplicable economy, arrange themselves so as to form the plan of a watch or house. Experience, therefore, proves that there is an original principle of order in mind, not in matter. From similar effects we infer similar causes. The adjustment of means to ends is alike in the universe, as in a machine of human contrivance. The causes, therefore, must be resembling.

I was from the beginning scandalized, I must own, with this resemblance which is asserted between the Deity and human creatures, and must conceive it to imply such a degradation of the Supreme Being as no sound theist could endure. With your assistance, therefore, *Demea,* I shall endeavor to defend what you justly call the adorable mysteriousness of the Divine Nature, and shall refute this reasoning of *Cleanthes,* provided he allows that I have made a fair representation of it.

When *Cleanthes* had assented, *Philo,* after a short pause, proceeded in the following manner.

That all inferences, *Cleanthes,* concerning fact are founded on experience, and that all experimental reasonings are founded on the supposition that similar causes prove similar effects, and similar effects similar causes, I shall not at present much dispute with you. But observe, I entreat you, with what extreme caution all just reasoners proceed in the transferring of experiments to similar cases. Unless the cases be exactly similar, they repose no perfect confidence in applying their past observation to any particular phenomenon. Every alteration of circumstances occasions a doubt concerning the event; and it requires new experiments to prove certainly that the new circumstances are of no moment or importance. A change in bulk, situation, arrangement, age, disposition of the air, or surrounding bodies; any of these particulars may be attended with the most unexpected consequences. And unless the objects be quite familiar to us, it is the highest temerity to expect with assurance, after any of these changes, an event similar to that which before fell under our observation. The slow and deliberate steps of philosophers here, if anywhere, are distinguished from the precipitate march of the vulgar, who, hurried on by the smallest similitude, are incapable of all discernment or consideration.

But can you think, *Cleanthes,* that your usual phlegm and philosophy have been preserved in so wide a step as you have taken when you compared to the universe houses, ships, furniture, machines; and, from their similarity in some circumstances, inferred a similarity in their causes? Thought, design, intelligence, such as we discover in men and other animals, is no more than one of the springs and principles of the universe, as well as heat or cold, attraction or repulsion, and a hundred others which fall under daily observation. It is an active cause by which some particular parts of nature, we find, produce alterations on other parts. But can a conclusion, with any propriety, be transferred from parts to the whole? Does not the great disproportion bar all comparison and inference? From observing the growth of a hair, can we learn anything concerning the generation of a man? Would the manner of a leaf's blowing, even though perfectly known, afford us any instruction concerning the vegetation of a tree?

But allowing that we were to take the *operations* of one part of nature upon another for the foundation of our judgment concerning the *origin* of the whole (which never can be admitted), yet why select so minute, so weak, so bounded a principle as the reason and design of animals is found to be upon this planet? What peculiar privilege has this little agitation of the brain which we call "thought," that we must thus make it the model of the whole universe? Our partiality in our own favor does indeed present it on all occasions, but sound philosophy ought carefully to guard against so natural an illusion.

So far from admitting, continued *Philo,* that the operations of a part can afford us any just conclusion concerning the origin of the whole, I will not allow any one part to form a rule for another part if

the latter be very remote from the former, is there any reasonable ground to conclude that the inhabitants of other planets possess thought, intelligence, reason, or anything similar to these faculties in men? When nature has so extremely diversified her manner of operation in this small globe, can we imagine that she incessantly copies herself throughout so immense a universe? And if thought, as we may well suppose, be confined merely to this narrow corner, and has even there so limited a sphere of action, with what propriety can we assign it for the original cause of all things? The narrow view of a peasant who makes his domestic economy the rule for the government of kingdoms is in comparison a pardonable sophism.

But were we ever so much assured that a thought and reason resembling the human were to be found throughout the whole universe, and were its activity elsewhere vastly greater and more commanding than it appears in this globe; yet I cannot see why the operations of a world constituted, arranged, adjusted, can with any propriety be extended to a world which is in its embryo state, and is advancing towards that constitution and arrangement. By observation we know somewhat of the economy, action, and nourishment of a finished animal; but we must transfer with great caution that observation to the growth of a fetus in the womb, and still more to the formation of an animalcule in the loins of its male parent. Nature, we find, even from our limited experience, possesses an infinite number of springs and principles which incessantly discover themselves on every change of her position and situation. And what new and unknown principles would actuate her in so new and unknown a situation as that of the formation of a universe, we cannot, without the utmost temerity, pretend to determine.

A very small part of this great system, during a very short time, is very imperfectly discovered to us; and do we thence pronounce decisively concerning the origin of the whole?

Admirable conclusion! Stone, wood, brick, iron, brass, have not, at this time, in this minute globe of earth, an order or arrangement without human art and contrivance; therefore, the universe could not originally attain its order and arrangement without something similar to human art. But is a part of nature a rule for another part very wide of the former? Is it a rule for the whole? Is a very small part a rule for the universe? Is nature in one situation a certain rule for nature in another situation vastly different from the former?

And can you blame me, *Cleanthes,* if I here imitate the prudent reserve of *Simonides,* who, according to the noted story, being asked by *Hiero, What God was?* desired a day to think of it, and then two days more; and after that manner continually prolonged the term, without ever bringing in his definition or description? Could you even blame me if I had answered, at first, *that I did not know,* and was sensible that this subject lay vastly beyond the reach of my faculties? You might cry out skeptic and raillier, as much as you pleased; but, having found in so many other subjects much more familiar the imperfections and even contradictions of human reason, I never should expect any success from its feeble conjectures in a subject so sublime and so remote from the sphere of our observation. When two species of objects have always been observed to be conjoined together, I can infer, by custom, the existence of one wherever I see the existence of the other; and this I call an argument from experience. But how this argument can have place where the objects, as in the present case, are single, individual, without parallel or specific resemblance, may be difficult to explain. And will any man tell me with a serious countenance that an orderly universe must arise from some thought and art like the human because we have experience of it? To ascertain this reasoning it were requisite that we had experience of the origin of worlds; and it is not sufficient, surely, that we have seen ships and cities arise from human art and contrivance....

Philo: But to show you still more inconveniences, continued *Philo,* in your anthropomorphism, please to take a new survey of your principles. *Like effects prove like causes.* This is the experimental argument; and this, you say too, is the sole theological argument. Now it is certain that the liker the effects are which are seen and the

liker the causes which are inferred, the stronger is the argument. Every departure on either side diminishes the probability and renders the experiment less conclusive. You cannot doubt of the principle; neither ought you to reject its consequences.

All the new discoveries in astronomy which prove the immense grandeur and magnificence of the works of nature are so many additional arguments for a Deity, according to the true system of theism; but, according to your hypothesis of experimental theism, they become so many objections, by removing the effect still farther from all resemblance to the effects of human art and contrivance. For if *Lucretius,* even following the old system of the world, could exclaim:

> Who is strong enough to rule the sum,
> who to hold in hand and control the
> mighty bridle of the unfathomable deep?
> who to turn about all the heavens at one
> time, and warm the fruitful worlds with
> ethereal fires, or to be present in all places
> and at all times.[1]

If Tully[2] esteemed this reasoning so natural as to put it into the mouth of his Epicurean:

> What power of mental vision enabled your
> master Plato to descry the vast and
> elaborate architectural process which, as he
> makes out, the deity adopted in building
> the structure of the universe? What
> method of engineering was employed?
> What tools and levers and derricks? What
> agents carried out so vast an
> understanding? And how were air, fire,
> water, and earth enabled to obey and
> execute the will of the architect?

If this argument, I say, had any force in former ages, how much greater must it have at present when the bounds of nature are so infinitely enlarged and such a magnificent scene is opened to us? It is still more unreasonable to form our idea of so unlimited a cause from our experience of the narrow productions of human design and invention.

The discoveries by microscopes, as they open a new universe in miniature, are still objections, according to you; arguments, according to me. The farther we push our researches of this kind, we are still led to infer the universal cause of all to be vastly different from mankind, or from any object of human experience and observation.

And what say you to the discoveries in anatomy, chemistry, botany?…

Cleanthes: These surely are no objections, replied *Cleanthes;* they only discover new instances of art and contrivance. It is still the image of mind reflected on us from innumerable objects. Philo: Add a mind like the human, said Philo. I know of no other, replied *Cleanthes. Philo:* And the liker, the better, insisted Philo. To be sure, said *Cleanthes.*

Philo: Now, *Cleanthes,* said *Philo,* with an air of alacrity and triumph, mark the consequences. First, by this method of reasoning you renounce all claim to infinity in any of the attributes of the Deity. For, as the cause ought only to be proportioned to the effect, and the effect, so far as it falls under our cognizance, is not infinite: What pretensions have we, upon your suppositions, to ascribe that attribute to the Divine Being? You will still insist that, by removing him so much from all similarity to human creatures, we give in to the most arbitrary hypothesis, and at the same time weaken all proofs of his existence.

Secondly, you have no reason, on your theory, for ascribing perfection to the Deity, even in his finite capacity; or for supposing him free from every error, mistake, or incoherence, in his undertakings. There are many inexplicable difficulties in the works of Nature which, if we allow a perfect author to be proved *a priori,* are easily solved, and become only seeming difficulties from the narrow capacity of man, who cannot trace infinite relations. But according to your method of reasoning, these difficulties become all real; and, perhaps, will be insisted on as new instances of likeness to human art and contrivance. At least, you must acknowledge that it is impossible for us to tell, from our limited views, whether this system contains any great faults or deserves any considerable praise if compared to other possible and even real systems. Could a peasant, if the *Aeneid* were read to him, pronounce that poem to be absolutely faultless, or

even assign to it its proper rank among the productions of human wit, he who had never seen any other production?

But were this world ever so perfect a production, it must still remain uncertain whether all the excellences of the work can justly be ascribed to the workman. If we survey a ship, what an exalted idea must we form of the ingenuity of the carpenter who framed so complicated, useful, and beautiful a machine? And what surprise must we feel when we find him a stupid mechanic who imitated others, and copied an art which, through a long succession of ages, after multiplied trials, mistakes, corrections, deliberations, and controversies, had been gradually improving? Many worlds might have been botched and bungled, throughout an eternity, ere this system was struck out; much labor lost; many fruitless trials made; and a slow but continued improvement carried on during infinite ages in the art of world-making. In such subjects, who can determine where the truth, nay, who can conjecture where the probability lies, amidst a great number of hypotheses which may be proposed, and a still greater which may be imagined?

And what shadow of an argument, continued Philo, can you produce from your hypothesis to prove the unity of the Deity? A great number of men join in building a house or ship, in rearing a city, in framing a commonwealth; why may not several deities combine in contriving and framing a world? This is only so much greater similarity to human affairs. By sharing the work among several, we may so much further limit the attributes of each, and get rid of that extensive power and knowledge which must be supposed in one deity, and which, according to you, can only serve to weaken the proof of his existence. And if such foolish, such vicious creatures as man can yet often unite in framing and executing one plan, how much more those deities or demons, whom we may suppose several degrees more perfect?

To multiply causes without necessity is indeed contrary to true philosophy, but this principle applies not to the present case. Were one deity antecedently proved by your theory who were possessed of every attribute requisite to the production of the universe, it would be needless, I own (though not absurd), to suppose any other deity existent. But while it is still a question whether all these attributes are united in one subject or dispersed among several independent beings; by what phenomena in nature can we pretend to decide the controversy? Where we see a body raised in a scale, we are sure that there is in the opposite scale, however concealed from sight, some counterpoising weight equal to it; but it is still allowed to doubt whether that weight be an aggregate of several distinct bodies or one uniform united mass. And if the weight requisite very much exceeds anything which we have ever seen conjoined in any single body, the former supposition becomes still more probable and natural. An intelligent being of such vast power and capacity as is necessary to produce the universe, or, to speak in the language of ancient philosophy, so prodigious an animal, exceeds all analogy and even comprehension.

But further, *Cleanthes,* men are mortal, and renew their species by generation; and this is common to all living creatures. The two great sexes of male and female, says *Milton,* animate the world. Why must this circumstance, so universal, so essential, be excluded from those numerous and limited deities? Behold, then, the theogony of ancient times brought back upon us.

And why not become a perfect anthropomorphite? Why not assert the deity or deities to be corporeal, and to have eyes, a nose, mouth, ears, etc.? *Epicurus* maintained that no man had ever seen reason but in a human figure; therefore, the gods must have a human figure. And this argument, which is deservedly so much ridiculed by *Cicero,* becomes, according to you, solid and philosophical.

In a word, *Cleanthes,* a man who follows your hypothesis is able, perhaps, to assert or conjecture that the universe sometime arose from something like design: But beyond that position he cannot ascertain one single circumstance, and is left afterwards to fix every point of his theology by the utmost license of fancy and hypothesis. This world, for aught he knows, is very faulty and imperfect, compared to a superior standard; and was only the first rude essay of some infant deity who afterwards abandoned it, ashamed of his lame performance: It is the work only of some dependent, inferior deity, and is the object of derision to his superiors: It is the production of old age and dotage in some superannuated deity; and ever since his death has run on at adventures, from the first impulse and active force which it received from him…. You justly give signs of horror, *Demea,* at these strange suppositions; but these, and a thousand more of the same kind, are *Cleanthes'* suppositions, not mine. From the moment the attributes of the Deity are supposed finite, all these have place. And I cannot, for my part, think that so wild and unsettled a system of theology is, in any respect, preferable to none at all.

Cleanthes: These suppositions I absolutely disown, cried *Cleanthes:* They strike me, however, with no horror, especially when proposed in that rambling way in which they drop from you. On the contrary, they give me pleasure when I see that, by the utmost indulgence of your imagination, you never get rid of the hypothesis of design in the universe, but are obliged at every turn to have recourse to it. To this concession I adhere steadily; and this I regard as a sufficient foundation for religion.

NOTES

1. *On the Nature of Things,* II, 1096–1099 (trans. by W. D. Rouse).

2. Tully was a common name for the Roman lawyer and philosopher, Marcus Tullius Cicero, 106–43 BC. The excerpt is from *The Nature of the Gods,* i, viii, 19 (trans. By H. Rackham).

II.C.3

The Argument from Design

RICHARD SWINBURNE

Richard Swinburne (1934–   ) was, until his retirement, the Nolloth Professor of the Philosophy of the Christian Religion at Oxford University. He has written extensively in philosophy of religion, and his body of work includes several pieces on the traditional arguments for the existence of God. The following selection is from The Existence of God *(1979) in which he rejects all deductive forms of arguments for the existence of God but sets in their place a series of inductive arguments. In this selection, he presents an inductive version of the argument from design. His strategy is to show that several of the arguments, although only minimally suggestive when taken in isolation, together make a cumulative case for the truth of theism.*

A few notes are crucial to an understanding of Swinburne's essay. First, he contrasts the "Hempelian account" of scientific explanation with the "powers-and-liabilities account" of scientific explanation. According to the Hempelian account—named after Carl Hempel—to provide a scientific explanation of an event is (roughly) to show that the occurrence of the event is logically implied by the occurrence of particular circumstances that obtained prior to the event together with facts about the laws of nature. On the other hand, the powers-and-liabilities account says that providing a scientific explanation for an event is a matter of showing that the event's cause had powers to bring about the event that it was liable to exercise under the given circumstances. Second, Hempel thinks that scientific explanations are not the only available explanations for events in the world. There are also what he calls "personal" explanations. Third, Swinburne places a great deal of weight on the notion of simplicity. Other things being equal, if a theory A is simpler than a theory B, theory A is to be preferred. Finally, Swinburne uses Bayes's theorem to sustain his argument: Let h be a theory or hypothesis, let e be the evidential phenomena, and let k be our background knowledge. P(h/e&k) represents the probability of h being true given the available evidence and our background knowledge. You do not need to understand the intricacies of Bayes's theorem in order to follow Swinburne's reasoning.

I understand by an argument from design one which argues from some general pattern of order in the universe or provision for the needs of conscious beings to a God responsible for these phenomena. An argument from a general pattern of order I shall call a teleological argument. In the definition of "teleological argument" I emphasize the words "general pattern"; I shall not count an argument to the existence of God from some particular pattern of order manifested on a unique occasion as a teleological argument.

TWO FORMS OF TELEOLOGICAL ARGUMENT

I begin with the distinction between spatial order and temporal order, between what I shall call regularities of co-presence and regularities of succession. An example of a regularity of co-presence would be a town with all its roads at right angles to each other, or a section of books in a library arranged in alphabetical order of authors. Regularities of succession are simple patterns of behaviour of objects, such as their behaviour in accordance with the laws of nature—for example, Newton's laws.

Many of the striking examples of order in the universe evince an order which is due both to a regularity of co-presence and to a regularity of succession. A working car consists of many parts so adjusted to each other that it follows the instructions of the driver delivered by his pulling and pushing a few levers and buttons and turning a wheel, to take passengers whither he wishes. Its order arises because its parts are so arranged at some instant (regularity of co-presence) that, the laws of nature being as they are (regularity of succession) it brings about the result neatly and efficiently. The order of living animals and plants likewise results from regularities of both types.

Men who marvel at the order of the universe may marvel at either or both of the regularities of co-presence and of succession. The thinkers of the eighteenth century to whom the argument from design appealed so strongly were struck almost exclusively by the regularities of co-presence. They marveled at the order in animals and plants; but since they largely took for granted the regularities of succession, what struck them about the animals and plants, as to a lesser extent about machines made by men, was the subtle and coherent arrangement of their millions of parts. Paley's *Natural Theology* dwells mainly on details of comparative anatomy, on eyes and ears and muscles and bones arranged with minute precision so as to operate with high efficiency, and in the *Dialogues* Hume's Cleanthes produces the same kind of examples: "Consider, anatomize the eye, survey its structure and contrivance, and tell me from your own feeling, if the idea of a contriver does not immediately flow in upon you with a force like that of sensation."

The eighteenth-century argument from spatial order seems to go as follows. Animals and plants have the power to reproduce their kind, and so, given the past existence of animals and plants, their present existence is to be expected. But what is vastly surprising is the existence of animals and plants at all. By natural processes they can only come into being through generation. But we know that the world has not been going on for ever, and so the great puzzle is the existence of the first animals and plants in 4004 BC or whenever exactly it was that animals and plants began to exist. Since they could not have come about by natural scientific processes, and since they are very similar to the machines, which certain rational agents, viz. men, make, it is very probable that they were made by a rational agent—only clearly one much more powerful and knowledgeable than men.

In the *Dialogues*, through the mouth of Philo, Hume made some classical objections to the argument in this form, some of which have some force against all forms of the argument; I shall deal with most of these as we come to appropriate places in this chapter. Despite Hume's objections, the argument is, I think, a very plausible one—given its premises. But one of its premises was shown by Darwin and his successors to be clearly false. Complex animals and plants can be produced through generation by less complex animals and plants— species are not eternally distinct; and simple animals and plants can be produced by natural processes from inorganic matter. This discovery led to the virtual disappearance of the argument from design from popular apologetic—mistakenly, I think, since it can easily be reconstructed in a form which does not rely on the premises shown to be false by Darwin. This can be done even for the argument from spatial order.

We can reconstruct the argument from spatial order as follows. We see around us animals and plants, intricate examples of spatial order in the ways which Paley set out, similar to machines of the kind which men make. We know that these animals and plants have evolved by natural processes from inorganic matter. But clearly this evolution can only have taken place, given certain special natural laws. These are first, the chemical laws stating how under certain circumstances inorganic molecules combine to make organic ones, and organic ones combine to make organisms. And secondly, there are the biological laws of evolution stating how organisms have very many offspring, some of which vary in one or more characteristics from their parents, and how some of these characteristics are passed on to most offspring, from which it follows that, given shortage of food and other environmental needs, there will be competition for survival, in which the fittest will survive. Among organisms very well fitted for survival will be organisms of such complex and subtle construction as to allow easy adaptation to a changing environment. These organisms will evince great spatial order. So the laws of nature are such as, under certain circumstances, to give rise to striking examples of spatial order similar to the machines which men make. Nature, that is, is a machine-making machine. In the twentieth century men make not only machines, but machine-making machines. They may therefore naturally infer from nature which produces animals and plants, to a creator of nature similar to men who make machine-making machines.

This reconstructed argument is now immune to having some crucial premises shown false by some biologist of the 1980s. The facts to which its premises appeal are too evident for that—whatever the details, natural laws are clearly such as to produce complex organisms from inorganic matter under certain circumstances. But although this is so, I do not find the argument a very strong one, and this is because of the evident paucity of organisms throughout the universe. The circumstances under which nature behaves as a machine-making machine are rare. For that reason nature does not evince very strongly the character of a machine-making machine and hence the analogies between the products of natural processes on the one hand and machines on the other are not too strong.

Perhaps they give a small degree of probability to the hypothesis that a rational agent was responsible for the laws of evolution in some ways similar to the rational agents who make machines, but the probability is no more than that.

I pass on to consider a form of teleological argument which seems to me a much stronger one—the teleological argument from the temporal order of the world. The temporal order of the universe is, to the man who bothers to give it a moment's thought, an overwhelmingly striking fact about it. Regularities of succession are all-pervasive. For simple laws govern almost all successions of events. In books of physics, chemistry, and biology we can learn how almost everything in the world behaves. The laws of their behavior can be set out by relatively simple formulae which men can understand and by means of which they can successfully predict the future. The orderliness of the universe to which I draw attention here is its conformity to formula, to simple, formulable, scientific laws. The orderliness of the universe in this respect is a very striking fact about it. The universe might so naturally have been chaotic, but it is not—it is very orderly.

That the world has this very peculiar characteristic may be challenged in various ways. It may be said of the order which we seem to see in the universe that we impose the order on the world, that it is not there independently of our imposition. Put another way all that this temporal order amounts to, it might be said, is a coincidence between how things have been so far in the world and the patterns which men can recognize and describe, a coincidence which is itself susceptible of an explanation in terms of natural selection. In fact, however, the temporal order of the world is something deeper than that. The premise of a good teleological argument is not that so far (within his life or within human history) things have conformed to a pattern which man can recognize and describe. The premiss is rather that things have and will continue to conform to such a pattern however initial conditions vary, however men interfere in the world. If induction is justified, we are justified in supposing that things will continue to behave as they have behaved in the kinds of respect which scientists and ordinary people recognize and describe. I assume that we are justified in believing that the laws of gravity and chemical cohesion will continue to hold tomorrow—that stones will fall, and desks hold together tomorrow as well as today—however initial conditions vary, however men interfere in the world. It may of course be doubted whether philosophers have given a very satisfactory account of what makes such beliefs justified (hence "the problem of induction"); but I assume the common-sense view that they are justified. So the teleologist's premiss is not just that there has been in nature so far an order which men can recognize and describe; but there has been and will continue to be in nature an order, recognizable and describable by men certainly, but one which exists independently of men. If men are correct in their belief that the order which they see in the world is an order which will hold in the future as in the past, it is clearly not an imposed or invented order. It is there in nature. For man cannot make nature conform subsequently to an order which he has invented. Only if the order is there in nature is nature's future conformity to be expected.

An objector may now urge that although the order of the universe is an objective matter, nevertheless, unless the universe were an orderly place, men would not be around to comment on the fact. (If there were no natural laws, there would be no regularly functioning organisms, and so no men.) Hence there is nothing surprising in the fact that men find order—they could not possibly find anything else. This conclusion is clearly a little too strong. There would need to be quite a bit of order in and around our bodies if men are to exist and think, but there could be chaos outside the earth, so long as the earth was largely unaffected by that chaos. There is a great deal more order in the world than is necessary for the existence of humans. So men could still be around to comment on the fact even if the world were a much less orderly place than it is. But quite apart from this minor consideration, the argument still fails totally for a reason which can best be brought out by an analogy. Suppose that a madman kidnaps a victim

and shuts him in a room with a card-shuffling machine. The machine shuffles ten packs of cards simultaneously and then draws a card from each pack and exhibits simultaneously the ten cards. The kidnapper tells the victim that he will shortly set the machine to work and it will exhibit its first draw, but that unless the draw consists of an ace of hearts from each pack, the machine will simultaneously set off an explosion which will kill the victim, in consequence of which he will not see which cards the machine drew. The machine is then set to work, and to the amazement and relief of the victim the machine exhibits an ace of hearts drawn from each pack. The victim thinks that this extraordinary fact needs an explanation in terms of the machine having been rigged in some way. But the kidnapper, who now reappears, casts doubt on this suggestion. "It is hardly surprising," he says, "that the machine draws only aces of hearts. You could not possibly see anything else. For you would not be here to see anything at all, if any other cards had been drawn." But of course the victim is right and the kidnapper is wrong. There is indeed something extraordinary in need of explanation in ten aces of hearts being drawn. The fact that this peculiar order is a necessary condition of the draw being perceived at all makes what is perceived no less extraordinary and in need of explanation. The teleologist's starting-point is not that we perceive order rather than disorder, but that order rather than disorder is there. Maybe only if order is there can we know what is there, but that makes what is there no less extraordinary and in need of explanation.

So the universe is characterized by vast, all-pervasive temporal order, the conformity of nature to formula, recorded in the scientific laws formulated by men. Now this phenomenon, like the very existence of the world, is clearly something "too big" to be explained by science. If there is an explanation of the world's order it cannot be a scientific one, and this follows from the nature of scientific explanation. For, in scientific explanation we explain particular phenomena as brought about by prior phenomena in accord with scientific laws; or we explain the operation of scientific laws in terms of more general scientific laws (and perhaps also particular phenomena). Thus we explain the operation of Kepler's laws in terms of the operation of Newton's laws (given the masses, initial velocities, and distances apart of the sun and planets); and we explain the operation of Newton's laws in terms of the operation of Einstein's field equations for space relatively empty of matter. Science thus explains particular phenomena and low-level laws in terms partly of high-level laws. But from the very nature of science it cannot explain the highest-level laws of all; for they are that by which it explains all other phenomena.

At this point we need to rephrase our premises in terms of the powers-and-liabilities account of science, which we have seen reason for preferring to the Hempelian account. On this account what the all-pervasive temporal order amounts to is the fact that throughout space and time there are physical objects of various kinds, every such object having the powers and liabilities which are described in laws of nature—e.g. the power of attracting each other physical object in the universe with a force of $\gamma mm^1/r^2$ dynes (where γ is the gravitational constant), the liability always to exercise this power, and the liability to be attracted by each other body in the universe with a force of $\gamma mm^1/r^2$ dynes and so on. From the fact that it has such general powers it follows that an object will have certain more specific powers, given the land of object that it is. For example, given that it has a mass of 1 gram, it will follow that it has the power of attracting each other body in the universe with a force of $\gamma m^1/r^2$ dynes. This picture allows us to draw attention to one feature of the orderliness of the universe which the other picture makes it easy to ignore. Unlike the feature to which I have drawn attention so far, it is not one of which men have always known; it is one which the atomic theory of chemistry strongly suggested, and the discovery of fundamental particles confirmed. It is this. The physical objects scattered throughout space and time are, or are composed of, particles of a few limited kinds, which we call fundamental particles. Whether the protons and electrons which we suppose to be the fundamental particles are in fact fundamental, or whether they are composed of yet more fundamental particles (e.g. quarks) which are capable of independent existence is not altogether clear—but what does seem clear is that if there are yet more fundamental particles, they too come in a few specific kinds. Nature only has building-blocks of a few lands. Each particle of a given kind has a few defining properties which determine its behaviour and which are specific to that kind. Thus all electrons have a mass of $1/2 MeV/c^2$, a charge of -1, a spin of $1/2$, etc. All positrons have other properties the same as electrons, but a charge of $+1$. All protons have a mass of $938 \ MeV/c^2$, a charge of $+1$, and a spin of $1/2$. And so on. There are innumerably many particles which belong to each of a few kinds, and no particles with characteristics intermediate between those of two kinds. The properties of fundamental kinds, that is, which give specific form to the general powers which all objects have, belong to a small class; and the powers and liabilities of large-scale objects are determined by those of their fundamental components. Particles have constant characteristics over time; they only change their characteristics, or are destroyed or converted into other particles by reason of their own liabilities (e.g. to decay) or the action of other particles acting in virtue of their powers.

Put in these terms then, the orderliness of nature is a matter of the vast uniformity in the powers and liabilities of bodies throughout endless time and space, and also in the paucity of kinds of components of bodies. Over centuries long, long ago and over distances distant in millions of light years from ourselves the same universal orderliness reigns. There are, as we have seen, explanations of only two kinds for phenomena—scientific explanation and personal explanation. Yet, although a scientific explanation can be provided of why the more specific powers and liabilities of bodies hold (e.g. why an electron exerts just the attractive force which it does) in terms of more general powers and liabilities possessed by all bodies (put in Hempelian terms—why a particular natural law holds in terms of more general natural laws), science cannot explain why all bodies do possess the same very general powers and liabilities. It is with this fact that scientific explanation stops. So either the orderliness of nature is where all explanation stops, or we must postulate an agent of great power and knowledge who brings about through his continuous action that bodies have the same very general powers and liabilities (that the most general natural laws operate); and, once again, the simplest such agent to postulate is one of infinite power, knowledge, and freedom, i.e. God. An additional consideration here is that it is clearly vastly simpler to suppose that the existence and the order of the world have the same cause, and the considerations which lead us to postulate a being of infinite power, knowledge, and freedom as the cause of the former reinforce the considerations which lead us to postulate such a cause for the latter.

In the *Dialogues* Hume made the objection—why should we not postulate many gods to give order to the universe, not merely one? "A great number of men join in building a house or a ship, in rearing a city, in framing a commonwealth, why may not several deities combine in framing a world?" Hume again is aware of the obvious counter-objection to his suggestion. "To multiply causes without necessity is … contrary to true philosophy." He claims, however, that the counter-objection does not apply here, because (in my terminology) although the supposition that there is one god is a simpler supposition than the supposition that there are many, in postulating many persons to be responsible for the order of the universe we are postulating persons more like to men in power and knowledge—that is we are putting forward a hypothesis which fits in better with our background knowledge of what there is in the world. That may be. But Hume's hypothesis is very complicated—we want to ask about it such questions as why are there just 333 deities (or whatever the number is), why do they have powers of just the strength which they do have, and what moves them to cooperate as closely as obviously they do; questions of a kind which obtrude far less with the far simpler and so less arbitrary theistic hypothesis. Even if Hume were right in supposing that the prior probability of his hypothesis were as great as that of theism (because the fit with background knowledge of the former cancels out the

simplicity of the latter) (and I do not myself think that he is right), the hypothesis of theism nevertheless has greater explanatory power than the Humean hypothesis and is for that reason more probable. For theism leads us to expect that we will find throughout nature one pattern of order. But if there were more than one deity responsible for the order of the universe, we would expect to see characteristic marks of the handiwork of different deities in different parts of the universe, just as we see different kinds of workmanship in the different houses of a city. We would expect to find an inverse square of law of gravitation obeyed in one part of the universe, and in another part a law which was just short of being an inverse square law—without the difference being explicable in terms of a more general law. It is enough to draw this absurd conclusion to see how wrong the Humean objection is.

So I shall take as the alternatives—the first, that the temporal order of the world is where explanation stops, and the second, that the temporal order of the world is due to the agency of God; and I shall ignore the less probable possibilities that the order is to be explained as due to the agency of an agent or agents of finite power. The proponent of the teleological argument claims that the order of nature shows an orderer—God.

THE FORCE OF THE SECOND FORM OF TELEOLOGICAL ARGUMENT

The teleological argument, whether from temporal or spatial order, is, I believe, a codification by philosophers of a reaction to the world deeply embedded in the human consciousness. Men see the comprehensibility of the world as evidence of a comprehending creator. The prophet Jeremiah lived in an age in which the existence of a creator-god of some sort was taken for granted. What was at stake was the extent of his goodness, knowledge, and power. Jeremiah argued from the order of the world that he was a powerful and reliable god, that god was God. He argued to the power of the creator from the extent of the creation—"The host of heaven cannot be numbered, neither the sand of the sea measured"; and he argued that its regular behaviour showed the reliability of the creator, and he spoke of the "covenant of the day and night" whereby they follow each other regularly, and "the ordinances of heaven and earth,"[1] and he used their existence as an argument for the trust-worthiness of the God of Jacob. The argument from temporal order has been with us ever since.

You get the argument from temporal order also in Aquinas's fifth way, which runs as follows:

> The fifth way is based on the guidedness of nature. An orderedness of actions to an end is observed in all bodies obeying natural laws, even when they lack awareness. For their behaviour hardly ever varies, and will practically always turn out well; which shows that they truly tend to a goal, and do not merely hit it by accident. Nothing however that lacks awareness tends to a goal, except under the direction of someone with awareness and with understanding; the arrow, for example requires an archer. Everything in nature, therefore is directed to its goal by someone with understanding and this we call "God."[2]

Aquinas argues that the regular behaviour of each inanimate thing shows that some animate being is directing it (making it move to achieve some purpose, attain some goal); and from that he comes—rather quickly—to the conclusion that one "being with understanding" is responsible for the behaviour of all inanimate things.

It seems to me fairly clear that no argument from temporal order—whether Aquinas's fifth way or any other argument can be a good deductive argument. For although the premiss is undoubtedly correct—a vast pervasive order characterizes the world—the step from premiss to conclusion is not a valid deductive one. Although the existence of order may be good

evidence of a designer, it is surely compatible with the non-existence of one—it is hardly a logically necessary truth that all order is brought about by a person. And although, as I have urged, the supposition that one person is responsible for the orderliness of the world is much simpler and so more probable than the supposition that many persons are, nevertheless, the latter supposition seems logically compatible with the data—so we must turn to the more substantial issue of whether the argument from the temporal order of the world to God is a good inductive argument. We had reached the conclusion that either the vast uniformity in the powers and liabilities of bodies was where explanation stopped, or that God brings this about by his continuous action, through an intention constant over time.

Let us represent by e this conformity of the world to order, and let h be the hypothesis of theism. It is not possible to treat a teleological argument in complete isolation from the cosmological argument. We cannot ask how probable the premiss of the teleological argument makes theism, independently of the premiss of the cosmological argument, for the premiss of the teleological argument entails in part the premiss of the cosmological argument. That there is order of the kind described entails at least that there is a physical universe. So let k be now, not mere tautological evidence, but the existence of a complex physical universe (the premiss of the version of the cosmological argument to which I devoted most attention). Let us ask how much more probable does the orderliness of such a universe make the existence of God than does the mere existence of the universe.

With these fillings, we ask whether $P(h/e\&k) > P(h/k)$ and by how much. As we have seen $P(h/e\&k)$ will exceed $P(h/k)$ if and only if $P(e/h\&k) > P(e/\sim h\&k)$. Put in words with our current fillings for h, e, and k, the existence of order in the world confirms the existence of God if and only if the existence of this order in the world is more probable if there is a God than if there is not. We saw in Chapter 6 that where h is the hypothesis that there is a God $P(e/h\&k)$ may exceed $P(e/\sim h\&k)$, either because e cannot be explained in any other way and is very unlikely to occur uncaused or because God has character such that he is more likely to bring about e than alternative states. With respect to the cosmological argument, I suggested that its case rested solely on the first consideration. Here I shall suggest that again the first consideration is dominant, but that the second has considerable significance also.

Let us start with the first consideration, e is the vast uniformity in the powers and liabilities possessed by material objects—$P(e/\sim h \& k)$ is the probability that there should be that amount of uniformity in a God-less world, that this uniform distribution of the powers of things should be where explanation terminates, that they be further inexplicable. That there should be material bodies is strange enough; but that they should all have such similar powers which they inevitably exercise, seems passing strange. It is strange enough that physical objects should have powers at all—why should they not just be, without being able to make a difference to the world? But that they should all, throughout infinite time and space, have some general powers identical to those of all other objects (and they all be made of components of very few fundamental kinds, each component of a given kind being identical in all characteristics with each other such component) and yet there be no cause of this at all seems incredible. The universe is complex as we urged, in the last chapter, in that there are so many bodies of different shapes, etc., and now we find an underlying orderliness in the identity of powers and paucity of kinds of components of bodies. Yet this orderliness, if there is no explanation of it in terms of the action of God, is the orderliness of coincidence—the fact that one body has certain powers does not explain the fact that a second body has—not the simplicity of a common underlying explanation. The basic complexity remains in the vast number of different bodies in which the orderliness of identical powers and components is embodied. It is a complexity too striking to occur unexplained. It cries out for explanation in terms of some single common source with the power to produce it. Just as we would seek to explain all the coins of the realm having an identical pattern in terms of their origin from a common

mould, or all of many pictures' having a common style in terms of their being painted by the same painter, so too should we seek to explain all physical objects' having the same powers in terms of their deriving them from a common source. On these grounds alone $P(e/h \& k) \gg P(e/k)$, and so $P(b/e \& k) \gg P(h/k)$.[3]

I think, however, that we can go further by bringing in considerations from God's character—we saw in Chapter 6 that God will bring about a state of affairs if it is over all a good thing that he should, he will not bring about a state of affairs if it is over all a bad thing that he should, and that he will only bring about a state of affairs if it is in some way a good thing that he should. Put in terms of reasons—he will always act on overriding reasons and cannot act except for a reason. Now there are two reasons why human beings produce order. One is aesthetic—beauty comes in the patterns of things, such as dances and songs. Some sort of order is a necessary condition of phenomena having beauty; complete chaos is just ugly—although of course not any order is beautiful. The second reason why a human being produces order is that when there is order he or other rational agents can perceive that order and utilize it to achieve ends. If we see that there is a certain pattern of order in phenomena we can then justifiably predict that that order will continue, and that enables us to make predictions about the future on which we can rely. A librarian puts books in an alphabetical order of authors in order that he and users of the library who come to know that the order is there may subsequently be able to find any book in the library very quickly (because, given knowledge of the order, we can predict whereabouts in the library any given book will be).

God has similar reasons for producing an orderly, as opposed to a chaotic universe. In so far as some sort of order is a necessary condition of beauty, and it is a good thing—as it surely is—that the world be beautiful rather than ugly, God has reason for creating an orderly universe. Secondly, I shall argue in Chapter 10 that it is good that God should make finite creatures with the opportunity to grow in knowledge and power. Now if creatures are going consciously to extend their control of the world, they will need to know how to do so. There will need to be some procedures which they can find out, such that if they follow those procedures, certain events will occur. This entails the existence of temporal order. There can only be such procedures if the world is orderly, and, I should add, there can only be such procedures ascertainable by men if the order of the world is such as to be discernible by men. To take a simple example, if hitting things leads to them breaking or penetrating other things, and heating things leads to them melting, men can discover these regularities and utilize them to make artefacts such as houses, tables, and chairs. They can heat iron ore to melt it to make nails, hammers, and axes, and use the latter to break wood into the right shapes to hammer together with nails to make the artefacts. Or, if light and other electro-magnetic radiation behave in predictable ways comprehensible by men, men can discover those ways and build telescopes and radio and television receivers and transmitters. A world must evince the temporal order exhibited by laws of nature if men are to be able to extrapolate from how things have behaved in the past, to how they will behave in the future, which extrapolation is necessary if men are to have the knowledge of how things will behave in the future, which they must have in order to be able to extend their control over the world. (There would not need to be complete determinism—agents themselves could be exempt from the full rigors of determinism, and there might be violations of natural laws from time to time. But basically the world has to be governed by laws of nature if agents are consciously to extend their control of the world.) If I am right in supposing that God has reason to create finite creatures with the opportunity to grow in knowledge and power, then he has reason to create temporal order. So I suggest that God has at least these two reasons for producing an orderly world. Maybe God has reasons for not making creatures with the opportunity to grow in knowledge and power, and so the second reason for his creating an orderly universe does not apply. But with one possible, and, I shall show, irrelevant qualification, the first surely does. God may choose whether or not to make a physical universe, but if he does, he has reason for making a beautiful and so an orderly one. God has reason, if he does make a physical universe, not to make a chaotic or botched-up one. The only reason of which I can think why God should make the universe in some respects ugly would be to give to creatures the opportunity to discover the aesthetic merits of different states of affairs and through cooperative effort to make the world beautiful for themselves. But then the other argument shows that if they are to be able to exercise such an opportunity the world will need to be orderly in some respects. (There will have to be predictable regularities which creatures may utilize in order to produce beautiful states of affairs.) So, either way, the world will need to be orderly. It rather looks as if God has overriding reason to make an orderly universe if he makes a universe at all. However, as I emphasized, human inquiry into divine reasons is a highly speculative matter. But it is nevertheless one in which men are justified in reaching tentative conclusions. For God is postulated to be an agent like ourselves in having knowledge, power, and freedom, although to an infinitely greater degree than we have. The existence of the analogy legitimizes us in reaching conclusions about his purposes, conclusions which must allow for the quantitative difference, as I have tried to do.

So I suggest that the order of the world is evidence of the existence of God both because its occurrence would be very improbable *a priori* and also because, in virtue of his postulated character, he has very good, apparently overriding, reason for making an orderly universe, if he makes a universe at all. It looks as if $P(e/h\&k)$ equals 1. For both reasons $P(e/h\&k) \gg P(e/{\sim}h\&k)$ and so $P(b/e\&k) \gg P(h/k)$. I conclude that the teleological argument from temporal order is a good C-inductive argument to the existence of God.[†]

Let us look at the argument from a slightly different angle. It is basically an argument by

---

[†]Earlier in the book Swinburne distinguishes a P-inductive argument from a C-inductive argument. A P-inductive argument is one in which the premises make the conclusion probable. A C-inductive argument is one in which the premises *add to the probability of the conclusion (i.e., makes it more probable than it would otherwise be).*

analogy, an analogy between the order in the natural world (the temporal order codified in laws of nature) and the patterns of order which men often produce (the ordered books on library shelves, or the temporal order in the movements of a dancer or the notes of a song). It argues from similarity between phenomena of two kinds B and B^* to similarity between their causes A and A^*. In view of the similarities between the two kinds of order B and B^*, the theist postulates a cause (A^*) in some respects similar to A (men); yet in view of the dissimilarities the theist must postulate a cause in other respects different. All arguments by analogy do and must proceed in this way. They cannot postulate a cause in all respects similar. They postulate a cause who is such that one would expect him to produce phenomena similar to B in the respects in which B^* are similar to B and different from B in the respects in which B^* are different from B.

All argument from analogy works like this. Thus various properties of light and sound were known in the nineteenth century, among them that both light and sound are reflected, refracted, diffracted, and show interference phenomena. In the case of sound these were known to be due to disturbance of the medium, air, in which it is transmitted. What could one conclude by analogy about the cause of the reflection, etc., of light? One could conclude that the propagation of light was, like the propagation of sound, the propagation of a wavelike disturbance in a medium. But one could not conclude that it was the propagation of a disturbance in the same medium—air, since light passed through space empty of air. Scientists had to postulate a separate medium—aether, the disturbance of which was responsible for the reflection, etc., of light. And not merely does all argument by analogy proceed like this, but all inductive inference can be represented as argument by analogy. For all inductive inference depends on the assumption that in certain respects things continue the same and in other respects they differ. Thus that crude inference from a number of observed swans all having been white to the next swan's being white is an argument by analogy. For it claims that the next swan will be like the observed swans

in one respect—color, while being unlike them in other respects.

In our case the similarities between the temporal order which men produce and the temporal order in nature codified in scientific laws mean postulating as cause of the latter a person who acts intentionally. The dissimilarities between the kinds of order include the world-wide extent of the order in nature in comparison with the very narrow range of order which men produce. This means postulating as cause of the former a person of enormous power and knowledge. Now, as we saw in Chapter 2, a person has a body if there is a region of the world under his direct control and if he controls other regions of the world only by controlling the former and by its movements having predictable effects on the outside world. Likewise he learns about the world only by the world having effects on this region. If these conditions are satisfied, the person has a body, and the stated region is that body. But if a person brings about directly the connections between things, including the predictable connections between the bodies of other persons and the world, there is no region of the world, goings-on in which bring about those connections. The person must bring about those connections as a basic action. His control of the world must be immediate, not mediated by a body. So the dissimilarities between the two kinds of order necessarily lead to the postulation of a non-embodied person (rather than an embodied person) as cause of the temporal order in nature.

These considerations should suffice to rebut that persistent criticism of the argument from design which we have heard ever since Hume that, taken seriously, the argument ought to be postulating an embodied god, a giant of a man. "Why not," wrote Hume, "become a perfect anthro-pomorphite? Why not assert the deity or deities to be corporeal, and, to have eyes, a nose, mouth, ears, etc.?" The answer is the simple one that dissimilarities between effects lead the rational man to postulate dissimilarities between causes, and that this procedure is basic to inductive inference.

It is true that the greater the dissimilarities between effects, the weaker is the argument to the existence of a similar cause; and it has been a traditional criticism of the argument from design represented as an argument by analogy that the analogy is weak. The dissimilarities between the natural world and the effects which men produce are indeed striking; but the similarities between these are also, I have been suggesting, striking—in both there is the conformity of phenomena to a simple pattern of order detectable by men. But although the dissimilarities are perhaps sufficiently great to make the argument not a good P-inductive argument, this chapter suggests that it remains a good C-inductive argument. The existence of order in the universe increases significantly the probability that there is a God, even if it does not by itself render it probable.

THE ARGUMENT FROM BEAUTY

We saw that God has reason, apparently overriding reason, for making, not merely any orderly world (which we have been considering so far) but a beautiful world—at any rate to the extent to which it lies outside the control of creatures. (And he has reason too, I would suggest, even in whatever respects the world does lie within the control of creatures, to give them experience of beauty to develop, and perhaps also some ugliness to annihilate.) So God has reason to make a basically beautiful world, although also reason to leave some of the beauty or ugliness of the world within the power of creatures to determine; but he would seem to have overriding reason not to make a basically ugly world beyond the powers of creatures to improve. Hence, if there is a God there is more reason to expect a basically beautiful world than a basically ugly one—by the principles of Chapter 6. A priori, however, there is no particular reason for expecting a basically beautiful rather than a basically ugly world. In consequence, if the world is beautiful, that fact would be evidence for God's existence. For, in this case, if we let k be "there is an orderly physical universe," e be "there is a beautiful universe," and h be "there is a God," $P(e/h\&k)$ will be greater than $P(e/k)$; and so by our previous principles the argument from e to h will be another good C-inductive argument.

Few, however, would deny that our universe (apart from its animal and human inhabitants, and aspects subject to their immediate control) has that beauty. Poets and painters and ordinary men down the centuries have long admired the beauty of the orderly procession of the heavenly bodies, the scattering of the galaxies through the heavens (in some ways random, in some ways orderly), and the rocks, sea, and wind interacting on earth, "The spacious firmament on high, and all the blue aethereal sky," the water lapping against "the old eternal rocks," and the plants of the jungle and of temperate climates, contrasting with the desert and the Arctic wastes. Who in his senses would deny that here is beauty in abundance? If we confine ourselves to the argument from the beauty of the inanimate and plant worlds, the argument surely works.

NOTES

1. Jer. 33: 20f. and 25f.
2. St. Thomas Aquinas, *Summa Theologiae,* 1 a, 2.3, trans. T. McDermott, OP (London, 1964).
3. "$\gg$" means "is much greater than," "$\ll$" means "is much less than."

II.C.4

A Scientific Argument for the Existence of God

ROBIN COLLINS

Robin Collins (1961–   ) is professor of philosophy at Messiah College, and he has written several articles on the argument from design. The article included here presents a simplified version of an argument that he has developed in much more technical detail elsewhere. He begins by noting that life would have been impossible had certain laws of nature and fundamental physical constants (such as the gravitational constant) been even slightly different. He then argues that since this apparent "fine-tuning" of the laws and constants is significantly more probable on the assumption that the universe was designed to be hospitable for life than on the assumption that it was not designed at all, such apparent fine-tuning counts as evidence in favor of the existence of a designer.

I. INTRODUCTION

The Evidence of Fine-Tuning

Suppose we went on a mission to Mars, and found a domed structure in which everything was set up just right for life to exist. The temperature, for example, was set around 70° F and the humidity was at 50 percent; moreover, there was an oxygen recycling system, an energy gathering system, and a whole system for the production of food. Put simply, the domed structure appeared to be a fully functioning biosphere. What conclusion would we draw from finding this structure? Would we draw the conclusion that it just happened to form by chance? Certainly not. Instead, we would unanimously conclude that it was designed by some intelligent being. Why would we draw this conclusion? Because an intelligent designer appears to be the only plausible explanation for the existence of the structure. That is, the only alternative explanation we can think of—that the structure was formed by some natural process—seems extremely unlikely. Of course, it is *possible* that, for example, through some volcanic eruption various metals and other compounds could have formed, and then separated out in just the right way to produce the "biosphere," but such a scenario strikes us as extraordinarily unlikely, thus making this alternative explanation unbelievable.

The universe is analogous to such a "biosphere," according to recent findings in physics. Almost everything about the basic structure of the universe—for example, the fundamental laws and parameters of physics and the initial distribution of matter and energy—is balanced on a razor's edge for life to occur. As the eminent Princeton physicist Freeman Dyson notes, "There are many ... lucky accidents in physics. Without such accidents, water could not exist as liquid, chains of carbon atoms could not form complex organic molecules, and hydrogen atoms could not form breakable bridges between molecules"[1]—in short, life as we know it would be impossible.

Scientists call this extraordinary balancing of the parameters of physics and the initial conditions of the universe the "fine-tuning of the cosmos." It has been extensively discussed by philosophers, theologians, and scientists, especially since the early 1970s, with hundreds of articles and dozens of books written on the topic. Today, it is widely regarded as offering by far the most persuasive current argument for the existence of God. For example, theoretical physicist and popular science writer Paul Davies—whose early writings were not particularly sympathetic to theism—claims that with regard to basic structure of the universe, "the impression of design is overwhelming."[2] Similarly, in response to the life-permitting fine-tuning of the nuclear resonances responsible for the oxygen and carbon synthesis in stars, the famous astrophysicist Sir Fred Hoyle declares that

> I do not believe that any scientists who examined the evidence would fail to draw the inference that the laws of nuclear physics have been deliberately designed with regard to the consequences they produce inside stars. If this is so, then my apparently random quirks have become part of a deep-laid scheme. If not then we are back again at a monstrous sequence of accidents.[3]

A few examples of this fine-tuning are listed below:

1. If the initial explosion of the big bang had differed in strength by as little as one part in 10^{60}, the universe would have either quickly collapsed back on itself, or expanded too rapidly for stars to form. In either case, life would be impossible. (As John Jefferson Davis points out, an accuracy of one part in 10^{60} can be compared to firing a bullet at a one-inch target on the other side of the observable universe, twenty billion light years away, and hitting the target.)[4]

2. Calculations indicate that if the strong nuclear force, the force that binds protons and neutrons together in an atom, had been stronger or weaker by as little as five percent, life would be impossible.[5]

3. Calculations by Brandon Carter show that if gravity had been stronger or weaker by one part in 10^{40}, then life-sustaining stars like the sun could not exist. This would most likely make life impossible.[6]

4. If the neutron were not about 1.001 times the mass of the proton, all protons would have decayed into neutrons or all neutrons would have decayed into protons, and thus life would not be possible.[7]

5. If the electromagnetic force were slightly stronger or weaker, life would be impossible, for a variety of different reasons.[8]

Imaginatively, one could think of each instance of fine-tuning as a radio dial: unless all the dials are set exactly right, life would be impossible. Or, one could think of the initial conditions of the universe and the fundamental parameters of physics as a dart board that fills the whole galaxy, and the conditions necessary for life to exist as a small one-foot-wide target: unless the dart hits the target, life would be impossible. The fact that the dials are perfectly set, or that the dart has hit the target, strongly suggests that someone set the dials or aimed the dart, for it seems enormously improbable that such a coincidence could have happened by chance.

Although individual calculations of fine-tuning are only approximate and could be in error, the fact that the universe is fine-tuned for life is almost beyond question because of the large number of independent instances of apparent fine-tuning. As philosopher John Leslie has pointed out, "Clues heaped upon clues can constitute weighty evidence despite doubts about each element in the pile."[9] What is controversial, however, is the degree to which the fine-tuning provides evidence for the existence of God. As impressive as the argument from fine-tuning seems to be, atheists have raised several significant objections to it. Consequently, those who are aware of these objections, or have thought of them on their own, often will find the argument unconvincing. This is not only true of atheists, but also many theists. I have known, for instance, both a committed Christian Hollywood filmmaker and a committed Christian biochemist who remained unconvinced because of certain atheist objections to the argument. This is unfortunate, particularly since the fine-tuning argument is probably the most powerful current argument for the existence of God. My goal in this chapter, therefore, is to make the fine-tuning argument as strong as possible. This will involve developing the argument in as objective and rigorous a way as I can, and then answering the major atheist objections to it. Before launching into this, however, I will need to make a preliminary distinction.

A Preliminary Distinction

To develop the fine-tuning argument rigorously, it is useful to distinguish between what I shall call the *atheistic single-universe hypothesis* and the *atheistic many-universes hypothesis*. According to the atheistic single-universe hypothesis, there is only one universe, and it is ultimately an inexplicable, "brute" fact that the universe exists and is fine-tuned. Many atheists, however, advocate another hypothesis, one which attempts to explain how the seemingly improbable fine-tuning of the universe could be the result of chance. We will call this hypothesis the *atheistic many-worlds hypothesis,* or *the atheistic many-universes hypothesis.* According to this hypothesis, there exists what could be imaginatively thought of as a "universe generator" that produces a very large or infinite number of universes, with each universe having a randomly selected set of initial conditions and values for the parameters of physics. Because this generator produces so many universes, just by chance it will eventually produce one that is fine-tuned for intelligent life to occur.

Plan of the Chapter

Below, we will use this distinction between the atheistic single-universe hypothesis and the atheistic many-universes hypothesis to present two separate arguments for theism based on the fine-tuning: one which argues that the fine-tuning provides strong reasons to prefer theism over the atheistic single-universe hypothesis and one which argues that we should prefer theism over the atheistic many-universes hypothesis. We will develop the argument against the atheistic single-universe hypothesis in section II below, referring to it as the core argument. Then we will answer objections to this *core* argument in section III, and finally develop the argument for preferring theism to the atheistic many-universes hypothesis in section IV. An appendix is also included that further elaborates and justifies one of the key premises of the core argument presented in section II.

II. CORE ARGUMENT RIGOROUSLY FORMULATED

General Principle of Reasoning Used

The Principle Explained We will formulate the fine-tuning argument against the atheistic single-universe hypothesis in terms of what I will call the *prime principle of confirmation*. The prime principle of confirmation is a general principle of reasoning which tells us when some observation counts as evidence in favor of one hypothesis over another. *Simply put, the principle says that whenever we are considering two competing hypotheses, an observation counts as evidence in favor of the hypothesis under which the observation has the highest probability (or is the least improbable).* (Or, put slightly differently, the principle says that whenever we are considering two competing hypotheses, H_1 and H_2, an observation, O, counts as evidence in favor of H_1 over H_2 if O is more probable under H_1 than it is under H_2.) Moreover, the degree to which the evidence counts in favor of one hypothesis over another is proportional to the degree to which the observation is more probable under the one hypothesis than the other.[10] For example, the fine-tuning is much, much more probable under theism than under the atheistic single-universe hypothesis, so it counts as strong evidence for theism over this atheistic hypothesis. In the next major subsection, we will present a more formal and elaborated rendition of the fine-tuning argument in terms of the prime principle. First, however, let's look at a couple of illustrations of the principle and then present some support for it.

Additional Illustrations of the Principle For our first illustration, suppose that I went hiking in the mountains, and found underneath a certain cliff a group of rocks arranged in a formation that clearly formed the pattern "Welcome to the mountains, Robin Collins." One hypothesis is that, by chance, the rocks just happened to be arranged in that pattern—ultimately, perhaps, because of certain initial conditions of the universe. Suppose the only viable alternative hypothesis is that my brother, who was in the mountains before me, arranged the rocks in this way. Most of us would immediately take the arrangements of rocks to be strong evidence in favor of the "brother" hypothesis over the "chance" hypothesis. Why? Because it strikes us as extremely *improbable* that the rocks would be arranged that way by chance, but *not improbable* at all that my brother would place them in that configuration. Thus, by the prime principle of confirmation we would conclude that the arrangement of rocks strongly supports the "brother" hypothesis over the chance hypothesis.

Or consider another case, that of finding the defendant's fingerprints on the murder weapon. Normally, we would take such a finding as strong evidence that the defendant was guilty. Why? Because we judge that it would be *unlikely* for these fingerprints to be on the murder weapon if the defendant was innocent, but *not unlikely* if the defendant was guilty. That is, we would go through the same sort of reasoning as in the above case.

Support for the Principle Several things can be said in favor of the prime principle of confirmation. First, many philosophers think that this principle can be derived from what is known as the *probability calculus,* the set of mathematical rules that are typically assumed to govern probability. Second, there does not appear to be any case of recognizably good reasoning that violates this principle. Finally, the principle appears to have a wide range of applicability, undergirding much of our reasoning in science and everyday life, as the examples above illustrate. Indeed, some have even claimed that a slightly more general version of this principle undergirds all scientific reasoning. Because of all these reasons in favor of the principle, we can be very confident in it.

Further Development of Argument

To further develop the core version of the fine-tuning argument, we will summarize the argument by explicitly listing its two premises and its conclusion:

- *Premise 1.* The existence of the fine-tuning is not improbable under theism.

- *Premise 2.* The existence of the fine-tuning is very improbable under the atheistic single-universe hypothesis.

- *Conclusion*: From premises (1) and (2) and the prime principle of confirmation, it follows that the fine-tuning data provide strong evidence to favor the design hypothesis over the atheistic single-universe hypothesis.

At this point, we should pause to note two features of this argument. First, the argument does not say that the fine-tuning evidence proves that the universe was designed, or even that it is likely that the universe was designed. In order to justify these sorts of claims, we would have to look at the full range of evidence both for and against the design hypothesis, something we are not doing in this chapter. Rather, the argument merely concludes that the fine-tuning strongly *supports* theism *over* the atheistic single-universe hypothesis.

In this way, the evidence of the fine-tuning argument is much like fingerprints found on the gun: although they can provide strong evidence that the defendant committed the murder, one could not conclude merely from them alone that the defendant is guilty; one would also have to look at all the other evidence offered. Perhaps, for instance, ten reliable witnesses claimed to see the defendant at a party at the time of the shooting. In this case, the fingerprints would still count as significant evidence of guilt, but this evidence would be counterbalanced by the testimony of the witnesses. Similarly the evidence of fine-tuning strongly supports theism over the atheistic single-universe hypothesis, though it does not itself show that, everything considered, theism is the most plausible explanation of the world. Nonetheless, as I argue in the conclusion of this chapter, the evidence of fine-tuning provides a much stronger and more objective argument for theism (over the atheistic single-universe hypothesis) than the strongest atheistic argument does against theism.

The second feature of the argument we should note is that, given the truth of *the prime principle of confirmation*, the conclusion of the argument follows from the premises. Specifically, if the premises of the argument are true, then we are guaranteed that the conclusion is true: that is, the argument is what philosophers call *valid*. Thus, insofar as we can show that the premises of the argument are true, we will have shown that the conclusion is true. Our next task, therefore, is to attempt to show that the premises are true, or at least that we have strong reasons to believe them.

Support for the Premises
Support for Premise (1) Premise (1) is easy to support and fairly uncontroversial. One major argument in support of it can be simply stated as follows: *since God is an all good being, and it is good for intelligent, conscious beings to exist, it is not surprising or improbable that God would create a world that could support intelligent life.* Thus, the fine-tuning is not improbable under theism, as premise (1) asserts.

Support for Premise (2) Upon looking at the data, many people find it very obvious that the fine-tuning is highly improbable under the atheistic single-universe hypothesis. And it is easy to see why when we think of the fine-tuning in terms of the analogies offered earlier. In the dart board analogy, for example, the initial conditions of the universe and the fundamental parameters of physics are thought of as a dart board that fills the whole

galaxy, and the conditions necessary for life to exist as a small one-foot-wide target. Accordingly, from this analogy it seems obvious that it would be highly improbable for the fine-tuning to occur under the atheistic single-universe hypothesis— that is, for the dart to hit the target by chance.

Typically, advocates of the fine-tuning argument are satisfied with resting the justification of premise (2), or something like it, on this sort of analogy. Many atheists and theists, however, question the legitimacy of this sort of analogy, and thus find the argument unconvincing. For these people, the appendix to this chapter offers a rigorous and objective justification of premise (2) using standard principles of probabilistic reasoning. Among other things, in the process of rigorously justifying premise (2), we effectively answer the common objection to the fine-tuning argument that because the universe is a unique, unrepeatable event, we cannot meaningfully assign a probability to its being fine-tuned.

III. SOME OBJECTIONS TO CORE VERSION

As powerful as the core version of the fine-tuning argument is, several major objections have been raised to it by both atheists and theists. In this section, we will consider these objections in turn.

Objection 1: More Fundamental Law Objection

One criticism of the fine-tuning argument is that, as far as we know, there could be a more fundamental law under which the parameters of physics *must* have the values they do. Thus, given such a law, it is not improbable that the known parameters of physics fall within the life-permitting range.

Besides being entirely speculative, the problem with postulating such a law is that it simply moves the improbability of the fine-tuning up one level, to that of the postulated physical law itself. Under this hypothesis, what is improbable is that of all the conceivable fundamental physical laws there could be, the universe just happens to have the one that constrains the parameters of physics in a life-permitting way. Thus, trying to explain the fine-tuning by postulating this sort of fundamental law is like trying to explain why the pattern of rocks below a cliff spell "Welcome to the mountains, Robin Collins" by postulating that an earthquake occurred and that all the rocks on the cliff face were arranged in just the right configuration to fall into the pattern in question. Clearly this explanation merely transfers the improbability up one level, since now it seems enormously improbable that of all the possible configurations the rocks could be in on the cliff face, they are in the one which results in the pattern "Welcome to the mountains, Robin Collins."

A similar sort of response can be given to the claim that the fine-tuning is not improbable because it might be *logically necessary* for the parameters of physics to have life-permitting values. That is, according to this claim, the parameters of physics must have life-permitting values in the same way 2 + 2 must equal 4, or the interior angles of a triangle must add up to 180 degrees in Euclidian geometry. Like the "more fundamental law" proposal above, however, this postulate simply transfers the improbability up one level: of all the laws and parameters of physics that conceivably could have been logically necessary, it seems highly improbable that it would be those that are life-permitting.[11]

Objection 2: Other Forms of Life Objection

Another objection people commonly raise to the fine-tuning argument is that as far as we know, other forms of life could exist even if the parameters of physics were different. So, it is claimed, the fine-tuning argument ends up presupposing that all forms of intelligent life must be like us. The answer to this objection is that most cases of fine-tuning do not make this presupposition. Consider, for instance, the case of the fine-tuning of the strong nuclear force. If it were slightly smaller, no atoms could exist other than hydrogen. Contrary to what one might see on *Star Trek*, an intelligent life-form cannot be composed merely of hydrogen gas: there

is simply not enough stable complexity. So, in general the fine-tuning argument merely presupposes that intelligent life requires some degree of stable, reproducible organized complexity. This is certainly a very reasonable assumption.

Objection 3: Anthropic Principle Objection

According to the weak version of the so-called *anthropic principle,* if the laws of nature were not fine-tuned, we would not be here to comment on the fact. Some have argued, therefore, that the fine-tuning is not really *improbable or surprising* at all under atheism, but simply follows from the fact that we exist. The response to this objection is to simply restate the argument in terms of our existence: our existence as embodied, intelligent beings is extremely unlikely under the atheistic single-universe hypothesis (since our existence requires fine-tuning), but not improbable under theism. Then, we simply apply the prime principle of confirmation to draw the conclusion that *our existence* strongly confirms theism over the atheistic single-universe hypothesis.

To further illustrate this response, consider the following "firing squad" analogy. As John Leslie points out, if fifty sharpshooters all miss me, the response "if they had not missed me I wouldn't be here to consider the fact" is not adequate. Instead, I would naturally conclude that there was some reason why they all missed, such as that they never really intended to kill me. Why would I conclude this? Because my continued existence would be very improbable under the hypothesis that they missed me by chance, but not improbable under the hypothesis that there was some reason why they missed me. Thus, by the prime principle of confirmation, my continued existence strongly confirms the latter hypothesis.[12]

Objection 4: The "Who Designed God?" Objection

Perhaps the most common objection that atheists raise to the argument from design, of which the fine-tuning argument is one instance, is that postulating the existence of God does not solve the problem of design, but merely transfers it up one level. Atheist George Smith, for example, claims that

> If the universe is wonderfully designed, surely God is even more wonderfully designed. He must, therefore, have had a designer even more wonderful than He is. If *God* did not require a designer, then there is no reason why such a relatively less wonderful thing as the universe needed one.[13]

Or, as philosopher J. J. C. Smart states the objection:

> If we postulate God in addition to the created universe we increase the complexity of our hypothesis. We have all the complexity of the universe itself, and we have in addition the at least equal complexity of God. (The designer of an artifact must be at least as complex as the designed artifact).... *If the theist can show the atheist that postulating God actually reduces the complexity of one's total world view, then the atheist should be a theist.*[14]

The first response to the above atheist objection is to point out that the atheist claim that the designer of an artifact must be as complex as the artifact designed is certainly not obvious. But I do believe that their claim has some intuitive plausibility: for example, in the world we experience, organized complexity seems only to be produced by systems that already possess it, such as the human brain/mind, a factory, or an organism's biological parent.

The second, and better, response is to point out that, at most, the atheist objection only works against a version of the design argument that claims that all organized complexity needs an explanation, and that God is the best explanation of the organized complexity found in the world. The version of the argument I presented against the atheistic single-universe hypothesis, however, only required that the fine-tuning be more probable under theism than under the atheistic single-universe hypothesis.

But this requirement is still met even if God exhibits tremendous internal complexity, far exceeding that of the universe. Thus, even if we were to grant the atheist assumption that the designer of an artifact must be as complex as the artifact, the fine-tuning would still give us strong reasons to prefer theism over the atheistic single-universe hypothesis.

To illustrate, consider the example of the "biosphere" on Mars presented at the beginning of this paper. As mentioned above, the existence of the biosphere would be much more probable under the hypothesis that intelligent life once visited Mars than under the chance hypothesis. Thus, by the prime principle of confirmation, the existence of such a "biosphere" would constitute strong evidence that intelligent, extraterrestrial life had once been on Mars, even though this alien life would most likely have to be much more complex than the "biosphere" itself.

The final response theists can give to this objection is to show that a supermind such as God would *not* require a high degree of unexplained organized complexity to create the universe. Although I have presented this response elsewhere, presenting it here is beyond the scope of this chapter.

IV. THE ATHEISTIC MANY-UNIVERSES HYPOTHESIS

The Atheistic Many-Universes Hypothesis Explained

In response to the theistic explanation of fine-tuning of the cosmos, many atheists have offered an alternative explanation, what I will call the atheistic many-universes hypothesis. (In the literature it is more commonly referred to as the *many-worlds hypothesis,* though I believe this name is somewhat misleading.) According to this hypothesis, there are a very large—perhaps infinite—number of universes, with the fundamental parameters of physics varying from universe to universe.[15] Of course, in the vast majority of these universes the parameters of physics would not have life-permitting values.

Nonetheless, in a small proportion of universes they would, and consequently it is no longer improbable that universes such as ours exist that are fine-tuned for life to occur.

Advocates of this hypothesis offer various types of models for where these universes came from. We will present what are probably the two most popular and plausible, the so-called *vacuum fluctuation* models and the *oscillating big bang* models. According to the vacuum fluctuation models, our universe, along with these other universes, were generated by quantum fluctuations in a preexisting superspace.[16] Imaginatively, one can think of this preexisting superspace as an infinitely extending ocean full of soap, and each universe generated out of this superspace as a soap bubble which spontaneously forms on the ocean.

The other model, the oscillating big bang model, is a version of the big bang theory. According to the big bang theory, the universe came into existence in an "explosion" (that is, a "bang") somewhere between ten and fifteen billion years ago. According to the *oscillating* big bang theory, our universe will eventually collapse back in on itself (what is called the "big crunch") and then from that "big crunch" will arise another "big bang," forming a new universe, which will in turn itself collapse, and so on. According to those who use this model to attempt to explain the fine-tuning, during every cycle, the parameters of physics and the initial conditions of the universe are reset at random. Since this process of collapse, explosion, collapse, and explosion has been going on for all eternity, eventually a fine-tuned universe will occur, indeed infinitely many of them.

In the next section, we will list several reasons for rejecting the atheistic many-universes hypothesis.

Reasons for Rejecting the Atheistic Many-Universes Hypothesis

First Reason The first reason for rejecting the atheistic many-universes hypothesis, and preferring the theistic hypothesis, is the following general rule: *everything else being equal, we should prefer hypotheses for which we have independent evidence or that are natural extrapolations from what we already know.* Let's first illustrate and support this principle, and then apply it to the case of the fine-tuning.

Most of us take the existence of dinosaur bones to count as very strong evidence that dinosaurs existed in the past. But suppose a dinosaur skeptic claimed that she could explain the bones by postulating a "dinosaur-bone-producing-field" that simply materialized the bones out of thin air. Moreover, suppose further that, to avoid objections such as that there are no known physical laws that would allow for such a mechanism, the dinosaur skeptic simply postulated that we have not yet discovered these laws or detected these fields. Surely, none of us would let this skeptical hypothesis deter us from inferring the existence of dinosaurs. Why? Because although no one has directly observed dinosaurs, we do have experience of other animals leaving behind fossilized remains, and thus the dinosaur explanation is a *natural extrapolation* from our common experience. In contrast, to explain the dinosaur bones, the dinosaur skeptic has invented a set of physical laws, and a set of mechanisms that are *not* a natural extrapolation from anything we know or experience.

In the case of the fine-tuning, we already know that minds often produce fine-tuned devices, such as Swiss watches. Postulating God—a supermind—as the explanation of the fine-tuning, therefore, is a natural extrapolation from what we already observe minds to do. In contrast, it is difficult to see how the atheistic many-universes hypothesis could be considered a natural extrapolation from what we observe. Moreover, unlike the atheistic many-universes hypothesis, we have some experiential evidence for the existence of God, namely religious experience. Thus, by the above principle, we should prefer the theistic explanation of the fine-tuning over the atheistic many-universes explanation, everything else being equal.

Second Reason

A second reason for rejecting the atheistic many-universes hypothesis is that the "many-universes generator" seems like it would need to be designed.

For instance, in all current worked-out proposals for what this "universe generator" could be—such as the oscillating big bang and the vacuum fluctuation models explained above—the "generator" itself is governed by a complex set of physical laws that allow it to produce the universes. It stands to reason, therefore, that if these laws were slightly different the generator probably would not be able to produce any universes that could sustain life. After all, even my bread machine has to be made just right in order to work properly, and it only produces loaves of bread, not universes! Or consider a device as simple as a mousetrap: it requires that all the parts, such as the spring and hammer, be arranged just right in order to function. It is doubtful, therefore, whether the atheistic many-universe theory can entirely eliminate the problem of design the atheist faces; rather, at least to some extent, it seems simply to move the problem of design up one level.[17]

Third Reason A third reason for rejecting the atheistic many-universes hypothesis is that the universe generator must not only select the parameters of physics at random, but must actually randomly create or select the very laws of physics themselves. This makes this hypothesis seem even more far-fetched since it is difficult to see what possible physical mechanism could select or create laws.

The reason the "many-universes generator" must randomly select the laws of physics is that, just as the right values for the parameters of physics are needed for life to occur, the right set of laws is also needed. If, for instance, certain laws of physics were missing, life would be impossible. For example, without the law of inertia, which guarantees that particles do not shoot off at high speeds, life would probably not be possible.[18] Another example is the law of gravity: if masses did not attract each other, there would be no planets or stars, and once again it seems that life would be impossible. Yet another example is the *Pauli Exclusion Principle*, the principle of quantum mechanics that says that no two fermions—such as electrons or protons—can share the same quantum state. As prominent Princeton physicist Freeman Dyson points out,[19]

without this principle all electrons would collapse into the nucleus and thus atoms would be impossible.

Fourth Reason The fourth reason for rejecting the atheistic many-universes hypothesis is that it cannot explain other features of the universe that seem to exhibit apparent design, whereas theism can. For example, many physicists, such as Albert Einstein, have observed that the basic laws of physics exhibit an extraordinary degree of beauty, elegance, harmony, and ingenuity. Nobel prize-winning physicist Steven Weinberg, for instance, devotes a whole chapter of his book *Dreams of a Final Theory*[20] explaining how the criteria of beauty and elegance are commonly used to guide physicists in formulating the right laws. Indeed, one of the most prominent theoretical physicists of this century, Paul Dirac, went so far as to claim that "it is more important to have beauty in one's equations than to have them fit experiment."[21]

Now such beauty, elegance, and ingenuity make sense if the universe was designed by God. Under the atheistic many-universes hypothesis, however, there is no reason to expect the fundamental laws to be elegant or beautiful. As theoretical physicist Paul Davies writes, "If nature is so 'clever' as to exploit mechanisms that amaze us with their ingenuity, is that not persuasive evidence for the existence of intelligent design behind the universe? If the world's finest minds can unravel only with difficulty the deeper workings of nature, how could it be supposed that those workings are merely a mindless accident, a product of blind chance?"[22]

Final Reason This brings us to the final reason for rejecting the atheistic many-universes hypothesis, which may be the most difficult to grasp: namely, neither the atheistic many-universes hypothesis (nor the atheistic single-universe hypothesis) can at present adequately account for the improbable initial arrangement of matter in the universe required by the second law of thermodynamics. To see this, note that according to the second law of thermodynamics, the entropy of the universe is constantly increasing. The standard way of understanding this entropy increase is to say that the universe is going from a state of order to disorder. We observe this entropy increase all the time around us: things, such as a child's bedroom, that start out highly organized tend to "decay" and become disorganized unless something or someone intervenes to stop it.

Now, for purposes of illustration, we could think of the universe as a scrabble-board that initially starts out in a highly ordered state in which all the letters are arranged to form words, but which keeps getting randomly shaken. Slowly, the board, like the universe, moves from a state of order to disorder. The problem for the atheist is to explain how the universe could have started out in a highly ordered state, since it is extraordinarily improbable for such states to occur by chance.[23] If, for example, one were to dump a bunch of letters at random on a scrabble-board, it would be very unlikely for most of them to form into words. At best, we would expect groups of letters to form into words in a few places on the board.

Now our question is, Could the atheistic many-universes hypothesis explain the high degree of initial order of our universe by claiming that given enough universes, eventually one will arise that is ordered and in which intelligent life occurs, and so it is no surprise that we find ourselves in an ordered universe? The problem with this explanation is that it is overwhelmingly more likely for local patches of order to form in one or two places than for the whole universe to be ordered, just as it is overwhelmingly more likely for a few letters on the scrabble-board randomly to form words than for all the letters throughout the board randomly to form words. Thus, the overwhelming majority of universes in which intelligent life occurs will be ones in which the intelligent life will be surrounded by a small patch of order necessary for its existence, but in which the rest of the universe is disordered. Consequently, even under the atheistic many-universes hypothesis, it would still be enormously improbable for intelligent beings to find themselves in a universe such as ours which is highly ordered throughout.[24]

Conclusion

Even though the above criticisms do not definitively refute the atheistic many-universes hypothesis, they do show that it has some severe disadvantages relative to theism. This means that if atheists adopt the atheistic many-universes hypothesis to defend their position, then atheism has become much less plausible than it used to be. Modifying a turn of phrase coined by philosopher Fred Dretske: these are inflationary times, and the cost of atheism has just gone up.

V. OVERALL CONCLUSION

In the above sections I showed there are good, objective reasons for claiming that the fine-tuning provides strong evidence for theism. I first presented an argument for thinking that the fine-tuning provides strong evidence for preferring theism over the atheistic single-universe hypothesis, and then presented a variety of different reasons for rejecting the atheistic many-universes hypothesis as an explanation of the fine-tuning. In order to help one appreciate the strength of the arguments presented, I would like to end by comparing the strength of the *core* version of the argument from the fine-tuning to what is widely regarded as the strongest atheist argument against theism, the argument from evil.[25]

Typically, the atheist argument against God based on evil takes a similar form to the core version of the fine-tuning argument. Essentially, the atheist argues that the existence of the kinds of evil we find in the world is very improbable under theism, but not improbable under atheism. Thus, by the prime principle of confirmation, they conclude that the existence of evil provides strong reasons for preferring atheism over theism.

What makes this argument weak in comparison to the core version of the fine-tuning argument is that, unlike in the case of the fine-tuning, the atheist does not have a significant objective basis for claiming that the existence of the kinds of evil we find in the world is highly improbable under theism. In fact, their judgment that it is improbable seems largely to rest on a mistake in reasoning. To see this, note that in order to show that it is improbable, atheists would have to show that it is *unlikely* that the types of evils we find in the world are necessary for any morally good, greater purpose, since if they are, then it is clearly not at all unlikely that an all good, all powerful being would create a world in which those evils are allowed to occur. But how could atheists show this without first surveying all possible morally good purposes such a being might have, something they have clearly not done? *Consequently, it seems, at most the atheist could argue that since no one has come up with any adequate purpose yet, it is unlikely that there is such a purpose.* This argument, however, is very weak, as I will now show.

The first problem with this atheist argument is that it assumes that the various explanations people have offered for why an all good God would create evil—such as the free will theodicy—ultimately fail. But even if we grant that these theodicies fail, the argument is still very weak. To see why, consider an analogy. Suppose someone tells me that there is a rattlesnake in my garden, and I examine a portion of the garden and do not find the snake. I would only be justified in concluding that there was probably no snake in the garden if either: i) I had searched at least half the garden; or ii) I had good reason to believe that if the snake were in the garden, it would likely be in the portion of the garden that I examined. If, for instance, I were randomly to pick some small segment of the garden to search and did not find the snake, I would be unjustified in concluding from my search that there was probably no snake in the garden. Similarly, if I were blindfolded and did not have any idea of how large the garden was (e.g., whether it was ten square feet or several square miles), I would be unjustified in concluding that it was unlikely that there was a rattlesnake in the garden, even if I had searched for hours with my rattlesnake-detecting dogs. Why? Because I would not have any idea of what percentage of the garden I had searched.

As with the garden example, we have no idea of how large the realm is of possible greater purposes for evil that an all good, omnipotent being

could have. Hence we do not know what proportion of this realm we have actually searched. Indeed, considering the finitude of our own minds, we have good reason to believe that we have so far only searched a small proportion, and we do not have significant reason to believe that all the purposes God might have for allowing evil would be in the proportion we searched. Thus, we have little objective basis for saying that the existence of the types of evil we find in the world is highly improbable under theism.

From the above discussion, therefore, it is clear that the relevant probability estimates in the case of the fine-tuning are much more secure than those estimates in the probabilistic version of the atheist's argument from evil, since unlike the latter, we can provide a fairly rigorous, objective basis for them based on actual calculations of the relative range of life-permitting values for the parameters of physics. (See the appendix to this chapter for a rigorous derivation of the probability of the fine-tuning under the atheistic single-universe hypothesis.) *Thus, I conclude, the core argument for preferring theism over the probabilistic version of the atheistic single-universe hypothesis is much stronger than the atheist argument from evil.*[26]

APPENDIX

In this appendix, I offer a rigorous support for premise (2) of the main argument: that is, the claim that the fine-tuning is very improbable under the atheistic single-universe hypothesis. Support for premise (2) will involve three major subsections. The first subsection will be devoted to explicating the fine-tuning of gravity since we will often use this to illustrate our arguments. Then, in our second subsection, we will show how the improbability of the fine-tuning under the atheistic single-universe hypothesis can be derived from a commonly used, objective principle of probabilistic reasoning called the *principle of indifference*. Finally, in our third subsection, we will explicate what it could mean to say that the fine-tuning is improbable given that the universe is a unique, unrepeatable event as assumed by the atheistic single-universe hypothesis. The appendix will in effect answer the common atheist objection that theists can neither *justify* the claim that the fine-tuning is improbable under the atheistic single-universe hypothesis, nor can they provide an account of what it could possibly *mean* to say that the fine-tuning is improbable.

i. The Example of Gravity

The force of gravity is determined by Newton's law $F = Gm_1m_2/r^2$. Here G is what is known as the *gravitational constant*, and is basically a number that determines the force of gravity in any given circumstance. For instance, the gravitational attraction between the moon and the earth is given by first multiplying the mass of the moon (m_1) times the mass of the earth (m_2), and then dividing by the distance between them squared (r^2). Finally, one multiplies this result by the number G to obtain the total force. Clearly the force is directly proportional to G: for example, if G were to double, the force between the moon and the earth would double.

In the previous section, we reported that some calculations indicate that the force of gravity must be fine-tuned to one part in 10^{40} in order for life to occur. What does such fine-tuning mean? To understand it, imagine a radio dial, going from 0 to $2G_0$, where G_0 represents the current value of the gravitational constant. Moreover, imagine the dial being broken up into 10^{40}—that is, ten thousand, billion, billion, billion, billion—evenly spaced tick marks. To claim that the strength of gravity must be fine-tuned to one part in 10^{40} is simply to claim that, in order for life to exist, the constant of gravity cannot vary by even one tick mark along the dial from its current value of G_0.

ii. The Principle of Indifference

In the following subsections, we will use the *principle of indifference* to justify the assertion that the fine-tuning is highly improbable under the atheistic single-universe hypothesis.

a. The Principle Stated Applied to cases in which there is a finite number of alternatives, the principle of indifference can be formulated as the claim that we should assign the same probability to what are called *equipossible alternatives*, where two or more alternatives are said to be equipossible if we have no reason to prefer one of the alternatives over any of the others. (In another version of the principle, alternatives that are relevantly symmetrical are considered equipossible and hence the ones that should be assigned equal probability.) For instance, in the case of a standard two-sided coin, we have no more reason to think that the coin will land on heads than that it will land on tails, and so we assign them each an equal probability. Since the total probability must add up to one, this means that the coin has a 0.5 chance of landing on heads and a 0.5 chance of landing on tails. Similarly, in the case of a standard six-sided die, we have no more reason to think that it will land on one number, say a 6, than any of the other numbers, such as a 4. Thus, the principle of indifference tells us to assign each possible way of landing an equal probability—namely ⅙.

The above explication of the principle applies only when there are a finite number of alternatives, for example six sides on a die. In the case of the fine-tuning, however, the alternatives are not finite but form a continuous magnitude. The value of G, for instance, conceivably could have been any number between 0 and infinity. Now, continuous magnitudes are usually thought of in terms of ranges, areas, or volumes depending on whether or not we are considering one, two, three, or more dimensions. For example, the amount of water in an 8 oz. glass could fall anywhere within the *range* 0 oz. to 8 oz., such as 6.012345645 oz. Or, the exact position that a dart hits a dart board can fall anywhere within the *area* of the dart board. With some qualifications to be discussed below, the principle of indifference becomes in the continuous case the principle that *when we have no reason to prefer any one value of a parameter over another, we should, assign equal probabilities to equal ranges, areas, or volumes*. So, for instance, suppose one aimlessly throws a dart at a dart board. Assuming the dart hits the board, what is the probability it will hit within the bull's eye? Since the dart is thrown aimlessly, we have no more reason to believe it will hit one part of the dart board than any other part. The principle of indifference, therefore, tells us that the probability of its hitting the bull's eye is the same as the probability of hitting any other part of the dart board of equal area. This means that the probability of its hitting the bull's eye is simply the ratio of the area of the bull's eye to the rest of the dart board. So, for instance, if the bull's eye forms only 5 percent of the total area of the board, then the probability of its hitting the bull's eye will be 5 percent.

b. Application to Fine-Tuning In the case of the fine-tuning, we have no more reason to think that the parameters of physics will fall within the life-permitting range than within any other range, given the atheistic single-universe hypothesis. Thus according to the principle of indifference, equal ranges of these parameters should be assigned equal probabilities. As in the case of the dart board mentioned in the last section, this means that the probability of the parameters of physics falling within the life-permitting range under the atheistic single-universe hypothesis is simply the ratio of the range of life-permitting values (the "area of the bull's eye") to the total *relevant* range of possible values (the "relevant area of the dart board").

Now physicists can make rough estimates of the range of *life-permitting* values for the parameters of physics, as discussed above in the case of gravity, for instance. But what is the "total *relevant* range of possible values"? At first one might think that this range is infinite, since the values of the parameters could conceivably be anything. This, however, is not correct, for although the possible range of values could be infinite, for most of these values we have no way of estimating whether they are life-permitting or not. We do not truly know, for example, what would happen if gravity were 10^{60} times stronger than its current value: as far as we know, a new form of matter might come into existence that could sustain life. Thus, as far as we

know, there could be other life-permitting ranges far removed from the actual values that the parameters have. Consequently, all we can say is that the life-permitting range is very, very small *relative* to the limited range of values for which we can make estimates, a range that we will here-after refer to as the "*illuminated*" range.

Fortunately, however, this limitation does not affect the overall argument. The reason is that, based on the principle of indifference, we can still say that it is very improbable for the values for the parameters of physics to have fallen in the life-permitting range *instead* of some other part of the "illuminated" range.[27] And this *improbability* is all that is actually needed for our main argument to work. To see this, consider an analogy. Suppose a dart landed on the bull's eye at the center of a huge dart board. Further, suppose that this bull's eye is surrounded by a very large empty, bull's-eye-free, area. Even if there were many other bull's eyes on the dart board, we would still take the fact that the dart landed on the bull's eye instead of some other part of the large empty area surrounding the bull's eye as strong evidence that it was aimed. Why? Because we would reason that *given that the dart landed in the empty area*, it was very improbable for it to land in the bull's eye by chance but not improbable if it were aimed. Thus, by the prime principle of confirmation, we could conclude that the dart landing on the bull's eye strongly confirms the hypothesis that it was aimed over the chance hypothesis.

c. The Principle Qualified Those who are familiar with the principle of indifference, and mathematics, will recognize that one important qualification needs to be made to the above account of how to apply the principle of indifference. (Those who are not mathematically adept might want to skip this and perhaps the next paragraph.) To understand the qualification, note that the ratio of ranges used in calculating the probability is dependent on how one parameterizes, or writes, the physical laws. For example, suppose for the sake of illustration that the range of life-permitting values for the gravitational constant is 0 to G_0, and the "illuminated" range of possible values for G is 0 to $2G_0$. Then, the ratio of life-permitting values to the range of "illuminated" possible values for the gravitational constant will be ½. Suppose, however, that one writes the law of gravity in the mathematically equivalent form of $F = \sqrt{Um_1m_2}/r^2$ instead of $F = Gm_1m_2/r^2$, where $U = G^2$. (In this way of writing Newton's law, U becomes the new gravitational constant.) This means that $U_0 = G_0{}^2$, where U_0, like G_0, represents the actual value of U in our universe. Then, the range of life-permitting values would be 0 to U_0, and the "illuminated" range of possible values would be 0 to $4U_0$ on the U scale (which is equivalent to 0 to $2G_0$ on the G scale). Hence, calculating the ratio of life-permitting values using the U scale instead of the G scale yields a ratio of ¼ instead of ½ Indeed, for almost any ratio one chooses—such as one in which the life-permitting range is about the same size as the "illuminated" range—there exist mathematically equivalent forms of Newton's law that will yield that ratio. So, why choose the standard way of writing Newton's law to calculate the ratio instead of one in which the fine-tuning is not improbable at all?

The answer to this question is to require that the proportion used in calculating the probability be between *real* physical ranges, areas, or volumes, not merely mathematical representations of them. That is, the proportion given by the scale used in one's representation must directly correspond to the proportions actually existing in physical reality. As an illustration, consider how we might calculate the probability that a meteorite will fall in New York state instead of somewhere else in the northern, contiguous United States. One way of doing this is to take a standard map of the northern, contiguous United States, measure the area covered by New York on the map (say 2 square inches) and divide it by the total area of the map (say 30 square inches). If we were to do this, we would get approximately the right answer because the proportions on a standard map directly correspond to the actual proportions of land areas in the United States.[28] On the other hand, suppose we had a map made by some lover of the east coast in

which, because of the scale used, the east coast took up half the map. If we used the proportions of areas as represented by this map we would get the wrong answer since the scale used would not correspond to real proportions of land areas. Applied to the fine-tuning, this means that our calculations of these proportions must be done using parameters that directly correspond to physical quantities in order to yield valid probabilities. In the case of gravity, for instance, the gravitational constant G directly corresponds to the force between two unit masses a unit distance apart, whereas U does not. (Instead, U corresponds to the square of the force.) Thus, G is the correct parameter to use in calculating the probability.[29]

d. Support for Principle   Finally, although the principle of indifference has been criticized on various grounds, several powerful reasons can be offered for its soundness if it is restricted in the ways explained in the last subsection. First, it has an extraordinarily wide range of applicability. As Roy Weatherford notes in his book, *Philosophical Foundations of Probability Theory*, "an astonishing number of extremely complex problems in probability theory have been solved, and usefully so, by calculations based entirely on the assumption of equiprobable alternatives [that is, the principle of indifference]."[30] Second, at least for the discrete case, the principle can be given a significant theoretical grounding in information theory, being derivable from Shannon's important and well-known measure of *information*, or *negative* entropy.[31] Finally, in certain everyday cases the principle of indifference seems the only justification we have for assigning probability. To illustrate, suppose that in the last ten minutes a factory produced the first fifty-sided die ever produced. Further suppose that every side of the die is (macroscopically) perfectly symmetrical with every other side, except for there being different numbers printed on each side. (The die we are imagining is like a fair six-sided die except that it has fifty sides instead of six.) Now, we all immediately know that upon being rolled the probability of the die coming up on any given side is one in fifty. Yet, we do not know this directly from experience with fifty-sided dice, since by hypothesis no one has yet rolled such dice to determine the relative frequency with which they come up on each side. Rather, it seems our only justification for assigning this probability is the principle of indifference: that is, given that every side of the die is relevantly macroscopically symmetrical with every other side, we have no reason to believe that the die will land on one side over any other side, and thus we assign them all an equal probability of one in fifty.[32]

iii. The Meaning of Probability

In the last section we used the principle of indifference to rigorously justify the claim that the fine-tuning is highly improbable under the atheistic single-universe hypothesis. We did not explain, however, what it could *mean* to say that it is improbable, especially given that the universe is a unique, unrepeatable event. To address this issue, we shall now show how the probability invoked in the fine-tuning argument can be straightforwardly understood either as what could be called *classical probability* or as what is known as *epistemic probability*.

Classical Probability The *classical conception of probability* defines probability in terms of the ratio of number of "favorable cases" to the total number of equipossible cases.[33] Thus, for instance, to say the probability of a die coming up "4" is one out of six is simply to say that the number of ways a die could come up "4" is one-sixth the number of equipossible ways it could come up. Extending this definition to the continuous case, classical probability can be defined in terms of the relevant ratio of ranges, areas, or volumes over which the principle of indifference applies. Thus, under this extended definition, to say that the probability of the parameters of physics falling into the life-permitting value is very improbable simply *means* that the ratio of life-permitting values to the range of possible values is very, very small. Finally, notice that this definition of probability implies the principle of indifference, and thus we can be certain

that the principle of indifference holds for classical probability.

Epistemic Probability *Epistemic probability* is a widely recognized type of probability that applies to claims, statements, and hypotheses—that is, what philosophers call propositions.[34] (A proposition is any claim, assertion, statement, or hypothesis about the world.) Roughly, the epistemic probability of a proposition can be thought of as the degree of credence—that is, degree of confidence or belief—we rationally should have in the proposition. Put differently, epistemic probability is a measure of our rational degree of belief under a condition of ignorance concerning whether a proposition is true or false. For example, when one says that the special theory of relativity is probably true, one is making a statement of epistemic probability. After all, the theory is actually either true or false. But, we do not know for sure whether it is true or false, so we say it is probably true to indicate that we should put more confidence in its being true than in its being false. It is also commonly argued that the probability of a coin toss is best understood as a case of epistemic probability. Since the side the coin will land on is determined by the laws of physics, it is argued that our assignment of probability is simply a measure of our rational expectations concerning which side the coin will land on.

Besides epistemic probability sumpliciter, philosophers also speak of what is known as the *conditional* epistemic probability of one proposition on another. The conditional epistemic probability of a proposition R on another proposition S—written as $P(R/S)$—can be defined as the degree to which the proposition S of itself should rationally lead us to expect that R is true. For example, there is a high conditional probability that it will rain today on the hypothesis that the weatherman has predicted a 100 percent chance of rain, whereas there is a low conditional probability that it will rain today on the hypothesis that the weatherman has predicted only a 2 percent chance of rain. That is, the hypothesis that the weatherman has predicted a 100 percent chance of rain today should strongly lead us to expect that it will rain, whereas the hypothesis that the weatherman has predicted a 2 percent chance should lead us to expect that it will not rain. Under the epistemic conception of probability, therefore, the statement that *the fine-tuning of the Cosmos is very improbable under the atheistic single-universe hypothesis* makes perfect sense: it is to be understood as making a statement about the degree to which the atheistic single-universe hypothesis would or should, of *itself*, rationally lead us to expect the cosmic fine-tuning.[35]

Conclusion

The above discussion shows that we have at least two ways of understanding improbability invoked in our main argument: as classical probability or epistemic probability. This undercuts the common atheist objection that it is meaningless to speak of the probability of the fine-tuning under the atheistic single-universe hypothesis since under this hypothesis the universe is not a repeatable event.

NOTES

1. Freeman Dyson, *Disturbing the Universe* (New York: Harper and Row, 1979), 251.

2. Paul Davies, *The Cosmic Blueprint: New Discoveries in Nature's Creative Ability to Order the Universe* (New York: Simon and Schuster, 1988), 203.

3. Fred Hoyle, in *Religion and the Scientists* (1959); quoted in *The Anthropic Cosmological Principle*, ed. John Barrow and Frank Tipler (Oxford: Oxford University Press, 1986), 22.

4. See Paul Davies, *The Accidental Universe* (Cambridge: Cambridge University Press, 1982), 90–91. John Jefferson Davis, "The Design Argument, Cosmic 'Fine-tuning,' and the Anthropic Principle," *The International Journal of Philosophy of Religion* 22 (1987): 140.

5. John Leslie, *Universes* (New York: Routledge, 1989), 4, 35; *Anthropic Cosmological Principle*, 322.

6. Paul Davies, *Superforce: The Search for a Grand Unified Theory of Nature* (New York: Simon and Schuster, 1984), 242.

7. Leslie, *Universes*, 39–40.

8. John Leslie, "How to Draw Conclusion from a Fine-Tuned Cosmos," in *Physics, Philosophy and Theology: A Common Quest for Understanding*, ed. Robert Russell et al. (Vatican City State: Vatican Observatory Press, 1988), 299.

9. Leslie, "How to Draw Conclusions," 300.

10. For those familiar with the probability calculus, a precise statement of the degree to which evidence counts in favor of one hypothesis over another can be given in terms of the odds form of Bayes's Theorem: that is, $P(H_1/E)/P(H_2/E) = [P(H_1/P$ $(H_2)] \times [P(E/H_1)/(E/H_2)]$. The general version of the principle stated here, however, does not require the applicability or truth of Bayes's Theorem.

11. Those with some training in probability theory will want to note that the kind of probability invoked here is what philosophers call *epistemic probability*, which is a measure of the rational degree of belief we should have in a proposition (see appendix, subsection iii). Since our rational degree of belief in a necessary truth can be less than 1, we can sensibly speak of it being improbable for a given law of nature to exist necessarily. For example, we can speak of an unproven mathematical hypothesis—such as Goldbach's conjecture that every even number greater than 6 is the sum of two odd primes—as being probably true or probably false given our current evidence, even though all mathematical hypotheses are either necessarily true or necessarily false.

12. Leslie, "How to Draw Conclusion," 304.

13. George Smith, "The Case Against God," reprinted in *An Anthology of Atheism and Rationalism*, ed. Gordon Stein (Buffalo: Prometheus Press, 1980), 56.

14. J. J. C. Smart, "Laws of Nature and Cosmic Coincidence," *The Philosophical Quarterly* 35 (July 1985): 275–76, italics added.

15. I define a "universe" as any region of space-time that is disconnected from other regions in such a way that the parameters of physics in that region could differ significantly from the other regions.

16. Quentin Smith, "World Ensemble Explanations," *Pacific Philosophical Quarterly* 67 (1986): 82.

17. Moreover, the advocate of the atheistic many-universes hypothesis could not avoid this problem by hypothesizing that the many universes always existed as "brute fact" without being produced by a universe generator. This would simply add to the problem: it would not only leave unexplained the fine-tuning or our own universe, but would leave unexplained the existence of these other universes.

18. Leslie, *Universes*, 59.

19. Dyson, *Disturbing the Universe*, 251.

20. Chapter 6, "Beautiful Theories."

21. Paul Dirac, "The Evolution of the Physicist's Picture of Nature," *Scientific American* (May 1963): 47.

22. Davies, *Superforce*, 235–36.

23. This connection between order and probability, and the second law of thermodynamics in general, is given a precise formulation in a branch of fundamental physics called *statistical mechanics*, according to which a state of high order represents a very improbable state, and a state of disorder represents a highly probable state.

24. See Lawrence Sklar, *Physics and Chance: Philosophical Issues in the Foundation of Statistical Mechanics* (Cambridge: Cambridge University Press, 1993), chapter 8, for a review of the nontheistic explanations for the ordered arrangement of the universe and the severe difficulties they face.

25. A more thorough discussion of the atheist argument from evil is presented in Daniel Howard-Snyder's chapter (pp. 76–115), and a discussion of other atheistic arguments is given in John O'Leary-Hawthorn's chapter (pp. 116–34).

26. This work was made possible in part by a Discovery Institute grant for the fiscal year 1997–1998.

27. In the language of probability theory, this sort of probability is known as a conditional probability. In the case of G, calculations indicate that this conditional probability of the fine-tuning would be less than 10^{-40} since the life-permitting range is less than 10^{-40} of the range 0 to $2G_0$, the latter range being certainly smaller than the total "illuminated" range for G.

28. I say "approximately right" because in this case the principle of indifference only applies to strips of land that are the same distance from the equator. The reason for this is that only strips of land equidistant from the equator are truly symmetrical with regard to the motion of the earth. Since the northern, contiguous United States are all about the same distance from the equator, equal land areas should be assigned approximately equal probabilities.

29. This solution will not always work since, as the well-known Bertrand Paradoxes illustrate (e.g., see Roy Weatherford, *Foundations of Probability Theory* [Boston: Routledge and Kegan Paul, 1982], 56), sometimes there are two equally good and conflicting parameters that directly correspond to a physical quantity and to which the principle of indifference applies. In these cases, at best we can say that the probability is somewhere between that given by the two conflicting parameters. This problem, however, typically does not seem to arise for most cases of fine-tuning. Also, it should be noted that the principle of indifference applies best to *classical* or *epistemic* probability, not other kinds of probability such as *relative frequency*. (See subsection iii below.)

30. Weatherford, *Probability Theory*, 35.

31. Sklar, *Physics and Chance*, 191; Bas van Fraassen, *Laws and Symmetry* (Oxford: Oxford University Press, 1989), 345.

32. Of course, one could claim that our experience with items such as coins and dice teaches us that whenever two alternatives are macroscopically symmetrical, we should assign them an equal probability, unless we have a particular reason not to. All this claim implies, however, is that we have experiential justification for the principle of indifference, and thus it does not take away from our main point that in certain practical situations we must rely on the principle of indifference to justify our assignment of probability.

33. See Weatherford, *Probability Theory*, ch. 2.

34. For an in-depth discussion of epistemic probability, see Richard Swinburne, *An Introduction to Confirmation Theory* (London: Methuen, 1973); Ian Hacking, *The Emergence of Probability: A Philosophical Study of Early Ideas About Probability, Induction and Statistical Inference* (Cambridge: Cambridge University Press, 1975); and Alvin Plantinga, *Warrant and Proper Function* (Oxford: Oxford University Press, 1993), chapters 8 and 9.

35. It should be noted here that this rational degree of expectation should not be confused with the degree to which one should expect the parameters of physics to fall within the life-permitting range if one believed the atheistic single-universe hypothesis. For even those who believe in this atheistic hypothesis should expect the parameters of physics to be life-permitting since this follows from the fact that we are alive. Rather, the conditional epistemic probability in this case is the degree to which the atheistic single-universe hypothesis *of itself* should lead us to expect parameters of physics to be life-permitting. This means that in assessing the conditional epistemic probability in this and other similar cases, one must exclude contributions to our expectations arising from other information we have, such as that we are alive. In the case at hand, one way of doing this is by means of the following sort of thought experiment. Imagine a disembodied being with mental capacities and a knowledge of physics comparable to that of the most intelligent physicists alive today, except that the being does not know whether the parameters of physics are within the life-permitting range. Further, suppose that this disembodied being believed in the atheistic single-universe hypothesis. Then, the degree that being should rationally expect the parameters of physics to be life-permitting will be equal to our conditional epistemic probability, since its expectation is solely a result of its belief in the atheistic single-universe hypothesis, not other factors such as its awareness of its own existence.

PART IV

The Problem of Evil

Is he willing to prevent evil, but not able? then is he impotent.
Is he able, but not willing? then is he malevolent. Is he both
able and willing? whence then is evil?
EPICURUS (341-270 BCE)

In Part II, we examined several arguments in favor of God's existence. The agnostic and atheist usually base their case on the *absence* of evidence for God's existence. But they do have at least one arrow in their own quiver, an argument for disbelief. It is the problem of evil. With it, the "atheologian" (one who argues against the existence of God) hopes either to neutralize any positive evidence for God's existence, based on whatever in the traditional arguments survives their criticism, or to demonstrate that it is unreasonable to believe in God.

The problem of evil arises from the apparent tension between the divine attributes of omnipotence, omniscience, and omnibenevolence on the one hand and the existence of evil on the other. The Judeo-Christian tradition has affirmed each of the following propositions:

1. God is all-powerful.
2. God is all-knowing.
3. God is perfectly good.
4. Evil exists.

But if God is perfectly good, it seems that God would not want evil to exist, and, being omniscient, God must surely know what potentials for evil lurk in the world and what evils will arise apart from divine intervention. Being omnipotent, God could prevent any evil that God knows about and wants to prevent. So, then, why does our world contain so much evil? Indeed, why does it contain any evil at all? It seems that the existence of God logically precludes the existence of evil, and vice versa.

Generally, Western thought has distinguished between two types of evil: moral and natural. "Moral evil" covers all those bad things for which creatures are morally responsible. "Natural evil" includes those terrible events that occur in nature of their own accord, such as hurricanes, tornadoes, earthquakes, volcanic eruptions, natural diseases, and so on, that cause suffering to humans and animals. However, some defenses of theism affirm that all evil is essentially moral evil, with the devil brought in as the cause of natural evil.

The main defense of theism in response to the problem of evil is the free will defense, going back as far as St. Augustine (354–430) and receiving modern treatment in the work of John Hick, Alvin Plantinga, and Richard Swinburne. The free will defense maintains that premises 1–4 are not inconsistent with one another since (a) it is logically impossible for God to create free creatures and guarantee that they will never do evil, and (b) for all we know, freedom might be a great enough good that God is justified in permitting evil in order to make room for freedom.

Those developing the free will defense typically assume a libertarian view of freedom. That is, they assume that humans are free to choose between good and evil acts and that freedom is inconsistent with determinism. This view is opposed to determinism as well as to compatibilism (a view that tries to reconcile freedom of action with determinism). It is widely believed that if either compatibilism or determinism is true, the free will defense will not be effective against the argument from evil. This matter is well treated in Chapter 9 of J. L. Mackie's *The Miracle of Theism.*

Proponents of the free will defense claim that all moral evil derives from creatures' freedom of will. But how does the theist account for natural evil? There are two different ways. The first one, suggested by Alvin Plantinga (see Part IV bibliography), is to attribute natural evil, such as disease and tornadoes, to the work of the devil and his angels. The second way, favored by Swinburne, argues that natural evil is part and parcel of the nature of things, resulting from the combination of deterministic physical laws that are necessary for consistent action and the responsibility given to humans to exercise their freedom.

There is one further distinction necessary to work through this problem: the distinction between *defense* and *theodicy*. A theodicy is a theory whose aim is to explain why God in fact permits evil; a defense is simply a demonstration of consistency—an effort to show that there is no formal contradiction in premises 1–4 above. The difference is that one can offer a defense without believing the details, and so without really having a *theory* about why God permits evil. For example: You are told that the defendant's fingerprints were found on the gun, and security cameras in an outside room place him at the scene of the crime within five minutes of when the crime took place. If (as is unlikely) your goal is simply to show that the evidence is logically consistent with the defendant's innocence, you might say, "Well, for all we know, he walked in, saw the crime being committed, went over and handled the gun right afterward, and then departed without calling the police." You probably won't believe this story, and you might even go on to qualify it by saying something like, "Of course, I really doubt that that's what happened; but my point is just that it's *possible*." But that doesn't matter if your goal is simply to demonstrate consistency. This is analogous to a defense. If, on the other hand, you tried to offer a theory explaining the evidence in a way consistent with the defendant's innocence— perhaps, say, a story, complete with suspects, motives and opportunities, according to which the defendant was framed, and which you were proposing for us actually to believe—you would be giving something analogous to a theodicy.

We begin our treatment of the problem of evil in the first section with three of the most important and widely discussed historical and literary treatments of the problem of evil. In the second section, we examine several contemporary formulations. Finally, in the third section, we look at replies.

IV.A. HISTORICAL AND LITERARY PERSPECTIVES

In the first reading, "The Argument from Evil," David Hume argues through his persona Philo that the existence of God is called into doubt not just by the mere existence of evil, but by the enormous amount of evil in the world. It is arguable that there is actually more evil than good in the world, and it is hard to reconcile this fact with the existence of an all-powerful, omnibenevolent deity.

In the second reading, "Theodicy: A Defense of Theism," Gottfried Leibniz (1646–1716) argues that the fact of evil in no way refutes theism, and he answers the kinds of objections raised by Hume. He contends that God permitted evil to exist in order to bring about greater goods and that Adam's fall was a *felix culpa* ("blessed fault") because it led to the incarnation of the Son of God, raising humanity to an ultimately higher destiny. (The *felix culpa* idea is also explored and defended in one of the essays by Alvin Plantinga later on in this part—reading IV.C.3.) Leibniz's response to the problem of evil also includes the idea that, as the creation of a perfectly good God, our world must be the best of all possible worlds. As we saw in Part I.B, this idea raises interesting questions about divine freedom.

Finally, in the third reading—the famous "Rebellion" chapter from Dostoevsky's *The Brothers Karamazov*—we find a poignant response to the Leibnizian idea that God is justified in permitting evil in order to bring about greater goods. The troubled Ivan Karamazov angrily describes cases of horrendous suffering on the part of children and then challenges his religious brother Alyosha to say whether, if *he* were the architect of the universe, he could bring himself to permit such suffering in order to bring about global happiness. The expected answer is "No"; and that is precisely the answer that Alyosha sadly gives.

IV.A.1

The Argument from Evil

DAVID HUME

A short biographical sketch of David Hume precedes selection II.C.2. In the present selection, Hume argues through his persona Philo that not merely the fact of evil, but the enormous amount of evil makes it dubious that a deity exists. It is arguable that there is actually more evil than good in the world, so it is hard to see how one can reconcile the existence of evil with the existence of an all-powerful, omnibenevolent deity.

PART X

It is my opinion, I own, replied Demea, that each man feels, in a manner, the truth of religion within his own breast, and, from a consciousness of his imbecility and misery rather than from any reasoning, is led to seek protection from that Being on whom he and all nature is dependent. So anxious or so tedious are even the best scenes of life that futurity is still the object of all our hopes and fears. We incessantly look forward and endeavour, by prayers, adoration, and sacrifice, to appease those unknown powers whom we find, by experience, so able to afflict and oppress us. Wretched creatures that we are! What resource for us amidst the innumerable ills of life did not religion suggest some methods of atonement, and appease those terrors with which we are incessantly agitated and tormented?

I am indeed persuaded, said Philo, that the best and indeed the only method of bringing everyone to a due sense of religion is by just representations of the misery and wickedness of men. And for that purpose a talent of eloquence and strong imagery is more requisite than that of reasoning and argument. For is it necessary to prove what everyone feels within himself? It is only necessary to make us feel it, if possible, more intimately and sensibly.

The people, indeed, replied Demea, are sufficiently convinced of this great and melancholy truth. The miseries of life, the unhappiness of man, the general corruptions of our nature, the unsatisfactory enjoyment of pleasures, riches, honours—these phrases have become almost proverbial in all languages. And who can doubt of what all men declare from their own immediate feeling and experience?

In this point, said Philo, the learned are perfectly agreed with the vulgar; and in all letters, *sacred* and *profane*, the topic of human misery has been insisted on with the most pathetic eloquence that sorrow and melancholy could inspire. The poets, who speak from sentiment, without a system, and whose testimony has therefore the more authority, abound in images of this nature. From Homer down to Dr. Young, the whole inspired tribe have ever been sensible that no other representation of things would suit the feeling and observation of each individual.

As to authorities, replied Demea, you need not seek them. Look round this library of Cleanthes. I shall venture to affirm that, except authors of

Reprinted from David Hume, *Dialogues Concerning Natural Religion* (1779); London: Longmans Green, 1878.

121

particular sciences, such as chemistry or botany, who have no occasion to treat of human life, there is scarce one of those innumerable writers from whom the sense of human misery has not, in some passage or other, extorted a complaint and confession of it. At least, the chance is entirely on that side; and no one author has ever, so far as I can recollect, been so extravagant as to deny it.

There you must excuse me, said Philo: Leibniz has denied it, and is perhaps the first[1] who ventured upon so bold and paradoxical an opinion; at least, the first who made it essential to his philosophical system.

And by being the first, replied Demea, might he not have been sensible of his error? For is this a subject in which philosophers can propose to make discoveries especially in so late an age? And can any man hope by a simple denial (for the subject scarcely admits of reasoning) to bear down the united testimony of mankind, founded on sense and consciousness?

And why should man, added he, pretend to an exemption from the lot of all other animals? The whole earth, believe me, Philo, is cursed and polluted. A perpetual war is kindled amongst all living creatures. Necessity, hunger, want stimulate the strong and courageous; fear, anxiety, terror agitate the weak and infirm. The first entrance into life gives anguish to the new-born infant and to its wretched parent; weakness, impotence, distress attend each stage of that life, and it is, at last, finished in agony and horror.

Observe, too, says Philo, the curious artifices of nature in order to embitter the life of every living being. The stronger prey upon the weaker and keep them in perpetual terror and anxiety. The weaker, too, in their turn, often prey upon the stronger, and vex and molest them without relaxation. Consider that innumerable race of insects, which either are bred on the body of each animal or, flying about, infix their stings in him. These insects have others still less than themselves which torment them. And thus on each hand, before and behind, above and below, every animal is surrounded with enemies which incessantly seek his misery and destruction.

Man alone, said Demea, seems to be, in part, an exception to this rule. For by combination in society he can easily master lions, tigers, and bears, whose greater strength and agility naturally enable them to prey upon him.

On the contrary, it is here chiefly, cried Philo, that the uniform and equal maxims of nature are most apparent. Man, it is true, can, by combination, surmount all his real enemies and become master of the whole animal creation; but does he not immediately raise up to himself *imaginary* enemies, the demons of his fancy, who haunt him with superstitious terrors and blast every enjoyment of life? His pleasure, as he imagines, becomes in their eyes a crime; his food and repose give them umbrage and offence; his very sleep and dreams furnish new materials to anxious fear; and even death, his refuge from every other ill, presents only the dread of endless and innumerable woes. Nor does the wolf molest more the timid flock than superstition does the anxious breast of wretched mortals.

Besides, consider, Demea: This very society by which we surmount those wild beasts, our natural enemies, what new enemies does it not raise to us? What woe and misery does it not occasion? Man is the greatest enemy of man. Oppression, injustice, contempt, contumely, violence, sedition, war, calumny, treachery, fraud—by these they mutually torment each other, and they would soon dissolve that society which they had formed were it not for the dread of still greater ills which must attend their separation.

But though these external insults, said Demea, from animals, from men, from all the elements, which assault us form a frightful catalogue of woes, they are nothing in comparison of those which arise within ourselves, from the distempered condition of our mind and body. How many lie under the lingering torment of diseases? Hear the pathetic enumeration of the great poet.

Intestine stone and ulcer, colic-pangs, Demoniac frenzy, moping melancholy, And moon-struck madness, pining atrophy, Marasmus, and

wide-wasting pestilence. Dire was the tossing,
deep the groans: Despair Tended the sick,
busiest from couch to couch. And over them
triumphant Death his dart Shook: but delay'd
to strike, though oft invok'd With vows, as their
chief good and final hope.[2]

The disorders of the mind, continued Demea, though more secret, are not perhaps less dismal and vexatious. Remorse, shame, anguish, rage, disappointment, anxiety, fear, dejection, despair—who has ever passed through life without cruel inroads from these tormentors? How many have scarcely ever felt any better sensations? Labour and poverty, so abhorred by everyone, are the certain lot of the far greater number; and those few privileged persons who enjoy ease and opulence never reach contentment or true felicity. All the goods of life united would not make a very happy man, but all the ills united would make a wretch indeed; and any one of them almost (and who can be free from every one?), nay, often the absence of one good (and who can possess all?) is sufficient to render life ineligible.

Were a stranger to drop on a sudden into this world, I would show him, as a specimen of its ills, an hospital full of diseases, a prison crowded with malefactors and debtors, a field of battle strewed with carcases, a fleet foundering in the ocean, a nation languishing under tyranny, famine, or pestilence. To turn the gay side of life to him and give him a notion of its pleasures—whither should I conduct him? To a ball, to an opera, to court? He might justly think that I was only showing him a diversity of distress and sorrow.

There is no evading such striking instances, said Philo, but by apologies which still further aggravate the charge. Why have all men, I ask, in all ages, complained incessantly of the miseries of life? ... They have no just reason, says one: these complaints proceed only from their discontented, repining, anxious disposition.... And can there possibly, I reply, be a more certain foundation of misery than such a wretched temper?

But if they were really as unhappy as they pretend, says my antagonist, why do they remain in life? ...

Not satisfied with life, afraid of death—

this is the secret chain, say I, that holds us. We are terrified, not bribed to the continuance of our existence.

It is only a false delicacy, he may insist, which a few refined spirits indulge, and which has spread these complaints among the whole race of mankind. ... And what is this delicacy, I ask, which you blame? Is it anything but a greater sensibility to all the pleasures and pains of life? And if the man of a delicate, refined temper, by being so much more alive than the rest of the world, is only so much more unhappy, what judgment must we form in general of human life?

Let men remain at rest, says our adversary, and they will be easy. They are willing artificers of their own misery. ... No! reply I: an anxious langour follows their repose; disappointment, vexation, trouble, their activity and ambition.

I can observe something like what you mention in some others, replied Cleanthes, but I confess I feel little or nothing of it in myself, and hope that it is not so common as you represent it.

If you feel not human misery yourself, cried Demea, I congratulate you on so happy a singularity. Others, seemingly the most prosperous, have not been ashamed to vent their complaints in the most melancholy strains. Let us attend to the great, the fortunate emperor, Charles V, when, tired with human grandeur, he resigned all his extensive dominions into the hands of his son. In the last harangue which he made on that memorable occasion, he publicly avowed *that the greatest prosperities which he had ever enjoyed had been mixed with so many adversities that he might truly say he had never enjoyed any satisfaction or contentment.* But did the retired life in which he sought for shelter afford him any greater happiness? If we may credit his son's account, his repentance commenced the very day of his resignation.

Cicero's fortune, from small beginnings, rose to the greatest lustre and renown; yet what pathetic complaints of the ills of life do his familiar letters, as well as philosophical discourses, contain? And suitably to his own experience, he introduces Cato, the great, the fortunate Cato protesting in his old age that had he a new life in his offer he would reject the present.

Ask yourself, ask any of your acquaintance, whether they would live over again the last ten or twenty years of their life. No! but the next twenty, they say, will be better:

> And from the dregs of life, hope to receive
> What the first sprightly running could not
>   give.[3]

Thus, at last, they find (such is the greatness of human misery, it reconciles even contradictions) that they complain at once of the shortness of life and of its vanity and sorrow.

And is it possible, Cleanthes, said Philo, that after all these reflections, and infinitely more which might be suggested, you can still persevere in your anthropomorphism, and assert the moral attributes of the Deity, his justice, benevolence, mercy, and rectitude, to be of the same nature with these virtues in human creatures? His power, we allow, is infinite; whatever he wills is executed; but neither man nor any other animal is happy; therefore, he does not will their happiness. His wisdom is infinite; he is never mistaken in choosing the means to any end; but the course of nature tends not to human or animal felicity; therefore, it is not established for that purpose. Through the whole compass of human knowledge there are no inferences more certain and infallible than these. In what respect, then, do his benevolence and mercy resemble the benevolence and mercy of men?

Epicurus' old questions are yet unanswered.

Is he willing to prevent evil, but not able? then is he impotent. Is he able, but not willing? then is he malevolent. Is he both able and willing? whence then is evil?

You ascribe, Cleanthes, (and I believe justly) a purpose and intention to nature. But what, I beseech you, is the object of that curious artifice and machinery which she has displayed in all animals—the preservation alone of individuals, and

propagation of the species? It seems enough for her purpose, if such a rank be barely upheld in the universe, without any care or concern for the happiness of the members that compose it. No resource for this purpose: no machinery in order merely to give pleasure or ease; no fund of pure joy and contentment; no indulgence without some want or necessity accompanying it. At least, the few phenomena of this nature are overbalanced by opposite phenomena of still greater importance.

Our sense of music, harmony, and indeed beauty of all kinds, gives satisfaction, without being absolutely necessary to the preservation and propagation of the species. But what racking pains, on the other hand, arise from gouts, gravels, megrims, toothaches, rheumatisms, where the injury to the animal machinery is either small or incurable? Mirth, laughter, play, frolic seem gratuitous satisfactions which have no further tendency; spleen, melancholy, discontent, superstition are pains of the same nature. How then does the Divine benevolence display itself, in the sense of you anthropomorphites? None but we mystics, as you were pleased to call us, can account for this strange mixture of phenomena, by deriving it from attributes infinitely perfect but incomprehensible.

And have you, at last, said Cleanthes smiling, betrayed your intentions, Philo? Your long agreement with Demea did indeed a little surprise me, but I find you were all the while erecting a concealed battery against me. And I must confess that you have now fallen upon a subject worthy of your noble spirit of opposition and controversy. If you can make out the present point, and prove mankind to be unhappy or corrupted, there is an end at once of all religion. For to what purpose establish the natural attributes of the Deity, while the moral are still doubtful and uncertain?

You take umbrage very easily, replied Demea, at opinions the most innocent and the most generally received, even amongst the religious and devout themselves; and nothing can be more surprising than to find a topic like this—concerning the wickedness and misery of man—charged with no less than atheism and profaneness. Have not all pious divines and preachers who have indulged their rhetoric on so fertile a subject, have they not easily, I say, given a solution of any difficulties which may attend it? This world is but a point in comparison of the universe; this life but a moment in comparison of eternity. The present evil phenomena, therefore, are rectified in other regions, and in some future period of existence. And the eyes of men, being then opened to larger views of things, see the whole connection of general laws, and trace, with adoration, the benevolence and rectitude of the Deity through all the mazes and intricacies of his providence.

No! replied Cleanthes, no! These arbitrary suppositions can never be admitted, contrary to matter of fact, visible and uncontroverted. Whence can any cause be known but from its known effects? Whence can any hypothesis be proved but from the apparent phenomena? To establish one hypothesis upon another is building entirely in the air; and the utmost we ever attain by these conjectures and fictions is to ascertain the bare possibility of our opinion, but never can we, upon such terms, establish its reality.

The only method of supporting Divine benevolence—and it is what I willingly embrace—is to deny absolutely the misery and wickedness of man. Your representations are exaggerated; your melancholy views mostly fictitious; your inferences contrary to fact and experience. Health is more common than sickness; pleasure than pain; happiness than misery. And for one vexation which we meet with, we attain, upon computation, a hundred enjoyments.

Admitting your position, replied Philo, which yet is extremely doubtful, you must at the same time allow that, if pain be less frequent than pleasure, it is infinitely more violent and durable. One hour of it is often able to outweigh a day, a week, a month of our common insipid enjoyments; and how many days, weeks, and months are passed by several in the most acute torments? Pleasure, scarcely in one instance, is ever able to reach ecstasy and rapture; and in no one instance can it continue for any time at its highest pitch and altitude. The spirits evaporate, the nerves relax, the fabric is disordered, and the enjoyment quickly degenerates

into fatigue and uneasiness. But pain often, good God, how often! rises to torture and agony; and the longer it continues, it becomes still more genuine agony and torture. Patience is exhausted, courage languishes, melancholy seizes us, and nothing terminates our misery but the removal of its cause or another event which is the sole cure of all evil, but which, from our natural folly, we regard with still greater horror and consternation.

But not to insist upon these topics, continued Philo, though most obvious, certain, and important, I must use the freedom to admonish you, Cleanthes, that you have put the controversy upon a most dangerous issue, and are unawares introducing a total scepticism into the most essential articles of natural and revealed theology. What! no method of fixing a just foundation for religion unless we allow the happiness of human life, and maintain a continued existence even in this world, with all our present pains, infirmities, vexations, and follies, to be eligible and desirable! But this is contrary to everyone's feeling and experience; it is contrary to an authority so established as nothing can subvert. No decisive proofs can ever be produced against this authority; nor is it possible for you to compute, estimate, and compare all the pains and all the pleasures in the lives of all men and of all animals; and thus, by your resting the whole system of religion on a point which, from its very nature, must forever be uncertain, you tacitly confess that that system is equally uncertain.

But allowing you what never will be believed, at least, what you never possibly can prove, that animal or, at least, human happiness in this life exceeds its misery, you have yet done nothing; for this is not, by any means, what we expect from infinite power, infinite wisdom, and infinite goodness. Why is there any misery at all in the world? Not by chance, surely. From some cause then. Is it from the intention of the Deity? But he is perfectly benevolent. Is it contrary to his intention? But he is almighty. Nothing can shake the solidity of this reasoning, so short, so clear, so decisive, except we assert that these subjects exceed all human capacity, and that our common measures of truth and falsehood are not applicable to them—a topic which I have all along insisted on, but which you have, from the beginning, rejected with scorn and indignation.

But I will be contented to retire still from this intrenchment, for I deny that you can ever force me in it. I will allow that pain or misery in man is *compatible* with infinite power and goodness in the Deity, even in your sense of these attributes: what are you advanced by all these concessions? A mere possible compatibility is not sufficient. You must prove these pure, unmixed, and uncontrollable attributes from the present mixed and confused phenomena, and from these alone. A hopeful undertaking! Were the phenomena ever so pure and unmixed, yet, being finite, they would be insufficient for that purpose. How much more, where they are also so jarring and discordant!

Here, Cleanthes, I find myself at ease in my argument. Here I triumph. Formerly, when we argued concerning the natural attributes of intelligence and design, I needed all my sceptical and metaphysical subtilty to elude your grasp. In many views of the universe and of its parts, particularly the latter, the beauty and fitness of final causes strike us with such irresistible force that all objections appear (what I believe they really are) mere cavils and sophisms; nor can we then imagine how it was ever possible for us to repose any weight on them. But there is no view of human life or of the condition of mankind from which, without the greatest violence, we can infer the moral attributes or learn that infinite benevolence, conjoined with infinite power and infinite wisdom, which we must discover by the eyes of faith alone. It is your turn now to tug the labouring oar, and to support your philosophical subtilties against the dictates of plain reason and experience.

NOTES

1. That sentiment had been maintained by Dr. King and some few others before Leibniz, though by none of so great fame as that German philosopher.

2. Milton: *Paradise Lost,* Bk. XI.

3. John Dryden, *Aureng-Zebe,* Act IV, sc. 1.

IV.A.2

Theodicy: A Defense of Theism

GOTTFRIED LEIBNIZ

Gottfried Wilhelm Leibniz (1646–1716) was a German idealist who tried to set forth a thoroughgoing theodicy, a justification of the ways of God. In this selection he argues that the fact of evil in no way refutes theism, and he answers the kinds of objections raised by

Reprinted from Gottfried Leibniz, *The Theodicy: Abridgement of the Argument Reduced to Syllogistic Form* (1710) in *The Philosophical Works of Leibnitz,* ed. & trans. by G. M. Duncan (New Haven: Tuttle, Morehouse, & Taylor, 1890).

Hume. He contends that God permitted evil to exist in order to bring about greater good and that Adam's fall was a felix culpa *(a "happy sin") because it led to the incarnation of the Son of God, raising humanity to an ultimately higher destiny. He argues that although God can foresee the future, humans are still free in that they act voluntarily.*

Some intelligent persons have desired that this supplement be made [to the Theodicy], and I have the more readily yielded to their wishes as in this way I have an opportunity again to remove certain difficulties and to make some observations which were not sufficiently emphasized in the work itself.

I. *Objection.* Whoever does not choose the best is lacking in power, or in knowledge, or in goodness.

God did not choose the best in creating this world.

Therefore, God has been lacking in power, or in knowledge, or in goodness.

Answer. I deny the minor, that is, the second premise of this syllogism; and our opponent proves it by this.

Prosyllogism. Whoever makes things in which there is evil, which could have been made without any evil, or the making of which could have been omitted, does not choose the best.

God has made a world in which there is evil; a world, I say, which could have been made without any evil, or the making of which could have been omitted altogether.

Therefore, God has not chosen the best.

Answer. I grant the minor of this prosyllogism; for it must be confessed that there is evil in this world which God has made, and that it was possible to make a world without evil, or even not to create a world at all, for its creation has depended on the free will of God; but I deny the major, that is, the first of the two premises of the prosyllogism, and I might content myself with simply demanding its proof; but in order to make the matter clearer, I have wished to justify this denial by showing that the best plan is not always that which seeks to avoid evil, since it may happen that *the evil is accompanied by a greater good.* For example, a general of an army will prefer a great victory with a slight wound to a condition without wound and without victory. We

have proved this more fully in the large work by making it clear, by instances taken from mathematics and elsewhere, that an imperfection in the part may be required for a greater perfection in the whole. In this I have followed the opinion of St. Augustine, who has said a hundred times, that God has permitted evil in order to bring about good, that is, a greater good; and that of Thomas Aquinas (in libr. II. sent. dist. 32, qu. I, art. 1), that the permitting of evil tends to the good of the universe. I have shown that the ancients called Adam's fall *felix culpa,* a happy sin, because it had been retrieved with immense advantage by the incarnation of the Son of God, who has given to the universe something nobler than anything that ever would have been among creatures except for it. For the sake of a clearer understanding, I have added, following many good authors, that it was in accordance with order and the general good that God allowed to certain creatures the opportunity of exercising their liberty, even when he foresaw that they would turn to evil, but which he could so well rectify; because it was not fitting that, in order to hinder sin, God should always act in an extraordinary manner. To overthrow this objection, therefore, it is sufficient to show that a world with evil might be better than a world without evil; but I have gone even farther, in the work, and have even proved that this universe must be in reality better than every other possible universe.

II. *Objection.* If there is more evil than good in intelligent creatures, then there is more evil than good in the whole work of God.

Now, there is more evil than good in intelligent creatures.

Therefore, there is more evil than good in the whole work of God.

Answer. I deny the major and the minor of this conditional syllogism. As to the major, I do not admit it at all, because this pretended deduction from a part to the whole, from intelligent creatures to all creatures, supposes tacitly and without proof that creatures destitute of reason cannot enter into comparison nor into account with those which possess it. But why may it not be that the surplus of good in the non-intelligent creatures which fill the world, compensates for, and even incomparably surpasses, the surplus of evil in the rational creatures? It is true that the value of the latter is greater; but, in compensation, the others are beyond comparison the more numerous, and it may be that the proportion of number and quantity surpasses that of value and of quality.

As to the minor, that is no more to be admitted; that is, it is not at all to be admitted that there is more evil than good in the intelligent creatures. There is no need even of granting that there is more evil than good in the human race, because it is possible, and in fact very probable, that the glory and the perfection of the blessed are incomparably greater than the misery and the imperfection of the damned, and that here the excellence of the total good in the smaller number exceeds the total evil in the greater number. The blessed approach the Divinity, by means of a Divine Mediator, as near as may suit these creatures, and make such progress in good as is impossible for the damned to make in evil, approach as nearly as they may to the nature of demons. God is infinite, and the devil is limited; the good may and does go to infinity, while evil has its bounds. It is therefore possible, and is credible, that in the comparison of the blessed and the damned, the contrary of that which I have said might happen in the comparison of intelligent and non-intelligent creatures, takes place; namely, it is possible that in the comparison of the happy and the unhappy, the proportion of degree exceeds that of number, and that in the comparison of intelligent and non-intelligent creatures, the proportion of number is greater than that of value. I have the right to suppose that a thing is possible so long as its impossibility is not proved; and indeed that which I have here advanced is more than a supposition.

But in the second place, if I should admit that there is more evil than good in the human race, I have still good grounds for not admitting that there is more evil than good in all intelligent creatures. For there is an inconceivable number of genii, and perhaps of other rational creatures. And an opponent could not prove that in all the City of God, composed as well of genii as of rational animals without number and of an infinity of kinds, evil exceeds good. And although in order to answer an objection, there is no need of proving that a thing is, when its mere possibility suffices; yet, in this work, I have not omitted to show that it is a consequence of the supreme perfection of the Sovereign of the universe, that the kingdom of God is the most perfect of all possible states or governments, and that consequently the little evil there is, is required for the consummation of the immense good which is found there.

III. _Objection._ If it is always impossible not to sin, it is always unjust to punish.

Now, it is always impossible not to sin; or, in other words, every sin is necessary.

Therefore, it is always unjust to punish.

The minor of this is proved thus:

1. _Prosyllogism._ All that is predetermined is necessary.

Every event is predetermined.

Therefore, every event (and consequently sin also) is necessary.

Again this second minor is proved thus:

2. _Prosyllogism._ That which is future, that which is foreseen, that which is involved in the causes, is predetermined.

Every event is such.

Therefore, every event is predetermined.

Answer. I admit in a certain sense the conclusion of the second prosyllogism, which is the minor of the first; but I shall deny the major of the first prosyllogism, namely, that every thing predetermined is necessary; understanding by the _necessity_ of sinning, for example, or by the impossibility of not sinning, or of not performing any action, the necessity with which we are here concerned, that is, that which is essential and absolute, and which destroys the morality of an action and the justice of punishments. For if anyone understood another necessity or impossibility, namely, a necessity which should be only moral, or which was only hypothetical (as will be explained shortly); it is clear that I should deny the major of the objection itself. I might content myself with this answer and demand the proof of the proposition denied; but I have again desired to explain my procedure in this work, in order to better elucidate the matter and to throw more light on the whole subject, by explaining the necessity which ought to be rejected and the determination which must take place. That *necessity* which is contrary to morality and which ought to be rejected, and which would render punishment unjust, is an insurmountable necessity which would make all opposition useless, even if we should wish with all our heart to avoid the necessary action, and should make all possible efforts to that end. Now, it is manifest that this is not applicable to voluntary actions, because we would not perform them if we did not choose to. Also their prevision and predetermination are not absolute, but presuppose the will: if it is certain that we shall perform them, it is not less certain that we shall choose to perform them. These voluntary actions and their consequences will not take place no matter what we do or whether we wish them or not; but, *through* that which we shall do and through that which we shall wish to do, which leads to them. And this is involved in prevision and in predetermination, and even constitutes their ground. And the necessity of such an event is called conditional or hypothetical, or the necessity of consequence, because it supposes the will, and the other *requisites*; whereas the necessity which destroys morality and renders punishment unjust and reward useless, exists in things which will be whatever we may do or whatever we may wish to do, and, in a word, is in that which is essential; and this is what is called an absolute necessity. Thus it is to no purpose, as regards what is absolutely necessary, to make prohibitions or commands, to propose penalties or prizes, to praise or to blame; it will be none the less. On the other hand, in voluntary actions and in that which depends upon them, precepts armed with power to punish and to recompense are very often of use and are included in the order of causes which make an action exist. And it is for this reason that not only cares and labors but also prayers are useful; God having had these prayers in view before he regulated things and having had that consideration for them which was proper. This is why the precept which says *ora et labora* (pray and work), holds altogether good; and not only those who (under the vain pretext of the necessity of events) pretend that the care which business demands may be neglected, but also those who reason against prayer, fall into what the ancients even then called the *lazy sophism*. Thus the predetermination of events by causes is just what contributes to morality instead of destroying it, and causes incline the will, without compelling it. This is why the *determination* in question is not a necessitation—it is certain (to him who knows all) that the effect will follow this inclination; but this effect does not follow by a necessary consequence, that is, one the contrary of which implies contradiction. It is also by an internal inclination such as this that the will is determined, without there being any necessity. Suppose that one has the greatest passion in the world (a great thirst, for example), you will admit to me that the soul can find some reason for resisting it, if it were only that of showing its power. Thus, although one may never be in a perfect indifference of equilibrium and there may be always a preponderance of inclination for the side taken, it, nevertheless, never renders the resolution taken absolutely necessary.

IV. Objection. Whoever can prevent the sin of another and does not do so, but rather contributes to it although he is well informed of it, is accessory to it.

God can prevent the sin of intelligent creatures; but he does not do so, and rather contributes to it by his concurrence and by the opportunities which he brings about, although he has a perfect knowledge of it.

Hence, etc.

Answer. I deny the major of this syllogism. For it is possible that one could prevent sin, but ought not, because he could not do it without himself committing a sin, or (when God is in question) without performing an unreasonable action. Examples have been given and the application to God himself has been made. It is possible also that we contribute to evil and that sometimes we even open the road to it, in doing things which we are obliged to do; and, when we do our duty or (in speaking of God) when, after thorough consideration, we do that which reason demands, we are not responsible for the results, even when we foresee them. We do not desire these evils; but we are willing to permit them for the sake of a greater good which we cannot reasonably help preferring to other considerations. And this is a *consequent* will, which results from *antecedent* wills by which we will the good. I know that some persons, in speaking of the antecedent and consequent will of God, have understood by the *antecedent* that which wills that all men should be saved; and by the consequent, that which wills, in consequence of persistent sin, that some should be damned. But these are merely illustrations of a more general idea, and it may be said for the same reason that God, by his antecedent will, wills that men should not sin; and by his consequent or final and decreeing will (that which is always followed by its effect), he wills to permit them to sin, this permission being the result of superior reasons. And we have the right to say in general that the antecedent will of God tends to the production of good and the prevention of evil, each taken in itself and as if alone (*particulariter et secundum quid*, Thom. I, qu. 19, art. 6), according to the measure of the degree of each good and each evil; but that the divine consequent or final or total will tends toward the production of as many goods as may be put together, the combination of which becomes in this way determined, and includes also the permission of some evils and the exclusion of some goods, as the best possible plan for the universe demands. Arminius, in his *Antiperkinsus*, has very well explained that the will of God may be called consequent, not only in relation to the action of the creature considered beforehand in the divine understanding, but also in relation to other anterior divine acts of will. But this consideration of the passage cited from Thomas Aquinas, and that from Scotus (I. dist. 46, qu. XI), is enough to show that they make this distinction as I have done here. Nevertheless, if anyone objects to this use of terms let him substitute *deliberating* will, in place of antecedent, and final or decreeing will, in place of consequent. For I do not wish to dispute over words.

V. *Objection.* Whoever produces all that is real in a thing, is its cause.

God produces all that is real in sin.

Hence, God is the cause of sin.

Answer. I might content myself with denying the major or the minor, since the term real admits of interpretations which would render these propositions false. But in order to explain more clearly, I will make a distinction. *Real* signifies either that which is positive only, or, it includes also privative beings: in the first case, I deny the major and admit the minor; in the second case, I do the contrary. I might have limited myself to this, but I have chosen to proceed still farther and give the reason for this distinction. I have been very glad therefore to draw attention to the fact that every reality purely positive or absolute is a perfection; and that imperfection comes from limitation, that is, from the privative: for to limit is to refuse progress, or the greatest possible progress. Now God is the cause of all perfections and consequently of all realities considered as purely positive. But limitations or privations result from the original imperfection of creatures, which limits their receptivity. And it is with them as with a loaded vessel, which the river causes to move more or less slowly according to the weight which it carries: thus its speed depends upon the river, but the retardation which limits this speed comes from the load. Thus in the *Theodicy*, we have shown how the creature, in causing sin, is a defective cause; how errors and evil inclinations are born of privation; and how privation is accidentally efficient; and I have justified the opinion of St. Augustine (lib. I, ad Simpl. qu. 2) who explains, for example, how God makes the soul obdurate, not by giving it something evil, but because the effect of his good impression is limited by the soul's resistance and by the circumstances which contribute to this resistance, so that he does not give it all the good which would overcome its evil. *Nec* (inquit) *ab illo erogatur aliquid quo homo fit deterior, sed tantum quo fit melior non erogatur.* But if God had wished to do more, he would have had to make either other natures for creatures or other miracles to change their natures, things which the best plan could not admit. It is as if the current of the river must be more rapid than its fall admitted or that the boats should be loaded more lightly, if it were necessary to make them move more quickly. And the original limitation or imperfection of creatures requires that even the best plan of the universe could not receive more good, and could not be exempt from certain evils, which, however, are to result in a greater good. There are certain disorders in the parts which marvelously enhance the beauty of the whole; just as certain dissonances, when properly used, render harmony more beautiful. But this depends on what has already been said in answer to the first objection.

VI. Objection. Whoever punishes those who have done as well as it was in their power to do, is unjust.

God does so.

Hence, etc.

Answer. I deny the minor of this argument. And I believe that God always gives sufficient aid and grace to those who have a good will, that is, to those who do not reject this grace by new sin. Thus, I do not admit the damnation of infants who have died without baptism or outside of the church; nor the damnation of adults who have acted according to the light which God has given them. And I believe that if *any one has followed the light which has been given him,* he will undoubtedly receive greater light when he has need of it, as the late M. Hulseman, a profound and celebrated theologian at Leipzig, has somewhere

remarked; and if such a man has failed to receive it during his lifetime he will at least receive it when at the point of death.

VII. Objection. Whoever gives only to some, and not to all, the means which produces in them effectively a good will and salutary final faith, has not sufficient goodness.

God does this.

Hence, etc.

Answer. I deny the major of this. It is true that God could overcome the greatest resistance of the human heart; and does it, too, sometimes, either by internal grace, or by external circumstances which have a great effect on souls; but he does not always do this. Whence comes this distinction? it may be asked, and why does his goodness seem limited? It is because, as I have already said in answering the first objection, it would not have been in order always to act in an extraordinary manner, and to reverse the connection of things. The reasons of this connection, by means of which one is placed in more favorable circumstances than another, are hidden in the depths of the wisdom of God; they depend upon the universal harmony. The best plan of the universe, which God could not fail to choose, made it so. We judge from the event itself; since God has made it, it was not possible to do better. Far from being true that this conduct is contrary to goodness, it is supreme goodness which led him to it. This objection with its solution might have been drawn from what was said in regard to the first objection; but it seemed useful to touch upon it separately.

VIII. Objection. Whoever cannot fail to choose the best, is not free.

God cannot fail to choose the best.

Hence, God is not free.

Answer. I deny the major of this argument; it is rather true liberty, and the most perfect, to be able to use one's free will for the best, and to always exercise this power, without ever being turned aside either by external force or by internal passions, the first of which causes slavery of the body, the second, slavery of the soul. There is nothing less servile, and nothing more in accordance with the highest degree of freedom, than to be always led toward the good, and always by one's own inclination, without any constraint and without any displeasure. And to object therefore that God had need of external things, is only a sophism. He created them freely; but having proposed to himself an end, which is to exercise his goodness, wisdom has determined him to choose the means best fitted to attain this end. To call this a need, is to take that term in an unusual sense which frees it from all imperfection, just as when we speak of the wrath of God.

Seneca has somewhere said that God commanded but once but that he obeys always, because he obeys laws which he willed to prescribe to himself: *semel jussit, semper paret*. But he might better have said that God always commands and that he is always obeyed; for in willing, he always follows the inclination of his own nature, and all other things always follow his will. And as this will is always the same, it cannot be said that he obeys only that will which he formerly had. Nevertheless, although his will is always infallible and always tends toward the best, the evil, or the lesser good, which he rejects, does not cease to be possible in itself; otherwise the necessity of the good would be geometrical (so to speak), or metaphysical, and altogether absolute; the contingency of things would be destroyed, and there would be no choice. But this sort of necessity, which does not destroy the possibility of the contrary, has this name only by analogy; it becomes effective, not by the pure essence of things, but by that which is outside of them, above them, namely, by the will of God. This necessity is called moral, because, to the sage, *necessity* and *what ought to be* are equivalent things; and when it always has its effect, as it really

has in the perfect sage, that is, in God, it may be said that it is a happy necessity. The nearer creatures approach to it, the nearer they approach to perfect happiness. Also this kind of necessity is not that which we try to avoid and which destroys morality, rewards and praise. For that which it brings, does not happen whatever we may do or will, but because we will it so. And a will to which it is natural to choose well, merits praise so much the more; also it carries its reward with it, which is sovereign happiness. And as this constitution of the divine nature gives entire satisfaction to him who possesses it, it is also the best and the most desirable for the creatures who are all dependent on God. If the will of God did not have for a rule the principle of the best, it would either tend toward evil, which would be the worst; or it would be in some way indifferent to good and to evil, and would be guided by chance: but a will which would allow itself always to act by chance, would not be worth more for the government of the universe than the fortuitous concourse of atoms, without there being any divinity therein. And even if God should abandon himself to chance only in some cases and in a certain way (as he would do, if he did not always work entirely for the best and if he were capable of preferring a lesser work to a greater, that is, an evil to a good, since that which prevents a greater good is an evil), he would be imperfect, as well as the object of his choice; he would not merit entire confidence; he would act without reason in such a case, and the government of the universe would be like certain games, equally divided between reason and chance. All this proves that this objection which is made against the choice of the best, perverts the notions of the free and of the necessary, and represents to us the best even as evil: which is either malicious or ridiculous.

IV.A.3

Rebellion

FYODOR DOSTOEVSKY

Fyodor Dostoevsky (1821–1881) was one of the greatest and most influential Russian novelists. He is the author of Crime and Punishment, Notes from the Underground, The Gambler, *and* The Brothers Karamazov, *from which the present selection is taken. In this chapter, Ivan Karamazov challenges the idea that some greater good might justify the horrendous suffering of even one small child, much less the vast amounts of such suffering that our world has so far seen.*

"I must admit one thing to you," Ivan began. "I could never understand how one can love one's neighbors. It's just one's neighbors, to my mind, that one can't love, though one might love those at a distance. I once read somewhere of 'John the Merciful,' a saint, that when a hungry, frozen beggar came to him, and asked him to warm him up, he took him into his bed, held him in his arms, and began breathing into his mouth, which was putrid and loathsome from some awful disease. I am convinced that he did that from the laceration of falsity, for the sake of the love imposed by duty, as a penance laid on him. For anyone to love a man, he must be hidden, for as soon as he shows his face, love is gone."

"Father Zosima has talked of that more than once," observed Alyosha; "he, too, said that the face of a man often hinders many people not practised in love, from loving him. But yet there's a great deal of love in mankind, and almost Christlike love. I know that myself, Ivan."

"Well, I know nothing of it so far, and can't understand it, and the innumerable mass of mankind are with me there. The question is, whether that's due to men's bad qualities or whether it's inherent in their nature. To my thinking, Christlike love for men is a miracle impossible on earth. He was God. But we are not gods. Suppose I, for instance, suffer intensely. Another can never know how much I suffer, because he is another and not I. And what's more, a man is rarely ready to admit another's suffering (as though it were a distinction). Why won't he admit it, do you think? Because I smell unpleasant, because I have a stupid face, because I once trod on his foot. Besides there is suffering and suffering; degrading, humiliating suffering such as humbles me—hunger, for instance—my benefactor will perhaps allow me; but when you come to higher suffering—for an idea, for instance—he will very rarely admit that, perhaps because my face strikes him not at all as what he fancies a man should have who suffers for an idea. And so he deprives me instantly of his favor, and not at all from badness of heart. Beggars, especially general beggars, ought never to show themselves, but to ask for charity through the newspapers. One can love one's neighbors in the abstract, or even at a distance, but at close quarters it's almost impossible.

PART IV • THE PROBLEM OF EVIL

If it were as on the stage, in the ballet, where if beggars come in, they wear silken rags and tattered lace and beg for alms dancing gracefully, then one might like looking at them. But even then we would not love them. But enough of that. I simply wanted to show you my point of view. I meant to speak of the suffering of mankind generally, but we had better confine ourselves to the sufferings of the children. That reduces the scope of my argument to a tenth of what it would be. Still we'd better keep to the children, though it does weaken my case. But, in the first place, children can be loved even at close quarters, even when they are dirty, even when they are ugly (I fancy, though, children never are ugly). The second reason why I won't speak of grown-up people is that, besides being disgusting and unworthy of love, they have retribution—they've eaten the apple and know good and evil, and they have become 'like God.' They go on eating it still. But the children haven't eaten anything, and are so far innocent. Are you fond of children, Alyosha? I know you are, and you will understand why I prefer to speak of them. If they, too, suffer horribly on earth, they must suffer for their fathers, they must be punished for their fathers, who have eaten the apple; but that reasoning is of the other world and is incomprehensible for the heart of man here on earth. The innocent must not suffer for another's sins, and especially such innocents! You may be surprised at me, Alyosha, but I am awfully fond of children, too. And observe, cruel people, the violent, the rapacious, the Karamazovs are sometimes very fond of children. Children while they are quite little—up to seven, for instance—are so remote from grown-up people; they are different creatures, as it were, of a different species. I knew a criminal in prison who had, in the course of his career as a burglar, murdered whole families, including several children. But when he was in prison, he had a strange affection for them. He spent all his time at his window, watching the children playing in the prison yard. He trained one little boy to come up to his window and made great friends with him…. You don't know why I am telling you all this, Alyosha? My head aches and I am sad."

"You speak with a strange air," observed Alyosha uneasily, "as though you were not quite yourself."

"By the way, a Bulgarian I met lately in Moscow," Ivan went on, seeming not to hear his brother's words, "told me about the crimes committed by Turks and Circassians in all parts of Bulgaria through fear of a general rising of the Slavs. They burn villages, murder, rape women and children, they nail their prisoners to the fences by the ears, leave them so till morning, and in the morning they hang them—all sorts of things you can't imagine. People talk sometimes of bestial cruelty, but that's a great injustice and insult to the beast; a beast can never be so cruel as a man, so artistically cruel. The tiger only tears and gnaws, that's all he can do. He would never think of nailing people by the ears, even if he were able to do it. These Turks took a pleasure in torturing children, too; cutting the unborn child from the mother's womb, and tossing babies up in the air and catching them on the points of their bayonets before their mother's eyes. Doing it before the mother's eyes was what gave zest to the amusement. Here is another scene that I thought very interesting. Imagine a trembling mother with her baby in her arms, a circle of invading Turks around her. They've planned a diversion; they pet the baby, laugh to make it laugh. They succeed, the baby laughs. At that moment a Turk points a pistol four inches from the baby's face. The baby laughs with glee, holds out its little hands to the pistol, and he pulls the trigger in the baby's face and blows out its brains. Artistic, wasn't it? By the way, Turks are particularly fond of sweet things, they say."

"Brother, what are you driving at?" asked Alyosha.

"I think if the devil doesn't exist, but man has created him, he has created him in his own image and likeness."

"Just as he did God, then?" observed Alyosha.

"It's wonderful how you can turn words, as Polonius says in *Hamlet*," laughed Ivan. "You turn my words against me. Well, I am glad. Yours must be a fine God, if man created Him in His image and likeness. You asked just now what I was driving at. You see, I am fond of collecting certain little facts, and, would you believe, I even copy anecdotes of a certain sort from newspapers and stories, and I've already got a fine collection. The Turks, of course, have gone into it, but they are foreigners. I have specimens from home that are even better than the Turks. You know we prefer beating—rods and scourges—that's our national institution. Nailing ears is unthinkable for us, for we are, after all, Europeans. But the rod and the scourge we have always with us and they cannot be taken from us. Abroad now they scarcely do any beating. Perhaps manners are more humane, or laws have been passed, so that they don't dare to flog men now. But they make up for it in another way just as national as ours. And so national that it would be practically impossible among us, though I believe we are being inoculated with it, since the religious movement began in our aristocracy. I have a charming pamphlet, translated from the French, describing how, quite recently, five years ago, a murderer, Richard, was executed—a young man, of twenty-three, I believe, who repented and was converted to the Christian faith at the very scaffold. This Richard was an illegitimate child who was *given* as a child of six by his parents to some shepherds on the Swiss mountains. They brought him up to work for them. He grew up like a little wild beast among them. The shepherds taught him nothing, and scarcely fed or clothed him, but sent him out at age seven to herd the flock in cold and wet, and no one hesitated or scrupled to treat him so. Quite the contrary, they thought they had every right, for Richard had been given to them as a chattel, and they did not even see the necessity of feeding him. Richard himself describes how in those years, like the Prodigal Son in the Gospel, he longed to eat of the mash given to the pigs, which were fattened for sale. But they wouldn't even give him that, and beat him when he stole from the pigs. And that was how he spent all his childhood and his youth, till he grew up and was strong enough to go away and be a thief. The savage began to earn his living as a day laborer in Geneva.

He drank what he earned, he lived like a monster, and finished by killing and robbing an old man. He was caught, tried, and condemned to death. They are not sentimentalists there. And in prison he was immediately surrounded by pastors, members of Christian brotherhoods, philanthropic ladies, and the like. They taught him to read and write in prison, and expounded the Gospel to him. They exhorted him, worked upon him, drummed at him incessantly, till at last he solemnly confessed his crime. He was converted. He wrote to the court himself that he was a monster, but that in the end God had vouchsafed him light and shown grace. All Geneva was in excitement about him— all philanthropic and religious Geneva. All the aristocratic and well-bred society of the town rushed to the prison, kissed Richard and embraced him; 'You are our brother, you have found grace.' And Richard does nothing but weep with emotion, 'Yes, I've found grace! All my youth and childhood I was glad of pigs' food, but now even I have found grace. I am dying in the Lord.' 'Yes, Richard, die in the Lord; you have shed blood and must die in the Lord. Though it's not your fault that you knew not the Lord, when you coveted the pig's food and were beaten for stealing it (which was very wrong of you, for stealing is forbidden); but you've shed blood and you must die.' And on the last day, Richard, perfectly limp, did nothing but cry and repeat every minute 'This is my happiest day. I am going to the Lord.' 'Yes,' cry the pastors and the judges and philanthropic ladies. 'This is the happiest day of your life, for you are going to the Lord!' They all walk or drive to the scaffold in procession behind the prison van. At the scaffold they call to Richard: 'Die, brother, die in the Lord, for even thou hast found grace!' And so, covered with his brothers' kisses, Richard is dragged on to the scaffold, and led to the guillotine. And they chopped off his head in brotherly fashion, because he had found grace. Yes, that's characteristic. That pamphlet is translated into Russian by some Russian philanthropists of aristocratic rank and evangelical aspirations, and has been distributed gratis for the enlightenment of the people. The case of Richard is interesting because it's national. Though to us it's absurd to cut off a man's head, because he has become our brother and has found grace, yet we have our own speciality, which is all but worse. Our historical pastime is the direct satisfaction of inflicting pain. There are lines in Nekrasov describing how a peasant lashes a horse on the eyes, 'on its meek eyes,' everyone must have seen it. It's peculiarly Russian. He describes how a feeble little nag had foundered under too heavy a load and cannot move. The peasant beats it, beats it savagely, beats it at last not knowing what he is doing in the intoxication of cruelty, thrashes it mercilessly over and over again. 'However weak you are, you must pull, if you die for it.' The nag strains, and then he begins lashing the poor defenseless creature on its weeping, on its 'meek eyes.' The frantic beast tugs and draws the load, trembling all over, gasping for breath, moving sideways, with a sort of unnatural spasmodic action—it's awful in Nekrasov. But that's only a horse, and God has given horses to be beaten. So the Tatars have taught us, and they left us the knout as a remembrance of it. But men, too, can be beaten. A well-educated, cultured gentleman and his wife beat their own child with a birch rod; a girl of seven. I have an exact account of it. The papa was glad that the birch was covered with twigs. 'It stings more,' said he, and so he began stinging his daughter. I know for a fact there are people who at every blow are worked up to sensuality, to literal sensuality, which increases progressively at every blow they inflict. They beat for a minute, for five minutes, for ten minutes, more often and more savagely. The child screams. At last the child cannot scream, it gasps, 'Daddy! daddy!' By some diabolical unseemly chance the case was brought into court. A lawyer is engaged. The Russian people have long called a lawyer 'a conscience for hire.' The lawyer protests in his client's defense. 'It's such a simple thing,' he says, 'an everyday domestic event. A father corrects his child. To our shame be it said, it is brought into court.' The jury, convinced by him, gives a

favorable verdict. The public roars with delight that the torturer is acquitted. Ah, pity I wasn't there! I would have proposed to raise a subscription in his honor! … Charming pictures.

"But I've still better things about children. I've collected a great, great deal about Russian children, Alyosha. There was a little girl of five who was hated by her father and mother, 'most worthy and respectable people, of good education and breeding.' You see, I must repeat again, it is a peculiar characteristic of many people, this love of torturing children, and children only. To all other types of humanity these torturers behave mildly and benevolently, like cultivated and humane Europeans; but they are very fond of tormenting children, even fond of children themselves in that sense. It's just their defenselessness that tempts the tormentor, just the angelic confidence of the child who has no refuge and no appeal, that sets his vile blood on fire. In every man, of course, a beast lies hidden—the beast of rage, the beast of lustful heat at the screams of the tortured victim, the beast of lawlessness let off the chain, the beast of diseases that follow on vice, gout, kidney disease, and so on.

"This poor girl of five was subjected to every possible torture by those cultivated parents. They beat her, thrashed her, kicked her for no reason till her body was one bruise. Then, they went to greater refinements of cruelty—shut her up all night in the cold and frost in a privy, and because she didn't ask to be taken up at night (as though a child of five sleeping its angelic, sound sleep could be trained to wake and ask), they smeared her face and made her eat that excrement, and it was her mother, her mother did this. And that mother could sleep, hearing the poor child's groans locked up in that vile place! Can you understand why a little creature, who can't even understand what's done to her, should beat her little aching heart with her tiny fist in that vile place, in the dark and the cold, and weep her sanguine meek, unresentful tears to dear, kind God to protect her? Do you understand that infamy, my friend and my brother, my pious and humble novice? Do you understand why this rigmarole must be and is permitted? Without it, I am told, man could not have existed on earth, for he could not have known good and evil. Why should he know that diabolical good and evil when it costs so much? Why, the whole world of knowledge is not worth that child's prayer to 'dear, kind God'! I say nothing of the sufferings of grown-up people, they have eaten the apple, damn them, and the devil take them all! But these little ones! I am making you suffer, Alyoshka, you are not yourself. I'll leave off if you like."

"Never mind, I want to suffer too," muttered Alyosha.

"One picture, only one more, because it's so curious, so characteristic, and I have only just read it in some collection of Russian antiquities in the *Archive*, or the *Past*. I've forgotten the name. I must look it up. It was in the darkest days of serfdom at the beginning of the century, and long live the Liberator of the People! There was in those days a general of aristocratic connections, the owner of great estates, one of those men—somewhat exceptional, I believe, even then—who, retiring from the service into a life of leisure, are convinced that they've earned the power of life and death over their subjects. There were such men then. So our general, settled on his property of two thousand souls, lives in pomp, and domineers over his poor neighbors as though they were dependents and buffoons. He has kennels of hundreds of hounds and nearly a hundred dog-boys—all mounted, and in uniform. One day a serf boy, a little child of eight, threw a stone in play and hurt the paw of the general's favorite hound. 'Why is my favorite dog lame?' He is told that the boy threw a stone that hurt the dog's paw. 'So you did it.' The general looked the child up and down 'Take him.' He was taken—taken from his mother and kept shut up all night. Early that morning the general comes out in full pomp, mounts his horse with the hounds, his dependents, dog-boys, and the huntsmen, all mounted around him. The servants are summoned for their edification, and in front of them all stands the mother of the child. The child is brought from the lockup. It's a gloomy cold, foggy autumn day, a capital day for hunting. The general

orders the child to be undressed; the child is stripped naked. He shivers, numb with terror, not daring to cry…. 'Make him run,' commands the general. 'Run! run!' shout the dog-boys. The boy runs…. 'At him!' yells the general, and he sets the whole pack of hounds on the child. The hounds catch him, and tear him to pieces before his mother's eyes! … I believe the general was afterwards declared incapable of administering his estates. Well—what did he deserve? To be shot? To be shot for the satisfaction of our moral feelings? Speak, Alyoshka!"

"To be shot," murmured Alyosha, lifting his eyes to Ivan with a pale, twisted smile.

"Bravo!" shouted Ivan delighted. "If even you say so, it means… You're a pretty monk! So there is a little devil sitting in your heart, Alyoshka Karamazov!"

"What I said was absurd, but—"

"That's just the point, that 'but'!" cried Ivan. "Let me tell you, novice, that the absurd is only too necessary on earth. The world stands on absurdities, and perhaps nothing would have come to pass in it without them. We know what we know!"

"What do you know?"

"I understand nothing," Ivan went on, as though in delirium. "I don't want to understand anything now. I want to stick to the fact. I made up my mind long ago not to understand. If I try to understand anything, I shall be false to the fact and I have determined to stick to the fact."

"Why are you trying me?" Alyosha cried out with a bitter outburst. "Will you say what you mean at last?"

"Of course, I will; that's what I've been leading up to. You are dear to me, I don't want to let you go, and I won't give you up to your Zosima."

Ivan for a minute was silent, his face became all at once very sad.

"Listen! I took the case of children only to make my case clearer. Of the other tears of humanity with which the earth is soaked from its crust to its center, I will say nothing. I have narrowed my subject on purpose. I am a bug, and I recognize in all humility that I cannot understand why the world is arranged as it is. Men are themselves to blame, I suppose; they were given paradise, they wanted freedom, and stole fire from heaven, though they knew they would become unhappy, so there is no need to pity them. With my pitiful, earthly, Euclidean understanding, all I know is that there is suffering and that there are none guilty; that cause follows effect, simply and directly; that everything flows and finds its level—but that's only Euclidean nonsense, I know that, and I can't consent to live by it! What comfort is it to me that there are none guilty and that cause follows effect simply and directly, and that I know it—I must have retribution, or I will destroy myself. And not retribution in some remote infinite time and space, but here on earth, and that I could see myself. I have believed in it. I want to see it, and if I am dead by then, let me rise again, for if it all happens without me, it will be too unfair. Surely I haven't suffered, simply that I, my crimes and my sufferings, may manure the soil of the future harmony for somebody else. I want to see with my own eyes the hind lie down with the lion and the victim rise up and embrace his murderer. I want to be there when everyone suddenly understands what it has all been for. All the religions of the world are built on this longing, and I am a believer. But then there are the children, and what am I to do about them? That's a question I can't answer. For the hundredth time I repeat, there are numbers of questions, but I've only taken the children, because in their case what I mean is so unanswerably clear. Listen! If all must suffer to pay for the eternal harmony, what have children to do with it, tell me, please? It's beyond all comprehension why they should suffer, and why they should pay for the harmony. Why should they, too, furnish material to enrich the soil for the harmony of the future? I understand solidarity in sin among men. I understand solidarity in retribution, too; but there can be no such solidarity in sin with children. And if it is really true that they must share responsibility for all their fathers' crimes, such a truth is not of this world and is beyond my comprehension. Some jester will say, perhaps, that the child would have grown up and have sinned, but you see he didn't grow up, he was torn to pieces by the dogs, at eight years old. Oh, Alyosha, I am not blaspheming! I understand, of course, what an upheaval of the universe it will be, when everything in heaven and earth blends in one hymn of praise and everything that lives and has lived cries aloud: 'Thou art just, O Lord, for Thy ways are revealed.' When the mother embraces the fiend who threw her child to the dogs, and all three cry aloud with tears, 'Thou art just, O Lord!' then, of course, the crown of knowledge will be reached and all will be made clear. But what pulls me up here is that I can't accept that harmony. And while I am on earth, I make haste to take my own measures. You see, Alyosha, perhaps it really may happen that if I live to that moment, or rise again to see it, I, too, perhaps, may cry aloud with the rest, looking at the mother embracing the child's torturer, 'Thou art just, O Lord!' but I don't want to cry aloud then. While there is still time, I hasten to protect myself and so I renounce the higher harmony altogether. It's not worth the tears of that one tortured child who beat itself on the breast with its little fist and prayed in its stinking outhouse, with its unexpiated tears to 'dear, kind God'! It's not worth it, because those tears are unatoned for. They must be atoned for, or there can be no harmony. But how? How are you going to atone for them? Is it possible? By their being avenged? But what do I care for avenging them? What do I care for a hell for oppressors? What good can hell do, since those children have already been tortured? And what becomes of harmony, if there is hell? I want to forgive. I want to embrace. I don't want more suffering. And if the sufferings of children go to swell the sum of sufferings which was necessary to pay for truth, then I protest that the truth is not worth such a price. I don't want the mother to embrace the oppressor who threw her son to the dogs! She dare not forgive him! Let her forgive him for herself, if she will, let her forgive the torturer for the immeasurable suffering of her mother's heart. But the sufferings of her tortured child she has no right to forgive; she dare not forgive the torturer, even if the child were to forgive him! And if that is so, if they dare not forgive, what becomes of harmony? Is there in the whole world a being who would have the right to forgive and could forgive?

I don't want harmony. From love for humanity I don't want it. I would rather be left with the unavenged suffering. I would rather remain with my unavenged suffering and unsatisfied indignation, *even if I were wrong*. Besides, too high a price is asked for harmony; it's beyond our means to pay so much to enter on it. And so I hasten to give back my entrance ticket, and if I am an honest man I am bound to give it back as soon as possible. And that I am doing. It's not God that I don't accept, Alyosha, only I most respectfully return Him the ticket."

"That's rebellion," murmured Alyosha, looking down.

"Rebellion? I am sorry you call it that," said Ivan earnestly. "One can hardly live in rebellion, and I want to live. Tell me yourself, I challenge you—answer. Imagine that you are creating a fabric of human destiny with the object of making men happy in the end, giving them peace and rest at last, but that it was essential and inevitable to torture to death only one tiny creature—that little child beating its breast with its fist, for instance—and to found that edifice on its unavenged tears, would you consent to be the architect on those conditions? Tell me, and tell the truth."

"No, I wouldn't consent," said Alyosha softly.

"And can you admit the idea that men for whom you are building it would agree to accept their happiness on the foundation of the unexpiated blood of a little victim? And accepting it would remain happy forever?"

"No, I can't admit it. Brother," said Alyosha suddenly, with flashing eyes, "you said just now, is there a being in the whole world who would have the right to forgive and could forgive? But there is a Being and He can forgive everything, all *and for all*, because He gave His innocent blood for all and everything. You have forgotten Him, and on Him is built the edifice, and it is to Him they cry aloud. 'Thou art just, O Lord, for Thy ways are revealed!'"

"Ah! the One without sin and his blood! No, I have not forgotten Him; on the contrary I've been wondering all the time how it was you did not bring Him in before, for usually all arguments on your side put Him in the foreground. Do you know, Alyosha—don't laugh! I composed a poem about a year ago. If you can waste another ten minutes on me, I'll tell it to you."

"You wrote a poem?"

"Oh, no, I didn't write it," laughed Ivan, "and I've never written two lines of poetry in my life. But I composed up this poem in prose and I remembered it. I was carried away when I composed it. You will be my first reader— that is, listener. Why should an author forego even one listener?" smiled Ivan. "Shall I tell it to you?"

"I am all attention," said Alyosha....

IV.B. CONTEMPORARY FORMULATIONS

The previous three essays presented two (rather different) historical formulations of the problem of evil and one of the most well-known historical replies. In the present section, we turn to contemporary philosophical formulations of the problem.

We begin with J. L. Mackie's classic statement of the "logical problem of evil"—an argument for the conclusion that the existence of the God of the Judeo-Christian tradition is logically inconsistent with the existence of evil. A perfectly good being, Mackie contends, always eliminates evil as far as it can; and an omnipotent and omniscient being, he argues, can eliminate evil entirely. He considers the response that the value of creating a world with free creatures might justify God in permitting the existence of evil. But he argues that since it is not *impossible* for there to be a world in which free creatures always do what is right, God must have been able to create such a world. And so, since a world in which free creatures always do what is right is clearly better than one in which free creatures sometimes do what is wrong, the appeal to freedom fails to solve the problem.

Despite the intuitive appeal of Mackie's argument, most philosophers nowadays agree that the argument fails. As William Rowe puts it in one of the endnotes to our next selection:

> *Some philosophers have contended that the existence of evil is logically inconsistent with the existence of the theistic God. No one, I think, has succeeded in establishing such an extravagant claim.*

Rowe goes on to credit Alvin Plantinga for showing in a clear and compelling way why Mackie's argument fails. (Plantinga's argument is given in selection IV. C.1 below.) Nevertheless, Rowe says,

> *[t]here remains…what we may call the evidential form—as opposed to the logical form—of the problem of evil; the view that the variety and profusion of evil in our world although perhaps not logically inconsistent with the existence of the theistic God, provides, nevertheless, rational support for atheism.*

It is the evidential form of the argument with which his article (selection IV.B.2) is concerned.

As it is typically presented, the "evidential problem of evil" relies on the premise that a good God would permit evil only if it contributed to some greater good, together with the claim that many of the evils we in fact observe seem not to contribute to any greater good. This is roughly the argument defended by Rowe; but Paul Draper, in the final reading of this section, takes a different tack. According to Draper, the "pattern of both pain and pleasure" in the world constitutes evidence against theism and in favor of naturalism. (As he defines it, naturalism is the hypothesis that the universe is a closed system, and it entails that there are no supernatural beings—divine or otherwise.) In his view, the pattern of pain and pleasure that we in fact observe isn't what we would naturally expect if pain existed (say) to serve the purpose of punishing sinners, or of building moral character. Rather, it is systematically connected with reproductive success, which is what we would expect on the supposition that naturalism and evolutionary theory are both true. Thus, on his view, the fact that pain and pleasure are systematically connected with reproductive success, together with the truth of evolutionary theory, provides evidence in support of naturalism.

IV.B.1

Evil and Omnipotence

J. L. MACKIE

John L. Mackie (1917–1981) was born in Australia and taught at Oxford University until his death. He made important contributions to the fields of metaphysics, epistemology, ethics, and philosophy of religion. Among his works are The Cement of the Universe *(1974),* Ethics: Inventing Right and Wrong *(1977), and* The Miracle of Theism *(1982). In this essay, Mackie argues that the argument from evil demonstrates the incoherence of theism. If there is a God who is all-powerful and completely good, he will be able and willing to eliminate all evil in the world. But there is evil, so no God exists.*

The traditional arguments for the existence of God have been fairly thoroughly criticised by philosophers. But the theologian can, if he wishes, accept this criticism. He can admit that no rational proof of God's existence is possible. And he can still retain all that is essential to his position, by holding that God's existence is known in some other, non-rational way. I think, however, that a more telling criticism can be made by way of the traditional problem of evil. Here it can be shown, not that religious beliefs lack rational support, but that they are positively irrational, that the several parts of the essential theological doctrine are inconsistent with one another, so that the theologian can maintain his position as a whole only by a much more extreme rejection of reason than in the former case. He must now be prepared to believe, not merely what cannot be proved, but what can be *disproved* from other beliefs that he also holds.

The problem of evil, in the sense in which I shall be using the phrase, is a problem only for someone who believes that there is a God who is both omnipotent and wholly good. And it is a logical problem, the problem of clarifying and reconciling a number of beliefs: it is not a scientific problem that might be solved by further observations, or a practical problem that might be solved by a decision or an action. These points are obvious; I mention them only because they are sometimes ignored by theologians, who sometimes parry a statement of the problem with such remarks as "Well, can you solve the problem yourself?" or "This is a mystery which may be revealed to us later" or "Evil is something to be faced and overcome, not to be merely discussed."

In its simplest form the problem is this: God is omnipotent; God is wholly good; and yet evil exists. There seems to be some contradiction between these three propositions, so that if any two of them were true the third would be false. But at the same time all three are essential parts of most theological positions: the theologian, it seems, at once *must* adhere and *cannot consistently* adhere to all three. (The problem does not arise only for theists, but I shall discuss it in the form in which it presents itself for ordinary theism.)

However, the contradiction does not arise immediately; to show it we need some additional

From *Mind*, 64 (1955): 200–212. Reprinted by permission of Oxford University Press.

premises, or perhaps some quasi-logical rules connecting the terms "good, evil," and "omnipotent." These additional principles are that good is opposed to evil, in such a way that a good thing always eliminates evil as far as it can, and that there are no limits to what an omnipotent thing can do. From these it follows that a good omnipotent thing eliminates evil completely, and then the propositions that a good omnipotent thing exists, and that evil exists, are incompatible.

A. ADEQUATE SOLUTIONS

Now once the problem is fully stated it is clear that it can be solved, in the sense that the problem will not arise if one gives up at least one of the propositions that constitute it. If you are prepared to say that God is not wholly good, or not quite omnipotent, or that evil does not exist, or that good is not opposed to the kind of evil that exists, or that there are limits to what an omnipotent thing can do, then the problem of evil will not arise for you.

There are, then, quite a number of adequate solutions of the problem of evil, and some of these have been adopted, or almost adopted, by various thinkers. For example, a few have been prepared to deny God's omnipotence, and rather more have been prepared to keep the term "omnipotence" but severely to restrict its meaning, recording quite a number of things that an omnipotent being cannot do. Some have said that evil is an illusion, perhaps because they held that the whole world of temporal, changing things is an illusion, and that what we call evil belongs only to this world, or perhaps because they held that although temporal things are much as we see them, those that we call evil are not really evil. Some have said that what we call evil is merely the privation of good, that evil in a positive sense, evil that would really be opposed to good, does not exist. Many have agreed with Pope that disorder is harmony not understood, and that partial evil is universal good. Whether any of these views is true is, of course, another question. But each of them gives

an adequate solution of the problem of evil in the sense that if you accept it this problem does not arise for you, though you may, of course, have *other* problems to face.

But often enough these adequate solutions are only *almost* adopted. The thinkers who restrict God's power, but keep the term "omnipotence," may reasonably be suspected of thinking, in other contexts, that his power is really unlimited. Those who say that evil is an illusion may also be thinking, inconsistently, that this illusion is itself an evil. Those who say that "evil" is merely privation of good may also be thinking, inconsistently, that privation of good is an evil. (The fallacy here is akin to some forms of the "naturalistic fallacy" in ethics, where some think, for example, that "good" is just what contributes to evolutionary progress, and that evolutionary progress is itself good.) If Pope meant what he said in the first line of his couplet, that "disorder" is only harmony not understood, the "partial evil" of the second line must, for consistency, mean "that which, taken in isolation, falsely appears to be evil," but it would more naturally mean "that which, in isolation, really is evil." The second line, in fact, hesitates between two views, that "partial evil" isn't really evil, since only the universal quality is real, and that "partial evil" is really an evil, but only a little one.

In addition, therefore, to adequate solutions, we must recognise unsatisfactorily inconsistent solutions, in which there is only a half-hearted or temporary rejection of one of the propositions which together constitute the problem. In these, one of the constituent propositions is explicitly rejected, but it is covertly re-asserted or assumed elsewhere in the system.

B. FALLACIOUS SOLUTIONS

Besides these half-hearted solutions, which explicitly reject but implicitly assert one of the constituent propositions, there are definitely fallacious solutions which explicitly maintain all the constituent propositions, but implicitly reject at least one of them in the course of the argument that explains away the problem of evil.

There are, in fact, many so-called solutions which purport to remove the contradiction without abandoning any of its constituent propositions. These must be fallacious as we can see from the very statement of the problem, but it is not so easy to see in each case precisely where the fallacy lies. I suggest that in all cases the fallacy has the general form suggested above: in order to solve the problem one (or perhaps more) of its constituent propositions is given up, but in such a way that it appears to have been retained, and can therefore be asserted without qualification in other contexts. Sometimes there is a further complication: the supposed solution moves to and fro between, say, two of the constituent propositions, at one point asserting the first of these but covertly abandoning the second, at another point asserting the second but covertly abandoning the first. These fallacious solutions often turn upon some equivocation with the words "good" and "evil," or upon some vagueness about the way in which good and evil are opposed to one another, or about how much is meant by "omnipotence." I propose to examine some of these so-called solutions, and to exhibit their fallacies in detail. Incidentally, I shall also be considering whether an adequate solution could be reached by a minor modification of one or more of the constituent propositions, which would, however, still satisfy all the essential requirements of ordinary theism.

(1)   "Good cannot exist without evil" or "Evil is necessary as a counterpart to good."

It is sometimes suggested that evil is necessary as a counterpart to good, that if there were no evil there could be no good either, and that this solves the problem of evil. It is true that it points to an answer to the question "Why should there be evil?" But it does so only by qualifying some of the propositions that constitute the problem.

First, it sets a limit to what God can do, saying that God *cannot* create good without simultaneously creating evil, and this means either that God is not omnipotent or that there are *some* limits to what an omnipotent thing can do. It may be replied that these limits are always presupposed, that omnipotence has never meant the power to do what is logically impossible, and on the present view the existence of good without evil would be a logical impossibility. This interpretation of omnipotence may, indeed, be accepted as a modification of our original account which does not reject anything that is essential to theism, and I shall in general assume it in the subsequent discussion. It is, perhaps, the most common theistic view, but I think that some theists at least have maintained that God can do what is logically impossible. Many theists, at any rate, have held that logic itself is created or laid down by God, that logic is the way in which God arbitrarily chooses to think. (This is, of course, parallel to the ethical view that morally right actions are those which God arbitrarily chooses to command, and the two views encounter similar difficulties.) And this account of logic is clearly inconsistent with the view that God is bound by logical necessities—unless it is possible for an omnipotent being to bind himself, an issue which we shall consider later, when we come to the Paradox of Omnipotence. This solution of the problem of evil cannot, therefore, be consistently adopted along with the view that logic is itself created by God.

But, secondly, this solution denies that evil is opposed to good in our original sense. If good and evil are counterparts, a good thing will not "eliminate evil as far as it can." Indeed, this view suggests that good and evil are not strictly qualities of things at all. Perhaps the suggestion is that good and evil are related in much the same way as great and small. Certainly, when the term "great" is used relatively as a condensation of "greater than so-and-so," and "small" is used correspondingly, greatness and smallness are counterparts and cannot exist without each other. But in this sense greatness is not a quality, not an intrinsic feature of anything; and it would be absurd to think of a movement in favour of greatness and against smallness in this sense. Such a movement would be self-defeating, since relative greatness can be promoted only by a simultaneous promotion of relative smallness. I feel sure that no theists would be content to regard God's goodness as analogous to this—as if what he supports were not the *good* but the *better*, and if he had the paradoxical aim that all things should be better than other things.

This point is obscured by the fact that "great" and "small" seem to have an absolute as well as a relative sense. I cannot discuss here whether there is absolute magnitude or not, but if there is, there could be an absolute sense for "great," it could mean of at least a certain size, and it would make sense to speak of all things getting bigger, of a universe that was expanding all over, and therefore it would make sense to speak of promoting greatness. But in *this* sense great and small are not logically necessary counterparts: either quality could exist without the other. There would be no logical impossibility in everything's being small or in everything's being great.

Neither in the absolute nor in the relative sense, then, of "great" and "small" do these terms provide an analogy of the sort that would be needed to support this solution of the problem of evil. In neither case are greatness and smallness *both* necessary counterparts *and* mutually opposed forces or possible objects for support and attack.

It may be replied that good and evil are necessary counterparts in the same way as any quality and its logical opposite: redness can occur, it is suggested, only if non-redness also occurs. But unless evil is merely the privation of good, they are not logical opposites, and some further argument would be needed to show that they are counterparts in the same way as genuine logical opposites. Let us assume that this could be given. There is still doubt of the correctness of the metaphysical principle that a quality must have a real opposite: I suggest that it is not really impossible that everything should be, say, red, that the truth is merely that if everything were red we should not notice redness, and so we should have no word "red"; we observe and give names to qualities only if they have real opposites. If so, the principle that a term must have an opposite would belong only to our language or to our thought, and would not be an ontological principle, and correspondingly, the rule that good cannot exist without evil would not state a logical

necessity of a sort that God would just have to put up with. God might have made everything good, though *we* should not have noticed it if he had.

But, finally, even if we concede that this is an ontological principle, it will provide a solution for the problem of evil only if one is prepared to say, "Evil exists, but only just enough evil to serve as the counterpart of good." I doubt whether any theist will accept this. After all, the ontological requirement that non-redness should occur would be satisfied even if all the universe, except for a minute speck, were red, and, if there were a corresponding requirement for evil as a counterpart to good, a minute dose of evil would presumably do. But theists are not usually willing to say, in all contexts, that all the evil that occurs is a minute and necessary dose.

(2) "Evil is necessary as a means to good."

It is sometimes suggested that evil is necessary for good not as a counterpart but as a means. In its simple form this has little plausibility as a solution of the problem of evil, since it obviously implies a severe restriction of God's power. It would be a *causal* law that you cannot have a certain end without a certain means, so that if God has to introduce evil as a means to good, he must be subject to at least some causal laws. This certainly conflicts with what a theist normally means by omnipotence. This view of God as limited by causal laws also conflicts with the view that causal laws are themselves made by God, which is more widely held than the corresponding view about the laws of logic. This conflict would, indeed, be resolved if it were possible for an omnipotent being to bind himself, and this possibility has still to be considered. Unless a favourable answer can be given to this question, the suggestion that evil is necessary as a means to good solves the problem of evil only by denying one of its constituent propositions, either that God is omnipotent or that "omnipotent" means what it says.

(3) "The universe is better with some evil in it than it could be if there were no evil."

Much more important is a solution which at first seems to be a mere variant of the previous one, that evil may contribute to the goodness of a whole in which it is found, so that the universe as a whole is better as it is, with some evil in it, than it would be if there were no evil. This solution may be developed in either of two ways. It may be supported by an aesthetic analogy, by the fact that contrasts heighten beauty, that in a musical work, for example, there may occur discords which somehow add to the beauty of the work as a whole. Alternatively, it may be worked out in connection with the notion of progress, that the best possible organization of the universe will not be static, but progressive, that the gradual overcoming of evil by good is really a finer thing than would be the eternal unchallenged supremacy of good.

In either case, this solution usually starts from the assumption that the evil whose existence gives rise to the problem of evil is primarily what is called physical evil, that is to say, pain. In Hume's rather half-hearted presentation of the problem of evil, the evils that he stresses are pain and disease, and those who reply to him argue that the existence of pain and disease makes possible the existence of sympathy, benevolence, heroism, and the gradually successful struggle of doctors and reformers to overcome these evils. In fact, theists often seize the opportunity to accuse those who stress the problem of evil of taking a low, materialistic view of good and evil, equating these with pleasure and pain, and of ignoring the more spiritual goods which can arise in the struggle against evils.

But let us see exactly what is being done here. Let us call pain and misery "first order evil" or "evil (1)." What contrasts with this, namely, pleasure and happiness, will be called "first order good" or "good (1)." Distinct from this is "second order good" or "good (2)" which somehow emerges in a complex situation in which evil (1) is a necessary component—logically not merely causally, necessary. (Exactly *how* it emerges does not matter: in the crudest version of this solution good (2) is simply the heightening of happiness by the contrast with misery, in other versions it includes sympathy with suffering, heroism in facing danger, and the gradual decrease of first order evil and increase of

first order good.) It is also being assumed that second order good is more important than first order good or evil, in particular that it more than outweighs the first order evil it involves.

Now this is a particularly subtle attempt to solve the problem of evil. It defends God's goodness and omnipotence on the ground that (on a sufficiently long view) this is the best of all logically possible worlds, because it includes the important second order goods, and yet it admits that real evils, namely first order evils, exist. But does it still hold that good and evil are opposed? Not, clearly, in the sense that we set out originally: good does not tend to eliminate evil in general. Instead, we have a modified, a more complex pattern. First order good (*e.g.* happiness) *contrasts with* first order evil (*e.g.* misery): these two are opposed in a fairly mechanical way; some second order goods (*e.g.* benevolence) try to maximize first order good and minimize first order evil; but God's goodness is not this, it is rather the will to maximize *second* order good. We might, therefore, call God's goodness an example of a third order goodness, or good (3). While this account is different from our original one, it might well be held to be an improvement on it, to give a more accurate description of the way in which good is opposed to evil, and to be consistent with the essential theist position.

There might, however, be several objections to this solution.

First, some might argue that such qualities as benevolence—and *a fortiori* the third order goodness which promotes benevolence—have a merely derivative value, that they are not higher sorts of good, but merely means to good (1), that is, to happiness, so that it would be absurd for God to keep misery in existence in order to make possible the virtues of benevolence, heroism, etc. The theist who adopts the present solution must, of course, deny this, but he can do so with some plausibility, so I should not press this objection.

Secondly, it follows from this solution that God is not in our sense benevolent or sympathetic: he is not concerned to minimize evil (1), but only to promote good (2); and this might be a disturbing conclusion for some theists.

But, thirdly, the fatal objection is this. Our analysis shows clearly the possibility of the existence of a *second* order evil, an evil (2) contrasting with good (2) as evil (1) contrasts with good (1). This would include malevolence, cruelty, callousness, cowardice, and states in which good (1) is decreasing and evil (1) increasing. And just as good (2) is held to be the important kind of good, the kind that God is concerned to promote, so evil (2) will, by analogy, be the important kind of evil, the kind which God, if he were wholly good and omnipotent, would eliminate. And yet evil (2) plainly exists, and indeed most theists (in other contexts) stress its existence more than that of evil (1). We should, therefore, state the problem of evil in terms of second order evil, and against this form of the problem the present solution is useless.

An attempt might be made to use this solution again, at a higher level, to explain the occurrence of evil (2); indeed the next main solution that we shall examine does just this, with the help of some new notions. Without any fresh notions, such a solution would have little plausibility: for example, we could hardly say that the really important good was a good (3), such as the increase of benevolence in proportion to cruelty, which logically required for its occurrence the occurrence of some second order evil. But even if evil (2) could be explained in this way, it is fairly clear that there would be third order evils contrasting with this third order good: and we should be well on the way to an infinite regress, where the solution of a problem of evil, stated in terms of evil (*n*), indicated the existence of an evil (*n* + 1), and a further problem to be solved.

(4) "Evil is due to human free will."

Perhaps the most important proposed solution of the problem of evil is that evil is not to be ascribed to God at all, but to the independent actions of human beings, supposed to have been endowed by God with freedom of the will. This solution may be combined with the preceding one: first order evil (*e.g.* pain) may be justified as a logically necessary component in second order good (*e.g.* sympathy) while second order evil (*e.g.* cruelty) is not *justified*, but is so ascribed to human beings

that God cannot be held responsible for it. This combination evades my third criticism of the preceding solution.

The free will solution also involves the preceding solution at a higher level. To explain why a wholly good God gave men free will although it would lead to some important evils, it must be argued that it is better on the whole that men should act freely, and sometimes err, than that they should be innocent automata, acting rightly in a wholly determined way. Freedom that is to say, is now treated as a third order good, and as being more valuable than second order goods (such as sympathy and heroism) would be if they were deterministically produced, and it is being assumed that second order evils, such as cruelty, are logically necessary accompaniments of freedom, just as pain is a logically necessary precondition of sympathy.

I think that this solution is unsatisfactory primarily because of the incoherence of the notion of freedom of the will: but I cannot discuss this topic adequately here, although some of my criticisms will touch upon it.

First I should query the assumption that second order evils are logically necessary accompaniments of freedom. I should ask this: if God has made men such that in their free choices they sometimes prefer what is good and sometimes what is evil, why could he not have made men such that they always freely choose the good? If there is no logical impossibility in a man's freely choosing the good on one, or on several, occasions, there cannot be a logical impossibility in his freely choosing the good on every occasion. God was not, then, faced with a choice between making innocent automata and making beings who, in acting freely, would sometimes go wrong: there was open to him the obviously better possibility of making beings who would act freely but always go right. Clearly, his failure to avail himself of this possibility is inconsistent with his being both omnipotent and wholly good.

If it is replied that this objection is absurd, that the making of some wrong choices is logically necessary for freedom, it would seem that "freedom" must here mean complete randomness or indeterminacy, including randomness with regard to the alternatives good and evil, in other words that men's choices and consequent actions can be "free" only if they are not determined by their characters. Only on this assumption can God escape the responsibility for men's actions; for if he made them as they are, but did not determine their wrong choices, this can only be because the wrong choices are not determined by men as they are. But then if freedom is randomness, how can it be a characteristic of *will?* And, still more, how can it be the most important good? What value or merit would there be in free choices if these were random actions which were not determined by the nature of the agent?

I conclude that to make this solution plausible two different senses of "freedom" must be confused, one sense which will justify the view that freedom is a third order good, more valuable than other goods would be without it, and another sense, sheer randomness, to prevent us from ascribing to God a decision to make men such that they sometimes go wrong when he might have made them such that they would always freely go right.

This criticism is sufficient to dispose of this solution. But besides this there is a fundamental difficulty in the notion of an omnipotent God creating men with free will, for if men's wills are really free this must mean that even God cannot control them, that is, that God is no longer omnipotent. It may be objected that God's gift of freedom to men does not mean that he *cannot* control their wills, but that he always *refrains* from controlling their wills. But why, we may ask, should God refrain from controlling evil wills? Why should he not leave men free to will rightly, but intervene when he sees them beginning to will wrongly? If God could do this, but does not, and if he is wholly good, the only explanation could be that even a wrong free act of will is not really evil, that its freedom is a value which outweighs its wrongness, so that there would be a loss of value if God took away the wrongness and the freedom together. But this is utterly opposed to what theists say about sin in other contexts. The present solution of the problem of evil, then, can be maintained only in the form that God has made men so free that he *cannot* control their wills.

This leads us to what I call the Paradox of Omnipotence: can an omnipotent being make things which he cannot subsequently control? Or, what is practically equivalent to this, can an omnipotent being make rules which then bind himself? (These are practically equivalent because any such rules could be regarded as setting certain things beyond his control, and *vice versa.*) The second of these formulations is relevant to the suggestions that we have already met, that an omnipotent God creates the rules of logic or causal laws, and is then bound by them.

It is clear that this is a paradox: the questions cannot be answered satisfactorily either in the affirmative or in the negative. If we answer "Yes," it follows that if God actually makes things which he cannot control, or makes rules which bind himself, he is not omnipotent once he has made them: there are then things which he cannot do. But if we answer "No," we are immediately asserting that there are things which he cannot do, that is to say that he is already not omnipotent.

It cannot be replied that the question which sets this paradox is not a proper question. It would make perfectly good sense to say that a human mechanic has made a machine which he cannot control: if there is any difficulty about the question it lies in the notion of omnipotence itself.

This, incidentally, shows that although we have approached this paradox from the free will theory, it is equally a problem for a theological determinist. No one thinks that machines have free will, yet they may well be beyond the control of their makers. The determinist might reply that anyone who makes anything determines its ways of acting, and so determines its subsequent behaviour: even the human mechanic does this by his *choice* of materials and structure for his machine, though he does not know all about either of these: the mechanic thus determines, though he may not foresee, his machine's actions. And since God is omniscient, and since his creation of things is total, he both determines and foresees the ways in which his creatures will act. We may grant this, but it is beside the point. The question is not whether God *originally* determined the future actions of his creatures, but whether he can *subsequently* control their actions, or whether he was able in his original creation to put things beyond his subsequent control. Even on determinist principles the answers "Yes" and "No" are equally irreconcilable with God's omnipotence.

Before suggesting a solution of this paradox, I would point out that there is a parallel Paradox of Sovereignty. Can a legal sovereign make a law restricting its own future legislative power? For example, could the British parliament make a law forbidding any future parliament to socialise banking, and also forbidding the future repeal of this law itself? Or could the British parliament, which was legally sovereign in Australia in, say, 1899, pass a valid law, or series of laws, which made it no longer sovereign in 1933? Again, neither the affirmative nor the negative answer is really satisfactory. If we were to answer "Yes," we should be admitting the validity of a law which, if it were actually made, would mean that parliament was no longer sovereign. If we were to answer "No," we should be admitting that there is a law, not logically absurd, which parliament cannot validly make, that is, that parliament is not now a legal sovereign. This paradox can be solved in the following way. We should distinguish between first order laws, that is laws governing the actions of individuals and bodies other than the legislature, and second order laws, that is laws about laws, laws governing the actions of the legislature itself. Correspondingly, we should distinguish two orders of sovereignty, first order sovereignty (sovereignty (1)) which is unlimited authority to make first order laws, and second order sovereignty (sovereignty (2)) which is unlimited authority to make second order laws. If we say that parliament is sovereign we might mean that any parliament at any time has sovereignty (1), or we might mean that parliament has both sovereignty (1) and sovereignty (2) at present, but we cannot without contradiction mean both that the present parliament has sovereignty (2) and that every parliament at every time has sovereignty (1), for if the present parliament has sovereignty (2) it

may use it to take away the sovereignty (1) of later parliaments. What the paradox shows is that we cannot ascribe to any continuing institution legal sovereignty in an inclusive sense.

The analogy between omnipotence and sovereignty shows that the paradox of omnipotence can be solved in a similar way. We must distinguish between first order omnipotence (omnipotence (1)), that is unlimited power to act, and second order omnipotence (omnipotence (2)), that is unlimited power to determine what powers to act things shall have. Then we could consistently say that God all the time has omnipotence (1), but if so no beings at any time have powers to act independently of God. Or we could say that God at one time had omnipotence (2), and used it to assign independent powers to act to certain things, so that God thereafter did not have omnipotence (1). But what the paradox shows is that we cannot consistently ascribe to any continuing being omnipotence in an inclusive sense.

An alternative solution of this paradox would be simply to deny that God is a continuing being, that any times can be assigned to his actions at all. But on this assumption (which also has difficulties of its own) no meaning can be given to the assertion that God made men with wills so free that he could not control them. The paradox of omnipotence can be avoided by putting God outside time, but the free will solution of the problem of evil cannot be saved in this way, and equally it remains impossible to hold that an omnipotent God *binds himself* by causal or logical laws.

CONCLUSION

Of the proposed solutions of the problem of evil which we have examined, none has stood up to criticism. There may be other solutions which require examination, but this study strongly suggests that there is no valid solution of the problem which does not modify at least one of the constituent propositions in a way which would seriously affect the essential core of the theistic position.

Quite apart from the problem of evil, the paradox of omnipotence has shown that God's omnipotence must in any case be restricted in one way or another, that unqualified omnipotence cannot be ascribed to any being that continues through time. And if God and his actions are not in time, can omnipotence, or power of any sort, be meaningfully ascribed to him?

IV.B.2

The Inductive Argument from Evil against the Existence of God

WILLIAM ROWE

A short biographical sketch of William Rowe appears before selection I.B.9. In the present selection, Rowe argues that an inductive or probabilistic version of the argument from evil justifies atheism. He concedes that deductive arguments against the existence of God on the basis of evil, such as J. L. Mackie uses (Reading IV. B. 1), do not succeed. Nevertheless, he says it is reasonable to believe that there is no God. In the last part of his essay, Rowe defines his position as "friendly atheism" since he admits that a theist may be justified in rejecting the probabilistic argument from evil.

This paper is concerned with three interrelated questions. The first is: Is there an argument for atheism based on the existence of evil that may rationally justify someone in being an atheist? To this first question I give an affirmative answer and try to support that answer by setting forth a strong argument for atheism based on the existence of evil.[1] The second question is: How can the theist best defend his position against the argument for atheism based on the existence of evil? In response to this question I try to describe what may be an adequate rational defense for theism against any argument for atheism based on the existence of evil. The final question is: What position should the informed atheist take concerning the rationality of theistic belief? Three different answers an atheist may give to this question serve to distinguish three varieties of atheism: unfriendly atheism, indifferent atheism, and friendly atheism. In the final part of the paper I discuss and defend the position of friendly atheism.

Before we consider the argument from evil, we need to distinguish a narrow and a broad sense of the terms "theist," "atheist," and "agnostic." By a "theist" in the narrow sense I mean someone who believes in the existence of an omnipotent, omniscient, eternal, supremely good being who created the world. By a "theist" in the

Reprinted from "The Problem of Evil and Some Varieties of Atheism," *American Philosophical Quarterly* 16 (1979) by permission. Footnotes edited.

broad sense I mean someone who believes in the existence of some sort of divine being or divine reality. To be a theist in the narrow sense is also to be a theist in the broad sense, but one may be a theist in the broad sense—as was Paul Tillich—without believing that there is a supremely good, omnipotent, omniscient, eternal being who created the world. Similar distinctions must be made between a narrow and a broad sense of the terms "atheist" and "agnostic." To be an atheist in the broad sense is to deny the existence of any sort of divine being or divine reality. Tillich was not an atheist in the broad sense. But he was an atheist in the narrow sense, for he denied that there exists a divine being that is all-knowing, all-powerful and perfectly good. In this paper I will be using the terms "theism," "theist," "atheism," "atheist," "agnosticism," and "agnostic" in the narrow sense, not in the broad sense.

I

In developing the argument for atheism based on the existence of evil, it will be useful to focus on some particular evil that our world contains in considerable abundance. Intense human and animal suffering, for example, occurs daily and in great plenitude in our world. Such intense suffering is a clear case of evil. Of course, if the intense suffering leads to some greater good, a good we could not have obtained without undergoing the suffering in question, we might conclude that the suffering is justified, but it remains an evil nevertheless. For we must not confuse the intense suffering in and of itself with the good things to which it sometimes leads or of which it may be a necessary part. Intense human or animal suffering is in itself bad, an evil, even though it may sometimes be justified by virtue of being a part of, or leading to, some good which is unobtainable without it. What is evil in itself may sometimes be good as a means because it leads to something that is good in itself. In such a case, while remaining an evil in itself, the intense

human or animal suffering is, nevertheless, an evil which someone might be morally justified in permitting.

Taking human and animal suffering as a clear instance of evil which occurs with great frequency in our world, the argument for atheism based on evil can be stated as follows:

1. There exist instances of intense suffering which an omnipotent, omniscient being could have prevented without thereby losing some greater good or permitting some evil equally bad or worse.[2]

2. An omniscient, wholly good being would prevent the occurrence of any intense suffering it could, unless it could not do so without thereby losing some greater good or permitting some evil equally bad or worse.

3. There does not exist an omnipotent, omniscient, wholly good being.

What are we to say about this argument for atheism, an argument based on the profusion of one sort of evil in our world? The argument is valid; therefore, if we have rotational grounds for accepting its premises, to that extent we have rational grounds for accepting atheism. Do we, however, have rational grounds for accepting the premises of this argument?

Let's begin with the second premise. Let s_1 be an instance of intense human or animal suffering which an omniscient, wholly good being could prevent. We will also suppose that things are such that s_1 will occur unless prevented by the omniscient, wholly good (OG) being. We might be interested in determining what would be a sufficient condition of OG failing to prevent s_1. But, for our purpose here, we need only try to state a necessary condition for OG failing to prevent s_1. That condition, so it seems to me, is this:

Either

(i) there is some greater good, G, such that G is obtainable by OG only if OG permits s_1,

or

(ii)   there is some greater good, G, such that G is obtainable by OG only if OG permits either s_1 or some evil equally bad or worse,

or

(iii) s_1 is such that it is preventable by OG only if OG permits some evil equally bad or worse.

It is important to recognize that (iii) is not included in (i). For losing a good greater than s_1 is not the same as permitting an evil greater than s_1. And this because the *absence* of a good state of affairs need not itself be an evil state of affairs. It is also important to recognize that s_1 might be such that it is preventable by OG *without* losing G (so condition (i) is not satisfied) but also such that if OG did prevent it, G would be lost unless OG permitted some evil equal to or worse than s_1. If this were so, it does not seem correct to require that OG prevent s_1. Thus, condition (ii) takes into account an important possibility not encompassed in condition (i).

Is it true that if an omniscient, wholly good being permits the occurrence of some intense suffering it could have prevented, then either (i) or (ii) or (iii) obtains? It seems to me that it is true. But if it is true then so is premise (2) of the argument for atheism. For that premise merely states in more compact form what we have suggested must be true if an omniscient, wholly good being fails to prevent some intense suffering it could prevent. Premise (2) says that an omniscient, wholly good being would prevent the occurrence of any intense suffering it could, unless it could not do so without thereby losing some greater good or permitting some evil equally bad or worse. This premise (or something not too distant from it) is, I think, held in common by many atheists and nontheists. Of course, there may be disagreement about whether something is good, and whether, if it is good, one would be morally justified in permitting some intense suffering to occur in order to obtain it. Someone might hold, for example, that no good is great enough to justify permitting an innocent child to suffer terribly. Again, someone might hold that the mere fact that a given good

outweighs some suffering and would be lost if the suffering were prevented, is not a morally sufficient reason for permitting the suffering. But to hold either of these views is not to deny (2). For (2) claims only that *if* an omniscient, wholly good being permits intense suffering *then* either there is some greater good that would have been lost, or some equally bad or worse evil that would have occurred, had the intense suffering been prevented. (2) does not purport to describe what might be a *sufficient* condition for an omniscient, wholly good being to permit intense suffering, only what is a *necessary* condition. So stated, (2) seems to express a belief that accords with our basic moral principles, principles shared by both theists and nontheists. If we are to fault the argument for atheism, therefore, it seems we must find some fault with its first premise.

Suppose in some distant forest lightning strikes a dead tree, resulting in a forest fire. In the fire a fawn is trapped, horribly burned, and lies in terrible agony for several days before death relieves its suffering. So far as we can see, the fawn's intense suffering is pointless. For there does not appear to be any greater good such that the prevention of the fawn's suffering would require either the loss of that good or the occurrence of an evil equally bad or worse. Nor does there seem to be any equally bad or worse evil so connected to the fawn's suffering that it would have had to occur had the fawn's suffering been prevented. Could an omnipotent, omniscient being have prevented the fawn's apparently pointless suffering? The answer is obvious, as even the theist will insist. An omnipotent, omniscient being could have easily prevented the fawn from being horribly burned, or, given the burning, could have spared the fawn the intense suffering by quickly ending its life, rather than allowing the fawn to lie in terrible agony for several days. Since the fawn's intense suffering was preventable and, so far as we can see, pointless, doesn't it appear that premise (1) of the argument is true, that there do exist instances of intense suffering which an omnipotent, omniscient being could have prevented without thereby losing some greater good or permitting some evil equally bad or worse?

It must be acknowledged that the case of the fawn's apparently pointless suffering does not prove that (1) is true. For even though we cannot see how the fawn's suffering is required to obtain some greater good (or to prevent some equally bad or worse evil), it hardly follows that it is not so required. After all, we are often surprised by how things we thought to be unconnected turn out to be intimately connected. Perhaps, for all we know, there is some familiar good outweighing the fawn's suffering to which that suffering is connected in a way we do not see. Furthermore, there may well be unfamiliar goods, goods we haven't dreamed of, to which the fawn's suffering is inextricably connected. Indeed, it would seem to require something like omniscience on our part before we could lay claim to *knowing* that there is no greater good connected to the fawn's suffering in such a manner than an omnipotent, omniscient being could not have achieved that good without permitting that suffering or some evil equally bad or worse. So the case of the fawn's suffering surely does not enable us to *establish* the truth of (1).

The truth is that we are not in a position to prove that (1) is true. We cannot know with certainty that instances of suffering of the sort described in (1) do occur in our world. But it is one thing to *know* or *prove* that (1) is true and quite another thing to have *rational grounds* for believing (1) to be true. We are often in the position where in the light of our experience and knowledge it is rational to believe that a certain statement is true, even though we are not in a position to prove or to know with certainty that the statement is true. In the light of our past experience and knowledge it is, for example, very reasonable to believe that neither Goldwater nor McGovern will ever be elected President, but we are scarcely in the position of knowing with certainty that neither will ever be elected President. So, too, with (1), although we cannot know with certainty that it is true, it perhaps can be rationally supported, shown to be a rational belief.

Consider again the case of the fawn's suffering. Is it reasonable to believe that there is some greater good so intimately connected to that suffering that even an omnipotent, omniscient being could not have obtained that good without permitting that suffering or some evil at least as bad? It certainly does not appear reasonable to believe this. Nor does it seem reasonable to believe that there is some evil at least as bad as the fawn's suffering such that an omnipotent being simply could not have prevented it without permitting the fawn's suffering. But even if it should somehow be reasonable to believe either of these things of the fawn's suffering, we must then ask whether it is reasonable to believe either of these things of *all* the instances of seemingly pointless human and animal suffering that occur daily in our world. And surely the answer to this more general question must be no. It seems quite unlikely that all the instances of intense suffering occurring daily in our world are intimately related to the occurrence of greater goods or the prevention of evils at least as bad; and even more unlikely, should they somehow all be so related, that an omnipotent, omniscient being could not have achieved at least some of those goods (or prevented some of those evils) without permitting the instances of intense suffering that are supposedly related to them. In the light of our experience and knowledge of the variety and scale of human and animal suffering in our world, the idea that none of this suffering could have been prevented by an omnipotent being without thereby losing a greater good or permitting an evil at least as bad seems an extraordinary absurd idea, quite beyond our belief. It seems then that although we cannot prove that (1) is true, it is, nevertheless, altogether *reasonable* to believe that (1) is true, that (1) is a *rational* belief.

Returning now to our argument for atheism, we've seen that the second premise expresses a basic belief common to many theists and nontheists. We've also seen that our experience and knowledge of the variety and profusion of suffering in our world provides *rational support* for the first premise. Seeing that the conclusion, "There does not exist an omnipotent, omniscient, wholly good being" follows from these two premises, it does seem that we have *rational support* for atheism, that it is reasonable for us to believe that the theistic God does not exist.

II

Can theism be rationally defended against the argument for atheism we have just examined? If it can, how might the theist best respond to that argument? Since the argument from (1) and (2) to (3) is valid, and since the theist, no less than the nontheist, is more than likely committed to (2), it's clear that the theist can reject this atheistic argument only by rejecting its first premise, the premise that states that there are instances of intense suffering which an omnipotent, omniscient being could have prevented without thereby losing some greater good or permitting some evil equally bad or worse. How, then, can the theist best respond to this premise and the considerations advanced in its support?

There are basically three responses a theist can make. First, he might argue not that (1) is false or probably false, but only that the reasoning given in support of it is in some way *defective*. He may do this either by arguing that the reasons given in support of (1) are *in themselves* insufficient to justify accepting (1), or by arguing that there are other things we know which, when taken in conjunction with these reasons, do not justify us in accepting (1). I suppose some theists would be content with this rather modest response to the basic argument for atheism. But given the validity of the basic argument and the theist's likely acceptance of (2), he is thereby committed to the view that (1) is false, not just that we have no good reasons for accepting (1) as true. The second two responses are aimed at showing that it is reasonable to believe that (1) is false. Since the theist is committed to this view, I shall focus the discussion on these two attempts, attempts which we can distinguish as "the direct attack" and "the indirect attack."

By a direct attack, I mean an attempt to reject (1) by pointing out goods, for example, to which suffering may well be connected, goods which an omnipotent, omniscient being could not achieve without permitting suffering. It is doubtful, however, that the direct attack can succeed. The theist may point out that some suffering leads to moral and spiritual development impossible without suffering. But it's reasonably clear that suffering often occurs in a degree far beyond what is required for character development. The theist may say that some suffering results from free choices of human beings and might be preventable only by preventing some measure of human freedom. But, again, it's clear that much intense suffering occurs not as a result of human free choices. The general difficulty with this direct attack on premise (1) is twofold. First, it cannot succeed; for the theist does not know what greater goods might be served, or evils prevented, by each instance of intense human or animal suffering. Second, the theist's own religious tradition usually maintains that in this life it is not given to us to know God's purpose in allowing particular instances of suffering. Hence, the direct attack against premise (1) cannot succeed and violates basic beliefs associated with theism.

The best procedure for the theist to follow in rejecting premise (1) is the indirect procedure. This procedure I shall call "the G. E. Moore shift," so-called in honor of the twentieth century philosopher G. E. Moore, who used it to great effect in dealing with the arguments of the skeptics. Skeptical philosophers such as David Hume have advanced ingenious arguments to prove that no one can know of the existence of any material object. The premises of their arguments employ plausible principles, principles which many philosophers have tried to reject directly, but only with questionable success. Moore's procedure was altogether different. Instead of arguing directly against the premises of the skeptic's arguments, he simply noted that the premises implied, for example, that he (Moore) did not know of the existence of a pencil. Moore then proceeded indirectly against the skeptic's premises by arguing:

I do know that this pencil exists.

If the skeptic's principles are correct I cannot know of the existence of this pencil.

∴ The skeptic's principles (at least one) must be incorrect.

Moore then noted that his argument is just as valid as the skeptic's, that both of their arguments contain the premise "If the skeptic's principles are correct Moore cannot know of the existence of this pencil," and concluded that the only way to choose between the two arguments (Moore's and the skeptic's) is by deciding which of the first premises it is more rational to believe—Moore's premise "I do know that this pencil exists" or the skeptic's premise asserting that his skeptical principles are correct. Moore concluded that his own first premise was the more rational of the two.

Before we see how the theist may apply the G. E. Moore shift to the basic argument of atheism, we should note the general strategy of the shift. We're given an argument: p, q, therefore, r. Instead of arguing directly against p, another argument is constructed not-r, q, therefore, not-p—which begins with the denial of the conclusion of the first argument, keeps its second premise, and ends with the denial of the first premise as its conclusion. Compare, for example, these two:

$$\text{I.} \quad p \qquad \text{II.} \quad \text{not-}r$$
$$\frac{q}{r} \qquad \qquad \frac{q}{\text{not-}p}$$

It is a truth of logic that if I is valid II must be valid as well. Since the arguments are the same so far as the second premise is concerned, any choice between them must concern their respective first premises. To argue against the first premise (p) by constructing the counter argument II is to employ the G. E. Moore shift.

Applying the G. E. Moore shift against the first premise of the basic argument for atheism, the theist can argue as follows:

not-3. There exists an omnipotent, omniscient, wholly good being.

2. An omniscient, wholly good being would prevent the occurrence of any intense suffering it could, unless it could not do so without thereby losing some greater good or permitting some evil equally bad or worse.

therefore,

not-1. It is not the case that there exist instances of intense suffering which an omnipotent, omniscient being could have prevented without thereby losing some greater good or permitting some evil equally bad or worse.

We now have two arguments: the basic argument for atheism from (1) and (2) to (3), and the theist's best response, the argument from (not-3) and (2) to (not-1). What the theist then says about (1) is that he has rational grounds for believing in the existence of the theistic God (not-3), accepts (2) as true, and sees that (not-1) follows from (not-3) and (2). He concludes, therefore, that he has rational grounds for rejecting (1). Having rational grounds for rejecting (1), the theist concludes that the basic argument for atheism is mistaken.

III

We've had a look at a forceful argument for atheism and what seems to be the theist's best response to that argument. If one is persuaded by the argument for atheism, as I find myself to be, how might one best view the position of the theist? Of course, he will view the theist as having a false belief, just as the theist will view the atheist as having a false belief. But what position should the atheist take concerning the *rationality* of the theist's belief? There are three major positions an atheist might take, positions which we may think of as some varieties of atheism. First, the atheist may believe that no one is rationally justified in believing that the theistic God exists. Let us call this position "unfriendly atheism." Second, the atheist may hold no belief concerning whether any theist is or isn't rationally justified in believing that the theistic God exists. Let us call this view "indifferent atheism." Finally, the atheist may believe that some theists are rationally justified in believing that the theistic God exists. This view we shall call "friendly atheism." In this final part of the paper I propose to discuss and defend the position of friendly atheism.

If no one can be rationally justified in believing a false proposition then friendly atheism is a paradoxical, if not incoherent position. But surely the truth of a belief is not a necessary condition of someone's being rationally justified in having that belief. So in holding that someone is rationally justified in believing that the theistic God exists, the friendly atheist is not committed to thinking that the theist has a true belief. What he is committed to is that the theist has rational grounds for his belief, a belief the atheist rejects and is convinced he is rationally justified in rejecting. But is this possible? Can someone, like our friendly atheist, hold a belief, be convinced that he is rationally justified in holding that belief, and yet believe that someone else is equally justified in believing the opposite? Surely this is possible. Suppose your friends see you off on a flight to Hawaii. Hours after take-off they learn that your plane has gone down at sea. After a twenty-four hour search, no survivors have been found. Under these circumstances they are rationally justified in believing that you have perished. But it is hardly rational for you to believe this, as you bob up and down in your life vest, wondering why the search planes have failed to spot you. Indeed, to amuse yourself while awaiting your fate, you might very well reflect on the fact that your friends are rationally justified in believing that you are now dead, a proposition you disbelieve and are rationally justified in disbelieving. So, too, perhaps an atheist may be rationally justified in his atheistic belief and yet hold that some theists are rationally justified in believing just the opposite of what he believes.

What sort of grounds might a theist have for believing that God exists? Well, he might endeavor to justify his belief by appealing to one or more of the traditional arguments: Ontological, Cosmological, Teleological, Moral, etc. Second, he might appeal to certain aspects of religious experience, perhaps even his own religious experience. Third, he might try to justify theism as a plausible theory in terms of which we can account for a variety of phenomena. Although an atheist must hold that the theistic God does not exist, can he not also believe, and be justified in so believing, that some of these "justifications of theism" do actually rationally justify some theists in their belief that there exists a supremely good, omnipotent, omniscient being? It seems to me that he can.

If we think of the long history of theistic belief and the special situations in which people are sometimes placed, it is perhaps as absurd to think that no one was ever rationally justified in believing that the theistic God exists as it is to think that no one was ever justified in believing that human beings would never walk on the moon. But in suggesting that friendly atheism is preferable to unfriendly atheism, I don't mean to rest the case on what some human beings might reasonably have believed in the eleventh or thirteenth century. The more interesting question is whether some people in modern society, people who are aware of the usual grounds for belief and disbelief and are acquainted to some degree with modern science, are yet rationally justified in accepting theism. Friendly atheism is a significant position only if it answers this question in the affirmative.

It is not difficult for an atheist to be friendly when he has reason to believe that the theist could not reasonably be expected to be acquainted with the grounds for disbelief that he (the atheist) possesses. For then the atheist may take the view that some theists are rationally justified in holding to theism, but would not be so were they to be acquainted with the grounds for disbelief—those grounds being sufficient to tip the scale in favor of atheism when balanced against the reasons the theist has in support of his belief.

Friendly atheism becomes paradoxical, however, when the atheist contemplates believing that the theist has all the grounds for atheism that he, the atheist, has, and yet is rationally justified in maintaining his theistic belief. But even so excessively friendly a view as this perhaps can be held by the atheist if he also has some reason to think that the grounds for theism are not as telling as the theist is justified in taking them to be.

In this paper I've presented what I take to be a strong argument for atheism, pointed out what I think is the theist's best response to that argument, distinguished three positions an atheist might take concerning the rationality of theistic belief, and made some remarks in defense of the position called "friendly atheism." I'm aware that the central points of the paper are not likely to be warmly received by many philosophers. Philosophers who are atheists tend to be tough minded—holding that there are no good reasons for supposing that theism is true. And theists tend either to reject the view that the existence of evil provides rational grounds for atheism or to hold that religious belief has nothing to do with reason and evidence at all. But such is the way of philosophy.

NOTES

1. Some philosophers have contended that the existence of evil is *logically inconsistent* with the existence of the theistic God. No one, I think, has succeeded in establishing such an extravagant claim. Indeed, granted incompatibilism, there is a fairly compelling argument for the view that the existence of evil is logically consistent with the existence of the theistic God. (For a lucid statement of this argument see Alvin Plantinga, *God, Freedom, and Evil* (New York, 1974), 29-59.) There remains, however, what we may call the *evidential* form—as opposed to the *logical* form—of the problem of evil; the view that the variety and profusion of evil in our world, although perhaps not logically inconsistent with the existence of the theistic God, provides, nevertheless, *rational support* for atheism. In this paper I shall be concerned solely with the evidential form of the problem, the form of the problem which, I think, presents a rather severe difficulty for theism. William L. Rowe,

"The Problem of Evil and Some Varieties of Atheism," first published in *American Philosophical Quarterly*, 16 (1979), pp. 335-41. Used with permission.

2. If there is some good, G, greater than any evil, (1) will be false for the trivial reason that no matter what evil, E, we pick the conjunctive good state of affairs consisting of G and E will outweigh E and be such that an omnipotent being could not obtain it without permitting E. (See Alvin Plantinga, *God and Other Minds* (Ithaca, 1967), 167.) To avoid this objection we may insert "unreplaceable" into our premises (1) and (2) between "some" and "greater." If E isn't required for G, and G is better than G plus E, then the good conjunctive state of affairs composed of G and E would be replaceable by the greater good of G alone. For the sake of simplicity, however, I will ignore this complication both in the formulation and discussion of premises (1) and (2).

IV.B.3

Evolution and the Problem of Evil

PAUL DRAPER

A short biographical sketch of Paul Draper appears before selection II.B.5. In the present article, Draper notes that traditionally the problem of evil has been, with few exceptions, the only atheological argument against the existence of God. He argues that the naturalistic account of evolution can provide a cogent alternative to theism and that by combining that with the problem of evil, one can begin to build a cumulative case against theism.

I. INTRODUCTION

Naturalism and theism are powerful and popular worldviews. They suggest very different conceptions of the nature of human beings, our relationship to the world, and our future. Though I hope that theism is true, I believe that it faces a number of evidential problems, problems that prevent my hope from becoming belief. In this paper I will examine two of those problems: evolution and evil. I will use certain known facts about the origin of complex life and the pattern of pain and pleasure in the world to construct a powerful *prima facie* case against theism.

By "theism" I mean the hypothesis[1] that God is the creator of the physical universe. I take the word "God" to be a title that, by definition, can be borne only by a perfect supernatural person. To claim that God is a "person" is to claim that God performs actions and has beliefs and purposes. "Supernatural" persons are not natural— they are neither a part nor a product of the physical universe—and yet they can affect natural objects. A "perfect" person is, among other things, perfect in power (omnipotent), perfect in knowledge

(omniscient), and perfect in moral goodness (morally perfect). While some have dismissed this conception of God as religiously insignificant, I am convinced that, for millions of Jews, Christians, and Muslims, factual belief in a perfect supernatural person is essential for making sense of their forms of worship. By "naturalism" I mean the hypothesis that the physical universe is a "closed system" in the sense that nothing that is neither a part nor a product of it can affect it. So naturalism entails the nonexistence of all supernatural beings, including the theistic God.

Arguments against theism can be divided into two main types. *Logical* arguments attempt to show that theism is either self-contradictory or logically inconsistent with some known fact. *Evidential* arguments attempt to show that certain known facts that are (at least so far as we can tell) consistent with theism nevertheless provide evidence against it.[2] The arguments in this paper will be evidential. I will show that certain known facts support the hypothesis of naturalism over the hypothesis of theism because we have considerably more reason to expect them to obtain on the assumption that naturalism is true than on the assumption that theism is true. This is a threat to theism because naturalism and theism are alternative hypotheses—they cannot both be true. Thus, if (after considering all of the evidence) naturalism turns out to be more probable than theism, then theism is probably false.

II. EVOLUTION

Ever since the publication of Darwin's *On the Origin of Species*, countless theologians, philosophers, and scientists have pointed out that evolution could be the means by which God has chosen to create human beings and the rest of the living world. This is thought to show that, while the truth of evolution does refute the biblical story of creation as told in the book of Genesis, it in no way threatens the more general belief that the universe was created by God. In other words, it provides no reason to doubt theism. The plausibility of this argument is reflected by the fact that many scientists are both evolutionists and theists. Commenting on this fact, Stephen Jay Gould says:

> Unless at least half my colleagues are dunces, there can be—on the most raw and direct empirical grounds—no conflict between science and religion. I know hundreds of scientists who share a conviction about the fact of evolution, and teach it in the same way. Among these people I note an entire spectrum of religious attitudes— from devout daily prayer and worship to resolute atheism. Either there's no correlation between religious belief and confidence in evolution—or else half these people are fools.[3]

What Gould neglects to mention is that many well-educated people, including many of Gould's colleagues on the irreligious end of the spectrum, reject theism precisely because they believe in evolution. For example, William B. Provine, a leading historian of science, maintains that those who retain their religious beliefs while accepting evolution "have to check [their] brains at the church-house door."[4]

So who is correct? Is it compatibilists like Gould and the liberal preacher Henry Ward Beecher, who claimed in 1885 that evolution "will change theology, but only to bring out the simple temple of God in clearer and more beautiful lines and proportions"[5]? Or is it incompatibilists like Provine and the fundamentalist preacher William Jennings Bryan, who once defined "theistic evolution" as "an anesthetic which deadens the patient's pain while atheism removes his religion"[6]? My own position, as my introductory remarks suggest, lies somewhere between the view that theistic evolution is a happy marriage and the view that it must end in divorce. I agree with the compatibilists that theism and evolution are logically consistent. What I disagree with is the compatibilist's inference from no inconsistency to no conflict. For while consistency implies that the truth of evolution does not disprove theism—that there is no good *logical* argument from evolution against theism just as there is no good logical argument from evil against theism—it does not imply that the truth of evolution is no evidence at all against theism. My position is that evolution is evidence favoring naturalism over theism. There is, in other words, a good *evidential* argument from evolution against theism.

By "evolution," I mean the conjunction of two theses. The first, which I will call "the genealogical thesis," asserts that evolution did in fact occur— complex life did evolve from relatively simple life. Specifically, it is the view that all multicellular organisms and all (relatively) complex unicellular organisms on earth (both present and past) are the (more or less) gradually modified descendents of a small number of relatively simple unicellular organisms. The second thesis, which I will call "the genetic thesis," addresses the issue of how evolution occurred. It states that all evolutionary change in populations of complex organisms either is or is the result of trans-generational genetic change (or, to be more precise, trans-generational change in nucleic acids). It is important to distinguish this claim about the mechanisms by which evolution takes place from the much more specific claim that natural selection operating on random genetic mutation is the principal mechanism driving evolutionary change (or the principal mechanism driving the evolutionary change that results in increased complexity). Let's call this more specific claim "Darwinism" and its conjunction with evolution "Darwinian evolution."

Many evolutionary arguments against theism appeal to Darwinian evolution rather than just to evolution. I believe that such arguments overestimate the strength of the evidence for Darwinism. Darwinism may be highly probable on the assumption that naturalism is true. But it is far less probable on the assumption that theism is true, because on theism it is a real possibility that God has guided evolution by directly causing various genetic changes to occur. Thus, any argument against theism that is based on the truth of Darwinism is at best question-begging. This is why my argument appeals only to evolution rather than to Darwinian evolution. It is my belief (which I won't defend here) that the evidence for evolution, unlike the evidence for Darwinian evolution, is overwhelming—so overwhelming that evolution can legitimately be taken as fact rather than mere theory for the purpose of arguing against theism.

The specific claim I wish to defend is the following:

> Antecedently, evolution is much more probable on the assumption that naturalism is true than on the assumption that theism is true.

By "antecedently" I mean "independent of the observations and testimony that together constitute the primary evidence upon which what we know about evolution, as well as the connection between pain and pleasure and reproductive success, is based." Thus, I intend to abstract from our information about selective breeding and other changes within populations of animals, as well as what we know about the geographical distribution of living things, homologies, the fossil record, genetic and biochemical evidence, imperfect adaptations, and vestigial organs. The additional abstraction concerning pain and pleasure is necessary because eventually I will combine my argument concerning evolution with an argument concerning the

systematic connection between pain and pleasure and reproductive success. The claim will be made that evolution and this connection are, taken together, antecedently much more likely on naturalism than on theism. One last point. No other abstraction from what we know is intended. For example, I do not intend to abstract from our knowledge that complex life of various forms exists nor from our knowledge that this life has not always existed. It is an interesting and difficult question whether these facts are evidence favoring theism over naturalism, but that issue is beyond the scope of this paper.

Let "T," "N," and "E" stand for theism, naturalism and evolution, let "Pr(p)" stand for the antecedent probability of p being true, and let "Pr(p/q)" stand for the antecedent probability of p being true on the assumption that q is true. Finally, let ">!" stand for "is much greater than." The claim I wish to defend can now be restated as follows:

$$Pr(E/N) \; >! \; Pr(E/T)$$

My strategy for proving this claim requires one more symbol and one more definition. Let "S" stand for special creationism, by which I mean the statement that some relatively complex living things did not descend from relatively simple single-celled organisms but rather were independently created by a supernatural person. (The use of the word "independently" here signifies not just that the creation in question violates genealogical continuity, but also that it involves the direct intervention of the deity in the natural order.) Since evolution entails that special creationism is false, some basic theorems of the probability calculus give us:

$Pr(E/N) \; >! \; Pr(E/T)$ if and only if $Pr(\sim S/N) \times Pr(E/\sim S\&N) \; >! \; Pr(\sim S/T) \times Pr(E/\sim S\&T)$[7]

My strategy for establishing that $Pr(E/N) \; >! \; Pr(E/T)$ will be to show both that $Pr(\sim S/N) \; >! \; Pr(\sim S/T)$ and that $Pr(E/\sim S\&N) \; >! \; Pr(E/\sim S\&T)$. In other words, I will show both that special creationism is antecedently much more likely to be false on naturalism than on theism and that, even on the assumption that special creationism is false, evolution is still antecedently at least as likely to be true on naturalism as it is on theism.

Since naturalism entails that no supernatural beings exist, it entails that special creationism is false. Thus, the falsity of special creationism is antecedently certain on naturalism: $Pr(\sim S/N) = 1$. But on theism special creationism might, for all we know antecedently, be true: $Pr(\sim S/T) < 1$. Thus, the falsity of special creationism is antecedently more probable on naturalism than on theism, which implies that the falsity of special creationism is some evidence favoring naturalism over theism—it raises the ratio of the probability of naturalism to the probability of theism. But how strong is this evidence? Is the falsity of special creationism *much* more probable on naturalism than on theism? I will show that $\sim S$ is at least twice as probable antecedently on naturalism as it is on theism, which implies that it at least doubles the ratio of the probability of naturalism to the probability of theism.[8] Since $Pr(\sim S/N) = 1$, my task is to show that $Pr(\sim S/T) \leq 1/2$, which is to say that $Pr(S/T) \geq 1/2$—that, independent of the evidence for evolution, special creationism is at least as likely as not on the assumption that theism is true. To defend this claim, I will first evaluate some antecedent reasons for believing that God, assuming he exists, did not create any complex living things independently. Then I will show that we have a very strong antecedent reason for believing that God, assuming he exists, did specially create.

At first glance, it seems that the evidence for evolution is the only strong reason theists have for believing that God is not a special creator (which is to say that we don't have any strong *antecedent* reasons for believing this). After all, for all we know antecedently, God might have chosen to create in a variety of different ways. For example, while he might have created life in a way consistent with genealogical continuity, he might also have created each species independently. Or he might have created certain basic types independently, allowing for evolutionary change, including change resulting in new species, within these types. Or he might have independently created

only a few species or even only a single species, humans perhaps. Antecedently—that is, independent of the evidence for evolution—it appears we have no reason at all to think that an omnipotent, omniscient, and morally perfect creator would prefer evolution or any other "naturalistic" approach to one of these forms of special creation.

Some theists, however, are quite confident on purely *a priori* grounds that God is not a special creator. According to Diogenes Allen and Howard J. Van Till, for example, special creationism was implausible even before the evidence for evolution was discovered, because it is an implication of God's "rationality" or his status as creator rather than as "member of the universe" that God "creates a universe with members that are coherently connected."[9] This coherence precludes God's intervening in the natural order and hence precludes any sort of special creation, including the creation of those first simple life forms from which all subsequent life has evolved. Thus, according to these theists, the only sort of explanations of natural phenomena that theistic scientists should look for are ones that are consistent with naturalism. In short, these theists are committed methodological naturalists.

I don't find these arguments at all convincing. What possible justification could be given for thinking that if God were the immediate cause of a natural event that would reduce God's status from creator to "member of the universe"? Also, what does God's rationality have to do with this? Perhaps the idea is that, just as a perfectly rational car manufacturer would produce a car that never needed its gas tank filled or its air filter replaced, a perfectly rational creator would make a universe that ran on its own. But such a car would be preferable because filling up with gas or replacing parts has a cost in terms of time, energy, and so on. An omnipotent and omniscient creator wouldn't have such worries. In general, what counts as a rational or perfect or defective universe depends on the creator's goals. What goal or plan of God would be better served by a universe in which God never intervenes? Of course, human freedom may place limitations on the amount and type of God's interventions. But it doesn't rule out special creation. For all we know, God may have some goal that is furthered by the laws of nature we have, but those laws are such that they will not by themselves produce the sort of complex life God wants. If this were the case, then God would independently create that life. Surely such intervention in the course of nature would not conflict with God's status as creator or with his rationality. Nor would it imply that the universe is in some way defective or inferior to universes in which God never intervenes.

Another theist who holds that we have antecedent reasons for believing that God would not perform any special creative acts is the philosopher Ernan McMullin. In response to Alvin Plantinga's defense of special creationism, McMullin says that "from the theological and philosophical standpoints, such intervention is, if anything, antecedently *improbable*."[10] McMullin claims that "the eloquent texts of *Genesis, Job, Isaiah,* and *Psalms*" support his position, because "The Creator whose powers are gradually revealed in these texts is omnipotent and all-wise, far beyond the reach of human reckoning. His Providence extends to all His creatures; they are all part of His single plan, only a fragment of which we know, and that darkly."[11] But how this is supposed to support his position is never explained. It seems to do the opposite, since any claim to know that God would never intervene in the natural order will be difficult to justify if we are as much in the dark about God's plans as these texts suggest.[12]

Incidentally, I find it interesting that, when confronted with arguments against theism based on the idea that it is antecedently unlikely that God would permit heinous evil, theistic philosophers are quick to suggest that, since God is omniscient, humans are not in a position to make such a judgment. Yet, if we are to believe Allen and Van Till (McMullin has his doubts), then humans are in a position to judge that it is antecedently unlikely that God would create any life forms independently! Personally, I find the claim that the torturing of innocent children is antecedently improbable on theism vastly more plausible than

the claim that special creationism is antecedently improbable on theism.

The problem with the theistic objections to special creationism considered so far is that they all involve *a priori* theological or philosophical speculation, the direction of which is influenced far too much by the conclusion desired.[13] Indeed, these attempts to make special creation seem incompatible with theism are no more objective and no more plausible than William B. Provine's attempt to make evolution seem incompatible with theism. While Allen, Van Till, and McMullin claim that God would never intervene in nature to create life, Provine claims that the idea of a God who "works through the laws of nature" is "worthless" and "equivalent to atheism."[14] How convenient!

A more serious attempt to show that special creationism is antecedently unlikely on theism is a posteriori in nature. We know by past experience that God, if he exists, has at least latent deistic tendencies. Teleology was, after all, eliminated from the physical sciences well before Darwin wrote *On the Origin of Species*. And even independent of the evidence for evolution there is considerable evidence that various biological processes work quite well without divine intervention. In general, even independent of the evidence on which evolution is based, the history of science is a history of success for naturalistic explanations and failure for supernaturalistic ones. Thus, we have a good antecedent *a posteriori* reason to believe that, assuming theism is true, God does not intervene in nature.

I believe that the past success of naturalistic science does provide some reason for theists to believe that God is not a special creator. But it is easy to overestimate the strength of this reason, especially for intellectual theists who must admit to living in a "post-mythological" era or else risk being held personally responsible for the plight of Galileo. But putting scientific propaganda aside, it is important to remember how little we actually know about the causal history of the universe! Were it not for the evidence for evolution, our sample of successful naturalistic explanations seems to me to be much too small to justify great confidence in the claim that, *assuming God exists*, God is not a special creator. Of course, it is worth mentioning that, if I am underestimating how successful the search for naturalistic explanations has been, then theists hardly escape unscathed. For if the search for such explanations has been so successful that any supernaturalistic explanation of a natural phenomenon is implausible even on the assumption that theism is true, then that would be powerful evidence against theism. For such extraordinary success would be antecedently much more likely on naturalism—which entails that all supernaturalistic explanations are false—than it would on theism.

More to the point, however, I believe theists have a very strong antecedent reason for believing that God did create at least some complex life independently. For the division between conscious and nonconscious life is enormously significant if theism is true. Theism implies an extreme metaphysical dualism—a mind existed prior to the physical world and was responsible for its existence. Thus, on the assumption that theism is true, it is antecedently likely that minds are fundamentally nonphysical entities and hence that conscious life is fundamentally different from nonconscious life. But this in turn makes it likely that conscious living things are not just the genetically modified descendents of nonconscious living things—that conscious life was created independently. And since special creationism is defined as the position that at least some complex life was created independently, it follows that, on the assumption that theism is true, it is antecedently likely that special creationism is true.

The dualism inherent in theism may explain why so many theists were drawn to the idea of special creationism before (and in many cases even after) the evidence for evolution was discovered. For this dualism supports a dualistic view of human nature—a view that must have made the idea that we are the effect of altering the nucleic acids of single-celled organisms seem ludicrous. Offspring don't have to be identical to their parents, but surely genetic change can't result in fundamental metaphysical lines being crossed! Thus, even if we know by past experience that God, assuming he or she exists, generally doesn't intervene in nature, the sort

of metaphysics presupposed by theism makes it antecedently likely that God did intervene in the physical world in order to create a mental world within it. So it's hardly surprising that, before Darwin, many theists were special creationists. They had a good reason and we have a good *antecedent* reason to believe that God, assuming he or she exists, performed at least one special creative act. Thus, $\Pr(S/T) \geq 1/2$. And this implies that the falsity of special creationism is at least twice as probable antecedently on naturalism as it is on theism: $\Pr(\sim S/N) \geq 2 \times \Pr(\sim S/T)$.

Recall that, in order to show that $\Pr(E/N) >! \Pr(E/T)$, it is sufficient to show first that $\Pr(\sim S/N) >! \Pr(\sim S/T)$ and second that $\Pr(E/\sim S\&N) \geq \Pr(E/\sim S\&T)$. I have completed the first of these two tasks. Turning to the second, we are now assuming that special creationism is false and asking how likely evolution is on naturalism and on theism. Of course, naturalism entails that special creationism is false, so the denial of special creationism conjoined with naturalism ($\sim S\&N$) just is naturalism (N). I will call the denial of special creationism conjoined with theism ($\sim S\&T$) "regular theism." So my task is to show that evolution is antecedently at least as probable on naturalism as it is on regular theism.

It is important to recognize that the probabilities in question are to be assessed relative to the background knowledge that various complex life forms do exist. Thus, the issue is not whether complex life together with the evolutionary mechanisms that produce it are more surprising on theism or on naturalism. (Again, whether or not there is a good anthropic design argument supporting theism is beyond the scope of this paper.) Given that complex life exists, what makes evolution so likely on naturalism is the lack of plausible naturalistic alternatives to evolution. On naturalism, it is antecedently much more likely that all complex organisms descended from a small number of relatively simple organisms than that complex life descended from a large number of relatively simple single-celled organisms all of which arose independently from nonliving matter or that complex life arose directly from nonliving matter. Furthermore, given the genealogical thesis, it is antecedently likely on naturalism that all evolutionary change in complex life is or results from one basic sort of change like genetic change. On regular theism, alternatives to evolution are somewhat more likely, simply because there is less reason to assume that the complex must arise from the simple. When one starts with omnipotence and omniscience, so much is possible!

Even if the regular theist grants that these considerations favor naturalism, she might counter that it has never been proven that naturalistic evolution is biologically possible. Perhaps evolution could not have produced complex life without supernatural assistance. For example, it might be argued that, without some intelligent being guiding genetic change, such magnificent ordered systems as the human eye would never have evolved. The stronger the evidence for this, the lower the antecedent probability of evolution on naturalism. I do not believe, however, that the evidence for this is very strong. Admittedly, no one can describe in detail exactly how the eye or any other complex organic system could have come about without supernatural assistance. And it's hard to see how anyone could prove that evolution could produce complex life in a naturalistic universe. But neither has anyone provided good reason for thinking that it couldn't either. (Some special creationists have tried, but their arguments are very weak.[15]) This is not to say that there are no real difficulties for naturalistic evolution. (For example, it's notoriously difficult to explain how sexual reproduction evolved.) It's just to say that no one has given a good reason to believe that naturalistic solutions to these problems will not be found. Indeed, the fact that plausible solutions have been found to some of these problems (e.g., the problem of altruistic behavior) gives the naturalist reason for optimism. So any advantage that the problems faced by naturalistic evolution give to regular theism is more than offset by the considerations favoring naturalism mentioned above. All things considered, then, the modest conclusion that evolution is at least as probable antecedently on naturalism as it is on regular theism is

justified. Therefore, since the falsity of special creationism is antecedently much more probable on naturalism than on theism, it follows for the reasons explained earlier that evolution is antecedently much more probable on naturalism than on theism.

III. PAIN AND PLEASURE

It is true by definition that a morally perfect God would permit an instance of pain only if he or she had a morally sufficient reason to do so. (By "pain" I mean any suffering, physical or mental.) Thus, the "logical" problem of pain is the problem of whether or not God's being both omnipotent and omniscient is logically compatible with God's having a morally sufficient reason to permit all of the suffering in the world. No one has been able to demonstrate an incompatibility because not even an omnipotent being can do the logically impossible and it might, for all we know or can prove, be logically impossible to bring about certain important goods without at least risking the existence of the suffering we find in our world. So demonstrative logical arguments from pain have been unsuccessful. And nondemonstrative or probabilistic logical arguments from pain have been challenged on the grounds that they involve questionable inductive generalizations, questionable inferences from there being no *known* morally sufficient reasons for an omnipotent and omniscient being to permit certain instances of suffering to their probably being no such morally sufficient reasons. But these discussions of the logical problem of pain leave unsettled the issue of whether or not the suffering in our world is evidence against theism or evidence favoring naturalism over theism. In other words, the failure of logical arguments from evil, including probabilistic ones, does not preclude a successful evidential argument from evil.

I do not, however, wish to consider suffering in isolation. Instead, I will address the issue of whether the pattern of both pain and pleasure in the world is evidence favoring naturalism over theism. The more common strategy of focusing only on evil, indeed only on a few particularly heinous evils, has its advantages. I choose not to pursue this strategy because the theist might counter such an argument by pointing out a few particularly glorious goods and plausibly claiming that they are equally strong evidence favoring theism over naturalism. So my argument will be based on both pain and pleasure. There may, of course, be other intrinsic evils and intrinsic goods besides pain and pleasure, but the issue of whether or not there are, and whether or not, if there are, their existence is evidence against theism, will not be addressed in this paper.

There are many facts about pain and pleasure that might provide the resources for an evidential argument against theism. Because I wish to explore how our knowledge of evolution affects the problem of evil, I will focus on the fact that much of the pain and pleasure we find in the world is systematically connected (in a variety of often complex ways) to reproductive success. For example, it is no accident that we find a warm fire on a cold night pleasurable and lying naked in a snowbank painful. Maintaining a constant body temperature increases our chances of (temporary) survival and thereby increases our chances of reproducing. Of course, the connections are not all this obvious or this direct. For example, children enjoy playing, which promotes the development of various physical, social, and intellectual skills, which in turn increases children's chances of surviving and reproducing. Even less obviously and less directly, adults find play pleasurable (though typically not as much as children do), which may or may not promote reproductive success, but which results from our capacity to enjoy play as children, which, as we have seen, does promote reproductive success. I could give countless other examples, but the connection between pain and pleasure and reproductive success and the systematic nature of that connection is so striking that additional examples aren't really needed. Instead, I will now turn to the task of showing that, antecedently, this connection is much more probable on evolutionary naturalism than it is on evolutionary theism. I will offer a two-part argument for this position, and then reply to two objections.

The first part of my argument appeals to natural selection. I suggested earlier that Darwinism is much more likely to be true if evolutionary naturalism is true than if evolutionary theism is true. Allow me to explain why. Darwinism is likely on evolutionary naturalism both because it explains the increase in the complexity of life over time better than other naturalistic mechanisms and, most importantly for our purposes, it solves an explanatory problem for naturalism: the problem of explaining teleological or "means–end" order in organic systems. Since evolutionary theism can explain teleological order in terms of God's conscious purposes, it wouldn't be at all surprising on theism if the principal mechanisms driving evolution themselves displayed teleological order—if, for example, organisms had built-in mechanisms that would produce precisely those genetic changes needed to solve a problem arising because of some environmental change. (Such mechanisms would have made William Paley a happy evolutionist!) On naturalism, natural selection is just the sort of process one would expect to drive evolution: a simple "blind" process that can explain the extremely complex teleological order in the living world without itself displaying such order. Notice also that, contrary to popular belief, natural selection does not generally promote the good of individual animals. Variations that result in reproductive success will be favored, regardless of the other consequences—good or bad—of the variation. For example, if walking upright gave our distant ancestors a reproductive advantage (e.g., by allowing them to carry tools while they walked), then this trait was selected despite the foot, back, heart, and numerous other ailments that resulted from it. Further, natural selection requires competition for scarce resources and thus entails that many living things will not flourish. So the claim that natural selection is the principal mechanism driving evolutionary change is much more probable on evolutionary naturalism than on evolutionary theism.

Of course, if natural selection is the principal mechanism driving evolution, then it is likely on evolutionary naturalism that it played a significant role in the evolution of pain and pleasure and so it is likely on evolutionary naturalism that pain and pleasure will, like anything produced by natural selection, be systematically connected to reproductive success. Thus, the fact that natural selection is antecedently much more likely to have governed the evolution of pain and pleasure if evolutionary naturalism is true than if evolutionary theism is true supports my position that the systematic connection between reproductive success and the pain and pleasure we find in the world is antecedently much more likely on evolutionary naturalism than on evolutionary theism.

This position is further supported by our antecedent knowledge that many other parts of organic systems are systematically connected to reproductive success. This gives us much more reason to believe that pain and pleasure will also be so connected if we assume that evolutionary naturalism is true than if we assume that evolutionary theism is true. To see why, consider the inductive inference from a sample consisting of other physical and mental parts of organic systems that are systematically connected to reproductive success to the conclusion that pain and pleasure are also systematically connected to reproductive success. Although a good number of parts of organic systems lack such a connection, this inference is potentially quite strong given the suitability of pain and pleasure for promoting reproductive success. But the assumption that evolutionary theism is true undermines this inference, while the assumption that evolutionary naturalism is true does not. To see why, notice that this inference is an inductive inference from a sample to another member of a population, and the strength of any such inference depends on how much reason one has to believe that this other member is relevantly different from the members of the sample. Now pain and pleasure are strikingly different from other parts of organic systems in one way: They have a specific sort of moral significance that other parts lack. (Other parts of organic systems may have moral significance, but not of the same sort.) But is this a relevant difference? We have much more reason to believe it is on the assumption that evolutionary theism is true than on the assumption that evolutionary naturalism is true.

For the biological goal of reproductive success does not provide an omnipotent omniscient creator with a morally sufficient reason for permitting humans and animals to suffer in the ways they do or for limiting their pleasure to the sorts and amounts we find. Thus, on evolutionary theism, pain and pleasure would be systematically connected to the biological goal of reproductive success only if this goal and some unknown justifying moral goal happened to coincide in such a way that each could be simultaneously satisfied. Such a coincidence is (to say the least) antecedently far from certain. So on the assumption that evolutionary theism is true, the inference to the conclusion that pain and pleasure are systematically connected to reproductive success from the premise that other parts of organic systems are so connected is very weak. This inference is much stronger on the assumption that evolutionary naturalism is true because evolutionary naturalism entails nothing that would undermine the inference—on evolutionary naturalism the moral significance of pain and pleasure provides no antecedent reason at all to doubt that they will resemble other parts of organic systems by being systematically connected to reproductive success. Therefore, our antecedent knowledge that pain and pleasure have a certain sort of moral significance adds further support to my position that the systematic connection between pain and pleasure and reproductive success is antecedently much more probable on evolutionary naturalism than on evolutionary theism.

One might object that my argument ignores the many instances of pain and pleasure that are, so far as we can tell, disconnected from the biological goal of reproductive success. For example, some aesthetic pleasures seem to have at most a very remote connection to reproductive success. But neither the existence of such pain and pleasure, nor the fact that, in general, such pain and pleasure is more common in animals that are psychologically complex, is at all surprising on evolutionary naturalism. For the greater the complexity of a system, the more likely that some of its characteristics will be epiphenomenal. Also, much biologically gratuitous pain and pleasure is pathological—it results from the failure of an organic system to function properly. And the existence of this sort of pain and pleasure is also unsurprising on evolutionary naturalism. So on evolutionary naturalism, what we know about biologically gratuitous pain and pleasure is not surprising, while on evolutionary theism, the excess pleasure is perhaps to be expected, but this advantage is offset by the limited amount of such pleasure, by the existence of biologically gratuitous pain, and by the fact that a significant amount of biologically gratuitous pleasure and pain is pathological.

One might also object that theodicies undermine my argument; for theodicies make certain facts about pain antecedently more likely than they would otherwise be. The problem with existing theodicies, however, is that they explain certain facts at the price of making others even more mysterious. That is, they make certain facts more likely only by making others less likely. For example, if one of God's reasons for permitting pain is to punish sinners, then why do the innocent suffer as much as the guilty? Or, if we assume that God wants to use pain to build moral character, then pain (and pleasure) that is demoralizing becomes even more surprising. If, instead of focusing on a few isolated cases, one looks at the overall pattern of pain and pleasure in the world, one cannot help but be struck by its apparent moral randomness. Pain and pleasure do not systematically promote justice or moral virtue. Nor are moral agents treated all that differently from nonmoral agents. Nonhuman animals suffer in many of the ways humans suffer (the more similar the animal, the more similar the suffering), despite the fact that such suffering cannot play a moral role in their lives, since they are not moral agents.

All of these facts, which might be summed up by saying that pain and pleasure do not systematically promote any discernible moral ends, are exactly what one would expect on evolutionary naturalism. For on evolutionary naturalism, the causes of good and evil are morally indifferent. Thus, on the assumption that evolutionary naturalism is true, it would be surprising in the extreme if pain and pleasure appeared to be anything but morally random. But a discernible moral pattern would be less surprising on theism even if, given the cognitive distance between humans and an omniscient being, it should not be expected. Notice that I am not claiming that the apparent moral randomness of pain and pleasure is antecedently unlikely on evolutionary theism. I'm just claiming that it is antecedently less likely on evolutionary theism than on evolutionary naturalism. And it seems to me that this is obvious. But that means that this apparent randomness adds to the evidence favoring evolutionary naturalism over evolutionary theism. It may not add a lot, but it certainly offsets any advantage evolutionary theism has as a result of the moral roles that pain and pleasure admittedly do play in human lives.

IV. CONCLUSION

I have argued both that evolution is antecedently much more probable on naturalism than on theism and that the systematic connection between pain, as well as pleasure, and reproductive success is antecedently much more probable on evolutionary naturalism than on evolutionary theism. This entails that the conjunction of evolution and the statement that pain and pleasure are systematically connected to reproductive success is antecedently very much more probable on naturalism than on theism. And since neither the truth nor falsity of naturalism or theism is certain, it follows that this conjunction substantially raises the ratio of the probability of naturalism to the probability of theism. Of course, if naturalism were far less plausible than theism (or if it were compatible with theism), then this sort of evidence would be worthless. But naturalism is a very serious alternative to theism. Neither evolution nor anything about pain and pleasure is built into it in an *ad hoc* way. (It is not as if I were claiming, for example, that *evolution* is antecedently more probable on *evolutionary* naturalism than on theism.) Also, naturalism doesn't deny the existence of all nonnatural beings—it only denies the existence of supernatural beings. And surely this is no less plausible than asserting the existence of a very specific sort of supernatural being. So naturalism is at least as plausible as theism.

Therefore, it follows from my arguments concerning evil and evolution that, other evidence held equal, naturalism is very much more probable than theism. And since naturalism and theism are alternative hypotheses—they cannot both be true—this implies that, other evidence held equal, it is highly likely that theism is false. So the evidence discussed in this paper provides a powerful *prima facie* case against theism. To put it another way, if one looks only at the evidence discussed here—evolution, the ability of natural selection to explain complex biological order without purpose, the systematic connection between pain and pleasure and reproductive success, and the apparent moral randomness of pain and pleasure—then Hume's words ring true: "The whole presents nothing but the idea of a blind nature, impregnated by a great vivifying principle, and pouring forth from her lap, without discernment or parental care, her maimed and abortive children.[16,17]

APPENDIX

My argument in this paper is based on the following two theorems of the probability calculus:

$$A: \frac{\Pr(N/E\&P)}{\Pr(T/E\&P)} = \frac{\Pr(N)}{\Pr(T)} \times \frac{\Pr(E\&P/N)}{\Pr(E\&P/T)}$$

$$B: \frac{\Pr(E\&P/N)}{\Pr(E\&P/T)} = \frac{\Pr(E/N)}{\Pr(E/T)} \times \frac{\Pr(P/E\&N)}{\Pr(P/E\&T)}$$

In using these two equations, I assume that neither naturalism nor theism is certainly true or certainly false.

$\Pr(N/E\&P)$ is the antecedent probability of naturalism given the conjunction of evolution and the statement (P) that pain and pleasure are systematically connected to reproductive success. In other words, it is the probability of naturalism, all things considered. (I assume here that the "given E&P" puts back everything of significance that the "antecedent" takes out.) Similarly, $\Pr(T/E\&P)$ is

the probability of theism, all things considered. So the left side of equation A is the ratio of the probability of naturalism to the probability of theism. If this ratio is greater than 1, then naturalism is more probable than theism and hence theism is probably false.

Now consider the right side of equation A. The main purpose of my paper was to evaluate the second ratio here: The ratio of the antecedent probability of evolution conjoined with P given naturalism to the antecedent probability of this conjunction given theism. This ratio was evaluated using equation B. The first of the two ratios on the right side of B is the ratio of the antecedent probability of evolution given naturalism to the antecedent probability of evolution given theism. And the second is the ratio of the antecedent probability of P given evolutionary naturalism to the antecedent probability of P given evolutionary theism. I argued that each of these two ratios is much greater than 1. From this it follows (using equation B) that the ratio of $\Pr(E\&P/N)$ to $\Pr(E\&P/T)$ is very much greater than 1.

Now look at the first ratio on the right side of equation A. $\Pr(N)$ is the antecedent probability of naturalism. In other words, it is the probability of naturalism independent of our knowledge of E&P. And $\Pr(T)$ is the probability of theism independent of our knowledge of E&P. So the first ratio on the right side of equation A depends on the plausibility of naturalism and theism as well as on other evidence (propositional or nonpropositional) for and against naturalism and theism (e.g., the existence of life on earth, the success of science, religious experiences, immorality, etc.). I argued very briefly that considerations of plausibility do not give us any reason to believe that this ratio is less than one. But I did not, of course, evaluate all of the other relevant evidence for and against theism and naturalism. So I did not come to any conclusion about this first ratio. This is why my case against theism is a *prima facie* one. I am entitled to conclude only that, other evidence held equal, the ratio on the left side of equation A is very much greater than 1. And this implies that, other evidence held equal, it is highly probable that theism is false.

The following summarizes my argument:

(1) Evolution is antecedently much more probable on the assumption that naturalism is true than on the assumption that theism is true [i.e., Pr(E/N) >! Pr(E/T)].

(2) The statement that pain and pleasure are systematically connected to reproductive success is antecedently much more probable on the assumption that evolutionary naturalism is true than on the assumption that evolutionary theism is true [i.e., Pr(P/E&N) >! Pr(P/E&T)].

(3) Therefore, evolution conjoined with this statement about pain and pleasure is antecedently very much more probable on the assumption that naturalism is true than on the assumption that theism is true [i.e., Pr(E&P/N) >!! Pr(E&P/T)]. (From 1 and 2)

(4) Naturalism is at least as plausible as theism [i.e., other evidence held equal, Pr(N) ≥ Pr(T)].

(5) Therefore, other evidence held equal, naturalism is very much more probable than theism [i.e., other evidence held equal, Pr(N/E&P) >!! Pr(T/E&P)]. (From 3 and 4)

(6) Naturalism entails that theism is false.

(7) Therefore, other evidence held equal, it is highly probable that theism is false [i.e., other evidence held equal, Pr(T/E&P) <!! 1/2. (From 5 and 6)

NOTES

1. By "hypothesis" I mean a statement that is neither certainly true nor certainly false.

2. It is worth noting that, although "probabilistic" arguments from evil are usually classified as evidential, many such arguments are logical—they attempt to show that theism is probably inconsistent with some known fact about evil.

3. "Darwinism Defined: The Difference Between Fact and Theory," *Discover*, Jan. 1987, p. 70. Quoted in James Rachels, *Created from Animals: The Moral Implications of Darwinism* (Oxford University Press, 1990), p. 100.

4. Quoted in Phillip E. Johnson, *Darwin on Trial* (InterVarsity Press, 1993), p. 126.

5. "The Two Revelations," in Gail Kennedy, *Evolution and Religion* (D. C. Heath and Company, 1957), p. 20. Also quoted on p. xiv.

6. Quoted in Kennedy, p. xiv.

7. Proof: Since E entails S, E is logically equivalent to ~S&E. Thus, since it is a theorem of the probability calculus that logically equivalent statements are equally probable, it follows that Pr(E/N) >! Pr(E/T) if and only if Pr(~S&E/N) >! Pr(~S&E/T). But it is also a theorem of the probability calculus that Pr(p&q/r) = Pr(p/r) × Pr(q/p&r). Therefore, Pr(E/N) >! Pr(E/T) if and only if Pr(~S/N) × Pr(E/~S&N) >! Pr(~S/T) × Pr(E/~S&T).

8. Of course, whether this strong evidence is also significant depends on what the ratio of the probability of naturalism to the probability of theism is prior to considering the fact that special creationism is false. If it is extremely high or low, then the falsity of special creationism will not be significant evidence favoring naturalism. If, on the other hand, the other evidence is nearly balanced and both hypotheses are plausible, then this evidence will be significant. For example, if theism starts out twice as probable as naturalism, then the two hypotheses will end up being equally probable.

9. Diogenes Allen, *Christian Belief in a Postmodern World* (Westminster: John Knox Press, 1989), p. 59. Quoted with approval in Howard J. Van Till, "When Faith and Reason Cooperate," *Christian Scholar's Review* 21.1 (1991), p. 43.

10. "Plantinga's Defense of Special Creation," *Christian Scholar's Review* 21.1 (1991), p. 74. Plantinga refers to McMullin's position as "semideism." McMullin complains that this terminology is loaded, yet he describes his own position as believing in "the integrity of the natural order." It would seem then that Christians have a dilemma. No good Christian wants to be called a "deist," but no good Christian would want to deny that God's creation has "integrity"!

11. Ibid., p. 75.

12. For additional criticisms of the positions of Van Till and McMullin, see Alvin Plantinga, "Evolution, Neutrality, and Antecedent Probability: A Reply to Van Till and McMullin," *Christian Scholar's Review* 21.1 (1991), pp. 80–109.

13. Cf. Plantinga, p. 100.

14. Review of "Trial and Error: The American Controversy over Creation and Evolution," *Academe* 73.1 (1987), 50–52. Quoted in McMullin, p. 58.

15. For an excellent defense of evolution against special creationist objections, see Philip Kitcher,

Abusing Science: The Case Against Creationism (Cambridge, Massachusetts: The MIT Press, 1982).

16. *Dialogues Concerning Natural Religion*, ed. Norman Kemp Smith (Macmillan Publishing Co., 1947), p. 211.

17. I am grateful to Kai Draper, Daniel Howard Snyder, James Keller, George Mavrodes, Wes Morriston, William L. Rowe, Michael Tooley, and Stephen J. Wykstra for helpful comments on earlier versions of this paper.

IV.C. REPLIES

Having now considered various different formulations of the problem of evil, we turn to replies.

In our first reading, Alvin Plantinga rebuts J. L. Mackie's defense of the "logical problem of evil." He argues that Mackie is wrong in thinking that the existence of evil is inconsistent with the existence of God, and he also argues that Mackie is wrong in thinking that every *possible* world is *creatable*. Unlike Leibniz, Plantinga is offering merely a defense rather than a theodicy. (See the main introduction to Part IV for the distinction between "defense" and "theodicy.") Central to Plantinga's defense are the following three ideas: (a) a perfectly good being might have morally sufficient reason to permit evil, (b) the value of free will might provide such a morally sufficient reason if it is impossible for God to guarantee that a world containing free creatures would be free from evil, and (c) for all we know, it *is* impossible for God to guarantee that a world containing free creatures would be free from evil. In defense of (c), Plantinga sets forth the hypothesis of *transworld depravity*. Roughly, to suffer from transworld depravity is to be such that, no matter what total creative act God had performed, if God had created you and left you free, you would freely have done something wrong. According to Plantinga, for all we know everyone in the actual world suffers from transworld depravity. If that's so, then no matter what creative act God had performed, if he had created just those creatures who in fact exist, the world would have contained moral evil. Thus, though there are *possible* worlds in which everyone freely does what is right, those worlds are not *creatable*. They are not creatable because, in effect, free creatures *cooperate* with God in determining what sort of world will exist; and (given the hypothesis of transworld depravity) no matter what God had done, his creatures would not have cooperated in such a way as to keep the world free from evil.

Our second reading, John Hick's "Evil and Soul-Making," is an example of a theodicy that is based on the free will defense. Hick distinguishes between two different types of theodicy. The Augustinian theodicy starts with the idea that God created humans without sin and set them in a sinless paradise and goes on to maintain that humanity fell into sin *through the misuse of free will*. So we are to blame, not God, for the existence of suffering in the world. God's grace will save some of us, but others will perish everlastingly. In this division, God's goodness is manifested, for his mercy redeems some and his justice is served on the rest. On the other hand, the Irenaean theodicy, stemming from Irenaeus (AD 120 – 202), views Adam not as a free agent rebelling against God, but as more akin to a very small child. The fall is humanity's first faulty step in the direction of freedom. God is still working with humanity in order to bring it from undeveloped life (*bios*) to a state of self-realization in divine love, spiritual life (*zoe*). This life is viewed as the "vale of soul-making." Spiritual development requires obstacles and the opportunity to fail as well as to succeed. Hick declares that those who are opposed to the challenge that our freedom grants us are looking for a hedonistic paradise in which every desire is gratified and we are treated by God as pet animals rather than autonomous agents. On the other hand, those who accept the challenge of freedom consider themselves to be coworkers with God in bringing forth the kingdom of God.

In our third selection, we revisit a line of response that came up in the selection by Leibniz in Section IV.A. As noted earlier, Leibniz regarded the fall of Adam as a "blessed fault" because it led to the incarnation of the Son of God. In our third selection, Alvin Plantinga takes up the same idea. Perhaps, Plantinga suggests, what justifies God in permitting the evils in our world is just that (a) our world (or something worse) is what would have resulted if God permitted humanity to fall into sin, (b) the incarnation of the Son of God and the subsequent redemption of humanity would not have happened had humanity not fallen into sin, and (c) any possible world which includes the Son of God becoming incarnate for the redemption of humanity is better, overall, than any world which doesn't include those events. If that is right, then, contrary to what is suggested by "free will theodicies" (and defenses), it is not the value of human freedom on its own that justifies God in permitting the evils we find in our world, but rather the value of the incarnation and atonement (perhaps in conjunction with the value of free will).

As should be clear by now, the typical strategy in both defense and theodicy is to look for *goods* that might somehow justify the *evil* of human suffering. The final three readings in this section each in their own way offer correctives to this trend. In the fourth selection, Eleonore Stump notes that a great deal of human suffering comes from unfulfilled "desires of the heart"—desires that matter to us a great deal but whose satisfaction isn't strictly necessary for our flourishing as human beings. Traditional theodicies fail to accord sufficient value to this sort of suffering—as if it is rather easily outweighed, offset, or defeated by global goods (like the value of freedom) or by "replacement goods" (like a new family, to replace the old one that was lost in some catastrophe). To the extent that they do fail in this way, she argues, such theodicies are, at best, incomplete.

In a somewhat similar vein, Marilyn Adams argues that traditional responses to the problem of evil do not deal adequately with *horrendous evil*, where horrendous evil is (roughly) evil that we might intuitively regard as life-wrecking. The problem, she argues, is that, when it comes to accounting for horrendous evils, the standard responses to the problem of evil fail to accord these evils the weight they deserve, or they fail in other ways to respect our moral intuitions or our intuitions about value. She then goes on to sketch a way of responding to the problem of evil that does deal adequately with horrors. At the heart of her response is the idea that horrors in our lives are, or can be, defeated by a kind of intimacy and identification with God which is made possible by the incarnation.

Finally, in our sixth reading, Laura Waddell Ekstrom explores the idea that, far from constituting evidence *against* the existence of God (as the atheologians would have it), suffering may in fact be an avenue *to* knowledge of God. Finding affinities between her own (partial) theodicy and responses to the problem of evil offered by Eleonore Stump and Marilyn Adams, Ekstrom argues that some instances of suffering satisfy standard conceptions of religious experience and serve as means of intimacy with God.

IV.C.1

The Free Will Defense

ALVIN PLANTINGA

A brief biographical sketch of Alvin Plantinga appears before selection I.B.8. In the present selection, Plantinga argues that Mackie and other atheologians (those who argue against the existence of God) are mistaken in thinking that the existence of evil is inconsistent with the existence of a perfectly good and powerful God.

2. DOES THE THEIST CONTRADICT HIMSELF?

In a widely discussed piece entitled "Evil and Omnipotence" John Mackie makes this claim:

I think, however, that a more telling criticism can be made by way of the traditional problem of evil. Here it can be shown, not that religious beliefs lack rational support, but that they are positively irrational, that the several parts of the

From *God, Freedom, and Evil* by Alvin Plantinga (Harper & Row, 1974). Reprinted by permission of the author. Footnotes edited.

essential theological doctrine are *inconsistent* with one another....[1]

Is Mackie right? Does the theist contradict himself? But we must ask a prior question: just what is being claimed here? That theistic belief contains an inconsistency or contradiction, of course. But what, exactly, is an inconsistency or contradiction? There are several kinds. An *explicit* contradiction is a *proposition* of a certain sort—a conjunctive proposition, one conjunct of which is the denial or negation of the other conjunct. For example:

> Paul is a good tennis player, and it's false that Paul is a good tennis player.

(People seldom assert explicit contradictions.) Is Mackie charging the theist with accepting such a contradiction? Presumably not; what he says is

> In its simplest form the problem is this: God is omnipotent; God is wholly good; yet evil exists. There seems to be some contradiction between these three propositions, so that if any two of them were true the third would be false. But at the same time all three are essential parts of most theological positions; the theologian, it seems, at once *must* adhere and *cannot consistently* adhere to all three.

According to Mackie, then, the theist accepts a group or set of three propositions; this set is inconsistent. Its members, of course, are

(1)   God is omnipotent

(2)   God is wholly good

and

(3)   Evil exists.

Call this set *A*; the claim is that *A* is an inconsistent set. But what is it for a *set* to be inconsistent or contradictory? Following our definition of an explicit contradiction, we might say that a set of propositions is explicitly contradictory if one of the members is the denial or negation of another member. But then, of course, it is evident that the set we are discussing is not explicitly contradictory; the denials of (1), (2), and (3), respectively, are

(1′)   God is not omnipotent (or it's false that God is omnipotent)

(2′)   God is not wholly good

and

(3′)   There is no evil

none of which is in set *A*.

Of course many sets are pretty clearly contradictory, in an important way, but not explicitly contradictory. For example, set *B*:

(4)   If all men are mortal, then Socrates is mortal

(5)   All men are mortal

(6)   Socrates is not mortal.

This set is not explicitly contradictory; yet surely *some* significant sense of that term applies to it. What is important here is that by using only the rules of ordinary logic—the laws of propositional logic and quantification theory found in any introductory text on the subject—we can deduce an explicit contradiction from the set. Or to put it differently, we can use the laws of logic to deduce a proposition from the set, which proposition, when added to the set, yields a new set that is explicitly contradictory. For by using the law *modus ponens* (if *p*, then *q*; *p*; therefore *q*) we can deduce

(7)   Socrates is mortal

from (4) and (5). The result of adding (7) to *B* is the set {(4), (5), (6), (7)}. This set, of course, is explicitly contradictory in that (6) is the denial of (7). We might say that any set which shares this characteristic with set *B* is *formally* contradictory. So a formally contradictory set is one from whose members an explicit contradiction can be deduced by the laws of logic. Is Mackie claiming that set *A* is formally contradictory?

If he is, he's wrong. No laws of logic permit us to deduce the denial of one of the propositions in *A* from the other members. Set *A* isn't formally contradictory either.

But there is still another way in which a set of propositions can be contradictory or inconsistent. Consider set *C*, whose members are

(8)   George is older than Paul

(9)   Paul is older than Nick

and

(10)   George is not older than Nick.

This set is neither explicitly nor formally contradictory; we can't, just by using the laws of logic, deduce the denial of any of these propositions from the others. And yet there is a good sense in which it is inconsistent or contradictory. For clearly it is *not possible* that its three members all be true. It is *necessarily true* that

(11)   If George is older than Paul, and Paul is older than Nick, then George is older than Nick.

And if we add (11) to set *C*, we get a set that is formally contradictory; (8), (9), and (11) yield, by the laws of ordinary logic, the denial of (10).

I said that (11) is *necessarily true*; but what does *that* mean? Of course we might say that a proposition is necessarily true if it is impossible that it be false, or if its negation is not possibly true. This would be to explain necessity in terms of possibility. Chances are, however, that anyone who does not know what necessity is, will be equally at a loss about possibility; the explanation is not likely to be very successful. Perhaps all we can do by way of explanation is to give some examples and hope for the best. In the first place many propositions can be established by the laws of logic alone—for example,

(12)   If all men are mortal and Socrates is a man, then Socrates is mortal.

Such propositions are truths of logic; and all of them are necessary in the sense of question. But truths of arithmetic and mathematics generally are also necessarily true. Still further, there is a host of propositions that are neither truths of logic nor truths of mathematics but are nonetheless necessarily true; (11) would be an example, as well as

(13)   Nobody is taller than himself

(14)   Red is a color

(15)   No numbers are persons

(16)   No prime number is a prime minister

and

(17)   Bachelors are unmarried.

So here we have an important kind of necessity—let's call it "broadly logical necessity." Of course there is a correlative kind of *possibility*: a proposition *p* is possibly true (in the broadly logical sense) just in case its negation or denial is not necessarily true (in that same broadly logical sense). This sense of necessity and possibility must be distinguished from another that we may call *causal* or *natural* necessity and possibility. Consider

(18)   Henry Kissinger has swum the Atlantic.

Although this proposition has an implausible ring, it is not necessarily false in the broadly logical sense (and its denial is not necessarily true in that sense). But there is a good sense in which it is impossible: it is *causally* or *naturally* impossible. Human beings, unlike dolphins, just don't have the physical equipment demanded for this feat. Unlike Superman, furthermore, the rest of us are incapable of leaping tall buildings at a single bound or (without auxiliary power of some kind) traveling faster than a speeding bullet. These things are *impossible* for us—but not *logically* impossible, even in the broad sense.

So there are several senses of necessity and possibility here. There are a number of propositions, furthermore, of which it's difficult to say whether they are or aren't possible in the broadly logical sense; some of these are subjects of philosophical controversy. Is it possible, for example, for a person never to be conscious during his entire existence? Is it possible for a (human) person to exist *disembodied*? If that's possible, is it possible that there be a person who *at no time at all* during his entire existence has a body? Is it possible to see without eyes? These are propositions about whose possibility in that broadly logical sense there is disagreement and dispute.

Now return to set *C*.... What is characteristic of it is the fact that the conjunction of its members—the proposition expressed by the result of putting "and's" between (8), (9), and (10)—is necessarily false. Or we might put it like this: what characterizes set *C* is the fact that we can get a formally contradictory set by adding a necessarily true proposition—namely (11). Suppose we say that a set is *implicitly contradictory* if it resembles *C* in this respect. That is, a set *S* of propositions is implicitly contradictory if there is a necessary proposition *p* such that the result of adding *p* to *S* is a formally contradictory set. Another way to put it: *S* is implicitly contradictory if there is some necessarily true proposition *p* such that by using just the laws of ordinary logic, we can deduce an explicit contradiction from *p* together with the members of *S*. And when Mackie says that set *A* is contradictory, we may properly take him, I think, as holding that it is implicitly contradictory in the explained sense. As he puts it:

> However, the contradiction does not arise immediately; to show it we need some additional premises, or perhaps some quasi-logical rules connecting the terms "good" and "evil" and "omnipotent." These additional principles are that good is opposed to evil, in such a way that a good thing always eliminates evil as far as it can, and that there are no limits to what an omnipotent thing can do. From these it follows that a good omnipotent thing elimi-nates evil completely, and then the propositions that a good omnipotent thing exists, and that evil exists, are incompatible.[2]

Here Mackie refers to "additional premises"; he also calls them "additional principles" and "quasi-logical rules"; he says we need them to show the contradiction. What he means, I think, is that to get a formally contradictory set we must add some more propositions to set *A*; and if we aim to show that set *A* is implicitly contradictory, these propositions must be necessary truths—"quasi-logi-cal rules" as Mackie calls them. The two additional principles he suggests are

(19) A good thing always eliminates evil as far as it can

and

(20) There are no limits to what an omnipotent being can do.

And, of course, if Mackie means to show that set *A* is implicitly contradictory, then he must hold that (19) and (20) are not merely *true* but *necessarily true*.

But, are they? What about (20) first? What does it mean to say that a being is omnipotent? That he is *all-powerful*, or *almighty*, presumably. But are there no limits at all to the power of such a being? Could he create square circles, for example, or married bachelors? Most theologians and theistic philosophers who hold that God is omnip-otent, do not hold that He can create round squares or bring it about that He both exists and does not exist. These theologians and philosophers may hold that there are no *nonlogical* limits to what an omnipotent being can do, but they concede that not even an omnipotent being can bring about logically impossible states of affairs or cause neces-sarily false propositions to be true. Some theists, on the other hand—Martin Luther and Descartes, perhaps—have apparently thought that God's power is unlimited even by the laws of logic. For these the-ists the question whether set *A* is contradictory will not be of much interest. As theists they believe (1) and (2), and they also, presumably, believe (3). But they remain undisturbed by the claim that (1), (2), and (3) are jointly inconsistent—because, as they say, God can do what is logically impossible. Hence He can bring it about that the members of set *A* are all true, even if that set is contradictory (concentrating very intensely upon this suggestion is likely to make you dizzy). So the theist who thinks that the power of God isn't *limited at all*, not even by the laws of logic, will be unimpressed by Mackie's argument and won't find any diffi-culty in the contradiction set *A* is alleged to con-tain. This view is not very popular, however, and for good reason; it is quite incoherent. What the theist typically means when he says that God is omnipotent is not that there are *no* limits to God's power, but at most that there are no non-logical limits to what He can do; and given this qualification, it is perhaps initially plausible to sup-pose that (20) is necessarily true.

But what about (19), the proposition that every good thing eliminates every evil state of affairs that it can eliminate? Is that necessarily true? Is it true at all? Suppose, first of all, that your friend Paul unwisely goes for a drive on a wintry day and runs out of gas on a deserted road. The temperature dips to −10°, and a miserably cold wind comes up. You are sitting comfortably at home (twenty-five miles from Paul) roasting chestnuts in a roaring blaze. Your car is in the garage; in the trunk there is the full five-gallon can of gasoline you always keep for emergencies. Paul's discomfort and danger are certainly an evil, and one which you could eliminate. You don't do so. But presumably you don't thereby forfeit your claim to being a "good thing"—you simply didn't know of Paul's plight. And so (19) does not appear to be necessary. It says that every good thing has a certain property—the property of eliminating every evil that it can. And if the case I described is possible—a good person's failing through ignorance to eliminate a certain evil he can eliminate—then (19) is by no means necessarily true.

But perhaps Mackie could sensibly claim that if you *didn't know* about Paul's plight, then in fact you were not, at the time in question, able to eliminate the evil in question; and perhaps he'd be right. In any event he could revise (19) to take into account the kind of case I mentioned:

(19a) Every good thing always eliminates every evil that *it knows about* and can eliminate.

{(1), (2), (3), (20), (19a)}, you'll notice is not a formally contradictory set—to get a formal contradiction we must add a proposition specifying that God *knows about* every evil state of affairs. But most theists do believe that God is omniscient or all-knowing; so if this new set—the set that results when we add to set A the proposition that God is omniscient—is implicitly contradictory then Mackie should be satisfied and the theist confounded. (And, henceforth, set A will be the old set A together with the proposition that God is omniscient.)

But is (19a) necessary? Hardly. Suppose you know that Paul is marooned as in the previous example, and you also know another friend is similarly marooned fifty miles in the opposite direction. Suppose, furthermore, that while you can rescue one or the other, you simply can't rescue both. Then each of the two evils is such that it is within your power to eliminate it; and you know about them both. But you can't eliminate *both*; and you don't forfeit your claim to being a good person by eliminating only one—it wasn't within your power to do more. So the fact that you don't doesn't mean that you are not a good person. Therefore (19a) is false; it is not a necessary truth or even a truth that every good thing eliminates every evil it knows about and can eliminate.

We can see the same thing another way. You've been rock climbing. Still something of a novice, you've acquired a few cuts and bruises by inelegantly using your knees rather than your feet. One of these bruises is fairly painful. You mention it to a physician friend, who predicts the pain will leave of its own accord in a day or two. Meanwhile, he says, there's nothing he can do, short of amputating your leg above the knee, to remove the pain. Now the pain in your knee is an evil state of affairs. All else being equal, it would be better if you had no such pain. And it is within the power of your friend to eliminate this evil state of affairs. Does his failure to do so mean that he is not a good person? Of course not; for he could eliminate this evil state of affairs only by bringing about another, much worse evil. And so it is once again evident that (19a) is false. It is entirely possible that a good person fail to eliminate an evil state of affairs that he knows about and can eliminate. This would take place, if, as in the present example, he couldn't eliminate the evil without bringing about a *greater* evil.

A slightly different kind of case shows the same thing. A really impressive good state of affairs G will outweigh a trivial E—that is, the conjunctive state of affairs G and E is itself a good state of affairs. And surely a good person would not be obligated to eliminate a given evil if he could do so only by eliminating a good that outweighed it. Therefore (19a) is not necessarily true; it can't be used to show that set A is implicitly contradictory.

These difficulties might suggest another revision of (19); we might try

(19b) A good being eliminates every evil E that it knows about and that it can eliminate without either bringing about a greater evil or eliminating a good state of affairs that outweighs E.

Is this necessarily true? It takes care of the second of the two difficulties afflicting (19a) but leaves the first untouched. We can see this as follows. First, suppose we say that a being *properly eliminates* an evil state of affairs if it eliminates that evil without either eliminating an outweighing good or bringing about a greater evil. It is then obviously possible that a person find himself in a situation where he could properly eliminate an evil E and could also properly eliminate another evil E', but couldn't properly eliminate them *both*. You're rock climbing again, this time on the dreaded north face of the Grand Teton. You and your party come upon Curt and Bob, two mountaineers stranded 125 feet apart on the face. They untied to reach their cigarettes and then carelessly dropped the rope while lighting up. A violent, dangerous thunderstorm is approaching. You have time to rescue one of the stranded climbers and retreat before the storm hits; if you rescue both, however, you and your party and the two climbers will be caught on the face during the thunderstorm, which will very likely destroy your entire party. In this case you can eliminate one evil (Curt's being stranded on the face) without causing more evil or eliminating a greater good; and you are also able to properly eliminate the other evil (Bob's being thus stranded). But you can't properly eliminate them *both*. And so the fact that you don't rescue Curt, say, even though you could have, doesn't show that you aren't a good person. Here, then, each of the evils is such that you can properly eliminate it; but you can't properly eliminate them both, and hence can't be blamed for failing to eliminate one of them.

So neither (19a) nor (19b) is necessarily true. You may be tempted to reply that the sort of counterexamples offered—examples where someone is able to eliminate an evil A and also able to eliminate a different evil B, but unable to eliminate them both—are irrelevant to the case of a being who, like God, is both omnipotent and omniscient.

That is, you may think that if an omnipotent and omniscient being is able to eliminate each of two evils, it follows that he can eliminate them *both*. Perhaps this is so; but it is not strictly to the point. The fact is the counterexamples show that (19a) and (19b) are not necessarily true and hence can't be used to show that set A is implicitly inconsistent. What the reply does suggest is that perhaps the atheologian will have more success if he works the properties of omniscience and omnipotence into (19). Perhaps he could say something like

(19c) An omnipotent and omniscient good being eliminates every evil that it can properly eliminate.

And suppose, for purposes of argument, we concede the necessary truth of (19c). Will it serve Mackie's purposes? Not obviously. For we don't get a set that is formally contradictory by adding (20) and (19c) to set A. This set (call it A') contains the following six members:

(1)   God is omnipotent

(2)   God is wholly good

(2')   God is omniscient

(3)   Evil exists

(19c) An omnipotent and omniscient good being eliminates every evil that it can properly eliminate

and

(20)   There are no nonlogical limits to what an omnipotent being can do.

Now if A' were formally contradictory, then from any five of its members we could deduce the denial of the sixth by the laws of ordinary logic. That is, any five would *formally entail* the denial of the sixth. So if A' were formally inconsistent, the denial of (3) would be formally entailed by the remaining five. That is, (1), (2), (2'), (19c), and (20) would formally entail

(3')   There is no evil.

But they don't; what they formally entail is not that there is no evil *at all* but only that

(3″) There is no evil that God can properly eliminate.

So (19c) doesn't really help either—not because it is not necessarily true but because its addition [with (20)] to set A does not yield a formally contradictory set.

Obviously, what the atheologian must add to get a formally contradictory set is

(21) If God is omniscient and omnipotent, then he can properly eliminate every evil state of affairs.

Suppose we agree that the set consisting in A plus (19c), (20), and (21) is formally contradictory. So if (19c), (20), and (21) are all necessarily true, then set A is implicitly contradictory. We've already conceded that (19c) and (20) are indeed necessary. So we must take a look at (21). Is this proposition necessarily true?

No. To see this let us ask the following question. Under what conditions would an omnipotent being be unable to eliminate a certain evil E without eliminating an outweighing good? Well, suppose that E is *included in* some good state of affairs that outweighs it. That is, suppose there is some good state of affairs G so related to E that it is impossible that G obtain or be actual and E fail to obtain. (Another way to put this: a state of affairs S includes S′ if the conjunctive state of affairs S *but not S′* is impossible, or if it is necessary that S′ obtains if S does.) Now suppose that some good state of affairs G includes an evil state of affairs E that it outweighs. Then not even an omnipotent being could eliminate E without eliminating G. But are there any cases where a good state of affairs includes, in this sense, an evil that it outweighs?[3] Indeed there are such states of affairs. To take an artificial example, let's suppose that E is Paul's suffering from a minor abrasion and G is your being deliriously happy. The conjunctive state of affairs, G *and E*—the state of affairs that obtains if and only if both G and E obtain—is then a good state of affairs: it is better, all else being equal, that you be intensely happy and Paul suffer a mildly annoying abrasion than that this state of affairs not obtain. So G *and E* is a good state of affairs. And clearly G *and E* includes E: obviously it is

necessarily true that if you are deliriously happy and Paul is suffering from an abrasion, then Paul is suffering from an abrasion.

But perhaps you think this example trivial, tricky, slippery, and irrelevant. If so, take heart; other examples abound. Certain kinds of values, certain familiar kinds of good states of affairs, can't exist apart from evil of some sort. For example, there are people who display a sort of creative moral heroism in the face of suffering and adversity—a heroism that inspires others and creates a good situation out of a bad one. In a situation like this the evil, of course, remains evil; but the total state of affairs—someone's bearing pain magnificently, for example—may be good. If it is, then the good present must outweigh the evil; otherwise the total situation would not be *good*. But, of course, it is not possible that such a good state of affairs obtain unless some evil also obtain. It is a necessary truth that if someone bears pain magnificently, then someone is in pain.

The conclusion to be drawn, therefore, is that (21) is not necessarily true. And our discussion thus far shows at the very least that it is no easy matter to find necessarily true propositions that yield a formally contradictory set when added to set A.[4] One wonders, therefore, why the many atheologians who confidently assert that this set is contradictory make no attempt whatever to *show* that it is. For the most part they are content just to *assert* that there is a contradiction here. Even Mackie, who sees that some "additional premises" or "quasi-logical rules" are needed, makes scarcely a beginning towards finding some additional premises that are necessarily true and that together with the members of set A formally entail an explicit contradiction.

3. CAN WE SHOW THAT THERE IS NO INCONSISTENCY HERE?

To summarize our conclusions so far: although many atheologians claim that the theist is involved in contradiction when he asserts the members of set *A*, this set, obviously, is neither *explicitly nor formally* contradictory; the claim, presumably, must be that it is *implicitly* contradictory. To make good this claim the atheologian must find some necessarily true proposition *p* (it could be a conjunction of several propositions) such that the addition of *p* to set *A* yields a set that is formally contradictory. No atheologian has produced even a plausible candidate for this role, and it certainly is not easy to see what such a proposition might be. Now we might think we should simply declare set *A* implicitly consistent on the principle that a proposition (or set) is to be presumed consistent or possible until proven otherwise. This course, however, leads to trouble. The same principle would impel us to declare the atheologian's claim—that set *A* is inconsistent—possible or consistent. But the claim that a given set of propositions is implicitly contradictory, is itself either necessarily true or necessarily false; so if such a claim is *possible*, it is not necessarily false and is, therefore, true (in fact, necessarily true). If we followed the suggested principle, therefore, we should be obliged to declare set *A* implicitly consistent (since it hasn't been shown to be otherwise), but we should have to say the same thing about the atheologian's claim, since we haven't shown *that* claim to be inconsistent or impossible. The atheologian's claim, furthermore, is necessarily true if it is possible. Accordingly, if we accept the above principle, we shall have to declare set *A* both implicitly consistent and implicitly inconsistent. So all we can say at this point is that set *A* has not been shown to be implicitly inconsistent.

Can we go any further? One way to go on would be to try to *show* that set *A* is implicitly consistent or possible in the broadly logical sense. But what is involved in showing such a thing? Although there are various ways to approach this matter, they all resemble one another in an important respect. They all amount to this: to show that a set *S* is consistent you think of a *possible state of affairs* (it needn't *actually obtain*) which is such that if it were actual, then all of the members of *S* would be true. This procedure is sometimes called *giving a model of S*. For example, you might

construct an axiom set and then show that it is consistent by giving a model of it; this is how it was shown that the denial of Euclid's parallel postulate is formally consistent with the rest of his postulates.

There are various special cases of this procedure to fit special circumstances. Suppose, for example, you have a pair of propositions *p* and *q* and wish to show them consistent. And suppose we say that a proposition *p*1 entails a proposition *p*2 if it is impossible that *p*1 be true and *p*2 false—if the conjunctive proposition *p*1 and not *p*2 is necessarily false. Then one way to show that *p* is consistent with *q* is to find some proposition *r* whose conjunction with *p* is both possible, in the broadly logical sense, and entails *q*. A rude and unlettered behaviorist, for example, might hold that thinking is really nothing but movements of the larynx; he might go on to hold that

P   Jones did not move his larynx after April 30 is inconsistent (in the broadly logical sense) with

Q   Jones did some thinking during May.

By way of rebuttal, we might point out that *P* appears to be consistent with

R   While convalescing from an April 30 laryngotomy, Jones whiled away the idle hours by writing (in May) a splendid paper on Kant's *Critique of Pure Reason*.

So the conjunction of *P* and *R* appears to be consistent; but obviously it also entails *Q* (you can't write even a passable paper on Kant's *Critique of Pure Reason* without doing some thinking); so *P* and *Q* are consistent.

We can see that this is a special case of the procedure I mentioned above as follows. This proposition *R* is consistent with *P*; so the proposition *P and R* is possible, describes a possible state of affairs. But *P* and *R* entails *Q*; hence if *P* and *R* were true, *Q* would also be true, and hence both *P* and *Q* would be true. So this is really a case of producing a possible state of affairs such that, if it were actual, all the members of the set in question (in this case the pair set of *P* and *Q*) would be true.

How does this apply to the case before us? As follows, let us conjoin propositions (1), (2), and (2′) and henceforth call the result (1):

(1)   God is omniscient, omnipotent, and wholly good.

The problem, then, is to show that (1) and (3) (evil exists) are consistent. This could be done, as we've seen, by finding a proposition *r* that is consistent with (1) and such that (1) and (*r*) together entail (3). One proposition that might do the trick is

(22)   God creates a world containing evil and has a good reason for doing so.

If (22) is consistent with (1), then it follows that (1) and (3) (and hence set *A*) are consistent. Accordingly, one thing some theists have tried is to show that (22) and (1) are consistent.

One can attempt this in at least two ways. On the one hand, we could try to apply the same method again. Conceive of a possible state of affairs such that, if it obtained, an omnipotent, omniscient, and wholly good God would have a good reason for permitting evil. On the other, someone might try to specify *what God's reason is* for permitting evil and try to show, if it is not obvious, that it is a good reason. St. Augustine, for example, one of the greatest and most influential philosopher-theologians of the Christian Church, writes as follows:

... some people see with perfect truth that a creature is better if, while possessing free will, it remains always fixed upon God and never sins; then, reflecting on men's sins, they are grieved, not because they continue to sin, but because they were created. They say: He should have made us such that we never willed to sin, but always to enjoy the unchangeable truth.

They should not lament or be angry. God has not compelled men to sin just because He created them and gave them the power to choose between sinning and not sinning. There are angels who have never sinned and never will sin.

Such is the generosity of God's goodness that He has not refrained from creating even that creature which He foreknew would not only sin, but remain in the will to sin. As a runaway horse is better than a stone which does not run away because it lacks self-movement and sense perception, so the creature is more excellent which sins by free will than that which does not sin only because it has no free will.[5]

In broadest terms Augustine claims that God could create a better, more perfect universe by permitting evil than He could by refusing to do so:

Neither the sins nor the misery are necessary to the perfection of the universe, but souls as such are necessary, which have the power to sin if they so will, and become miserable if they sin. If misery persisted after their sins had been abolished, or if there were misery before there were sins, then it might be right to say that the order and government of the universe were at fault. Again, if there were sins but no consequent misery, that order is equally dishonored by lack of equity.[6]

Augustine tries to tell us *what God's reason is* for permitting evil. At bottom, he says, it's that God can create a more perfect universe by permitting evil. A really top-notch universe requires the existence of free, rational, and moral agents; and some of the free creatures He created went wrong. But the universe with the free creatures it contains and the evil they commit is better than it would have been had it contained neither the free creatures nor this evil. Such an attempt to specify God's reason for permitting evil is what I earlier called a *theodicy*; in the words of John Milton it is an attempt to "justify the ways of God to man," to show that God is just in permitting evil. Augustine's kind of theodicy might be called a Free Will Theodicy, since the idea of rational creatures with free will plays such a prominent role in it.

A theodicist, then, attempts to tell us why God permits evil. Quite distinct from a Free Will

Theodicy is what I shall call a Free Will Defense. Here the aim is not to say what God's reason *is*, but at most what God's reason *might possibly be*. We could put the difference like this. The Free Will Theodicist and Free Will Defender are both trying to show that (1) is consistent with (22), and of course if so, then set *A* is consistent. The Free Will Theodicist tries to do this by finding some proposition *r* which in conjunction with (1) entails (22); he claims, furthermore, that this proposition is true, not just consistent with (1). He tries to tell us what God's reason for permitting evil *really is*. The Free Will Defender, on the other hand, though he also tries to find a proposition *r* that is consistent with (1) and in conjunction with it entails (22), does *not* claim to know or even believe that *r* is true. And here, of course, he is perfectly within his rights. His aim is to show that (1) is consistent with (22); all he need do then is find an *r* that is consistent with (1) and such that (1) and (*r*) entail (22); whether *r* is true is quite beside the point.

So there is a significant difference between a Free Will Theodicy and a Free Will Defense. The latter is sufficient (if successful) to show that set *A* is consistent; in a way a Free Will Theodicy goes beyond what is required. On the other hand, a theodicy would be much more satisfying, if possible to achieve. No doubt the theist would rather know what God's reason is for permitting evil than simply that it's possible that He has a good one. But in the present context (that of investigating the consistency of set A), the latter is all that's needed. Neither a defense or a theodicy, of course, gives any hint to what God's reason for some *specific* evil—the death or suffering of someone close to you, for example—might be. And there is still another function[7]—a sort of pastoral function—in the neighborhood that neither serves. Confronted with evil in his own life or suddenly coming to realize more clearly than before the *extent* and *magnitude* of evil, a believer in God may undergo a crisis of faith. He may be tempted to follow the advice of Job's "friends"; he may be tempted to "curse God and die." Neither a Free Will Defense nor a Free Will Theodicy is designed to be of much help or comfort to one suffering from such a storm in the soul (although in a specific case, of course, one or the other could prove useful). Neither is to be thought of first of all as a means of pastoral counseling. Probably neither will enable someone to find peace with himself and with God in the face of the evil the world contains. But then, of course, neither is intended for that purpose.

4. THE FREE WILL DEFENSE

In what follows I shall focus attention upon the Free Will Defense. I shall examine it more closely, state it more exactly, and consider objections to it; and I shall argue that in the end it is successful. Earlier we saw that among good states of affairs there are some that not even God can bring about without bringing about evil: those goods, namely, that *entail* or *include* evil states of affairs. The Free Will Defense can be looked upon as an effort to show that there may be a very different kind of good that God can't bring about without permitting evil. These are good states of affairs that don't include evil; they do not entail the existence of any evil whatever; nonetheless God Himself can't bring them about without permitting evil.

So how does the Free Will Defense work? And what does the Free Will Defender mean when he says that people are or may be free? What is relevant to the Free Will Defense is the idea of *being free with respect to an action*. If a person is free with respect to a given action, then he is free to perform that action and free to refrain from performing it; no antecedent conditions and/or causal laws determine that he will perform the action, or that he won't. It is within his power, at the time in question, to take or perform the action and within his power to refrain from it. Freedom so conceived is not to be confused with unpredictability. You might be able to predict what you will do in a given situation even if you are free, in that situation, to do something else. If I know you well, I may be able to predict what action you will take in response to a certain set of conditions; it does not follow that you are not free with respect to that action. Secondly, I shall say that an action is *morally significant*, for a given person, if it would be wrong for him to perform the action but right to refrain or vice versa. Keeping a promise, for example, would ordinarily be morally significant for a person, as would refusing induction into the army. On the other hand, having Cheerios for breakfast (instead of Wheaties) would not normally be morally significant. Further, suppose we say that a person is *significantly free*, on a given occasion, if he is then free with respect to a morally significant action. And finally we must distinguish between *moral evil* and *natural evil*. The former is evil that results from free human activity; natural evil is any other kind of evil.[8]

Given these definitions and distinctions, we can make a preliminary statement of the Free Will Defense as follows. A world containing creatures who are significantly free (and freely perform more good than evil actions) is more valuable, all else being equal, than a world containing no free creatures at all. Now God can create free creatures, but He can't *cause* or *determine* them to do only what is right. For if He does so, then they aren't significantly free after all; they do not do what is right *freely*. To create creatures capable of *moral good*, therefore, He must create creatures capable of moral evil; and He can't give these creatures the freedom to perform evil and at the same time prevent them from doing so. As it turned out, sadly enough, some of the free creatures God created went wrong in the exercise of their freedom; this is the source of moral evil. The fact that free creatures sometimes go wrong, however, counts neither against God's omnipotence nor against His goodness; for He could have forestalled the occurrence of moral evil only by removing the possibility of moral good.

I said earlier that the Free Will Defender tries to find a proposition that is consistent with

(1)   God is omniscient, omnipotent, and wholly good

and together with (1) entails that there is evil. According to the Free Will Defense, we must find this proposition somewhere in the above story. The heart of the Free Will Defense is the claim that it is *possible* that God could not have created a universe containing moral good (or as much moral good as this world contains) without creating one that also contained moral evil. And if so, then it is possible that God has a good reason for creating a world containing evil.

Now this defense has met with several kinds of objections. For example, some philosophers say that *causal determinism* and *freedom*, contrary to what we might have thought, are not really incompatible.[9] But if so, then God could have created free creatures who were free, and free to do what is wrong, but nevertheless were causally determined to do only what is right. Thus He could have created creatures who were free to do what was wrong, while nevertheless preventing them from ever performing any wrong actions—simply by seeing to it that they were causally determined to do only what is right. Of course this contradicts the Free Will Defense, according to which there is inconsistency in supposing that God determines free creatures to do only what is right. But is it really possible that all of a person's actions are causally determined while some of them are free? How could that be so? According to one version of the doctrine in question, to say that George acts freely on a given occasion is to say only this: *if George had chosen to do otherwise, he would have done otherwise*. Now George's action A is causally determined if some event E— some event beyond his control—has already occurred, where the state of affairs consisting in E's occurrence conjoined with George's *refraining* from performing A, is a causally impossible state of affairs. Then one can consistently hold both that all of a man's actions are causally determined and that some of them are free in the above sense. For suppose that all of a man's actions are causally determined and that he *couldn't*, on any occasion, have made any choice or performed any action different from the ones he did make and perform. It could still be true that if he *had* chosen to do otherwise, he would have done otherwise. Granted, he couldn't have chosen to do otherwise; but this is consistent with saying that *if* he had, things would have gone differently.

This objection to the Free Will Defense seems utterly implausible. One might as well claim that being in jail doesn't really limit one's freedom on the grounds that if one were *not* in jail, he'd be free to come and go as he pleased. So I shall say no more about this objection here.[10]

A second objection is more formidable. In essence it goes like this. Surely it is possible to do only what is right, even if one is free to do wrong. It is *possible*, in that broadly logical sense, that there would be a world containing free creatures who always do what is right. There is certainly no *contradiction* or *inconsistency* in this idea. But God is omnipotent; his power has no nonlogical limitations. So if it's possible that there be a world containing creatures who are free to do what is wrong but never in fact do so, then it follows that an omnipotent God could create such a world. If so, however, the Free Will Defense must be mistaken in its insistence upon the possibility that God is omnipotent but unable to create a world containing moral good without permitting moral evil.). J. L. Mackie ... states this objection:

> If God has made men such that in their free choices they sometimes prefer what is good and sometimes what is evil, why could he not have made men such that they always freely choose the good? If there is no logical impossibility in a man's freely choosing the good on one, or on several occasions, there cannot be a logical impossibility in his freely choosing the good on every occasion. God was not, then, faced with a choice between making innocent automata and making beings who, in acting freely, would sometimes go wrong; there was open to him the obviously better possibility of making beings who would act freely but always go right. Clearly, his failure to avail himself of this possibility is inconsistent with his being both omnipotent and wholly good.[11]

Now what, exactly, is Mackie's point here? This. According to the Free Will Defense, it is possible both that God is omnipotent and that He was unable to create a world containing moral good without creating one containing moral evil. But,

replies Mackie, this limitation on His power to create is inconsistent with God's omnipotence. For surely it's *possible* that there be a world containing perfectly virtuous persons—persons who are significantly free but always do what is right. Surely there are *possible worlds* that contain moral good but no moral evil. But God, if He is omnipotent, can create any possible world He chooses. So it is *not* possible, contrary to the Free Will Defense, both that God is omnipotent and that He could create a world containing moral good only by creating one containing moral evil. If He is omnipotent, the only limitations of His power are *logical* limitations; in which case there are no possible worlds He could not have created.

This is a subtle and important point. According to the great German philosopher G. W. Leibniz, *this* world, the actual world, must be the best of all possible worlds. His reasoning goes as follows. Before God created anything at all, He was confronted with an enormous range of choices; He could create or bring into actuality any of the myriads of different possible worlds. Being perfectly good, He must have chosen to create the best world He could; being omnipotent, He was able to create any possible world He pleased. He must, therefore, have chosen the best of all possible worlds; and hence *this* world, the one He did create, must be the best possible. Now Mackie, of course, agrees with Leibniz that God, if omnipotent, could have created any world He pleased and would have created the best world he could. But while Leibniz draws the conclusion that this world, despite appearances, must be the best possible, Mackie concludes instead that there is no omnipotent, wholly good God. For, he says, it is obvious enough that this present world is not the best of all possible worlds.

The Free Will Defender disagrees with both Leibniz and Mackie. In the first place, he might say, what is the reason for supposing that there is such a thing as the best of all possible worlds? No matter how marvelous a world is—containing no matter how many persons enjoying unalloyed bliss—isn't it possible that there be an even better world containing even more persons enjoying even more unalloyed bliss? But what is really characteristic and central to the Free Will Defense is the claim that God, though omnipotent, could not have actualized just any possible world He pleased.

5. WAS IT WITHIN GOD'S POWER TO CREATE ANY POSSIBLE WORLD HE PLEASED?

This is indeed the crucial question for the Free Will Defense. If we wish to discuss it with insight and authority, we shall have to look into the idea of *possible worlds*. And a sensible first question is this: what sort of thing is a possible world? The basic idea is that a possible world is *a way things could have been*; it is a *state of affairs* of some kind. Earlier we spoke of states of affairs, in particular of good and evil states of affairs. Suppose we look at this idea in more detail. What sort of thing is a state of affairs? The following would be examples:

Nixon's having won the 1972 election

7 + 5's being equal to 12

All men's being mortal

and

Gary, Indiana's, having a really nasty pollution problem.

These are *actual* states of affairs: states of affairs that do in fact obtain. And corresponding to each such actual state of affairs there is a true proposition—in the above cases, the corresponding propositions would be *Nixon won the 1972 presidential election, 7 + 5 is equal to 12, all men are mortal,* and *Gary, Indiana, has a really nasty pollution problem.* A proposition *p corresponds* to a state of affairs s_1, in this sense, if it is impossible that *p* be true and s_1 fail to obtain and impossible that s_1 obtain and *p* fail to be true.

But just as there are false propositions, so there are states of affairs that do *not* obtain or are *not* actual. *Kissinger's having swum the Atlantic* and *Hubert Horatio Humphrey's having run a mile in four minutes* would be examples. Some states of affairs that do

not obtain are impossible: e.g., *Hubert's having drawn a square circle, 7 + 5's being equal to 75,* and *Agnew's having a brother who was an only child.* The propositions corresponding to these states of affairs, of course, are necessarily false. So there are states of affairs that *obtain* or are *actual* and also states of affairs that don't obtain. Among the latter some are *impossible* and others are possible. And a possible world is a possible state of affairs. Of course not every possible state of affairs is a possible world; *Hubert's having run a mile in four minutes* is a possible state of affairs but not a possible world. No doubt it is an *element* of many possible worlds, but it isn't itself inclusive enough to be one. To be a possible world, a state of affairs must be very large—so large as to be *complete* or *maximal.*

To get at this idea of completeness we need a couple of definitions. As we have already seen … a state of affairs *A includes* a state of affairs *B* if it is not possible that *A* obtain and *B* not obtain or if the conjunctive state of affairs *A but not B*—the state of affairs that obtains if and only if *A* obtains and *B* does not—is not possible. For example, *Jim Whittaker's being the first American to climb Mt. Everest* includes *Jim Whittaker's being an American.* It also includes *Mt. Everest's being climbed, something's being climbed, no American's having climbed Everest before Whittaker did,* and the like. *Inclusion* among states of affairs is like *entailment* among propositions; and where a state of affairs *A* includes a state of affairs *B,* the proposition corresponding to *A* entails the one corresponding to *B.* Accordingly, *Jim Whittaker is the first American to climb Everest* entails *Mt. Everest has been climbed, something has been climbed,* and *no American climbed Everest before Whittaker did.* Now suppose we say further that a state of affairs *A precludes* a state of affairs *B* if it is not possible that *both* obtain, or if the conjunctive state of affairs *A and B* is impossible. Thus *Whittaker's being the first American to climb Mt. Everest* precludes *Luther Jerstad's being the first American to climb Everest,* as well as Whittaker's never having climbed any mountains. If *A* precludes *B,* than *A's* corresponding proposition entails the denial of the one corresponding to *B.* Still further, let's say that the *complement* of a state of affairs is the state of affairs that obtains just in case *A* does not obtain. [Or we might say that the complement (call it $\bar{A}$) of A is the state of affairs corresponding to the *denial* or *negation* of the proposition corresponding to A.] Given these definitions, we can say what it is for a state of affairs to be *complete*: A is a complete state of affairs if and only if for every state of affairs B, either A *includes* B or A *precludes* B. (We could express the same thing by saying that if A is a complete state of affairs, then for every state of affairs B, either A includes B or A includes $\bar{B}$, the complement of B.) And now we are able to say what a possible world is: a possible world is any possible state of affairs that is complete. If A is a possible world, then it says something about everything; every state of affairs S is either included in or precluded by it.

Corresponding to each possible world W, furthermore, there is a set of propositions that I'll call the book on W. A proposition is in the book on W just in case the state of affairs to which it corresponds is included in W. Or we might express it like this. Suppose we say that a proposition P *is true in a world W* if and only if P *would have been true if W had been actual*—if and only if, that is, it is not possible that W be actual and P be false. Then the book on W is the set of propositions true in W. Like possible worlds, books are *complete*; if B is a book, then for any proposition P, either P or the denial of P will be a member of B. A book is a *maximal consistent set* of propositions; it is so large that the addition of another proposition to it always yields an explicitly inconsistent set.

Of course, for each possible world there is exactly one book corresponding to it (that is, for a given world W there is just one book B such that each member of B is true in M; and for each book there is just one world to which it corresponds). So every world has its book.

It should be obvious that exactly one possible world is actual. At *least* one must be, since the set of true propositions is a maximal consistent set and hence a book. But then it corresponds to a possible world, and the possible world corresponding to this set of propositions (since it's the set of *true* propositions) will be actual. On the other hand there is at *most* one actual world. For suppose there were two:

W and W'. These worlds cannot include all the very same states of affairs; if they did, they would be the very same world. So there must be at least one state of affairs S such that W includes S and W' does not. But a possible world is maximal; W', therefore, includes the complement $\bar{S}$ of S. So if both W and W' were actual, as we have supposed, then both S and $\bar{S}$ would be actual—which is impossible. So there can't be more than one possible world that is actual.

Leibniz pointed out that a proposition p is necessary if it is true in every possible world. We may add that p is possible if it is true in one world and impossible if true in none. Furthermore, *p entails q* if there is no possible world in which p is true and q is false, and *p is consistent with q* if there is at least one world in which both p and q are true.

A further feature of possible worlds is that people (and other things) exist in them. Each of us exists in the actual world, obviously; but a person also exists in many worlds distinct from the actual world. It would be a mistake, of course, to think of all of these worlds as somehow "going on" at the same time, with the same person reduplicated through these worlds and actually existing in a lot of different ways. This is not what is meant by saying that the same person exists in different possible worlds. What is meant, instead, is this: a person Paul exists in each of those possible worlds W which is such that, if W *had been actual,* Paul would have existed—actually existed. Suppose Paul had been an inch taller than he is, or a better tennis player. Then the world that does in fact obtain would not have been actual; some other world— W', let's say—would have obtained instead. If W' had been actual, Paul would have existed; so Paul exists in W'. (Of course there are still other possible worlds in which Paul does not exist—worlds, for example, in which there are no people at all.) Accordingly, when we say that Paul exists in a world W, what we mean is that Paul *would have* existed had W been actual. Or we could put it like this: Paul exists in each world W that includes the state of affairs consisting in Paul's existence. We can put this still more simply by saying that Paul exists in those worlds whose books contain the proposition *Paul exists.*

But isn't there a problem here? *Many* people are named "Paul": Paul the apostle, Paul J. Zwier, John Paul Jones, and many other famous Pauls. So who goes with "Paul exists"? Which Paul? The answer has to do with the fact that books contain *propositions*—not sentences. They contain the sort of thing sentences are used to express and assert. And the same sentence—"Aristotle is wise," for example—can be used to express many different propositions. When Plato used it, he asserted a proposition predicating wisdom of his famous pupil; when Jackie Onassis uses it, she asserts a proposition predicating wisdom of her wealthy husband. These are distinct propositions (we might even think they differ in truth value); but they are expressed by the same sentence. Normally (but not always) we don't have much trouble determining which of the several propositions expressed by a given sentence is relevant in the context at hand. So in this case a given person, Paul, exists in a world *W* if and only if *W'* book contains the proposition that says that *he*— that particular person—exists. The fact that the sentence we use to express this proposition can also be used to express *other* propositions is not relevant.

After this excursion into the nature of books and worlds we can return to our question. Could God have created just any world He chose? Before addressing the question, however, we must note that God does not, strictly speaking, *create* any possible worlds or states of affairs at all. What He creates are the heavens and the earth and all that they contain. But He has not created states of affairs. There are, for example, the state of affairs consisting in God's existence and the state of affairs consisting in His nonexistence. That is, there is such a thing as the state of affairs consisting in the existence of God, and there is also such a thing as the state of affairs consisting in the nonexistence of God, just as there are the two propositions *God exists* and *God does not exist*. The theist believes that the first state of affairs is actual and the first proposition true; the atheist believes that the second state of affairs is actual and the second proposition true. But, of course, both propositions *exist*, even though just one is true. Similarly, there are two states of affairs

here, just one of which is actual. So both states of affairs *exist*, but only one *obtains*. And God has not created either one of them since there never was a time at which either did not exist. Nor has he created the state of affairs consisting in the earth's existence; there was a time when *the earth* did not exist, but none when the state of affairs consisting in the earth's existence didn't exist. Indeed, God did not bring into existence any states of affairs at all. What He did was to perform actions of a certain sort—creating the heavens and the earth, for example—which resulted in the *actuality* of certain states of affairs. God *actualizes* states of affairs. He actualizes the possible world that does in fact obtain; He does not create it. And while He has created Socrates, He did not create the state of affairs consisting in Socrates' existence.[12]

Bearing this in mind, let's finally return to our question. Is the atheologian right in holding that if God is omnipotent, then he could have actualized or created any possible world He pleased? Not obviously. First, we must ask ourselves whether God is a *necessary* or a *contingent* being. A necessary being is one that exists in every possible world—one that would have existed no matter which possible world had been actual; a contingent being exists only in some possible worlds. Now if God is not a necessary being (and many, perhaps most, theists think that He is not), then clearly enough there will be many possible worlds He could not have actualized—all those, for example, in which He does not exist. Clearly, God could not have created a world in which He doesn't even exist.

So, if God is a contingent being then there are many possible worlds beyond His power to create. But this is really irrelevant to our present concerns. For perhaps the atheologian can maintain his case if he revises his claim to avoid this difficulty; perhaps he will say something like this: if God is omnipotent, then He could have actualized any of these possible worlds *in which He exists*. So if He exists and is omnipotent, He could have actualized (contrary to the Free Will Defense) any of those possible worlds in which He exists and in which there exist free creatures who do no wrong. He could have actualized worlds containing moral good but no moral evil. Is this correct?

Let's begin with a trivial example. You and Paul have just returned from an Australian hunting expedition: your quarry was the elusive double-waffled cassowary. Paul captured an aardvark, mistaking it for a cassowary. The creature's disarming ways have won it a place in Paul's heart; he is deeply attached to it. Upon your return to the States you offer Paul $500 for his aardvark, only to be rudely turned down. Later you ask yourself, "What would he have done if I'd offered him $700?" Now what is it, exactly, that you are asking? What you're really asking in a way is whether, under a *specific set of conditions*, Paul would have sold it. These conditions include your having offered him $700 rather than $500 for the aardvark, everything else being as much as possible like the conditions that did in fact obtain. Let S' be this set of conditions or state of affairs. S' includes the state of affairs consisting in your offering Paul $700 (instead of the $500 you did offer him); of course it does not include his *accepting* your offer, and it does not include his *rejecting* it; for the rest, the conditions it includes are just like the ones that did obtain in the actual world. So, for example, S' includes Paul's being free to accept the offer and free to refrain; and if in fact the going rate for an aardvark was $650, then S' includes the state of affairs consisting in the going rate's being $650. So we might put your question by asking which of the following conditionals is true:

(23) If the state of affairs S' had obtained, Paul would have accepted the offer

(24) If the state of affairs S' had obtained, Paul would not have accepted the offer.

It seems clear that at least one of these conditionals is true, but naturally they can't both be; so exactly one is.

Now since S' includes neither Paul's accepting the offer not his rejecting it, the antecedent of (23) and (24) does not entail the consequent of either. That is,

(25) S' *obtains* does not entail either

(26) Paul accepts the offer

   or

(27) Paul does not accept the offer.

So there are possible worlds in which both (25) and (26) are true, and other possible worlds in which both (25) and (27) are true.

We are now in a position to grasp an important fact. Either (23) or (24) is in fact true; and either way there are possible worlds God could not have actualized. Suppose, first of all, that (23) is true. Then it was beyond the power of God to create a world in which (1) Paul is free to sell his aardvark and free to refrain, and in which the other states of affairs included in S' obtain, and (2) Paul does not sell. That is, it was beyond His power to create a world in which (25) and (27) are both true. There is at least one possible world like this, but God, despite His omnipotence, could not have brought about its actuality. For let W be such a world. To actualize W, God must bring it about that Paul is free with respect to this action, and that the other states of affairs included in S' obtain. But (23), as we are supposing, is true; so if God had actualized S' and left Paul *free* with respect to this action, he would have sold: in which case W would not have been actual. If, on the other hand, God had *brought it about* that Paul didn't sell or had *caused him to* refrain from selling, then Paul would not have been free with respect to this action; then S' would not have been actual (since S' includes Paul's being free with respect to it), and W would not have been actual since W includes S'.

Of course if it is (24) rather than (23) that is true, then another class of worlds was beyond God's power to actualize—those, namely, in which S' obtains and Paul *sells* his aardvark. These are the worlds in which both (25) and (26) are true. But either (23) or (24) is true. Therefore, there are possible worlds God could not have actualized. If we consider whether or not God could have created a world in which, let's say, both (25) and (26) are true, we see that the answer depends upon a peculiar kind of fact; it depends upon what Paul would have freely chosen to do in a certain situation. So there are any number of possible worlds such that it is partly up to Paul whether God can create them.[13]

That was a past tense example. Perhaps it would be useful to consider a future tense case, since this might seem to correspond more closely to God's situation in choosing a possible world to actualize. At some time *t* in the near future Maurice will be free with respect to some insignificant action—having freeze-dried oatmeal for breakfast, let's say. That is, at time *t* Maurice will be free to have oatmeal but also free to take something else—shredded wheat, perhaps. Next, suppose we consider *S'*, a state of affairs that is included in the actual world and includes Maurice's being free with respect to taking oatmeal at time *t*. That is, *S'* includes Maurice's being free at time *t* to take oatmeal and free to reject it. *S'* does not include Maurice's taking oatmeal, however; nor does it include his rejecting it. For the rest *S'* is as much as possible like the actual world. In particular there are many conditions that do in fact hold at time *t* and are *relevant* to his choice—such conditions, for example, as the fact that he hasn't had oatmeal lately, that his wife will be annoyed if he rejects it, and the like; and *S'* includes each of these conditions. Now God no doubt knows what Maurice will do at time *t*, if *S* obtains; He knows which action Maurice would freely perform if *S* were to be actual. That is, God knows that one of the following conditionals is true:

(28) If *S'* were to obtain, Maurice will freely take the oatmeal

or

(29) If *S'* were to obtain, Maurice will freely reject it.

We may not know which of these is true, and Maurice himself may not know; but presumably God does.

So either God knows that (28) is true, or else He knows that (29) is. Let's suppose it is (28). Then there is a possible world that God, though omnipotent, cannot create. For consider a possible world *W'* that shares *S'* with the actual world (which for

ease of reference I'll name "Kronos") and in which Maurice does not take oatmeal. (We know there is such a world, since *S'* does not include Maurice's taking the oatmeal.) *S'* obtains in *W'* just as it does in Kronos. Indeed, everything in *W'* is just as it is in Kronos up to time *t*. But whereas in Kronos Maurice takes oatmeal at time *t*, in *W'* he does not. Now *W'* is a perfectly possible world; but it is not within God's power to create it or bring about its actuality. For to do so He must actualize *S'*. But (28) is in fact true. So if God actualizes *S'* (as He must to create *W'*) and leaves Maurice free with respect to the action in question, then he will take the oatmeal; and then, of course, *W'* will not be actual. If, on the other hand, God causes Maurice to *refrain* from taking the oatmeal, then he is not free to take it. That means, once again, that *W'* is not actual; for in *W'* Maurice is free to take the oatmeal (even if he doesn't do so). So if (28) is true, then this world *W'* is one that God can't actualize, it is not within His power to actualize it even though He is omnipotent and it is a possible world.

Of course, if it is (29) that is true, we get a similar result; then too there are possible worlds that God can't actualize. These would be worlds which share *S'* with Kronos and in which Maurice *does* take oatmeal. But either (28) or (29) is true; so either way there is a possible world that God can't create. If we consider a world in which *S'* obtains and in which Maurice freely chooses oatmeal at time *t*, we see that whether or not it is within God's power to actualize it depends upon what Maurice would do if he were free in a certain situation. Accordingly, there are any number of possible worlds such that it is partly up to Maurice whether or not God can actualize them. It is, of course, up to God whether or not to create Maurice and also up to God whether or not to make him free with respect to the action of taking oatmeal at time *t*. (God could, if He chose, cause him to succumb to the dreaded *equine obsession*, a condition shared by some people and most horses, whose victims find it *psychologically impossible* to refuse oats or oat products.) But if He creates Maurice and creates him free with respect to this action, then whether or not he actually performs the action is up to Maurice—not God.[14]

Now we can return to the Free Will Defense and the problem of evil. The Free Will Defender, you recall, insists on the possibility that it is not within God's power to create a world containing moral good without creating one containing moral evil. His atheological opponent—Mackie, for example—agrees with Leibniz in insisting that *if* (as the theist holds) God is omnipotent, then it *follows* that He could have created any possible world He pleased. We now see that this contention—call it "Leibniz' Lapse"—is a mistake. The atheologian is right in holding that there are many possible worlds containing moral good but no moral evil; his mistake lies in endorsing Leibniz' Lapse. So one of his premises—that God, if omnipotent, could have actualized just any world He pleased—is false.

6. COULD GOD HAVE CREATED A WORLD CONTAINING MORAL GOOD BUT NO MORAL EVIL?

Now suppose we recapitulate the logic of the situation. The Free Will Defender claims that the following is possible:

(30)   God is omnipotent, and it was not within His power to create a world containing moral good but no moral evil.

By way of retort the atheologian insists that there are possible worlds containing moral good but no moral evil. He adds that an omnipotent being could have actualized any possible world he chose. So if God is omnipotent, it follows that He could have actualized a world containing moral good but no moral evil, hence (30), contrary to the Free Will Defender's claim, is not possible. What we have seen so far is that his second premise—Leibniz' Lapse—is false.

Of course, this does not settle the issue in the Free Will Defender's favor. Leibniz' Lapse (appropriately enough for a lapse) is false; but this doesn't show that (30) is possible. To show this latter we must demonstrate the possibility that among the worlds God could not have actualized are all the worlds containing moral good but no moral evil. How can we approach this question?

Instead of choosing oatmeal for breakfast or selling an aardvark, suppose we think about a morally significant action such as taking a bribe. Curley Smith, the mayor of Boston, is opposed to the proposed freeway route; it would require destruction of the Old North Church along with some other antiquated and structurally unsound buildings. L. B. Smedes, the director of highways, asks him whether he'd drop his opposition for $1 million. "Of course," he replies. "Would you do it for $2?" asks Smedes. "What do you take me for?" comes the indignant reply. "That's already established," smirks Smedes; "all that remains is to nail down your price." Smedes then offers him a bribe of $35,000; unwilling to break with the fine old traditions of Bay State politics, Curley accepts. Smedes then spends a sleepless night wondering whether he could have bought Curley for $20,000.

Now suppose we assume that Curley was free with respect to the action of taking the bribe— free to take it and free to refuse. And suppose, furthermore, that he would have taken it. That is, let us suppose that

(31)   If Smedes had offered Curley a bribe of $20,000, he would have accepted it.

If (31) is true, then there is a state of affairs S' that (1) includes Curley's being offered a bribe of $20,000; (2) does not include either his accepting the bribe or his rejecting it; and (3) is otherwise as much as possible like the actual world. Just to make sure S' includes every relevant circumstance, let us suppose that it is a *maximal world segment*. That is, add to S' any state of affairs compatible with but not included in it, and the result will be an entire possible world. We could think of it roughly like this: S' is included in at least one world W in which Curley takes the bribe and in at least one world W'

in which he rejects it. If S' is a maximal world segment, then S' is what remains of W when *Curley's taking the bribe* is deleted; it is also what remains of W' when *Curley's rejecting the bribe* is detected. More exactly, if S' is a maximal world segment, then every possible state of affairs that includes S', but isn't included by S', is a possible world. So if (31) is true, then there is a maximal world segment S' that (1) includes Curley's being offered a bribe of \$20,000; (2) does not include either his accepting the bribe or his rejecting it; (3) is otherwise as much as possible like the actual world—in particular, it includes Curley's being free with respect to the bribe; and (4) is such that if it were actual then Curley would have taken the bribe. That is

(32) if S' were actual, *Curley would have accepted the bribe* is true.

Now, of course, there is at least one possible world W' in which S' is actual and Curley does not take the bribe. But God could not have created W'; to do so, he would have been obliged to actualize S', leaving Curley free with respect to the action of taking the bribe. But under these conditions Curley, as (32) assures us, would have accepted the bribe, so that the world thus created would not have been S'.

Curley, as we see, is not above a bit of Watergating. But there may be worse to come. Of course, there are possible worlds in which he is significantly free (i.e., free with respect to a morally significant action) and never does what is wrong. But the sad truth about Curley may be this. Consider W', any of these worlds: in W' Curley is significantly free, so in W' there are some actions that are morally significant for him and with respect to which he is free. But at least one of these actions—call it A—has the following peculiar property. There is a maximal world segment S' that obtains in W' and is such that (1) S' includes Curley's being free *re* A but neither his performing A nor his refraining from A; (2) S' is otherwise as much as possible like W' and (3) if S' had been actual, Curley would have gone wrong with respect to A.[15] (Notice that this third condition holds in fact, in the actual world; it does not hold in that world W'.)

This means, of course, that God could not have actualized W'. For to do so He'd have been obliged to bring it about that S' is actual; but then Curley would go wrong with respect to A. Since in W' he always does what is right, the world thus actualized would not be W'. On the other hand, if God *causes* Curley to go right with respect to A or *brings it about* that he does so, then Curley isn't free with respect to A; and so once more it isn't W' that is actual. Accordingly God cannot create W'. But W' was just any of the worlds in which Curley is significantly free but always does only what is right. It therefore follows that it was not within God's power to create a world in which Curley produces moral good but no moral evil. Every world God can actualize is such that if Curley is significantly free in it, he takes at least one wrong action.

Obviously Curley is in serious trouble. I shall call the malady from which he suffers transworld depravity. (I leave as homework the problem of comparing transworld depravity with what Calvinists call "total depravity.") By way of explicit definition:

(33) A person P *suffers from transworld depravity* if and only if the following holds: for every world W such that P is significantly free in W and P does only what is right in W, there is an action A and a maximal world segment S' such that

(1) S' includes A's being morally significant for P

(2) S' includes P's being free with respect to A

(3) S' is included in W and includes neither P's performing A nor P's refraining from performing A

and

(4) If S' were actual, P would go wrong with respect to A.

(In thinking about this definition, remember that (4) is to be true in fact, in the actual world—not in that world W.)

What is important about the idea of transworld depravity is that if a person suffers from it, then it wasn't within God's power to actualize any world in which that person is significantly free but does no wrong—that is, a world in which he produces moral good but no moral evil.

We have been here considering a crucial contention of the Free Will Defender: the contention, namely, that

(30) God is omnipotent, and it was not within His power to create a world containing moral good but no moral evil.

How is transworld depravity relevant to this? As follows. Obviously it is possible that there be persons who suffer from transworld depravity. More generally, it is possible that *everybody* suffers

from it. And if this possibility were actual, then God, though omnipotent, could not have created any of the possible worlds containing just the persons who do in fact exist, and containing moral good but no moral evil. For to do so He'd have to create persons who were significantly free (otherwise there would be no moral good) but suffered from transworld depravity. Such persons go wrong with respect to at least one action in any world God could have actualized and in which they are free with respect to morally significant actions; so the price for creating a world in which they produce moral good is creating one in which they also produce moral evil.

NOTES

1. John Mackie, "Evil and Omnipotence," in *The Philosophy of Religion*, ed. Basil Mitchell (London Oxford University Press:, 1971), p. 92. [See previous reading.]

2. Ibid., p. 93. [*Philosophy of Religion: Selected Readings, Second Edition*, p. 224.]

3. More simply, the question is really just whether any good state of affairs includes an evil; a little reflection reveals that no good state of affairs can include an evil that it does not outweigh.

4. In Plantinga, *God and Other Minds* (Ithaca, N.Y.: Cornell University Press, 1967), chap. 5, I explore further the project of finding such propositions.

5. *The Problem of Free Choice*, Vol. 22 of *Ancient Christian Writers* (Westminster, Md.: The Newman Press, 1955), bk. 2, pp. 14–15.

6. Ibid., bk. 3, p. 9.

7. I am indebted to Henry Schuurman (in conversation) for helpful discussion of the difference between this pastoral function and those served by a theodicy or a defense.

8. This distinction is not very precise (how, exactly, are we to construe "results from"?), but perhaps it will serve our present purposes.

9. See, for example, A. Flew, "Divine Omnipotence and Human Freedom," in *New Essays in Philosophical Theology*, eds. A. Flew and A. MacIntyre (London SCM:, 1955), pp. 150–53.

10. For further discussion of it see Plantinga, *God and Other Minds*, pp. 132–35.

11. Mackie, in *The Philosophy of Religion*, pp. 100–101.

12. Strict accuracy demands, therefore, that we speak of God as actualizing rather than creating possible worlds. I shall continue to use both locutions, thus sacrificing accuracy to familiarity. For more about possible worlds see my book *The Nature of Necessity* (Oxford The Clarendon Press:, 1974), chaps. 4–8.

13. For a fuller statement of this argument see Plantinga, *The Nature of Necessity*, chap. 9, secs. 4–6.

14. For a more complete and more exact statement of this argument see Plantinga, *The Nature of Necessity*, chap. 9, secs. 4–6.

15. A person goes wrong with respect to an action if he either wrongfully performs it or wrongfully fails to perform it.

IV.C.2

Evil and Soul-Making

JOHN HICK

John Hick (1922–) was for many years professor of theology at the University of Bir-mingham in England and, until his retirement, was professor of philosophy at Claremont Graduate School. His book Evil and the God of Love *(1966), from which the following selection is taken, is considered one of the most thorough treatises on the problem of evil. "Evil and Soul-Making" is an example of a theodicy argument that is based on the free will defense. Theodicies can be of two differing types depending on how they justify the ways of God in the face of evil. The Augustinian position is that God created humans without sin and set them in a sinless, paradisical world. However, humanity fell into sin through the misuse of free will. God's grace will save some of us, but others will perish everlastingly. The second type of theodicy stems from the thinking of Irenaeus (120–202), of the Greek Church. The Irenaean tradition views Adam not as a free agent rebelling against God but as more akin to a small child. The fall is humanity's first faulty step in the direction of freedom. God is still working with humanity in order to bring it from undeveloped life (bios) to a state of self-realization in divine love, spiritual life (zoe). This life is viewed as the "vale of soul-making." Hick favors this version and develops it in this reading.*

Fortunately there is another and better way. As well as the "majority report" of the Augustinian tradition, which has dominated Western Christendom, both Catholic and Protestant, since the time of Augustine himself, there is the "minority report" of the Irenaean tradition. This latter is both older and newer than the other, for it goes back to Sr. Irenaeus and others of the early Hellenistic Fathers of the Church in the two centuries prior to St. Augustine, and it has flourished again in more developed forms during the last hundred years.

Instead of regarding man as having been created by God in a finished state, as a finitely perfect being fulfilling the divine intention for our human level of existence, and then falling disastrously away

from this, the minority report sees man as still in process of creation. Irenaeus himself expressed the point in terms of the (exegetically dubious) distinction between the "image" and the "likeness" of God referred to in Genesis i.26: "Then God said, Let us make man in our image, after our likeness." His view was that man as a personal and moral being already exists in the image, but has not yet been formed into the finite likeness of God. By this "likeness" Irenaeus means something more than personal existence as such; he means a certain valuable quality of personal life which reflects finitely the divine life. This represents the perfecting of man, the fulfillment of God's purpose for humanity, the "bringing of many sons to glory," the creating of "children of God" who are "fellow heirs with Christ" of his glory.

And so man, created as a personal being in the image of God, is only the raw material for a further and more difficult stage of God's creative work. This is the leading of men as relatively free and autonomous persons, through their own dealings with life in the world in which He has placed them, towards that quality of personal existence that is the finite likeness of God. The features of this likeness are revealed in the person of Christ, and the process of man's creation into it is the work of the Holy Spirit. In St. Paul's words, "And we all, with unveiled faces, beholding the glory of the Lord, are being changed into his likeness (εικών) from one degree of glory to another; for this comes from the Lord who is the Spirit";[1] or again, "For God knew his own before ever they were, and also ordained that they should be shaped to the likeness (εικών) of his Son."[2] In Johannine terms, the movement from the image to the likeness is a transition from one level of existence, that of animal life (*Bios*), to another and higher level, that of eternal life (*Zoe*), which includes but transcends the first. And the fall of man was seen by Irenaeus as a failure within the second phase of this creative process, a failure that has multiplied the perils and complicated the route of the journey in which God is seeking to lead mankind.

In the light of modern anthropological knowledge some form of two-stage conception of the creation of man has become an almost unavoidable Christian tenet. At the very least we must acknowledge as two distinguishable stages the fashioning of *homo sapiens* as a product of the long evolutionary process, and his sudden or gradual spiritualization as a child of God. But we may well extend the first stage to include the development of man as a rational and responsible person capable of personal relationship with the personal Infinite who has created him. This first stage of the creative process was, to our anthropomorphic imaginations, easy for divine omnipotence. By an exercise of creative power God caused the physical universe to exist, and in the course of countless ages to bring forth within it organic life, and finally to produce out of organic

life personal life; and when man had thus emerged out of the evolution of the forms of organic life, a creature had been made who has the possibility of existing in conscious fellowship with God. But the second stage of the creative process is of a different kind altogether. It cannot be performed by omnipotent power as such. For personal life is essentially free and self-directing. It cannot be perfected by divine fiat, but only through the uncompelled responses and willing co-operation of human individuals in their actions and reactions in the world in which God has placed them. Men may eventually become the perfected persons whom the New Testament calls "children of God," but they cannot be created ready-made as this.

The value-judgment that is implicitly being invoked here is that one who has attained to goodness by meeting and eventually mastering temptations, and thus by rightly making responsible choices in concrete situations, is good in a richer and more valuable sense than would be one created *ab initio* in a state either of innocence or of virtue. In the former case, which is that of the actual moral achievements of mankind, the individual's goodness has within it the strength of temptation overcome, a stability based upon an accumulation of right choices, and a positive and responsible character that comes from the investment of costly personal effort. I suggest, then, that it is an ethically reasonable judgment, even though in the nature of the case not one that is capable of demonstrative proof, that human goodness slowly built up through personal histories of moral effort has a value in the eyes of the Creator which justifies even the long travail of the soul-making process.

The picture with which we are working is thus developmental and teleological. Man is in process of becoming the perfected being whom God is seeking to create. However, this is not taking place—it is important to add—by a natural and inevitable evolution, but through a hazardous adventure in individual freedom. Because this is a pilgrimage within the life of each individual, rather than a racial evolution, the progressive fulfillment of God's purpose does not entail any corresponding progressive improvement in the moral state of the world. There is no doubt a development in man's ethical situation from generation to generation through the building of individual choices into public institutions, but this involves an accumulation of evil as well as of good. It is thus probable that human life was lived on much the same moral plane two thousand years ago or four thousand years ago as it is today. But nevertheless during this period uncounted millions of souls have been through the experience of earthly life, and God's purpose has gradually moved towards its fulfillment within each one of them, rather than within a human aggregate composed of different units in different generations.

If, then, God's aim in making the world is "the bringing of many sons to glory," that aim will naturally determine the kind of world that He has created. Antitheistic writers almost invariably assume a conception of the divine purpose which is contrary to the Christian conception. They assume that the purpose of a loving God must be to create a hedonistic paradise; and therefore to the extent that the world is other than this, it proves to them that God is either not loving enough or not powerful enough to create such a world. They think of God's relation to the earth on the model of a human being building a cage for a pet animal to dwell in. If he is humane he will naturally make his pet's quarters as pleasant and healthful as he can. Any respect in which the cage falls short of the veterinarian's ideal, and contains possibilities of accident or disease, is evidence of either limited benevolence or limited means, or both. Those who use the problem of evil as an argument against belief in God almost invariably think of the world in this kind of way. David Hume, for example, speaks of an architect who is trying to plan a house that is to be as comfortable and convenient as possible. If we find that "the windows, doors, fires, passages, stairs, and the whole economy of the building were the source of noise, confusion, fatigue, darkness, and the extremes of heat and cold" we should have no hesitation in blaming the architect. It would be in vain for him to prove that if this or that defect were corrected greater ills would result: "still you would assert in general, that, if the architect had had skill and good

intentions, he might have formed such a plan of the whole, and might have adjusted the parts in such a manner, as would have remedied all or most of these inconveniences."[3]

But if we are right in supposing that God's purpose for man is to lead him from human *Bios*, or the biological life of man, to that quality of *Zoe*, or the personal life of eternal worth, which we see in Christ, then the question that we have to ask is not, Is this the kind of world that an all-powerful and infinitely loving being would create as an environment for his human pets? or, Is the architecture of the world the most pleasant and convenient possible? The question that we have to ask is rather, Is this the kind of world that God might make as an environment in which moral beings may be fashioned, through their own free insights and responses, into "children of God"?

Such critics as Hume are confusing what heaven ought to be, as an environment for perfected finite beings, with what this world ought to be, as an environment for beings who are in process of becoming perfected. For if our general conception of God's purpose is correct the world is not intended to be a paradise, but rather the scene of a history in which human personality may be formed towards the pattern of Christ. Men are not to be thought of on the analogy of animal pets, whose life is to be made as agreeable as possible, but rather on the analogy of human children, who are to grow to adulthood in an environment whose primary and overriding purpose is not immediate pleasure but the realizing of the most valuable potentialities of human personality.

Needless to say, this characterization of God as the heavenly Father is not a merely random illustration but an analogy that lies at the heart of the Christian faith. Jesus treated the likeness between the attitude of God to man, and the attitude of human parents at their best towards their children, as providing the most adequate way for us to think about God. And so it is altogether relevant to a Christian understanding of this world to ask, How does the best parental love express itself in its influence upon the environment in which children are to grow up? I think it is clear that a parent who loves his children, and wants them to become the best human beings that they are capable of becoming, does not treat pleasure as the sole and supreme value. Certainly we seek pleasure for our children, and take great delight in obtaining it for them; but we do not desire for them unalloyed pleasure at the expense of their growth in such even greater values as moral integrity, unselfishness, compassion, courage, humour, reverence for the truth, and perhaps above all the capacity for love. We do not act on the premise that pleasure is the supreme end of life; and if the development of these other values sometimes clashes with the provision of pleasure, then we are willing to have our children miss a certain amount of this, rather than fail to come to possess and to be possessed by the finer and more precious qualities that are possible to the human personality. A child brought up on the principle that the only or the supreme value is pleasure would not be likely to become an ethically mature adult or an attractive or happy personality. And to most parents it seems more important to try to foster quality and strength of character in their children than to fill their lives at all times with the utmost possible degree of pleasure. If, then, there is any true analogy between God's purpose for his human creatures, and the purpose of loving and wise parents for their children, we have to recognize that the presence of pleasure and the absence of pain cannot be the supreme and overriding end for which the world exists. Rather, this world must be a place of soul-making. And its value is to be judged, not primarily by the quantity of pleasure and pain occurring in it at any particular moment, but by its fitness for its primary purpose, the purpose of soul-making.

In all this we have been speaking about the nature of the world considered simply as the God given environment of man's life. For it is mainly in this connection that the world has been regarded in Irenaean and in Protestant thought. But such a way of thinking involves a danger of anthropocentrism from which the Augustinian and Catholic tradition has generally been protected by its sense of the relative insignificance of man within the totality of the created universe. Man was dwarfed within the medieval worldview by the innumerable hosts of angels and archangels above him—unfallen rational natures which rejoice in the immediate presence of God, reflecting His glory in the untarnished mirror of their worship. However, this higher creation has in our modern world lost its hold upon the imagination. Its place has been taken, as the minimizer of men, by the immensities of outer space and by the material universe's unlimited complexity transcending our present knowledge. As the spiritual environment envisaged by Western man has shrunk, his physical horizons have correspondingly expanded. Where the human creature was formerly seen as an insignificant appendage to the angelic world, he is now seen as an equally insignificant organic excrescence, enjoying a fleeting moment of consciousness on the surface of one of the planets of a minor star. Thus the truth that was symbolized for former ages by the existence of the angelic hosts is today impressed upon us by the vastness of the physical universe, countering the egoism of our species by making us feel that this immense prodigality of existence can hardly all exist for the sake of man—though, on the other hand, the very realization that it is not all for the sake of man may itself be salutary and beneficial to man!

However, instead of opposing man and nature as rival objects of God's interest, we should perhaps rather stress man's solidarity as an embodied being with the whole natural order in which he is embedded. For man is organic to the world; all his acts and thoughts and imaginations are conditioned by space and time; and in abstraction from nature he would cease to be human. We may, then, say that the beauties and sublimities and powers, the microscopic intricacies and macroscopic vastnesses, the wonders and the terrors of the natural world and of the life that pulses through it, are willed and valued by their Maker in a creative act that embraces man together with nature. By means of matter and living flesh God both builds a path and weaves a veil between Himself and the creature made in His image. Nature thus has permanent significance; for God has set man in a creaturely environment, and the final fulfilment of our nature in relation to God will accordingly take the form of an embodied life within "a new heaven and a new earth." And as in the present age man moves slowly towards that fulfillment through the pilgrimage of his earthly life, so also "the whole creation" is "groaning in travail," waiting for the time when it will be "set free from its bondage to decay."

And yet however fully we thus acknowledge the permanent significance and value of the natural order, we must still insist upon man's special character as a personal creature made in the image of God; and our theodicy must still centre upon the soul-making process that we believe to be taking place within human life.

This, then, is the starting-point from which we propose to try to relate the realities of sin and suffering to the perfect love of an omnipotent Creator. And as will become increasingly apparent, a theodicy that starts in this way must be eschatological in its ultimate bearings. That is to say, instead of looking to the past for its clue to the mystery of evil, it looks to the future, and indeed to that ultimate future to which only faith can look. Given the conception of a divine intention working in and through human time towards a fulfilment that lies in its completeness beyond human time, our theodicy must find the meaning of evil in the part that it is made to play in the eventual outworking of that purpose; and must find the justification of the whole process in the magnitude of the good to which it leads. The good that outshines all ill is not a paradise long since lost but a kingdom which is yet to come in its full glory and permanence.

NOTES

1. II Corinthians iii. 18.
2. Romans viii. 29. Other New Testament passages expressing a view of man as undergoing a process of spiritual growth within God's purpose are: Ephesians ii. 21, iii. 16; Colossians ii. 19; I John iii. 2; II Corinthians iv. 16.
3. *Dialogues Concerning Natural Religion*, pt. xi. Kemp-Smith's ed. (Oxford: Clarendon Press, 1935), p.251.

IV.C.3

Supralapsarianism, or "O Felix Culpa"

ALVIN PLANTINGA

A short biographical sketch of Alvin Plantinga precedes selection I.B.8. In the present article, Plantinga develops the idea that humanity's fall into sin is a felix culpa ("blessed fault"). Plantinga suggests that a world that includes the incarnation of the Son of God and the subsequent redemption of humanity might be better than any world that lacks these events. If that is right, then perhaps the great good of the incarnation and atonement is sufficient to justify God's allowing humanity to fall into sin.

Reprinted from Peter van Inwagen, ed, *Christian Faith and the Problem of Evil* (Grand Rapids, Mich.: Wm. B. Eerdmans, 2009), pp. 1–25. Used by permission of Wm. B. Eerdmans.

Among the tenets of a certain sort of Calvinism is supralapsarianism, a claim about the order of the decrees of God. God has decreed to permit humanity to fall into sin; he has also decreed to save at least some of the fallen.[1] Does the former decree precede or succeed the latter? According to supralapsarianism the decree to save some of the fallen precedes the decree to permit sin; according to infralapsarianism, it's the other way around. The debate between Supra and Infra has sometimes been held up as an example of Protestant scholasticism run amok. That is because, in part, it is extremely hard to see just what the debate is. The main problem here is the "precede" and "succeed." As the disputants saw, the question isn't about temporal precedence (it isn't that God promulgated part of his decree at one time and part at a later); they therefore suggested that the precedence in question is logical. As Carl Henry says, "The terms supra and infra stipulate whether the divine decree to elect some to salvation comes logically before or after the decrees to create and to permit the fall."[2] But what would that mean? Would the idea be that one of the decrees entailed but was not entailed by the other? But then, apparently, the Infras would have to think the decree to permit the fall entails but is not entailed by the decree to save some of the fallen. The Infras may have been misguided, but they weren't as obtuse as all that; surely they saw that the proposition *God decrees to save some of the fallen* entails but is not entailed by the proposition *God decrees to permit some to fall*; but then presumably that's compatible with their infralapsarianism. So what does this dispute amount to?

One understandable reaction is that it doesn't much matter what the dispute amounts to; the question concerns wholly arcane matters where Scripture is for the most part silent; why waste time on something like that? Isn't this something like arguing about how many angels can dance on the head, or maybe even the point, of a pin? I have some sympathy for this reaction. Nevertheless, I think we can see which of these is right and what kind of priority is relevant. And we can see which is right by thinking about the problem of evil.

SUFFERING AND EVIL

The late and unlamented twentieth century displayed an absolutely appalling amount and variety both of suffering and of evil; no previous century rivals it. As I'm thinking of the matter, suffering encompasses any kind of pain or discomfort: pain or discomfort that results from disease, injury, oppression, overwork, old age, sorrow for one's sins, disappointment with one's self or with one's lot in life (or that of persons close to one), the pain of loneliness, isolation, betrayal, unrequited love, and awareness of the suffering of others. I'm thinking of evil, on the other hand, as, fundamentally, a matter of free creatures' doing what is wrong and/or displaying vicious character traits. Often pain and suffering is a result of evil, as in some of the events for which our century will be remembered—the horrifying seventy-year-long Marxist experiments in eastern Europe and China with their many millions of victims, the Holocaust, genocide in late twentieth-century Europe and Africa, and the like. Of course much suffering and evil is banal, prosaic, commonplace, and is none the better for that.

It isn't only the twentieth century that has featured suffering and evil. Christians and other believers in God have long been baffled and perplexed by its presence, or by the amount of it, or by certain especially heinous displays of it, some of which are so horrifying that it seems callous and unfeeling to bring them up in the context of a scholarly discussion. Why does God permit evil, or why does he permit so much of it, or why does he permit those horrifying varieties of it? This bafflement and perplexity is widely represented in the Bible: perhaps especially in the Psalms and the book of Job, but elsewhere as well. And the perplexity is by no means merely theoretical: faced with an especially abhorrent example of suffering or evil in her own life, or the life of someone she loves, a believer can find herself tempted to take towards God an attitude she herself hates—an attitude of mistrust, or suspicion, or bitterness, or rebellion. A person in this condition may not be much tempted to doubt the existence or even the goodness of God;

nevertheless she may resent God, fail to trust him, be wary of him, be unable to think of him as a loving father, think of him as distant and indifferent.

Now many have urged that knowledge of the extent, variety, duration and distribution of suffering and evil ("the facts of evil," for short) confronts the believer with a problem of quite another sort.[3] The facts of evil, they argue, can serve as the premise of a powerful argument against the very existence of God—against the existence, that is, of an all-powerful, all-knowing, and wholly good person who has created the world and loves the creatures he has created. Call such an argument "atheological"; atheological arguments go all the way back to the ancient world—at least to Epicurus, whose argument is repeated in the eighteenth century by Hume: Epicurus' old questions are yet unanswered.

Is he willing to prevent evil, but not able? then is he impotent. Is he able, but not willing? then is he malevolent. Is he both able and willing? whence then is evil?[4]

And the claim is that the facts of evil constitute a defeater for theistic belief for those theists who are fully aware of them—and if for theistic belief, then also for Christian belief. Christians may find this argument less than compelling;[5] nevertheless they may also find the facts of evil disturbing, both from a practical and from a theoretical point of view; understanding of evil and its place in God's world is an important goal for Christians, one where philosophers can perhaps be of some help.

Christian philosophers have for the most part concentrated on the apologetic effort of rebutting the various versions of the argument from evil. These rebuttals have taken several forms. One sort of response specifies some particular kind of good, and suggests that God could not have created a world displaying that kind of good without permitting evil. Thus perhaps the world is a vale of soul-making, with evil and suffering permitting human beings to achieve certain desirable spiritual states they couldn't otherwise attain. Alternatively, evil arises from creaturely free will: God wanted a world in which there are free creatures who freely

obey his commands and enter into personal relationship with him; but of course whether a creature freely obeys God's commands is not up to God: it is up to the creature in question; and the counterfactuals of freedom are such that God couldn't actualize a really good world with free creatures without permitting evil. There is also the "no-see-um re-sponse":[6] God has his reasons for permitting evil, but the epistemic distance between him and us is such that we can't really hope to know what those reasons are, or why they require him to permit the evil we see.[7] Still another response: Donald Turner suggests that (to put it roughly and inaccurately) perhaps God creates concrete worlds or cosmoi corresponding to all of the possible worlds that are on balance good.[8] Some of these worlds, of course, will contain a great deal of evil (and even more good); our world is one of those worlds.

These responses are useful and important. But in addition to rebutting these arguments, Christian philosophers should also turn to a different task: that of understanding the evil our world displays from a Christian perspective. Granted, the atheological arguments are unsuccessful; but how should Christians think about evil?[9] I therefore want to suggest still another response, or rather I want to reinvent the wheel and propose for further consideration a response that has been with us for a long time. I don't claim that this response answers all our questions or relieves all of our perplexity. It does make a contribution along these lines, however, and in what follows I want to explore it, to see what it has to offer us.

Suppose initially we think about the matter as follows. God intends to create a world; to do so, he must weakly actualize a possible world.[10] He considers all the uncountably many possible worlds, each with its own degree of excellence or value. How shall we think of the value or goodness of a possible world? Well, what sorts of things are good or valuable or excellent, on the one hand, or bad or unhappy or deplorable on the other? The answer is easy; states of affairs (perhaps among other things) are good or bad.[11] John's being in pain is a bad state of affairs, and John's suffering pain magnificently, a good one; there being many people who treat each other in accord with the law of love is a good state of affairs; there being people who hate God and each other is a bad. Since possible worlds are states of affairs, they are precisely the sorts of things that are good or bad, valuable or disvaluable. Perhaps there is no best possible world (there is a tie, or for each world, no matter how good, there is another better yet) but in any event what God intended, in creating, was to actualize (weakly actualize) a really good possible world.

Now many of these possible worlds, I take it, are such that it is not within God's power to weakly actualize them. I've argued for this elsewhere;[12] here I'll just sketch the argument. For a given possible world W, let T(W) be the largest state of affairs God strongly actualizes in W.[13] Assuming that there are nontrivial true counterfactuals of freedom,[14] God would be able to weakly actualize a given possible world W only if the counterfactual

(1)   If God were to strongly actualize T(W), then W would be actual

were true. Now there are possible worlds W and W★ such that God strongly actualizes the same states of affairs in W as in W★; that is, there are many possible worlds W and W★ such that T(W) = T(W★). Where T(W) = T(W★), it is of course impossible that both (1) and

(2)   If God were to strongly actualize T(W★), then W★ would be actual

be true; that is because it is not possible that both W and W★ be actual. Accordingly, either W or W★ is a world God could not have actualized. Following Thomas Flint, we could say that the worlds God could have weakly actualized are the feasible worlds. God's aim in creating, then, is to create an extremely good feasible world.

So far so good; but what are good-making qualities among worlds—what sort of features will make one world better than another? Here one thinks, for example, of the amount of creaturely happiness; a world with a great deal of creaturely happiness (i.e., a world such that if it were actual, there would be a great deal of creaturely happiness) is so far forth a better world than one in which there is little such happiness. Other characteristics on which the goodness of a world depends would be the amount of beauty, justice, creaturely goodness, performance of duty, and the like. The existence of creatures who conform to the divine law to love God above all and their neighbor as themselves (which presumably holds not just for humans but for other rational creatures—angels, other rational species in our universe, if there are any others) would also be an important determinant of a world's goodness or excellence. And of course there are also badmaking characteristics of a world: containing much suffering, pain, creaturely rejection of God, hatred, sin, and the like. Fundamentally, a world W is a better world than a world W★ just if God would prefer the actuality of W to the actuality of W★.

The above list of good-making characteristics, however, omits the two most important. First, any world in which God exists is enormously more valuable than any world in which he does not exist. According to the traditional doctrine of God's necessary existence, of course, God is both concrete and necessarily existent, and the only being who displays both those characteristics. If this doctrine is correct, then there aren't any worlds in which God does not exist. Still further, regardless of whether there are any such worlds, God will be able to choose only among those in which he exists; hence this great-making characteristic, trivially, will be present in any world he chooses for weak actualization.

Given the truth of Christian belief, however, there is also a contingent good-making characteristic of our world—one that isn't present in all worlds—that towers enormously above all the rest of the contingent states of affairs included in our world: the unthinkably great good of divine incarnation and atonement. Jesus Christ, the second person of the divine Trinity, incomparably good, holy, and sinless, was willing to empty himself, to take on our flesh and become incarnate, and to suffer and die so that we human beings can have life and be reconciled to the Father. In order to accomplish this, he was willing to undergo suffering of a depth and intensity we cannot so much as imagine, including even the shattering climax of being abandoned by God the Father himself: "My God, my God, why have you forsaken me?" God the Father, the first being of the whole universe, perfectly good and holy, all-powerful and all-knowing, was willing to permit his Son to undergo this suffering, and to undergo enormous suffering himself, in order to make it possible for us human beings to be reconciled to him. And this in face of the fact that we have turned our back upon God, have rejected him, are sunk in sin, indeed, are inclined to resent God and our neighbor. Could there be a display of love to rival this? More to the present purpose, could there be a goodmaking feature of a world to rival this?

Suppose we think about these points a bit further. We are considering just the worlds in which God exists; for present purposes, let's assume that traditional theism is true, and that these are all the worlds there are. The first thing to note, I think, is that all of these worlds—all possible worlds, then—are very good. For God is unlimited in goodness and holiness, as well as in power and knowledge; these properties, furthermore, are essential to him; and this means, I believe, that God not only has created a world that is very good, but that there aren't any conditions under which he would have created a world that is less than very good. It isn't possible that he create such a world; every possible world in which God creates is very good. For every possible world containing creatures is a world such that it is possible, in the broadly logical sense, that God weakly actualize it;[15] none is such that God's goodness or love or mercy would make it impossible for him to actualize it. There is therefore no level of value among possible worlds such that God couldn't actualize possible worlds whose value falls below that level (and such that some possible worlds fall below that level). The class of possible worlds God's love and goodness prevents him from actualizing is empty. All possible worlds, we might say, are eligible worlds: worlds that God's goodness, mercy, and love would permit him to actualize.

Now I don't mean to suggest that every imaginable or in some sense conceivable world is a very good world. Perhaps we can imagine or in some sense conceive of worlds in which the only things that exist are persons always in excruciating pain. No such world is in fact possible, however, if God, as we are assuming, is a necessary being who has essentially such properties as unlimited goodness, love, knowledge, and power. For first, of course, every world includes the existence of God. But neither would any world contain just God and creatures always in excruciating pain: God wouldn't create such worlds. So perhaps there are imaginable or even conceivable worlds that are not very good; the fact is, however, no such world is possible. All possible worlds are very good.

Of course it is also possible that God refrain from creating altogether. If he had done so, however, the world still would have been very good; for his own existence, of course, would have been actual. Indeed, any world in which God exists is in a good sense infinitely valuable. I don't mean to suggest that we can apply Cantorian infinitary mathematics to these topics. I don't mean to suggest that there are proper units of goodness—felicifics, for example—such that any world containing God displays infinitely many of those units of goodness. Still, God himself, who is unlimited in goodness, love, knowledge, power, and the like, exists in any such world; it follows, I suggest, that the value of any state of affairs in which God alone exists is itself unlimited.

But what is the force of "unlimited" here? I take it to mean that there are no nonlogical limits to God's display of these great-making properties: no nonlogical limit to his goodness, love, knowledge, and power. From this it follows, I believe, that any state of affairs containing God alone—any state of affairs that would have been actual had God not created anything at all—is also in a sensible sense infinite in value. It is not that any such world W is of maximal value, so that there are no possible worlds better than W. On the contrary: a world that also contains very good creatures—free creatures, perhaps, who always do what is right—would be a better world than W. No: it's something else. To see what, consider a possible world W and then consider the state of affairs W-consisting just in the existence and properties of the free creatures W contains. Let us also suppose that we have a coherent sense of entailment in which W- does not entail the existence of God, even though the latter is a necessary state of affairs. (I believe there are such senses, but don't have the space to pursue the matter here.) Now the way in which such a world W is unlimited in value is that W-, no matter how good, and no matter how many wonderful creatures with splendid properties it displays, is not as good as the state of affairs consisting in the existence of God. We might say that in this way the good of God's existence is incommensurable with creaturely goods. But it is also incommensurable with creaturely evils. No matter how much sin and suffering and evil W-contains, it is vastly outweighed by the goodness of God, so that W is a good world, and indeed a very good world. It follows, once more, that every possible world is a very good world.

But that doesn't mean that none are more valuable than others. The fact is: some possible worlds are much better than others. For there is a second and enormously impressive good-making feature of our world, a feature to be found only in some and not in all possible worlds. This is the towering and magnificent good of divine incarnation and atonement. According to the traditional Christian way of looking at the matter, God was in no way obliged to provide a way of salvation for his erring creatures. It would have been consistent with his love, goodness, and mercy not to institute this marvelous plan by which we sinful creatures can have life and be reconciled with God. Hence there are possible worlds in which there are free creatures who go wrong, and in which there is no atonement; in these worlds all these free creatures suffer the consequences of their sin and are ultimately cut off from God. Such a world, I say, is not as good—perhaps not nearly as good—as a world in which sinful creatures are offered redemption and salvation from their sins.

In fact I believe we can go further. I believe that any world with incarnation and atonement is a better world than any without it—or at any rate better than any world in which God does nothing comparable to incarnation and atonement. It is hard to imagine what God could do that is in fact comparable to incarnation and atonement; but perhaps this is just a limitation of our imagination. But since this is so hard to imagine, I propose that we ignore those possible worlds, if there are any, in which God does not arrange for incarnation and atonement, but does something else of comparable excellence. So consider the splendid and gracious marvel of incarnation and atonement. I believe that the great goodness of this state of affairs, like that of the divine existence itself, makes its value incommensurable with the value of states of affairs involving creaturely good and bad. Thus the value of incarnation and atonement cannot be matched by any aggregate of creaturely goods. No matter how many excellent creatures there are in a world, no matter how rich and beautiful and sinless their lives, the aggregated value of their lives would not match that of incarnation and atonement; any world with incarnation and atonement would be better yet. And no matter how much evil, how much sin and suffering a world contains, the aggregated badness would be outweighed by the goodness of incarnation and atonement, outweighed in such a way that the world in question is very good. In this sense, therefore, any world with incarnation and atonement is of infinite value by virtue of containing two goods of infinite value: the existence of God, and incarnation and atonement. Under this assumption, there will be a certain level L of excellence or goodness, among possible worlds, such that all the worlds at that level or above contain incarnation and atonement. Call this "the strong value assumption," and say that any world whose value equals or exceeds it, is a highly eligible world.

I am inclined to accept the strong value assumption, but I don't need anything quite as powerful as all that for my argument. I can hold something weaker. Contrast two kinds of possible worlds. In the first kind, there are free creatures who always do only what is right, who live in love and harmony with God and each other, and do so, let's add, through all eternity. Now for each of these worlds W of this kind, there is a world W★ of the second kind. In W★ God creates the very same creatures as in W; but in W★ these free creatures rebel against him, fall into sin and wickedness, turn their backs upon God. In W★, however, God graciously provides a means of salvation by way of incarnation and atonement. My claim is that for any such worlds W and W★, W★ is a better world than W. Unlike the strong value assumption, this claim does not entail that every world with incarnation and atonement is better than any world without them, and it does not entail that there is a level of value such that every world at or above that level contains incarnation and atonement. What it does imply, however, is that there is no level of value such that none of the worlds at or above that level contain incarnation and atonement. Call this the moderate value assumption.

But my argument doesn't require even the moderate value assumption.[16] All it really requires is that among the worlds of great value, there be some that include incarnation and atonement. Indeed, we can go further: given that all of the possible worlds including creatures are worlds sufficiently good for God to actualize them, all that is really required, for my argument, is that incarnation and atonement be possible, i.e., that there be possible worlds that include them. Since, according to Christian thought, this state of affairs is actual, it is a fortiori possible.

I shall conduct the argument under the strong value assumption, merely reminding the reader that the argument can also be conducted under the moderate or weak assumptions. Under the strong assumption, the value of any world which displays incarnation and atonement will exceed that of any world without those features. Perhaps, even, the value of incarnation and atonement, (i.e., the complex event involving the actions of God the Father and God the Son) is so great that any world in which it occurs is as valuable as any other world, so that the value of all the worlds in which atonement occurs is equal. We needn't go as far as all that, however; more modestly, we can

say that the value of the worlds with atonement exceeds that of worlds without atonement, and the value of the former are clumped together in such a way that while some may be more valuable than others, none is very much more valuable than any other. More modestly still, we can say simply that all the worlds in which incarnation and atonement are present are worlds of very great goodness, achieving that level L of goodness such that no world without incarnation and atonement achieves that level.

Accordingly, if God proposes to actualize a really good possible world, one whose value exceeds L, he will create a world with incarnation and atonement. But of course all the worlds with incarnation and atonement contain evil. For atonement is among other things a matter of creatures' being saved from the consequences of their sin; therefore if there were no evil, there would be no sin, no consequences of sin to be saved from, and hence no atonement. Therefore a necessary condition of atonement is sin and evil. But all the highly eligible worlds contain atonement; hence all the highly eligible worlds contain sin and evil, and the suffering consequent upon them. You can't have a world whose value exceeds L without sin and evil; sin and evil is a necessary condition of the value of every really good possible world. O Felix Culpa indeed![17] But then this gives us a very straightforward and simple response to the question "Why is there evil in the world?" The response is that God wanted to create a highly eligible world, wanted to actualize one of the best of all the possible worlds; all those worlds contain atonement, hence they all contain sin and evil. I've claimed elsewhere that theodicies are unsuccessful: "And here I must say that most attempts to explain why God permits evil—theodicies, as we may call them—strike me as tepid, shallow, and ultimately frivolous."[18] But doesn't the above furnish us with an answer to the question "Why does God permit evil?" The answer is: because he wanted to actualize a possible world whose value was greater than L; but all those possible worlds contain incarnation and atonement; hence all those worlds contain evil. So if a theodicy is an attempt to explain why God permits evil, what we have here is a theodicy—and, if I'm right, a successful theodicy.

And as a bonus, we get a clear resolution of the Supra/Infra debate: the Supras are right. God's fundamental and first intention is to actualize an extremely good possible world, one whose value exceeds L; but all those worlds contain incarnation and atonement and hence also sin and evil; so the decree to provide incarnation and atonement and hence salvation is prior to the decree to permit fall into sin. The priority in question isn't temporal, and isn't exactly logical either; it is a matter, rather, of ultimate aim as opposed to proximate aim. God's ultimate aim, here, is to create a world of a certain level of value. That aim requires that he aim to create a world in which there is incarnation and atonement—which, in turn, requires that there be sin and evil. So there is a clear sense in which the decree to provide salvation precedes the decree to permit sin; but there is no comparable sense in which the decree to permit sin precedes the decree to permit evil.

One final point before we turn to objections. In "Salvifici Doloris," a recent apostolic letter from Pope John Paul II on the Christian meaning of suffering, we read that

> Each one is also called to share in that suffering through which the Redemption was accomplished. He is called to share in that suffering through which all human suffering has also been redeemed.... Thus each man, in his suffering, can also become a sharer in the redemptive suffering of Christ. (p. 31)

Here the suggestion seems to be that we human beings, by virtue of suffering, can participate and take part in, can contribute to the divine suffering by which humankind is redeemed. Now this seems to suggest that Christ's suffering and sacrifice was somehow incomplete: if my contribution is genuinely useful, must there not be something in some sense lacking in what Christ himself did in the Atonement? From a Christian perspective, this seems a bit suspect. But the same suggestion is made by the apostle Paul, whose credentials here are certainly beyond question: "Now I rejoice in what was suffered for you, and I fill up in my flesh what is still lacking in regard to Christ's afflictions, for the sake of his body which is the church" (Colossians 1:24).[19] "What is still lacking in regard to Christ's affliction"? What could still be lacking? What could this lack be?

From the present perspective there is an answer: highly eligible possible worlds, those whose value exceeds level L, also contain creaturely suffering, suffering on the part of victims and perpetrators of sin. This suffering is a necessary condition of the goodness of the world in question. In suffering, then, we creatures can be like Christ. We get to take part and participate in his redemptive activity. So, for a highly eligible world to be actualized, more is needed than just the suffering of Christ. All of these worlds contain atonement; so they all contain divine suffering; but they also all contain creaturely suffering. Creatures, therefore, can fill up what is lacking in regard to Christ's suffering in the following way: there is a necessary condition of the goodness of truly good (highly eligible) possible worlds that is not and cannot be satisfied by Christ's suffering; it requires creaturely suffering as well. It is in this sense that Paul as well as the rest of us can fill up what is still lacking in regard to Christ's suffering.

OBJECTIONS

Accordingly, the Felix Culpa approach can perhaps provide us with a theodicy. But of course it does so properly only if it isn't itself subject to fatal flaws. Is it? What might be objections to it? There are at least three principal objections to this line of thought, or perhaps three kinds of difficult questions to answer. First, why does God permit suffering as well as sin and evil? Second, why does God permit so much suffering and evil? And third, if God permitted human suffering and evil in order to achieve a world in which there is incarnation and atonement, wouldn't he be manipulative, calculating, treating his creatures like means instead of ends? There is a sort of psychological disorder called "Munchausen syndrome by proxy"[20] in which parents harm their children and then rush them to the hospital in order to look heroic and get attention; wouldn't this be a bit like that? In the interests of decency and good order I will take these up one at a time and in order.

Why Suffering?

I said above that the Felix Culpa line of thought offers a theodicy: an answer to the question "Why does God permit evil?" But perhaps a serious theodicy would have to answer other questions as well: for example, why does God permit so much evil, and why does God permit suffering? Concede that you can't have atonement without evil; why do you also need suffering? Incarnation and atonement requires sin and evil: why think it also requires suffering? Wouldn't the cosmos have been better if God had permitted sin and evil, so that there was occasion for incarnation and atonement, but no suffering? Maybe the Felix Culpa line of thought explains the existence of sin and evil; how does it help with respect to suffering?

The answer is twofold: (a) significantly free creatures are free to do evil, and some of them in fact do evil, causing suffering; (b) suffering itself is instrumentally valuable. So first, one good-making feature of a world is the existence, in it, of free and rational creatures. But free creatures come in a variety of versions, and not all free creatures are equal with respect to value, i.e., to the value of the worlds in which they exist. In general, the more free creatures resemble God, the more valuable they are and the more valuable are the worlds in which they exist. In particular, creatures that have a great deal of power, including power to do both good and evil, are more valuable than creatures who are free, but whose power is limited or meager. God therefore created a world in which there are creatures with at least two features: (a) a great deal of power, including the power to work against God, and (b) the freedom to turn their backs upon God, to rebel against him, fight against what he values. Thus Milton's Satan declares "Evil, be Thou my

Good!"; in so doing he announces his intention to take up arms against God, to resist him, to try to destroy what God values, to do his best to wreck God's world, to promote what God hates. Suffering is intrinsically a bad thing; accordingly God hates it; Satan therefore aims to promote suffering, to cause as much of it as he can. Much of the suffering in the world results in this way from the free actions of creatures who actively oppose God and what he values. But free creatures also cause suffering, sometimes, not because they intend in this way actively to oppose God, but just because they don't have any objection to inflicting suffering on others in order to achieve their own selfish or foolish ends. Here one thinks of the enormous suffering inflicted, in the twentieth century, on the population of the former Soviet Union in order to attain that Marxist paradise; Stalin and his henchmen recklessly ran roughshod over the rights and goods of others in order to achieve something they saw as valuable. At least some of the suffering the world displays results from the free actions of significantly free creatures.

But what about so-called natural evil, evil that cannot be attributed to the free actions of human beings? What about the suffering due to disease, earthquake, flood, famine, pestilence, and the like? What about animal suffering and the savagery displayed in the natural world? What about the Ichneumonid wasp Darwin found so upsetting, a wasp that lays its eggs in a live caterpillar, so that when the eggs hatch, the pupae eat the caterpillar alive from the inside? Well, perhaps, as Peter van Inwagen suggests, this is the price God had to pay for a regular world. But there is another and more traditional suggestion here. Perhaps the term "natural evil" is something of a misnomer, or perhaps, at any rate, the contrast between natural evil and moral evil is misleading in that the former is really an instance of the latter. It is plausible to think that there are deeper layers to the sin and evil the world displays, than that exhibited by human beings and embodied in their actions. According to the apostle Paul, the whole creation is groaning, and groaning because of sin.[21] Here a traditional suggestion is that suffering and evil of this sort is to be attributed to the actions of Satan and his cohorts; Satan is a mighty non-human free creature who rebelled against the Lord long before human beings were on the scene; and much of the natural evil the world displays is due to the actions of Satan and his cohorts.[22]

This suggestion is not at present widely popular in Western academia, and not widely endorsed by the contemporary intellectual elite. But it is less than clear that Western academia has much to say by way of evidence against the idea. That beings of these sorts should be involved in the history of our world seems to me (as to, e.g., C. S. Lewis and many others) not at all unlikely, in particular not unlikely with respect to Christian theism. The thought that much evil is due to Satan and his cohorts is of course entirely consistent with God's being omnipotent, omniscient, and perfectly good; furthermore it isn't nearly as improbable with respect to "what we now know" as most philosophers seem to assume. Objections to it consist much more in amused contempt or instinctive revulsion than in reasoned refutation. They are like those incredulous stares David Lewis complains of—not much by way of considered thought. But how much evidential value should be attached to a thing like that?

> So the fallen angels which have power over the universe and over this planet in particular, being motivated by an intense angelic hatred of God and of all creatures, have acted upon the forces of matter, actuating them in false proportions so far as lay in their power, and this from the very outset of evolution, thus producing a deep-set disorder in the very heart of the universe which manifests itself today in the various physical evils which we find in nature, and among them the violence, the savagery, and the suffering of animal life. This does not mean that, for instance, an earthquake or a thunderstorm is due directly to satanic action. It is due to purely natural causes, but these causes are what they now are owing to the deep-set disorder in the heart of nature resulting from this action of fallen spirits, most subtly mingled with the action of good spirits, throughout the long ages of the world's formation—"an enemy came and sowed tares also amid the wheat."

Why Does God Permit Evil? (London: Burns, Oates & Washbourne Ltd., 1941), pp. 49–50. Aquinas approvingly quotes Damascene to the same effect: "The devil was one of the angelic powers who presided over the terrestrial order" (ST I, Q. 110, a. 1, ad 3).

So suffering results, at least in part, from the actions of free creatures; and perhaps it wasn't within the power of God to create free creatures who are both capable of causing suffering and turning to evil, but never in fact do cause suffering. But further, perhaps even if God could create such creatures, he wouldn't want to, or wouldn't want to create only them. Perhaps worlds with free powerful creatures who sin but do not cause suffering are not as good as worlds in which they create suffering; for suffering is also itself of instrumental value. First, some suffering has the effect of improving our character and preparing God's people for life in his kingdom;[23] this world is in part a vale of soul-making, as John Hick and many others (including the apostle Paul) before him have suggested. Some suffering may also be the price of a regular world, as Peter van Inwagen suggests.[24] But according to the apostle Paul, there are other subtle ways in which suffering is of instrumental value. He suggests, for example, that our present suffering is a means to the eternal weight of glory prepared for those who follow him:

> We always carry around in our body the death of Jesus, so that the life of Jesus may also be revealed in our body. For we who are alive are always being given over to death so that his life may be revealed in our mortal body. (2 Corinthians 4:10–11, 14)

> We are … fellow heirs with Christ, provided we suffer with him in order that we may also be glorified with him. I consider that the sufferings of this present

time are not worthy to be compared.... (Romans 8)

For our light and momentary troubles are achieving for us an eternal glory that far outweighs them all. (2 Corinthians 4:17)

Our suffering can enable us to be glorified, and achieve for us an eternal glory; but we aren't told how this works: how is it that our suffering is a means to this eternal glory? Elsewhere there are tantalizing suggestions:

I want to know Christ and the power of his resurrection, and the fellowship of sharing in his sufferings, becoming like him in his death, and so, somehow, to attain to the resurrection from the dead. (Philippians 3:10–11)

I believe three things are suggested. First, there is the suggestion that sharing in the suffering of Christ is a means to attain "the resurrection from the dead," i.e., salvation. Second, it is a good thing that the followers of Christ share in his sufferings because this is a means of fellowship with him at a very profound level and a way in which they achieve a certain kind of solidarity with him; and third, in thus sharing his suffering, his followers come to resemble Christ in an important respect, thus displaying more fully the image of God.[25] Although these are deep waters, I'd like to say just a bit about the second and third suggestions. Consider the idea of fellowship with Christ in his suffering, then: what is valuable about fellowship in sharing in the sufferings of Christ? The suggestion, I think, is just that our suffering with Christ, thus joining him in the most profound expression of his love and enjoying solidarity with him in his central mission, is a good state of affairs; it is good that creatures, whose sins require this activity on his part, join him in it. Secondly, those who suffer resemble Christ in an important respect, thus displaying more fully the image of God, i.e., displaying that image more fully than they could have without the suffering. An absolutely central part of Christ's mission is his suffering; it is through this suffering that he atones for human sin and

enables human beings to achieve union with God. But then if it is a good thing that creatures resemble Christ, it is a good thing that they resemble him in this respect as well. According to Jonathan Edwards, by virtue of our fall and subsequent redemption, we can achieve a level of intimacy with God that can't be achieved in any other way; by virtue of suffering we are invited to join the charmed circle of the Trinity itself. And according to Abraham Kuyper, the angels see this and are envious.[26] Perhaps another part of what is required for membership in this circle is solidarity with Christ and resemblance to him with respect to suffering. The really mature Christian, furthermore, one like St. Paul, will welcome this opportunity. Furthermore, perhaps all of us who suffer will welcome the opportunity in retrospect. Julian of Norwich suggests that those who suffer will receive God's gratitude[27] and will of course much rather have had the suffering and received the divine gratitude than to have had neither. That too is a good state of affairs.

I say that our fellowship and solidarity in Christ's suffering and our resembling him in suffering are good states of affairs; I do not say that we can clearly see that they are indeed good states of affairs. My reason for saying that they are in fact good is not that it is simply obvious and apparent to us that they are good states of affairs, in the way in which it is simply apparent that severe suffering is intrinsically a bad thing. Perhaps this is indeed apparent to some especially mature or especially favored human beings, but it isn't to the rest of us. So I don't say this because it is evident to us, but rather because we learn from Scripture that these are good states of affairs—or, more modestly, we learn this from what seems to me to be the best understanding of the scriptural passages in question. Someone might object that in a theodicy, one cannot appeal to goods we can't ourselves recognize to be goods; but why think a thing like that? A theodicy will of course make reference to states of affairs that are known to be good, or reasonably thought to be good. How this information is acquired is neither here nor there.

So why is suffering present in the really good possible worlds; why is it that they contain not just sin, evil, and rebellion, but also suffering? Because, first, some of the free creatures God has created have turned their backs on God and behaved in such a way as to cause suffering; and second, because suffering is itself of instrumental value, and thus will be found in really good worlds. Suffering is of instrumental value, furthermore, in several different ways. In addition to the ways suggested by Hick, Swinburne, and van Inwagen, there is also the fact that the suffering of God's children enables them to be in fellowship and solidarity with the Lord Jesus Christ; it also enhances the image of God in them.

Why So Much Sin and Suffering?

But why is there so much sin and suffering? Concede that every really good world contains both evil and suffering; but why does there have to be as much of these dubious quantities as our world in fact manifests?

Wouldn't a world with much less sin and suffering than ours be a better world, even if it contains both incarnation and atonement and also some sin and suffering? Here there are two considerations. First, perhaps the counterfactuals of freedom come out in such a way that a world as good as ours will contain as much sin and suffering as ours. But secondly, there is the question how much sin and suffering a highly eligible world contains. This is not an easy question. As I've argued, the best worlds contain incarnation and atonement. But for all we know, there isn't any maximal amount of sin and suffering contained in such worlds; that is, there isn't an amount a of sin and suffering such that some world in this class contains a units (turps, perhaps) of sin and suffering and no world in this class contains more. Perhaps for every degree of sin and suffering contained in some highly eligible world, there is another highly eligible world with more. In the same way, for all we know there is no minimum degree of suffering among these highly eligible worlds. Perhaps for every degree of sin and suffering contained in some highly eligible world, there is another highly eligible world with less.

This is compatible with the degree of sin and suffering, in such worlds, being bounded both above and below: perhaps there is a degree of suffering and evil a such that every highly eligible world contains at least that much suffering and evil, and a degree $a^\star$ such that no highly eligible world contains more than that amount of suffering and evil. Then it could also be that for any given evil, God could have actualized a highly eligible world without permitting that evil; it doesn't follow that he would be unjustified in permitting it. It could also be that God could have actualized a world that is better than alpha, the actual world; it doesn't follow that he ought to have done so, since perhaps for every possible world there is a better he could have actualized.

A second complication: how much sin is required to warrant incarnation and atonement? Suppose the extent of sin were one small misstep on the part of an otherwise admirably disposed angel: would that be sufficient to warrant such drastic and dramatic action on the part of God? Wouldn't such a response on the part of God be somehow inappropriate, something like overkill, perhaps? Probably, although one hardly knows what to say. It might be objected that God, given the unlimited extent of his love, would be willing to undergo the suffering involved in incarnation and atonement, even to save just one sinner. Perhaps so; but that is compatible with its being more appropriate that God's magnificent action here save many, perhaps indefinitely many. Christian doctrine includes, of course, the teaching that human beings are immortal, and can spend eternity with God; the more creatures who attain that state, presumably, the better. Jonathan Edwards and Abraham Kuyper believe, as we saw above, that fallen creatures who are redeemed can be admitted to a greater degree of intimacy with God (can join that charmed circle) than creatures who have not fallen. If so, the highly eligible worlds would no doubt contain a good deal of sin and evil—and, also, consequently, a good deal of suffering. How much sin and evil, then, will a highly eligible world contain? That is hard to say; and again, of course, there may be no answer.

Considering all of these then—our lack of knowledge of the relevant counterfactuals of freedom, the fact that suffering is of instrumental value in a variety of ways—it seems to me that we have no way at all of estimating how much suffering the best worlds will contain, or where the amount of suffering and evil contained in alpha stands in comparison with those worlds. This objection, therefore, is inconclusive.

Munchausen Syndrome by Proxy?

Finally, an objection that has no doubt been clamoring for attention; this objection is powerful, but a little hard to state. The basic idea, however, goes something like this: wouldn't God, in the scenario we're thinking about, be using his creatures, treating them like means, not ends?[28] God has this magnificent end of actualizing a highly eligible possible world (one in which he incidentally plays the stellar role); this requires suffering and evil on the part of his creatures, and apparently requires a good deal of innocent suffering and evil: is that fair, or right? More crucially, would this be consistent with God's loving these creatures,[29] as according to Christian belief he certainly does? If he loved them, would he compel them to suffer in this way so that he can achieve these fine ends? Or perhaps we could put it like this: isn't there something unduly calculating about this procedure? Isn't this a scenario for a sort of cosmic Munchausen syndrome by proxy?[30] Isn't it too much like a father who throws his children into the river so that he can then heroically rescue them, or a doctor who first spreads a horrifying disease so that he can then display enormous virtue in fighting it in heroic disregard of his own safety and fatigue? Could we really think God would behave in this way? How could it be in character for God to riffle through the whole range of possible creatures he could create and the circumstances in which he could create them, to find some who would freely sin, and then create them, so that he could display his great love by saving them? How could God be so manipulative?

According to my dictionary, manipulation, in the currently relevant sense, is "management with the use of unfair, scheming, or underhanded methods, especially for one's own advantage"; and calculating behavior is "marked by coldhearted calculation as to what will most promote self-interest." Manipulation thus involves seeking one's own advantage by unfair means; and the problem with calculating behavior is that it is "coldhearted." The idea, then, is that if God acted according to the Felix Culpa line of thought, he would be unfair to his creatures and would be acting in a coldhearted, i.e., unloving way. This coldheartedness part of the present strand of the objection, therefore, reduces to the charge of unlovingness, the other strand in the objection. This leaves the charge of unfairness. But why would it be unfair of God to behave in this way toward his creatures? For two reasons, perhaps: (a) this way of behaving on God's part requires suffering on the part of his creatures; and it is unfair of God to act in such a way as to require suffering on the part of his creatures in order to attain or achieve his own ends as opposed to what is good for them; and (b) involving his creatures in this way is unfair because it fails to respect their autonomy. And both of these could be thought of as treating his creatures as means, not ends.

Of course it isn't always wrong for you to treat me as a means rather than an end. You hire me to weed your garden or repair your car or instruct your children: are you not then treating me as a means rather than an end? You are not thinking first, or perhaps at all, of my needs and interests, but of your own; and you get me to do something that serves your ends. Of course I am perhaps also treating you as means under those conditions: I take the job so that I can earn some money, enabling me to accomplish some of my own ends. So exactly why would it be out of character for God to treat his creatures as a means? Perhaps the problem is along the following lines: you offer to hire me to weed your garden, and of course I can refuse; similarly, I don't force you to hire me. But with God, of course, it is quite different. He doesn't ask our permission before creating us, before actualizing this world in which we are called upon to suffer. We don't accept the suffering voluntarily; we don't get a choice; God doesn't consult us before actualizing this world, this world that requires our suffering. Obviously he couldn't have consulted us about whether we wish to be created in a world such as this, but still he doesn't; and isn't that somehow unfair? So with respect to this strand of the objection, the charge is twofold: (a) God requires his creatures to suffer, not for their own good, but in order to advance some aims or ends of his own; and (b) God does this without asking their permission.

The second strand of the objection—the strand according to which if God loved his creatures, he would not act in accord with the Felix Culpa scenario—reduces to the same charge: God's love for his creatures is incompatible with his requiring them to suffer in order to advance divine aims or ends that do not advance the creatures' good or welfare. The claim is that if God loves creatures the way he is said to, he would not treat them in that fashion. Marilyn Adams and Eleonore Stump, both extraordinarily thoughtful writers on evil and suffering, have both proposed what Adams calls "agent centered restrictions" on the way in which a holy, just and loving God would treat us. Asking how Christian philosophers can now best contribute to the solution of the problem of evil, she replies that they "should focus on God's agent centered goodness: the very dimension rendered so baffling in the face of horrific individual sufferings." And Stump says … The thought is that Christian philosophers should recognize that God is wholly good, but also perfectly loving, loves each of his creatures with a perfect love. If so, could it be that he would permit a person S to suffer for the good of someone else (or, more abstractly, permit S to suffer because S's suffering is an element in the best world God can actualize)? If God perfectly loves his creatures, he would not require one of them to suffer in order to advance an end or aim that wasn't directly connected with that agent's own welfare. God wouldn't require me to suffer in order to benefit someone else; he wouldn't even require me to suffer in order to actualize an extremely good world; he wouldn't require me to suffer, unless that suffering was necessary for some good for me myself.

Now as we have seen, some suffering is directly connected with the agent's good. But it doesn't appear that all suffering is. So suppose some suffering is not. How shall we think about this? Here we must make some distinctions. First, of course, God might, in perfect consonance with his love, permit me to suffer in order to benefit someone else or to achieve a highly eligible good world if I freely consent to it and (like Christ) voluntarily accept the suffering. But suppose I don't voluntarily accept it: perhaps I am unable, for one reason or another, to make the decision whether or not to accept the suffering in question. (Perhaps the suffering is childhood suffering.) Well, of course we sometimes quite properly make important decisions for someone (in a coma, say) who can't make the decision for herself; we try to determine what the person in question would decide if she could make the decision herself. So suppose further that God knew that if I were able to make that decision, I would freely accept the suffering: then too, so far as I can see, his being perfectly loving wouldn't at all preclude his permitting me to suffer for the benefit of others, or to enable him to achieve his end of actualizing a highly eligible good world. But suppose still further, that I am able to make the decision and in fact would not accept the suffering; but suppose God knows that this unwillingness on my part would be due only to ignorance: if I knew the relevant facts, then I would accept the suffering. In that case too, God's perfect love, as far as I can see, would not preclude his permitting me to suffer. Finally, suppose further yet that God knows that I would not accept the suffering in question, but only because of disordered affections; if I had the right affections (and also knew enough), then I would accept the suffering: in this case too, as far as I can see, his being perfectly loving would not preclude his allowing me to suffer. In this case God would be like a mother who, say, insists that her eight-year-old child take piano lessons or go to church or school.

There is another distinction that must be made. Perhaps God's reason for permitting me to suffer is not that by undergoing this suffering I can thus achieve a greater good (the good of enjoying his gratitude, for example: see footnote 27) but because he can thus achieve a better world overall. Nevertheless, perhaps it is also true that he would not permit me to suffer for that end, an end outside my own good, unless he could also bring good for me out of the evil. Then his reason for permitting me to suffer would not be that this suffering contributes to my own improvement; nevertheless he would not permit me to suffer unless the suffering could somehow be turned to my own good.[31] A constraint on God's reasons (induced, perhaps, by his being perfectly loving) is one thing; a constraint on the conditions under which he would permit involuntary and innocent suffering is another. To return to an earlier example (above, p. 7), perhaps God sees that the best worlds he can actualize are ones that include the unthinkably great good of divine incarnation and atonement. Suppose he therefore actualizes a highly eligible world that includes incarnation and atonement, and in which human beings fall into sin, evil, and consequent suffering. Suppose also that the final condition of human beings, in this world, is better than it is in the worlds in which there is no fall into sin but also no incarnation and redemption; they receive God's thanks, enjoy a greater intimacy with him, are invited to join that charmed circle. Then God's actualizing the world in question involves suffering for many human beings; his reason for permitting that suffering is not that thereby the suffering individuals will be benefited (his reason is that he wishes to actualize a highly eligible world, one with the great goods of incarnation, atonement, and redemption). Nevertheless his perfect love perhaps mandates that he actualize a world in which those who suffer are benefited in such a way that their condition is better than it is in those worlds in which they do not suffer.

By way of conclusion: the Felix Culpa approach does not dispel all the perplexity surrounding human suffering and evil; I suppose nothing can do that. But perhaps it reduces the perplexity, and perhaps it provides the means for a deeper grasp of the salvific meaning of suffering and evil.

NOTES

1. Many Supras also held that God's first decree included that some should be damned as well as that some should be saved; perhaps this accounts for the association of supralapsarianism with the sterner sort of Calvinism.

2. *God Who Stands and Stays,* vol. VI of *God, Revelation, and Authority* (Waco, Tex.: Word, 1983), p. 88.

3. It is worth noting that there are many *different* problems, questions, and topics that fall under the rubric of the problem of evil. There are, for example, the problems of *preventing* suffering and evil, that of *alleviating* it (knowing how to comfort and help those that suffer from it), that of maintaining the right attitude towards those who suffer, the pastoral or spiritual problem I mentioned above, and more; and of course a proper response to one of these problems might be totally inappropriate as a response to another.

4. *Dialogues concerning Natural Religion,* ed. Richard Popkin (Indianapolis: Hackett Publishing, 1980), p. 63. Hume puts the argument in the mouth of Philo, widely thought to represent Hume's own views.

5. See, e.g., Chapter 14 of my book *Warranted Christian Belief* (New York: Oxford University Press, 2000).

6. A no-see-um is a very small midge with a bite out of all proportion to its size. The reference is to the fact that your failing to see a no-see-um in your tent is no evidence that there aren't any there; similarly, failing to see what God's reason is for a given evil is no reason to think he doesn't or couldn't have a reason.

7. See, e.g., Steve Wykstra, "Difficulties in Rowe's Argument for Atheism, and in One of Plantinga's Fustigations against It," read on the *Queen Mary* at the Pacific Division Meeting of the American

Philosophical Association, 1983, and "The Humian Obstacle to Evidential Arguments from Suffering: On Avoiding the Evils of 'Appearance,'" *International Journal for Philosophy of Religion* 16 (1984): 73–94.

8. See Donald Turner's 1994 Ph.D. dissertation *God and the Best of All Possible Worlds* (University of Pittsburgh). Here we must be careful: there is a good world W where you wear your blue shirt today, and another that differs from W only (substantially) in that you wear your yellow shirt today; a good world W where you have a Coke with lunch and another just like it except that you have coffee. God does not, of course, create cosmoi corresponding to all of these. That is because you yourself could not be in more than one cosmos; so while he creates cosmoi corresponding to each of the good possible worlds, the appropriate function is many-one. For details see Turner's dissertation.

9. Here Marilyn Adams and Eleonore Stump have led the way: see, for example. Stump's "Aquinas on the Sufferings of Job" in *The Evidential Argument from Evil*, ed. Daniel Howard-Snyder (Bloomington, Ind.: Indiana University Press, 1996) and "Second Person Accounts and the Problem of Evil," in *Faith and the Problem of Evil*, Stob Lectures at Calvin College, January 1999 (Grand Rapids: Calvin College, 1999), and Adams' "Horrendous Evils and the Goodness of God" in *The Problem of Evil*, ed. Marilyn McCord Adams and Robert Merrihew Adams (New York: Oxford University Press, 1990).

10. For the notion of possible worlds in play here, see my *The Nature of Necessity* (Oxford: Clarendon Press, 1974), Chapter 4, and "Actualism and Possible Worlds," *Theoria* 1976: 139ff., reprinted in Michael Loux, *The Actual and the Possible* (Ithaca, N.Y.: Cornell University Press, 1979). For the notions of strong and weak actualization, see the Profiles volume *Alvin Plantinga*, ed. James Tomberlin and Peter van Inwagen (Dordrecht: D. Reidel Publishing Co., 1985) (hereafter Profiles), pp. 49ff.

11. I don't mean to address here the question whether it is states of affairs or objects or events that are the primary locus of value; in either case states of affairs will be good or bad.

12. *The Nature of Necessity*, pp. 18off., and Profiles, pp. 50ff.

13. God strongly actualizes a given state of affairs S just if he causes S to be actual.

14. I don't have the space here to respond to objections to this assumption. Perhaps the most important of these objections is the so-called "grounding" objection offered by Robert Adams in "Middle Knowledge and the Problem of Evil," *American Philosophical Quarterly, 1977*, and William Hasker in "A Refutation of Middle Knowledge," *Noûs*, December 1986. This objection goes all the way back to the Jesuit/Dominican controversy in the sixteenth century, a dispute whose increasing rancor finally induced the Pope to forbid the disputants to vilify one another in public (although he apparently didn't object to vilification among consenting adults in the privacy of their own quarters). The grounding and founding objection has been dealt with in magisterial fashion in my colleague Thomas Flint's book *Divine Providence: The Molinist Account* (Ithaca, N.Y.: Cornell University Press, 1998).

15. This is trivial; every possible world W containing creatures is such that there is some possible world in which God actualizes W: W itself.

16. As was pointed out to me by Tom Flint, for whose penetrating comments on this and other topics of this paper I am extremely grateful.

17. The Roman Catholic Easter Vigil liturgy contains the words, "O felix culpa, quae talem ac tantum meruit habere Redemptorem."

18. Profiles, p. 35.

19. The same idea is to be found elsewhere in Paul's writings: see, e.g., Romans 1:17.

20. Here I am indebted for a correction to Tom Flint.

21. "For the creation was subjected to frustration, not by its own choice, but by the will of the one who subjected it, in hope that the creation itself will be liberated from its bondage to decay and brought into the glorious freedom of the children of God. We know that the whole creation has been groaning as in the pains of childbirth right up to the present time" (Romans 1:18–22).

22. Thus, for example, Dom Bruno Well:

23. "God disciplines us for our good, that we may share in his holiness. No discipline seems pleasant at the time, but painful. Later on, however, it produces a harvest of righteousness and peace for

those who have been trained by it" (Hebrews 12:10–11).

24. See, e.g., "The Magnitude, Duration, and Distribution of Evil" in *God, Knowledge, and Mystery* (Ithaca, N.Y.: Cornëll University Press, 1995), p. 118.

25. Simone Weil: "… the distress of the abandoned Christ is a good. There cannot be a greater good for us on earth than to share in it." "The Love of God and Affliction" in *On Science, Necessity and the Love of God* (London: Oxford University Press, 1968), p. 177.

26. *To Be Near unto God*, trans. John Hendrik de Vries (Grand Rapids: Wm. B. Eerdmans, 1918,) p. 307.

27. *Revelation of Divine Love*, Chapter 14.

28. This way of putting the objection was suggested to me by Michael Schryna-macher.

29. See Marilyn Adams, "Horrendous Evils and the Goodness of God" in *The Problem of Evil*, ed. Marilyn McCord Adams and Robert Merrihew Adams (New York: Oxford University Press, 1990).

30. "[Child abuse] includes not only children who have suffered physical abuse with fractures and bruises ('the battered child') but also those who have experienced emotional abuse, sexual abuse, deliberate poisoning, and the infliction of fictitious illness on them by their parents (Munchausen syndrome …)" *Encyclopedia Britannica*, 11th ed., s.v. "child abuse."

31. See, e.g., Romans 8:28.

IV.C.4

The Problem of Evil and the Desires of the Heart

ELEONORE STUMP

Eleonore Stump (1947–) is professor of philosophy at St. Louis University. She has written extensively in the areas of medieval philosophy, metaphysics, and philosophy of religion. In this article, she argues that traditional theodicies often fail to accord proper importance to the suffering that results from unsatisfied "desires of the heart." She maintains that, to the extent that they fail in this way, such theodicies are, at best, incomplete.

I. INTRODUCTION

The problem of evil is raised by the existence of suffering in the world. Can one hold consistently both chat the world has such suffering in it and that it is governed by an omniscient, omnipotent, perfectly good God, as the major monotheisms claim? An affirmative answer to this question has often enough taken the form of a theodicy. A theodicy is an attempt to show that these claims are

Reprinted from *Oxford Studies in Philosophy of Religion*, vol. 1 (2008), pp. 196–215, edited by Jonathan Kvanvig. Used by permission of Oxford University Press.

consistent by providing a morally sufficient reason for God to allow suffering. In the history of the discussions of the problem of evil, a great deal of effort has been expended on proposing and defending, or criticizing and attacking, theodicies and the putative morally sufficient reasons which theodicies propose.

Generally, a putative morally sufficient reason for God to allow suffering is centred on a supposed benefit which could not be gotten without the suffering and which outweighs it. And the benefit is most commonly thought of as some intrinsically valuable thing supposed to be essential to general human flourishing, such as the significant use of free will or virtuous character, either for human beings in general or for the sufferer in particular.[1]

So, for example, in his insightful reflections on the sort of sufferings represented by the afflictions of Job, the impressive tenth-century Jewish thinker Saadiah Gaon says,

> Now He that subjects the soul to its trials is none other than the Master of the universe, who is, of course, acquainted with all its doings. This testing of the soul [that is, the suffering of Job] has been compared to the assaying by means of fire of [lumps of metal] that have been referred to as gold or silver. It is thereby that the true nature of their composition is clearly established. For the original gold and silver remain, while the alloys that have been mingled with them are partly burned and partly take flight... The pure, clear souls that have been refined are thereupon exalted and ennobled.[2]

The same approach is common in contemporary times. So, for example, John Hick has proposed a soul-making theodicy, which justifies suffering as building the character of the sufferer and thereby contributing to the flourishing of the sufferer.[3] Or, to take a very different example which nonetheless makes the same point, Richard Swinburne has argued that suffering contributes to the flourishing of sufferers because, among other things, a person's suffering makes him useful to others, and

being useful to others is an important constituent of human well-being in general.[4]

Those who have attacked theodicies such as these have tended to focus on the theodicist's claims about the connections between the putative benefit and the suffering. Opponents of theodicy have argued that the proposed benefit could have been obtained without the suffering, for example, or that the suffering is not a morally acceptable means to that (or any other) benefit. But these attacks on theodicy share an assumption with the attempted theodicies themselves. Both the attacks and the attempted theodicies suppose that a person's generic human flourishing would be sufficient to justify God in allowing that a person's suffering if only the suffering and the flourishing were connected in the right way. In this paper, I want to call this assumption into question.

I will argue that the sufferings of unwilling innocents cannot be justified only in terms of the intrinsically valuable things which make for general human flourishing (however that flourishing is understood). I will argue that even if such flourishing is connected in the appropriate ways to the suffering in a person's life, intrinsically valuable things essential to flourishing are not by themselves sufficient to constitute a morally sufficient reason for God to allow human suffering. That is because human beings can set their hearts on things which are not necessary for such flourishing, and they suffer when they lose or fail to get what they set their hearts on.[5] That suffering also needs to be addressed in consideration of the problem of evil.

II. THE DESIRES OF THE HEART

The suffering to which I want to call attention can be thought of in terms of what the Psalmist calls "the desires of the heart."[6] When the Psalmist says, "Delight yourself in the Lord, and he will give you the desires of your heart,"[7] we all have some idea what the Psalmist is promising. We are clear, for example, that some abstract theological good which a person does not care much about does not count as one of the desires of that person's heart. Suffering also arises when a human being fails to get a desire of her heart or has and then loses a desire of her heart.

I do not know how to make the notion of a desire of the heart precise; but, clearly, we do have some intuitive grasp of it, and we commonly use the expression or others related to it in ordinary discourse. We say, for example, that a person is heartsick because he has lost his heart's desire. He is filled with heartache because his heart's desire is kept from him. He loses heart, because something he had put his heart into is taken from him. It would have been different for him if he had wanted it only half-heartedly; but since it was what he had at heart, he is likely to be heartsore a long time over the loss of it, unless, of course, he has a change of heart about it—and so on, and on.

Perhaps we could say that a person's heart's desire is a particular kind of commitment on her part to something—a person or a project—which matters greatly to her but which need not be essential to her flourishing, in the sense that human flourishing for her may be possible without it. So, for example, Coretta Scott King's life arguably exemplifies flourishing, on any ordinary measure of human flourishing and yet her husband's assassination was undoubtedly heartbreaking for her. If there is such a thing as a web of belief, with some beliefs peripheral and others central to a person's set of beliefs, maybe there is also a web of desire. A desire of a person's heart is a desire which is at or near the centre of the web of desire for her. If she loses what she wants when her desire is at or near the centre of the web, then other things which she had wanted begin to lose their ability to attract her because what she had most centrally wanted is gone. The web of desire starts to fall apart when the centre does not hold, we might say. That is why the ordinary good things of life, like food and work, fail to draw a person who has lost the desires of her heart. She is heartbroken, we say, and that is why she has no heart for anything else now.

If things essential to general human flourishing are intrinsically valuable for all human beings, then those things which are the desires of the heart can be thought of as the things which have the value they do for a particular person primarily because she has set her heart on them, like the value a child has for its parents, the value they have *for her* is derivative from her love of them, not the other way around. A loving father, trying to deal gently with his small daughter's childish tantrums, finally said to her with exasperated adult feeling, "It isn't reasonable to cry about these things!" Presumably, the father means that the things for which his little daughter was weeping did not have much value on the scale which measures the intrinsic value of good things essential to human flourishing; and, no doubt, he was right in that assessment. But there is another scale by which to measure, too, and that is the scale which measures the value a thing has for a particular person because of the love she has for it. The second scale cannot be reduced to the first. Clearly, we care not just about general human flourishing and the intrinsically valuable things essential to it. We also care about those things which are the desires of our hearts, and we suffer when we are denied our heart's desires. I would say that it is not reasonable to say to a weeping child that it is not reasonable for her to weep about the loss of something she had her heart set on.

Suffering which stems from a loss of the heart's desires is often enough compatible with flourishing.[8] As far as that goes, for any particular historical person picked as an exemplar of a flourishing life, it is certainly arguable that, at some time in her life, that person will have lost or failed to get something on which she had fixed her heart. Think, for example, not only of Coretta Scott King but also of Sojourner Truth, who was sold away from her parents at the age of nine, or Harriet Tubman, who suffered permanent neurological damage from the beatings she sustained in adolescence. If any human lives manifest flourishing, the lives of these women certainly do. Each of them is an exemplar of a highly admirable, meaningful life. Yet each of these women undoubtedly experienced heartbreak.

In fact, stern-minded thinkers in varying cultures, including some Stoics, Buddhists, and many in the Christian tradition, have been fiercely committed to the position that human flourishing is independent of the vicissitudes of fortune. On their view, human flourishing ought to be understood in a way which makes it compatible even with such things as poverty, disease and disabilities, the death of loved ones, betrayal by intimate friends, estrangements from friends or family, and imprisonment. But it certainly seems as if each of these is sufficient to break the heart of a person who suffers them if the person is not antecedently in the grip of such a stern-minded attitude.

So, for example, in the history of the medieval Christian tradition, for example, human flourishing was commonly taken as a matter of a certain relationship with God, mediated by the indwelling of the Holy Spirit. On this view of flourishing, most of the evils human beings suffer are compatible with flourishing. That is because, as Christian confessional literature makes clear, a human person can feel that she is in such a relationship with God, even when she is afflicted with serious suffering of body or mind.

This sort of position is also common among the reflective in our own culture. In a moving passage reflecting on his long experience of caring for and living with the severely disabled, Jean Vanier says about the disabled and about himself, too,

> we can only accept ... [the] pain [in our lives] if we discover our true self beneath all the masks and realize that if we are broken, we are also more beautiful than we ever dared to suspect. When we realize our brokenness, we do not have to fall into depression ... Seeing our own brokenness and beauty allows us to recognize, hidden under the brokenness and self-centeredness of others, their beauty, their value, and their sacredness. This discovery is ... a blessed moment, a moment of grace, and a moment of enlightenment that comes in a meeting with the God of love, who

reveals to us that we are beloved and so is everyone else ... We can start to live the pain of loss and accept anguish because a new love and a new consciousness of self are being given to us.[9]

A particularly poignant example of such an attitude is given by John Hull in his memoir about his own blindness. After many pages of documenting the great suffering caused him by blindness, Hull summarizes his attitude towards his disability in this powerful passage:

> the thought keeps coming back to me ... Could there be a strange way in which blindness is a dark, paradoxical gift? Does it offer a way of life, a purification, an economy? Is it really like a kind of painful purging through a death? ... If blindness is a gift, it is not one that I would wish on anybody ... [But in the midst of the experience of music in church] as the whole place and my mind were filled with that wonderful music, I found myself saying, "I accept the gift. I accept the gift." I was filled with a profound sense of worship. I felt that I was in the very presence of God, that the giver of the gift had drawn near to me to inspect his handiwork ... If I hardly dared approach him, he hardly dared approach me.... He had, as it were, thrown his cloak of darkness around me from a distance, but had now drawn near to seek a kind of reassurance from me that everything was all right, that he had not misjudged the situation, that he did not have to stay. "It's all right," I was saying to him, "There's no need to wait. Go on, you can go now; everything's fine."[10]

Everything *is* fine, in some sense having to do with relationship to God, and so with flourishing, on this understanding of flourishing. I have no wish to undermine the appealing attitude exemplified in this powerful text. And yet something more needs to be said. The problem is that suffering is not confined to things which undermine a person's flourishing and keep him from being *fine*, in this deep sense of "fine." What is bad about the evils human beings suffer is not just that they can undermine a person's flourishing, but also that they can keep her from having the desires of her heart, when the desires of her heart are for something which is not essential for general human flourishing. Suffering arises also from the loss of the desires of one's heart; and, in considerations of the problem of evil and proposed theodicies, this suffering needs to be addressed as well. This suffering also needs to be justified.

III. THE STERN-MINDED ATTITUDE

Stated so baldly, this last claim looks less open to question than it really is. We do not ordinarily suppose that a parent's goodness is impugned if the parent refuses to provide for the child anything at all which the child happens to set its heart on. But, as regards the problem of evil, what is at issue is apparently analogous, namely, God's allowing some human being to fail to have the desires of her heart when those desires are focused on something not essential to her flourishing. Why, someone might ask, should we suppose that a good God must provide whatever goods not necessary for her flourishing a human person has fixed her heart on?

Now it is certainly true that there can be very problematic instances of heart's desires. A person could set his heart on very evil things, for example, or a person might set his heart in random ways on trivial things or on a set of mutually incompossible things. And no doubt, there are other examples as well. In cases such as these, reasonable people are unlikely to suppose that some explanation is needed for why a good God would fail to give a person the desires of his heart. Even if we exclude such cases, however, there remain many instances in which a person sets his heart, in humanly understandable and appropriate ways, on something which is not essential to his flourishing and whose value for him

is derivative of his love for it.[11] Surely, in that restricted class of cases, some justification is needed for God's allowing a person to suffer heartbreak.

But even this weaker claim will strike some people as false. Some people will object, for example, that human flourishing is a very great good, sufficient to outweigh suffering. For those who think of human flourishing as a relationship to God, it can seem an infinite good or a good too great to be commensurable with other goods; and this good is possible even when many other goods are lost or denied.[12] If God provides *this* good for a human being, then, an objector might claim, that is or ought to be enough for her. A person who does not find this greatest of all goods good enough, an objector might say, is like a person who wins the lottery but who is nonetheless unhappy because she did not get exactly what she wanted for Christmas.

In the history of Christianity in particular, there have been stern-minded thinkers who would not accept the claim that the suffering caused by any loss of the heart's desires requires justification. In effect, this stern-minded attitude is unwilling to assign a positive value to anything which is not essential to general human flourishing. For this reason, the stern-minded approach is, at best, unwilling to accord any value to the desires of the heart and, at worst, eager to extirpate the desires themselves. Such an attitude is persistent in the history of Christian thought from the Patristic period onwards.

In its Patristic form, it can be seen vividly in a story which Cassian tells about a monk named "Patermutus." It is worth quoting at length the heartrendingly horrible story which Cassian recounts with so much oblivious admiration:

> Patermutus's constant perseverance [in his request to be admitted into the monastery finally] induced [the monks] to receive him along with his little son, who was about eight years old.... To test [Patermutus] the more, and see if he would be more moved by family affection and the love of his own brood

than by the obedience and mortification of Christ, which every monk should prefer to his love, [the monks] deliberately neglected the child, dressed him in rags ... and even subjected [the child] to cuffs and slaps, which ... the father saw some of them inflict on the innocent for no reason, so that [the father] never saw [his son] without [the son's] cheeks being marked by the signs of tears. Although he saw the child being treated like this day after day before his eyes, the father's feelings remained firm and unmoving, for the love of Christ ... The superior of the monastery ... decided to test [the father's] strength of mind still further: one day when he noticed the child weeping, he pretended to be enraged at [the child], and ordered the father to pick up [his son] and throw him in the Nile. The father, as if the command had been given him by our Lord, at once ran and snatched up his son and carried him in his own arms to the river bank to throw him in. The deed would have been done ... had not some of the brethren been stationed in advance to watch the riverbank carefully; as the child was thrown they caught him ... Thus they prevented the command, performed as it was by the father's obedience and devotion, from having any effect.[13]

Cassian plainly prizes Patermutus's actions and attitude; but surely most of us will find it chilling and reprehensible. For my part, I would say that one can only wonder why the monks bothered to catch the child, if the father's willingness to kill the child was so praiseworthy in their eyes. Can it be morally praiseworthy to will an act whose performance is morally prohibited?

An attitude similar to Cassian's but less appalling can still be found more than a millenium later in some texts (but not others) of the work of Teresa of Avila, to take just one example from among a host of thinkers who could have been selected. Writing to her sister nuns, Teresa says,

Oh, how desirable is ... [the] union with God's will! Happy the soul that has reached it. Such a soul will live tranquilly in this life, and in the next as well. Nothing in earthly events afflicts it unless it finds itself in some danger of losing God ...: neither sickness, nor poverty, nor death ... For this soul sees well that the Lord knows what He is doing better than ... [the soul] knows what it is desiring ... But alas for us, how few there must be who reach [union with God's will!] ... I tell you I am writing this with much pain upon seeing myself so far away [from union with God's will]—and all through my own fault .... Don't think the matter lies in my being so conformed to the will of God that if my father or brother dies I don't feel it, or that if there are trials or sicknesses I suffer them happily.[14]

Not feeling it when one's father dies, not weeping with grief over his death, is, in Teresa's view, a good spiritual condition which she is not yet willing to attribute to herself. Teresa is here echoing a tradition which finds its prime medieval exemplar in Augustine's *Confessions*. Augustine says that, at the death of his mother, by a powerful command of his will, he kept himself from weeping at her funeral, only to disgrace himself in his own eyes later by weeping copiously in private.[15]

In the same text from which I just quoted, Teresa emphasizes the importance of love of neighbour; but it is hard to see how love of neighbour coheres with the stern-minded attitude manifested by Teresa and Augustine in the face of the death (real or imagined) of a beloved parent. As I have argued elsewhere, it is the nature of love to desire the good of the beloved and union with him.[16] But the desire for the good of the beloved is frustrated if the beloved gets sick or dies. Or, if the stern-minded attitude is unwilling to concede that point, then this much is incontrovertible even on the stern-minded attitude: the desire for union with the beloved is frustrated when the beloved dies and so is absent. One way or another, then, the desires of love are frustrated when the beloved dies.

Consequently, there is something bad and lamentable, something worth tears, something whose loss brings affliction with it, about the death of any person whom one loves—one's father, or even one's neighbour, whom one is bound to love too, as Teresa thinks.

Unmoved tranquillity at the death of another person is thus incompatible with love of that person. To the extent to which one loves another person, one cannot be unmoved at his death. And so love of neighbour is in fact incompatible with the stern-minded attitude.

The stance Teresa wishes she might take towards her father's death, as she imagines it, can be usefully contrasted with Bernard of Clairvaux's reaction to the death of his brother. Commenting on his grief at that death, Bernard says to his religious community, "You, my sons, know how deep my sorrow is, how galling a wound it leaves."[17] And, addressing himself, he says, "Flow on, flow on, my tears ... Let my tears gush forth like fountains."[18] Reflecting on his own failure to repudiate his great sorrow over his brother's death, his failure, that is, to follow Augustine's model, Bernard says,

> It is but human and necessary that we respond to our friends with feeling, that we be happy in their company, disappointed in their absence. Social intercourse, especially between friends, cannot be purposeless: the reluctance to part and the yearning for each other when separated indicate how meaningful their mutual love must be when they are together.[19]

And Bernard is hardly the only figure in the Christian tradition who fails to accept and affirm Cassian's attitude. Aquinas is another.

There are isolated texts which might suggest to some readers that Aquinas himself is an adherent of Cassian's attitude. So, for example, in his commentary on Christ's line that he who loves his life will lose it, Aquinas reveals that he recognizes the concept of the desires of the heart; but, in this same passage, he also seems to suggest that such desires should be stamped out. He says.

> Everyone loves his own soul, but some love it *simpliciter* and some *secundum quid*. To love someone is to will the good for him; and so he who loves his soul wills the good for it. A person who wills for his soul the good *simpliciter* also loves his soul *simpliciter*. But a person who wills some particular good for his soul loves his soul *secundum quid*. The goods for the soul *simpliciter* are those things by which the soul is good, namely, the highest good, which is God. And so he who wills for his soul the divine good, a spiritual good, loves his soul *simpliciter*. But he who wills for his soul earthly goods such as riches and honors, pleasures, and things of that sort, he loves his soul [only] *secundum quid* ... He who loves his soul *secundum quid* namely with regard to temporal goods, will lose it.[20]

And the implication seems to be that, for Aquinas, the person who does not want to lose his soul should extirpate from himself all desires for any good other than the highest good, which is, as Aquinas says, God.

But it is important to see that what is at issue for Aquinas in this passage is the desire for worldly things, that is for those goods, such as money or fame, which diminish when they are distributed. On Aquinas' scale of values, any good which diminishes when it is distributed is only a small good. When it comes to the desires of the heart for things which are earthly goods but great goods, such as the love of a particular person, Aquinas' attitude differs sharply from Cassian's. So, for example, in explaining why Christ told his disciples that he was going to the father in order to comfort them when they were sad at the prospect of being separated from him, Aquinas says,

> It is common among friends to be less sad over the absence of a friend when the friend is going to something which exalts him.

That is why the Lord gives them this reason [for his leaving] in order to console them.[21]

Unlike Teresa's repudiation of grief at the prospect of losing her father, Aquinas is here, as in many other places, accepting the appropriateness of a person's grief at the loss of a loved person and validating the need for consolation for such grief

So Aquinas is not to be ranked among the members of the stern-minded group, any more than Bernard is; and, of course, in other moods, when she is not self-consciously evaluating her own spiritual progress, Teresa herself sounds more like Bernard and Aquinas than like Cassian. As far as that goes, the Psalmist who authored Psalm 37 is not on Cassian's side. The Psalmist claims that God will give the desires of the heart to those who delight in the Lord; so the Psalmist is supposing that, for those who trust in God, God himself honours the desires of the heart. On this subject, then, the Christian tradition is of two minds. Not all its influential figures stand with Cassian; and, even among those who do, many are double-minded about it.

IV. A POSSIBLE CONFUSION

But, someone will surely object, isn't it a part of Christian doctrine that God allows the death of any person who dies? Does anyone die when God wills that that person live? So when a person dies, on Christian theology, isn't it the will of God that that person die? In what sense, then, could Teresa be united with God in will if she grieved over her father's death? How could she be united with God, as she explains she wants to be, if her will is frustrated in what God's will accepts or commands?

The position presupposed by the questions of this putative objector, in my view, rests on too simple an understanding of God's will and union with God's will.

To see why, assume that at death Teresa's father is united with God in heaven. Then the death which unites Teresa's father permanently with God has the opposite effect for Teresa: at least for the time being, it deprives Teresa of her father's presence and so keeps her from union with him, at least for the rest of Teresa's earthly life. For this reason, on the Christian doctrine Teresa accepts, love's desire for union with the beloved cannot be fulfilled in the same way for Teresa as for God. If Teresa's will is united with God's will in desiring union with a beloved person, then Teresa's will must also be frustrated at the very event, her father's dying, which fulfils God's will with respect to this desire.

Something analogous can be said about the other desire of love, for the good of the beloved. If Teresa desires the good of her father, she can only desire what her own mind sees as that good; but her mind's ability to see the good is obviously much smaller than God's. To the extent to which Teresa's will is united with God's will in desiring the good of the beloved, then Teresa will also desire for the beloved person things different from those desired by God, in virtue of Teresa's differing ability to see the good for the beloved person.

It is easy to become confused here because the phrase "the good" can be used either attributively or referentially.[22] In this context, "the good of the beloved" can be used either to refer to particular things which are conducive to the beloved's well-being; or it can be used opaquely, to refer to anything whatever, under the description *the good of the beloved*. A mother who is baffled by the quarrels among her adult children and clueless about how to bring about a just peace for them may say, despairingly, "I just want the good for everybody". She is then using the phrase "the good" attributively, with no idea of how to use it referentially.

If Teresa were tranquil over any affliction which happens to her father, because she thinks that in this tranquillity her will is united to God's will and that she is therefore willing the good for her father,[23] "the good" in this thought of hers is being used attributively, to designate *whatever* God thinks is good. But this cannot be the way "the good" is used in any thought of God's, without relativizing the good entirely to God's will. If we eschew such relativism, then it is not the case that anything God desires is good just because God desires it. And so it is also not true that God desires as the good of a beloved person *whatever* it is that God desires for her. When God desires the good for someone, then, God must desire it by desiring particular things as good for that person. Consequently, to say that God desires the good for a person is to use "the good" referentially.

For this reason, when, in an effort to will what God wills, Teresa desires *whatever* happens to her father as the good for her father, she thereby actually *fails* to will what God wills. To be united with God in willing the good requires willing for the beloved particular things which are in fact the good for the beloved, and doing so requires recognizing those things which constitute that good.

At the death of Mao Tse-tung, one of the groups competing for power was called "the Whatever Faction," because the members of that group were committed to maintaining as true, and compulsory for all Chinese to believe, anything Mao said, whatever it was.[24] In trying to desire whatever happens as good because God wills it, a person is as it were trying to be part of a Whatever Faction for God. She is trying to maintain as good anything that happens, whatever it is, on the grounds that it is what God wills. By contrast, in his great lament over the death of his brother, Bernard of Clairvaux is willing to affirm both his passionate grief over the loss of his brother and his acceptance of God's allowing that death. Bernard says, "Shall I find fault with [God's] judgment because I wince from the pain?";[25] "I have no wish to repudiate the decrees of God, nor do I question that judgment by which each of us has received his due ...."[26] Bernard grieves over this particular death as a bad thing, even while he accepts that God's allowing this bad thing is a good thing.

Understanding the subtle but important difference in attitude between Teresa and Bernard on this score helps to elucidate the otherwise peculiar part of the book of Job in which God rebukes Job's comforters because they did not say of God the thing which is right, unlike God's servant Job, who did. What the comforters had said was that God is justified in allowing Job's suffering. Job, on the other hand, had complained bitterly that his suffering is unjust and that God should not have allowed it to happen. How is it that, in the story, God affirms Job's position and repudiates that of the comforters? The answer lies in seeing that the comforters took Job's suffering to be good just because, in their view. Job's suffering was willed by God. In effect, then, the comforters were (and wanted to be) part of the Whatever Faction of God. Job, by contrast, was intransigent in his refusal to be partisan in this way. And so, on the apparently paradoxical view of the book of Job, in opposing God, Job is more allied with God's will than are the comforters, who were taking God's part. That is why when in the story God comes to adjudicate, he sides with Job, who had opposed him, and not with the comforters, who were trying to be his partisans.

The apparent paradox here can be resolved by the scholastic distinction between God's antecedent and consequent will. On this distinction, whatever happens in the world happens only because it is in accordance with God's will, but that will is God's *consequent* will. God's consequent will, however, is to be distinguished from his antecedent will; and many of the things which happen in the world are not in accordance with God's *antecedent* will. Roughly put, God's *antecedent* will is what God would have willed if things in the world had been up to God alone. God's *consequent* will is what God in fact will, given what he knows that his creatures will. God's consequent will is his will for the greatest good available in the circumstances which are generated through creaturely free will.

To try to be in accord with God's will by taking as acceptable, as unworthy of sorrow, everything that happens is to confuse the consequent will of God with the antecedent will. It is to accept as intrinsically good even those things which God wills as good only secundum quid, that is, as the best available in the circumstances. But God does not will as intrinsically good everything he wills; what he wills in his consequent will, what is the best available in the circumstances, might be only the lesser of evils, not the intrinsically good.

And so to accept as good whatever happens on the grounds that it is God's will is the wrong way to try to be united with God's will. One can desire as intrinsically good what one sees for oneself is good in the circumstances, or one can desire[27] as intrinsically good whatever happens, on the grounds that it is God's will. But only the former desire can be in accordance with God's will, given that God's consequent will is not the same as his antecedent will. For the same reasons, only the former desire is conductive to union with God. Although it appears paradoxical, then, the closest a human person may be able to come, in this life, to uniting her will with God's will may include her willing things (say, that a beloved person not die) which are opposed to God's (consequent) will.

It is also important to see in this connection that, in principle, there cannot be any competition between the love of God and the love of other persons. On the contrary, if one does not love one's neighbour, then one does not love God either. That is because to love God is to desire union with him; and union with God requires being united in will with him. But a person who does not love another, his father or brother, for example, cannot be united in will with a God who does love these people. So, in being tranquil and unmoved in the face of the death of a beloved father or mother, a person is not more united with God, or more in harmony with God's will, but less.

V. DENYING ONESELF

Something also needs to be said in this connection about the Christian doctrine mandating denial of the self. This much understanding of the two different ways in which one can try to will what God wills shows that there are also two correspondingly different interpretations of that doctrine.

Cassian and others who hold the stern-minded attitude manifest one such understanding. A person who shares Cassian's attitude will attempt to deny his self by, in effect, refusing to let his own mind and his own will exercise their characteristic functions. That is because a person who attempts to see as good whatever happens, on the grounds that whatever happens is willed by God, is trying to suppress, or trying to fail to acquire, his own

understanding of the good. And a person who attempts to will as good whatever happens, on the same grounds, is trying to suppress the desires his own will forms, or trying not to acquire the desires his will would have formed if he were not in the grip of the stern-minded attitude. To attempt to deny the self in the stern-minded way is thus to try not to have a self at all. A woman who says sincerely to her father, "I want only what you want," and "whatever you think is good is good in my view, too," is a woman who is trying to be at one with her father by having no self of her own.

On the other hand, it is possible to let one's own faculties of intellect and will have their normal functioning and still deny oneself. This is a stance with which we are all familiar from our experiences of ordinary, daily life. Consider, for example, a mother with the stomach flu who creeps out of bed to care for her baby who also has the flu. When she leaves her bed to tend the baby, she is preferring to meet the baby's needs rather than her own. That is, she desires to stay in bed, but she also desires that the baby's needs take precedence over her own needs and desires. In her desire about the rank-ordering of desires, she does not cease to desire to stay in bed. She still has that desire; she just acts counter to it. This is to deny the self by first having a self to deny. Unlike the no-self position, this position is compatible with sorrow, and tears, for the things lost in the desires denied.

On reflection, it is clear that, contrary to first appearances, the no-self position is actually incompatible with the Christian injunction of self-denial. That is because one cannot crucify a self one does not have. To crucify one's self is to have desires and to be willing to act counter to them. An adherent to the Whatever Faction of God cannot deny his self, however, because he has constructed his desires in such away that, whatever he wills, he does not will counter to his own desires. A person who is a partisan of the no-self position has a first-order desire for whatever it may be that is God's will, and he attempts to have no first-order desires which are in conflict with whatever it may be that is God's will. That is why (unlike the real Teresa, who was full of very human emotions) such a person would not weep if her father died. In theory, at any rate, whatever happens to her is in accordance with her first-order will and is therefore not a source of sorrow to her. In virtue of the fact that she has tried to extirpate from herself all desires except the one desire for whatever it may be that is God's will, such a person has no desires which are frustrated by whatever happens, as long as she herself remains committed to willing whatever God wills.[28]

The self-crucifying denier of the self, by contrast, has first-order desires for things his own intellect finds good, so that he is vulnerable to grief in the frustration of those desires. But he prefers his grief and frustration to the violation of God's will. In this sense, he also wills that God's will be done. His second-order desire is that God's desires take precedence over his own. When Christ says, "not my will but yours be done," he is not expressing the no-self position, because he is admitting that he has desires in conflict with God's desires. On the other hand, in virtue of preferring his pain to the violation of God's will, he is also willing that God's desires take precedence over his. This is the sense, then, in which he is willing that God's will be done.

VI. THE DESIRES OF THE HEART AND THE FLOURISHING OF A PERSON

So, for all these reasons, the stern-minded attitude is to be repudiated. Whatever its antiquity and ancestry, such influential thinkers as Bernard and Aquinas do not accept it. More importantly, it is an unpalatable position, even from the point of view of an ascetically minded Christianity. It underlies the repellent and lamentable mind-set exemplified in Cassian's story, and it is incompatible with the love of one's neighbour and consequently also with love of God. There are things worth desiring other than the intrinsically valuable things necessary for human flourishing, and the desires for these things should not be suppressed or stamped out. On the contrary, as Cassian's story makes plain, the attempt to extirpate any desires of the heart

does not lead to human excellence, as Cassian thought it did, but to a kind of inhumanity willing to murder one's own child in the service of a confused and reprehensible attempt at self-denial.

There is an apparent paradox here, however. As I introduced the phrase, the desires of the heart are desires which are central to a person's web of desires but whose objects have the value they do for her because of her desire for them, not because of their connection to general human flourishing. On the face of it, then, losing the objects of such desires or giving up those desires themselves is compatible with general human flourishing for that person. But the rejection of the stern-minded attitude seems to imply that a person's flourishing requires that he have desires of the heart and that he strive to have what he desires. Consequently, it also seems to imply that it is essential to a person's flourishing that he have desires of the heart. But, then, if the desires of the heart are required for his flourishing, it seems that the objects of those desires are as well. And so it seems to follow, paradoxically, that it is essential to human flourishing that a person desire and seek to have things at least some of which are not necessary to human flourishing.

In recent work, Harry Frankfurt has argued that it is useful for a person to have final ends.[29] The central idea of his argument is the thought that a person with no final ends at all will have a life which lacks flourishing. And so final ends *are* useful as a means to an end, namely, human flourishing. The apparently paradoxical claim about the desires of the heart can be understood analogously. Human beings are constructed in such a way that they naturally set their hearts on things in addition to and different from intrinsically valuable things essential to general human flourishing. That is why confining a person's desires just to human flourishing has something inhuman about it. A person's flourishing therefore also requires that he care about and seek to have things besides those that are intrinsically valuable components of or means to human flourishing.[30] On Frankfurt's view, having a desire for something which is not a means to anything else is a means to a person's flourishing.

On the view I have argued for here, having a desire for things which are not essential to flourishing and seeking to have those things is also necessary as a means to flourishing.

And so, although no particular thing valued as a desire of the heart is essential to a person's flourishing, human flourishing is not possible in the absence of the desires of the heart.

VII. CONCLUSION

For all these reasons, we can safely leave the objections of the stern-minded attitude to one side. It therefore remains the case that justification is also needed for suffering stemming from unfulfilled or frustrated desires of the heart. For this reason, theodicies which focus just on one or another variety of general human flourishing as the morally sufficient reason for God's allowing evil are, at best, incomplete. Even if we give a theodicy such as Hick's or Swinburne's everything it wants as regards the relation between suffering and flourishing, however flourishing is understood in their theodicies, there remains the problem of suffering stemming from the loss of the desires of one's heart.

Take the story of Job, for example. For the sake of argument, let it be the case, as Saadiah Gaon appears to hold in his excellent and impressive commentary, that Job's suffering is necessary to his ennobling and purification, morally acceptable as a means to these things, and outweighed by them, in the sense that (on some objective measure) Job's ennobling and purification are a greater good than his suffering is an evil. Even if this were entirely so, and even if it were right that ennobling and purification constituted consummate human flourishing, something more would be needed for theodicy in Job's case. Job might care about his children at least as much as about his own ennobling and purification; and he might be heartbroken at the loss of his children, even with the benefit to him of his ennobling and purification. Something also needs to be said about the moral justification for God's allowing such heartbreak.

Someone might object that if the benefit to Job really is connected to his suffering in the way I have just described, then nothing more is needed for theodicy, because the good given to Job through his suffering defeats the suffering. But this is to accord no value to the desires of Job's heart. It is, in effect, to say with regard to Job a much sterner version of what the loving but exasperated father said to his daughter: It is not reasonable to weep about these things. But, as I have been at pains to show, disregarding or downplaying the desires of the heart is itself unreasonable. Suffering is a function of what we care about, and we care not only about human flourishing; we care also about the things on which we have set our hearts. The suffering stemming from the loss of the heart's desires also needs to be redeemed. The benefit which outweighs the suffering for Job, as Saadiah Gaon sees it, outweighs that suffering only on the scale of values which measures the intrinsic worth of things essential to human flourishing in general. It does not outweigh it on the scale which measures things that have the value they do for a particular person only because he has set his heart on them.

That this is so helps to explain why so many people feel uneasy or disappointed at attempted solutions to the problem of evil which focus on some global good (for humanity in general—the significant use of free will, for example—as a morally sufficient reason for God to allow suffering. If a person's own flourishing is not sufficient to justify God in allowing her to be heartbroken, then, a fortiori, some component of or contribution to the flourishing of the human species considered as a whole cannot do so either.

And so the desires of the heart also need to be considered in connection with the problem of evil. For my part, I think it is possible to find a way to develop traditional theodicies to include satisfactory consideration of the problem posed by the desires of the heart;[31] but, clearly, that complicated and challenging task lies outside the scope of this paper.

REFERENCES

Adams, Marilyn, *Horrendous Evils and the Goodness of God* (Ithaca, NY: Cornell University Press, 1999).

Astell, Ann, *The Song of Songs in the Middle Ages* (Ithaca, NY: Cornell University Press, 1990).

Cassian, *The Monastic Institutes*, tr. Jerome Bertram (London: Saint Austin Press, 1999).

Frankfurt, Harry, "On the Usefulness of Final Ends," *Necessity, Volition, and Love* (Princeton, NJ: Princeton University Press, 1998).

Hick, John, *Evil and the God of Love* (New York: Harper and Row, 1966).

___ "God, Evil and Mystery," *Religious Studies* 3 (1968a): 539–46.

___ "The Problem of Evil in the First and Last Things," *Journal of Theological Studies* 19 (1968b): 591–602.

Hull, Jonathan, *Touching the Rock. An Experience of Blindness* (New York: Vintage Books, 1991).

MacFarquhar, Roderick, "The Succession to Mao and the End of Maoism," in *The Cambridge History of China*, vol. 15, *The People's Republic, pt.2: Revolutions within the Chinese Revolution: 1966–1982* (Cambridge: Cambridge University Press, 1991).

Saadiah Gaon, *The Book of Beliefs and Opinions*, tr. Samuel Rosenblatt (New Haven, CT: Yale University Press, 1948).

Stump, Eleonore, "Love, By All Accounts," Proceedings and Addresses of The American Philosophical Association, Vol. 80, No. 2, November 2006.

_____ *Wandering in Darkness: Narrative and the Problem of Suffering* (Oxford: Oxford University Press, forthcoming).

Swinburne, Richard, *Providence and the Problem of Evil* (Oxford: Oxford University Press, 1998).

Teresa of Avila, *The Interior Castle* (Mahwah, NJ: Paulist Press, 1979).

Vanier, Jean, *Becoming Human* (Mahwah, NJ: Paulist Press, 1998).

NOTES

For helpful comments on earlier drafts of this paper or on its contents, I am grateful to Jeffrey Brower, Frank Burch Brown, John Foley, John Kavanaugh, Scott MacDonald, Michael Murray, Michael Rea, Theodore Vitali, and anonymous reviewers for *Oxford Studies in Philosophy of Religion*.

1. There is a large, contentious philosophical literature on the nature of human flourishing or well-being, and it is not part of my purpose to try to engage that literature here. For my purposes in this paper, I will understand flourishing to consist in just those things necessary in a person's life for that person's life to be admirable and meaningful.

2. Saadiah Gaon 1948: 246–7.

3. Hick 1966. For Hick's defence of his solutions against objections, see, for example, Hick 1968a: 539–46, and Hick 1968b: 591–602.

4. See Swinburne 1998.

5. In Adams 1999, Marilyn Adams makes a distinction which is at least related to the distinction I am after here. She says, "the value of a person's life may be assessed from the inside (in relation to that person's own goals, ideals, and choices) and from the outside (in relation to the aims, tastes, values, and preferences of others)... My notion is that for a person's life to be a great good to him/her on the whole, the external point of view (even if it is God's) is not sufficient" (p. 145).

6. The expression "the desire of the heart" is also ambiguous. It can mean either a particular kind of desire or else the thing which is desired in that way. When we say, "the desire of his heart was to be a great musician," the expression refers to a desire; when we say, "In losing her, he lost the desire of his heart," the expression refers to the thing desired. I will not try to sort out this ambiguity here; I will simply trust to the context to disambiguate the expression.

7. Ps. 37: 4–5.

8. Except for conceptions of flourishing which make flourishing identical to the satisfaction of desires, but equating flourishing just with desire satisfaction is problematic enough that it can be left to one side here.

9. Vanier 1998: 158–9.

10. Hull 1991: 205–6.

11. Elsewhere I consider the complication of cases in which an apparently appropriate heart's desire is such that its fulfilment would undermine the flourishing of the person who has it. So, for example, the great English poet John Milton apparently had a heart's desire to be an administrator in the Puritan government of his time; but his government work kept him from writing poetry. All his greatest poetry was written after the fail of the Puritan regime. There are also cases in which a person sets his heart on what he himself takes to be essential to his flourishing, when in fact he is mistaken on this score. Viktor Klemperer supposed that his flourishing was dependent on his writing a great study of eighteenth-century French literature, and he describes his own sense of the blight of his life in consequence of his inability to write a great book in his stunningly excellent diaries, published now to rave reviews. For consideration of complicated cases such as these, see my *Wandering in Darkness: Narrative and the Problem of Suffering* (Oxford, forthcoming).

12. For a persuasive statement of a case for such a view, see Adams 1998.

13. Cassian 1999: 55–6.

14. Teresa of Avila 1979: 98, 99, 100.

15. *Confessions* IX.12.

16. Stump 2006.

17. Cited in Astell 1990: 126.

18. Cited in Astell 1990: 130.

19. Cited in Astell 1990: 133.

20. *Super Evangelium S.Ioannis Lectura,* John 12: 24–5, Lectio IV.7, 1643–1644.

21. *Super Evangelium S.Ioannis Lectura,* John 14: 27–31, Lectio VIII.l, 1966.

22. "The commander of the armed forces" is used referentially when it refers to the particular person who is the President; it is used attributively when it refers to anyone who holds the office of commander without reference to a particular person who in fact currently holds the office.

23. It is important to put the point in terms of what *happens* to her father, rather than in terms of any state or condition of her father, since there are certainly things her father might do which cause Teresa a grief she would approve of having.

24. The official formula was "Whatever policy Chairman Mao decided upon, we shall resolutely defend; whatever directives Chairman Mao issued, we shall steadfastly obey." See MacFarquhar 1991: 372

25. Cited in Astell 1990: 133.

26. Cited in Astell 1990: 130.

27. Or try to accept—a distinction manifested by Teresa's own description of herself.

28. The last clause is a necessary caveat because, presumably, even an adherent to the position would be distressed at finding sin in himself (and maybe even at finding sin in others), since sin cannot be considered in accordance with God's will.

29. Frankfurt 1998.

30. In this respect, the desires of the heart are to human flourishing what accidents are to a primary substance. Any particular accident is not necessary to a substance, but it is necessary to a substance that it have accidents. Analogously, no particular desire of the heart is necessary for a person's flourishing, but it is necessary for her flourishing that she have desires of die heart.

31. I argue for this claim in detail in my *Wandering in Darkness. Narrative and the Problem of Suffering* (Oxford, forthcoming).

IV.C.5

Horrendous Evils and the Goodness of God

MARILYN McCORD ADAMS

Marilyn McCord Adams (1943–) is a research professor of philosophy at the University of North Carolina, Chapel Hill. She has held positions in philosophy and theology at Oxford University, Yale University, and the University of California, Los Angeles, and has written extensively on topics at the intersection of both disciplines. In this article, Adams argues that standard responses to the problem of evil fall short in their ability to deal with "horrendous evil." She then argues that God could defeat such evils only by somehow "integrating participation in horrendous evils into a person's relationship with God."

1. INTRODUCTION

Over the past thirty years, analytic philosophers of religion have defined "the problem of evil" in terms of the prima-facie difficulty in consistently maintaining

(1)   God exists, and is omnipotent, omniscient, and perfectly good

and

(2)   Evil exists.

In a crisp and classic article, "Evil and Omnipotence,"[1] J. L. Mackie emphasized that the problem is not that (1) and (2) are logically inconsistent by themselves, but that they together with quasi-logical rules formulating attribute-analyses—such as

(P1)   A perfectly good being would always eliminate evil so far as it could,

and

(P2)   There are *no limits* to what an omnipotent being can do—

constitute an inconsistent premiss-set. He added, of course, that the inconsistency might be removed by substituting alternative and perhaps more subtle analyses, but cautioned that such replacements of (P1) and (P2) would save "ordinary theism" from his charge of positive irrationality, only if true to its "essential requirements."[2]

In an earlier paper, "Problems of Evil: More Advice to Christian Philosophers,"[3] I underscored Mackie's point and took it a step further. In debates about whether the argument from evil can establish the irrationality of religious belief, care must be taken, both by the atheologians who deploy it and by the believers who defend against it, to ensure that the operative attribute-analyses accurately reflect that religion's understanding of divine power and goodness. It does the atheologian no good to argue for the falsity of Christianity on the ground that the existence of an omnipotent, omniscient, pleasure-maximizer is incompossible with a

Marilyn McCord Adams, 'Horrendous Evils and The Goodness of God', first published in *Proceedings of the Aristotelian Society*, Supplementary Vol. 63 (1989), pp. 297–310, with revisions and additional notes from the revised version in The Problem of Evil, ed. Robert Merrihew Adams and Marilyn McCord Adams (Oxford University Press, 1990), pp. © The Aristotelian Society 1989. Reprinted by permission of the Aristotelian Society and Oxford University Press.

world such as ours, because Christians never believed God was a pleasure-maximizer anyway. But equally, the truth of Christianity would be inadequately defended by the observation that an omnipotent, omniscient egoist could have created a world with suffering creatures, because Christians insist that God loves other (created) persons than Himself. The extension of "evil" in (2) is likewise important. Since Mackie and his successors are out to show that "the several parts of the *essential* theological doctrine are inconsistent with *one another*,"[4] they can accomplish their aim only if they circumscribe the extension of "evil" as their religious opponents do. By the same token, it is not enough for Christian philosophers to explain how the power, knowledge, and goodness of God could coexist with some evils or other; a full account must exhibit the compossibility of divine perfection with evils in the amounts and of the kinds found in the actual world (and evaluated as such by Christian standards).

The moral of my earlier story might be summarized thus: where the internal coherence of a system of religious beliefs is at stake, successful arguments for its inconsistency must draw on premises (explicitly, or implicitly) internal to that system or obviously acceptable to its adherents; likewise for successful rebuttals or explanations of consistency. The thrust of my argument is to push both sides of the debate towards more detailed attention to and subtle understanding of the religious system in question.

As a Christian philosopher, I want to focus in this paper on the problem for the truth of Christianity raised by what I shall call "horrendous" evils. Although our world is riddled with them, the biblical record punctuated by them, and one of them—namely, the passion of Christ; according to Christian belief, the judicial murder of God by the people of God—is memorialized by the Church on its most solemn holiday (Good Friday) and in its central sacrament (the Eucharist), the problem of horrendous evils is largely skirted by standard treatments for the good reason that they are intractable by them. After showing why, I will draw on other Christian materials to sketch ways of meeting this, the deepest of religious problems.

2. DEFINING THE CATEGORY

For present purposes, I define "horrendous evils" as "evils the participation in (the doing or suffering of) which gives one reason prima facie to doubt whether one's life could (given their inclusion in it) be a great good to one on the whole."[5] Such reasonable doubt arises because it is so difficult humanly to conceive how such evils could be overcome. Borrowing Chisholm's contrast between *balancing off* (which occurs when the opposing values of *mutually exclusive* parts of a whole partially or totally cancel each other out) and *defeat* (which cannot occur by the mere addition to the whole of a new part of opposing value, but involves some "organic unity" among the values of parts and wholes, as when the positive aesthetic value of a whole painting defeats the ugliness of a small colour patch),[6] horrendous evils seem prima facie, not only to balance off but to engulf the positive value of a participant's life. Nevertheless, that very horrendous proportion, by which they threaten to rob a person's life of positive meaning, cries out not only to be engulfed, but to be made meaningful through positive and decisive defeat.

I understand this criterion to be objective, but relative to individuals. The example of habitual complainers, who know to make the worst of a good situation, shows individuals not to be incorrigible experts on what ills would defeat the positive value of their lives. Nevertheless, nature and experience endow people with different strengths; one bears easily what crushes another. And a major consideration in determining whether an individual's life is/has been a great good to him/her on the whole, is invariably and appropriately how it has seemed to him/her.[7]

I offer the following list of paradigmatic horrors: the rape of a woman and axing off of her arms, psychophysical torture whose ultimate goal is the disintegration of personality, betrayal of one's deepest loyalties, cannibalizing one's own offspring, child abuse of the sort described by Ivan Karamazov, child pornography, parental incest, slow death by starvation, participation in the Nazi death camps, the explosion of nuclear bombs over populated areas, having to choose which of one's children shall live and which be executed by terrorists, being the accidental and/or unwitting agent of the disfigurement or death of those one loves best. I regard these as *paradigmatic*, because I believe most people would find in the doing or suffering of them prima-facie reason to doubt the positive meaning of their lives.[8] Christian belief counts the crucifixion of Christ another: on the one hand, death by crucifixion seemed to defeat Jesus' Messianic vocation; for according to Jewish law, death by hanging from a tree made its victim ritually accursed, definitively excluded from the compass of God's people, *a fortiori* disqualified from being the Messiah. On the other hand, it represented the defeat of its perpetrators' leadership vocations, as those who were to prepare the people of God for the Messiah's coming, killed and ritually accursed the true Messiah, according to later theological understanding, God Himself.

3. THE IMPOTENCE OF STANDARD SOLUTIONS

For better and worse, the by now standard strategies for "solving" the problem of evil are powerless in the face of horrendous evils.

3.1. Seeking the Reason-Why

In his model article "Hume on Evil,"[9] Pike takes up Mackie's challenge, arguing that (P1) fails to reflect ordinary moral intuitions (more to the point, I would add, Christian beliefs), and traces the abiding sense of trouble to the hunch that an omnipotent, omniscient being could have no reason compatible with perfect goodness for permitting (bringing about) evils, because all legitimate excuses arise from ignorance or weakness. Solutions to the problem of evil have thus been sought in the form of counter-examples to this latter claim, i.e. logically possible reasons-why that would excuse even an omnipotent, omniscient God! The putative logically possible reasons offered have tended to be *generic* and *global*: generic in so far as some *general* reason is sought to cover all sorts of evils; global in so far as they seize upon some feature of the world as a whole. For example, philosophers have alleged that the desire to make a world with one of the following properties—"the best of all possible worlds,"[10] "a world more perfect than which is impossible," "a world exhibiting a perfect balance of retributive justice,"[11] "a world with as favorable a balance of (created) moral good over moral evil as God can weakly actualize"[12]—would constitute a reason compatible with perfect goodness for God's creating a world with evils in the amounts and of the kinds found in the actual world. Moreover, such general reasons are presented as so powerful as to do away with any need to catalogue types of evils one by one, and examine God's reason for permitting each in particular. Plantinga explicitly hopes that the problem of horrendous evils can thus be solved without being squarely confronted.[13]

3.2. The Insufficiency of Global Defeat

A pair of distinctions is in order here: (i) between two dimensions of divine goodness in relation to creation—namely, "producer of global goods" and "goodness to" or "love of individual created persons"; and (ii) between the overbalance/defeat of evil by good on the global scale, and the overbalance/ defeat of evil by good within the context of an individual person's life.[14] Correspondingly, we may separate two problems of evil parallel to the two sorts of goodness mentioned in (i).

In effect, generic and global approaches are directed to the first problem: they defend divine goodness along the first (global) dimension by suggesting logically possible strategies for the global defeat of evils. But establishing God's excellence as a producer of global goods does not automatically solve the second problem, especially in a world containing horrendous evils. For God cannot be said to be good or loving to any created persons the positive meaning of whose lives He allows to be engulfed in and/or defeated by evils—that is, individuals within whose lives horrendous evils remain undefeated. Yet, the only way unsupplemented global and generic approaches could have to explain the latter, would be by applying their general reasons-why to particular cases of horrendous suffering.

Unfortunately, such an exercise fails to give satisfaction. Suppose for the sake of argument that horrendous evil could be included in maximally perfect world orders; its being partially constitutive of such an order would assign it that generic and global positive meaning. But would knowledge of such a fact defeat for a mother the prima-facie reason provided by her cannibalism of her own infant to wish that she had never been born? Again, the aim of perfect retributive balance confers meaning on evils imposed. But would knowledge that the torturer was being tortured give the victim who broke down and turned traitor under pressure any more reason to think his/her life worth while? Would it not merely multiply reasons for the torturer to doubt that his/her life could turn out to be a good to him/her on the whole? Could the truck-driver who accidentally runs over his beloved child find consolation in the idea that this middle-known[15] but unintended side-effect was part of the price God accepted for a world with the best balance of moral good over moral evil he could get?

Not only does the application to horrors of such generic and global reasons for divine permission of evils fail to solve the second problem of evil; it makes it worse by adding *generic prima-facie* reasons to doubt whether human life would be a great good to individual human beings in possible worlds where such divine motives were operative. For, taken in isolation and made to bear the weight of the whole explanation, such reasons-why draw a picture of divine indifference or even hostility to the human plight. Would the fact that God permitted horrors because they were constitutive means to His end of global perfection, or that He tolerated them because He could obtain that global end anyway, make the participant's life more tolerable, more worth living for him/her? Given radical human vulnerability to

horrendous evils, the ease with which humans participate in them, whether as victim or perpetrator, would not the thought that God visits horrors on anyone who caused them, simply because he/she deserves it, provide one more reason to expect human life to be a nightmare?

Those willing to split the two problems of evil apart might adopt a divide-and-conquer strategy, by simply denying divine goodness along the second dimension. For example, many Christians do not believe that God will ensure an overwhelmingly good life to each and every person He creates. Some say the decisive defeat of evil with good is promised only within the lives of the obedient, who enter by the narrow gate. Some speculate that the elect may be few. Many recognize that the sufferings of this present life are as nothing compared to the hell of eternal torment, designed to defeat goodness with horrors within the lives of the damned.

Such a road can be consistently travelled only at the heavy toll of admitting that human life in worlds such as ours is a bad bet. Imagine (adapting Rawls's device) persons in a pre-original position, considering possible worlds containing managers of differing power, wisdom, and character, and subjects of varying fates. The question they are to answer about each world is whether they would willingly enter it as a human being, from behind a veil of ignorance as to which position they would occupy. Reason would, I submit, dictate a negative verdict for worlds whose omniscient and omnipotent manager permits ante-mortem horrors that remain undefeated within the context of the human participant's life; *a fortiori*, for worlds in which some or most humans suffer eternal torment.

3.3. Inaccessible Reasons

So far, I have argued that generic and global solutions are at best incomplete: however well their account of divine motivating reasons deals with the first problem of evil, the attempt to extend it to the second fails by making it worse. This verdict might seem prima facie tolerable to standard generic and global approaches and indicative of only a minor modification in their strategy: let the above-mentioned generic and global reasons cover divine permission of non-horrendous evils, and find other *reasons* compatible with perfect goodness *why* even an omnipotent, omniscient God would permit horrors.

In my judgement, such an approach is hopeless. As Plantinga[16] points out, where horrendous evils are concerned, not only do we not know God's *actual* reason for permitting them; we cannot even *conceive* of any plausible candidate sort of reason consistent with worthwhile lives for human participants in them.

4. THE HOW OF GOD'S VICTORY

Up to now, my discussion has given the reader cause to wonder whose side I am on anyway. For I have insisted, with rebels like Ivan Karamazov and John Stuart Mill, on spotlighting the problem horrendous evils pose. Yet, I have signalled my preference for a version of Christianity that insists on both dimensions of divine goodness, and maintains not only (a) that God will be good enough to created persons to make human life a good bet, but also (b) that each created person will have a life that is a great good to him/her on the whole. My critique of standard approaches to the problem of evil thus seems to reinforce atheologian Mackie's verdict of "positive irrationality" for such a religious position.

4.1. Whys Versus Hows

The inaccessibility of reasons-why seems especially decisive. For surely an all-wise and all-powerful God, who loved each created person enough (a) to defeat any experienced horrors within the context of the participant's life, and (b) to give each created person a life that is a great good to him/her on the whole, would not permit such persons to suffer horrors for no reason.[17] Does not our inability even to conceive of plausible candidate reasons suffice to make belief in such a God

positively irrational in a world containing horrors? In my judgement, it does not.

To be sure, motivating reasons come in several varieties relative to our conceptual grasp: There are (i) reasons of the sort we can readily understand when we are informed of them (e.g. the mother who permits her child to undergo painful heart surgery because it is the only humanly possible way to save its life). Moreover, there are (ii) reasons we would be cognitively, emotionally, and spiritually equipped to grasp if only we had a larger memory or wider attention span (analogy: I may be able to memorize small town street plans; memorizing the road networks of the entire country is a task requiring more of the same, in the way that proving Gödel's theorem is not). Some generic and global approaches insinuate that divine permission of evils has motivating reasons of this sort. Finally, there are (iii) reasons that we are cognitively, emotionally, and/or spiritually too immature to fathom (the way a two-year-old child is incapable of understanding its mother's reasons for permitting the surgery). I agree with Plantinga that our ignorance of divine reasons for permitting horrendous evils is not of types (i) or (ii), but of type (iii).

Nevertheless, if there are varieties of ignorance, there are also varieties of reassurance.[18] The two-year-old heart patient is convinced of its mother's love, not by her cognitively inaccessible reasons, but by her intimate care and presence through its painful experience. The story of Job suggests something similar is true with human participation in horrendous suffering: God does not give Job His reasons-why, and implies that Job isn't smart enough to grasp them; rather Job is lectured on the extent of divine power, and sees God's goodness face to face! Likewise, I suggest, to exhibit the logical compossibility of both dimensions of divine goodness with horrendous suffering, it is not necessary to find logically possible reasons *why* God might permit them. It is enough to show *how* God can be good enough to created persons despite their participation in horrors—by defeating them within the context of the individual's life and by giving that individual a life that is a great good to him/her on the whole.

4.2. What Sort of Valuables?

In my opinion, the reasonableness of Christianity can be maintained in the face of horrendous evils only by drawing on resources of religious value theory. For one way for God to be *good to* created persons is by relating them appropriately to relevant and great goods. But philosophical and religious theories differ importantly on what valuables they admit into their ontology. Some maintain that "what you see is what you get," but nevertheless admit a wide range of valuables, from sensory pleasures, the beauty of nature and cultural artefacts, the joys of creativity, to loving personal intimacy. Others posit a transcendent good (e.g. the Form of the Good in Platonism, or God, the Supremely Valuable Object, in Christianity). In the spirit of Ivan Karamazov, I am convinced that the depth of horrific evil cannot be accurately estimated without recognizing it to be incommensurate with any package of merely non-transcendent goods and so unable to be balanced off, much less defeated, thereby.

Where the *internal* coherence of Christianity is the issue, however, it is fair to appeal to its own store of valuables. From a Christian point of view God is a being greater than which cannot be conceived, a good incommensurate with both created goods and temporal evils. Likewise, the good of beatific, face-to-face intimacy with God is simply incommensurate with any merely non-transcendent goods or ills a person might experience, Thus, the good of beatific face-to-face intimacy with God would *engulf* (in a sense analogous to Chisholmian balancing off) even the horrendous evils humans experience in this present life here below, and overcome any prima-facie reasons the individual had to doubt whether his/her life would or could be worth living.

4.3. Personal Meaning, Horrors
Defeated

Engulfing personal horrors within the context of the participant's life would vouchsafe to that individual a life that was a great good to him/her on the whole. I am still inclined to think it would

guarantee that immeasurable divine goodness to any person thus benefited. But there is good theological reason for Christians to believe that God would go further, beyond engulfment to defeat. For it is the nature of persons to look for meaning, both in their lives and in the world. Divine respect for and commitment to created personhood would drive God to make all those sufferings which threaten to destroy the positive meaning of a person's life meaningful through positive defeat.[19]

How could God do it? So far as I can see, only by integrating participation in horrendous evils into a person's relationship with God. Possible dimensions of integration are charted by Christian soteriology. I pause here to sketch three:[20] (i) First, because God in Christ participated in horrendous evil through His passion and death, human experience of horrors can be a means of *identifying* with Christ, either through *sympathetic* identification (in which each person suffers his/her own pains, but their similarity enables each to know what it is like for the other) or through *mystical* identification (in which the created person is supposed literally to experience a share of Christ's pain[21]). (ii) Julian of Norwich's description of heavenly welcome suggests the possible defeat of horrendous evil through divine gratitude. According to Julian, before the elect have a chance to thank God for all He has done for them, God will say, "Thank you for all your suffering, the suffering of your youth." She says that the creature's experience of divine gratitude will bring such full and unending joy as could not be merited by the whole sea of human pain and suffering throughout the ages.[22] (iii) A third idea identifies temporal suffering itself with a vision into the inner life of God, and can be developed several ways. Perhaps, contrary to medieval theology, God is not impassible, but rather has matched capacities for joy and for suffering. Perhaps, as the Heidelberg catechism suggests, God responds to human sin and the sufferings of Christ with an agony beyond human conception.[23] Alternatively, the inner life of God may be, strictly speaking and in and of itself, beyond both joy and sorrow. But, just as (according to Rudolf Otto) humans experience divine presence now as *tremendum* (with deep dread and anxiety), now as *fascinans* (with ineffable attraction), so perhaps our deepest suffering as much as our highest joys may themselves be direct visions into the inner life of God, imperfect but somehow less obscure in proportion to their intensity. And if a face-to-face vision of God is a good for humans incommensurate with any non-transcendent goods or ills, so any vision of God (including horrendous suffering) would have a good aspect in so far as it is a vision of God (even if it has an evil aspect in so far as it is horrendous suffering). For the most part, horrors are not recognized as experiences of God (any more than the city slicker recognizes his visual image of a brown patch as a vision of Beulah the cow in the distance). But, Christian mysticism might claim, at least from the post-mortem perspective of the beatific vision, such sufferings will be seen for what they were, and retrospectively no one will wish away any intimate encounters with God from his/her life-history in this world. The created person's experience of the beatific vision together with his/her knowledge that intimate divine presence stretched back over his/her ante-mortem life and reached down into the depths of his/her worst suffering, would provide retrospective comfort independent of comprehension of the reasons-why akin to the two-year-old's assurance of its mother's love. Taking this third approach, Christians would not need to commit themselves about what in any event we do not know: namely, whether we will (like the two-year-old) ever grow up enough to understand the reasons why God permits our participation in horrendous evils. For by contrast with the best of earthly mothers, such divine intimacy is an incommensurate good and would cancel out for the creature any need to know why.

5. CONCLUSION

The worst evils demand to be defeated by the best goods. Horrendous evils can be overcome only by the goodness of God. Relative to human nature, participation in horrendous evils and loving intimacy with God are alike disproportionate: for the former threatens to engulf the good in an individual human life with evil, while the latter guarantees the reverse engulfment of evil by good. Relative to one another, there is also disproportion, because the good that God *is*, and intimate relationship with Him, is incommensurate with created goods and evils alike. Because intimacy with God so outscales relations (good or bad) with any creatures, integration into the human person's relationship with God confers significant meaning and positive value even on horrendous suffering. This result coheres with basic Christian intuition: that the powers of darkness are stronger than humans, but they are no match for God!

Standard generic and global solutions have for the most part tried to operate within the territory common to believer and unbeliever, within the confines of religion-neutral value theory. Many discussions reflect the hope that substitute attribute-analyses, candidate reasons-why, and/or defeaters could issue out of values shared by believers and unbelievers alike. And some virtually make this a requirement on an adequate solution. Mackie knew better how to distinguish the many charges that may be levelled against religion. Just as philosophers may or may not find the existence of God plausible, so they may be variously attracted or repelled by Christian values of grace and redemptive sacrifice. But agreement on truth-value is not necessary to consensus on internal consistency. My contention has been that it is not only legitimate, but, given horrendous evils, necessary for Christians to dip into their richer store of valuables to exhibit the consistency of (1) and (2).[24] I would go one step further: assuming the pragmatic and/or moral (I would prefer to say, broadly speaking, religious) importance of believing that (one's own) human life is worth living, the ability of Christianity to exhibit how this could be so despite human vulnerability to horrendous evil, constitutes a pragmatic/moral/religious consideration in its favour, relative to value schemes that do not.

To me, the most troublesome weakness in what I have said lies in the area of conceptual under-development. The contention that God suffered in Christ or that one person can experience another's pain requires detailed analysis and articulation in metaphysics and philosophy of mind. I have shouldered some of this burden elsewhere,[25] but its full discharge is well beyond the scope of this paper.

NOTES

1. J. L. Mackie, "Evil and Omnipotence," *Mind*, 64 (1955) [Chapter 1 in this collection]; repr. in Nelson Pike (ed.), *God and Evil* (Englewood Cliffs, NJ: Prentice-Hall, 1964), 46–60.

2. Ibid. 47 [pp. 26–7, 37 above].

3. Marilyn McCord Adams, "Problems of Evil: More Advice to Christian Philosophers," *Faith and Philosophy* (Apr. 1988), 121–43.

4. Mackie, "Evil and Omnipotence," pp. 46–7 [p. 25 above], (emphasis mind).

5. Stewart Sutherland (in his comment "Horrendous Evils and the Goodness of God—II," *Proceedings of the Aristotelian Society*, suppl. vol. 63 (1989), 311–23; esp. 311) takes my criterion to be somehow "first-person." This was not my intention. My definition may be made more explicit as follows: an evil *e* is horrendous if and only if participation in *e* by person *p* gives everyone prima-facie reason to doubt whether *p*'s life can, given *p*'s participation in *e*, be a great good to *p* on the whole.

6. Roderick Chisholm, "The Defeat of Good and Evil" [Chapter III in this collection].

7. Cf. Malcolm's astonishment at Wittgenstein's dying exclamation that he had had a wonderful life, *Ludwig Wittgenstein: A Memoir* (London: Oxford University Press, 1962), 100.

8. Once again, more explicitly, most people would agree that a person *p*'s doing or suffering of them constitutes prima-facic reason to doubt whether *p*'s life can be, given such participation, a great good to *p* on the whole.

9. "Hume on Evil," *Philosophical Review*, 72 (1963), 180–97 [Chapter II in this collection]; reprinted in Pike (ed.), *God and Evil*, p. 88 [pp. 40–1 above].

10. Following Leibniz, Pike draws on this feature as part of what I have called his Epistemic Defence ("Problems of Evil: More Advice to Christian Philosophers," pp. 124–5).

11. Augustine, *On Free Choice of Will*, iii. 93–102, implies that there is a maximum value for created worlds, and a plurality of worlds that meet it. All of these contain rational free creatures; evils are foreseen but unintended side-effects of their creation. No matter what they choose, however, God can order their choices into a maximally perfect universe by establishing an order of retributive justice.

12. Plantinga takes this line in numerous discussions, in the course of answering Mackie's objection to the Free Will Defence, that God should have made sinless free creatures. Plantinga insists that, given incompatibilist freedom in creatures, God cannot strongly actualize any world He wants. It is logically possible that a world with evils in the amounts and of the kinds found in this world is the best that He could do, Plantinga argues, given His aim of getting some moral goodness in the world.

13. Alvin Plantinga, "Self-Profile," in James E. Tomberlin and Peter van Inwagcn (eds.). *Profiles: Alvin Plantinga* (Dordrecht, Boston, Mass., and Lancaster, Pa.: Reidel, 1985), 38.

14. I owe the second of these distinctions to a remark by Keith De Rose in our Fall 1987 seminar on the problem of evil at UCLA.

15. Middle knowledge, or knowledge of what is "in between" the actual and the possible, is the sort of knowledge of what a free creature *would do* in every situation in which that creature could possibly find himself. Following Luis de Molina and Francisco Suarez, Alvin Plantinga ascribes such knowledge to God, prior in the order of explanation to God's decision about which free creatures to actualize (in *The Nature of Necessity* (Oxford: Clarendon Press, 1974), pp. 164–93 [Chapter V in this collection]). Robert Merrihew Adams challenges this idea in his article "Middle Knowledge and the Problem of Evil," *American Philosophical Quarterly*, 14 (1977) [Chapter VI in this collection]; repr. in *The Virtue of*

Faith (New York: Oxford University Press, 1987), 77–93.

16. Alvin Plantinga, "Self-Profile," pp. 34–5.

17. This point was made by William Fitzpatrick in our Fall 1987 seminar on the problem of evil at UCLA.

18. Contrary to what Sutherland suggests ("Horrendous Evils," pp. 314–15), so far as the compossibility problem is concerned, I intend no illicit shift from reason to emotion. My point is that intimacy with a loving other is a good, participation in which can defeat evils, and so provide everyone with reason to think a person's life can be a great good to his/her on the whole, despite his/her participation in evils.

19. Note, once again, contrary to what Sutherland suggests ("Horrendous Evils," pp. 321–3) "horrendous evil *e* is defeated" entails *none* of the following propositions: "*e* was not horrendous," "*e* was not unjust," "*e* was not so bad after all." Nor does my suggestion that even horrendous evils can be defeated by a great enough (because incommensurate and uncreated) good, in any way impugn the reliability of our moral intuitions about injustice, cold-bloodedness, or horror. The judgement that participation in *e* constitutes prima-facie reason to believe that *p*'s life is ruined, stands and remains a daunting measure of *e*'s horror.

20. In my paper "Redemptive Suffering: A Christian Solution to the Problem of Evil," in Robert Audi and William J. Wainwright (eds.). *Rationality, Religious Belief, and Moral Commitment: New Essays in Philosophy of Religion* (Cornell University Pres., 1986), 248–67, I sketch how horrendous suffering can be meaningful by being made a vehicle of divine redemption for victim, perpetrator, and onlooker, and thus an occasion of the victim's collaboration with God. In "Separation and Reversal in Luke-Acts," in Thomas Morris (ed.).

Philosophy and the Christian Faith (Notre Dame, Ind.: Notre Dame University Press, 1988), 92–117, I attempted to chart the redemptive plot-line whereby horrendous sufferings are made meaningful by being woven into the divine redemptive plot. My considered opinion is that such collaboration would be too strenuous for the human condition were it not to be supplemented by a more explicit and beatific divine intimacy.

21. For example, Julian of Norwich tells us that she prayed for and received the latter (*Revelations of Divine Love*, ch. 17). Mother Theresa of Calcutta seems to construe Matthew 25: 31–46 to mean that the poorest and the least *are* Christ, and that their sufferings *are* Christ's (Malcolm Muggeridge, *Something Beautiful for God* (New York; Harper & Row, 1960), 72–5).

22. *Revelations of Divine Love*, ch. 14. I am grateful to Houston Smit for recognizing this scenario of Julian's as a case of Chisholmian defeat.

23. Cf. Plantinga, "Self-Profile," p. 36.

24. I develop this point at some length in "Problems of Evil: More Advice to Christian Philosophers," pp. 127–35.

25. For example in "The Metaphysics of the Incarnation in Some Fourteenth Century Franciscans," in William A. Frank and Girard J. Etzkorn (eds.), *Essays Honoring Allan B. Walter* (St. Bonaventure, NY: The Franciscan Institute, 1985), 21–57.

26. In the development of these ideas, I am indebted to the members of our Fall 1987 seminar on the problem of evil at UCLA—especially to Robert Merrihew Adams (its co-leader) and to Keith De Rose, William Fitzpatrick, and Houston Smit. I am also grateful to the Very Rcvd. Jon Hart Olson for many conversations in mystical theology.

IV.C.6

Suffering as Religious Experience

LAURA WADDELL EKSTROM

Laura Waddell Ekstrom is a professor of philosophy at the College of William and Mary, specializing primarily in ethics and agency theory. In this article, Ekstrom argues that some instances of suffering might reasonably be viewed as religious experiences that serve as a means of intimacy with God. Thus, whereas atheologians typically take suffering as evidence against the existence of God, Ekstrom argues that it might in fact be a route to knowledge of God.

INTRODUCTION

Works of literature, accounts of human history, and the events of everyday life confront us directly with the reality of pain and suffering. Some of us of a melancholy (some might say morbid) disposition are overcome with worry over this reality. Light-hearted neighbors and friends perplex us. How do they carry on so, trimming their yards and enjoying the weather, all the while maintaining faith in a perfect and provident Lord of the universe? Is it out of callousness, shallowness, blessedness, or wisdom? Have they any dark nights of the soul or anguish over the cries and shed blood of their fellow creatures? The worry leads some of us to academic study of the problem of evil. But our answers are incomplete and fail fully to satisfy. O God, where are you through the violent violation of a woman? Why tarry when a child falls feverish and is ripped from life too soon? Why still your hand through war, betrayal, and pain?

Yet through our own suffering, confusion and bitterness may take a startling turn. Job's heartrending cries of injustice against the Almighty become the breathtaking utterance, "My ears had heard of you but now my eyes have seen you."[1] In his

suffering, Job reports, he has met God. God has shown himself, made himself known to the sufferer. The philosopher Nicholas Wolterstorff gives something of a similar account in his report of a vision of God. As we strain to discern an explanation for divine permission of suffering, "instead of hearing an answer," Wolterstorff writes, "we catch sight of God himself scraped and torn." He attests: "Through the prism of my tears I have seen a suffering God."[2] God is seen, God is known, in suffering.

The aim of this paper is to explore the idea of suffering as a kind of religious experience. It is argued by David Hume, William Rowe, and Paul Draper, among others, that pain and suffering constitute evidence against the existence of God.[3] But perhaps at least some such instances of pain and suffering are, rather, avenues to knowledge of God. Many individuals, Wolterstorff and Job among them, report that the times during which they have suffered the most deeply are the occasions of the most vivid of whatever glimpses they have been given into the character of God. The experiences are marked, that is, by intimacy with the divine. Is not precisely this the mark of (at least one important type of) religious experience? And is not suffering as a means to intimacy with God exactly what one

Reprinted from Peter van Inwagen, ed., *Christian Faith and the Problem of Evil* (Grand Rapids, Mich.: Wm. B. Eerdmans, 2009), pp. 95–110. Used by permission of Wm. B. Eerdmans.

would expect of a God who, on Christian scripture and tradition, took on human form and suffered along with and for the world?[4]

Understanding some instances of human suffering as means to intimacy with the divine makes available a line of partial theodicy distinct from the traditional soul-making, punishment, and free will theodicies. I call it the *divine intimacy theodicy*. The theodicy is suggested to an extent in the work of such contemporary philosophers as Marilyn Adams, Nicholas Wolterstorff, and Eleonore Stump, as well as in the writings of many Christian mystics of the medieval and later periods, including, for instance, Therese of Lisieux (1873–1897).[5] Why would the divine agent permit instances of evil? Perhaps a reply applicable to some instances of personal suffering is this: in order to provide occasions in which we can perceive God, understand him to some degree, know him, even meet him directly. In this essay I explore the plausibility of this line of thought.[6]

THE NATURE OF RELIGIOUS EXPERIENCE

Religious experience is variously characterized. Rudolf Otto (1869–1937) describes it as experience in which the soul is "held speechless, trembles inwardly to the farthest fiber of its being," as it faces something so forceful and overwhelming that one feels oneself to be "dust and ashes as against majesty." The experience is one of "fear and trembling" but also of "wonderfulness and rapture."[7] The Christian mystic Teresa of Avila (1515–1582) reports an experience in which the mystic is

> conscious of having been most delectably wounded.... [The soul] complains to its Spouse with words of love, and even cries aloud, being unable to help itself, for it realizes that he is present but will not manifest himself in such a way as to allow it to enjoy him, and this is a great grief, though a sweet and delectable one.... So powerful is the effect of this upon the soul that it becomes consumed with desire, yet

cannot think what to ask, so clearly conscious is it of the presence of God.[8]

John of the Cross (1542–1591) describes experience in which the understanding of the soul "is now moved and informed by ... the supernatural light of God, and has been changed into the divine, for its understanding and that of God are now both one."[9]

One way of understanding religious experience is on analogy with sensory experience of the physical world. One might say that religious experience is experience of the divine by way of some perceptual faculties, perhaps including a special spiritual faculty or a *sensus divinitatus*. So as not to beg any questions concerning the veridicality of the experience, religious experience might be defined more cautiously as experience that the agent *takes to be* of the divine: experience perceived by the perceiver as acquaintance or intimacy with God. William Alston, for instance, understands religious experience as "(putative) direct awareness of God."[10]

I propose to understand the category of religious experience rather broadly. I consider the term "religious experience" to apply appropriately to at least the following three types of experience. First, a religious experience may be an experience in which it seems to one that one perceives God. Examples include a vision of divinity, a sense of God's presence during prayer or worship, and a feeling of God's nearness and comfort. Such experiences are regularly had by some theists. But an atheist may have them as well, as in Paul's experience on the road to Damascus.

Second, the category of religious experience includes experiences *like* those of God — experiences of the same sort as God's own experiences. In the Christian tradition, we could describe religious experience of the second sort as experience like that of one of the three persons comprising God. Or perhaps, so as not to beg any questions, we should describe the second type of religious experience as experience like what God would experience were God to exist with a nature as depicted by Christian scripture and tradition.

Third, an experience counts as a religious experience if it brings to consciousness the issue of

God's nature and existence and makes vivid one's own attitude regarding this issue. Religious experiences of the third sort may include, for example, experience showing us ugly, horrifying or frightening aspects of the world; experience of our own capacity for evil; and experience of our frailty. Such experiences tend to bring to mind questions concerning the existence of God, as well as questions concerning the goodness, power, and knowledge of God. Religious experiences of the third type also include experiences carrying a sense of awe or wonder, such as witnessing the birth of a child or feeling moved by the beauty of a natural scene: the vista from a mountaintop or a seashore, for example.

Each of these types of experience has a legitimate claim to being religious in character. Consider an atheist who was raised in a religious family. She might sensibly describe her observations of pervasive poverty and disease during a visit to India as a *religious experience:* the experience raised vividly for her the problem of evil and occasioned her realization that she had become an atheist. A theist's sense of the majestic presence of God during worship is religious experience of a different (the first) sort: it is experience in which one is putatively aware of God. Further, insofar as it makes sense to describe experience like an eagle's (say, soaring above the rooftops) as *avian experience,* and insofar as it makes sense to describe experiences of running, jumping, and playing with toys *childhood experience,* so too there seems room for counting experiences similar to those of the divine being—if there is any—*religious experience.*

WHY COUNT SUFFERING AS RELIGIOUS EXPERIENCE?

Is it plausible to suppose that some instances of suffering qualify as religious experiences as characterized above? Testimonial evidence supports the claim that instances of suffering are sometimes instances of religious experience of the first type: experience in which it seems to the perceiver that he or she is aware of the presence of God. Consider, as one example, the divine vision recounted by Julian of Norwich in the midst of suffering a severe illness for which she had received last rites: "At once I saw the red blood trickling down under the garland, hot, fresh, and plentiful, just as it did at the time of his passion when the crown of thorns was pressed on to the blessed head of God-and-Man.... And I had a strong, deep, conviction that it was he himself,"[11] She reports of the divine being: "I saw that he is to us everything which is good and comforting for our help. He is our clothing, who wraps and enfolds us for love, embraces us and shelters us, surrounds us for his love."[12] Many individuals in sorrow and pain have reported a vision of the divine or a feeling of God's nearness and comfort in their distress.

It is likewise reasonable to consider some occasions of suffering as religious experiences of the third type: experiences that vividly raise fundamental religious questions and illuminate one's commitments regarding them. One's becoming the victim of a crime, for instance, or suffering a debilitating physical injury, commonly brings to one's mind the question of God's existence and nature. The experience of hardship is often a sort of testing experience in which one "shows one's true colors," demonstrating one's deepest commitments. Suffering is a religious experience of the third sort in driving us to seek God or in causing doubt, reinforcing unbelief, or in generating questions concerning God's nature and existence.

I would like to focus more attention on the notion that some instances of suffering qualify as religious experience of the second type: experiences *like* those of God.

Suppose that, as on traditional Christian doctrine, God created persons in order for them to love and to be intimate with him and to glorify him forever. Suppose that persons were once in a state of intimacy with God, but that we rebelled by choice, with the consequence that we suffer physical and emotional pain, as well as the spiritual pain of being out of harmony with the Creator. Suppose that God enacted a plan for reestablishing our harmony with him involving his taking on human form and suffering rejection, torture, and execution.

From the perspective of one who adopts this account, some human suffering may be viewed, in fact, as a kind of privilege, in that it allows us to share in some of the experiences of God and thus gives us a window into understanding his nature. Some instances of suffering are avenues for intimacy, oneness, with God. One cannot love what one does not know, and one means of knowing someone is to have experience like hers. Naturally we feel affinity toward and grow to understand and to cherish other persons with experiences similar to our own. These include educational, career, and family experiences, but also experiences of illness and adversity. A person whose experiences are quite different from one's own is difficult for one to come deeply to understand and fully to appreciate. Shared experiences facilitate dialogue in providing something in common about which to converse, and they make possible understanding that is beyond words, communicated perhaps with understanding looks or gestures. The parent of an ill newborn knows something about the other parents in the emergency room without their exchanging any words. Lovers become intimate through sharing experiences. Victims of a similar sort of oppression or injustice understand each other in a way that outsiders to their experience cannot.

For the Christian, then, instances of suffering can be occasions for identification with the person of Jesus Christ. Intimacy with Christ gained through suffering provides deeper appreciation of his passion.[13] I understand the notion of *identification with Christ* in a sympathetic rather than a mystical sense: the claim is not that the sufferer bears Christ's *actual* sufferings, as, first, it is unclear what the point of that bearing would be and, second, the mystical view would seem to require quite peculiar views concerning pain. Rather, I mean to suggest that the sufferer may sympathetically identify with Christ in sharing similar experience, as any other two persons identify with each other in the loose sense that they connect with, appreciate, or understand each other better when they share experiences of the same type or similar types.

Several objections immediately arise. The first is that this aspect of the theodicy is so thoroughgoingly Christian. Since I accept the truth of orthodox Christian doctrine, this objection is from my perspective otiose. But to widen the appeal of the theodicy, we can set aside reference to the person of Christ and understand suffering as experience like that of God, like that of the divine being, if we join Wolterstorff and others in affirming, against tradition, that God is not impassible but is, rather, a God who suffers. Suppose, for instance, that God grieves over human sin. Then in feeling deep sorrow over the neglect and abuse of children, and in having regret and disapproval over the poverty and arrogance in our world, a person may have experience *like* God's and so may have a glimpse into the divine nature. An individual's own sorrow and suffering may, then, be a means to understanding and having intimacy with the divine being.

DIVINE PASSIBILITY

On the traditional conception of the divine nature, God is not affected by anything and so cannot suffer.[14] The doctrine of impassibility is defended primarily by appeal to philosophical considerations, including reflection on the natures of perfection, immutability, and transcendence. But the doctrine of divine impassibility has been recently criticized by a number of philosophers, including Alvin Plantinga, Charles Hartshore, Charles Taliaferro, Kelly James Clark, Nicholas Wolterstorff, and Richard Swinburne. Like Wolterstorff's avowal of a suffering God, Plantinga, for instance, affirms the existence of a God who "enters into and shares our suffering." Plantinga writes: "Some theologians claim that God cannot suffer. I believe they are wrong. God's capacity for suffering, I believe, is proportional to his greatness; it exceeds our capacity for suffering in the same measure as his capacity for knowledge exceeds ours."[15]

Of the considerations in favor of rejecting divine impassibility, the most salient from my perspective are the scriptural evidence and the natures of goodness and love. Many biblical passages depict God as experiencing emotions that entail suffering. Consider the following: "The LORD was grieved that he had made man on the earth, and his heart was filled with pain" (Gen. 6:6). "I have seen these people, the LORD said to Moses, and they are a stiff-necked people. Now leave me alone so that my anger may burn against them and that I may destroy them" (Exod. 32:9–10). The writer of Psalm 78 describes how the Israelites "grieved [God] … they vexed the Holy One of Israel" (41–42) and speaks of God's "wrath, indignation and hostility" (49). Consider, as well: "Praise be to the Lord, to God our Savior, who daily bears our burdens" (Ps. 68:19).

Impassibilists dismiss such passages as mere anthropomorphism. Commenting on Genesis 6:6, for example, John Calvin writes:

> Since we cannot comprehend [God] as he is, it is necessary that, for our sake, he should, in a certain sense, transform himself… . Certainly God is not sorrowful or sad; but remains forever like himself in his celestial and happy repose; yet because it could not otherwise be known how great is God's hatred and detestation of sin, therefore the spirit accommodates himself to our capacity… . God was so offended by the atrocious wickedness of men, [he speaks] as if they had wounded his heart with mortal grief.[16]

According to Calvin, God permits biblical writers to use figures of speech about himself in accommodation to humanity's limited capacities of understanding. Given interpretive differences, the impassibility issue cannot be settled, of course, simply by citing biblical material. Nonetheless, a passibilist conception of God, it must be admitted, fits most naturally with the scriptural account of God's activities and involvement with human beings. The impassibilist must explain away or reinterpret numerous passages that, on their face, suggest that God is affected by and suffers over his creation.

On the traditional conception of the divine agent, God is not only omnipotent and omniscient, but also wholly good and perfectly loving. A number of philosophers, including Wolterstorff and Taliaferro, have registered their rejection of the Greek-influenced medieval conception of divine

love as non-suffering benevolence. The argument is that apathy, unperturbed emotional indifference to the plight of humanity, is incompatible with God's love of humanity.

Here is why the incompatibility claim seems right. Suppose that we understand love, rather uncontroversially, as consisting in or at least essentially involving concern for the well-being or flourishing of a beloved object. This understanding of love applies equally to love of a cause or of an ideal or of a person, but I am concerned particularly with love of persons. In his recent work on love, Harry Frankfurt adds that the lover's concern for the beloved is disinterested, in the sense that the good of the beloved is desired by the lover for its own sake rather than for the sake of promoting any other interests.[17] Frankfurt emphasizes that lovers are not merely concerned for the interests of their beloveds; further, they *identify* the interests of the beloveds as their own.[18] And he argues that if the lover "comes to believe that his beloved is not flourishing, then it is unavoidable that this causes him harm."[19] Lack of flourishing in the beloved, by the nature of love, causes harm in the lover.

Of course, it could be claimed that this account applies only to instances of human love and not to divine love. But the move appears *ad hoc*. If love of someone consists in or essentially involves concern for her well-being, then it involves valuing, or having concerned approval for, her flourishing and disvaluing, or having concerned disapproval for, her harm. To say that I love my daughter, yet that I experience no sorrow, grief, or passion of any kind at her pain or disgrace, stretches the concept of love beyond comprehensibility. Furthermore, since one can love something only insofar as one is acquainted with it, it would seem that God cannot love us fully without knowing us fully. But our being fully known requires acquaintance on the part of the knower with our suffering and with the evil in our world.[20] Thus, reflection on the nature of love supports the conception of a God who suffers.

Further support for the passibility of God comes from the consideration of the nature of goodness. A morally good being grieves over evil. In a recent book offering an extended defense of the traditional doctrine of divine impassibility,[21] Richard Creel argues in part that it serves no *purpose* to attribute suffering to God, as God may act out of love and justice without being sorrowful. But to the contrary, we question the goodness of an agent who acts correctly towards victims of crime or disease, yet wholly without sorrow or empathy for the persons served. Passibilism, Creel argues, makes God worthy of our pity rather than our worship. But a great moral character, one worthy of worship, shows itself great in part by its sorrow, what it sorrows over and to what degree. Noble sorrow at witnessing a tragic occurrence is a good. Hence it would seem that God's goodness and love include sorrow, as well as joy, over the world. This sorrow is arguably not a defect, but a strength or an asset, a part of being supremely good.

Taliaferro understands divine sorrow as "concerned disapproval." "God disapproves of our cruelty and malice," he writes, "God cares about our failures, and this concerned disapproval may rightly be counted as an instance of sorrow."[22] Consider, for instance, Miriam's rape. Taliaferro writes: "Part of what it means to be sorrowful here is that you do disapprove of it, the harming of someone who matters to you, and you disapprove of this profoundly. Any tenable notion of the goodness of the God of Christian theism must include the supposition that God exercises profound, concerned disapproval of creaturely ills."[23] It does seem reasonable to suppose that the God who is love, the God who is perfectly good, is deeply concerned for persons and suffers profound sorrow over their sins and afflictions. It is facile to presume oneself too sophisticated to go in for such supposed "sentimentalism." Proponents of the divine impassibility doctrine must defend it further against substantive religious and moral reasons for concluding that God suffers.

OBJECTIONS: PATHOLOGY, CRUELTY, AND INEFFICACY

In this section, I consider four central objections to a divine intimacy theodicy. The first, which I will address only briefly, comes from the direction of one unconvinced of the passibility of God. I have suggested that there is reason to think that God does suffer, provided by scripture and by reflection on the natures of goodness and love. But should the considerations in favor of the attribute of impassibility prove in the end more powerful, the divine intimacy theodicy is not thereby defeated. If suffering cannot be religious experience in the sense of being experience like that of God himself, it can qualify still as religious experience of the first and third sorts, and thus it can be justified as a means to intimacy with the divine. Furthermore, should traditional impassibilism survive recent attacks. Christian theism can yet make sense of suffering as experience shared with the person of Jesus Christ and so can count some occasions of suffering as avenues to intimacy with God through sympathetic identification with Christ.

A second and potentially more damaging objection is this: To view suffering as religious experience is evidence of a personality disturbance or psychological disorder. That is, it seems to indicate not right thinking but pathology that a person would glory in suffering or see spiritual dimensions to pain. The objection gains force from considering the physical conditions of the lives of some Christian mystics of the medieval and later periods who viewed suffering in such a manner. For instance, the Cistercian nun Beatrice of Nazareth (1200–1268), the author of *The Seven Manners of Love*, is reported to have deprived herself of food, worn uncomfortable garments, scourged herself, and slept on thorns.[24] Other religious figures may strike us as melodramatic and distressingly passive in their welcoming attitudes toward suffering. Consider the remarks of Therese of Lisieux concerning the onset of symptoms of the tuberculosis that took her life at the age of twenty-four:

> Oh! how sweet this memory really is! After remaining at the Tomb until midnight, I returned to our cell, but I had scarcely laid my head upon the pillow when I felt something like a bubbling stream mounting to my lips. I didn't know what

it was, but I thought that perhaps I was going to die and my soul was flooded with joy. However, as our lamp was extinguished, I told myself I would have to wait until the morning to be certain of my good fortune, for it seemed to me that it was blood I had coughed up. The morning was not long in coming; upon awakening, I thought immediately of the joyful thing that I had to learn, and so I went over to the window. I was able to see that I was not mistaken. Ah! my soul was filled with a great consolation; I was interiorly persuaded that Jesus, on the anniversary of his own death, wanted to have me hear his first call. It was like a sweet and distant murmur that announced the Bridegroom's arrival.[25]

Therese welcomes the blood in her cough as the answer to her prayer that God consume her with his love, that God carry her to him quickly, and that she be allowed to share in the suffering of Christ. She declares in her "Act of Oblation to Merciful Love":

I thank you, O my God! for all the graces you have granted me, especially the grace of making me pass through the crucible of suffering. It is with joy I shall contemplate you on the last day carrying the scepter of your cross. Since you deigned to give me a share in this very precious cross, I hope in heaven to resemble you and to see shining in my glorified body the sacred stigmata of your passion.[26]

In light of such passages, it may strike one as at best wishful thinking and, worse, indicative of a psychiatric condition, to believe that God is with one or is providing one intimacy with himself through suffering.

But of course those who report experience of supernatural phenomena are notoriously subject to the charge of being delusional. And certainly adopting the proposed partial theodicy need not lead one to self-mutilation or to other eccentric or damaging

behaviors. The view under consideration is perfectly consistent with a mandate to *alleviate* suffering so far as possible and with a mandate not to self-impose pain. Furthermore, which views indicate spiritual insight and which indicate a condition in need of medical or psychological treatment is a matter of opinion. As it stands, the objection from pathology amounts to no more than the claim that it seems to the objector that the proposed view is crazy or, in other words, false. Without any further positive reasons to doubt the sanity of the proponent of the divine intimacy theodicy, other than that she believes the view, the objection is dismissible.

The objector might respond by pointing to such factors as social isolation, inadequate sleep, poor nutrition, and lack of medical care in the lives of some religious mystics. These circumstances, it may be argued, indicate that the view of suffering as religious experience is pathological and not reasonable. Yet surely these considerations are inconclusive. Recall C. D. Broad's remark that a person "might need to be slightly 'cracked' in order to have some peep-holes into the super-sensible world."[27] Difficult living conditions might in fact facilitate spiritual insight. Furthermore, a charge of insanity against every adherent to a divine intimacy theodicy is grandiose.

A third objection is an objection from cruelty. Why would a loving God create such a cruel way of our getting to know him? Why would suffering as a *means* to knowing God be preferable to direct divine self-revelation? Since permitting suffering is a cruel way of fostering intimacy, the objection goes, the perfect being would not be justified in this permission and so the account of suffering as religious experience fails as a partial theodicy.

It is surely troubling to conceive of God as declaring to created beings in a tone of sinister delight, "Suffer, and then I will let you know me," as if enduring a crucible of suffering were a passkey. But this image inaccurately reflects the divine intimacy theodicy. A perfect being does not, of course, delight over suffering, but rather causes or allows it when it is necessary to bringing about a greater good or preventing a worse evil.

And the suggestion I am exploring is that, perhaps, some occasions of suffering are necessary for certain individuals' coming to love of and intimacy with God. The objector may counter that some persons experience God in moments of great joy and beauty. Yet this may be true while it is also true that other persons' paths to God are paths through suffering. And it may be that the good thereby achieved could not be achieved in any other way: namely, the profound good of appreciation for and intimacy with a loving and suffering God.

The objector might be troubled with the question of why God would not simply show himself at all times, to everyone. Here the right line of response may be that for God to directly, constantly, and obviously manifest his presence would be coercive.[28] Perhaps God's remaining somewhat hidden protects our freedom, preserving our independence of thought and action. The rationale behind divine hiddenness may be something like this: I (the divine agent) will not intervene in the natural course of events to prevent your difficulties and your suffering, in part because perhaps then you will appreciate the ways in which I have loved and provided for you all along; perhaps you will freely come to recognize that acting wholly by your own lights is unsuccessful and that you need my help; perhaps you will be rid of some of your arrogance and will recognize your limitations. Suffering, that is, may be for some persons the most effective non-coercive means to achieving the end of love of and intimacy with God. Additionally, it may be that it is impossible fully to know God without personally experiencing suffering, because God himself suffers. If God is passible in emotion, then there is something that a person could not know about God if she did not suffer, one aspect of God's being that would remain entirely mysterious.

The fourth and final objection I will consider is this: a common reaction to suffering is not a sense of intimacy with the divine but rather confusion and rejection of God's existence. Suffering is easily interpreted as evidence that God does not exist or does not care about the sufferer. Hence, many cases of suffering, particularly those of non-theists, cannot plausibly be construed as religious experience.

In response, first, the divine intimacy theodicy is not designed to apply to all cases of suffering. Second, from the fact that some persons reject the existence of God on the basis of suffering, it does not follow that some occasions of suffering do not provide an *opportunity* for intimacy with God. We can choose, it seems, the manner in which we respond to suffering, including which types of attitudes we adopt in the midst of it. The thesis at issue is not that meaning *is* always found in suffering by everyone who suffers, but rather that a certain kind of meaning *can* be found in suffering, through divine intimacy.

Suffering might be religious experience without the sufferer recognizing it as such. This claim seems unproblematic, since a person can have an experience of a certain type without ever recognizing it as an experience of that type. Consider the following examples. First, suppose that Keith thinks that he is devising a novel line of reasoning. But in fact he is remembering a conversation in which someone else recounted a certain line of thought. Keith is having a memory experience, but he does not, and need not ever, recognize it as such. Second, suppose that Sandra begins thinking about chance and providence. Although she need not ever recognize the experience as such, she may be having a telepathic experience of the thoughts of Peter, who is across the room. Third, imagine a husband who begins to have indigestion, headaches, and back pain during the pregnancy of his wife. He consults his doctor, who finds his symptoms mysterious. He is, perhaps, having an empathic experience without realizing it. The concept of a religious experience, unrecognized as such, appears cogent.

CONCLUSION

A full justificatory account of suffering may be unattainable for us. I have simply sketched here and begun to explore the suggestion that one justifying reason for certain instances of suffering is that those occasions constitute religious experiences. Some cases of suffering may be viewed as kinds of experience that can bring a person closer to God, such that the good either in or resulting from them is intimacy with the divine agent.

The account of suffering as religious experience may have use not only as a partial theodicy, but also as a method for the theist for dealing with the existential problem of evil. That is, one way of enduring unchangeable occasions of pain and suffering may be to adopt an attitude of acceptance and, oddly, enjoyment in identifying with God. Consider how this might work, in particular, for a Christian theist. One in the midst of dealing with a deep betrayal of loyalty, for instance, might call to mind the thought, "As I have been rejected, Christ was rejected even by his close friend, Peter," and take comfort in the sympathetic identification. Likewise, although perhaps Christ never experienced precisely the particular physical pain from which one suffers, the sufferer is in part able to appreciate something about the person of Christ that perhaps not all others fully can: the sacrifice of his passion.[29]

NOTES

1. Job 42:5.

2. Nicholas Wolterstorff, *Lament for a Son* (Grand Rapids: Eerdmans Publishing Co., 1987), pp. 80–81.

3. David Hume, *Dialogues Concerning Natural Religion*, ed. Richard Popkin (Indianapolis: Hackett, 1980); William Rowe, "The Problem of Evil and Some Varieties of Atheism," *American Philosophical Quarterly* 16 (1979): 335–41; Paul Draper, "Pain and Pleasure: An Evidential Problem for Theists," *Noûs* 23 (1989).

4. According to orthodox Christian tradition, the person of Jesus Christ suffered for us, yet God the Father is not capable of suffering.

5. Marilyn McCord Adams, "Redemptive Suffering: A Christian Solution to the Problem of Evil," *in Rationality, Religious Belief, and Moral Commitment*, ed. Robert Audi and William J. Wainwright (Ithaca, N.Y.: Cornell University Press, 1986), and "Horrendous Evils and the Goodness of God," *Proceedings of the Aristotelian Society*, supplementary vol. 63 (1989), pp. 297–310; Wolterstorff, *Lament for a Son*, and "Suffering Love," in *Philosophy and the Christian Faith*, ed. Thomas V. Morris (Notre Dame, Ind.: University of Notre Dame Press, 1988); Eleonore Stump, *Faith and the Problem of Evil: The Stob Lectures, 1998–99* (Grand Rapids: The Stob Lectures Endowment, 1999), and "The Mirror of Evil," in *God and the Philosophers*, ed. Thomas V. Morris (New York: Oxford University Press, 1994), pp. 235–47, arid "The Problem of Evil," *Faith and Philosophy* 2:4 (1985): 392–418.

6. The divine intimacy theodicy most likely has some measure of plausibility only when applied to human suffering and not to the suffering of non-human animals. Nonetheless, the matter is open in the absence of conclusive information concerning the capacities of members of other species.

7. Rudolf Otto, *The Idea of the Holy* (London: Oxford University Press, 1936), pp. 17–26, 31–33.

8. *The Interior Castle*, trans. and ed. E. Allison Peers (Garden City, N.Y.: Doubleday Image, 1961), pp. 135–36.

9. *The Living Flame of Love*, trans. and ed. E. Allison Peers (Garden City, N.Y.: Doubleday Image, 1962), p. 78.

10. William Alston, *Perceiving God: The Epistemology of Religious Experience* (Ithaca, N.Y.: Cornell University Press, 1991), p. 35.

11. Julian of Norwich, *Revelations of Divine Love* (New York: Penguin Books, 1984), p. 66.

12. Julian of Norwich, Long Text 5, quoted in *Enduring Grace: Living Portraits of Seven Women Mystics* (New York: HarperCollins, 1993), p. 88.

13. Marilyn McCord Adams similarly suggests that instances of suffering, even horrendous ones, might be made *meaningful* by being integrated into the sufferer's relationship with God through identification with Christ, understood either as sympathetic identification (in which each person suffers her own pain, enabling her to understand something of Christ's suffering) or as mystical

identification (in which the human sufferer literally experiences a share of Christ's pain). Alternately, Adams suggests, meaningfulness may derive from suffering serving as a vision into the inner life of God, either because God is not impassible, or because the sheer intensity of the experience gives one a glimpse of what it is like to be beyond joy and sorrow. She proposes, as well, that sufferings might be made meaningful through defeat by divine gratitude which, when expressed by God in the afterlife, gives one full and unending joy. "Horrendous Evils and the Goodness of God," *Proceedings of the Aristotelian Society*, supplementary vol. 63 (1989), pp. 297–310; reprinted in *The Problem of Evil*, ed. Marilyn McCord Adams and Robert Merrihew Adams (New York: Oxford University Press, 1990), pp. 209–21.

14. The Westminster Confession of Faith (II.1) states: "There is but one ... true God, who is infinite in being and perfection, a most pure spirit, invisible, without body, parts, or passions...."

15. "Self-Profile," in *Alvin Plantinga*, ed. James E. Tomberlin and Peter van Inwagen (Dordrecht: D. Reidel, 1985), p. 36.

16. *Calvin's Commentaries*, vol. 1, trans, and ed. John Owen (Grand Rapids: Baker Book House, 1979), p. 249.

17. Harry Frankfurt, "On Caring," in *Necessity, Volition, and Love* (Cambridge: Cambridge University Press, 1999), p. 165.

18. Frankfurt, "On Caring," p. 168.

19. Frankfurt, "On Caring," p. 170.

20. Cf. Nicholas Wolterstorff, "Suffering Love," in *Philosophy and the Christian Faith*, ed. Thomas V. Morris (Notre Dame, Ind.: University of Notre Dame Press, 1988), p. 223.

21. Richard E. Creel, *Divine Impassibility* (Cambridge: Cambridge University Press, 1986).

22. Charles Taliaferro, "The Passibility of God," *Religious Studies*, vol. 25: 220.

23. Taliaferro, "Passibility," p. 220.

24. *Women Mystics in Medieval Europe*, ed. Emilie Zum Brunn and Georgette Epiney-Burgard, trans. Sheila Hughes (New York: Paragon House, 1989), p. 72.

25. *Story of a Soul: The Autobiography of St. Therese of Lisieux*, trans. John Clarke O.C.D. (Washington, D.C.: ICS Publications, 1996), pp. 210–11.

26. *Story of a Soul*, p. 277.

27. C. D. Broad, "Arguments for the Existence of God. II," *Journal of Theological Studies* 40 (1939): 164.

28. Michael J. Murray, "Coercion and the Hiddenness of God," *American Philosophical Quarterly* 30 (1993): 27–38.

29. I am grateful to Michael Murray and Kelly James Clark for comments on an earlier version of this essay.

PART VII

Faith and Reason

One of the most important and widely discussed issues in the philosophy of religion is the relationship of faith to reason. Is religious belief rational? And if so, is that because we have something like evidence or proof for the religious claims that we believe? Or might our religious beliefs be rendered rational in some other way?

In this section, we focus on two key issues in the debate over faith and reason. The first question, which is taken up by the essays in Part A, is the question whether it is appropriate to hold religious beliefs, or to engage in religious practices, simply because we find it in our best interests to do so. According to Blaise Pascal, even if we don't yet have *evidence* for believing in God, we do have strong pragmatic, or practical, reason to believe in God. Though this by itself doesn't necessarily render belief in God rational, Pascal does think it gives us good reason to live as if there is a God and to try to cultivate belief in God. But is he right? Many are inclined to think that cultivating a belief simply because it is in our best interests to hold it is positively irrational. Indeed, some would say it is morally repugnant. Cultivating beliefs on important matters for reasons of self-interest rather than as a result of hard-nosed objective inquiry might seem grossly irresponsible; and when acting on those beliefs has serious consequences for others (as is often the case with religious belief) such irresponsibility might also seem terribly immoral. Just imagine how you would feel if you discovered that many of your surgeon's beliefs about surgery were cultivated not as a result of reading medical journals but rather because she discovered that she would feel better if she thought that it was sensible to follow this or that surgical procedure.

The second question is the question of how, if at all, religious belief might come to be rationally justified. Many suppose that in order for our religious beliefs to be rational, we would need to have *arguments* to support them. Suppose you have the experience of seeming to see a boat on a lake; and suppose that, on the basis of this experience, you form the belief that there is a boat on a lake in front of you. In this case, you have no argument for your belief. Your only evidence is experiential. You haven't inferred that there is a boat on a lake in front of you from anything else you believe; you have simply formed it on the basis of an experience. But, of course, we don't at all think that *this* fact renders your belief unjustified. In fact, we think that most of our perceptual beliefs are prime examples of justified belief. Might the same be the case for religious belief? Might religious belief be rationally grounded in experience? If not, then what would it take for religious belief to be justified? These and related questions are taken up in Part B of this section.

VII.A. PRAGMATIC JUSTIFICATION OF RELIGIOUS BELIEF

THIS SECTION CONTAINS readings that deal with the practical reasonableness of religious belief. Even if we cannot find good evidence for religious beliefs, would it perhaps be in our interest to get ourselves to believe in these propositions anyway? And would such believing be morally permissible? In the first reading, "The Wager," the renowned French physicist and mathematician Blaise Pascal (1623–1662) argues that if we do a cost–benefit analysis of the matter, we find that it is eminently reasonable to take steps to put ourselves in a position to believe that God exists—and this regardless of whether we have good evidence for that belief.

The argument goes something like this: Regarding the proposition "God exists," reason is neutral. It can neither prove nor disprove the proposition. But we must wager. That is, we must live as if God exists or as if he does not exist— where living as if God exists involves acting as if theistic doctrines (and, for Pascal, specifically Christian doctrines) are true. Living as if God exists doesn't guarantee that belief will follow; but, on Pascal's view, it makes belief more likely. And since the benefits associated with belief promise to be infinite (and the loss equally infinite if we bet against God's existence and turn out to be wrong), we might set forth the possibilities shown in Table 7.1. There is some sacrifice of earthly pleasures involved in betting on God. But the fact is, no matter how enormous the *finite* gain associated with betting against God's existence, the mere possibility of *infinite* gain associated with betting in favor of God's existence will always make the latter preferable to the former. In short, we have a clear self-interested reason for betting on God.

TABLE 7.1

	God exists	God does not exist
Bet that God exists	A. Infinite gain with minimal finite loss	B. Overall finite loss in terms of sacrifice of earthly goods
Bet that God doesn't exist	C. Infinite loss with finite gain	D. Overall finite gain

Pascal is commonly understood as suggesting that we ought to *believe* in God (as opposed to simply living as if God exists in the hope or expectation that evidentially grounded belief will follow) because it is in our interests to do so. In the second reading, "The Ethics of Belief," the British philosopher W. K. Clifford (1845–1879) assembles reason's roadblocks to such pragmatic justifications for religious belief. Clifford argues that there is an ethics to belief that makes it immoral to believe something without sufficient evidence. Pragmatic justifications are not justifications at all but counterfeits of genuine justifications, which must always be based on evidence.

Clifford illustrates his thesis with the example of a shipowner who sends an emigrant ship to sea. He knows that the ship is old and not well built but fails to have the ship inspected. Dismissing from his mind all doubts about the vessel's seaworthiness, the owner trusts in Providence to care for his ship. He acquires a sincere and comfortable conviction in this way and collects his insurance money without a trace of guilt after the ship sinks and all the passengers drown. Clifford comments that although the shipowner sincerely believed that all was well with the ship, his sincerity in no way exculpates him because "he had no right to believe on such evidence as was before him." One has an obligation to get oneself in a position in which one will believe propositions only on sufficient evidence.

Some may object that the shipowner simply had an obligation to *act* in a certain way (viz., inspect the ship), not to *believe* in a certain way. Granted, the shipowner does have an obligation to inspect the ship; but the objection overlooks the function of believing in guiding action. "No man holding a strong belief on one side of a question, or even wishing to hold a belief on one side, can investigate it with such fairness and completeness as if he were really in doubt and unbiased; so that the existence of a belief not founded on fair inquiry unfits a man for the performance of this necessary duty." The general conclusion is that it is always wrong for anyone to believe anything on insufficient evidence.

The classic response to Clifford's ethics of belief is William James's "The Will to Believe" (1896), the last reading in this section. James argues that life would be greatly impoverished if we confined our beliefs to such a Scrooge-like epistemology as Clifford proposes. In everyday life, where the evidence for important propositions is often unclear, we must live by faith or cease to act at all. Although we may not make leaps of faith just anywhere, sometimes practical considerations force us to make decisions about propositions that do not have their truth value written on their faces.

In "The Sentiment of Rationality" (1879), James defines "faith" as follows: "a belief in something concerning which doubt is still theoretically possible: and as the test of belief is willingness to act, one may say that faith is the readiness to act in a cause the prosperous issue of which is not certified to us in advance." In "The Will to Believe" he argues on behalf of the rationality of believing, even with insufficient evidence, certain kinds of hypotheses—namely, those where the choice between the hypothesis and its denial is *live, momentous,* and *unavoidable.* For, he argues, to withhold belief on such momentous matters until sufficient evidence is forthcoming may, in the end, be too costly.

There is a good illustration of this notion of faith in "The Sentiment of Rationality." A mountain climber in the Alps finds himself in a position from which he can escape only by means of an enormous leap. If he tries to calculate the evidence, believing only on sufficient evidence, he will be paralyzed by emotions of fear and mistrust and hence will be lost. Without evidence that he is capable of performing this feat successfully, the climber would be better off getting himself to believe that he can and will make the leap. "In this case ... the part of wisdom clearly is to believe what one desires; for the belief is one of the indispensable preliminary conditions of the realization of its object. *There are then cases where faith creates its own verification.*" James claims that religion may be such an optional hypothesis for many people, and in this case one has the right to believe the better story rather than the worse. To do so, one must will to believe what the evidence alone is inadequate to support.

There are two questions, one descriptive and the other normative, that you should keep in mind when you are reading these essays. The first is whether it is possible to believe propositions at will. In what sense can we get ourselves to believe propositions that the evidence doesn't force upon us. Surely we can't believe that the world is flat or that two plus two equals five simply by willing to do so, but which propositions (if any) are subject to volitional influences? Is it, then, psychologically impossible to believe something simply because it is in our interests to do so? Does it involve self-deception? If we know that the primary cause for our belief in a religious proposition is our desire to believe, can we rationally continue to believe that proposition?

The second question involves the ethics of belief, stressed by Clifford. Supposing that we can get ourselves to believe or disbelieve propositions for self-interested reasons, is this morally permissible? What are the arguments for and against integrity of belief? Note too that Pascal, unlike James, does not seem to suppose that we have *direct* voluntary control over our beliefs. Pascal's advice, again, is to *cultivate* belief—to *act* as if you believe (e.g., by going to church, participating in Mass, taking holy water, etc.) in the hope and expectation that belief will naturally follow. James, on the other hand, seems to be defending the rationality of acquiring beliefs simply by fiat of the will.

VII.A.1

The Wager

BLAISE PASCAL

Blaise Pascal (1623–1662) was a renowned French physicist and mathematician. In 1654, at the age of 31, Pascal had an intense religious experience that completely changed his life. After this experience, he devoted himself to prayer and the study of Scripture, abandoned his mathematical and scientific endeavors, and set himself to the task of writing a defense of the Christian faith. The book was never finished, but the present selection is taken from Pascal's notes, compiled under the title Pensées. Here he argues that if we do a cost–benefit analysis of the matter, we find that it is eminently reasonable to take steps to put ourselves in a position to believe that God exists, regardless of whether we now have good evidence for that belief.

Infinite—nothing.—Our soul is cast into a body, where it finds number, time, dimension. Thereupon it reasons, and calls this nature, necessity, and can believe nothing else.

Unity joined to infinity adds nothing to it, no more than one foot to an infinite measure. The finite is annihilated in the presence of the infinite, and becomes a pure nothing. So our spirit before God, so our justice before divine justice. There is not so great disproportion between our justice and that of God, as between unity and infinity.

The justice of God must be vast like His compassion. Now, justice to the outcast is less vast, and ought less to offend our feelings than mercy towards the elect.

We know that there is an infinite, and are ignorant of its nature. As we know it to be false that numbers are finite, it is therefore true that there is an infinity in number. But we do not know what it is. It is false that it is even, it is false that it is odd; for the addition of a unit can make no change in its nature. Yet it is a number, and every number is odd or even (this is certainly true of every finite number). So we may well know that there is a God without knowing what He is. Is there not one substantial truth, seeing there are so many things which are not the truth itself?

We know then the existence and nature of the finite, because we also are finite and have extension. We know the existence of the infinite, and are ignorant of its nature, because it has extension like us, but not limits like us. But we know neither the existence nor the nature of God, because He has neither extension nor limits.

But by faith we know His existence; in glory we shall know His nature. Now, I have already shown that we may well know the existence of a thing, without knowing its nature.

Let us now speak according to natural lights.

If there is a God, He is infinitely incomprehensible, since, having neither parts nor limits, He has no affinity to us. We are then incapable of knowing either what He is or if He is. This being so, who will dare to undertake the decision of the question? Not we, who have no affinity to Him.

Who then will blame Christians for not being able to give a reason for their belief, since they

Reprinted from Blaise Pascal, *Thoughts*, translated by W. F. Trotter (New York: Collier & Son, 1910).

profess a religion for which they cannot give a reason? They declare, in expounding it to the world, that it is a foolishness, *stultitiam*; and then you complain that they do not prove it! If they proved it, they would not keep their words; it is in lacking proofs, that they are not lacking in sense. "Yes, but although this excuses those who offer it as such, and takes away from them the blame of putting it forward without reason, it does not excuse those who receive it." Let us then examine this point, and say, "God is, or He is not." But to which side shall we incline? Reason can decide nothing here. There is an infinite chasm which separates us. A game is being played at the extremity of this infinite distance where heads or tails will turn up. What will you wager? According to reason, you can do neither the one thing nor the other, according to reason, you can defend neither of the propositions.

Do not then reprove for error those who have made a choice; for you know nothing about it. "No, but I blame them for having made, not this choice, but a choice; for again both he who chooses heads and he who chooses tails are equally at fault, they are both in the wrong. The true course is not to wager at all."

—Yes; but you must wager. It is not optional. You are embarked. Which will you choose then; let us see. Since you must choose, let us see which interests you least. You have two things to lose, the true and the good; and two things to stake, your reason and your will, your knowledge and your happiness; and your nature has two things to shun, error and misery. Your reason is no more shocked in choosing one rather than the other, since you must of necessity choose. This is one point settled. But your happiness? Let us weigh the gain and the loss in wagering that God is. Let us estimate these two chances. If you gain, you gain all; if you lose, you lose nothing. Wager them without hesitation that He is.—"That is very fine. Yes, I must wager; but I may perhaps wager too much."—Let us see.

Since there is an equal risk of gain and of loss, if you had only to gain two lives, instead of one, you might still wager. But if there were three lives to

gain, you would have to play (since you are under the necessity of playing), and you would be imprudent, when you are forced to play, not to chance your life to gain three at a game where there is an equal risk of loss and gain. But there is an eternity of life and happiness. And this being so, if there were an infinity of chances, of which one only would be for you, you would still be right in wagering one to win two, and you would act stupidly, being obliged to play, by refusing to stake one life against three at a game in which out of an infinity of an infinitely happy life to gain. But there is here an infinity of an infinitely happy life to gain a chance of gain against a finite number of chances of loss, and what you stake is infinite. It is all divided; wherever the infinite is and there is not an infinity of chances of loss against that of gain, there is no time to hesitate, you must give all. And thus, when one is forced to play, he must renounce reason to preserve his life, rather than risk it for infinite gain, as likely to happen as the loss of nothingness.

For it is no use to say it is uncertain if we will gain, and it is certain that we risk, and that the infinite distance between the *certainty* of what is staked and the *uncertainty* of what will be gained, equals the finite good which is certainly staked against the uncertain infinite. It is not so, as every player stakes a certainty to gain an uncertainty, and yet he stakes a finite certainty to gain a finite uncertainty, without transgressing against reason. There is not an infinite distance between the certainty staked and the uncertainty of the gain; that is untrue. In truth, there is an infinity between the certainty of gain and the certainty of loss. But the uncertainty of the gain is proportioned to the certainty of the stake according to the proportion of the chances of gain and loss. Hence it comes that, if there are as many risks on one side as on the other, the course is to play even; and then the certainty of the stake is equal to the uncertainty of the gain, so far is it from the fact that there is an infinite distance between them. And so our proposition is of infinite force, when there is the finite to stake in a game where there are equal risks of gain and loss, and the infinite to gain. This is demonstrable; and if men are capable of any truths, this is one.

VII.A.2

The Ethics of Belief

W. K. CLIFFORD

W. K. Clifford (1845–1879) was a British philosopher and mathematician. The selection that follows is perhaps his best known and most widely discussed philosophical essay. Clifford argues that there is an ethics to belief that makes it always wrong for anyone to believe anything on insufficient evidence. Pragmatic justifications are not justifications at all but counterfeits of genuine justifications, which must always be based on evidence.

A shipowner was about to send to sea an emigrant ship. He knew that she was old, and not over-well built at the first; that she had seen many seas and climes, and often had needed repairs. Doubts had been suggested to him that possibly she was not seaworthy. These doubts preyed upon his mind and made him unhappy; he thought that perhaps he ought to have her thoroughly overhauled and refitted, even though this should put him to great expense. Before the ship sailed, however, he succeeded in overcoming these melancholy reflections. He said to himself that she had gone safely through so many voyages and weathered so many storms that it was idle to suppose she would not come safely home from this trip also. He would put his trust in Providence, which could hardly fail to protect all these unhappy families that were leaving their fatherland to seek for better times elsewhere. He would dismiss from his mind all ungenerous suspicions about the honesty of builders and contractors. In such ways he acquired a sincere and comfortable conviction that his vessel was thoroughly safe and seaworthy; he watched her departure with a light heart, and benevolent wishes for the success of the exiles in their strange new home that was to be; and he got his insurance money when she went down in midocean and told no tales.

What shall we say of him? Surely this, that he was verily guilty of the death of those men. It is admitted that he did sincerely believe in the soundness of his ship; but the sincerity of his conviction can in no wise to help him, because he had no right to believe on such evidence as was before him. He had acquired his belief not by honestly earning it in patient investigation, but by stifling his doubts. And although in the end he may have felt so sure about it that he could not think otherwise, yet inasmuch as he had knowingly and willingly worked himself into that frame of mind, he must be held responsible for it.

Let us alter the case a little, and suppose that the ship was not unsound after all; that she made her voyage safely, and many others after it. Will that diminish the guilt of her owner? Not one jot. When an action is once done, it is right or wrong forever; no accidental failure of its good or evil fruits can possibly alter that. The man would not have been innocent, he would only have been not found out. The question of right or wrong has to do with the origin of his belief, not the matter of it; not what it was, but how he got it; not whether

Reprinted from W. K. Clifford, *Lecturers and Essays* (London: Macmillan, 1879).

it turned out to be true or false, but whether he had a right to believe on such evidence as was before him.

There was once an island in which some of the inhabitants professed a religion teaching neither the doctrine of original sin nor that of eternal punishment. A suspicion got abroad that the professors of this religion had made use of unfair means to get their doctrines taught to children. They were accused of wresting the laws of their country in such a way as to remove children from the care of their natural and legal guardians; and even of stealing them away and keeping them concealed from their friends and relations. A certain number of men formed themselves into a society for the purpose of agitating the public about this matter. They published grave accusations against individual citizens of the highest position and character, and did all in their power to injure those citizens in the exercise of their professions. So great was the noise they made, that a Commission was appointed to investigate the facts; but after the Commission had carefully inquired into all the evidence that could be got, it appeared that the accused were innocent. Not only had they been accused on insufficient evidence, but the evidence of their innocence was such as the agitators might easily have obtained, if they had attempted a fair inquiry. After these disclosures the inhabitants of that country looked upon the members of the agitating society, not only as persons whose judgment was to be distrusted, but also as no longer to be counted honorable men. For although they had sincerely and conscientiously believed in the charges they had made, yet they had no right to believe on such evidence as was before them. Their sincere convictions, instead of being honestly earned by patient inquiring, were stolen by listening to the voice of prejudice and passion.

Let us vary this case also, and suppose, other things remaining as before, that a still more accurate investigation proved the accused to have been really guilty. Would this make any difference in the guilt of the accusers? Clearly not; the question is not whether their belief was true or false, but whether they entertained it on wrong grounds. They would no doubt say, "Now you see that we were right

after all; next time perhaps you will believe us." And they might be believed, but they would not thereby become honorable men. They would not be innocent, they would only be not found out. Every one of them, if he chose to examine himself *in foro conscientiae*, would know that he had acquired and nourished a belief, when he had no right to believe on such evidence as was before him; and therein he would know that he had done a wrong thing.

It may be said, however, that in both of these supposed cases it is not the belief which is judged to be wrong, but the action following upon it. The shipowner might say, "I am perfectly certain that my ship is sound, but still I feel it my duty to have her examined, before trusting the lives of so many people to her." And it might be said to the agitator, "However convinced you were of the justice of your cause and the truth of your convictions, you ought not to have made a public attack upon any man's character until you had examined the evidence on both sides with the utmost patience and care."

In the first place, let us admit that, so far as it goes, this view of the case is right and necessary; right, because even when a man's belief is so fixed that he cannot think otherwise, he still has a choice in regard to the action suggested by it, and so cannot escape the duty of investigating on the ground of the strength of his convictions; and necessary, because those who are not yet capable of controlling their feelings and thoughts must have a plain rule dealing with overt acts.

But this being premised as necessary, it becomes clear that it is not sufficient, and that our previous judgment is required to supplement it. For it is not possible so to sever the belief from the action it suggests as to condemn the one without condemning the other. No man holding a strong belief on one side of a question, or even wishing to hold a belief on one side, can investigate it with such fairness and completeness as if he were really in doubt and unbiased; so that the existence of a belief not founded on fair inquiry unfits a man for the performance of this necessary duty.

Nor is that truly a belief at all which has not some influence upon the actions of him who holds it.

He who truly believes that which prompts him to an action has looked upon the action to lust after it, he has committed it already in his heart. If a belief is not realized immediately in open deeds, it is stored up for the guidance of the future. It goes to make a part of that aggregate of beliefs which is the link between sensation and action at every moment of all our lives, and which is so organized and compacted together that no part of it can be isolated from the rest, but every new addition modifies the structure of the whole. No real belief, however trifling and fragmentary it may seem, is ever truly insignificant; it prepares us to receive more of its like, confirms those which resembled it before, and weakens others; and so gradually it lays a stealthy train in our inmost thoughts, which may some day explode into overt action, and leave its stamp upon our character forever.

And no one man's belief is in any case a private matter which concerns himself alone. Our lives are guided by that general conception of the course of things which has been created by society for social purposes. Our words, our phrases, our forms and processes and modes of thought are common property, fashioned and perfected from age to age; an heirloom which every succeeding generation inherits as a precious deposit and a sacred trust to be handed on to the next one, not unchanged but enlarged and purified, with some clear marks of its proper handiwork. Into this, for good or ill, is woven every belief of every man who has speech of his fellows. An awful privilege, and an awful responsibility, that we should help to create the world in which posterity will live.

In the two supposed cases which have been considered, it has been judged wrong to believe on insufficient evidence, or to nourish belief by suppressing doubts and avoiding investigation. The reason of this judgment is not far to seek: it is that in both these cases the belief held by one man was of great importance to other men. But for as much as no belief held by one man, however seemingly trivial the belief, and however obscure the believer, is ever actually insignificant or without its effect on the fate of mankind, we have no choice but to extend our judgment to all cases of belief whatever. Belief, that sacred faculty which prompts

the decisions of our will, and knits into harmonious working all the compacted energies of our being, is ours not for ourselves, but for humanity. It is rightly used on truths which have been established by long experience and waiting toil, and which have stood in the fierce light of free and fearless questioning. Then it helps to bind men together, and to strengthen and direct their common action. It is desecrated when given to unproved and unquestioned statements, for the solace and private pleasure of the believer; to add a tinsel splendor to the plain straight road of our life and display a bright mirage beyond it; or even to drown the common sorrows of our kind by a self-deception which allows them not only to cast down, but also to degrade us. Whoso would deserve well of his fellows in this matter will guard the purity of his belief with a very fanaticism of jealous care, lest at any time it should rest on an unworthy object, and catch a stain which can never be wiped away.

It is not only the leader of men, statesman, philosopher or poet, that owes this bounden duty to mankind. Every rustic who delivers in the village alehouse his slow, infrequent sentences, may help to kill or keep alive the fatal superstitions which clog his race. Every hard-worked wife of an artisan may transmit to her children beliefs which shall knit society together, or rend it in pieces. No simplicity of mind, no obscurity of station, can escape the universal duty of questioning all that we believe.

It is true that this duty is a hard one, and the doubt which comes out of it is often a very bitter thing. It leaves us bare and powerless where we thought that we were safe and strong. To know all about anything is to know how to deal with it under all circumstances. We feel much happier and more secure when we think we know precisely what to do, no matter what happens, than when we have lost our way and do not know where to turn. And if we have supposed ourselves to know all about anything, and to be capable of doing what is fit in regard to it, we naturally do not like to find that we are really ignorant and powerless, that we have to begin again at the beginning, and try to learn what the thing is and how it is to be dealt with—if indeed anything can be learned about it. It is the sense of power attached to a sense of knowledge that makes men desirous of believing, and afraid of doubting.

This sense of power is the highest and best of pleasures when the belief on which it is founded is a true belief, and has been fairly earned by investigation. For then we may justly feel that it is common property, and holds good for others as well as for ourselves. Then we may be glad, not that I have learned secrets by which I am safer and stronger, but that we men have got mastery over more of the world; and we shall be strong, not for ourselves, but in the name of Man and in his strength. But if the belief has been accepted on insufficient evidence, the pleasure is a stolen one. Not only does it deceive ourselves by giving us a sense of power which we do not really possess, but it is sinful, because it is stolen in defiance of our duty to mankind. That duty is to guard ourselves from such beliefs as from a pestilence, which may shortly master our own body and then spread to the rest of the town. What would be thought of one who, for the sake of a sweet fruit, should deliberately run the risk of bringing a plague upon his family and his neighbors?

And, as in other such cases, it is not the risk only which has to be considered; for a bad action is always bad at the time when it is done, no matter what happens afterwards. Every time we let ourselves believe for unworthy reasons, we weaken our powers of self-control, of doubting, of judicially and fairly weighing evidence. We all suffer severely enough from the maintenance and support of false beliefs and the fatally wrong actions which they lead to, and the evil born when one such belief is entertained is great and wide. But a greater and wider evil arises when the credulous character is maintained and supported, when a habit of believing for unworthy reasons is fostered and made permanent. If I steal money from any person, there may be no harm done by the mere transfer of possession; he may not feel the loss, or it may prevent him from using the money badly. But I cannot help doing this great wrong towards Man, that I make myself dishonest. What hurts society is not that it should lose its property, but that it should become a den of thieves; for then it must cease to be society. This is why we ought not to do evil that good may come; for at any rate this great evil has come, that we have done evil and are made wicked thereby. In like manner, if I let myself believe anything on insufficient evidence, there may be no great harm done by the mere belief; it may be true after all, or I may never have occasion to exhibit it in outward acts. But I cannot help doing this great wrong toward Man, that I make myself credulous. The danger to society is not merely that it should believe wrong things, though that is great enough; but that it should become credulous, and lose the habit of testing things and inquiring into them; for then it must sink back into savagery.

The harm which is done by credulity in a man is not confined to the fostering of a credulous character in others, and consequent support of false beliefs. Habitual want of care about what I believe leads to habitual want of care in others about the truth of what is told to me. Men speak the truth to one another when each reveres the truth in his own mind and in the other's mind; but how shall my friend revere the truth in my mind when I myself am careless about it, when I believe things because I want to believe them, and because they are comforting and pleasant? Will he not learn to cry, "Peace," to me, when there is no peace? By such a course I shall surround myself with a thick atmosphere of falsehood and fraud, and in that must live. It may matter little to me, in my closed castle of sweet illusions and darling lies; but it matters much to Man that I have made my neighbors ready to deceive. The credulous man is father to the liar and the cheat; he lives in the bosom of this his family, and it is no marvel if he should become even as they are. So closely are our duties knit together, that whoso shall keep the whole law, and yet offend in one point, he is guilty of all.

To sum up: it is wrong always, everywhere and for anyone, to believe anything upon insufficient evidence.

If a man, holding a belief which he was taught in childhood or persuaded of afterwards, keeps down and pushes away any doubts which arise about it in his mind, purposely avoids the reading of books and the company of men that call in question or discuss it, and regards as impious those questions which cannot easily be asked without disturbing it—the life of that man is one long sin against mankind.

If this judgment seems harsh when applied to those simple souls who have never known better, who have been brought up from the cradle with a horror of doubt, and taught that their eternal welfare depends on what they believe, then it leads to the very serious question, Who hath made Israel to sin? ...

Inquiry into the evidence of a doctrine is not to be made once for all, and then taken as finally settled. It is never lawful to stifle a doubt; for either it can be honestly answered by means of the inquiry already made, or else it proves that the inquiry was not complete.

"But," says one, "I am a busy man; I have no time for the long course of study which would be necessary to make me in any degree a competent judge of certain questions, or even able to understand the nature of the arguments." Then he should have no time to believe....

VII.A.3

The Will to Believe

WILLIAM JAMES

William James (1842–1910) was a philosopher and psychologist, the elder brother of novelist Henry James, and one of the central figures in the American pragmatist school of philosophy. Among his more important works are The Varieties of Religious Experience *(1902),* Pragmatism *(1907), and* The Meaning of Truth *(1909). In the present essay James argues, against W. K. Clifford, that sometimes practical considerations force us to make decisions on propositions for which we do not yet and, indeed, may never have sufficient evidence.*

I

Let us give the name of hypothesis to anything that may be proposed to our belief; and just as the electricians speak of live and dead wires, let us speak of any hypothesis as either *live* or *dead*. A live hypothesis is one which appeals as a real possibility to him to whom it is proposed. If I ask you to believe in the Mahdi, the notion makes no electric connection with your nature—it refuses to scintillate with any credibility at all. As an hypothesis it is completely dead. To an Arab, however (even if he be not one of the Mahdi's followers), the hypothesis is among the mind's possibilities: It is alive. This shows that deadness and liveness in an hypothesis are not intrinsic properties, but relations to the individual thinker. They are measured by his willingness to act. The maximum of liveness in an hypothesis means willingness to act irrevocably. Practically, that means belief; but there is some believing tendency wherever there is willingness to act at all.

Reprinted from William James, *The Will to Believe* (New York: Longmans Green & Co., 1897).

Next, let us call the decision between two hypotheses an option. Options may be of several kinds. They maybe first, *living* or *dead*; secondly, *forced* or *avoidable*; thirdly, *momentous* or *trivial*; and for our purposes we may call an option a *genuine* option when it is of a forced, living, and momentous kind.

1. A living option is one in which both hypotheses are live ones. If I say to you: "Be a theosophist or be a Mohammedan," it is probably a dead option, because for you neither hypothesis is likely to be alive. But if I say: "Be an agnostic or be a Christian," it is otherwise: trained as you are, each hypothesis makes some appeal, however small, to your belief.

2. Next, if I say to you: "Choose between going out with your umbrella or without it," I do not offer you a genuine option, for it is not forced. You can easily avoid it by not going out at all. Similarly, if I say, "Either love me or hate me," "Either call my theory true or call it false," your option is avoidable. You may remain indifferent to me, neither loving nor hating, and you may decline to offer any judgment as to my theory. But if I say, "Either accept this truth or go without it," I put on you a forced option, for there is no standing place outside of the alternative. Every dilemma based on a complete logical disjunction, with no possibility of not choosing, is an option of this forced kind.

3. Finally, if I were Dr. Nansen and proposed to you to join my North Pole expedition, your option would be momentous; for this would probably be your similar opportunity, and your choice now would either exclude you from the North Pole sort of immortality altogether or put at least the chance of it into your hands. He who refuses to embrace a unique opportunity loses the prize as surely as if he tried and failed. Per contra, the option is trivial when the opportunity is not unique, when the stake is insignificant, or when the decision is reversible if it later proves unwise. Such trivial options abound in the scientific

life. A chemist finds an hypothesis live enough to spend a year in its verification: he believes in it to that extent. But if his experiments prove inconclusive either way, he is quit for his loss of time, no vital harm being done.

It will facilitate our discussion if we keep all these distinctions well in mind.

II

The next matter to consider is the actual psychology of human opinion. When we look at certain facts, it seems as if our passional and volitional nature lay at the root of all our convictions. When we look at others, it seems as if they could do nothing when the intellect had once said its say. Let us take the latter facts up first.

Does it not seem preposterous on the very face of it to talk of our opinions being modifiable at will? Can our will either help or hinder our intellect in its perceptions of truth? Can we, by just willing it, believe that Abraham Lincoln's existence is a myth, and that the portraits of him in *McClure's Magazine* are all of some one else? Can we, by any effort of our will, or by any strength of wish that it were true, believe ourselves well and about when we are roaring with rheumatism in bed, or feel certain that the sum of the two one-dollar bills in our pocket must be a hundred dollars? We can say any of these things, but we are absolutely impotent to believe them; and of just such things is the whole fabric of the truths that we do believe in made up—matters of fact, immediate or remote, as Hume said, and relations between ideas, which are either there or not there for us if we see them so, and which if not there cannot be put there by any action of our own.

In Pascal's *Thoughts* there is a celebrated passage known in literature as Pascal's Wager. In it he tries to force us into Christianity by reasoning as if our concern with truth resembled our concern with the stakes in a game of chance. Translated freely his words are these: You must either believe or not believe that God is—which will you do? Your human reason cannot say. A game is going on between you and the nature of things which at the day of judgment will bring out either heads or tails. Weigh what your gains and your losses would be if you should stake all you have on heads, or God's existence: if you win in such case you gain eternal beatitude; if you lose, you lose nothing at all. If there were an infinity of chances and only one for God in this wager, still you ought to stake your all on God; for though you surely risk a finite loss by this procedure, any finite loss is reasonable, even a certain one is reasonable, if there is but the possibility of infinite gain. Go then, and take holy water, and have masses said: belief will come and stupefy your scruples.... Why should you not? At bottom, what have you to lose?

You probably feel that when religious faith expresses itself thus, in the language of the gaming-table, it is put to its last trumps. Surely Pascal's own personal belief in masses and holy water had far other springs; and this celebrated page of his is but an argument for others, a last desperate snatch at a weapon against the hardness of the unbelieving heart. We feel that a faith in masses and holy water adopted wilfully after such a mechanical calculation would lack the inner soul of faith's reality; and if we were ourselves in the place of the Deity, we should probably take particular pleasure in cutting off believers of this pattern from their infinite reward. It is evident that unless there be some preexisting tendency to believe in masses and holy water, the option offered to the will by Pascal is not a living option. Certainly no Turk ever took to masses and holy water on its account and even to us Protestants these means of salvation seem such foregone impossibilities that Pascal's logic, invoked for them specifically, leaves us unmoved. As well might the Mahdi write to us saying, "I am the Expected One whom God has created in his effulgence. You shall be infinitely happy if you confess me; otherwise you shall be cut off from the light of the sun. Weigh, then, your infinite gain if I am genuine against your finite sacrifice if I am not!" His logic would be that of Pascal; but he would vainly use it on us, for the hypothesis he offers us is dead. No tendency to act on it exists in us to any degree.

The talk of believing by our volition seems, then from one point of view, simply silly. From another point of view it is worse than silly, it is vile. When one turns to the magnificent edifice of the physical sciences, and sees how it was reared; what thousands of disinterested moral lives of men lie buried in its mere foundations; what patience and postponement, what choking down of preference, what submission to the icy laws of outer fact are wrought into its very stones and mortar; how absolutely impersonal it stands in its vast augustness—then how besotted and contemptible seems every little sentimentalist who comes blowing his voluntary smoke-wreaths, and pretending to decide things from out of his private dream! Can we wonder if those bred in the rugged and manly school of science should feel like spewing such subjectivism out of their mouths? The whole system of loyalties which grow up in the schools of science go dead against its toleration; so that it is only natural that those who have caught the scientific fever should pass over to the opposite extreme, and write sometimes as if the incorruptibly truthful intellect ought positively to prefer bitterness and unacceptableness to the heart in its cup.

It fortifies my soul to know
That though I perish, truth is so

sings Clough, while Huxley exclaims: "My only consolation lies in the reflection that, however bad our posterity may become, so far as they hold by the plain rule of not pretending to believe what they have no reason to believe, because it may be to their advantage so to pretend [the word "pretend" is surely here redundant], they will not have reached the lowest depths of immorality." And that delicious *enfant terrible* Clifford writes: "Belief is desecrated when given to unproved and unquestioned statements for the solace and private pleasure of the believer.... Whoso would deserve well of his fellows in this matter will guard the purity of his belief with a very fanaticism of jealous care, lest at any time it should rest on an unworthy object, and catch a stain which can never be wiped away.... If [a] belief has been accepted on insufficient evidence [even though the belief be true, as Clifford on the same page explains] the pleasure is a stolen one.... It is sinful because it is stolen in defiance of our duty to mankind. That duty is to guard ourselves from such beliefs as from a pestilence which may shortly master our own body and then spread to the rest of the town.... It is wrong always, everywhere, and for every one, to believe anything upon insufficient evidence."

III

All this strikes one as healthy, even when expressed, as by Clifford, with somewhat too much of robustious pathos in the voice. Free will and simple wishing do seem, in the matter of our credences, to be only fifth wheels to the coach. Yet if any one should thereupon assume that intellectual insight is what remains after wish and will and sentimental preference have taken wing, or that pure reason is what then settles our opinions, he would fly quite as directly in the teeth of the facts.

It is only our already dead hypotheses that our willing nature is unable to bring to life again. But what has made them dead for us is for the most part a previous action of our willing nature of an antagonistic kind. When I say "willing nature," I do not mean only such deliberate volitions as may have set up habits of belief that we cannot now escape from—I mean all such factors of belief as fear and hope, prejudice and passion, imitation and partisanship, the circumpressure of our caste and set. As a matter of fact we find ourselves believing, we hardly know how or why. Mr. Balfour gives the name of "authority" to all those influences, born of the intellectual climate, that make hypotheses possible or impossible for us, alive or dead. Here in this room, we all of us believe in molecules and the conservation of energy, in democracy and necessary progress, in Protestant Christianity and the duty of fighting for "the doctrine of the immortal Monroe," all for no reasons worthy of the name. We see into these matters with no more inner clearness, and probably with much less, than any disbeliever in them might possess. His unconventionality would probably have

some grounds to show for its conclusions; but for us, not insight, but the *prestige* of the opinions, is what makes the spark shoot from them and light up our sleeping magazines of faith. Our reason is quite satisfied, in nine hundred and ninety-nine cases out of every thousand of us, if it can find a few arguments that will do to recite in case our credulity is criticized by some one else. Our faith is faith in some one else's faith, and in the greatest matters this is the most the case. Our belief in truth itself, for instance, that there is a truth, and that our minds and it are made for each other,—what is it but a passionate affirmation of desire, in which our social system backs us up? We want to have a truth; we want to believe that our experiments and studies and discussions must put us in a continually better and better position towards it; and on this line we agree to fight out our thinking lives. But if a pyrrhonistic sceptic asks *us how we know* all this, can our logic find a reply? No! certainly it cannot. It is just one volition against another,—we willing to go in for life upon a trust or assumption which he, for his part, does not care to make.

As a rule we disbelieve all facts and theories for which we have no use. Clifford's cosmic emotions find no use for Christian feelings. Huxley belabors the bishops because there is no use for sacerdotalism in his scheme of life. Newman, on the contrary, goes over to Romanism, and finds all sorts of reasons good for staying there, because a priestly system is for him an organic need and delight. Why do so few "scientists" even look at the evidence for telepathy, so called? Because they think, as a leading biologist, now dead, once said to me, that even if such a thing were true, scientists ought to band together to keep it suppressed and concealed. It would undo the uniformity of Nature and all sorts of other things without which scientists cannot carry on their pursuits. But if this very man had been shown something which as a scientist he might *do* with telepathy, he might not only have examined the evidence, but even have found it good enough.

This very law which the logicians would impose upon us—if I may give the name of logicians to those who would rule out our willing nature here—is based on nothing but their own natural wish to exclude all elements for which they, in their professional quality of logicians, can find no use.

Evidently, then, our non-intellectual nature does influence our convictions. There are passional tendencies and volitions which run before and others which come after belief, and it is only the latter that are too late for the fair; and they are not too late when the previous passional work has been already in their own direction. Pascal's argument, instead of being powerless, then seems a regular clincher, and is the last stroke needed to make our faith in masses and holy water complete. The state of things is evidently far from simple; and pure insight and logic, whatever they might do ideally, are not the only things that really do produce our creeds.

IV

Our next duty, having recognized this mixed up state of affairs, is to ask whether it be simply reprehensible and pathological, or whether, on the contrary, we must treat it as a normal element in making up our minds. The thesis I defend is, briefly stated, this: *Our passional nature not only lawfully may, but must, decide an option between propositions, whenever it is a genuine option that cannot by its nature be decided on intellectual grounds; for to say, under such circumstances, "Do not decide, but leave the question open," is itself a passional decision—just like deciding yes or no—and is attended with the same risk of losing the truth....*

VII

One more point, small but important, and our preliminaries are done. There are two ways of looking at our duty in the matter of opinion—ways entirely different, and yet ways about whose difference the theory of knowledge seems hitherto to have shown very little concern. *We must know the truth; and we must avoid error*—these are our first and great commandments as would-be knowers; but they are not two ways of stating an identical commandment, they are two separable laws. Although it may indeed happen that when we believe the truth A, we escape as an incidental consequence from believing the falsehood B, it hardly ever happens that by merely disbelieving B we necessarily believe A. We may in escaping B fall into believing other falsehoods, C or D, just as bad as B; or we may escape B by not believing anything at all, not even A.

Believe truth! Shun error!—these, we see, are two materially different laws; and by choosing between them we may end by coloring differently our whole intellectual life. We may regard the chase for truth as paramount, and the avoidance of error as secondary; or we may, on the other hand, treat the avoidance of error as more imperative, and let truth take its chance. Clifford, in the instructive passage which I have quoted, exhorts us to the latter course. Believe nothing, he tells us, keep your mind in suspense forever, rather than by closing it on insufficient evidence incur the awful risk of believing lies. You, on the other hand, may think that the risk of being in error is a very small matter when compared with the blessings of real knowledge, and be ready to be duped many times in your investigation rather than postpone indefinitely the chance of guessing true. I myself find it impossible to go with Clifford. We must remember that these feelings of our duty about either truth or error are in any case only expressions of our passional life. Biologically considered, our minds are as ready to grind out falsehood as veracity, and he who says, "Better go without belief forever than believe a lie!" merely shows his own preponderant private horror of becoming a dupe. He may be critical of many of his desires and fears, but this fear he slavishly obeys. He cannot imagine any one questioning its binding force. For my own part, I have also a horror of being duped; but I can believe that worse things than being duped may happen to a man in this world; so Clifford's exhortation has to my ears a thoroughly fantastic sound. It is like a general informing his soldiers that it is better to keep out of battle forever than to risk a single wound. Not so are victories either over enemies or over nature gained. Our errors are surely not such awfully solemn things. In a world where we are so certain to incur them in spite of all our caution, a certain lightness of heart seems healthier than this excessive nervousness on their behalf. At any rate, it seems the fittest thing for the empiricist philosopher.

VIII

And now, after all this introduction, let us go straight at our question. I have said, and now repeat it, that not only as a matter of fact do we find our passional nature influencing us in our opinions, but that there are some options between opinions in which this influence must be regarded both as an inevitable and as a lawful determinant of our choice.

I fear here that some of you my hearers will begin to scent danger, and lend an inhospitable ear. Two first steps of passion you have indeed had to admit as necessary—we must think so as to avoid dupery, and we must think so as to gain truth; but the surest path to those ideal consummations, you will probably consider, is from now onwards to take no further passional step.

Well, of course, I agree as far as the facts will allow. Wherever the option between losing truth and gaining it is not momentous, we can throw the chance of *gaining truth* away, and at any rate save ourselves from any chance of *believing falsehood*, by not making up our minds at all till objective evidence has come. In scientific questions, this is almost always the case; and even in human affairs in general, the need of acting is seldom so urgent that a false belief to act on is better than no belief at all. Law courts, indeed, have to decide on the best evidence attainable for the moment, because a judge's duty is to make law as well as to ascertain it, and (as a learned judge once said to me) few cases are worth spending much time over: the great thing is to have them decided on *any* acceptable principle,

and got out of the way. But in our dealings with objective nature we obviously are recorders, not makers, of the truth; and decisions for the mere sake of deciding promptly and getting on to the next business would be wholly out of place. Throughout the breadth of physical nature facts are what they are quite independently of us, and seldom is there any such hurry about them that the risks of being duped by believing a premature theory need be faced. The questions here are always trivial options, the hypotheses are hardly living (at any rate not living for us spectators), the choice between believing truth or falsehood is seldom forced. The attitude of sceptical balance is therefore the absolutely wise one if we would escape mistakes. What difference, indeed, does it make to most of us whether we have or have not a theory of the Röntgen rays, whether we believe or not in mind-stuff, or have a conviction about the causality of conscious states? It makes no difference. Such options are not forced on us. On every account it is better not to make them, but still keep weighing reasons *pro et contra* with an indifferent hand.

I speak, of course, here of the purely judging mind. For purposes of discovery such indifference is to be less highly recommended, and science would be far less advanced than she is if the passionate desires of individuals to get their own faiths confirmed had been kept out of the game. See for example the sagacity which Spencer and Weismann now display. On the other hand, if you want an absolute duffer in an investigation, you must, after all, take the man who has no interest whatever in its results: he is the warranted incapable, the positive fool. The most useful investigator, because the most sensitive observer, is always he whose eager interest in one side of the question is balanced by an equally keen nervousness lest he become deceived.[1] Science has organized this nervousness into a regular *technique*, her so-called method of verification; and she has fallen so deeply in love with the method that one may even say she has ceased to care for truth by itself at all. It is only truth as technically verified that interests her. The truth of truths might come in merely affirmative form, and she would decline to touch it. Such truth as that, she might repeat with Clifford, would be stolen in defiance of her duty to mankind. Human passions, however, are stronger than technical rules. *"Le coeur a ses raisons,"* as Pascal says, *"que la raison ne connait pas"*;[2] and however indifferent to all but the bare rules of the game the umpire, the abstract intellect, may be, the concrete players who furnish him the materials to judge of are usually, each one of them, in love with some pet "live hypothesis" of his own. Let us agree, however, that wherever there is no forced option, the dispassionately judicial intellect with no pet hypothesis, saving us, as it does, from dupery at any rate, ought to be our ideal.

The question next arises: Are there not somewhere forced options in our speculative questions, and can we (as men who may be interested at least as much in positively gaining truth as in merely escaping dupery) always wait with impunity till the coercive evidence shall have arrived? It seems *a priori* improbable that the truth should be so nicely adjusted to our needs and powers as that. In the great boarding-house of nature, the cakes and the butter and the syrup seldom come out so even and leave the plates so clean. Indeed, we should view them with scientific suspicion if they did.

IX

Moral questions immediately present themselves as questions whose solution cannot wait for sensible proof. A moral question is a question not of what sensibly exists, but of what is good, or would be good if it did exist. Science can tell us what exists; but to compare the *worths*, both of what exists and of what does not exist, we must consult not science, but what Pascal calls our heart....

Turn now from these wide questions of good to a certain class of questions of fact, questions concerning personal relations, states of mind between one man and another. *Do you like me or not?*—for example. Whether you do or not depends, in countless instances, on whether I meet you halfway, am willing to assume that you must like me, and show you trust and expectation. The previous faith on my part in your liking's

existence is in such cases what makes your liking come. But if I stand aloof, and refuse to budge an inch until I have objective evidence, until you shall have done something apt, as the absolutists say, *ad extorquendum assensum meum*, ten to one your liking never comes. How many women's hearts are vanquished by the mere sanguine insistence of some man that they must love him! He will not consent to the hypothesis that they cannot. The desire for a certain kind of truth here brings about that special truth's existence; and so it is in innumerable cases of other sorts.... *And where faith in a fact can help create the fact*, that would be an insane logic which should say that faith running ahead of scientific evidence is the "lowest kind of immorality" into which a thinking being can fall. Yet such is the logic by which our scientific absolutists pretend to regulate our lives!

X

In truths dependent on our personal action, then faith based on desire is certainly a lawful and possibly an indispensable thing.

But now, it will be said, these are all childish human cases, and have nothing to do with great cosmical matters, like the question of religious faith. Let us then pass on to that. Religions differ so much in their accidents that in discussing the religious question we must make it very generic and broad. What then do we now mean by the religious hypothesis? Science says things are; morality says some things are better than other things; and religion says essentially two things.

First, she says that the best things are the more eternal things, the overlapping things, the things in the universe that throw the last stone, so to speak and say the final word. "Perfection is eternal"—this phrase of Charles Secrétan seems a good way of putting this first affirmation of religion, an affirmation which obviously cannot yet be verified scientifically at all.

The second affirmation of religion is that we are better off even now if we believe her first affirmation to be true.

Now, let us consider what the logical elements of this situation are *in case the religious hypothesis in both its branches be really true.* (Of course, we must admit that possibility at the outset. If we are to discuss the question at all, it must involve a living option. If for any of you religion be a hypothesis that cannot, by any living possibility, be true, then you need go no farther. I speak to the "saving remnant" alone.) So proceeding, we see, first, that religion offers itself as a *momentous* option. We are supposed to gain, even now, by our belief, and to lose by our non-belief, a certain vital good. Secondly religion is a *forced* option, so far as that good goes. We cannot escape the issue by remaining sceptical and waiting for more light, because, although we do avoid error in that way *if religion be untrue,* we lose the good, *if it be true,* just as certainly as if we positively chose to disbelieve. It is as if a man should hesitate indefinitely to ask a certain woman to marry him because he was not perfectly sure that she would prove an angel after he brought her home. Would he not cut himself off from that particular angel-possibility as decisively as if he went and married some one else? Scepticism, then, is not avoidance of option; it is option of a certain particular kind of risk. *Better risk loss of truth than chance of error*—that is your faith-vetoer's exact position. He is actively playing his stake as much as the believer is; he is backing the field against the religious hypothesis, just as the believer is backing the religious hypothesis against the field. To preach scepticism to us as a duty until "sufficient evidence" for religion to be found is tantamount therefore to telling us, when in presence of the religious hypothesis, that to yield to our fear of its being error is wiser and better than to yield to our hope that it may be true. It is not intellect against all passions, then; it is only intellect with one passion laying down its law. And by what, forsooth, is the supreme wisdom of this passion warranted? Dupery for dupery, what proof is there that dupery through hope is so much worse than dupery through fear? I, for one, can see no proof; and I simply refuse obedience to the scientist's command to imitate his kind of option, in a case where my own stake is important enough to give me the right to choose my own form of risk. If religion be true and the evidence for it be still insufficient, I do not wish, by putting your extinguisher upon my nature (which feels to me as if it had after all some business in this matter), to forfeit my sole chance in life of getting upon the winning side—that chance depending, of course, on my willingness to run the risk of acting as if my passional need of taking the world religiously might be prophetic and right.

All this is on the supposition that it really may be prophetic and right, and that, even to us who are discussing the matter, religion is a live hypothesis which may be true. Now, to most of us religion comes in a still further way that makes a veto on our active faith even more illogical. The more perfect and more eternal aspect of the universe is represented in our religions as having personal form. The universe is no longer a mere *It* to us, but a *Thou,* if we are religious; and any relation that may be possible from person to person might be possible here. For instance, although in one sense we are passive portions of the universe, in another we show a curious autonomy, as if we were small active centers on our own account. We feel, too, as if the appeal of religion to us were made to our own active goodwill, as if evidence might be forever withheld from us unless we met the hypothesis halfway to take a trivial illusion; just as a man who in a company of gentlemen made no advances, asked a warrant for every concession, and believed no one's word without proof, would cut himself off by such churlishness from all the social rewards that a more trusting spirit would earn—so here, one who should shut himself up in snarling logicality and try to make the gods extort his recognition willy-nilly, or not get it at all, might cut himself off forever from his only opportunity of making the gods' acquaintance. This feeling, forced on us we know not whence that by obstinately believing that there are gods (although not to do so would be so easy both for our logic and our life) we are doing the universe the deepest service we can, seems part of the living essence of the religious hypothesis. If the hypothesis were true in all its parts, including this one, then pure intellectualism, with its veto on our making willing advances, would be an absurdity; and some participation of our sympathetic nature would be logically required. I therefore, for one, cannot see my way to accepting the agnostic rules for truth-seeking, or wilfully agree to keep my willing nature out of the game. I cannot do so for this plain reason, that *a rule of thinking which would absolutely prevent me from acknowledging certain kinds of truth if those kinds of truth were really there, would be an irrational rule.* That for me is the long and short of the formal logic of the situation, no matter what the kinds of truth might materially be.

I confess I do not see how this logic can be escaped. But sad experience makes me fear that some of you may still shrink from radically saying with me, *in abstracto*, that we have the right to believe at our own risk any hypothesis that is live enough to tempt our will. I suspect, however, that if this is so, it is because you have got away from the abstract logical point of view altogether, and are thinking (perhaps without realizing it) of some particular religious hypothesis which for you is dead. The freedom to "believe what we will" you apply to the case of some patent superstition; and the faith you think of is the faith defined by the schoolboy when he said, "Faith is when you believe something that you know ain't true." I can only repeat that this is misapprehension. *In concreto*, the freedom to believe can only cover living options which the intellect of the individual cannot by itself resolve; and living options never seem absurdities to him who has them to consider. When I look at the religious question as it really puts itself to concrete men, and when I think of all the possibilities which both practically and theoretically it involves, then this command that we shall put a stopper on our heart, instincts, and courage, and *wait*—acting of course meanwhile more or less as if religion were not true[3]—till doomsday, or till such time as our intellect and senses working together may have raked in evidence enough—this command, I say, seems to me the queerest idol ever manufactured in the philosophic cave. Were we scholastic absolutists, there might be more excuse. If we had an infallible intellect with its objective certitudes, we might feel ourselves disloyal to such a perfect organ or knowledge in not trusting to it exclusively, in not

waiting for its releasing word. But if we are empiricists, if we believe that no bell in us tolls to let us know for certain when truth is in our grasp, then it seems a piece of idle fantasticality to preach so solemnly our duty of waiting for the bell. Indeed we may wait if we will—I hope you do not think that I am denying that—but if we do so, we do so at our peril as much as if we believed. In either case we act, taking our life in our hands. No one of us ought to issue vetoes to the other, nor should we bandy words of abuse. We ought, on the contrary, delicately and profoundly to respect one another's mental freedom: then only shall we bring about the intellectual republic; then only shall we have that spirit of inner tolerance without which all our outer tolerance is soulless, and which is empiricism's glory; then only shall we live and let live, in speculative as well as in practical things.

I began by a reference to Fitz-James Stephen; let me end by a quotation from him. "What do you think of yourself? What do you think of the world? ... These are questions with which all must deal as it seems good to them. They are riddles of the Sphinx, and in some way or other we must deal with them.... In all important transactions of life we have to take a leap in the dark.... If we decide to leave the riddles unanswered, that is a choice; if we waver in our answer, that, too, is a choice: but whatever choice we make, we make it at our peril. If a man chooses to turn his back altogether on God and the future no one can prevent him; no one can show beyond reasonable doubt that he is mistaken. If a man thinks otherwise and acts as he thinks, I do not see that any one can prove that he is mistaken. Each must act as he thinks best; and if he is wrong, so much the worse for him. We stand on a mountain pass in the midst of whirling snow and blinding mist, through which we get glimpses now and then of paths which may be deceptive. If we stand still we shall be frozen to death. If we take the wrong road we shall be dashed to pieces. We do not certainly know whether there is any right one. What must we do? 'Be strong and of a good courage.' Act for the best, hope for the best, and take what comes.... If death ends all, we cannot meet death better."

NOTES

1. Compare Wilfrid Ward's Essay "The Wish to Believe," in his *Witnesses to the Unseen* (Macmillan & Co., 1893).

2. "The heart has its reasons which reason does not know."

3. Since belief is measured by action, he who forbids us to believe religion to be true, necessarily also forbids us to act as we should if we did believe it to be true. The whole defence of religious faith hinges upon action. If the action required or inspired by the religious hypothesis is in no way different from that dictated by the naturalistic hypothesis, then religious faith is a pure superfluity, better pruned away, and controversy about its legitimacy is a piece of idle trifling, unworthy of serious minds. I myself believe, of course, that the religious hypothesis gives to the world an expression which specifically determines our reactions, and makes them in a large part unlike what they might be on a purely naturalistic scheme of belief.

VII.B. EVIDENCE, RELIGIOUS BELIEF, AND FAITH

The previous section focused on the *practical* rationality of religious belief. Now, in this section, we turn to issues about the *epistemic* status of religious belief. To talk about the epistemic status of a belief is just to talk about whether the belief has whatever it takes (besides *truth*) to count as knowledge. If, for example, you believe that aliens from outer space have landed in New Mexico for no reason other than the fact that your favorite comic book series is premised on that claim, your belief has rather low, or poor, epistemic status—and this regardless of whether the belief is true. Believing things just because one's favorite comic book series is premised upon them just isn't a good way of forming beliefs if one is interested in maximizing one's knowledge of the world. In other words, forming beliefs in that way is epistemically irrational. On the other hand, if you believe that aliens have landed in New Mexico because CNN, MSNBC, the BBC, and a variety of other respectable news outlets are all presently doing "Breaking News" reports on the occurrence, your belief will have quite a bit more by way of positive epistemic status, or epistemic rationality. For purposes here, we are concerned with two main questions about the epistemic status of religious belief: (1) whether religious beliefs can be epistemically rational even if they aren't based on arguments, and (2) whether one might still have religious *faith* even in the absence of religious *belief.* Both are questions about the relation between evidence, religious belief, and faith. The first asks what sort of evidence (if any) is needed in order to make religious belief rational. The second asks whether faith is possible for those whose evidential situation leaves them unable to believe.

In the first reading, "Rational Theistic Belief Without Proof," John Hick discusses the relevance of the proofs or arguments for theistic beliefs that we studied in Part IV. He argues that the proofs are largely irrelevant to religion. They are neither sufficient nor necessary for the religious life. Not only do the so-called proofs for the existence of God fail to accomplish what they set out to do, but even if they did demonstrate what they purported to demonstrate, this would at best only force our notional assent. They would not bring about the deep devotion and sense of worship necessary for a full religious life. Furthermore, they are not necessary because believers have something *better*—an intense, coercive, indubitable experience—which convinces them of the reality of the being in question. For believers, God is not a hypothesis brought in ex machina to explain the world, but a living presence, closer to them than the air they breathe.

Hick develops a notion of religious experience as analogous to our experience of an external world. Neither the existence of an external world nor the existence of an external religious reality can be proven, but belief in each is a natural response to our experience. The main difference between the two kinds of experiences is that virtually everyone has external-world experiences, but only a relatively small minority of humankind have noticeable religious experiences. Should this undermine the argument from religious experience? Not necessarily, for it may be the case that the few have access to a higher reality. They cannot easily be dismissed as insane or simply hallucinating, for the "general intelligence and exceptionally high moral quality of the great religious figures clashes with any analysis of their experience in terms of abnormal psychology." At the end of his article Hick applies his thesis about the sense of the presence of God to the problem of the plurality of religions. He suggests that there is a convergence of religious experience, indicating the existence of a common higher reality.

In our next reading, Anthony Flew defends the view that debate about the existence of God should start with a "presumption of atheism." As Flew uses the term, an "atheist" is anyone who isn't a theist, and the *presumption of atheism* is akin to the presumption of innocence in a criminal trial: It is the procedural idea that one should not move from the "presumed" position unless sufficient proof has been given. One might think that proof is not needed if one agrees with Hick that religious belief can be justified on the basis of experience rather than argument. But, Flew argues, even if one can (in principle) be justified in believing in God on the basis of experience, this does not remove the burden of proof: One must still provide an argument for the claim that "having religious experience really is a kind of perceiving, and hence a sort of being in a position to know about its putative object." Absent an argument for that claim, he thinks, it is "impossible to vindicate [one's] claims to be harbouring rational beliefs."

One might look to the work of William Alston on perceiving God (see Selection III.3) for a reply to Flew. Along similar lines, one might look to what has come to be called "Reformed epistemology." Reformed epistemology—so called because it traces its roots through the Protestant Reformed tradition to John Calvin—maintains (with both Alston and Hick) that religious beliefs, like the belief that God exists, can be rationally held on the basis of experience and in the absence of argument. The main difference between Reformed epistemology as such and the sorts of views defended by Alston and Hick is that Reformed epistemologists are concerned with a wider range of experiences than the ones that might plausibly count as perceptual experiences of God.

The foremost contemporary developer and defender of Reformed epistemology is Alvin Plantinga; and the two most important sources for the view are his "Reason and Belief in God" and the magisterial conclusion to his *Warrant* trilogy: *Warranted Christian Belief.* Doing justice to the view in the short space that we have here, however, requires either a patchwork quilt of excerpts from these and perhaps other works by Plantinga or a brand new essay written with the aim of providing an accessible overview. We have gone the latter route, with a specially commissioned essay by Michael Bergmann. In "Rational Religious Belief Without Arguments," Bergmann presents the essentials of Reformed epistemology, along with replies to some of the most important objections. Along the way, he considers the question whether religious believers are indeed under a burden to defend with arguments the claim that their experiences are genuinely experiences *of God.* Drawing on an analogy with sense perception, Bergmann argues (contrary to Flew) that they are not.

In the final reading, "Faith, Hope, and Doubt," Louis Pojman examines the relationship between belief and faith and argues that religious faith can exist and flourish in the absence of belief. One may not be able to believe in God because of an insufficiency of evidence, but one may still live committed to a theistic worldview, in hope. Pojman argues that this is an authentic religious position, too often neglected in the literature.

VII.B.1

Rational Theistic Belief Without Proof

JOHN HICK

A short biographical sketch of John Hick precedes selection IV.C.2. In the present article, Hick argues that the so-called proofs for the existence of God are largely irrelevant for religion. Religious belief, he argues, can be rationally grounded in religious experience.

Reprinted from John Hick, *Arguments for the Existence of God* (Macmillan: London and Basingstoke, 1971) by permission of the author. Footnotes edited.

(A) THE RELIGIOUS REJECTION OF THE THEISTIC ARGUMENTS

We have seen that the major theistic arguments are all open to serious philosophical objections. Indeed we have in each case concluded, in agreement with the majority of contemporary philosophers, that these arguments fail to do what they profess to do. Neither those which undertake strictly to demonstrate the existence of an absolute. Being, nor those which profess to show divine existence to be probable, are able to fulfil their promise. We have seen that it is impossible to demonstrate the reality of God by *a priori* reasoning, since such reasoning is confined to the realm of concepts; impossible to demonstrate it by *a posteriori* reasoning, since this would have to include a premise begging the very question at issue; and impossible to establish it as in a greater or lesser degree probable, since the notion of probability lacks any clear meaning in this context. A philosopher unacquainted with modern developments in theology might well assume that theologians would, *ex officio*, be supporters of the theistic proofs and would regard as a fatal blow this conclusion that there can be neither a strict demonstration of God's existence nor a valid probability argument for it. In fact however such an assumption would be true only of certain theological schools. It is true of the more traditional Roman Catholic theology, of sections of conservative Protestantism, and of most of those Protestant apologists who continue to work within the tradition of nineteenth-century idealism. It has never been true, on the other hand, of Jewish religious thought; and it is not true of that central stream of contemporary Protestant theology which has been influenced by the "neo-orthodox" movement, the revival of Reformation studies and the "existentialism" of Kierkegaard and his successors; or of the most significant contemporary Roman Catholic thinkers, who are on this issue (as on so many others) in advance of the official teaching of the magisterium. Accordingly we have now to take note of this theological rejection of the theistic

proofs, ranging from a complete lack of concern for them to a positive repudiation of them as being religiously irrelevant or even harmful. There are several different considerations to be evaluated.

1. It has often been pointed out that for the man of faith, as he is depicted in the Bible, no theistic proofs are necessary. Philosophers in the rationalist tradition, holding that to know means to be able to prove, have been shocked to find that in the Bible, which is supposed to be the basis of Western religion, no attempt whatever is made to demonstrate the existence of God. Instead of professing to establish the divine reality by philosophical reasoning the Bible throughout takes this for granted. Indeed to the biblical writers it would have seemed absurd to try to establish by logical argumentation that God exists. For they were convinced that they were already having to do with him and he with them in all the affairs of their lives. They did not think of God as an inferred entity but as an experienced reality. Many of the biblical writers were (sometimes, though doubtless not all times) as vividly conscious of being in God's presence as they were of living in a material world. It is impossible to read their pages without realising that to them God was not a proposition completing a syllogism, or an idea adopted by the mind, but the supreme experiential reality. It would be as sensible for a husband to desire a philosophical proof of the existence of the wife and family who contribute so much of the meaning and value of his life as for the man of faith to seek for a proof of the existence of the God within whose purpose he believes that he lives and moves and has his being.

As Cook Wilson wrote:

> If we think of the existence of our friends; it is the "direct knowledge" which we want: merely inferential knowledge seems a poor affair. To most men it would be as surprising as unwelcome to hear it could not be directly known whether there were such existences as their friends, and that it was only a matter of (probable) empirical argument and inference from facts which are directly known. And even

if we convince ourselves on reflection that this is really the case, our actions prove that we have a confidence in the existence of our friends which can't be derived from an empirical argument (which can never be certain) for a man will risk his life for his friend. We don't want merely inferred friends. Could we possibly be satisfied with an inferred God?

In other words the man of faith has no need of theistic proofs; for he has something which for him is much better. However it does not follow from this that there may not be others who do need a theistic proof, nor does it follow that there are in fact no such proofs. All that has been said about the irrelevance of proofs to the life of faith may well be true, and yet it might still be the case that there are valid arguments capable of establishing the existence of God to those who stand outside the life of faith.

2. It has also often been pointed out that the God whose existence each of the traditional theistic proofs professes to establish is only an abstraction from and a pale shadow of the living God who is the putative object of biblical faith. A First Cause of the Universe might or might not be a deity to whom an unqualified devotion, love and trust would be appropriate; Aquinas's *Et hoc omnes intelligunt Deum* ("and this all understand to be God") is not the last step in a logical argument but merely an exercise of the custom of overlooking a gap in the argument at this point. A Necessary Being, and indeed a being who is metaphysically absolute in every respect—omnipotent, omniscient, eternal, uncreated—might be morally good or evil. As H. D. Aitken has remarked, "Logically, there is no reason why an almighty and omniscient being might not be a perfect stinker." A divine Designer of the world whose nature is read off from the appearances of nature might, as Hume showed, be finite or infinite, perfect or imperfect, omniscient or fallible, and might indeed be not one being but a veritable pantheon. It is only by going beyond what is proved, or claimed to have been proved, and

identifying the First Cause, Necessary Being, or Mind behind Nature with the God of biblical faith that these proofs could ever properly impel to worship. By themselves and without supplementation of content and infusion of emotional life from religious traditions and experiences transcending the proofs themselves they would never lead to the life of faith.

The ontological argument on the other hand is in this respect in a different category. If it succeeds it establishes the reality of a being so perfect in every way that no more perfect can be conceived. Clearly if such a being is not worthy of worship none ever could be. It would therefore seem that, unlike the other proofs, the ontological argument, if it were logically sound, would present the relatively few persons who are capable of appreciating such abstract reasoning with a rational ground for worship. On the other hand, however, whilst this is the argument that would accomplish most if it succeeded it is also the argument which is most absolutely incapable of succeeding; for it is, as we have seen, inextricably involved in the fallacy of professing to deduce existence from a concept.

3. It is argued by some religious writers that a logical demonstration of the existence of God would be a form of coercion and would as such be incompatible with God's evident intention to treat his human creatures as free and responsible persons. A great deal of twentieth-century theology emphasises that God as the infinite personal reality, having made man as person in his own image, always treats men as persons, respecting their relative freedom and autonomy. He does not override the human mind by revealing himself in overwhelming majesty and power, but always approaches us in ways that leave room for an uncompelled response of human faith. Even God's own entry into our earthly history, it is said, was in an "incognito" that could be penetrated only by the eyes of faith. As Pascal put it, "willing to appear openly to those who seek him with all their heart and to be hidden from those who flee from him with all their heart, he so regulates the knowledge of himself that he has given indications of himself

which are visible to those who seek him and not to those who do not seek him. There is enough light for those to see who only desire to see, and enough obscurity for those who have a contrary disposition." God's self-revealing actions are accordingly always so mediated through the events of our temporal experience that men only become aware of the divine presence by interpreting and responding to these events in the way which we call religious faith. For if God were to disclose himself to us in the coercive manner in which our physical environment obtrudes itself we should be dwarfed to nothingness by the infinite power thus irresistibly breaking open the privacy of our souls. Further, we should be spiritually blinded by God's perfect holiness and paralysed by his infinite energy; "for human kind cannot bear very much reality." Such a direct, unmediated confrontation breaking in upon us and shattering the frail autonomy of our finite nature would leave no ground for a free human response of trust, self-commitment and obedience. There could be no call for a man to venture upon a dawning consciousness of God's reality and thus to receive this consciousness as an authentic part of his own personal existence precisely because it has not been injected into him or clamped upon him by magisterial exercise of divine omnipotence.

The basic principle invoked here is that for the sake of creating a personal relationship of love and trust with his human creatures God does not force an awareness of himself upon them. And (according to the view which we are considering) it is only a further application of the same principle to add that a logically compelling demonstration of God's existence would likewise frustrate this purpose. For men—or at least those of them who are capable of following the proof—could then be forced to know that God is real. Thus Alasdair MacIntyre, when a Christian apologist, wrote: "For if we could produce logically cogent arguments we should produce the kind of certitude that leaves no room for decision; where proof is in place, decision is not. We do not decide to accept Euclid's conclusions; we merely look to the rigour of his arguments. If the existence of God were

demonstrable we should be as bereft of the possibility of making a free decision to love God as we should be if every utterance of doubt or unbelief was answered by thunderbolts from heaven." This is the "religious coercion" objection to the theistic proofs.

To what extent is it a sound objection? We may accept the theological doctrine that for God to force men to know him by the coercion of logic would be incompatible with his purpose of winning the voluntary response and worship of free moral beings. But the question still remains whether the theistic proofs could ever do this. Could a verbal proof of divine existence compel a consciousness of God comparable in coerciveness with a direct manifestation of his divine majesty and power? Could anyone be moved and shaken in their whole being by the demonstration of a proposition, as men have been by a numinous experience of overpowering impressiveness? Would the things that have just been said about an overwhelming display of divine glory really apply to verbal demonstrations—that infinite power would be irresistibly breaking in upon the privacy of our souls and that we should be blinded by God's perfect holiness and paralysed by his infinite energy? Indeed could a form of words, culminating in the proposition that "God exists," ever have power by itself to produce more than what Newman calls a notional assent in our minds?

It is of course true that the effect of purely rational considerations such as those which are brought to bear in the theistic proofs are much greater in some minds than in others. The more rational the mind the more considerable is the effect to be expected. In many persons—indeed taking mankind as a whole, in the great majority—the effect of a theistic proof, even when no logical flaw is found in it, would be virtually nil! But in more sophisticated minds the effect must be greater, and it is at least theoretically possible that there are minds so rational that purely logical considerations can move them as effectively as the evidence of their senses. It is therefore conceivable that someone who is initially agnostic might be presented with a philosophical proof of divine existence—

say the ontological argument, with its definition of God as that than which no more perfect can be conceived—and might as a result be led to worship the being whose reality has thus been demonstrated to him. This seems to be possible; but I believe that even in such a case there must, in addition to an intelligent appreciation of the argument, be a distinctively religious response to the idea of God which the argument presents. Some propensity to respond to unlimited perfection as holy and as rightly claiming a response of unqualified worship and devotion must operate, over and above the purely intellectual capacity for logical calculation. For we can conceive of a purely or merely logical mind, a kind of human calculating machine, which is at the same time devoid of the capacity for numinous feeling and worshipping response. Such a being might infer that God exists but be no more existentially interested in this conclusion than many people are in, say, the fact that the Shasta Dam is 602 feet high. It therefore seems that when the acceptance of a theistic proof leads to worship, a religious reaction occurs which turns what would otherwise be a purely abstract conclusion into an immensely significant and moving fact. In Newman's terminology, when a notional assent to the proposition that God exists becomes a real assent, equivalent to an actual living belief and faith in God, there has been a free human response to an idea which could instead have been rejected by being held at the notional level. In other words, a verbal proof of God's existence cannot by itself break down our human freedom; it can only lead to a notional assent which has little or no positive religious value or substance.

I conclude, then, that the theological objections to the theistic proofs are considerably less strong than the philosophical ones; and that theologians who reject natural theology would therefore do well to do so primarily on philosophical rather than on theological grounds. These philosophical reasons are, as we have seen, very strong; and we therefore now have to consider whether, in the absence of any theistic proofs, it can nevertheless be rational to believe in the existence of God.

(B) CAN THERE BE RATIONAL THEISTIC BELIEF WITHOUT PROOFS?

During the period dominated by the traditional theistic arguments the existence of God was often treated by philosophers as something to be discovered through reasoning. It was seen as the conclusion of an inference; and the question of the rationality of the belief was equated with that of the soundness of the inference. But from a religious point of view, as we have already seen, there has always been something very odd about this approach. The situation which it envisages is that of people standing outside the realm of faith, for whom the apologist is trying to build a bridge of rational inference to carry them over the frontier into that realm. But of course this is not the way in which religious faith has originally or typically or normally come about. When the cosmological, ontological, teleological and moral arguments were developed, theistic belief was already a functioning part of an immemorially established and developing form of human life. The claims of religion are claims made by individuals and communities on the basis of their experience—and experience which is none the less their own for occurring within an inherited framework of ideas. We are not dealing with a merely conceivable metaphysical hypothesis which someone has speculatively invented but which hardly anyone seriously believes. We are concerned, rather, with convictions born out of experience and reflection and living within actual communities of faith and practice. Historically, then, the philosophical proofs of God have normally entered in to support and confirm but not to create belief. Accordingly the proper philosophical approach would seem to be a probing of the actual foundations and structure of a living and operative belief rather than of theoretical and nonoperative arguments subsequently formulated for holding those beliefs. The question is not whether it is possible to prove, starting from zero, that God exists; the question is whether the religious man, given the distinctively religious form of human existence in which he participates, is properly entitled as a rational person to believe what he does believe?

At this point we must consider what we mean by a rational belief. If by a belief we mean a proposition believed, then what we are to be concerned with here are not rational beliefs but rational believings. Propositions can be well-formed or ill-formed, and they can be true or false, but they cannot be rational or irrational. It is *people* who are rational or irrational, and derivatively their states and their actions, including their acts and states of believing. Further, apart from the believing of analytic propositions, which are true by definition and are therefore rationally believed by anyone who understands them, the rationality of acts (or states) of believing has to be assessed separately in each case. For it is a function of the relation between the proposition believed and the evidence on the basis of which the believer believes it. It might conceivably be rational for Mr. *X* to believe *p* but not rational for Mr. *Y* to believe *p*, because in relation to the data available to Mr. *X p* is worthy of belief but not in relation to the data available to Mr. *Y*. Thus the question of the rationality of belief in the reality of God is the question of the rationality of a particular person's believing given the data that he is using; or that of the believing of a class of people who share the same body of data. Or putting the same point the other way round, any assessing of the belief-worthiness of the proposition that God exists must be an assessing of it in relation to particular ranges of data.

Now there is one area of data or evidence which is normally available to those who believe in God, and that provides a very important part of the ground of their believing, but which is normally not available to and therefore not taken into account by those who do not so believe; and this is religious experience. It seems that the religious man is in part basing his believing upon certain data of religious experience which the non-religious man is not using because he does not have them. Thus our question resolves itself into one about the theist's right, given his distinctively religious experience, to be certain that God exists.

It is the question of the rationality or irrationality, the well-groundedness or ill-groundedness, of the religious man's claim to know God. The theist cannot hope to prove that God exists; but despite this it may nevertheless be possible for him to show it to be wholly reasonable for him to believe that God exists.

What is at issue here is not whether it is rational for someone else, who does not participate in the distinctively religious mode of experience, to believe in God on the basis of the religious man's reports. I am not proposing any kind of "argument from religious experience" by which God is inferred as the cause of the special experiences described by mystics and other religious persons. It is not the non-religious man's theoretical use of someone else's reported religious experience that is to be considered, but the religious man's own practical use of it. The question is whether he is acting rationally in trusting his own experience and in proceeding to live on the basis of it.

In order to investigate this question we must consider what counts as rational belief in an analogous case. The analogy that I propose is that between the religious person's claim to be conscious of God and any man's claim to be conscious of the physical world as an environment, existing independently of himself, of which he must take account.

In each instance a realm of putatively cognitive experience is taken to be veridical and is acted upon as such, even though its veridical character cannot be logically demonstrated. So far as sense experience is concerned this has emerged both from the failure of Descartes' attempt to provide a theoretical guarantee that our senses relate us to a real material environment, and from the success of Hume's attempt to show that our normal non-solipsist belief in an objective world of enduring objects around us in space is neither a product of, nor justifiable by, philosophical reasoning but is what has been called in some expositions of Hume's thought (though the term does not seem to have been used by Hume himself) a natural belief. It is a belief which naturally and indeed inevitably arises in the normal human mind in response to normal human perceptual experience. It is a belief on the basis of which we live and the rejection of which, in favour of a serious adoption of the solipsist alternative, would so disorient our relationship to other persons within a common material environment that we should be accounted insane. Our insanity would consist in the fact that we should no longer regard other people as independent centres of consciousness, with their own purposes and wills, with whom interpersonal relationships are possible. We should instead be living in a one-person world.

It is thus a basic truth in, or a presupposition of, our language that it is rational or sane to believe in the reality of the external world that we inhabit in common with other people, and irrational or insane not to do so.

What are the features of our sense experience in virtue of which we all take this view? They would seem to be twofold: the givenness or the involuntary character of this form of cognitive experience, and the fact that we can and do act successfully in terms of our belief in an external world. That is to say, being built and circumstanced as we are we cannot help initially believing as we do, and our belief is not contradicted, but on the contrary continuously confirmed, by our continuing experience. These characteristics jointly constitute a sufficient reason to trust and live on the basis of our perceptual experience in the absence of any positive reason to distrust it; and our inability to exclude the theoretical possibility of our experience as a whole being purely subjective does not constitute such a reason. This seems to be the principle on which, implicitly, we proceed. And it is, by definition, rational to proceed in this way. That is to say, this is the way in which all human beings do proceed and have proceeded, apart from a very small minority who have for that very reason been labelled by the majority as insane. This habitual acceptance of our perceptual experience is thus, we may say, part of our operative concept of human rationality.

We can therefore now ask whether a like principle may be invoked on behalf of a parallel response to religious experience. "Religious experience" is of course a highly elastic concept. Let us restrict attention, for our present purpose, to the theistic "sense of the presence of God," the putative awareness of a transcendent divine Mind within whose field of consciousness we exist and with whom therefore we stand in a relationship of mutual awareness. This sense of "living in the divine presence" does not take the form of a direct vision of God, but of experiencing events in history and in our own personal life as the medium of God's dealings with us. Thus religious differs from non-religious experience, not as the awareness of a different world, but as a different way of experiencing the same world. Events which can be experienced as having a purely natural significance are experienced by the religious mind as having also and at the same time religious significance and as mediating the presence and activity of God.

It is possible to study this type of religious experience either in its strongest instances, in the primary and seminal religious figures, or in its much weaker instances in ordinary adherents of the traditions originated by the great exemplars of faith. Since we are interested in the question of the claims which religious experience justifies it is appropriate to look at that experience in its strongest and purest forms. A description of this will accordingly apply only very partially to the ordinary rank-and-file believer either of today or in the past.

If then we consider the sense of living in the divine presence as this was expressed by, for example, Jesus of Nazareth, or by St. Paul, St. Francis, St. Anselm or the great prophets of the Old Testament, we find that their "awareness of God" was so vivid that he was as indubitable a factor in their experience as was their physical environment. They could no more help believing in the reality of God than in the reality of the material world and of their human neighbours. Many of the pages of the Bible resound with the sense of God's presence as a building might reverberate from the tread of some gigantic being walking through it. God was known to the prophets and apostles as a dynamic will interacting with their own wills; a sheerly given personal reality, as inescapably to be reckoned with as destructive storm and life-giving sunshine, the fixed contours of the land, or the hatred of their enemies and the friendship of their neighbours.

Our question concerns, then, one whose "experience of God" has this compelling quality, so that he is no more inclined to doubt its veridical character than to doubt the evidence of his senses. Is it rational for him to take the former, as it is certainly rational for him to take the latter, as reliably cognitive of an aspect of his total environment and thus as knowledge in terms of which to act? Are the two features noted above in our sense experience—its givenness, or involuntary character, and the fact that we can successfully act in terms of it—also found here? It seems that they are. The sense of the presence of God reported by the great religious figures has a similar involuntary and compelling quality; and as they proceed to live on the basis of it they are sustained and confirmed by their further experiences in the conviction that they are living in relation, not to illusion, but to reality. It therefore seems prima facie, that the religious man is entitled to trust his religious experience and to proceed to conduct his life in terms of it.

The analogy operating within this argument is between our normal acceptance of our sense experiences as perception of an objective external world, and a corresponding acceptance of the religious experience of "living in God's presence" as the awareness of a divine reality external to our own minds. In each case there is a solipsist alternative in which one can affirm *solus ipse* to the exclusion of the transcendent—in the one case denying a physical environment transcending our own private consciousness and in the other case denying a divine Mind transcending our own private consciousness. It should be noted that this analogy is not grounded in die perception of particular material objects and does not turn upon the contrast between veridical and illusory sense perceptions, but is grounded in our awareness of an objective external world as such and turns upon the contrast between this and a theoretically possible solipsist interpretation of the same stream of conscious experience.

(C) RELIGIOUS AND PERCEPTUAL BELIEF

Having thus set forth the analogy fairly boldly and starkly I now want to qualify it by exploring various differences between religious and sensory experience. The resulting picture will be more complex than the first rough outline presented so far; and yet its force as supporting the rationality of theistic faith will not, I think, in the end have been undermined.

The most obvious difference is that everyone has and cannot help having sense experiences, whereas not everyone has religious experiences, at any rate of the very vivid and distinct kind to which we have been referring. As bodily beings existing in a material environment, we cannot help interacting consciously with that environment. That is to say, we cannot help "having" a stream of sense experiences; and we cannot help accepting this as the perception of a material world around us in space. When we open our eyes in daylight we cannot but receive the visual experiences that come to us; and likewise with the other senses. And the world which we thus perceive is not plastic to our wishes but presents itself to us as it is, whether we like it or not. Needless to say, our senses do not coerce us in any sense of the word "coerce" that implies unwillingness on our part, as when a policeman coerces an unwilling suspect to accompany him to the police station. Sense experience is coercive in the sense that we cannot when sane believe that our material environment is not broadly as we perceive it to be, and that if we did momentarily persuade ourselves that what we experience is not there we should quickly be penalised by the environment and indeed, if we persisted, destroyed by it.

In contrast to this we are not obliged to interact consciously with a spiritual environment. Indeed it is a commonplace of much contemporary theology that God does not force an awareness of himself upon mankind but leaves us free to know him by an uncompelled response of faith. And yet once a man has allowed himself freely to become conscious of God—it is important to note—that experience is, at its top levels of intensity, coercive. It creates the situation of the person who *cannot help* believing in the reality of God. The apostle, prophet or saint may be so vividly aware of God that he can no more doubt the veracity of his religious awareness than of his sense experience. During the periods when he is living consciously in the presence of God, when God is to him the divine Thou, the question whether God exists simply does not arise. Our cognitive freedom in relation to God is not to be found at this point but at the prior stage of our coming to be aware of him. The individual's own free receptivity and responsiveness plays an essential part in his dawning consciousness of God; but once he *has* become conscious of God that consciousness can possess a coercive and indubitable quality.

It is a consequence of this situation that whereas everyone perceives and cannot help perceiving the physical world, by no means everyone experiences the presence of God. Indeed only rather few people experience religiously in the vivid and coercive way reported by the great biblical figures. And this fact immediately suggests a sceptical question. Since those who enjoy a compelling religious experience form such a small minority of mankind, ought we not to suspect that they are suffering from a delusion comparable with that of the paranoiac who hears threatening voices from the walls or the alcoholic who sees green snakes?

This is of course a possible judgment to make. But this judgment should not be made *a priori*, in the absence of specific grounds such as we have in the other cases mentioned. And it would in fact be difficult to point to adequate evidence to support this hypothesis. On the contrary the general intelligence and exceptionally high moral quality of the great religious figures clashes with any analysis of their experience in terms of abnormal psychology. Such analyses are not indicated, as is the parallel view of paranoiacs and alcoholics, by evidence of general disorientation to reality or of incapacity to live a productive and satisfying life. On the contrary, Jesus of Nazareth, for example, has been

regarded by hundreds of millions of people as the fulfilment of the ideal possibilities of human nature. A more reasonable negative position would therefore seem to be the agnostic one that whilst it is proper for the religious man himself, given his distinctive mode of experience, to believe firmly in the reality of God, one does not oneself share that experience and therefore has no ground upon which to hold that belief. Theism is then not positively denied, but is on the other hand consciously and deliberately not affirmed. This agnostic position must be accepted by the theist as a proper one. For if it is reasonable for one man, on the basis of his distinctively religious experience, to affirm the reality of God it must also be reasonable for another man, in the absence of any such experience, not to affirm the reality of God.

The next question that must be raised is the closely connected one of the relation between rational belief and truth. I suggested earlier that, strictly, one should speak of rational believings rather than of rational beliefs. But nevertheless it is sometimes convenient to use the latter phrase, which we may then understand as follows. By a rational belief we shall mean a belief which it is rational for the one who holds it to hold, given the data available to him. Clearly such beliefs are not necessarily or always true. It is sometimes rational for an individual to have, on the basis of incomplete data, a belief which is in fact false. For example, it was once rational for people to believe that the sun revolves round the earth; for it was apparently perceived to do so, and the additional theoretical and observational data were not yet available from which it has since been inferred that it is the earth which revolves round the sun. If, then, a belief may be rational and yet false, may not the religious man's belief be of this kind? May it not be that when the data of religious experience are supplemented in the believer's mind by further data provided by the sciences of psychology or sociology, it ceases to be rational for him to believe in God? Might it not then be rational for him instead to believe that his "experience of the presence of God" is to be understood as an effect of a buried infancy memory of his father as a benevolent higher power; or of the pressure upon him of the human social organism of which he is a cell; or in accordance with some other naturalistic theory of the nature of religion?

Certainly this is possible. Indeed we must say, more generally, that all our beliefs, other than our acceptance of logically self-certifying propositions, are in principle open to revision or retraction in the light of new data. It is always conceivable that something which it is now rational for us to believe, it may one day not be rational for us to believe. But the difference which this general principle properly makes to our present believing varies from a maximum in relation to beliefs involving a considerable theoretical element, such as the higher-level hypotheses of the sciences, to a minimum in relation to perceptual beliefs, such as the belief that I now see a sheet of paper before me. And I have argued that so far as the great primary religious figures are concerned, belief in the reality of God is closer to the latter in that it is analogous to belief in the reality of the perceived material world. It is not an explanatory hypothesis, logically comparable with those developed in the sciences, but a perceptual belief. God was not, for Amos or Jeremiah or Jesus of Nazareth, an inferred entity but an experienced personal presence. If this is so, it is appropriate that the religious man's belief in the reality of God should be no more provisional than his belief in the reality of the physical world. The situation is in each case that given the experience which he has and which is part of him, he cannot help accepting as "there" such aspects of his environment as he experiences. He cannot help believing either in the reality of the material world which he is conscious of inhabiting, or of the personal divine presence which is overwhelmingly evident to him and to which his mode of living is a free response. And I have been suggesting that it is as reasonable for him to hold and to act upon the one belief as the other.

VII.B.2

The Presumption of Atheism

ANTHONY FLEW

Anthony Flew (1923–2010) was one of the most well known and influential atheistic philosophers of religion of the twentieth century. He was a professor of philosophy at the University of Keele, among other places, and was co-editor of the 1963 volume New Essays in Philosophical Theology, *which is widely credited as marking the revival of philosophy of religion in the latter half of the twentieth century. In 2004, he stirred up controversy with the book* There Is a God: How the World's Most Notorious Atheist Changed His Mind. *In the present essay, he argues that dispute over God's existence should start from a "presumption of atheism" (akin to the "presumption of innocence" that is the starting point of criminal trials). In other words, the "burden of proof" lies on the theist.*

Flew, Antony, *"The Presumption of Atheism," Canadian Journal of Philosophy,* 2 (1972). p. 29–46. Used by permission of University of Calgary Press. Some footnotes deleted.

A. INTRODUCTORY

At the beginning of Book X of his last work *The Laws* Plato turns his attention from violent and outrageous actions in general to the particular case of undisciplined and presumptuous behaviour in matters of religion: "We have already stated summarily what the punishment should be for temple-robbing, whether by open force or secretly. But the punishments for the various sorts of insolence in speech or action with regard to the gods, which a man can show in word or deed, have to be proclaimed after we have provided an exordium. Let this be it: 'No one believing, as the laws prescribe, in the existence of the gods has ever yet performed an impious action willingly, or uttered a lawless word. Anyone acting in such a way is in one of three conditions: either, first, he does not believe the proposition aforesaid; or, second, he believes that though the gods exist they have no concern about men; or, third, he believes that they can easily be won over by the bribery of prayer and sacrifice," (§ 885B).[1]

So Plato in this notorious treatment of heresy might be said to be rebuking the presumption of atheism. The word "presumption" would then be employed as a synonym for "presumptuousness." But, interesting though the questions here raised by Plato are, the word has in my title a different interpretation. The presumption of atheism which I want to discuss is not a form of presumptuousness; indeed it might be regarded as an expression of the very opposite, a modest teachability. My presumption of atheism is closely analogous to the presumption of innocence in the English Law; a comparison which we shall later find it illuminating to develop. What I want to examine in this paper is the contention that the debate about the existence of God should properly begin from a presumption of atheism, that the onus of proof must lie on the theist.

The word "atheism," however, has in this contention to be construed unusually. Whereas nowadays the usual meaning of "atheist" in English is "someone who asserts that there is no such being as God," I want the word to be understood here much less positively. I want the originally Greek

prefix "a" to be read in the same way in "atheist" as it customarily is read in such other Greco-English words as "amoral," "atypical," and "asymmetrical." In this interpretation an atheist becomes: not someone who positively asserts the non-existence of God; but someone who is simply not a theist. Let us, for future ready reference, introduce the labels "positive atheism" for the former doctrine and "negative atheism" for the latter.

The introduction of this new sense of the word "atheism" may appear to be a piece of perverse Humpty-Dumptyism,[2] going arbitrarily against established common usage. "Whyever," it could be asked, "don't you make it not the presumption of atheism but the presumption of agnosticism?" But this pardonably petulant reaction fails to appreciate just how completely noncommittal I intend my negative atheist to be. For in this context the agnostic—and it was, of course, in this context that Thomas Henry Huxley first introduced the term[3]—is by the same criterion of established common usage someone who, having entertained the existence of God as at least a theoretical possibility, now claims not to know either that there is or that there is not such a being. To be in this ordinary sense an agnostic you have already to have conceded that there is, and that you have, a legitimate concept of God; such that, whether or not this concept does in fact have application, it theoretically could. But the atheist in my peculiar interpretation, unlike the atheist in the usual sense, has not as yet and as such conceded even this.

This point is important, though the question whether the word "agnosticism" can bear the meaning which I want now to give to the word "atheism" is not. What the protagonist of the presumption of atheism, in my sense, wants to show is: that the debate about the existence of God ought be conducted in a particular way; and that the issue should be seen in a certain perspective. His thesis about the onus of proof involves that it is up to the theist: first, to introduce and to defend his proposed concept of God; and, second, to provide sufficient reason for believing that this concept of his does in fact have an application. It is the first of these two stages which needs perhaps to be emphasized even more strongly than the second. Where the question of existence concerns, for instance, a Loch Ness Monster or an Abominable Snowman this stage may perhaps reasonably be deemed to be more or less complete before the argument begins. But in the controversy about the existence of God this is certainly not so: not only for the quite familiar reason that the word "God" is used—or misused—in more than one way; but also, and much more interestingly, because it cannot be taken for granted that even the would-be mainstream theist is operating with a legitimate concept which theoretically could have an application to an actual being.

This last suggestion is not really as new-fangled and factitious as it is sometimes thought to be. But its pedigree has been made a little hard to trace. For the fact is that, traditionally, issues which should be seen as concerning the legitimacy or otherwise of a proposed or supposed concept have by philosophical theologians been discussed: either as surely disposable difficulties in reconciling one particular feature of the Divine nature with another; or else as aspects of an equally surely soluble general problem of saying something about the infinite Creator in language intelligible to his finite creatures. These traditional and still almost universally accepted forms of presentation are fundamentally prejudicial. For they assume: that there is a Divine being, with an actual nature the features of which we can investigate; and that there is an infinite Creator, whose existence—whatever difficulties we finite creatures may have in asserting anything else about Him— we may take for granted.

The general reason why this presumption of atheism matters is that its acceptance must put the whole question of the existence of God into an entirely fresh perspective. Most immediately relevant here is that in this fresh perspective problems which really are conceptual are seen as conceptual problems; and problems which have tended to be regarded as advanced and, so to speak, optional extras now discover themselves as both elementary and indispensable. The theist who wants to build a systematic and thorough apologetic finds that he is required to begin absolutely from the beginning; and this absolute beginning is to ensure that the

word "God" is provided with a meaning such that it is theoretically possible for an actual being to be so described.

Although I shall later be arguing that the presumption of atheism is neutral as between all parties to the main dispute, in as much as to accept it as determining a procedural framework is not to make any substantive assumptions, I must give fair warning now that I do nevertheless believe that in its fresh perspective the whole enterprise of theism appears even more difficult and precarious than it did before. In part this is a corollary of what I have just been suggesting; that certain difficulties and objections, which may previously have seemed peripheral or even factitious, are made to stand out as fundamental and unavoidable. But it is also in part, as we shall be seeing soon, a consequence of the emphasis which it places on the imperative need to produce some sort of sufficient reason to justify theist belief.

B. THE PRESUMPTION OF ATHEISM AND THE PRESUMPTION OF INNOCENCE

1. One thing which helps to conceal this need is a confusion about the possible varieties of proof, and this confusion is one which can be resolved with the help of the first of a series of comparisons between my proposed presumption of atheism and the legal presumption of innocence. It is frequently said nowadays, even by professing Roman Catholics, that everyone knows that it is impossible to prove the existence of God. The first objection to this putative truism is, as my reference to Roman Catholics should have suggested, that it is not true. For it is an essential dogma of Roman Catholicism, defined as such by the First Vatican Council, that "the one and true God our creator and lord can be known for certain through the creation by the natural light of human reason".[4] So even if this dogma is, as I myself believe, false, it is certainly not known

to be false by those many Roman Catholics who remain, despite all the disturbances consequent upon the Second Vatican Council, committed to the complete traditional faith.

To this a sophisticated objector might reply that the definition of the First Vatican Council speaks of knowing for certain rather than of proving or demonstrating; adding perhaps, if he was very sophisticated indeed, that the word "demonstrari" in an earlier draft was eventually replaced by the expression "*certo cognosci*." But though this is, I am told,[5] correct it is certainly not enough to vindicate the conventional wisdom. For the word "proof" is not ordinarily restricted in its application to demonstratively valid arguments; arguments, that is, in which the conclusion cannot be denied without thereby contradicting the premises. So it is too flattering to suggest that most of those who make this facile claim, that everyone knows that it is impossible to prove the existence of God, are intending only the strictly limited assertion that one special sort of proof is impossible.

The truth, and the danger, is that wherever there is any awareness of such a limited and specialized interpretation, there will be a quick and illegitimate move to the much wider general conclusion that it is impossible and, furthermore, unnecessary to provide any sufficient reason for believing. It is, therefore, worth underlining that when the presumption of atheism is explained as insisting that the onus of proof must be on the theist, the word "proof" is being used in the ordinary wide sense in which it can embrace any and every variety of sufficient reason. It is, of course, in this and only this sense that the word is interpreted when the presumption of innocence is explained as laying the onus of proof on the prosecution.

2. A second element of positive analogy between these two presumptions is that both are defeasible; and that they are, consequently, not to be identified with assumptions. The presumption of innocence indicates where the court should start and how it must proceed. Yet the prosecution is still able, more often than not, to bring forward what is in the end accepted as sufficient reason to warrant the verdict "Guilty"; which appropriate

sufficient reason is properly characterized as a proof of guilt. The defeasible presumption of innocence is thus in this majority of cases in fact defeated; whereas, were the indefeasible innocence of all accused persons an assumption of any legal system, there could not be within that system any provision for any verdict other than "Not Guilty." To the extent that it is, for instance, an assumption of the English Common Law that every citizen is cognizant of all that the law requires of him, that law cannot admit the fact that this assumption is, as in fact it is, false.

The presumption of atheism is similarly defeasible. It lays it down that thorough and systematic inquiry must start from a position of negative atheism, and that the burden of proof lies on the theist proposition. Yet this is not at all the same thing as demanding that the debate should proceed on a positive atheist assumption, which must preclude a theist conclusion. Counsel for theism no more betrays his client by accepting the framework determined by this presumption than counsel for the prosecution betrays the state by conceding the legal presumption of innocence. The latter is perhaps in his heart unshakeably convinced of the guilt of the defendant. Yet he must, and with complete consistency and perfect sincerity may, insist that the proceedings of the court should respect the presumption of innocence. The former is even more likely to be persuaded of the soundness of his brief. Yet he too can with a good conscience allow that a thorough and complete apologetic must start from, meet, and go on to defeat, the presumption of atheism.

Put as I have just been putting it the crucial distinction between a defeasible presumption and a categorical assumption will, no doubt, seem quite obvious. But I know from experience that many do find it difficult to grasp, at least in its application to the present highly controversial case. Theists fear that if once they allow this procedural presumption they will have sold the pass to the atheist enemy. Most especially when the proponent of this procedure happens to be a known opponent of theism, the theist is inclined to mistake it that the procedure itself prejudicially assumes an atheist conclusion. But this, as the comparison with the legal presumption of innocence surely makes clear, is wrong. Such presumptions are procedural and not substantive; they assume no conclusion, either positive or negative.

3. However, and here we come to a third element in the positive analogy, to say that such presumptions are in themselves procedural and not substantive is not to say that the higher-order questions of whether to follow this presumption or that are trifling and merely formal rather than material and substantial. These higher-order questions are not questions which can be dismissed cynically as "issues of principle as opposed to issues of substance." It can matter a lot which presumption is adopted. Notoriously there is a world of difference between legal systems which follow the presumption of innocence, and those which do not. And, as I began to indicate at the end of Part A, to adopt the presumption of atheism does put the whole argument into a distinctive perspective.

4. Next, as a fourth element in the positive analogy, it is a paradoxical consequence of the fact that these presumptions are procedural and not substantive that particular defeats do not constitute any sort of reason, much less a sufficient reason, for a general surrender. The fact that George Joseph Smith was in his trial proved guilty of many murders defeats the original presumption of his innocence. But this particular defeat has no tendency at all to show that even in this particular case the court should not have proceeded on this presumption. Still less does it tend to establish that the legal system as a whole was at fault in incorporating this presumption as a general principle. It is the same with the presumption of atheism. Suppose that someone is able to prove the existence of God. This achievement must, similarly, defeat our presumption. But it does not thereby show that the original contention about the onus of proof was mistaken.

One may, therefore, as a mnemonic think of the word "defeasible" (=defeatable) as implying precisely this capacity to survive defeat. A substantive generalization—such as, for instance, the assertion that all persons accused of murder are in fact innocent—is falsified decisively by the production of even one authentic counter-example. That is part of what is meant by the Baconian slogan: "Magis est vis instantiae negativae."[6] But a defeasible presumption is not shown to have been the wrong one to have made by being in a particular case in fact defeated. What does show the presumption of atheism to be the right one to make is what we have now to investigate.

C. THE CASE FOR THE PRESUMPTION OF ATHEISM

1. An obvious first move is to appeal to the old legal axiom: "Ei incumbit probatio qui dicit, non qui negat." Literally and unsympathetically translated this becomes: "The onus of proof lies on the man who affirms, not on the man who denies." To this the objection is almost equally obvious. Given just a very little verbal ingenuity, contrary motions can be rendered alternatively in equally positive forms: either, "That this house affirms the existence of God"; or, "That this house takes its stand for positive atheism." So interpreted, therefore, our axiom provides no determinate guidance.[7]

Suppose, however, that we take the hint already offered in the previous paragraph. A less literal but more sympathetic translation would be: "The onus of proof lies on the proposition, not on the opposition." The point of the change is to bring out that this maxim was offered in a legal context, and that our courts are institutions of debate. An axiom providing no determinate guidance outside that framework may nevertheless be fundamental for the effective conduct of orderly and decisive debate. Here the outcome is supposed to be decided on the merits of what is said within the debate itself, and of that alone. So no opposition can set about demolishing the proposition case until and unless that proposition has first provided them with a case for demolition.

Of course our maxim even when thus sympathetically interpreted still offers no direction on which contending parties ought to be made to undertake which roles. Granting that courts are to operate as debating institutions, and granting that this maxim is fundamental to debate, we have to appeal to some further premise principle before we become licensed to infer that the prosecution must propose and the defence oppose. This further principle is, once again, the familiar presumption of innocence. Were we, while retaining the conception of a court as an institution for reaching decisions by way of formalized debate, to embrace the opposite presumption, the presumption of guilt, we should need to adopt the opposite arrangements. In these the defence would first propose that the accused is after all innocent, and the prosecution would then respond by struggling to disintegrate the case proposed.

2. The first move examined cannot, therefore, be by itself sufficient. To have considered it does nevertheless help to show that to accept such a presumption is to adopt a policy. And policies have to be assessed by reference to the aims of those for whom they are suggested. If for you it is more important that no guilty person should ever be acquitted than that no innocent person should ever be convicted, then for you a presumption of guilt must be the rational policy. For you, with your preference structure, a presumption of innocence becomes simply irrational. To adopt this policy would be to adopt means calculated to frustrate your own chosen ends; which is, surely paradigmatically irrational. Take, as an actual illustration, the controlling elite of a ruling Leninist party, which must as such refuse to recognize any individual rights if these conflict with the claims of the party, and which in fact treats all those suspected of actual or potential opposition much as if they were already known "counter-revolutionaries," "enemies of socialism," "friends of the United States," "advocates of free elections," and all other like things bad. I can, and do, fault this policy and its agents on many counts. Yet I cannot say that for them, once granted their scale of values, it is irrational.

What then are the aims by reference to which an atheist presumption might be justified? One key word in the answer, if not the key word, must be "knowledge." The context for which such a policy is proposed is that of enquiry about the existence of God; and the object of the exercise is, presumably, to discover whether it is possible to establish that the word "God" does in fact have application. Now to establish must here be either to show that you know or to come to know. But knowledge is crucially different from mere true belief. All knowledge involves true belief; not all true belief constitutes knowledge. To have a true belief is simply and solely to believe that something is so, and to be in fact right. But someone may believe that this or that is so, and his belief may in fact be true, without its thereby and necessarily constituting knowledge. If a true belief is to achieve this more elevated status, then the believer has to be properly warranted so to believe. He must, that is, be in a position to know.

Obviously there is enormous scope for disagreement in particular cases: both about what is required in order to be in a position to know; and about whether these requirements have actually been satisfied. But the crucial distinction between believing truly and knowing is recognized as universally as the prior and equally vital distinction between believing and believing what is in fact true. If, for instance, there is a question whether a colleague performed some discreditable action, then all of us, though we have perhaps to admit that we cannot help believing that he did, are rightly scrupulous not to assert that this is known unless we have grounds sufficient to warrant the bolder claim. It is, therefore, not only incongruous but also scandalous in matters of life and death, and even of eternal life and death, to maintain that you know either on no grounds at all, or on grounds of a kind which on other and comparatively minor issues you yourself would insist to be inadequate.

It is by reference to this inescapable demand for grounds that the presumption of atheism is justified. If it is to be established that there is a God, then we have to have good grounds for believing that this is indeed so. Until and unless some such grounds are produced we have literally no reason at all for believing; and in that situation the only reasonable posture must be that of either the negative atheist or the agnostic. So the onus of proof has to rest on the proposition. It must be up to them: first, to give whatever sense they choose to the word "God," meeting any objection that so defined it would relate only to an incoherent pseudo-concept; and, second, to bring forward sufficient reasons to warrant their claim that, in their present sense of the word "God," there is a God. The same applies, with appropriate alterations, if what is to be made out is, not that atheism is known to be true, but only—more modestly—that it can be seen to be at least more or less probable.

D. OBJECTIONS TO THE PRESUMPTION OF ATHEISM

1. Once the nature of this presumption is understood, the supporting case is short and simple. One reason why it may appear unacceptable is a confusion of contexts. In a theist or post-theist society it comes more easily to ask why a man is not a theist than why he is. Provided that the question is to be construed biographically this is no doubt methodologically inoffensive. But our concern here is not all with biographical questions of why people came to hold whatever opinions they do hold. Rather it is with the need for opinions to be suitably grounded if they are to be rated as items of knowledge, or even of probable belief. The issue is: not what does or does not need to be explained biographically; but where the burden of theological proof should rest.

2. A more sophisticated objection of fundamentally the same sort would urge that our whole discussion has been too artificial and too general, and that any man's enquiries have to begin from wherever he happens to be. "We cannot begin," C. S. Peirce wrote, "with complete doubt. We must begin with all the prejudices which we actually have.... These prejudices are not to be dispelled by a maxim...."[8] With particular present reference Professor John Hick has urged: "The right question is whether it is rational for the religious man himself, given that his religious experience is coherent, persistent, and compelling, to affirm the reality of

God. What is in question is not the rationality of an inference from certain psychological events to God as their cause; for the religious man no more infers the existence of God than we infer the existence of the visible world around us. What is in question is the rationality of the one who has the religious experiences. If we regard him as a rational person we must acknowledge that he is rational in believing what, given his experiences, he cannot help believing."[9]

To the general point drawn from Peirce the answer comes from further reading of Peirce himself. He was in the paper from which I quoted arguing against the Cartesian programme of simultaneous, systematic, and (almost) universal doubt. Peirce did not want to suggest that it is impossible or wrong to subject any of our beliefs to critical scrutiny. In the same paragraph he continues: "A person may, it is true, find reason to doubt what he began by believing; but in that case he doubts because he has a positive reason for it, and not on account of the Cartesian maxim." One positive reason for being especially leery towards religious opinions is that these vary so very much from society to society; being, it seems, mainly determined, in Descartes' phrase, "by custom and example."[10]

To Hick it has at once to be conceded: that it is one thing to say that a belief is unfounded or well-founded; and quite another to say that it is irrational or rational for some particular person, in his particular time and circumstances, and with his particular experience and lack of experience, to hold or to reject that belief. Granted that his usually reliable Intelligence were sure that the enemy tank brigade was in the town, it was entirely reasonable for the General also to believe this. But the enemy tanks had in fact pulled back. Yet it was still unexceptionably sensible for the General on his part to refuse to expose his flank to those tanks which were in fact not there. This genuine and important distinction cannot, however, save the day for Hick.

In the first place, to show that someone may reasonably hold a particular belief, and even that he may properly claim that he knows it to be true, is at best still not to show that that belief is indeed well-grounded, much less that it constitutes an item of his knowledge.

Nor, second, is to accept the presumption of atheism as a methodological framework, as such: either to deprive anyone of his right "to affirm the reality of God"; or to require that to be respectable every conviction should first have been reached through the following of an ideally correct procedure. To insist on the correctness of this presumption as an initial presumption is to make a claim which is itself procedural rather than substantive; and the context for which this particular procedure is being recommended is that of justification rather than of discovery.

Once these fundamentals are appreciated those for whom Hick is acting as spokesman should at first feel quite content. For on his account they consider that they have the very best of grounds for their beliefs. They regard their "coherent, consistent, and compelling" religious experience as analogous to perception; and the man who can see something with his own eyes and feel it in his own hands is in a perfect position to know that it exists. His position is indeed so perfect that, as Hick says, it is wrong to speak here of evidence and inference. If he saw his wife in the act of intercourse with a lover then he no longer needs to infer her infidelity from bits and pieces of evidence. He has now what is better than inference; although for the rest of us, who missed this display, his testimony still constitutes an important part of the evidence in the case. The idiomatic expression "the evidence of my own eyes" derives its paradoxical piquancy from the fact that to see for oneself is better than to have evidence.

All this is true. Certainly too anyone who thinks that he can as it were see God must reject the suggestion that in so doing he infers "from certain psychological events to God as their cause." For to accept this account would be to call down upon his head all the insoluble difficulties which fall to the lot of all those who maintain that what we see, and all we ever really and directly see, is visual sense-data. And, furthermore, it is useful to be reminded that when we insist that

knowledge as opposed to mere belief has to be adequately warranted, this grounding may be a matter either of having sufficient evidence or of being in a position to know directly and without evidence. So far, therefore it might seem that Hick's objection was completely at cross-purposes; and that anyway his protégés have no need to appeal to the distinction between actual knowledge and what one may rationally and properly claim to know.

Wait a minute. The passage of Hick which has been under discussion was part of an attempt to show that criticism of the Argument from Religious Experience is irrelevant to such claims to as it were see God. But on the contrary: what such criticism usually challenges is just the vital assumption that having religious experience really is a kind of perceiving, and hence a sort of being in a position to know about its putative object. So this challenge provides just exactly that positive reason, which Peirce demanded, for doubting what, according to Hick, "one who has the religious experiences ... cannot help believing." If therefore he persists in so believing without even attempting to overcome this criticism, then it becomes impossible to vindicate his claims to be harbouring rational beliefs; much less items of authentic knowledge.

3. A third objection, of a different kind, starts from the assumption, mentioned in section B(1) earlier, that any programme to prove the existence of God is fundamentally misconceived; that this enterprise is on all fours with projects to square the circle or to construct a perpetual motion machine. The suggestion then is that the territory which reason cannot inhabit may nevertheless be freely colonized by faith:

"The world was all before them, where to choose."[11]

Ultimately perhaps it is impossible to establish the existence of God, or even to show that it is more or less probable. But, if so, this is not the correct moral: the rational man does not thereby become in this area free to believe, or not to believe, just as his fancy takes him. Faith, surely, should not be a leap in the dark but a leap towards the light. Arbitrarily to plump for some particular conviction, and then stubbornly to cleave to it, would be—to borrow the term which St. Thomas employed in discussing natural reason, faith, and revelation[12]—frivolous. If your venture of faith is not to be arbitrary, irrational, and frivolous, you must have presentable reasons: first for making any such commitment in this area, an area in which by hypothesis the available grounds are insufficient to warrant any firm conclusion; and second for opting for one particular possibility rather than any of the other available alternatives. To most such offerings of reasons the presumption of atheism remains relevant. For though, again by the hypothesis, these cannot aspire to prove their conclusions they will usually embrace some estimation of their probability. If the onus of proof lies on the man who hopes definitively to establish the existence of God, it must also by the same token rest on the person who plans to make out only that this conclusion is more or less probable.

I put in the qualifications "most" and "usually" in order to allow for apologetic in the tradition of Pascal's Wager.[13] Pascal makes no attempt in this most famous argument to show that his Roman Catholicism is true or probably true. The reasons which he suggests for making the recommended bet on his particular faith are reasons in the sense of motives rather than reasons in our previous sense of grounds. Conceding, if only for the sake of the present argument, that we can have no knowledge here, Pascal tries to justify as prudent a policy of systematic self-persuasion, rather than to provide grounds for thinking that the beliefs recommended are actually true.

Another instructive feature of Pascal's argument is his unwarranted assumption that there are only two betting options, neither of which, on the assumption of total ignorance, can be awarded any measure of positive probability. Granted all this it then appears compulsively reasonable to wager one's life on the alternative which promises and threatens so inordinately much. But the number of theoretically possible world-systems is infinite, and the subset of those making similar promises and threats is also infinite. The immediate relevance of this to us is that it will not do, without further reason given, to set up as the two mutually exclusive and together exhaustive alternatives (one sort of) theism and (the corresponding sort of) positive atheism; and then to suggest that, since neither position can be definitely established, everyone is entitled simply to take their pick. The objection that this way of constructing the book leaves out a third, agnostic, opinion is familiar; and it is one which Pascal himself tried to meet by arguing that to refuse to decide is in effect to decide against religion. The objection based on the point that the number of theoretically possible Hell-threatening and Heaven-promising world-systems is infinite, is quite different and against the Wager as he himself sets it up decisive. The point is that on the given assumption of total ignorance, combined with our present recognition of the infinite range of alternative theoretical possibilities; to bet on any one of the, so to speak, positive options, none of which can by the hypothesis be awarded any measure of positive probability, must be in the last degree arbitrary and capricious.

E. THE FIVE WAYS AS AN ATTEMPT TO DEFEAT THE PRESUMPTION OF ATHEISM

I have tried, in the first four sections, to explain what I mean by "the presumption of atheism," to bring out by comparison with the presumption of innocence in law what such a presumption does and does not involve, to deploy a case for adopting my presumption of atheism, and to indicate the lines on which two sorts of objection may be met. Now, finally, I want to point out that St. Thomas Aquinas presented the Five Ways in his *Summa Theologica* as an attempt to defeat just such a presumption. My hope in this is, both to draw attention to something which seems generally to be overlooked, and by so doing to summon a massive authority in support of a thesis which many apparently find scandalous.

These most famous arguments were offered there originally, without any inhibition or equivocation, as proofs, period: "I reply that we must say that God can be proved in five ways"; and the previous second Article, raising the question "Whether the existence of God can be demonstrated?," gives the categorical affirmative answer that "the existence of God … can be demonstrated."[14] Attention usually and understandably concentrates on the main body of the third Article, which is the part where Aquinas gives his five supposed proofs. But, as so often, it is rewarding to read the entire Article, and especially the second of the two Objections to which these are presented as a reply: "Furthermore, what can be accounted for by fewer principles is not the product of more. But it seems that everything which can be observed in the world can be accounted for by other principles, on the assumption of the non-existence of God. Thus natural effects are explained by natural causes, while contrived effects are referred to human reason and will. So there is no need to postulate the existence of God."[15]

The Five Ways are thus at least in one aspect an attempt to defeat this presumption of (an Aristotelian) atheist naturalism, by showing that the things "which can be observed in the world" cannot "be accounted for … on the assumption of the non-existence of God," and hence that there is "need to postulate the existence of God."[16] One must never forget that Aquinas composed his own Objections, and hence that it was he who introduced into his formulation here the idea of (this Aristotelian) scientific naturalism. No such idea is integral to the presumption of atheism as that has been construed in the present paper. When the addition is made the presumption can perhaps be labelled "Stratonician." (Strato was the next but one in succession to Aristotle as head of the Lyceum, and was regarded by Bayle and Hume as the archetypal ancient spokesman for an atheist scientific naturalism.)

By suggesting, a century before Ockham, an appeal to an Ockhamist principle of postulational economy Aquinas also indicates a reason for adopting such a presumption. The fact that the Saint cannot be suspect of wanting to reach atheist conclusions can now be made to serve as a spectacular illustration of a point laboured in Part B, above, that to adopt such a presumption is not to make an assumption. And the fact, which has been put forward as an objection to this reading of Aquinas, that "Thomas himself was never in the position of a Stratonician, nor did he live in a milieu in which Stratonicians were plentiful,"[17] is simply irrelevant. For the thesis that the onus of proof lies upon the theist is entirely independent of these biographical and sociological facts.

What is perhaps slightly awkward for present purposes is the formulation of the first Objection: "It seems that God does not exist. For if of two contrary things one were to exist without limit the other would be totally eliminated. But what is meant by this word 'God' is something good without limit. So if God were to have existed no evil would have been encountered. But evil is encountered in the world. Therefore, God does not exist."

It would from my point of view have been better had this first Objection referred to possible difficulties and incoherencies in the meaning proposed for the word "God." Unfortunately it does not, although Aquinas is elsewhere acutely aware of such problems. The changes required, however, are, though important, not extensive. Certainly, the Objection as actually given is presented as one of the God hypothesis falsified by familiar fact. Yet a particular variety of the same general point could be represented as the detection of an incoherence, not in the proposed concept of God as such, but between that concept and another element in the theoretical structure in which it is normally involved.

The incoherence—or perhaps on this occasion I should say only the ostensible incoherence—is between the idea of creation, as necessarily involving complete, continual and absolute dependence of creature upon Creator, and the idea that creatures may nevertheless be sufficiently autonomous for their faults not to be also and indeed primarily His fault. The former idea, the idea of creation, is so essential that it provides the traditional criterion for distinguishing theism from deism. The latter is no less central to the three great theist systems of Judaism, Christianity, and Islam, since all three equally insist that creatures of the immaculate Creator are corrupted by sin. So where Aquinas put as his first Objection a statement of the traditional Problem of Evil, conceived as a problem of squaring the God hypothesis with certain undisputed facts, a redactor fully seized of the presumption of atheism as expounded in the present paper would refer instead to the ostensible incoherence, within the system itself, between the concept of creation by a flawless Creator and the notion of His creatures flawed by their sins.

NOTES

1. This and all later translations from the Greek and Latin are by me.

2. See Chapter VI of Lewis Carroll's *Through the Looking Glass*:

   "But 'glory doesn't mean 'a nice knock-down argument,'" Alice objected.

   "When I use a word," Humpty Dumpty said in rather a scornful tone, "it means just what I choose it to mean—neither more nor less."

   "The question is," said Alice, "whether you can make words mean so many different things."

   "The question is," said Humpty Dumpty, "which is to be master—that's all."

3. See the essay 'Agnosticism', and also that on "Agnosticism and Christianity," in Volume V of his *Collected Essays* (MacMillan: London, 1894). I may perhaps also refer to my own article on "Agnosticism" for the 1972 revision of the *Encyclopaedia Britannica*.

4. H. Denzingerd (Ed.) *Enchiridion Symbolorum* (Twenty-ninth Revised Edition, Herder: Freiburg im Breisgau, 1953), section 1806.

5. By Professor P. T. Geach of Leeds.

6. "The force of the negative instance is greater." For, whereas a single positive, supporting instance can do only a very little to confirm an universal generalization, one negative, contrary example would be sufficient decisively to falsify that generalization.

7. See the paper "Presumptions" by my former colleague Patrick Day in the *Proceedings of the XIVth International Congress of Philosophy* (Vienna, 1968), Vol. V, at p. 140. I am pleased that it was I who first suggested to him an exploration of this unfrequented philosophical territory.

8. In "Some Consequences of Four incapacities" at pp. 156–157 of Volume V of the *Collected Papers* (Harvard University Press; Cambridge (Mass.), 1934).

9. In his review of *God and Philosophy* in *Theology Today* 1967, pp. 86–87. He makes his point not against the general presumption but against one particular application.

10. *Discourse on the Method*, Part II. It occurs almost immediately after his observation: "I took into account also the very different character which a person brought up from infancy in France or Germany exhibits, from that which... he would have possessed had he lived among the Chinese or with savages."

11. *Paradise Lost*, Bk. XII, line 646.

12. *Summa contra Gentiles*, Bk. I, Ch. VI. The whole passage, in which Aquinas gives his reasons for believing that the Christian candidate does, and that of Mohammed does not, constitute an authentic revelation of God, should be compared with some defence of the now widely popular *assumption* that the contents of a religious faith must be without evidential warrant.

    Professor A. C. Macintyre, for instance, while he was still himself a Christian argued with great vigour for the Barthian thesis that "Belief cannot argue with unbelief: it can only preach to it." Thus, in his paper on 'The Logical Status of Religious Belief' in *Metaphysical Beliefs* (Student Christian Movement press: London, 1957), Macintyre urged: "...suppose religion could be provided with a method of proof…since the Christian faith sees true religion only in a free decision made in faith and love, the religion would by this vindication be destroyed, For all possibility of free choice would have been done away. Any objective justification of belief would have the same effect … faith too would have been eliminated" (p. 209).

Now, first, in so far as this account is correct any commitment to a system of religious belief has to be made altogether without evidencing reasons. Macintyre himself concludes with a quotation from John Donne to illustrate the "confessional voice" of faith, commenting: "The man who speaks like this is beyond argument" (p. 211). But this, we must insist, would be nothing to be proud off. It is certainly no compliment, even if it were a faithful representation, to partray the true believer as necessarily irrational and a bigot. Furthermore, second, it is not the case that where sufficient evidence is available there can be no room for choice. Men can, and constantly do, choose to deceive themselves about the most well-evidenced, inconvenient truths. Also no recognition of any facts, however clear, is by itself sufficient to guarantee one allegiance and to preclude its opposite. MacIntyre needs to extend his reading of the Christian poets to the greatest of them all. For the hero of Milton's *Paradise Lost* had the most enviably full and direct knowledge of God. Yet Lucifer, if any creature could, chose freely to rebel.

13. *Pensées*, section 233 in the Brunschvicg arrangement. For a discussion of Pascal's argument see Chapter VI, section 7 of my *An Introduction to Western Philosophy* (Thames & Hudson, and Bobbs-Merrill: London and New York, 1971).

14. It is worth stressing this point, since nowadays it is frequently denied. Thus L. C. Velecky in an article in *Philosophy* 1968 asserts: "He did not prove here the existence of God, nor indeed, did the prove it anywhere else, for a very good reason. According to Thomas, God's existence is unknowable and, hence, cannot be proved" (p. 226). The quotations from Aquinas given in my text ought to be decisive. Yet there seems to be quite a school of devout interpretation which waives aside what the Saint straightforwardly said as almost irrelevant to the question of what he really meant.

15. I, Q2 A3.

16. In this perspective it becomes easier to see why Aquinas makes so much use of Aristotelian scientific ideas in his arguments. That they are in fact much more dependent on these now largely obsolete ideas is usefully emphasized in Anthony Kenny's *The Five Ways* (Routledge and Kegan Paul, and Schocken Books: London and New York, 1969). But Kenny does not bring out that they were deployed against a presumption of atheist naturalism.

17. Velecky *loc. cit.*, pp. 225–226.

VII.B.3

Rational Religious Belief Without Arguments

MICHAEL BERGMANN

Michael Bergmann (1964–) is professor of philosophy at Purdue University and works primarily in the fields of epistemology and philosophy of religion. In this chapter, Bergmann explains and defends the view (held by Alvin Plantinga and other so-called "Reformed epistemologists") that religious beliefs—like the belief that God exists—can be rational even if they are not based on arguments.

There have been many different attempts, by philosophers and others, to show that religious belief of various kinds is irrational. And there have been at least as many attempts by religious people to defend the rationality of their beliefs. Perhaps the most common religious belief to be attacked and defended in this way is belief in God—an omniscient, omnipotent, immaterial, eternal, perfectly good, wholly loving person on whom everything else depends. It will be convenient to focus our attention on belief in God, though much of our discussion will be relevant to other religious beliefs as well. Believers in God (theists) have for centuries now offered a variety of arguments for God's existence: they've argued that there must be a first cause (an uncaused cause) of the existence of things; they've argued that there must be a designer to account for the apparent design found in the natural world; they've argued that we can't make sense of morality without appealing to the existence of God; they've even argued that simply by reflecting on the concept of God we can see that God exists because such reflection reveals that God is the sort of being that *must* exist. The goal of these arguments is, at least in part, to show

that belief in God is rational. Reliance on these sorts of arguments is supposed by many to be what *makes* belief in God rational. In fact, it is commonly thought that belief in God *couldn't* be rational unless it is held on the basis of such arguments. But is that last thought right? Could a person's belief in God be rational even if it is not held on the basis of any of these alleged theistic proofs? Could there be rational religious belief without arguments?

For the past few decades, a prominent position within the philosophy of religion literature is that belief in God *can* be rational even if it isn't based on any arguments. This position is often called "Reformed Epistemology" to signify its roots in the writings of John Calvin (1509–1564), the great Protestant theologian and the main source of the Reformed tradition within Christendom. But one can find developments of the same idea in the writings of earlier figures such as Aquinas, Augustine, and even the apostle Paul. The central thesis of Reformed Epistemology is simply that religious belief, including belief in God, can be rational (sensible, reasonable, justified) even if it is not inferred from any other beliefs—even if it is not held on the basis of any argument at all. In what follows, I will

This essay was commissioned for the 6th edition of this anthology, and is published here for the first time.

explain this view in greater detail and then consider and respond to a number of objections to it.

I. UNDERSTANDING REFORMED EPISTEMOLOGY

A. A Little Background in Epistemology

In order to understand Reformed Epistemology, it will be helpful to begin with a little background in epistemology, which is the study of knowledge and rational belief. Epistemologists typically aren't concerned with religious belief in particular. Their concern is more general. They are trying to understand the nature of knowledge and rationality as these concepts apply to any belief whatsoever, regardless of the belief's topic or the means by which it was produced.

Let's begin by highlighting two distinctions. The first, which we've already been employing, is the distinction between rational and irrational beliefs. This is an *evaluative* distinction insofar as rational beliefs are, by definition, epistemically *better* than irrational beliefs. The second distinction is between basic beliefs and nonbasic beliefs. A basic belief is a belief that is not based on or inferred from another belief. A nonbasic belief is a belief that *is* based on or inferred from another belief. This is a *psychological* distinction, not an evaluative one. It has to do with how the beliefs are formed. Let's consider some examples of basic and nonbasic beliefs. Suppose you're visiting your doctor after being in a minor car accident and she is trying to determine the extent of your injuries. She gently presses on various parts of your back and neck, asking if it hurts when she does so. At one point you feel a very sharp pain and you tell her that it hurts. You tell her that because you *believe* that it hurts. That belief isn't inferred from other beliefs you have. (You don't first believe that you flinched when she pressed that spot and then infer that, because you flinch only when you're in pain, you must be in pain now). Instead, that belief is an automatic

noninferential response to the feeling of pain you experience; it is based on that experience, even though it isn't based on another belief. Because it is not based on another belief of yours, it is a basic (or noninferential) belief. Nonbasic (or inferential) beliefs are different. Suppose you want to figure out in your head what 9×53 equals. To do this, you typically will come first to believe that $9 \times 50 = 450$, that $9 \times 3 = 27$, and that $450 + 27 = 477$. Then you infer from those beliefs the further belief that $9 \times 53 = 477$. Since that last belief is inferred from other beliefs, it is a nonbasic belief.

An important question that has been of interest to philosophers as early as Aristotle (384–322 BCE) is whether any basic beliefs are rational. It's natural to think that for a belief to be rational, you must have a reason for holding it, where your reason is another belief of yours. But to hold a belief for a reason is to base it on or infer it from that other belief that is your reason. These considerations might incline a person to endorse *Inferentialism*, the view that a belief can be rational only if it's inferred from another belief. But there is a powerful and influential objection to Inferentialism, first proposed by Aristotle (*Posterior Analytics*, Book I, Chapters 2–3). This objection starts by noting that it's implausible to think that a belief can be rational in virtue of being inferred from an *irrational belief*. Hence, Inferentialism implies that a belief is rational only if it's inferred from another *rational* belief. But according to Inferentialism, for that second belief to be rational, it too must be inferred from another belief—which also must be rational. And so on. Thus, Inferentialism implies that in order for a belief to be rational, you must either base it on an infinite chain of reasoning or else reason in a circle. But it's obvious that reasoning in a circle cannot make a belief rational. And none of us is able to carry out an infinite chain of reasoning. (And even if we could, an infinite chain of reasoning cannot, by itself, make a belief rational without some original rationality to be transferred along the chain.) The upshot is that if Inferentialism is true, then it's impossible to have rational beliefs. Given that most philosophers think that it isn't impossible to have rational beliefs, it's widely believed that

Inferentialism is false: basic beliefs can be, and often are, rational. These rational basic beliefs are often called "properly basic beliefs."

Not just any basic belief is *properly* basic (i.e., both rational and noninferential). The reckless gambler who is having a run of terrible luck in the casino and who believes on a whim, not on the basis of any other beliefs, that his luck is about to improve, is thereby forming an irrational basic belief. Unlike your basic belief that you're in pain (when the doctor presses on your neck), the gambler's basic belief is not *properly* basic. So although some basic beliefs are properly basic, not all of them are. Which of our basic beliefs *are* properly basic? The answer to this question has to do with which belief-forming abilities we have. We humans have the ability to tell, without inference, that we're in pain. But we don't have the ability to tell, without inference, that our gambling luck is about to improve. We also have the ability to tell, without inference, what our own thoughts are. But we don't have the ability to tell, without inference, what others are thinking. Likewise, we have the ability to tell just by looking, without inference from other beliefs, that there's a book on the table in front of us. But we don't have the ability to tell in complete darkness, without inference, that there's a pillar six feet in front of us (though if we had the echolocation abilities that bats have, we could reasonably form such basic beliefs in the darkness). So which beliefs can be properly basic for us depends on which noninferential belief-forming abilities we have.

Which noninferential belief-forming abilities do we have? Which of our basic beliefs can be rational? There is wide agreement that we can tell noninferentially via introspection what we're thinking and feeling. In addition, there's wide agreement that we can tell noninferentially via rational intuition that one thing is logically implied by another, though this ability is limited for most people to very simple logical implications. (For example, we can tell noninferentially via rational intuition that if Jack and Jill are at the party then it logically follows that Jack is at the party.) Suppose that those were the only sorts of

properly basic beliefs we had and that the only way for us to have rational beliefs in addition to beliefs of those kinds would be to draw inferences from them. The famous philosopher René Descartes (1596–1650) began with only those sorts of basic belief—i.e., those formed via introspection and rational intuition—and tried from there to see what he could learn by inference. He thought that in that way, starting from those meager foundations, he could prove that God exists and that there is a physical world surrounding us. Most philosophers think that he failed in this attempt and that the problem had a lot to do with the fact that he allowed so few beliefs to count as properly basic. Today, most epistemologists think that in addition to the ability to form noninferential beliefs via introspection and rational intuition, we also have the ability to form noninferential beliefs via perception and memory. When, upon glancing at a nearby basketball, I believe there's a ball in front of me, I don't do this via inference: I don't first notice that it visually appears to me as if there's a ball there and that such appearances are good indicators that there is a ball there and from this infer that there's a ball in front of me. I can just tell noninferentially via perception that there's a ball in front of me. Likewise, I can tell noninferentially via memory that I had orange juice at breakfast. I don't infer this from the fact that there's a glass on the kitchen counter that looks as if it contained orange juice a few hours ago and that no one else in the house likes orange juice. Thus, it's very common for epistemologists to think we have the ability to form noninferential beliefs via perception, memory, introspection, and rational intuition. Because we have these abilities, the beliefs so produced are properly basic (i.e., noninferentially rational). And from these starting points, we can make inferences via good reasoning to the many other beliefs we hold; these other beliefs are then inferentially rational.

It's important to emphasize that although these properly basic beliefs aren't inferred from other beliefs, it doesn't follow that they are groundless or that we hold them without any evidence. Take for example the belief that you are in pain. It's true you don't infer that from other beliefs. But it's not groundless. Instead, it's based on your experience of pain. It's that experience, not another belief, which is the ground of your belief that you're in pain—that experience is your evidence for that belief. Other introspective beliefs are also based on experiences (such as the belief that you're happy or sad, which is based on your experience of feeling happy or sad).[1] Likewise, although perceptual beliefs aren't inferred from other beliefs, they aren't lacking in grounds or evidence. My belief that there's a ball in front of me is based on my visual experience at the moment (not on the belief that I'm having such a visual experience—I typically don't form such beliefs about my visual experience). That visual experience is my evidence—it is the ground of that visual belief. In the case of beliefs formed via memory or rational intuition, it's more difficult to say what they are based on. According to one common way of thinking about memory beliefs, they are based on memory seemings. It seems to me—in a remembering sort of way—that I had orange juice for breakfast. On the basis of that seeming (that memory seeming) I hold the memory belief that I had orange juice for breakfast. Similarly, beliefs in simple logical truths, formed via rational intuition are based on rational intuitions. I can just *see* (intellectually) that one thing logically follows from another. This "seeing" is a sort of insight, a rational intuition; it's an experience of something's seeming to me a certain way—it's an experience of its seeming obvious to me that this thing logically follows from that thing. And my belief that the one thing follows from the other is based on this rational intuition. Both the memory seeming and the rational intuition are experiences. They aren't themselves beliefs. So beliefs based on them still count as basic.

The resulting picture, widely endorsed by contemporary epistemologists, is the following. Some beliefs are rational and some are not. Those that are rational are either basic or not. The rational beliefs that aren't basic are inferred from other rational beliefs. These inference chains are ultimately traced back to properly basic beliefs—i.e., rational beliefs that aren't based on any other beliefs. What makes a basic belief rational has to do with which noninferential belief-forming abilities we have. At the very least, we humans seem to have the ability to form beliefs via perception, memory, rational intuition, and introspection. And the beliefs produced by these noninferential belief-forming abilities are based not on other beliefs but on experiences of various kinds—perceptual experiences, memory seemings, rational intuitions, and introspectable experiences such as pain, pleasure, happiness, sadness, etc.

There is one further "background epistemology" question that often gets discussed by philosophers and which will be relevant to our discussion of religious belief. The question is this: can a belief be properly basic for a person who has never thought at all about the epistemology of such beliefs in anything like the way we just have? For example, can a sad child be rational in remembering that his mother left the room a moment ago even if the child has no idea that that belief is based on a memory seeming? The answer, it seems, is "yes." One can be rational in forming noninferential beliefs via memory even if one has never thought about how memory works or what memory beliefs are based on or whether memory beliefs are basic or nonbasic.

However, given that rationality seems to rule out haphazard or careless belief formation, some might be tempted by a contrary view that we can call "Confirmationalism," which requires for a belief's rationality that we confirm that it was produced in the right way:

> *Confirmationalism:* In order for a belief to be rational, the person holding it needs a further belief that the first belief has an adequate basis.

So, for example, Confirmationalism would say that I can't be rational in my memory belief that I was in Florida last year unless I have an additional belief that that memory belief of mine has an adequate basis. Of course that second belief—required to confirm the adequacy of the first belief's basis—must itself be rational. But according to Confirmationalism, that second belief (like any other belief) is rational only if the person holding it has yet another belief that the second belief has an adequate basis. And that third belief must be rational too, which will require a fourth belief confirming the adequacy of its basis. And so on. Thus, Confirmationalism implies that in order for a simple belief—such as the belief that *there is a ball in front of me*—to be rational, I need to have an infinite number of other beliefs, each of which is about the previous belief having an adequate basis. (Because each belief is about the previous belief, this chain of beliefs will not circle back on itself.) But people aren't able to have an infinite number of extra beliefs for each of the simple beliefs they hold. Given Confirmationalism, this implies that people aren't able to have any rational beliefs. For this reason, most epistemologists reject Confirmationalism.[2]

B. Reformed Epistemology

Let us turn now to the task of trying to gain a better understanding of Reformed Epistemology, the view that belief in God can be rational even if it is not inferred from any other beliefs. Our background reflections in epistemology will benefit us as our discussion proceeds.

A helpful way to begin our more careful examination of Reformed Epistemology is to consider the context in which it was introduced into the contemporary philosophy of religion literature. A prominent twentieth-century objection to the rationality of belief in God runs as follows:

The Evidentialist Objection

1. *The Evidentialist Thesis*: Belief in God is rational only if it is inferred from other rational beliefs via good arguments.

2. But there aren't any good arguments for God's existence.

3. Therefore, belief in God is irrational.

The reason this objection is called "The Evidentialist Objection" is that it relies on the Evidentialist Thesis as its first premise.[3] According to that premise, theistic belief is rational only if it is based on

good evidence in the form of good theistic arguments. The proponent of this objection to theism will, of course, endorse the Evidentialist Thesis but will not believe in God. Let's call such a proponent a "Nontheistic Evidentialist." For most of the twentieth century, the most common response to this argument, by those who wanted to defend theistic belief, was the response given by Theistic Evidentialists. Like Nontheistic Evidentialists, they accept the first premise, the Evidentialist Thesis. But they reject the second premise. They think there *are* good arguments for God's existence. And they spend a lot of time devising such arguments and defending those arguments against objections. It was in just this context of disagreement (between Theistic Evidentialists and Nontheistic Evidentialists over whether there are good theistic arguments) that a second theistic response to the Evidentialist Objection was offered, this time by Reformed Epistemologists. They turned their sights on the first premise, the Evidentialist Thesis itself. Their claim was that belief in God—like the belief that I had orange juice for breakfast or the belief that there's a ball in front of me—can be properly basic. (As for the second premise, some Reformed Epistemologists join Nontheistic Evidentialists in accepting it; others join Theistic Evidentialists in rejecting it. But all Reformed Epistemologists reject the first premise; and that is what they tend to focus on in responding to the Evidentialist Objection.)

Given that Reformed Epistemologists think belief in God is properly basic (and in light of our background excursion into epistemology in the previous section), you would expect Reformed Epistemologists to also think that we have a noninferential belief-forming ability enabling us to tell, without inference, that God exists. And that's just what we find in their writings. Alvin Plantinga, perhaps the most prominent of contemporary Reformed Epistemologists, suggests that we have a "sense of divinity" enabling us to form properly basic beliefs about God. And just as noninferential beliefs formed via perception and memory are not groundless but instead based on experience, so also properly basic beliefs about God are, according to the Reformed Epistemologist, not groundless but based on experience. Plantinga gives some examples of the sort of experiential grounds on which noninferential beliefs about God are based:

> [T]here is in us a disposition to believe propositions of the sort *this flower was created by God* or *this vast and intricate universe was created by God* when we contemplate the flower or behold the starry heavens or think about the vast reaches of the universe…. Upon reading the Bible, one may be impressed with a deep sense that God is speaking to him. Upon having done what I know is cheap, or wrong, or wicked I may feel guilty in God's sight and form the belief *God disapproves of what I've done*. Upon confession and repentance, I may feel forgiven, forming the belief *God forgives me for what I've done*. A person in grave danger may turn to God asking for his protection and help; and of course he or she then forms the belief that God is indeed able to hear and help if he sees fit. When life is sweet and satisfying, a spontaneous sense of gratitude may well up within the soul; someone in this condition may thank and praise the Lord for his goodness, and will of course form the accompanying belief that indeed the Lord is to be thanked and praised.[4]

The proposal here is that experiences of awe, guilt, forgiveness, fear, and gratitude can operate as grounds for beliefs about God. The beliefs so formed aren't usually of the form "God exists." They're more often of the form "God does this" or "God has done that" or "God is able to do such and such." In this way, they're like our more ordinary beliefs about the world around us. We typically don't form beliefs like "that lake exists." Instead, we think "that lake is cold" or "that lake is beautiful" or some such thing. But it's a short step from the belief about the lake (or God) to the further belief that the lake (or God) exists.[5]

It's important to emphasize (because it's so common for people to mistakenly think otherwise)

that Reformed Epistemologists hold that ordinary unsophisticated religious believers who know nothing of the epistemological views discussed in this paper can have properly basic belief in God. As I already noted, most epistemologists (whether religious or not) think that a child's memory-produced belief that his mother left the room a few moments ago is rational even if the child can give no account of what that memory belief is based on or why it is rational. What matters for the rationality of that memory belief is that the child *has* the ability to form beliefs using his memory, not whether the child can give an account of the epistemology of memory beliefs. Likewise, Reformed Epistemologists say that what matters for properly basic belief in God is that the believer *has* the ability to form beliefs via the sense of divinity, not that the person can give an account of the epistemology of noninferential theistic beliefs. So a belief in God can be rational even if the person holding it doesn't have the further belief that her belief in God has an adequate basis via the sense of divinity. Some objectors will insist that your belief via this alleged sense of divinity won't be rational without a further belief, based on good reasons, that the experiences on which you base your belief in God provide an adequate basis for such a belief. In response, the Reformed Epistemologist will point out that this complaint seems to rely on an appeal to Confirmationalism discussed above—a principle which most philosophers reject, and for good reason.

Here is a simple way to think of the Reformed Epistemologist's position: *belief in God is more like belief in other people than it is like belief in electrons.* We are able to form properly basic beliefs that there are people around us because, by using our vision, we can tell noninferentially that there are people nearby. But we aren't able to tell noninferentially, just by looking, that there are electrons nearby. We don't have that sort of ability. Instead, humans arrived at the belief in electrons via inference: we inferred their existence because it provided the best explanation of all the experimental evidence collected by scientists. According to the Evidentialist Thesis, belief in God—like belief in electrons—is rational only if we infer it as the best explanation of the available evidence (in the case of belief in God, the evidence in question is what gets cited in the premises of theistic arguments). But according to the Reformed Epistemologist, belief in God is more like belief in other people.[6] We don't first notice that it visually appears to us as if there are other people and then conclude that the best explanation of these visual appearances is that there really are other people that are the causes of these visual appearances. Rather, we just have the visual experiences and believe on the basis of them, without inference, that there are people around us. Likewise, the Reformed Epistemologist thinks that for many people, belief in God is not an inferred explanatory hypothesis but a noninferential response to experience. It's worth noting that it wouldn't be surprising for a loving God who wants all people to believe in him to give us the ability to believe in him noninferentially through a sense of divinity. That way of believing in God seems to be easier and less affected by differences in intelligence than inferential belief-formation, which requires an expertise (that isn't widely shared) in formulating and evaluating arguments.

As I signaled at the beginning of this essay, the Reformed Epistemologist's views don't apply only to the belief that God exists. Other religious beliefs as well can be rational in a similar way—beliefs in specific doctrines of this or that religion. There are a number of accounts of how these other religious beliefs are formed.[7] But ultimately it comes down to something very much like the views described above concerning properly basic belief in God.

II. OBJECTIONS TO REFORMED EPISTEMOLOGY

Let's turn now to some objections to Reformed Epistemology and consider what sorts of response are available.

Objection 1: Religious Interpretation of Experiential Evidence Needs Defense. The Reformed Epistemologist says that beliefs about God are based on experiences such as feeling forgiven after confession and repentance. On the basis of such an experience a person believes "God forgives me for what I've done." But this is to *interpret* the experience within a particular theological framework—it's to impose one interpretation among many possible ones on a raw experience consisting of a feeling of being forgiven replacing a feeling of guilt. In order for the belief about God's forgiveness to be rational, one needs some reason for favoring that particular theological interpretation over some other nontheistic interpretation of that same raw experience.

Consider a parallel complaint lodged against perceptual beliefs: "When you believe, on the basis of visual experience, that there is a chair and a desk nearby, you are imposing one interpretation among many possible interpretations on the raw experience consisting of a visual appearance that seems to be of a chair and desk nearby. You've adopted the "standard" interpretation according to which there really is a chair and a desk nearby causing you to have that visual appearance. But perhaps you are dreaming. Or perhaps you are the victim of an experiment in which computers are connected to your brain causing you to have that visual appearance. You aren't rational in believing there really is a chair and desk nearby unless you first have a reason for favoring the standard interpretation over the dreaming interpretation and the computer–simulation interpretation."

How have epistemologists responded to this parallel complaint about perception? One common response is to note the following things. First, if this complaint were legitimate, then most people wouldn't be rational in their beliefs about the world around them since most people simply don't have any reasons they could produce for favoring the standard interpretation of perceptual experience. Second, epistemologists have worked very hard for centuries trying to come up with good reasons for preferring the standard interpretation of perceptual experience to its rivals and have yet to come up with an argument acknowledged to be convincing. Because of this failure, it is widely believed that there is no good argument for preferring the standard interpretation of perceptual experience that doesn't itself rely on perceptual experience to tell us about the world around us.[8] Third, it seems that, in looking around us and forming visual beliefs about our environment, we don't first have a visual experience and then consider various ways to interpret it, ultimately selecting the standard interpretation. Instead, the world seems to present itself to us in visual experience as if the standard interpretation is true—the standard interpretation comes along unbidden with the visual experience. In light of all this, many epistemologists conclude that our perceptual beliefs are rational not because we've got a good reason for preferring the standard interpretation of our perceptual experience but because the rational response to having such experiences is to form beliefs, without inference, in accord with the standard interpretation.

The Reformed Epistemologist will say similar things about belief in God based on things such as an experience of feeling forgiven.[9] Many who believe, on the basis of such an experience, that God has forgiven them don't have any arguments available for favoring a theistic interpretation of that experience over a nontheistic one. Moreover, in many cases, they don't first have the experience and then consider various ways of interpreting it, ultimately selecting the theistic interpretation. Instead, that theistic interpretation comes along unbidden with that experience of feeling forgiven. And just as the rational response to perceptual experience is to form noninferential beliefs in the objects one takes oneself to see nearby, so also (says the Reformed Epistemologist) the rational response to the experience of feeling forgiven is to believe, without inference, that God is as one takes God to be on the basis of that experience.

Objection 2: The Great Pumpkin Objection.
The Reformed Epistemologist's strategy for defending the rationality of religious belief is seriously problematic because the same strategy could be used to defend any bizarre belief you like, including Linus's belief (in the Charlie Brown comics) that the gift-delivering Great Pumpkin rises each Halloween over the most sincere pumpkin patch. When challenged to give reasons for their belief, Great Pumpkinites could simply point out that their belief is properly basic so they don't need to give any arguments for it. The fact that this strategy can be used to defend such a bizarre view reveals the bankruptcy of the strategy. But it seems that the Reformed Epistemologist, in endorsing this sort of strategy for defending the rationality of her belief in God, cannot offer any principled objection to this same strategy used by others in defense of silly views like belief in the Great Pumpkin.

Here too we can consider a parallel complaint, this time against those who think introspective beliefs are rational. Suppose you tell me that you're feeling a little hungry and I ask you what your argument is for that claim. You tell me that you don't need an argument in order to be rational in believing that claim; you have the ability to tell, just by thinking about it, what sorts of feelings you are having. In response I say "Oh really? Well, with that sort of reasoning, you could have no objection to a person who claimed to be a mind-reader with the special ability to tell, just by thinking about it, what those around her are thinking and feeling." Notice what I would be suggesting by that response. I'd be suggesting that because you claim to be able to tell *one* thing without argument (namely, what sorts of feelings you're having), you can have no objection to a person who claims to be able to tell *another* thing without argument (namely, what those around her are thinking and feeling). But that suggestion of mine would be silly. It's perfectly sensible to say there are some things people can tell without argument and other things they can't tell without argument.

Reformed Epistemologists respond to the Great Pumpkin Objection in a similar manner.

They think there are some things people can tell without argument and other things people can't tell without argument. They think people can tell without argument that God exists but they can't tell without argument that the Great Pumpkin exists. There is nothing remarkable about the suggestion that people have abilities to tell some things, but not others, without inference. We already know that people can tell, just by looking and without inference, that there are people around them; but they can't tell just by looking and without inference that there are electrons. People can also tell, just by thinking about it and without inference, what thoughts they are having; but they can't in the same way tell, without inference, what thoughts others are having. They can, without inference, remember what happened in the recent past; but they can't in the same way tell, without inference, what is going to happen in the future. The Reformed Epistemologist's claim—that we have the ability to tell noninferentially that God exists but we don't have any such ability with respect to the Great Pumpkin—is just another claim of this sort. The "strategy" of claiming to have an ability to know something noninferentially can be employed in defending the rationality of a belief even by those who think there are many things we don't have the ability to know noninferentially. So Reformed Epistemologists aren't committed to approving of others who use the same sort of strategy to defend all sorts of silly views.

Objection 3: Why Doesn't Everyone Believe in God? The previous two responses have compared basic belief in God to properly basic perceptual beliefs or properly basic introspective beliefs. But this ignores a very important difference between basic belief in God, on the one hand, and basic perceptual and introspective beliefs, on the other: pretty much everybody forms basic beliefs about their surroundings via perception and basic beliefs about their thoughts and feelings via introspection; but there are many people who don't believe in God at all. That's an important

difference. If we have the ability to tell, without inference, that God exists, why are there so many people who don't believe in God?

The first thing to note here is that belief in some sort of deity is very widespread throughout human history, across many different cultures.[10] This of course doesn't prove that it's true. But it's important to keep in mind that it's not as if only a small minority of the world's population believes in God. Nevertheless, there are many people who don't seem to have any belief in God, and this is strikingly different from what we see when we compare basic belief in God with basic perceptual belief in the world around us or introspective belief in our mental states. What does the Reformed Epistemologist have to say about this?

The natural thing to say is that the *sense of divinity* isn't working equally well in all people. It is either damaged or hindered in its operation in many people and this has been so for a long time. It would be as if all humans had their vision damaged or otherwise hindered from normal operation and this condition of humanity lasted for many centuries. If that were to happen, some humans wouldn't be able to see at all and others would have only distorted or unclear vision. It might then happen that some who could see better than others would believe that the moon existed, but those who were blind or couldn't see as well, might not believe that the moon existed. Of course this analogy breaks down after a while.[11] But the main point of it, according to Reformed Epistemologists, is just that the sense of divinity is more damaged in some people than it is in others, and this explains why some people don't have properly basic belief in God whereas others do.[12]

Objection 4: Sinfulness Doesn't Explain Atheism. In responding to the last objection, Reformed Epistemologists say that the sense of divinity is more damaged in some people than in others. But what is it that causes this damage? A common suggestion by some Reformed Epistemologists is that "sinfulness" is the cause of this damage. But that's both insulting and implausible. It's easy to give examples of nontheists and theists where the nontheists are, morally speaking, much better behaved than the theists.

It's true that many in the Reformed tradition say that operational deficiencies in the sense of divinity are caused by sinfulness. And it's also clear that some morally well-behaved people are nontheists and that some theists behave terribly (the Bible itself points to fallen angels as well as to many humans in giving examples of badly behaved theists). So how can anyone take seriously the suggestion that sinfulness explains why many people don't believe in God?

What follows is one possible way to make sense of the suggestion that sinfulness can explain lack of belief in God. (Notice that the goal here isn't to prove the truth of the explanation of unbelief in terms of sinfulness or of this particular way of making sense of it. Rather, it's to show how explaining unbelief by pointing to sinfulness can be consistent with the observation that nontheists often seem to be better behaved than theists.) We first need to distinguish inherited sinfulness from willful sinfulness. Ever since humans fell into sin, the result (according to Christians, including those in the Reformed tradition) has been that *all* of their descendents have been born with an inherited tendency to selfishness and pride.[13] This inherited tendency seems to come in various degrees. Because it is inherited, this tendency is not something we've chosen. Nor did we choose how severe it is in our own case.[14] In addition to inherited sinfulness, which we don't choose, there is also willful sinfulness. This occurs when we freely choose to act in a way that is contrary to our conscience. We are responsible for our willful sinfulness even though we aren't responsible for our inherited sinfulness. The explanation I want to consider for why not all people believe in God appeals, in part, to both inherited sinfulness and willful sinfulness.

There are really two things that need explaining: how sinfulness can keep people from believing

in God and why, despite that first explanation, there isn't a tight correlation between one's belief status (as theist or nontheist) and one's moral status (as well-behaved or badly behaved). As for the first explanation, there are two ways sinfulness can hinder belief in God: it can hinder it in a way for which the unbeliever is *not* to blame; and it can hinder it in a way for which the unbeliever *is* to blame. Let's consider how it might hinder it in ways for which the unbeliever is not to blame. For starters, the inherited tendency to selfishness and pride damages the sense of divinity in all people so that it doesn't work as it was originally intended.[15] It's as if all of us have blurred vision when it comes to detecting God noninferentially. And because our inherited sinfulness comes in varying degrees, the damage it causes to the sense of divinity also comes in varying degrees. On top of that, due to both the inherited and willful sinfulness of those in our family and our larger society, our upbringing can cause further damage or hindrance to the operation of the sense of divinity in us. Here too, the resulting damage will come in varying degrees, depending on what has happened in our family and society, on what damage was caused by our own inherited sinfulness, and on how those two kinds of damage interact. All of these sin-caused effects on our sense of divinity hinder belief in God in a way for which the unbeliever is *not* to blame.

But, in addition to the above-mentioned things that affect what we might think of as our unchosen "starting point," there are other things that hinder belief in God. These other things affect how we progress from our starting point either further from or closer to belief in God. One contributor here could be willful sinfulness. By choosing to go against my conscience, I can perhaps further contribute to the damage to my sense of divinity. This is a case in which I am partially to blame for the way in which sin hinders my belief in God. But there are other possible contributors as well. God may choose to give experiential evidence for theistic belief to some people and not to others— evidence on which a properly basic belief in God can be based without inference.[16] (This might involve giving experiences to a person that the person wouldn't otherwise have had. Or it might involve correcting damage to the sense of divinity so that the person treats as evidence for belief about God experiences that the person wouldn't otherwise have treated in that way.) God's decision to give or delay giving such evidence might be based on the willful sinfulness of the person in question. But it might be based on other things as well. Perhaps God thinks the person isn't yet ready to respond correctly to such evidence. Or perhaps God has a reason for wanting this person to progress further morally than others before coming to believe in God. And there may be other good reasons God has for delay in giving evidence, reasons that we don't know of.

In light of the above explanation for how sinfulness can hinder belief in God, we can see why it might be that there isn't a tight correlation between one's theistic-belief status and one's moral-behavior status. For, as we've just noted, though unbelief may be due to sinfulness in the ways described, God might give or delay giving evidence for properly basic belief in God on the basis of considerations that aren't correlated with how well-behaved the person is. And we aren't well placed to discern why there is unbelief in a particular case.

Moreover, appearances can be deceiving when we consider the moral goodness of those around us. It's natural to think that if God existed and were just and fair, he would judge people based on how well they did with the moral resources they were given. Consider two people, one of whom is given the opportunities of a naturally pleasant and cooperative personality and excellent moral training in her home and society while the other naturally has a more irritable and stubborn personality and is raised in a terrible home environment and influenced by a morally depraved society. It's easy to see how it might turn out that the person with the less fortunate background *might* be judged by God to have done much better, morally speaking, with what she was given than the more fortunate person; and this could be so even though the more fortunate person appears in many ways to behave better than the one with the less fortunate background. The point

here is just that we really aren't able to tell how people are to be judged unless we can look into their hearts and backgrounds to see how well they are doing with what they were given, something we are rarely, if ever, able to do with much accuracy. This point is reinforced when we consider that motives matter tremendously. A person may perform many seemingly kind and generous actions but be doing them from motives of selfishness and pride. Again, it seems that if God existed and were to judge us fairly, he would take that into account. Because we can't always tell how good people are (in terms of their motives or how well they've done with what they've been given), we aren't well placed to draw conclusions about how belief in God is in fact correlated with goodness in people. There might be more of a correlation there than meets the eye. But even if there isn't (and Reformed Epistemologists certainly aren't committed to thinking there is), there are the other considerations noted above explaining why there needn't be any such correlation even if sinfulness (both inherited and willful) does go some way toward explaining why people don't believe in God.

Objection 5: Religious Disagreement as a Reason for Doubt. In addition to the problem of people who don't believe in God, there's the problem of people who do believe in God but hold very different views about God. If each of them is relying on the sense of divinity and yet getting such different beliefs as a result, doesn't that give a person good reason to mistrust this alleged belief-forming ability in herself, especially given that many don't seem to have it at all? This problem is especially disconcerting when we consider that intelligent, thoughtful people who are sincerely seeking the truth discuss their disagreements about theism at length, explaining their evidence to each other, and yet continue to disagree.

There are three points to make in response to this objection.[17] The first has to do with the principle on which the objection seems to be based. The principle focuses on disagreement with someone who is intellectually virtuous (let's say a person is intellectually virtuous when he or she is intelligent, thoughtful, and sincerely seeking the truth). The basic idea seems to be that when someone who is intellectually virtuous disagrees with you, especially if you recognize that this person is about as intellectually virtuous as you are, then you thereby have a good reason to give up your belief. We can call this principle on which this objection seems to rely "the Withholding Principle." It can be formulated as follows:

> *Withholding Principle:* If an intellectually virtuous person (whom you realize is about as intellectually virtuous as you are) disagrees with you on a controversial topic even after each of you has tried your best to disclose all your relevant evidence to the other (where this evidence falls short of being a knockdown proof that every intelligent thoughtful truth-seeker would accept), then to be rational each of you should give up your contentious belief on this topic and, instead, withhold judgment on the matter.

The problem is that intelligent, thoughtful truth-seekers disagree about the Withholding Principle itself. Some think you should withhold judgment whenever you're in the circumstances described in the principle; but others think that's not so. Moreover, those who endorse the Withholding Principle don't have a knockdown proof for the principle, one that every intelligent, thoughtful truth-seeker would accept. The result is that if the principle is true, then rationality requires you to reject it—since you can't *prove* the principle's truth to intelligent, thoughtful truth-seekers who think it's false. And that means that the principle is self-undermining, saying about itself that it's irrational to accept it.

A second thing worth pointing out is that the Reformed Epistemologist can distinguish internal rationality from external rationality, conceding the former but not the latter to those who disagree about religious matters. This distinction highlights the fact that there are two stages in the formation of noninferential beliefs based on experiential evidence rather than on arguments. The first stage is where the person comes to have the experiential evidence; the second stage is where the person bases the noninferential belief in question on that experiential evidence. The belief so based is *internally rational* if it is an appropriate (reasonable, sensible) response for a person to have to that sort of experiential evidence. One way to put this point is to say that, in the formation of an internally rational belief, all is going well *downstream* from (i.e., in response to) the experience on which it is based. The belief is *externally* rational if, in addition to being internally rational, it's also the case that all is going well *upstream* from that experience—that is to say, the experiential evidence arises in the right way in the person who has it and is not due, for example, to any sort of cognitive malfunction. With this distinction in hand, the Reformed Epistemologist can point out that those who disagree with her may well be internally rational even if they aren't externally rational. Thus, for example, a Jewish theist who denies the divinity of Christ and who endorses the Reformed Epistemologist approach[18] can say (i) the Christian is internally rational in believing, on the basis of her experiential evidence in support of the doctrine, that *Jesus is God incarnate* and (ii) the atheist who lacks any experiential evidence in support of belief in God is internally rational in believing there is no God. But the Jewish believer can go on to add that the Christian is externally *irrational* because it is only due to some sort of cognitive malfunction that the Christian has that experiential evidence supporting the doctrine that Jesus is God incarnate; likewise, the Jewish believer can say that the atheist is externally irrational in believing there is no God because it is only due to some sort of cognitive malfunction (affecting the sense of divinity) that the atheist lacks any experiential evidence in support of belief in God.[19] In this way, those who endorse the Reformed Epistemologist approach can recognize that there is a sense in which the intelligent, thoughtful truth-seekers who disagree with them may be rational—they may be internally rational. But the Reformed Epistemologist can also explain why her beliefs are epistemically better than the religious beliefs of those who disagree—her own beliefs are externally rational whereas the beliefs of those who disagree with her are externally irrational.

The third point to make is that there seem to be examples where it is entirely appropriate to say—of intelligent, thoughtful truth-seekers whose views you disagree with but can't prove wrong—that their contrary views are externally irrational and mistaken whereas yours are externally rational and correct. Consider a case of moral disagreement about how to evaluate the following very disturbing behavior of Jack's. Jack takes pleasure in torturing and killing children, and he has found a way to do this without getting caught. I assume that you think this behavior of Jack's is morally wrong (extremely so). But you have a friend—who, like you, is an intelligent, thoughtful truth-seeker—who disagrees. She is a moral nihilist, someone who thinks it's false that Jack's behavior is morally wrong because there are no moral facts and nothing is morally wrong—or morally right. Like you, this friend is utterly disgusted by Jack's behavior and very strongly wishes that Jack wouldn't engage in it. But, unlike you, your friend doesn't think it is morally wrong. Now suppose you and your friend try to share with each other all your evidence for your opposing views. You point to your properly basic belief (based on some sort of intuitive seeming[20]) that actions of the sort Jack performs are morally wrong, which shows that moral nihilism is false. Your friend points to her properly basic belief (also based on some sort of intuitive seeming) in a key premise used to support her belief in moral nihilism—a view implying that Jack's behavior is neither morally wrong nor morally right. Unfortunately, even after you each try your best to share your relevant evidence, the disagreement persists. Does rationality require that, upon learning of this persistent disagreement with your friend, you should give up your belief that Jack's behavior is wrong? No. Instead of being moved to doubt the reliability of our own beliefs on this topic, we are sensibly moved to feel badly for the friend who disagrees with us and to be glad that we are fortunate enough not to lack the moral insight we have or to have the misleading moral views that our moral nihilist friend has.

Moreover, you can acknowledge that your moral nihilist friend may be *internally* rational in thinking Jack's behavior isn't wrong. After all, your friend has strong experiential evidence (i.e., *her* intuitive seemings) in support of that noninferential belief in the premise supporting moral nihilism. And your friend doesn't have the additional evidence you have which would outweigh this—namely, stronger experiential evidence (i.e., *your* intuitive seemings) in support of the view that Jack's behavior is wrong. You can concede that the right response to the evidence your friend has may be to believe in moral nihilism; so all may be going well downstream from your friend's experiential evidence. But you will insist that your friend isn't externally rational because something has gone wrong upstream from her experiential evidence. The very fact that moral nihilism seems intuitively more plausible to your friend than the claim that Jack's behavior is morally wrong shows that your friend is suffering from some sort of cognitive malfunction or problem, despite your friend's intelligence, thoughtfulness, and sincere interest in discovering the truth.[21]

The Reformed Epistemologist can, therefore, insist that, in the above scenario, it is appropriate for you to think Jack's behavior is wrong despite the fact that your intelligent, thoughtful, and truth-seeking friend continues to disagree with you about this, even after you share all your evidence. Moreover, it seems sensible for you to think that your friend is mistaken and externally irrational in her moral nihilist view that Jack's behavior is not wrong, though you could allow that that view of hers may be internally rational. And the Reformed Epistemologist can then point out that something similar is going on in the case of religious disagreement. Those who disagree with her religious beliefs might be *internally* rational in their beliefs in a different religion or against all religions. But the beliefs of those who disagree with her are both mistaken and *externally* irrational, despite the fact that they are held by intelligent, thoughtful truth-seekers. The point here is most definitely *not* that there is any connection between rejecting moral nihilism and endorsing a religious view. Rather, the point is that *if*—in the case of your belief that Jack's behavior is wrong—you can sensibly think your friend is mistaken and externally irrational despite the fact that she's also an internally rational, intelligent, thoughtful truth-seeker, *then* there is, in principle, no bar to your sensibly thinking something similar of a friend in the case of a religious disagreement. In addition, the fact that you and your friend are both relying on intuitive seemings in arriving at your opposing views about the morality of Jack's behavior doesn't show that you rationally ought to give up all views you have that are based on intuitive seemings. Likewise, the fact that you and someone else differ in your views about God even though you both rely on the sense of divinity doesn't show that you rationally ought to give up all your views based on the sense of divinity.

Of course, it's true that the nontheist will be inclined to think that her nontheistic beliefs are externally rational and that it's the *theist* that is externally irrational. But why think this should be a problem for the theist? After all, your moral nihilist friend will be inclined to think that she is externally rational and that *you* are externally irrational in thinking Jack's behavior is morally wrong. Should the fact that the moral nihilist views you this way lead you to give up your view that you, not her, are the one that is holding the externally rational belief on this matter? It seems not. Even if your moral nihilist friend thinks that of you, it seems perfectly reasonable for you to continue holding your belief and thinking that you are externally rational in doing so.[22] In the same way, even if the nontheist will be inclined to view the theist as externally irrational, it doesn't follow that the theist should give up her view that she, and not the nontheist, is externally rational.

CONCLUSION

We've considered in this paper the Reformed Epistemologist's position that belief in God can be rational even if it is not based on any argument. We've tried to understand what her view is—the sense in which she thinks belief in God is more like belief in other people like belief in electrons. And we've considered several challenging objections to the Reformed Epistemologist's proposal. There is a lot more that could be said in explaining and trying to make plausible the Reformed Epistemologist's position, especially as it applies to religious beliefs other than belief in God. And more should also be said in response to the above objections and to others besides.[23] Nevertheless, I hope what has been said here helps the reader to appreciate why many people take this sort of view seriously.[24]

NOTES

1. What about your introspective beliefs about what you're thinking? What are they based on? They're based on your experience of having those thoughts. They aren't inferred from other beliefs of yours.

2. Confirmationalism is similar to Inferentialism; in fact, it seems to be one version of Inferentialism.

3. Notice, by the way, that the Evidentialist Thesis is different from Inferentialism. The latter says that *no* belief can be rational unless it is inferred from other rational beliefs; the former says merely that *belief in*

God cannot be rational unless it is inferred from other beliefs.

4. Plantinga (1983:80).

5. For this reason, Plantinga suggests (1983:81-82) that it is beliefs about what God does or is like, not the belief that God exists, that are properly basic. But for simplicity's sake, I'll speak as if he and others think belief in God is properly basic.

6. Interestingly, current research in the cognitive science of religion has arrived at a similar conclusion in its attempts to explain the origins of

religious belief (which is widespread across times and cultures). One common theme in this research is that belief in God is a natural and instinctive reaction to a variety of stimuli; it is not the result of inferences or arguments. See Clark and Barrett (2010) for a summary of this research and a discussion of how it compares to the views of Reformed Epistemologists.

7. See Plantinga (2000) for one prominent example.

8. See Alston (1993) where this point is defended at length.

9. See, for example, Alston (1983).

10. For an extended explanation, from the perspective of cognitive science, of why this is so, see Barrett (2004).

11. Some might think that the analogy breaks down because vision can be cross-checked with other perceptual faculties such as sense of touch whereas we can't cross-check the sense of divinity in that same way. But see Alston (1991, ch. 5) for a discussion of how something like the sense of divinity might be subject to cross-checking.

12. Additional explanations for differences between properly basic religious belief and properly basic perceptual belief are given in Alston (1983) and Alston (1991).

13. Must one believe in a literal reading of early Genesis to believe that there was a time that humans fell into sin? And doesn't that literal reading conflict with the well-established theory of evolution? A literal reading of early Genesis does seem to conflict with evolutionary theory. But many religious people who accept the teachings of the Bible as authoritative think that (i) early Genesis is not best interpreted in that literal way, (ii) evolutionary theory is true, and (iii) one thing we can learn from early Genesis is that humanity fell into sin in some way or other, even if not in the precise way described there. For a discussion of how inherited sinfulness can be combined with an evolutionary account of human origin, see Collins (2003).

14. Is it fair for Gold to let the immoral choices of our ancestors cause us to have this inherited tendency? This is just an instance of the more general question: is it fair for God to let the wrong choices of some people negatively affect the lives of others? It's not implausible to think that, so long as God has some justifying reason for doing so (one that

treats those negatively affected with love and respect), it is fair for God to do that.

15. How does selfishness and pride cause damage to the sense of divinity? This might happen in any number of ways: perhaps selfishness and pride make one less inclined to believe in a being to whom they owe worship and service; or perhaps the sense of divinity works by way of divine blessing that is withheld from those who are selfish and proud; or perhaps the damage to the sense of divinity caused by selfishness and pride comes about in some other way.

16. Recall that, although basic beliefs are ones that are not inferred from other beliefs, they might still be based on evidence of some kind.

17. These three points are developed at greater length in a different context in Bergmann (2009).

18. To endorse the Reformed Epistemologist approach is *not* to endorse the teachings of the Reformed tradition within Christendom or any other distinctively Christian doctrines. Rather, it's to say that belief in God (or other religious beliefs) can be properly basic.

19. This example is not meant to suggest that Jewish believers must or often do explain Christian and atheistic belief in this way. The point is just to give an illustration of how one *could* explain the beliefs of those with whom one disagrees on religious matters. Moreover, in explaining that Christian and atheistic belief involve cognitive malfunction, the Jewish believer needn't think the Christian and the atheist are insane or brain-damaged. Instead, the Jewish believer would just be saying that the sense of divinity isn't working property in the Christian or in the atheist.

20. An intuitive seeming that p is true is an experience of it seeming intuitively to you that p is true.

21. Again, the point isn't that your friend is insane or brain-damaged but just that the process by which her moral intuitions are formed is not working properly.

22. But won't the same hold for your moral nihilist friend? Won't the fact that you view her as externally irrational fail to show that she should give up her view that she, not you, is the one that is externally rational? That may be right. But if that's right, which of you *really is* externally rational? Presumably it could only be the one whose views on this matter are correct. Which one of you is

that? Unfortunately, that's a matter of dispute. But you (and many others) will sensibly think that your view (that Jack's behavior is morally wrong) is both true and externally rational. Questions parallel to those raised here can be raised in the case of disagreement over theistic belief and parallel answers can be given.

23. The main places to look for further discussion of these topics are Alston (1991) and Plantinga (2000).

24. Thanks to Jeffrey Brower and Michael Rea for helpful comments on earlier drafts of this paper.

REFERENCES

Alston, William, "Christian Experience and Christian Belief" pp. 103–34 in *Faith and Rationality*, eds. Alvin Plantinga and Nicholas Wolterstorff (Notre Dame: University of Notre Dame Press, 1983).

Alston, William, *Perceiving God* (Ithaca: Cornell University Press, 1991).

Alston, William, *The Reliability of Sense Perception* (Ithaca: Cornell University Press, 1993).

Barrett, Justin. *Why Would Anyone Believe in God?* (Lanham, MD: AltaMira Press, 2004).

Bergmann, Michael, "Rational Disagreement after Full Disclosure," *Episteme* 6(2009): 336–53.

Clark, Kelly James and Justin Barrett. "Reformed Epistemology and the Cognitive Science of Religion." *Faith and Philosophy* 27 (2010): 174–89.

Collins, Robin. "Evolution and Original Sin" pp. 469–501 in *Perspectives on an Evolving Creation*, ed. Keith B. Miller 2006, (Grand Rapids: Eerdmans Publishing Company, 2003).

Plantinga, Alvin, "Reason and Belief in God" pp. 16–93 in *Faith and Rationality*, eds. Alvin Plantinga and Nicholas Wolterstorff (Notre Dame: University of Notre Dame Press, 1983).

Plantinga, Alvin, *Warranted Christian Belief* (New York: Oxford University Press, 2000).

VII.B.4

Faith, Hope, and Doubt

LOUIS P. POJMAN

Louis Pojman (1935–2005), the original editor of this anthology, was professor of philosophy at the United States Military Academy, West Point, New York. In this selection, Pojman examines the relationship between belief and faith and argues that belief is not necessary for religious faith. One may not be able to believe in God because of an insufficiency of evidence, but one may still live in hope, committed to a theistic worldview.

Many religious people have a problem because they doubt various credal statements contained in their religions. Propositional beliefs are often looked upon as necessary, though not sufficient, conditions for salvation. This doubt causes great anxiety and raises the question of the importance of belief in religion and in life in general. It is a question that has been neglected in the philosophy of religion and theology. In this paper I shall explore the question of the importance of belief as a religious attitude and suggest that there is at least one other attitude which may be adequate for religious faith, even in the absence of belief—that attitude being hope. I shall develop a concept of *faith as hope* as an alternative to the usual notion that makes a propositional belief that God exists a necessary condition for faith, as Plantinga implies in the following quotation. For simplicity's sake I shall concentrate on the most important proposition in Western religious creeds, which states that God exists (defined broadly as a benevolent, supreme Being, who is responsible for the creation of the universe), but the analysis could be applied *mutatis mutandis* to many other important propositions in religion (e.g., the Incarnation and the doctrine of the Trinity).

> It is worth noting, by way of conclusion, that the mature believer, the mature theist, does not typically accept belief in God tentatively, or hypothetically, or until something better comes along. Nor, I think, does he accept it as a conclusion from other things he believes; he accepts it as basic, as a part of the foundations of his noetic structure. The mature theist commits himself to belief in God: this means that he accepts belief in God as basic (Alvin Plantinga, "Is Belief in God Rational?").

Entombed in a secure prison, thinking our situation quite hopeless, we may find unutterable joy in the information that there is, after all, the slimmest possibility of escape. Hope provides comfort, and hope does not always require probability. But we must be believe that what we hope for is at least possible (Gretchen Weirob in John Perry's *A Dialogue on Personal Identity and Immortality*).

INTRODUCTION

Traditionally, orthodox Christianity has claimed (1) that faith in God and Christ entails belief that God exists and that Christ is God incarnate and (2) that without faith we are damned to eternal hell. Thus doubt is an unacceptable propositional attitude. I argue that this thesis is misguided. One may doubt—that is, lack propositional belief—and yet have faith in God and Christ.

Let me preface my remarks with a confession. I am a religious doubter. Doubt has haunted my life as long as I can remember. My mother was a devout Roman. Catholic and my father an equally convinced rationalistic atheist. From an early age metaphysical tension produced in me a sense of wonder about religion. In the process of seeking a solution to this conflict, at the age of seven I became a Protestant. But doubts continued to haunt me. I recall coming home from my high school biology class, where we had studied naturalistic evolution, and weeping over the Bible, trying to reconcile evolution with the creation account in Genesis 1 through 3. Finally, when I was about 15, I went to a minister and confessed my doubts about God and Christianity. He listened carefully1 and said the situation was grave indeed. My eternal soul was at stake. Thus I must will myself to believe the message of Christianity. He quoted Romans 14:23: "He that doubteth is damned... for whatsoever is not of faith is sin." I was thrown into paroxysms of despair, for the attempt to get myself to believe that God exists or that Christ is perfect God and perfect man failed. Yet, I wanted to believe with all my heart, and some days I would find myself believing—only to wake up the next day with doubts. Hence, this preoccupation with faith and doubt. Hence, this paper.

I. IS BELIEF A NECESSARY CONDITION FOR SALVATION?

According to traditional Christianity, belief is a necessary condition for salvation. Paul says in Romans 10:10, "If you confess with your lips that Jesus is Lord and believe in your heart that God raised him from the dead, you will be saved." In Hebrews 11 we are told that he who would please God must believe that He exists and is a rewarder of them that seek Him. The Athanasian Creed, an official doctrine of orthodox Christianity, states that salvation requires that one believe not only that God exists but also that God is triune and that Christ is perfect God and perfect man.[1] Most theologians and philosophers hold, at the least, that Christian faith requires propositional belief.[2] You can be judged and condemned according to your beliefs. As Romans 14:23 states, "He that doubteth is damned."

The basic argument goes Like this:

1. Faith in God through Christ is a necessary and sufficient condition for eternal salvation.

2. Belief that God exists is a necessary condition for faith.

3. Therefore belief is a necessary condition for salvation.

4. Therefore, doubt—the absence of belief—is an unacceptable attitude for salvation. No doubter will be saved.

Let us begin with some definitions:

1. **Belief**—an involuntary assenting of the mind to a proposition (a "yessing" to a proposition), a feeling of conviction about *p*—a *nonvolitional event.*

Consider the following belief line, defined in terms of subjective probability, the degree to which I think the proposition is probable. Let "*S*" stand for the believer or *subject,* "*B*" for *believe,* and "*p*" for the *proposition* in question. Then we can roughly locate our beliefs on the Belief Line. Greater than 0.5 equals various degrees of positive belief that *p*. Less than 0.5 equals various degrees of unbelief (or belief that the complement, "not-*p*" is true). 0.5 equals agnosticism or suspension of judgment.

Belief Line

$$0 \underline{\hspace{4cm}} 0.5 \underline{\hspace{4cm}} 1$$

SB not-*p*   Not-*SBp* & Not-*SB* not-*p*   *SBp*

2. **Acceptance**—deciding to include *p* in the set of propositions that you are willing to act on in certain contexts—*a volitional act.*

For example, in a *legal* context—say a jury, where there is insufficient evidence to convict an accused criminal—I may believe the subject is guilty but accept the proposition that he is not because the high standards of criminal justice have not been met; or in a *scientific* context—say, in testing the hypothesis that a formula will lead to the development of cold fusion—I may not believe the hypothesis I am testing is true but accept it for purposes of the experiment. Acceptance is different from belief in that we have some direct control over our acceptances, whereas we don't over our beliefs. We may or may not believe our acceptances and we may or may not accept our beliefs.

3. **Faith**—a commitment to something *X* (e.g., a person, hypothesis, religion, or worldview).

Faith is a *deep* kind of acceptance. An acceptance can be tentative. For example, when I make a marriage vow, I will to be faithful until death to my beloved, whether or not I believe that I will succeed. If my marriage vow were merely an acceptance, I suppose, it would be "I promise to be faithful to you for at least three years or until I lose interest in you." Faith involves commitment to its object. Under normal circumstances, it involves trusting and obeying the object of faith or doing what has the best chance of bringing its goals to fulfillment. It is a *volitional act.*

We may note at this point that the New Testament word *pistis* can be translated as either belief or faith. The distinction is discernible only by the context.

II. PHENOMENOLOGY OF BELIEF

First we must understand what is involved in direct volitionalism (the act of acquiring a belief directly by willing to have it). The following features seem to be necessary and jointly sufficient conditions for a minimally interesting thesis of volitionalism:

1. The acquisition is a basic act. That is, some of our beliefs are obtained by acts of will directly upon being willed. Believing itself need not be an action. It may be dispositional. The volitionalist need not assert that all belief acquisitions occur via the fiat of the will, only that some of them do.

2. The acquisition must be done in full consciousness of what one is doing. The paradigm cases of acts of will are those in which the agent deliberates over two courses of action and decides on one of them. However, acts of will may take place with greater or lesser awareness. Here our notion of will is ambiguous between two meanings: "desiring" and "deciding." Sometimes by "act of will" we mean simply a desire that manifests itself in action, such as my being hungry and finding myself going to the refrigerator or tired and finding myself heading for bed. We are not always aware of our desires or intentions. There is a difference between this type of willing and the sort where we are fully aware of a decision to perform an act. If we obtain beliefs via the will in the weaker sense of desiring, of which we are only dimly aware, how can we ever be sure that it was really an act of will that caused the belief directly rather than the will simply being an accompaniment of the belief? That is, there is a difference between willing to believe and believing willingly. The latter case is not an instance of acquiring a belief by fiat of the will; only the former is. In order for the volitionalist

to make his case, he must assert that the acts of will that produce beliefs are decisions of which he is fully aware.

3. The belief must be acquired independently of evidential considerations. That is, the evidence is not what is decisive in forming the belief. Perhaps the belief may be influenced by evidence (testimony, memory, inductive experience, and the like), so that the leap of faith cannot occur at just any time over any proposition, but only over propositions that have some evidence in their favor, though still inadequately supported by that evidence. They have an initial subjective probability of—or just under—0.5. According to Descartes, we ought to withhold belief in such situations where the evidence is exactly equal, whereas with Kierkegaard religious and existential considerations may justify leaps of believing even when the evidence is weighted against the proposition in question. William James prescribes such leaps only when the option is forced, living, and momentous. It may not be possible to volit* in the way Kierkegaard prescribes without a miracle of grace, as he suggests, but the volitionalist would have to assert that volitional belief goes beyond all evidence at one's disposal and hence the believer must acquire the belief through an act of choice that goes beyond evidential considerations. It is as though we place our volitional finger on the mental scales of evidence assessment, tipping the scale one way or the other.

In sum, then, a volit must be an act of will whereby I acquire a belief directly upon willing to have the belief, and it is an act made in full consciousness and independently of evidential considerations. The act of acquiring a belief may itself not be a belief but a way of moving from mere entertainment of a proposition to the disposition of having the belief. There is much to be said in

---

*Volit: (v.) to acquire a belief by choosing to have it or (n.) a belief acquired by exercising one's will. Voliting: obtaining beliefs by choosing to have them.

favor of volitionalism. It seems to extend the scope of human freedom to an important domain, and it seems to fit our experience o f believing where we are conscious of having made a choice. The teacher who sees that the evidence against a pupil's honesty is great and yet decides to trust him, believing that somehow he is innocent in spite of the evidence, and the theist who believes in God in spite of insufficient evidence, seem to be everyday examples confirming our inclination toward a volitional account of belief formation. We suspect, at times, that many of our beliefs, while not formed through *fully conscious* volits, have been formed through *half-aware* desires, for on introspection we note that past beliefs have been acquired in ways that could not have taken the evidence seriously into consideration. Volitionalism seems a good explanatory theory to account for a great deal of our cognitive experience.

Nonetheless, there are considerations which may make us question whether, upon reflection, volitionalism is the correct account of our situation. I will argue that choosing is not the natural way in which we acquire beliefs, and that whereas it may not be logically *impossible* that some people volit, it seems psychologically odd and even conceptually incoherent.

1. Beliefs-Are-Not-Chosen Argument against Volitionalism

Beliefs are not chosen but occur involuntarily as responses to states of affairs in the world. Beliefs are, to use Frank Ramsey's metaphor, mappings in the mind by which we steer our lives. As such, the states of affairs that beliefs represent exist independently of the mind; they exist independently of whether we want them to exist. Insofar as beliefs presume to represent the way the world is, and hence serve as effective guides to action, the will seems superfluous. Believing seems more like seeing than looking, falling than jumping, catching a cold than catching a ball, getting drunk than taking a drink, blushing than smiling, getting a headache than giving one to someone else. Indeed, this involuntary, passive aspect seems true on introspection of most propositional attitudes: anger, envy, fearing, suspecting, and doubting—although not necessarily of imagining or entertaining a proposition, where an active element may often be present.

When a person acquires a belief, the world forces itself upon him. Consider perceptual beliefs. If I am in a normal physiological condition and open my eyes, I cannot help but see certain things— for example, this piece of white paper in front of me. It seems intuitively obvious that I don't have to choose to have a belief that I see this piece of white paper before I believe I see it. Here "seeing is believing." This is not to deny a certain active element in perception. I can explore my environment— focus on certain features and turn from others. I can direct my perceptual mechanism, but once I do this the perceptions I obtain come of themselves whether or not I will to have them. I may even have an aversion to white paper and not want to have such a perception, but I cannot help having it. Likewise, if I am in a normal physiological state and someone nearby turns on loud music, I hear it. I cannot help believing that I hear it. Belief is forced on me.[3]

2. Logic-of-Belief Argument against Volitionalism

The notion of volitional believing involves a conceptual confusion; it is broadly speaking a logical mistake. There is something incoherent in stating that one can obtain or sustain a belief in full consciousness *simply* by a basic act of the will—that is, purposefully disregarding the evidence connection. This strategy does not altogether rule out the possibility of voliting when one is less than fully conscious (although one is not truly voliting if one is not fully conscious), but it asserts that when full consciousness enters, the "belief" will wither from one's noetic structure. One cannot believe in full consciousness "that *p* and I believe that *p* for other than truth considerations." If you understand that to believe that *p* is to believe that *p* is true and that *wishing never makes it so*, then there is simply no epistemic reason for believing *p*. Suppose I say that I believe I have $1,000,000 in my checking account, and suppose that when you point out to me that there is no reason to believe this, I respond, "I know that there is not the slightest reason to suppose that there is $1,000,000 in my checking account, but I believe it anyway, simply because I want to." If you were convinced that I was not joking, you would probably conclude that I was insane or didn't know what I was talking about.

If I said that I somehow find myself believing that I have $1,000,000 but don't know why, you might suppose that there is a memory trace of my having deposited $1,000,000 into my account or evidence to that effect in the guise of an intuition that caused my belief. But if I denied that and said—"No, I don't have any memory trace of depositing of $1,000,000 in my account; in fact, I'm sure that I never deposited $1,000,000 in the account; I just find it good to believe that it's there, so I have chosen to believe it,"—you would be stumped.

The point is that because beliefs are just about the way the world is and are made true (or false) depending on the way the world is, it is a confusion to believe that any given belief is true simply on the basis of being its being willed. As soon as the believer—assuming that he understands these basic concepts—discovers the basis of his belief as being caused by the will alone, he must drop the belief. In this regard, saying "I believe that *p*, but I believe it only because I want to believe it," has the same incoherence attached to it as G. E. Moore's paradoxical, "I believe *p* but it is false that *p*." Structurally, neither is a strictly logical contradiction, but both show an incoherence that might be broadly called contradictory.

If this reasoning is sound, then we cannot be judged for our beliefs because beliefs are not actions. That is, if *ought* implies *can*, and we cannot acquire beliefs directly by choosing them, we cannot be judged according to our beliefs. Of course, we can be judged by our actions and by how well we have investigated the evidence and paid attention to the arguments on the various sides of the issue. That leads to the matter of the ethics of belief.

III. THE ETHICS OF BELIEF

Of course we can obtain beliefs indirectly by willing to have them. I can desire to believe that I am innocent of an unjust act against my neighbor—say directing my drain pipes to drain onto his property. I can bring to mind all the nasty things my neighbor may have done and use autosuggestion to convince myself that I am justified in redirecting may drain pipes toward his property, thus bringing about the desired belief. This manipulation of the mind is immoral. At the least, there is a strong case against indirect volitionalism.

W. K. Clifford has given a classic absolutist injunction against voliting: "It is wrong always, everywhere and for anyone to believe anything on insufficient evidence." This may have the sound of too "robustious pathos in the voice" as James notes, but it may sound hyperbolic only because we have not taken truth seriously enough. Nevertheless, I defend the principle of an ethic of belief only as a *prima facie* moral principle—one which can be overridden by other moral principles—but which has strong presumptive force.[4]

Why do we want true justified beliefs— beliefs based on the best evidence available?

We want true justified beliefs because beliefs make up our road map of life; they guide our desires. If I believe that I can fly and jump out of the top of the Empire State Building to take a short cut to Columbia University, I'm likely to be disappointed. If I want to live a long life and believe that living on alcohol and poison ivy will enable me to do so, I will not attain my desire.

The importance of having well-justified beliefs is connected with truth-seeking in general. We believe that these two concepts are closely related, so the best way to assure ourselves of having true beliefs is to seek to develop one's belief-forming mechanisms in such ways as to become good judges of various types of evidence, attaining the best possible justification of our beliefs. The value of having the best possible justified beliefs can be defended on both deontological grounds with regard to the individual and on teleological or utilitarian grounds with regard to society as a whole. The deontological argument is connected with our notion of autonomy. To be an autonomous person is to have at one's disposal a high degree of warranted beliefs upon which to base one's actions. There is a tendency to lower one's freedom of choice as one lowers the repertoire of well-justified beliefs regarding a plan of action, and because it is a generally accepted moral principle that it is wrong to lessen one's autonomy or personhood, it is wrong to lessen the degree of justification of one's beliefs on important matters. Hence, there is a general presumption against beliefs by *willing* to have them. Cognitive voliting is a sort of lying or cheating in that it enjoins believing against what has the best guarantee of being the truth. When a friend or doctor lies to a terminally ill patient about her condition, the patient is deprived of the best evidence available for making decisions about her limited future. She is being treated less than fully autonomously. Whereas a form of paternalism may sometimes be justified, there is always a presumption against it and in favor of truth-telling. We even say that the patient has a *right* to know what the evidence points to. Cognitive voliting is a sort of lying to oneself, which, as such, decreases one's own freedom and personhood. It is a type of doxastic suicide that may be justified only in extreme circumstances. If there is something intrinsically wrong about lying (malting it *prima facie* wrong), then there is something intrinsically wrong with cognitive voliting, either directly or indirectly. Whether it be Pascal, William James, John Henry Newman, or Søren Kierkegaard, all prescriptive volitionalists (consciously or not) seem to undervalue the principle of truthfulness and its relationship to personal autonomy.

The utilitarian, or teleological, argument against cognitive voliting is fairly straightforward. General truthfulness is a *desideratum* without which society cannot function. Without it language itself would not be possible because it depends on faithful use of words and sentences to stand for appropriately similar objects and states of affairs. Communication depends on a general adherence to accurate reporting. More specifically, it is very important that a society have true beliefs with regard to important issues so that actions that are based on beliefs have a firm basis.

The doctor who cheated her way through medical school and who, as a consequence, lacks appropriate beliefs about certain symptoms may endanger a patient's health. A politician who fails to take into consideration the amount of pollutants being discharged into the air or water by large corporations that support his candidacy may endanger the health and even the lives of his constituents. Even the passer-by who gives wrong information to a stranger who asks for directions may seriously inconvenience the stranger. Here Clifford's point about believing against the evidence is well taken, despite its all-too-robustious tone: the shipowner who failed to make necessary repairs on his vessel and "chose" to believe that the ship was seaworthy is guilty of the deaths of the passengers. "He had no right to believe on such evidence as was before him." It is because beliefs are action-guiding maps by which we steer and, as such, tend to cause actions, that society has a keen interest in our having the best justified beliefs possible regarding important matters.

Some people object to my model of the verific person, the truth-seeker, as being neutral on the matter of religion. They point out that the issue is too important to permit neutrality as an appropriate attitude. Let me clear this up by making a distinction between *neutrality* and *impartiality*. The verific person is not neutral but impartial. For a proper model of the verific person—one seeking to proportion his or her beliefs to the strength of the evidence—consider the referee in an Army vs. Notre Dame football game. The veterans of foreign wars and Army alumni will tend to be biased toward Army, considering close calls against "their" team by the referee as clear instances of poor officiating—even of injustice. Roman Catholics throughout the nation will tend to be biased toward Notre Dame, seeing close calls against "their" team by the referee as clear instances of poor officiating—even of injustice. The neutral person is the atheist pacifist in the crowd—the one who doesn't care who wins the game. But the impartial person is the referee who, knowing that his wife has just bet their family fortune on the underdog, Notre Dame, still manages to call a fair game. He is able to separate his concerns about his financial security from his ability to discern the right calls in appropriate situations. The verific person is one who can be trusted to reach sound judgments where others are driven by bias, prejudice, and self-interest.

If we have a moral duty not to volit but to seek the truth impartially and passionately, then we ought not to obtain religious beliefs by wiling to have them; instead we should follow the best evidence we can get.

IV. HOPE AS THE PROPER RELIGIOUS PROPOSITIONAL ATTITUDE FOR DOUBTERS

For those who find it impossible to believe directly that God exists and who follow an ethic of belief acquisition (voliting), hope may be a sufficient substitute for belief. I can hope that God exists without believing that He does.

Let us first analyze the concept of hope in order to determine whether it is a viable option. Consider some examples of hope.

1. Ryan hopes that he will get an A in his philosophy course.

2. Mary hopes that Tom will marry her.

3. Susan hopes that Happy Dancer will win the Kentucky Derby next week.

4. Steve hopes that the Cubs won their game yesterday.

5. Although Bill desires a cigarette, he hopes he will not give into his desire.

6. Christy hopes her saying "no" to Ron's proposal of marriage is the right decision.

If we look closely at these examples of hoping, we can pick out salient features of the concept. First

of all, hope involves *belief in the possibility* that a state of affairs obtains or can obtain. We cannot hope for what we believe to be impossible. If Ryan hopes to get an A in philosophy, he must believe that it is possible to do so, and if Mary hopes that Tom will marry her, she must deem it possible. The *Oxford English Dictionary* defines *hope* as an "expectation of something desired," but this seems too strong. Expectation implies belief that something will occur, whereas we may hope even when we do not expect the object to obtain, as when Mary hopes that Tom will marry her or when Steve hopes the languishing Cubs won their game against the awesome Atlanta Braves. Susan may hope that Happy Dancer will win the race even though she doesn't expect that to happen. Thus belief that the object of desire will obtain does not seem necessary for hope. It is enough that the hoper believe that the proposition in question is possible, though not necessarily probable (it has a subjective probability of greater than 0 but not necessarily greater than 0.5).

Second, hope precludes certainty. Mary is not certain that Tom will marry her, and Susan is not certain that Happy Dancer will win the race. There must be an apparent possibility that the state of affairs will not obtain. We would think it odd to say, "Steve knows that the Cubs won the game yesterday, for he was there, but he still hopes that the Cubs won the game." As Paul wrote in Romans 8:24, "For hope that is seen is not hope: for what a man sees, why does he yet hope for?" Hope entails uncertainty, a subjective probability index of greater than 0 but less than 1.

Third, hope entails desire (or a pro-attitude) for the state of affairs in question to obtain or for the proposition to be true. In all of the preceding examples a propositional content can be seen as the object of desire. The states of affairs envisaged evoke a pro-attitude. The subject wants some proposition p to be true. It matters not whether the state of affairs is past (case 4) or present (cases 5 and 6) or future (cases 1 through 3), although it generally turns out, because of the role hope plays in goal orientation, that the state of affairs will be a future situation.

Fourth, the desire involved in hoping must be motivational—greater than mere *wishing*. I may wish to live forever, but if I don't think it is suffi-ciently probable or possible, it will not serve as a spring for action. I can wish, but not hope, for what I believe to be impossible—as when I wish I were twenty-years-old again. If I hope for some state of affairs to occur, under appropriate circumstances I will do what I can to bring it about—as Ryan will study hard to earn his A in philosophy. Bill's hope that he will not give in to his first-order desire for a cigarette will lead him to strive to reject the weed now being offered to him.

In this regard, hoping involves a willingness to run some risk because of the positive valuation of the object in question. Consider case 3 (Susan hopes Happy Dancer will win the Kentucky Derby). For this to be the case, Susan must be dis-posed to act in some way as to manifest trust in Happy Dancer. She may bet on the horse without believing he will win the race, and the degree to which she hopes Happy Dancer will win the race may be reflected in how much she is willing to bet.

Fifth, hoping—unlike believing—is typically under our direct control. I may decide to hope that the Cubs will win, but it doesn't make sense to decide to believe that they will win. I hear that my enemy is suffering and find myself hoping that he will suffer great harm. Then I reflect that this *schadenfreude* is a loathsome attitude and decide to change it (to hoping he will suffer only as he deserves!). I may or may not be able to give up a hope, but, unlike a belief, normally I am able to alter the degree to which I hope for something. I may find that I am hoping too strongly that I will get an A—I notice that I am preoccupied with it to the point of distraction—and decide to invest less hope in that goal. It seems that the degree of hope has something to do with cost-benefit analysis about the pay-off involved in obtaining a goal. The greater the combination of the (perceived) probability of p obtaining and the value to me of its obtaining, the more likely I am to hope for p. So reflection on the cost-benefits of p will affect hope. Still, I can exercise some voluntary control over my hopes in a way that I can't over beliefs.

Sixth, hoping—like wanting—is evaluative in a way that believing is not. We may have morally

unacceptable hopes, but not morally unacceptable beliefs. Consider the difference between:

i. "I believe that we are heading toward World War III in which nuclear weap-ons will destroy the world."

and

ii. "I hope that we are heading toward World War III in which nuclear weap-ons will destroy the world."

Beliefs may be formed through a culpable lack of attention and thus have a moral dimension, but a belief itself cannot be judged moral or immoral. This is applicable to beliefs about racial or gender differences. Sometimes being a "racist" or a "sexist" is defined by holding that people of different races or genders have different native cognitive abilities. The inference is then made that because racism and sexism are immoral, anyone holding these beliefs is immoral. Such beliefs may be false, but unless the believer has obtained the belief through immoral activities, there is nothing immoral in having such beliefs, as such. So either racism and sexism should be defined differently (as immoral actions) or the charge of immorality should be dropped (if it is simply the cognitive feature that is in question).

Finally, we must make a distinction between ordinary hope (such as hoping you will receive a high grade) and deep hope. Consider Susan's situa-tion as she hopes that Happy Dancer will win. She may believe that horse has only a 1-in-10 chance of winning the Kentucky Derby, but she may judge this to be significantly better than the official odds of 100-to-1 against him. Suppose that she has only $10 but wants desperately to enter a professional program that costs $1,000. She has no hope of get-ting the money elsewhere, and if she bets on Happy Dancer and wins, she will get the required amount. Because she believes that the real odds are better than the official odds and that winning will enable her to get into the professional program, she bets her $10 on the horse. She commits herself to Happy Dancer although she never *believes* that he will win. We might call such cases where one is disposed to risk something significant on the possibility of the proposition's being true *deep* or *profound* hope. When the risk involves something of enormous value, we might call it *desperate* hope.

We conclude, then, that *hoping is distinguished from believing* in that it may involve a strong volitional or affective aspect in a way that believing does not and that, as such, it is subject to moral assessment in a way that believing is not. Hoping is desiderative, but it is more inclined to action than mere wishing. Hope may be ordinary or profound.

Let us apply this distinction to religious faith. Can hope serve as a *type of faith* in a religion like Christianity without the belief that the object of faith exists? Let me tell a story to help focus our discussion.

Suppose that when Moses decides to launch a pre-emptive strike against the Amalekites in obedience to the command of Yahweh (in the book of Exodus in the Hebrew Bible), his brother Aaron doubts whether such a pre-emptive strike is morally right, let alone the command of God. Aaron is inclined to make a treaty with the neighboring tribe. He doubts whether Yahweh has revealed such a command to Moses, doubts whether God appeared to Moses in the burning bush, and wonders whether Moses is hallucinating. When Moses points out that God annihilated the Egyptian pharaoh's army, Aaron is inclined to see that deed as merely the army's getting caught in a flash flood. When Moses offers the fact that a cloud pillar leads them by day and that a pillar of fire leads them by night, Aaron entertains the supposition that the clouds are natural phenomena and the appearance of "fire" is simply the effect of the rays of the setting sun on the distant sands. Aaron is agnostic about both the existence of Yahweh and His "revelation" to Moses. Although he cannot bring himself to overcome his doubts, he opts for the better story. He decides to accept the proposition that Yahweh exists and has revealed himself to Moses, and so he lives according to this hypothesis as an experimental faith. He assists Moses in every way in carrying out the campaign. He proclaims the need for his people to fight against the enemy, helps hold up Moses's arms during the battle,

and urges the warriors on to victory in the name of God.

True, Aaron may not act out of spontaneous abandon as Moses does. On the other hand, his scrupulous doubt may help him to notice problems and evidence that might otherwise be neglected and to which the true believer may be impervious. This awareness may signal danger that may be avoided, thus saving the tribe from disaster. Doubt may have as many virtues as belief, although they may be different.

Moses is the true believer, whereas Aaron—the doubter—lives in hope, *profound* hope. He believes that it would be a good thing if Moses's convictions are true and that it is possible that they are true, and so he decides to throw in his lot with his brother, living as if God exists and has revealed his plans to Moses.

The point may be put more simply. Suppose you are fleeing a murderous gang of desperados—perhaps members of the Mafia—who are bent on your annihilation. You come to the edge of a cliff that overlooks a yawning gorge. You find a rope spanning the gorge—tied to a tree on the cliff on the opposite side—and a man who announces that he is a tight-rope walker and can carry you over the gorge on the rope. He doesn't look as if he can do it, so you wonder whether he is insane or simply overconfident. He takes a few steps on the rope to assure you that he can balance himself. You agree that it's possible that he can navigate the rope across the gorge, but you have grave doubts about whether he can carry you. But your options are limited. Soon your pursuers will be upon you. You must decide. Whereas you still don't believe that the "tight-rope walker" can save you, you decide to trust him. You place your faith in his ability, climb on his back, close your eyes (so as not to look down into the yawning gorge), and do your best to relax and obey his commands in adjusting your body as he steps onto the rope. You have a profound, even *desperate*, hope that he will be successful.

This is how I see religious hope functioning in the midst of doubt. The verific person recognizes the tragedy of existence, that unless there is a God and life after death, the meaning of life is less than glorious, but if there is a God and life after death, the meaning of that life is glorious. There is just enough evidence to whet his or her appetite, to inspire hope, a decision to live according to theism or Christianity as an experimental hypothesis, but not enough evidence to cause belief. So keeping his or her mind open, the hoper opts for the better story, gets on the back of what may be the Divine Tight-Rope Walker, and commits to the pilgrimage. Perhaps the analogy is imperfect, for it may be possible to get off the tight-rope walker's back in actual existence and to get back to the cliff. Perhaps the Mafia men make a wrong turn or take their time searching for you. Still, the alternative to the tight-rope walker is not exactly welcoming: death and the extinction of all life in a solar system that will one day be extinguished. We may still learn to enjoy the fruits of finite love and resign ourselves to a final, cold fate. As Russell wrote:

Brief and powerless is man's life; on him and all his race the slow, sure doom falls pitiless and dark. Blind to good and evil, reckless of destruction, omnipotent matter rolls on its relentless way; for man, condemned today to lose his dearest, tomorrow himself to pass through the gate of darkness, it remains only to cherish, ere yet the blow fall, the lofty thoughts that ennoble his little day; disdaining the coward terrors of the slave of Fate, to worship at the shrine that his own hands have built; undismayed by the empire of chance, to preserve a mind free from the wanton tyranny that rules his outward life; proudly defiant of the irresistible forces that tolerate, for a moment, his knowledge and his condemnation, to sustain alone, a weary but unyielding Atlas, the world that his own ideals have fashioned despite the trampling march of unconscious power.[5]

But if there is some evidence for something better, something eternal, someone benevolent who rules the universe and will redeem the world from evil and despair, isn't it worth betting on that worldview? Shouldn't we, at least, consider getting on the back of the tight-rope walker and letting him carry us across the gorge?

CONCLUSION

1. What's so great about belief? Note that the Epistle of James tells us that belief is insufficient for salvation, for "the devils believe and also tremble" (James 2:19). Note too that the verse quoted by the minister to me as a 15-year-old (Romans 14:23) was taken out of context. The passage reads: "For meat destroy not the work of God. All things are pure; but it is evil for that man who eateth with offense. It is good neither to eat flesh, nor to drink wine, nor any thing whereby thy brother stumbleth, or is offended, or is made weak. Hast thou faith? Have it to thyself before God. Happy is he that condemneth not himself in that thing which he alloweth. And he that doubteth is damned if he eats, because he eateth not of faith, for whatsoever is not of faith is sin." The passage is not about one's eternal salvation but about eating meat previously offered to idols. Paul is saying, "Let your conscience be your guide here. If your conscience condemns you—if you have doubts about this act—then refrain!"

2. Can we be judged (condemned) for our beliefs? No, not for our beliefs, as such, for they are not things we choose, so we're not (directly) responsible for them; we can be judged only according to what we have responsibly done (ought implies can).

   a. We can be judged only for things over which we have control.

   b. We only have control over our actions.

c. Beliefs are not actions.

d. Therefore we cannot be judged for our beliefs, but only for our actions.

Although we have some *indirect* control over acquiring beliefs, we ought not violate the ethics of belief and force ourselves to believe more than the evidence warrants.

3. We can be judged by how faithful we have been to the light we have, to how well we have lived, including how well we have impartially sought the truth. We may adopt theism and/or Christianity as experimental faith, living by hope in God, yet keeping our minds open to new evidence that may confirm or disconfirm our decision.

If this argument is sound, the people who truly have faith in God are those who live with moral integrity within their lights—some unbelievers will be in heaven and some religious, true believers, who never doubted, will be absent. My supposition is that they will be in purgatory. What is purgatory? It is a large philosophy department where people who compromised the truth and the good will be taught to think critically and morally, according to the ethics of belief. The faculty, God's servants in truth-seeking, will be David Hume, John Stuart Mill, Voltaire, Immanuel Kant, and Bertrand Russell.

NOTES

1. Whoever desires to be saved must above all things hold the Catholic faith. Unless a man keeps it in its entirety, inviolate, he will assuredly perish eternally. Now this is the Catholic faith, that we worship one God in Trinity and Trinity in unity without either confusing the persons or dividing the substance.... So he who desires to be saved should think thus of the Trinity.

   It is necessary, however, to eternal salvation that he should also faithfully believe in the Incarnation of our Lord Jesus Christ. Now the right faith is that we should believe and confess that our Lord Jesus Christ, the Son of God, is equally both God and man.

   This is the Catholic faith. Unless a man believes it faithfully and steadfastly, he will not be able to be saved. (Athanasian Creed).

2. Most theologians and Christian philosophers hold that belief is a necessary condition for faith. For example, Alvin Plantinga writes, "The mature theist does not typically accept belief in God tentatively or hypothetically or until something better comes along. Nor, I think, does he accept it as a conclusion from other things he believes; he accepts it as basic, as a part of the foundations of his

noetic structure. The mature theist commits himself to belief in God: this means that he accepts belief in God as basic." ("Is Belief in God Rational" in *Rationality and Religious Belief*, ed. C. F. Delaney, Notre Dame University Press, 1979, p. 27). See Reading VII.A.2 in this book.

3. Much more needs to be said than can be said here. I have developed a fuller argument against direct volitionalism in my book *What Can We Know?* (Wadsworth Publishing Co., 2001).

4. Many philosophers have criticized Clifford's advice as being self-referentially incoherent. It doesn't have sufficient evidence for itself. But, suitably modified, I think this problem can be overcome. We can give reasons why we ought generally to try to believe according to the evidence, and if these reasons are sound, then we do have sufficient evidence for accepting the principle. See W. K. Clifford, Reading VII.A.2 in this book.

5. Bertrand Russell, "A Free Man's Worship," pp. 104–116 in his *Why I Am Not A Christian and Other Essays on Religion and Related Subjects*, edited by Paul Edwards (Simon & Schuster, 1967) reading X.3 in this book.